T0305354

Data Science Fundamentals with R, Python, and Open Data

Data Science Fundamentals with R, Python, and Open Data

Marco Cremonini
University of Milan
Italy

Published by John Wiley & Sons, Inc., Hoboken, New Jersey.
Published simultaneously in Canada.

For general information on our other products and services or for technical support, please contact our Customer
Care Department within the United States at (800) 762-2974, outside the United States at (317) 572-3993 or
fax (317) 572-4002.

Wiley also publishes its books in a variety of electronic formats. Some content that appears in print may not be
available in electronic formats. For more information about Wiley products, visit our web site at www.wiley.com.

Library of Congress Cataloging-in-Publication Data Applied for:

Hardback ISBN: 9781394213245

Cover Design: Wiley
Cover Image: © Andriy Onufriyenko/Getty Images

Set in 9.5/12.5pt STIXTwoText by Straive, Chennai, India

Contents

Preface *xiii*
About the Companion Website *xvii*
Introduction *xix*

1   **Open-Source Tools for Data Science** *1*
1.1   R Language and RStudio *1*
1.1.1   R Language *2*
1.1.2   RStudio Desktop *2*
1.1.3   Package Manager *2*
1.1.4   Package Tidyverse *4*
1.2   Python Language and Tools *5*
1.2.1   Option A: Anaconda Distribution *6*
1.2.2   Option B: Manual Installation *6*
1.2.3   Google Colab *7*
1.2.4   Packages NumPy and Pandas *7*
1.3   Advanced Plain Text Editor *8*
1.4   CSV Format for Datasets *8*
    Questions *10*

2   **Simple Exploratory Data Analysis** *13*
2.1   Missing Values Analysis *13*
2.2   R: Descriptive Statistics and Utility Functions *15*
2.3   Python: Descriptive Statistics and Utility Functions *17*
    Questions *19*

3   **Data Organization and First Data Frame Operations** *23*
3.1   R: Read CSV Datasets and Column Selection *24*
3.1.1   Reading a CSV Dataset *26*
3.1.1.1   Reading Errors *27*
3.1.2   Selection by Column Name *29*
3.1.3   Selection by Column Index Position *30*
3.1.4   Selection by Range *31*
3.1.5   Selection by Exclusion *32*
3.1.6   Selection with Selection Helper *35*
3.2   R: Rename and Relocate Columns *36*

3.3   R: Slicing, Column Creation, and Deletion   *38*
3.3.1   Subsetting and Slicing   *39*
3.3.2   Column Creation   *42*
3.3.3   Column Deletion   *43*
3.3.4   Calculated Columns   *44*
3.3.5   Function `mutate()` and Data Masking   *44*
3.4   R: Separate and Unite Columns   *45*
3.4.1   Separation   *46*
3.4.2   Union   *48*
3.5   R: Sorting Data Frames   *49*
3.5.1   Sorting by Multiple Columns   *50*
3.5.2   Sorting by an External List   *51*
3.6   R: Pipe   *55*
3.6.1   Forward Pipe   *55*
3.6.2   Pipe in Base R   *57*
3.6.2.1   Variant   *57*
3.6.3   Parameter Placeholder   *58*
3.7   Python: Column Selection   *59*
3.7.1   Selecting Columns from Dataset Read   *61*
3.7.2   Selecting Columns from a Data Frame   *62*
3.7.3   Selection by Positional Index, Range, or with Selection Helper   *63*
3.7.4   Selection by Exclusion   *64*
3.8   Python: Rename and Relocate Columns   *67*
3.8.1   Standard Method   *67*
3.8.2   Functions `rename()` and `reindex()`   *67*
3.9   Python: NumPy Slicing, Selection with Index, Column Creation and Deletion   *69*
3.9.1   NumPy Array Slicing   *69*
3.9.2   Slicing of Pandas Data Frames   *70*
3.9.3   Methods `.loc` and `.iloc`   *73*
3.9.4   Selection with Selection Helper   *77*
3.9.5   Creating and Deleting Columns   *79*
3.9.6   Functions `insert()` and `assign()`   *80*
3.10   Python: Separate and Unite Columns   *81*
3.10.1   Separate   *81*
3.10.2   Unite   *84*
3.11   Python: Sorting Data Frame   *85*
3.11.1   Sorting Columns   *85*
3.11.2   Sorting Index Levels   *86*
3.11.3   From Indexed to Non-indexed Data Frame   *88*
3.11.4   Sorting by an External List   *89*
           Questions   *91*

4   Subsetting with Logical Conditions   *99*
4.1   Logical Operators   *99*
4.2   R: Row Selection   *101*
4.2.1   Operator `%in%`   *104*
4.2.2   Boolean Mask   *105*

4.2.3   Examples   *106*
4.2.3.1   Wrong Disjoint Condition   *107*
4.2.4   Python: Row Selection   *114*
4.2.5   Boolean Mask, Base Selection Method   *115*
4.2.6   Row Selection with `query()`   *119*
          Questions   *121*

5   Operations on Dates, Strings, and Missing Values   *127*
5.1   R: Operations on Dates and Strings   *129*
5.1.1   Date and Time   *129*
5.1.1.1   Datetime Data Type   *129*
5.1.2   Parsing Dates   *130*
5.1.3   Using Dates   *132*
5.1.4   Selection with Logical Conditions on Dates   *133*
5.1.5   Strings   *136*
5.2   R: Handling Missing Values and Data Type Transformations   *141*
5.2.1   Missing Values as Replacement   *142*
5.2.1.1   Keywords for Missing Values   *142*
5.2.2   Introducing Missing Values in Dataset Reads   *143*
5.2.3   Verifying the Presence of Missing Values   *144*
5.2.3.1   Functions `any()`, `all()`, and `colSums()`   *146*
5.2.4   Replacing Missing Values   *147*
5.2.5   Omit Rows with Missing Values   *149*
5.2.6   Data Type Transformations   *150*
5.3   R: Example with Dates, Strings, and Missing Values   *154*
5.3.1   When an Invisible Hand Mess with Your Data   *158*
5.3.2   Base Method   *159*
5.3.3   A Better Heuristic   *162*
5.3.4   Specialized Functions   *162*
5.3.4.1   Function `parse_date_time()`   *162*
5.3.5   Result Comparison   *165*
5.4   Pyhton: Operations on Dates and Strings   *165*
5.4.1   Date and Time   *165*
5.4.1.1   Function `pd.to_datetime()`   *165*
5.4.1.2   Function `datetime.datetime.strptime()`   *167*
5.4.1.3   Locale Configuration   *168*
5.4.1.4   Function `datetime.datetime.strftime()`   *169*
5.4.1.5   Pandas Timestamp Functions   *169*
5.4.2   Selection with Logical Conditions on Dates   *171*
5.4.3   Strings   *172*
5.5   Python: Handling Missing Values and Data Type Transformations   *173*
5.5.1   Missing Values as Replacement   *173*
5.5.1.1   Function `pd.replace()`   *175*
5.5.2   Introducing Missing Values in Dataset Reads   *175*
5.5.3   Verifying the Presence of Missing Values   *176*
5.5.4   Selection with Missing Values   *178*
5.5.5   Replacing Missing Values with Actual Values   *179*

5.5.6   Modifying Values *by View* or *by Copy*   *180*
5.5.7   Data Type Transformations   *182*
5.6   Python: Examples with Dates, Strings, and Missing Values   *182*
5.6.1   Example 1: Eurostat   *182*
5.6.2   Example 2: Open Data Berlin   *186*
         Questions   *190*

6   Pivoting and Wide-long Transformations   *195*
6.1   R: Pivoting   *197*
6.1.1   From Long to Wide   *197*
6.1.2   From Wide to Long   *199*
6.1.3   GOV.UK: Gender Pay Gap   *200*
6.2   Python: Pivoting   *202*
6.2.1   From Wide to Long with Columns   *203*
6.2.2   From Long to Wide with Columns   *204*
6.2.3   Wide-long Transformation with Index Levels   *206*
6.2.4   Indexed Data Frame   *207*
6.2.4.1 Function `unstack()`   *208*
6.2.4.2 Function `stack()`   *211*
6.2.5   From Long to Wide with Elements of Numeric Type   *213*
         Questions   *216*

7   Groups and Operations on Groups   *221*
7.1   R: Groups   *222*
7.1.1   Groups and Group Indexes   *224*
7.1.1.1 Function `group_by()`   *224*
7.1.1.2 Index Details   *226*
7.1.2   Aggregation Operations   *227*
7.1.2.1 Functions `group_by()` and `summarize()`   *227*
7.1.2.2 Counting Rows: function `n()`   *228*
7.1.2.3 Arithmetic Mean: function `mean()`   *228*
7.1.2.4 Maximum and Minimum Values: Functions `max()` and `min()`   *230*
7.1.2.5 Summing Values: function `sum()`   *231*
7.1.2.6 List of Aggregation Functions   *232*
7.1.3   Sorting Within Groups   *232*
7.1.4   Creation of Columns in Grouped Data Frames   *234*
7.1.5   Slicing Rows on Groups   *236*
7.1.5.1 Functions `slice_*()`   *236*
7.1.5.2 Combination of Functions `filter()` and `rank()`   *238*
7.1.6   Calculated Columns with Group Values   *242*
7.2   Python: Groups   *244*
7.2.1   Group Index and Aggregation Operations   *247*
7.2.1.1 Functions `groupby()` and `aggregate()`   *247*
7.2.1.2 Counting Rows, Computing Arithmetic Means, and Sum for Each Group   *247*
7.2.2   Names on Columns with Aggregated Values   *251*
7.2.3   Sorting Columns   *252*
7.2.4   Sorting on Index Levels   *254*

7.2.5	Slicing Rows on Groups	*255*
7.2.5.1	Functions `nlargest()` and `nsmallest()`	*259*
7.2.6	Calculated Columns with Group Values	*259*
7.2.7	Sorting Within Groups	*261*
	Questions	*265*

8	**Conditions and Iterations**	*271*
8.1	R: Conditions and Iterations	*272*
8.1.1	Conditions	*272*
8.1.1.1	Function `if_else()`	*275*
8.1.1.2	Function `case_when()`	*276*
8.1.1.3	Function `if()` and Constructs If-else and If-else If-else	*277*
8.1.2	Iterations	*278*
8.1.2.1	Function `for()`	*278*
8.1.2.2	Function Foreach()	*280*
8.1.3	Nested Iterations	*280*
8.1.3.1	Replacing a Single-Element Value	*282*
8.1.3.2	Iterate on the First Column	*283*
8.1.3.3	Iterate on all Columns	*283*
8.2	Python: Conditions and Iterations	*284*
8.2.1	Conditions	*284*
8.2.1.1	Function `if()`	*285*
8.2.1.2	Constructs If-else and If-elif-else	*285*
8.2.1.3	Function `np.where()`	*286*
8.2.1.4	Function `np.select()`	*287*
8.2.1.5	Functions `pd.where()` and `pd.mask()`	*289*
8.2.2	Iterations	*291*
8.2.2.1	Functions `for()` and `while()`	*291*
8.2.3	Nested Iterations	*294*
8.2.3.1	Execution Time	*296*
8.2.4	Iterating on Multi-index	*297*
8.2.4.1	Function `join()`	*300*
8.2.4.2	Function `items()`	*301*
	Questions	*302*

9	**Functions and Multicolumn Operations**	*307*
9.1	R: User-defined Functions	*308*
9.1.1	Using Functions	*309*
9.1.2	Data Masking	*312*
9.1.3	Anonymous Functions	*315*
9.2	R: Multicolumn Operations	*316*
9.2.1	Base Method	*316*
9.2.1.1	Functions `apply()`, `lapply()`, and `sapply()`	*316*
9.2.1.2	Mapping	*319*
9.2.2	Mapping and Anonymous Functions: *purrr-style* Syntax	*321*
9.2.3	Conditional Mapping	*321*
9.2.4	Subsetting Rows with Multicolumn Logical Condition	*323*

9.2.4.1   Combination of Functions `filter()` and `if_any()`   *323*
9.2.5   Multicolumn Transformations   *324*
9.2.5.1   Combination of Functions `mutate()` and `across()`   *324*
9.2.6   Introducing Missing Values   *325*
9.2.7   Use Cases and Execution Time Measurement   *326*
9.2.7.1   Case 1   *327*
9.2.7.2   Case 2   *328*
9.3   Python: User-defined and Lambda Functions   *330*
9.3.1   User-defined Functions   *330*
9.3.1.1   Lambda Functions   *333*
9.3.2   Python: Multicolumn Operations   *334*
9.3.2.1   Execution Time   *336*
9.3.3   General Case   *337*
9.3.3.1   Function `apply()`   *337*
           Questions   *342*

10   **Join Data Frames**   *347*
10.1   Basic Concepts   *348*
10.1.1   Keys of a Join Operation   *349*
10.1.2   Types of Join   *350*
10.1.3   R: Join Operation   *351*
10.1.4   Join Functions   *354*
10.1.4.1   Function `inner_join()`   *354*
10.1.4.2   Function `full_join()`   *356*
10.1.4.3   Functions `left_join()` and `right_join()`   *357*
10.1.4.4   Function `merge()`   *357*
10.1.5   Duplicated Keys   *358*
10.1.6   Special Join Functions   *363*
10.1.6.1   Semi Join   *363*
10.1.6.2   Anti Join   *365*
10.2   Python: Join Operations   *369*
10.2.1.1   Function `merge()`   *371*
10.2.1.2   Inner Join   *372*
10.2.1.3   Outer/Full Join   *374*
10.2.2   Join Operations with Indexed Data Frames   *375*
10.2.3   Duplicated Keys   *378*
10.2.4   Special Join Types   *384*
10.2.4.1   Semi Join: Function `isin()`   *384*
10.2.4.2   Anti Join: Variants   *386*
           Questions   *389*

11   **List/Dictionary Data Format**   *393*
11.1   R: List Data Format   *395*
11.1.1   Transformation of List Columns to Ordinary Rows and Columns   *401*
11.1.1.1   Other Options   *403*
11.1.2   Function `map` in List Column Transformations   *406*
11.2   R: JSON Data Format and Use Cases   *410*

11.2.1   Memory Problem when Reading Very Large Datasets   *421*

11.3   Python: Dictionary Data Format   *422*

11.3.1   Methods   *424*

11.3.2   From Dictionary to Data Frame With a Single Level of Nesting   *427*

11.3.2.1   Functions `pd.Dataframe()` and `pd.Dataframe.from_dict()`   *427*

11.3.3   From Dictionary to Data Frame with Several Levels of Nesting   *429*

11.3.3.1   Function `pd.json_normalize()` and Join Operation   *429*

11.3.4   Python: Use Cases with JSON Datasets   *436*

Questions   *443*

Index   *447*

Preface

Two questions come along with every new text that aims to teach someone something. The first is, Who is it addressed to? and the second is, Why does it have precisely those contents, organized in that way? These two questions, for this text, have perhaps even greater relevance than they usually do, because for both, the answer is unconventional (or at least not entirely conventional) and to some, it may seem surprising. It shouldn't be, or even better, if the answers will make the surprise a pleasant surprise.

Let's start with the first question: Who is the target of a text that introduces the fundamentals of two programming languages, R and Python, for the discipline called data science? Those who study to become data scientists, computer scientists, or computer engineers, it seems obvious, right? Instead, it is not so. For sure, future data scientists, computer scientists, and computer engineers could find this text useful. However, the real recipients should be others, simply all the others, the non-specialists, those who do not work or study to make IT or data science their main profession. Those who study to become or already are sociologists, political scientists, economists, psychologists, marketing or human resource management experts, and those aiming to have a career in business management and in managing global supply chains and distribution networks. Also, those studying to be biologists, chemists, geologists, climatologists, or even physicians. Then there are law students, human rights activists, experts of traditional and social media, memes and social networks, linguists, archaeologists, and paleontologists (I'm not joking, there really are fabulous data science works applied to linguistics, archeology, and paleontology). Certainly, in this roundup, I have forgotten many who deserved to be mentioned like the others. Don't feel left out. The artists I forgot! There are contaminations between art, data science, and data visualization of incredible interest. Art absorbs and re-elaborates, and in a certain way, this is also what data science does: it absorbs and re-elaborates. Finally, there are also all those who just don't know yet what they want to be; they will figure it out along the way, and having certain tools can come in handy in many cases.

Everyone can successfully learn the fundamentals of data science and the use of these computational tools, even with a few basic computer skills, with some efforts and time, of course, necessary but reasonable. Everyone could find opportunities for application in all, or almost all, existing professions, sciences, humanities, and cultural fields. And above all, without the need to take on the role of computer scientist or data scientist when you already have other roles to take on, which rightly demand time and dedication.

Therefore, the fact of not considering computer scientists and data scientists as the principal recipients of this book is not to diminish their role for non-existent reasons, but because for them there is no need to explain why a book that presents programming languages for data science has, at least in theory, something to do with what they typically do.

It is to the much wider audience of non-specialists that the exhortation to learn the fundamentals of data science should be addressed to, explaining that they do not have to transform themselves into computer scientists to be able to do so (or even worse, into geeks), which, with excellent reasons that are difficult to dispute, have no intention to do. It doesn't matter if they have always been convinced to be "unfit for computer stuff," and that, frankly, the rhetoric of past twenty years about "digital natives," "being a coder," or "joining the digital revolution" sounds just annoying. None of this should matter, time to move on. How? Everyone should look at what digital skills and technologies would be useful for their own discipline and do the training for those goals. Do you want to be a computer scientist or a data scientist? Well, do it; there is no shortage of possibilities. Do you want to be an economist, a biologist, or a marketing expert? Very well, do it, but you must not be cut off from adequate training on digital methodologies and tools from which you will benefit, as much as you are not cut off from a legal, statistical, historical, or sociological training if this knowledge is part of the skills needed for your profession or education. What is the objection that is usually made? No one can know everything, and generalists end up knowing a little of everything and nothing adequately. It's as true as clichés are, but that's not what we're talking about. A doctor who acquires statistical or legal training is no less a doctor for this; on the contrary, in many cases she/he is able to carry out the medical profession in a better way. No one reproaches an economist who becomes an expert in statistical analysis that she/he should have taken a degree in statistics. And soon (indeed already now), to the same economist who will become an expert in machine learning techniques for classification problems for fintech projects, no one, hopefully, will reproach that as an economist she/he should leave those skills to computer scientists. Like it or not, computer skills are spreading and will do so more and more among non-computer scientists, it's a matter of base rate, notoriously easy to be misinterpreted, as all students who have taken an introductory course in statistics know.

Let's consider the second question: Why this text presents two languages instead of just one as it is usually done? Isn't it enough to learn just one? Which is better? A friend of mine told me he's heard that Python is famous, the other one he has never heard of. Come on, seriously two? It's a miracle if I learn half of just one! Stop. That's enough.

It's not a competition or a beauty contest between programming languages, and not even a question of cheering, as with sports teams, where you have to choose one, none is admissible, but you can't root for two. R and Python are tools, in some ways complex, not necessarily complicated, professional, but also within anyone's reach. Above all, they are the result of the continuous work of many people; they are evolving objects and are extraordinary teaching aids for those who want to learn. Speaking of evolution, a recent and interesting one is the increasingly frequent convergence between the two languages presented in this text. Convergence means the possibility of coordinated, alternating, and complementary use: Complement the benefits of both, exploit what is innovative in one and what the other has, and above all, the real didactic value, learning not to be afraid to change technology, because much of what you learned with one will be found and will be useful with the other. There is another reason, this one is more specific. It is true that Python is so famous that almost everyone has heard its name while only relatively few know R, except that practically everyone involved in data science knows it and most of them uses it, and that's for a pretty simple reason: It's a great tool with a large community of people who have been contributing new features for many years. What about Python? Python is used by millions of people, mainly to make web services, so it has enormous application possibilities. A part of Python has specialized in data science and is growing rapidly, taking advantage of the ease of extension to dynamic and web-oriented applications. One last piece of information: Learning the first programming language could look difficult. The learning curve, so-called how fast you learn, is steep at first, you struggle at the very beginning, but after a while it softens, and you run. This is for the first one. Same ramp to climb with the second one too? Not at all. Attempting an estimate, I would say that just one-third of the effort is needed to learn the second, a bargain that probably few are aware of. Therefore, let's do both of them.

One last comment because one could certainly think that this discussion is only valid in theory, putting it into practice is quite another thing. Over the years I have required hundreds of social science students to learn the fundamentals of both R and Python for data science and I can tell you that it is true that most of them struggled initially, some complained more or less aloud that they were unfit, then they learned very quickly and ended up demonstrating that it was possible for them to acquire excellent computational skills without having to transform into computer scientists or data scientists (to tell the truth, someone transformed into one, but that's fine too), without possessing nonexistent digital native geniuses, without having to be anything other than what they study for, future experts in social sciences, management, human resources, or economics, and what is true for them is certainly true for everyone. This is the pleasant surprise.

Milan, Italy   *Marco Cremonini*
2023

About the Companion Website

This book is accompanied by student companion website.

www.wiley.com/go/DSFRPythonOpenData

The student website includes:
- MCQs
- Software

Introduction

This text introduces the fundamentals of data science using two main programming languages and open-source technologies : R and Python. These are accompanied by the respective application contexts formed by tools to support coding scripts, i.e. logical sequences of instructions with the aim to produce certain results or functionalities. The tools can be of the command line interface (CLI) type, which are consoles to be used with textual commands, and integrated development environment (IDE), which are of interactive type to support the use of languages. Other elements that make up the application context are the supplementary libraries that contain the additional functions in addition to the basic ones coming with the language, package managers for the automated management of the download and installation of new libraries, online documentation, cheat sheets, tutorials, and online forums of discussion and help for users. This context, formed by a language, tools, additional features, discussions between users, and online documentation produced by developers, is what we mean when we say "R" and "Python," not the simple programming language tool, which by itself would be very little. It is like talking only about the engine when instead you want to explain how to drive a car on busy roads.

R and Python, together and with the meaning just described, represent the knowledge to start approaching data science, carry out the first simple steps, complete the educational examples, get acquainted with real data, consider more advanced features, familiarize oneself with other real data, experiment with particular cases, analyze the logic behind mechanisms, gain experience with more complex real data, analyze online discussions on exceptional cases, look for data sources in the world of open data, think about the results to be obtained, even more sources of data now to put together, familiarize yourself with different data formats, with large datasets, with datasets that will drive you crazy before obtaining a workable version, and finally be ready to move to other technologies, other applications, uses, types of results, projects of ever-increasing complexity. This is the journey that starts here, and as discussed in the preface, it is within the reach of anyone who puts some effort and time into it. A single book, of course, cannot contain everything, but it can help to start, proceed in the right direction, and accompany for a while.

With this text, we will start from the elementary steps to gain speed quickly. We will use simplified teaching examples, but also immediately familiarize ourselves with the type of data that exists in reality, rather than in the unreality of the teaching examples. We will finish by addressing some elaborate examples, in which even the inconsistencies and errors that are part of daily reality will emerge, requiring us to find solutions.

Approach

It often happens that students dealing with these contents, especially the younger ones, initially find it difficult to figure out the right way to approach their studies in order to learn effectively. One of the main causes of this difficulty lies in the fact that many are accustomed to the idea that the goal of learning is to never make mistakes. This is not surprising, indeed, since it's the criteria adopted by many exams, the more mistakes, the lower the grade. This is not the place to discuss the effectiveness of exam methodologies or teaching philosophies; we are pragmatists, and the goal is to learn R and Python, computational logic, and everything that revolves around it. But it is precisely from a wholly pragmatic perspective that the problem of the inadequacy of the approach that seeks to minimize errors arises, and this for at least two good reasons. The first is that inevitably the goal of never making mistakes leads to mnemonic study. Sequences of passages, names, formulas, sentences, and specific cases are memorized, and the variability of the examples considered is reduced, tending toward schematism. The second reason is simply that trying to never fail is exactly the opposite of what it takes to effectively learn R and Python and any digital technology.

Learning computational skills for the data science necessarily requires a hands-on approach. This involves carrying out many practical exercises, meticulously redoing those proposed by the text, but also varying them, introducing modifications, and replicating them with different data. All those of the didactic examples can obviously be modified, but also all those with open data can easily be varied. Instead of certain information, others could be used, and instead of a certain result, a slightly different one could be sought, or different data made available by the same source could be tried. Proceeding methodically (being methodical, meticulous, and patient are fundamental traits for effective learning) is the way to go. Returning to the methodological doubts that often afflict students when they start, the following golden rule applies, which must necessarily be emphasized because it is of fundamental importance: exercises are used to make mistakes, an exercise without errors is useless.

Open Data

The use of open data, right from the first examples and to a much greater extent than examples with simplified educational datasets, is one of the characteristics, perhaps the main one, of this text. The datasets taken from open data are 26, sourced from the United States and other countries, large international organizations (the World Bank and the United Nations), as well as charities and independent research institutes, gender discrimination observatories, and government agencies for air traffic control, energy production and consumption, pollutant emissions, and other environmental information. This also includes data made available by cities like Milan, Berlin, and New York City. This selection is just a drop in the sea of open data available and constantly growing in terms of quantity and quality.

Using open data to the extent it has been done in this text is a precise choice that certainly imposes an additional effort on those who undertake the learning path, a choice based both on personal experience in teaching the fundamentals of data science to students of social and political sciences (every year I have increasingly anticipated the use of open data), and on the fundamental drawback of carrying out examples and exercises mainly with didactic cases, which are inevitably unreal and unrealistic. Of course, the didactic cases, also present in this text, are perfectly fit for showing a specific functionality, an effect or behavior of the computational tool. As mentioned before, though, the issue at stake is about learning to drive in urban traffic, not just understanding some engine mechanics, and at the end the only way to do that is … driving in traffic, there's no alternative. For us it is the same, anyone who works with data knows that one of the fundamental skills is to prepare the data for analysis (first there would be that of finding the data) and also that this task can easily be the most time- and effort-demanding part of the whole job. Studying mainly with simplified teaching examples erases this fundamental part of knowledge and experience, for this reason, they are always unreal and unrealistic, however you try to fix them. There is no alternative to putting your hands and banging your head on real data, handling datasets even of hundreds of thousands or millions of rows (the largest one we use in this text has more than 500 000 rows, the data of all US domestic flights of January 2022) with their errors, explanations that must be read and sometimes misinterpreted, even with cases where data was recorded inconsistently (we will see one of this kind quite amusing). Familiarity with real data should be achieved as soon as possible, to figure out their typical characteristics and the fact that behind data there are organizations made up of people, and it is thanks to them if we can extract new information and knowledge. You need to arm yourself with patience and untangle, one step at a time, each knot. This is part of the fundamentals to learn.

What You Don't Learn

One book alone can't cover everything; we've already said it and it's obvious. However, the point to decide is what to leave out. One possibility is that the author tries to discuss as many different topics as she/he can think of. This is the encyclopedic model, popular but not very compatible with a reasonably limited number of pages. It is no coincidence that the most famous of the encyclopedias have dozens of ponderous volumes. The short version of the encyclopedic model is a "synthesis," i.e. a reasonably short overview that is necessarily not very thorough and has to simplify complex topics. Many educational books choose this form, which has the advantage of the breadth of topics combined with a fair amount of simplification.

This book has a hybrid form, from this point of view. It is broader than the standard because it includes two languages instead of one, but it doesn't have the form of synthesis because it focuses on a certain specific type of data and functionality: data frames, with the final addition of lists/dictionaries, transformation and pivoting operations, group indexing, aggregation, advanced transformations and data frame joins, and on these issues, it goes into the details. Basically, it offers the essential toolbox for data science.

What's left out? Very much, indeed. The techniques and tools for data visualization, descriptive and predictive models, including machine learning techniques, obviously the statistical analysis part (although this is traditionally an autonomous part), technologies for "Big Data," i.e. distributed, scalable software infrastructures capable of managing not only a lot of data but above all data streams, i.e. real-time data flows, and the many web-oriented extensions, starting from data collection techniques from websites up to integration with dynamic dashboards and web services, are not included. Again, there are specialized standards, such as those for climate data, financial data, biomedical data, and coding used by some of the large international institutions that are not treated. The list could go on.

This additional knowledge, which is part of data science, deserves to be learned. For this, you need the fundamentals that this book presents. Once equipped with them, it's the personal interests and the cultural and professional path of each one to play the main role, driving in a certain direction or in another. But again, once it has been verified firsthand that it is possible, regardless of one's background, to profitably acquire the fundamentals of the discipline with R and Python, any further insights and developments can be tackled, in exactly the same way, with the same approach and spirit used to learn the fundamentals.

1

Open-Source Tools for Data Science

1.1 R Language and RStudio

In this first section, we introduce the main tools for the R environment: the **R language** and the **RStudio IDE** (interactive development environment). The first is an open-source programming language developed by the community, specifically for statistical analysis and data science; the second is an open-source development tool produced by *Posit* (www.posit.com), formerly called RStudio, representing the standard IDE for R-based data science projects. Posit offers a freeware version of RStudio called *RStudio Desktop* that fully supports all features for R development; it has been used (v. 2022.07.2) in the preparation of all the R code presented in this book. Commercial versions of RStudio add supporting features typical of managing production software in corporate environments. An alternative to RStudio Desktop is **RStudio Cloud**, the same IDE offered as a service on a cloud premise. Graphically and functionally, the cloud version is exactly the same as the desktop one; however, its free usage has limitations.

The official distribution of the R language and the RStudio IDE are just the starting points though. This is what distinguishes an open-source technology from a proprietary one. With an open-source technology actively developed by a large online community, as is the case for R, the official distribution provides the basic functionality and, on top of that, layers of additional, advanced, or specialistic features could be stacked, all of them developed by the open-source community. Therefore, it is a constantly evolving environment, not a commercial product subject to the typical life cycle mostly mandated by corporate marketing. What is better, an open-source or a proprietary tool? This is an ill-posed question, mostly irrelevant in generic terms because the only reasonable answer is, "It depends." The point is that they are different in a number of fundamental ways.

With R, we will use many features provided by additional packages to be installed on top of the base distribution. This is the normal course of action and is exactly what everybody using this technology is supposed to do in order to support the goal of a certain data analysis or data science project. Clearly, the additional features employed in the examples of this book are not all those available, and neither are all those somehow important, that would be simply impossible to cover. New features come out continuously, so in learning the fundamentals, it is important to practice with the approach, familiarize yourself with the environment, and exercise with the most fundamental tools, so as to be perfectly able to explore the new features and tools that become available.

Just keep in mind that these are professional-grade tools, not merely didactic ones to be abandoned after the training period. Thousands of experienced data scientists use these tools in their daily jobs and for top-level data science projects, so the instruments you start knowing and handling are powerful.

Data Science Fundamentals with R, Python, and Open Data, First Edition. Marco Cremonini.
© 2024 John Wiley & Sons, Inc. Published 2024 by John Wiley & Sons, Inc.
Companion website: www.wiley.com/go/DSFRPythonOpenData

1.1.1 R Language

CRAN (the Comprehensive R Archive Network, https://cloud.r-project.org/) is the official online archive for all R versions and software packages available to install. CRAN is mirrored on a number of servers worldwide, so, in practice, it is always available.

The R base package is basically compliant with all desktop platforms: Windows, MacOS, and Linux. The installation is guided through a standard wizard and is effortless. Mobile platforms such as iOS and Android, as well as hybrid products, like the Chromebook, are not supported. For old operating system versions, the currently available version of R might not be compatible. In that case, under *R Binaries*, all previous versions of R are accessible, the most recent compatible one can be installed with confidence, and all the important features will be available.

At the end of the installation, a link to an R execution file will be created in the programs or applications menu/folder. That is not the R language, but an old-fashioned IDE that comes with the language. You do not need that if you use RStudio, as is recommended. You just need to install the R language, that is all.

1.1.2 RStudio Desktop

The *RStudio Desktop* is an *integrated development environment* (IDE) for R programming, recently enhanced with features to interpret Python scripts too (https://posit.co/download/rstudio-desktop/). In short, this means that it is a tool offering a graphical interface that accommodates most of the necessary functionalities for developing projects using R, which is a separate component, as we have seen in the previous section. The RStudio IDE is unanimously considered one of the best available IDEs, being complete, robust, and consistent throughout the versions. For this reason, there is not much competition in that market, at least until now. It is simply the safest and best choice. Icons of R and of RStudio might be confusing at first, but they both show a big R.

It is important to familiarize yourself with RStudio's layout because of the many functionalities available and useful in data science projects. The layout is divided into four main *quadrants*, as shown in Figure 1.1, with quadrant *Q1* that appears only when an R Script is created from the drop-down menu of the top-left icon.

- *Q1*: The quadrant for editing the *R code*, with different scripts is shown in separate tabs on top.
- *Q2*: The main feature is the *R Console,* where single command line instructions can be executed and the output of the execution of an R script appears.
- *Q3*: Information about the environment is provided through this quadrant, such as R objects (variables) created in memory during the execution of code; Python objects too could be shown if software allowing for integration between the two languages is used.
- *Q4*: A multifunction quadrant allowing for exploring the local file system (tab *Files*), visualizing graphics (tab *Plots*), the R package manager (tab *Packages*), and online documentation (tab *Help*).

1.1.3 Package Manager

The package manager is a key component of open-source environments, frequently used for updating a configuration, adding new functionalities, duplicating a configuration for testing purposes, and so forth. Installing new components is a common and recurrent activity in environments like R and Python, so it has to be simple and efficient. This is the crucial role of a package manager.

A package manager is typically a piece of software with few functionalities that basically revolve around listing the installed packages, updating them, searching for new ones, installing them, and removing useless packages. Everything else is basically accessory features that are not

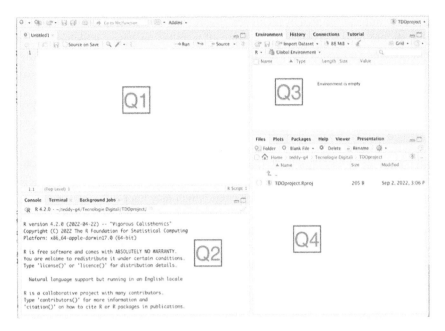

Figure 1.1 RStudio Desktop's standard layout

strictly necessary. Given the few specialized features a package manager must have, it should come without any surprise that modern package managers have their origins in classical command line tools. Actually, they still exist and thrive; they are often used as command line tools both in R and Python environments, just because they are simple to use and have limited options.

At any rate, a graphical interface exists, and RStudio offers it with the tab *Packages* in the Q4 quadrant. It is simple, just a list of installed packages and a selection box indicating if a package is also loaded or not. Installing and loading a package are two distinct operations. *Installing* means retrieving the executable code, for example, by downloading it from CRAN and configuring it in the local system. *Loading a package means making its functionalities available for a certain script*, which translates into the fundamental function `library(`<name of the package to load>`)`. Ticking the box beside a package in the RStudio package manager will execute on the R Console (quadrant Q2) the corresponding `library()` instruction. Therefore, using the console or ticking the box for loading a package is exactly the same.

However, neither of them is a good way to proceed, when we are writing R scripts, because a script should be reproducible, or at least understandable by others, at a later time, possibly a long time later. This means that all information necessary for reproducing it should be explicit, and if the list of packages to be loaded is defined externally by ticking selection boxes or running commands on the console, that knowledge is hidden, and it will be more difficult to understand exactly all the features of the script. So *the correct way to proceed is to explicitly write all necessary* `library()` *instructions in the script, loading all required packages.*

The opposite operation of loading a package is unloading it, which is certainly less frequent; normally, it is not needed in scripts. From the RStudio interface, it could be executed by unticking a package or by executing the corresponding instruction `detach("package:`<name of the package>`", unload=TRUE)`.

A reasonable doubt may arise about the reason why installed packages are not just all loaded by default. Why bother with this case-by-case procedure? The reason is memory, the RAM, in particular, that is not only finite and shared by all processes executed on the computer, but is often a scarce resource that should be used efficiently. Loading all installed packages, which could be dozens or even hundreds, when normally just a few are needed by the script in execution, is clearly a very inefficient way of using the RAM. In short, we bother with the manual loading of packages to save memory space, which is good when we have to execute computations on data.

Installing R packages is straightforward. The interactive button **Install** in tab *Packages* is handy and provides all the functionalities we need. From the window that opens, the following choices should be made:

- *Install from*: From which repository should the package be downloaded? Options are: **CRAN**, the official online repository, this is the default and the normal case. **Package Archive File** is only useful if the package to install has been saved locally, which may happen for experimental packages not available from GitHub, which is a rare combination. Packages available from GitHub could be retrieved and installed with a specialized command (`githubinstall ("PackageName")`).
- *Packages*: The name of the package(s) to install; the autocomplete feature looks up names from CRAN.
- *Install to library*: The installation path on the local system depends on the R version currently installed.
- *Install dependencies*: Dependencies are logical relationships between different packages. It is customary for new to packages exploit features of previous packages for many reasons, either because they are core or ancillary functionalities with respect to the features provided by the package. In this case, those functionalities are not reimplemented, but the package providing them is logically linked to the new one. This, in short, is the meaning of dependencies. It means that when a package is installed if it has dependencies, those should be installed too (with the required version). This option, when selected, automatically takes care of all dependencies, downloading and installing them, if not present. The alternative is to manually download and install the packages required as dependencies by a certain package. The automatic choice is usually the most convenient. Errors may arise because of dependencies, for example, when for any reason, the downloading of a package fails, or the version installed is not compatible. In those cases, the problem should be fixed manually, either by installing the missing dependencies or the one with the correct version.

1.1.4 Package Tidyverse

The main package we use in this book is called ***tidyverse*** (https://www.tidyverse.org/). It is a particular package because it does not directly provide new features, but rather groups a bunch of other packages, which are then installed all at once, and these provide the additional features. In a way, *tidyverse* is a shortcut created to simplify the life of people approaching data science with R, instead of installing a certain number of packages individually, common to the majority of projects, they have been encapsulated in just one package that does the whole job.

There are criticisms of this way of doing things based on the assumption that only necessary packages should be installed and, most of all, loaded. This principle is correct and should be followed as a general rule. However, a trade-off is also reasonable in most cases. Therefore, you may install *tidyverse* and then load only specific packages in a script, or just load the whole lot contained in *tidyverse*. Usually, it does not make much difference; you can choose without worrying too much about this.

In any case, *tidyverse* is widely used, and for this, it is useful to spend some time reading the description of the packages included in it because this provides a glimpse into what most data science projects use, the types of operations and more general features. In our examples, most of the functions we will use are defined in one of the *tidyverse* packages, with some exceptions that will be introduced.

The installation of *tidyverse* is the standard one, through the RStudio package manager, or the console with command `install.packages("tidyverse")`. Loading it in a script is done with `library(tidyverse)` for a whole lot of packages, or alternatively, for single packages such as `library(readr)`, where *readr* is the name of a package contained in *tidyverse*. In all cases, after the execution of a `library` instruction, the console shows if and what packages have been loaded.

In all our examples, it should be assumed that the first instruction to be executed is `library(tidyverse)`, even when not explicitly specified.

1.2   Python Language and Tools

Python's environment is more heterogeneous than R's, mostly because of the different scope of the language – Python is a general-purpose language mostly used for web and mobile applications, and in a myriad of other cases, data science is among them – which implies that several options are available as a convenient setup for data science projects. Here, one of the most popular is considered, but there are good reasons to make different choices.

The first issue to deal with is that, until now, there is not a data science Python IDE comparable to RStudio for R, which is the *de facto* standard and offers almost everything that is needed. In Python, you have to choose if you want to go with a classical IDE for coding; there are many, which is fine, but they are not much tailored for data science wrangling operations; or if you want to go with an IDE based on the **computational notebook** format (just *notebook* for short). The notebook format is a hybrid document that combines *formatted text*, usually based on a **Markdown** syntax and blocks of executable code. For several reasons, mostly related to utility in many contexts to have both formatted text and executable code, and the ease of use of these tools, IDEs based on the notebook format have become popular for Python data science and data analysis. The code in the examples of the following chapters has been produced and tested using the main one of these IDEs, **JupyterLab** (https://jupyterlab.readthedocs.io/en/latest/). It is widely adopted, well-documented, easy to install, and free to use. If you are going to write short blocks of Python code with associated descriptions, a typical situation in data science, it is a good choice. If you have to write a massive amount of code, then a classical IDE is definitely better. Jupyter notebooks are textual files with canonical extension **.ipynb** and an internal structure close to JSON specifications.

So, the environment we need has the *Python base distribution*, a *package manager*, for the same reasons we need it with R, the two packages specifically developed for data science functionalities called **NumPy** and **pandas**, and the *notebook-based IDE **JupyterLab***. These are the pieces. In order to have them installed and set up, there are two ways of proceeding: one is easy but inefficient, and the other is a little less easy but more efficient. Below, with *A* and *B,* the two options are summarized.

A.   A single installer package, equipped with a graphical wizard, installs and sets up everything that is needed, but also much more than you will likely ever use, for a total required memory space of approximately 5 GB on your hard disk or SSD memory.

B. A manual procedure individually installs the required components: first Python and the package manager, then the data science libraries *NumPy* and *pandas*, and finally the JupyterLab IDE. This requires using the command line shell (or terminal) to run the few installation instructions for the package manager, but the occupied memory space is just approximately 400 MB.

Both ways, the result is the Python setup for learning the fundamentals of data science, getting ready, and working. The little difficulty of the B option, i.e. using the command line to install components, is truly minimal and, in any case, the whole program described in this book is about familiarizing with command line tools for writing R or Python scripts, so nobody should be worried for a few almost identical commands to run with the package manager.

So, the personal suggestion is to try the *B* option, as described in the following, operationally better and able to teach some useful skills. At worst, it is always possible to backtrack and go with the easier *A* option on a second try.

1.2.1 Option A: Anaconda Distribution

Option A is easy to explain. There is a tool called **Anaconda Distribution** (https://www.anaconda.com/products/distribution) that provides everything needed for an initial Python data science environment. It contains all the components we have listed as well as tons of other tools and libraries. In addition, it offers a desktop application called *Anaconda Navigator*, which is basically a graphical interface to the package manager **conda**. Unfortunately, this interface is quite bulky. From this interface, it is also possible to launch the **JupyterLab** IDE.

1.2.2 Option B: Manual Installation

Option B requires a few steps:

Step 1: Python and package manager installation.
From the official repository of Python distribution (https://www.python.org/downloads/), the installer for the latest (or previous) distribution could be downloaded and launched. A graphical wizard guides the process. In the end, the Python language with its basic libraries and two package managers will be installed: **pip,** the standard Python package manager, and **conda,** the Anaconda's one. The differences between the two are minimal, and for all our concerns, they are equivalent. Even the syntax of the commands is basically the same. The only recommendation is to choose one and continue using that one for package management; this avoids some possible problems with dependencies. We show the examples using *pip*, but *conda* is fine as well.

Step 2: Installing data science packages *NumPy, pandas*, and *JupyterLab* IDE.
From a shell (e.g. *Terminal* on MacOS, *Powershell* on Windows), to run the package manager, it suffices to digit `pip` (or `conda`, for the other one) and return.

This way, a list of the options is shown. The most useful are:

- `pip list`: list all installed packages with the version.
- `pip install <package_name>`: install a package.
- `pip uninstall <package_name>`: uninstall a package.

When a package is installed or uninstalled, on the command line appears a request to confirm the operation; the syntax is `[n/Y]`, with *n* for No and *Y* for Yes.

```
(my-env)    :~    User$ jupyter lab  ◄─────────────────── Start Jupyter Lab
[I 18:30:05.974 LabApp] 2 kernels found
[I 18:30:06.658 LabApp] JupyterLab extension loaded from /Users/NomeUser/opt/lib/python3.9/site-
packages/jupyterlab
[I 18:30:06.658 LabApp] JupyterLab application directory is
/Users/NomeUser/opt/share/jupyter/lab
[I 18:30:06.662 LabApp] Serving notebooks from local directory: /Users/NomeUser  ◄── Working directory
[I 18:30:06.662 LabApp] The Jupyter Notebook is running at:
[I 18:30:06.662 LabApp]
http://localhost:8888/?token=a60f15cecd2e485c46f12350cd421a410735e2c3d0b4ec72
[I 18:30:06.663 LabApp]  or
http://127.0.0.1:8888/?token=a60f15cecd2e485c46f12350cd421a410735e2c3d0b4ec72
[I 18:30:06.663 LabApp] Use Control-C to stop this server and shut down all kernels (twice to
skip confirmation).
[C 18:30:06.701 LabApp]       ⌐ Control-C to stop

    To access the notebook, open this file in a browser:
        file:///Users/NomeUser/Library/Jupyter/runtime/nbserver-43274-open.html  ── URL to reopen
    Or copy and paste one of these URLs:                                             a closed tab
        http://localhost:8888/?token=a60f15cecd2e485c46f12350cd421a410735e2c3d0b4ec72
    or http://127.0.0.1:8888/?token=a60f15cecd2e485c46f12350cd421a410735e2c3d0b4ec72  ◄─
```

Figure 1.2 Example of starting JupyterLab

The commands we need to run are easy:

```
pip install numpy
pip install pandas
pip install jupyterlab
```

That is all, not difficult at all.

To start JupyterLab, again it is from the shell by executing **jupyterlab**. You will see the local service has started and, after a little while, a new tab is opened in the predefined browser with the JupyterLab interface. Figure 1.2 shows a screenshot of starting JupyterLab with some useful information that is presented, such as how to stop it (use Control-C and confirm the decision to stop it), where the working directory is, and the URL to copy and paste into the browser to reopen the tab if it was accidentally closed.

1.2.3 Google Colab

An alternative to JupyterLab is the cloud platform ***Google Colaboratory*** or ***Colab*** for short (https://colab.research.google.com/). It is accessible with a Google account and makes use of Google Drive for managing files and storing notebook documents. It is fully compatible with Jupyter notebooks. Those produced by Colab still have extension *ipynb* and are perfectly shareable between JupyterLab and Colab. The service is reliable, has quickly improved in just a few years, and is free to use at the moment of writing, so it should definitely be considered as a viable option, with pros and cons of a cloud platform evaluated for convenience.

1.2.4 Packages NumPy and Pandas

As already mentioned, *NumPy* (https://numpy.org/) and *pandas* (https://pandas.pydata.org/) are the data science-specific packages for Python. The first handles arrays and matrices, while the second is completely devoted to managing data frames, so we will make extensive use of the functionalities it offers. Both sites have updated and searchable technical documentation, which can also be downloaded, representing an indispensable supplement to the material, explanations, and examples of this book. In all cases of programming languages, the technical documentation should be at hand and regularly consulted, no matter whether the handbook is used for learning. A handbook and the technical documentation serve different purposes and complete each other; they are never alternatives.

All the Python scripts and fragments of code presented in the following chapters assume that both libraries have been loaded with the following instructions, which should appear as the first ones to be executed:

```
import numpy as np
import pandas as pd
```

1.3   Advanced Plain Text Editor

Another very useful, almost necessary, tool is an ***advanced plain text editor***. We will often need to inspect a dataset, which is a file containing data, whose format in our case is almost always a tabular text. We will use proprietary formats only to show how to use Microsoft Excel datasets, which are common for very small datasets, but many other proprietary formats exist and have specific ways to be accessed. However, in our reference environments, the standard format for datasets is the text file, and we will focus on it.

Text files could be opened with many common tools present in the standard configurations of all platforms, from Windows *Notepad* to MacOS *Text Edit* and others. However, those are basic tools for generic text files. Inspecting a very large dataset has different requirements; we need more features, like an advanced search and replace feature, line numbers, pattern matching features, and so on. The good news is that these advanced features are supported by many *advanced plain text editors*, readily available for all platforms. Among others, two widely used are **Notepad++** (https://notepad-plus-plus.org/), only for Windows, and **Sublime Text** (https://www.sublimetext .com/download), for Windows and MacOS. But again, many others exist, and readers are encouraged to explore the different alternatives and test them before choosing one.

1.4   CSV Format for Datasets

Finally, we reach one key component of the data science arsenal with R and Python, which is the **CSV format** (comma-separated values), the gold standard for all open data. This does not mean that all open data one could find is available in CSV format, of course not, they could be offered in different formats, open or proprietary, but if there is a format for datasets that could be considered the standard, that is CSV.

The format is extremely simple and has the minimum of requirements:

- It is a tabular format composed of rows and columns.
- Each row has an equal number of values separated by a common separator symbol and ended by a return (i.e. new line).
- Columns, defined by values in the same position for each row, have the same number of elements.

That is all it needs to define a CSV. Its simplicity is its main feature, of course, making it platform- and vendor-independent, not subject to versioning, human-readable, and also efficiently processable by computational means.

Its name reminds me of the original symbol used as a separator, the ***comma***, perfectly adapted to the Anglo-Saxon convention for floating point numbers and mostly numerical data. With the diffusion to European users and textual data, the comma became problematic, being used for the numeric decimal part and often in sentences, so the ***semicolon*** appeared as an alternative separator, less frequently used, and unrelated to numbers. But again, even the semicolon might be problematic when used in sentences, so the ***tabulation*** (tab character) became another typical separator. These three are the normal ones, so to say, since there is no formal specification mandating what symbols could act as separators and that we should expect to find them used. But other uncommon symbols could be encountered, such as the vertical bar (|) and others.

Ultimately, the point is that whatever separator is used in a certain CSV dataset, we could easily recognize it, for example, by visually inspecting the text file and easily accessing the dataset correctly. So, it needs to pay attention, but the separator is never a problem.

As a convention, not a strict rule, CSV files use the extension *.csv* (e.g. *dataset1.csv*), meaning that it is a text-based, tabular dataset. When the *tab* is used as a separator, it is common to indicate it by means of the *.tsv* file extension (e.g. *dataset2.tsv*), which is just good practice and a kind way to inform a user that tab characters have been placed in the dataset. In case they are not very evident at first sight, expect to also find datasets using tabs as separators named with the *.csv* extension.

Ambiguous cases arise anyway. A real example is shown in the fragment of Figure 1.3. This is a real dataset with information about countries, a type of widely common information. Countries have official denominations that have to be respected, especially in works with a certain degree of formality. If you look closely, you will notice something strange about the *Democratic Republic of the Congo.*

The name is written differently in order to maintain the coherence of the alphabetic order, so it became *Congo, Democratic Republic of the*. Fine for what concerns the order, but it complicates things for the CSV syntax because now the comma after *Congo* is part of the official name. It cannot be omitted or replaced with another symbol; that is the official name when the alphabetic order must be preserved. But commas also act as separators in this CSV, and now they are no longer unambiguously defined as separators.

How can we resolve this problem? We have already excluded the possibility of arbitrarily changing the denomination of the country, that is not possible. Could we replace all the commas as separators with another symbol, like a semicolon, for example? In theory yes, we could, but in practice, it might be much more complicated than a simple replacement because there could be other cases like *Congo, Democratic Republic of the,* and for all of them, the comma in the name should not be replaced. It is not that easy to make sure to not introduce further errors.

Looking at Figure 1.3, we see the standard solution for this case – *double quotes have been used to enclose the textual content with the same symbol used as a separator* (comma, in this case). This tells the function reading the CSV to consider the whole text within double quotes as a single element value and ignore the presence of symbols used as separators. *Single quotes* work fine too unless they are used as apostrophes in the text.

This solution solves most cases, but not all. What if the text contains all of them, double quotes, single quotes, and commas? For example, a sentence like this: *First came John "The Hunter" Western;*

```
50  Colombia,CO,COL,170,ISO 3166-2:CO,Americas,Latin America and the Caribbean,South America,019,419,005
51  Comoros,KM,COM,174,ISO 3166-2:KM,Africa,Sub-Saharan Africa,Eastern Africa,002,202,014
52  Congo,CG,COG,178,ISO 3166-2:CG,Africa,Sub-Saharan Africa,Middle Africa,002,202,017
53  "Congo, Democratic Republic of the",CD,COD,180,ISO 3166-2:CD,Africa,Sub-Saharan Africa,Middle Africa,002,202,017
54  Cook Islands,CK,COK,184,ISO 3166-2:CK,Oceania,Polynesia,"",009,061,""
55  Costa Rica,CR,CRI,188,ISO 3166-2:CR,Americas,Latin America and the Caribbean,Central America,019,419,013
56  Côte d'Ivoire,CI,CIV,384,ISO 3166-2:CI,Africa,Sub-Saharan Africa,Western Africa,002,202,011
```

Figure 1.3 Ambiguity between textual character and separator symbol

then his friend Bill li'l Rat Thompson, followed by the dog Sausage. How could we possibly put this in a CSV in a way that it is recognized as a unique value? There is a comma and a semicolon; single or double quotes do not help in this case because they are part of the sentence. We might replace all commas as separators with tabs or other symbols, but as already said, it could be risky and difficult.

There is a universal solution called ***escaping***, which makes use of the ***escape symbol***, which typically is the ***backslash*** (\). The escape symbol is interpreted as having a special meaning, which is *to consider the following character just literally, destitute of any syntactical meaning*, such as a separator symbol or any other meaning. Thus, our sentence could be put into a CSV and considered as a single value again by using double quotes, but being careful to escape the double quotes inside the sentence: "First came John \"The Hunter\" Western; then his friend Bill li'l Rat Thompson, followed by the dog Sausage." This way, the CSV syntax is unambiguous.

Finally, what if the textual value contains a backslash? For example: *The sentient AI wrote "Hi Donna, be ready, it will be a bumpy ride," and then executed \start.*

We know we have to escape the double quotes, but what about the backslash that will be interpreted as an escape symbol? *Escape the escape symbol,* so it will be interpreted literally: "The sentient AI wrote \"Hi, Donna, be ready, it will be a long ride\" and then executed \\start." Using single quotes, we do not need to escape double quotes in this case: 'The sentient AI wrote, "Hi, Donna, be ready, it will be a long ride" and then executed \\start.'

Questions

1.1 (R/Python)
CSV is ...
A A proprietary data format, human-readable
B An open data format, human-readable
C A proprietary format, not human-readable
D An open data format, not human-readable
(R: B)

1.2 (R/Python)
A CSV dataset has ...
A A tabular data organization
B A hierarchical data organization
C Metadata for general information
D An index
(R: A)

1.3 (R/Python)
A valid CSV dataset has ...
A No value with spaces
B Possibly different separators
C No missing value
D Equal number of elements for each row
(R: D)

1.4 (R/Python)
Which are considered legitimate separators in a CSV dataset?

A Only comma, semicolon, and tab

B Only comma and semicolon

C Comma, semicolon, and tab are the most typical, but other symbols are possible (e.g. pipe, dash)

D All sorts of characters, symbols, or strings

(R: C)

1.5 (R/Python)

What is the usage case for quotes and double quotes in a CSV dataset?

A There is no usage case for them

B As separators

C As commonly used symbols in strings

D To embrace an element value containing the same symbol used as separator

(R: D)

1.6 (R/Python)

What is the *escape* character?

A It is quotes or double quotes

B It is the separator symbol

C It is the symbol used to specify that the following character/symbol should be considered at face value, not interpreted as having a special meaning

D It is the symbol used to specify that the following word should be considered at face value, not interpreted as having a special meaning

(R: C)

2

Simple Exploratory Data Analysis

Having read a dataset, the first activity usually made afterward is to figure out the main characteristics of those data and make sense of them. This means understanding the organization of the data, their types, and some initial information on their values. For data of numerical type, simple statistical information can be obtained; these are usually called **descriptive statistics** and often include basic information like the arithmetic mean, the median, maximum and minimum values, and quartiles. Clearly, other, more detailed statistical information could be easily obtained from a series of numerical values.

This activity is often called *simple exploratory data analysis*, where the adjective "simple" distinguishes this basic and quick analysis performed to grasp the main features of a dataset with respect to thorough exploratory data analyses performed with more sophisticated statistical tools and methods.

However, the few requirements of this initial approach to a new dataset should not be erroneously considered unimportant. On the contrary, basic descriptive statistics offered by common tools may reveal important features of a dataset that could help decide how to proceed, show the presence of anomalous values, or indicate specific data wrangling operations to execute. It is important to dedicate attention to the information provided by a simple exploratory data analysis. Real datasets are typically too large to be visually inspected; therefore, in order to start collecting some information about the data, tools are needed, and descriptive statistics are the first among them.

R and Python offer common functionalities to obtain descriptive statistics together with other **utility functions**, which allow getting information on a dataset, from its size to the unique values of a column/variable, names, indexes, and so forth. These are simple but essential features and familiarity with them should be acquired.

Before presenting the first list of these functions, all of them will be used in the numerous examples that will follow throughout the book. Another very relevant issue is introduced – the *almost inevitable presence of missing values*.

2.1   Missing Values Analysis

Missing values are literally what their name means – some elements of a dataset may have no value. This must be understood literally, not metaphorically – a missing value is *the absence of value*, not a value with an undefined meaning like a space, a tab, some symbols like ?, ---, or *, or something like the string "Unknown," "Undefined," and the like. All these cases are not missing values; they are actual values with a possibly undefined meaning.

Data Science Fundamentals with R, Python, and Open Data, First Edition. Marco Cremonini.
© 2024 John Wiley & Sons, Inc. Published 2024 by John Wiley & Sons, Inc.
Companion website: www.wiley.com/go/DSFRPythonOpenData

Missing values are very common in real datasets to the point that it is a much safer assumption to expect their presence than the opposite. The absence of values may happen for a number of reasons, from a sensor that failed to take a measurement to an observer that failed to collect a certain data point. Errors of any sort may result in missing values, or they might be just the expected result of a certain data collection process, for example, a dataset reporting road incident may have values only if there has been at least one incident on a certain road in the reference period of time; otherwise, the element remains empty. Many other reasons for the presence of missing values could be envisioned. The important point when dealing with real datasets is *not to exclude the presence of missing values. That could lead to severe errors if missing values are unaccounted for. For this reason, the presence of missing values must always be carefully verified, and appropriate actions for dealing with them are decided on a case-by-case basis.*

We will dedicate a specific section in the following chapter on the tools and methods to analyze and manage missing values in R and Python. Here, it is important to get the fact that they are important to analyze, and their presence forces us to decide what to do with them. There is no general recipe to apply, it has to be decided on a case-by-case basis.

Once we have ascertained that missing values are present in a dataset, we should gather more information about them – where are they? (in which columns/variables, rows/observations), and how many are they? Special functions will assist us in answering these questions, but then it will be our turn to evaluate how to proceed. Three general alternatives typically lie in front of us:

1. Write an actual value for elements with missing values.
2. Delete rows/observations or columns/variables with missing values.
3. Do not modify the data and handle missing values explicitly in each operation.

For the first one, the obvious problem is to decide what value should be written in place of the missing values. In the example of the road incidents dataset, *if we know for sure* that when a road reports zero incidents, the corresponding element has no value, we may reasonably think to write zero in place of missing values. The criterion is correct, given the fact that we know for sure how values are inserted. Is there any possible negative consequence? Is it possible that we are arbitrarily and mistakenly modifying some data? Maybe. What if a missing value was instead present because there was an error in reporting or entering the data? We are setting zero for incidents on a certain road when the true value would have been a certain number, possibly a relevant one. Is the fact of having replaced the missing value with a number a better or worse situation than having kept the original missing value? This is something we should think about and decide.

Similar is the second alternative. If we omit rows or columns with *all missing values in their elements*, then we are likely simplifying the data without any particular alteration. But what if, as it is much more common, a certain row or column has only *some elements with missing values* and others with valid values? When we omit that row or column, we are omitting the valid values too, so we are definitely altering the data. Is that alteration relevant to our analysis? Did we clearly understand the consequences? Again, these are questions we should think about and decide on a case-by-case basis because it would depend on the specific context and data and the particular analysis we are carrying out.

So, is the third alternative always the best one? Again, it depends. With that option, we have the burden of dealing with missing values at every operation we perform on data. Functions will get a little complicated, the logic could also become somehow more complicated, chances of making mistakes increase with the increased complications, time increases, the level of attention should be higher, and so forth. It is a trade-off, meaning there is no general recipe; we have to think about it and decide. But yes, the third alternative is the safest in general; the data are not modified, which is always a golden rule, but even being the safest, it does not guarantee to avoid errors.

2.2   R: Descriptive Statistics and Utility Functions

Table 2.1 lists some of the main R utility functions to gather descriptive statistics and other general information on data frames.

It is useful to familiarize yourself with these functions and, without anticipating how to read datasets, which is the subject of the next chapter, predefined data frames made available by base R and several packages are helpful for exercising. For example, package *datasets* are installed with the base R configuration and contain small didactic datasets, most of them being around for quite a long time. It was a somewhat vintage-style experience to use those data, to be honest.

Additional packages, for example, those installed with *tidyverse*, often contain didactic datasets and are usually definitely more recent than those from package *datasets*. For example, readers affectionate to classical sci-fi might appreciate dataset *starwars* included in package *dplyr*, with data about the Star Wars saga's characters. It is a nice dataset for exercising. For other options, exists command **data()** to be executed on the RStudio console. It produces the list of predefined datasets contained in all *loaded* packages (pay attention to this, it is not sufficient to have the package installed, it has to be loaded with **library()**).

Table 2.1   R utility functions.

Function	Description
summary()	It is the main function for collecting simple descriptive statistics on data frame columns. For each column, it returns the data type (numerical, character, and logical). For numerical columns, it adds maximum and minimum values, mean and median, 1st and 3rd quartiles, and if present, the number of missing values.
str() glimpse()	They are equivalent in practice, with str() defined in package *utils* of R base configuration and glimpse() defined in package *dplyr*, included in *tidyverse*. They provide a synthetic representation of information on a data frame, like its size, column names, types, and values of the first elements.
head() tail()	They are among the most basic R functions and allow visualizing the few topmost (*head*) or bottommost (*tail*) rows of a command output. For example, we will often use head() to watch the first rows of a data frame and its header with column names. It is possible to specify the number of rows to show (e.g. head(10)); otherwise, the default applies (i.e. six rows).
View() view()	Basically, the same and, when package *tibble*, included in *tidyverse*, is loaded, the first is an alias of the second. They visualize a data frame and other structured data like lists by launching the native RStudio viewer, which offers a graphical spreadsheet-style representation and few features. It is useful for small data frames, but it becomes quickly unusable when the size increases.
unique()	It returns the list of unique values in a series. Particularly useful when applied to columns as unique(df$col_name).
names()	It returns column names of a data frame with *names(df)* and variable names with lists. It is particularly useful.
class()	It returns the data type of an R object, like *numeric*, *character*, *logical*, and *data frame*.
length()	It returns the length of an R object (careful, this is not the number of characters), like the number of elements in a vector or the number of columns.
nrow() ncol()	They return, respectively, the number of rows and columns in a data frame.

To read the data of a preinstalled dataset, it suffices to write its name in the RStudio console and return or to use `View(dataset_name)`.

Here, we see an example, with dataset ***msleep*** included in package *ggplot2*, part of *tidyverse*. It contains data regarding sleep times and weights for some mammal species. More information could be obtained by accessing help online by executing **?msleep** on the RStudio console.

Below is the textual visualization on the command console.

```
library(tidyverse)

msleep

# A tibble: 83 × 11
     name          genus vore  order conse...¹ sleep...² sleep...³ sleep...⁴ awake
     <chr>         <chr> <chr> <chr> <chr>        <dbl>    <dbl>    <dbl> <dbl>
 1 Cheetah       Acin... carni Carn... lc          12.1       NA       NA    11.9
 2 Owl monkey    Aotus omni  Prim... <NA>        17          1.8      NA     7
 3 Mountain be... Aplo... herbi Rode... nt         14.4        2.4      NA     9.6
 4 Greater sho... Blar... omni  Sori... lc         14.9        2.3      0.133  9.1
 5 Cow           Bos   herbi Arti... domest...    4          0.7      0.667 20
 6 Three-toed ... Brad... herbi Pilo... <NA>       14.4        2.2      0.767  9.6
 7 Northern fu... Call... carni Carn... vu          8.7        1.4      0.383 15.3
 8 Vesper mouse  Calo... <NA>  Rode... <NA>        7          NA       NA    17
 9 Dog           Canis carni Carn... domest...   10.1        2.9      0.333 13.9
10 Roe deer      Capr... herbi Arti... lc          3          NA       NA    21
# ... with 73 more rows, 1 more variable: bodywt <dbl>, and abbreviated variable
#   names ¹conservation, ²sleep_total, ³sleep_rem, ⁴sleep_cycle
```

Here is the equivalent tabular visualization.

name	genus	vore	order	conserva-tion	sleep_ total	sleep_ rem	sleep_ cycle	awake	brainwt	bodywt
Cheetah	Acinonyx	carni	Carnivora	lc	12.1	*NA*	*NA*	11.9	*NA*	50
Owl monkey	Aotus	omni	Primates	*NA*	17.0	1.8		7.0	0.0155	0.48
Cow	Bos	herbi	Artiodactyla	domesticated	4.0	0.7	0.67	20.0	0.423	6000
...	...	...	...	...	...	...		...	...	...
Human	Homo	omni	Primates	*NA*	8.0	1.9	1.500	16.0	1.320	62
Mongoose lemur	Lemur	herbi	Primates	vu	9.5	0.9	*NA*	14.5	*NA*	1.67
African elephant	Loxodonta	herbi	Proboscidea	vu	3.3	*NA*	*NA*	20.7	5.712	6,654

From the two visualizations, a detail should be noted – some values are indicated as **NA**, which stands for **Not Available**. *It is the visual notation R uses to indicate a missing value.* It may have some variation like **<NA>**.

The meaning is that there is no value corresponding to the element. It is a user-friendly notation to make it more evident where missing values are. It does not mean that in a certain element, there is a value corresponding to the two letters **N** and **A**, **NA**. Not at all, it is a missing value, there is nothing there, a void.

Then, as is often the case, there are exceptions, but we are not anticipating them. The important thing is that the notation **NA** is just a visual help to see where missing values are.

Let us see what function **summary()** returns.

```
summary(msleep)

      name               genus              vore
 Length:83          Length:83          Length:83
 Class :character   Class :character   Class :character
 Mode  :character   Mode  :character   Mode  :character


...


 conservation        sleep_total        sleep_rem          sleep_cycle
 Length:83          Min.   : 1.90      Min.    :0.100     Min.    :0.1167
 Class :character   1st Qu.: 7.85      1st Qu.:0.900      1st Qu.:0.1833
 Mode  :character   Median :10.10      Median :1.500      Median :0.3333
                    Mean   :10.43      Mean    :1.875     Mean    :0.4396
                    3rd Qu.:13.75      3rd Qu.:2.400      3rd Qu.:0.5792
                    Max.   :19.90      Max.    :6.600     Max.    :1.5000
                                       NA's    :22        NA's    :51

...
```

The result shows the columns of data frame *msleep,* and, for each one, some information. Columns of type character show very little information; numerical columns have the descriptive statistics that we have mentioned before and, where present, the number of missing values (e.g. column *sleep_cycle, NA's: 51*).

With function **str()**, we obtain a general overview. Same with function **glimpse()**.

```
str(msleep)

tibble [83 x 11] (S3: tbl_df/tbl/data.frame)
 $ name        : chr [1:83] "Cheetah" "Owl monkey" ...
 $ genus       : chr [1:83] "Acinonyx" "Aotus" ...
 $ vore        : chr [1:83] "carni" "omni" ...
 $ order       : chr [1:83] "Carnivora" "Primates" ...
 $ conservation: chr [1:83] "lc" NA ...
 $ sleep_total : num [1:83] 12.1 17 14.4 14.9 ...
 $ sleep_rem   : num [1:83] NA 1.8 2.4 2.3 0.7 2.2 ...
 $ sleep_cycle : num [1:83] NA NA NA 0.133 0.667 ...
 $ awake       : num [1:83] 11.9 7 9.6 9.1 20 9.6 15.3 ...
 $ brainwt     : num [1:83] NA 0.0155 NA 0.00029 ...
 $ bodywt      : num [1:83] 50 0.48 1.35 0.019 600 ...
```

2.3 Python: Descriptive Statistics and Utility Functions

With Python, we have similar utility functions providing descriptive statistics and other general information about a data frame or a series. In Table 2.2, some of the main utility functions are listed.

Table 2.2 Python utility functions.

Function	Description
.describe()	Its main function is to obtain descriptive statistics. For each numerical column, it shows the number of values, maximum and minimum values, arithmetic mean and median, and quartiles.
.info()	It provides particularly useful information like the size of the data frame, and for each column its name, the type (*object* for characters, *int64* for integers, *float64* for floating point numbers, and *lgl* if logical), and the number of *non-null values* (meaning that the column length minus the number of non-null values gives the number of missing values in a column).
.head() .tail()	They visualize the topmost (*head*) or bottommost (*tail*) rows of a data frame. It is possible to specify the number of rows to show (e.g. df.head(10)); otherwise the default applies (i.e. five rows).
.unique()	It returns a list of unique values in a series. Particularly useful when applied to columns as df['col_name'].unique().
.columns .index	They return, respectively, the list of column names and the list of names of the row index. Column names are formally the names of the column index, and both the row and the column index may have multi-index names.
.dtypes	It returns the list of columns with the corresponding data type. The same information is included in those returned by .info().
.size	It returns the length of a Python object, such as the number of elements in an array or a data frame. If missing values are present, they are included in the total length.
.shape	It returns the number of rows and columns of a data frame. To retrieve a single dimension, it could be referenced as .shape(0) for the number of rows, and .shape(1) for the number of columns.

In the standard configuration of Python and of its typical data science libraries, there are no predefined datasets to use for exercising.

Pandas versions *previous to 2.0.0* make it possible to create test data frames with random values by means of functions **pd.util.testing.makeMixedDataFrame()** and **pd.util.testing.makeMissingDataframe()**. With the first one, a small and very simple data frame is produced, and the second produces a little larger data frame with also missing values.

To try the utility functions before reading actual datasets, we could try the two generating functions, save the result, and test the utility functions.

```
test1= pd.util.testing.makeMixedDataFrame()
test1
     A    B     C          D
0  0.0  0.0  foo1  2009-01-01
1  1.0  1.0  foo2  2009-01-02
2  2.0  0.0  foo3  2009-01-05
3  3.0  1.0  foo4  2009-01-06
4  4.0  0.0  foo5  2009-01-07
```

```
test2= pd.util.testing.makeMissingDataframe()
test2
                 A         B         C         D
tW1QQvy0vf  0.451947  0.595209  0.233377       NaN
UCIUoAMHgo -1.627037 -1.116419 -0.393027  0.188878
SCc6D4RLxc  0.077580 -0.884746  0.688926  1.475203
OgTyFDzQli -0.125091 -0.533044  0.847568 -0.110436
InfV0yg8IH  0.575489       NaN -0.070264 -0.928023
SOo4brfQXb -0.965100 -1.368942 -0.358428  0.487762
CDmeMkic4o -0.348701 -0.427534  1.636490 -1.444168
OCi7RQZXaB  1.271422  1.216927 -0.232399 -0.985385
XEQvFbfp0X  0.207598       NaN -0.417492 -0.087897
UBt6uuJrsi -0.571392 -2.824272  0.200751 -0.778646
XPQTn1MN1N  0.725473  0.554177  1.520446  0.599409
saxiRCPV8f -0.351244  1.338322 -0.514414 -0.333148
```

The two results, data frames *test1* and *test2,* could be inspected with the functions we have presented; particular attention should be paid to the number of columns of *test2* (four, not five, as could be mistakenly believed at first sight) and the index, which has no name but several values (e.g. *tW1QQvy0vf*, *UCIUoAMHgo*, and *SCc6D4RLxc*). The unique() method in this case will not be useful because values, being random, are likely all different; it is better to use it only on *test1*.

It is to be observed that the notation used by Python to visually represent the missing values in *test2* is **NaN**, which stands for **Not a Number**. This may induce one to think that there should be different representations for the different data types. Luckily, this is not the case, so we will still see **NaN** even when missing values are in an *object* (character) or *logical* (Boolean) column. We may see **NaT** (*Not a Time*) for missing values in *datetime* column, but **NaN** and **NaT** are fully compatible, so we should not worry too much. Python provides a more general keyword for missing values – **None**, which does not carry the heritage of **NaN** as a numeric data type. Strictly speaking, **NaN** should be used for numerical data types, while **None** for nonnumerical ones; however, in practice, they have become much like equivalent notations, and especially when using pandas, **NaN** is the default for all missing values. In short, **NaN** is fine, it could be **None** too.

In the newer Pandas version 2.0.0+, the two functions for testing have been deprecated and are no longer available in the official *testing* module. It is still possible to use them by accessing the internal _*testing* module, such as – test= pd._testing.makeMixedDataFrame().

This could easily change in future versions of pandas; therefore, it might be better to be patient a little longer and test the utility functions on real datasets when, in the next chapter, we will learn how to read them.

Questions

2.1   (R/Python)

A Simple exploratory data analysis is ...

A Needed when a thorough statistical analysis is required

B Sometimes useful

C Always useful to gather general information about the data

D Always useful and specific to the expected result of the project

(R: C)

2.2 (R/Python)

Descriptive statistics ...

A Require good statistical knowledge

B Is the synonym for full statistical analysis

C Performed with specific statistical tools

D Require just basic statistical knowledge

(R: D)

2.3 (R/Python)

Missing values analysis is ...

A Needed when a thorough statistical analysis is required

B Sometimes useful

C Always useful to gather general information about the data

D Always useful and specific to the expected result of the project

(R: C)

2.4 (R/Python)

Missing values should be managed...

A By replacing them with actual values

B By replacing them with actual values, deleting corresponding observations, or case-by-case basis

C By deleting corresponding observations

D Do not care, they are irrelevant

(R: B)

2.5 (R/Python)

When handling missing values, what is the most important aspect to consider?

A Arbitrarily modifying data (either by replacing missing values or deleting corresponding observations) is a critical operation to perform, requiring extreme care for the possible consequences

B Being sure to replace them with true values

C Being sure not to delete observations without missing values

D There are no important aspects to consider

(R: A)

2.6 (R/Python)

What is the typical usage case for *head* and *tail* functions/methods?

A To extract the first few or the last few rows of a data frame

B To sort values in ascending or descending order

C To check the first few or the last few rows of a dataset

D To visually inspect the first few or the last few rows of a data frame

(R: D)

2.7 (R/Python)

What is the typical usage case for the *unique* function/method?

A To select unique values from a data frame

B To sort unique values in ascending or descending order

C To show the unique values of a column/variable

D To check the first few or the last few unique values of a data frame

(R: C)

2.8 **(R/Python)**

The notations NA (R) or NaN (Python) for missing values mean that ...

A A missing value is represented by the string NA (R) or NaN (Python)

B They are formal notations, but an element with a missing value has no value at all

C They are functions for handling missing values

D They are special kinds of missing values

(R: B)

3

Data Organization and First Data Frame Operations

Tabular data could be organized in different forms, with rows, columns, and values associated with information of various natures and carrying different meanings. Often, a specific organization of data is chosen to enhance readability; in other cases, it merely reflects characteristics of the data source or the data ingestion process (e.g. an automatic measurement process, an online data stream, a manual data entry), or it is functional for a certain transformation, computation, or visualization to be executed.

There exists a particular organization of data called *tidy* that is typically considered the reference model to be rational and suitable for further manipulations with computational or analytical tools. It has three main characteristics:

- Each **row** represents a single observation of the phenomenon.
- Each **column** represents a specific property (also called *variable*) of the phenomenon.
- Each **value** represents a single information rather than an aggregate.

For example, consider datasets with personal information on students enrolled in courses or employees working at a certain office. Each row would likely correspond to a single individual (*observation*), with columns representing relevant information (*variables*) for the specific context for which data have been produced. Values would carry single information like the initial name, the middle name or the surname, place of birth, birth date, and so on, each one associated with a distinct column rather than being glued together. This, in short, is the logic governing the data organization called *tidy*.

Tip

Regarding *date* and *time*, it would be possible to object that they are combinations of multiple information, not single, atomic information. Therefore, following the logic of a tidy data organization, they should be decomposed into day, month, and year for the date, and hour, minutes, and seconds for time.

In theory, that would be logically correct, but in practice, it is not the usual way to handle them because dates and times are considered atomic information, although of a special kind. The reason is that decomposing date and time into their parts makes it a lot more complicated to perform simple operations on them, such as finding the number of days between two dates, summing up two times, and so on. Dates and times are then considered as single information and they always have dedicated functions for operating on them.

Data Science Fundamentals with R, Python, and Open Data, First Edition. Marco Cremonini.
© 2024 John Wiley & Sons, Inc. Published 2024 by John Wiley & Sons, Inc.
Companion website: www.wiley.com/go/DSFRPythonOpenData

Untidy data organizations exhibit variations over the tidy model, such as:

- *Multiple information* combined into values (e.g. product codes, lists).
- *Columns as specific values* of a certain feature instead of the general feature; typical cases are time periods (e.g. years, months), names (e.g. brand names), components (e.g. ingredients, modules), and so on.
- *Rows as multiple observations*: examples are the same as the previous point; for example, if years are represented as different columns, the corresponding rows represent multiple observations of a certain characteristic repeated for all column years.

Many other variants are possible. It is important to highlight, however, that untidy organizations of data do not imply that they are somehow wrong or worse than tidy ones. Which data organization is better suited depends on the operations we are planning to perform on data, the expected results, and the recipients of those data. The data organization is the analyst's choice, and because it is context-dependent, it should be possible to efficiently modify it when needed or convenient for the goals of analysis. We will often use both tidy and untidy data frames, for good reasons.

In this chapter, we consider some of the most basic data wrangling operations, first focusing on columns:

- How to read a CSV dataset.
- How to select data frame columns.
- How to rename and relocate them.
- The standard mechanisms for creation and deletion.
- How to split column values into different columns and how to join separate columns into one.

Datasets

IBM HR Analytics Employee Attrition & Performance is available through the Kaggle platform. Data once produced by IBM for educational purposes regarding fictitious employees with typical human resources information. Accessed April 21, 2023. *Copyright*: Database Contents License (DbCL) v1.0. (https://opendatacommons.org/licenses/dbcl/1-0/).

Youth Behavior Risk Survey (YBRS) (High School), from the NYC Open Data, https://data .cityofnewyork.us/Health/Youth-Behavior-Risk-Survey-High-School-/3qty-g4aq. Accessed April 21, 2023. *Copyright*: NYC Open Data, Open Data Law (https://opendata.cityofnewyork.us/open-data-law/).

Air Data: Air Quality Data Collected at Outdoor Monitors Across the US, EPA – United States Environmental Protection Agency https://aqs.epa.gov/aqsweb/airdata/download_files.html. Data are referred to Particulates – PM2.5 FRM/FEM Mass (88101), Year 2022, https://aqs.epa.gov/aqsweb/ airdata/daily_88101_2022.zip. Accessed May 5, 2023. *Copyright*: Public domain (https://edg.epa .gov/epa_data_license.html)

3.1 R: Read CSV Datasets and Column Selection

We start by reading the dataset *IBM HR Analytics Employee Attrition & Performance*. First, we load the *tidyverse* library, as we always assume to do in this book, then we read the dataset into data frame *df* and look at some properties and descriptive statistics. Below is an extract of the first columns and rows.

```
library(tidyverse)
df= read_csv("datasets/IBM_Kaggle/WA_Fn-UseC_-HR-Employee-Attrition.csv")
```

Age	Attrition	BusinessTravel	Daily Rate	Department	Distance From Home	Education	Education Field
41	Yes	Travel_Rarely	1102	Sales	1	2	Life Sciences
49	No	Travel_Frequently	279	Research & Development	8	1	Life Sciences
37	Yes	Travel_Rarely	1373	Research & Development	2	2	Other
33	No	Travel_Frequently	1392	Research & Development	3	4	Life Sciences
27	No	Travel_Rarely	591	Research & Development	2	1	Medical
32	No	Travel_Frequently	1005	Research & Development	2	2	Life Sciences
59	No	Travel_Rarely	1324	Research & Development	3	3	Medical
30	No	Travel_Rarely	1358	Research & Development	24	1	Life Sciences
38	No	Travel_Frequently	216	Research & Development	23	3	Life Sciences
36	No	Travel_Rarely	1299	Research & Development	27	3	Medical

With utility functions `glimpse()` and `summary()`, we can obtain some information and simple statistics.

```
glimpse(df)
Rows: 1,470
Columns: 35
$ Ag               <dbl> 41, 49, 37, 33, 27, 32, 59, 30, 38, 36, 35, 2ı
$ Attrition        <chr> "Yes", "No", "Yes", "No", "No", "No", "No", "…
$ BusinessTravel   <chr> "Travel_Rarely", "Travel_Frequently", "Travel…
$ DailyRate        <dbl> 1102, 279, 1373, 1392, 591, 1005, 1324, 1358,…
$ Department       <chr> "Sales", "Research & Development", "Research …
$ DistanceFromHome <dbl> 1, 8, 2, 3, 2, 2, 3, 24, 23, 27, 16, 15, 26, …
$ Education        <dbl> 2, 1, 2, 4, 1, 2, 3, 1, 3, 3, 3, 2, 1, 2, 3, …
$ EducationField   <chr> "Life Sciences", "Life Sciences", "Other", "L…
…
```

```
summary(df)
      Age            DailyRate       DistanceFromHome    Education
 Min.   :18.00   Min.   : 102.0   Min.   : 1.000    Min.   :1.000
 1st Qu.:30.00   1st Qu.: 465.0   1st Qu.: 2.000    1st Qu.:2.000
 Median :36.00   Median : 802.0   Median : 7.000    Median :3.000
 Mean   :36.92   Mean   : 802.5   Mean   : 9.193    Mean   :2.913
 3rd Qu.:43.00   3rd Qu.:1157.0   3rd Qu.:14.000    3rd Qu.:4.000
 Max.   :60.00   Max.   :1499.0   Max.   :29.000    Max.   :5.000
…
```

From data frame characteristics, we now know that it has 1470 rows (observations) and 35 columns (variables). We also know columns' data types, with **dbl** for *double*, meaning a numerical data type, and **chr** for *character*, meaning strings possibly composed of alphabetic characters, digits, symbols, and punctuation. Looking at descriptive statistics, we mostly learn information about numeric columns. For example, we know that the minimum and maximum employees' ages are 18 and 60, and the median and mean age are 36 and 36.92, which is quite close, we may assume an age distribution is not much different from a normal distribution, just a little skewed toward older ages, with 50% of employees (difference between third and first quartile) between 30 and 43 years old.

With regard to the meaning of column values, when column names are not self-explanatory, the supplementary documentation provided together with a dataset should be consulted. This is often the case with datasets from public and governmental agencies, international organizations, or derived from large surveys, which typically adopt naming conventions and code names for variables.

3.1.1 Reading a CSV Dataset

Reading a comma separated values (CSV) dataset is so similar between R and Python that it makes sense to show both cases together. The main function is `read_csv()` in both environments. For R, the function is defined in *readr* package, which is part of *tidyverse*, while for Python, it is included in package *pandas*. The syntax is the following:

- R: `read_csv('path and file name', optional attributes)`
- Python: `pd.read_csv('path and file name', optional attributes)`

The execution will visualize the tabular content of the CSV dataset, *without creating an R or a Python object*. To make use of the data in subsequent operations, the result of the `read_csv()` function should be assigned to a variable. For example, we may instantiate variable *df1* (the choice of the name is free, as for every variable):

- R: `df1 = read_csv('path and file name', optional attributes)`
- Python: `df1 = pd.read_csv('path and file name', optional attributes)`

Object *df1*will be, in both cases, of type *data.frame*, with a content equivalent to the CSV dataset. Therefore, it is called *dataset,* the actual file containing data, and *data frame,* the object, R or Python, instantiated after reading the dataset. With R, we have some alternative notations for assigning a value to a variable, while with Python, the equal symbol (=) is the standard syntax. Listed below are the equivalent R notations:

- `VARIABLE = value`
- `VARIABLE <- value`
- `value -> VARIABLE`

So, reading a CSV dataset is generally easy, provided that the notion of CSV *separator*, as presented in previous chapter, is well understood, because a CSV dataset is read correctly *only if* the correct separator is specified. A typical error is trying to read a dataset with the wrong separator, a case that may easily confuse the user, especially a beginner. With a little practice, that would not be a hassle, just a minuscule nuisance.

As we already know from previous chapter, a CSV dataset may adopt different separator symbols with *comma* being the most common, *semicolon* being very common, *tabulation* being less common but not rare, and possibly other symbols like the *vertical bar*. The only rule is that for each CSV dataset, the separator adopted is unique. When a CSV dataset is read, you should tell R or Python which symbol to consider as the separator. The default is always the comma.

With R (*readr* package, suggested for use), we receive some help because, while it provides a generic function called `read_delim()` that requires explicitly stating which symbol is the separator (attribute `delim`), it also offers special versions that already have configured a certain separator, namely:

- *comma:* `read_csv('file.csv')`
- *semicolon:* `read_csv2('file.csv')`
- *tabulation:* `read_tsv('file.csv')`

These are particularly handy since almost always you have to choose between those three separators; exceptions are very rare.

Base R has similar functions called `read.csv()`, `read.csv2()`, and `read.delim()`, with only one difference, `read.delim()` has tabulation preconfigured as the separator, but all of them provide attribute `sep` to specify a different separator symbol. The other differences between read functions from *readr* and from base R are that the former produces a *tibble* data frame, which is still an ordinary data frame type but with some more information visualized, while the latter produces standard data frames. Also, they transform differently column names composed only by digits (e.g. years) or including spaces; *readr* read functions keep the original name embraced by backticks (e.g. `'2024'`, `'Product Code'`), so to consider them as strings, while base R read functions add an X as prefix to names composed by digits (e.g. X2024) and replace spaces with points (e.g. Product.Code). These are small differences that should be noticed though.

Python, instead, does not provide alternatives to `pd.read_csv()` and offers attribute `sep` to specify separators different than the comma, as follows:

- *comma:* `pd.read_csv('file.csv')`
- *semicolon:* `pd.read_csv('file.csv', sep=';')`
- *tabulation:* `pd.read_csv('file.csv', sep='\t')`
- *vertical bar:* `pd.read_csv('file.csv', sep='|')`

3.1.1.1 Reading Errors

Making errors in reading CSV dataset is very common for beginners; usually, they are trivial, but you should learn to recognize and fix them. More tricky errors would depend on something odd within the organization of the dataset, which requires directly inspecting the dataset and figuring out what is not compliant with CSV syntax. There could be many sources of this kind of error, from incompatible charsets (an old story coming from competing standards in defining charsets), spurious rows (e.g. titles or others due to CSV produced by some tools), to missing, misplaced, or incoherent quotes (as we discussed in previous chapters).

However, excluding problems of the data syntax or organization (unfortunately not rare), more frequently you will see errors due to two reasons:

- The path or file name is wrong (i.e. misspelled, incorrectly defined, or the file is missing).
- The separator used in read function does not correspond to the one in the dataset.

If the error is due to a *wrong path or file name*, the read function always produces a blocking error (unless you involuntarily read a different dataset), so you know there is something wrong and you need to fix it. Both R and Python interactive development environments (IDEs) allow using relative file names, provided the correct working directory is set, which eases the specification of the dataset file. The same for the *tab autocomplete* feature, which lets you navigate the file system and select a file by pressing the *tab* key (in order to use it, you must write the read function and the quotes without the file name, then move the cursor between the quotes and press tab).

The error raised when the file name is wrong is easily understandable and very typical, such as:

- R: *Error: 'file1.csv' does not exist in current working directory*
- Python: *FileNotFoundError: [Errno 2] No such file or directory: 'file1.csv'*

Different is the case of the *wrong separator*. In this case, both R and Python do not raise a blocking error, on the contrary, they do not raise any error because formally there is nothing wrong; the dataset has been read, just not in the correct way for using its data. This is why beginners get confused; they do not see errors on the console, so they assume everything is fine. You should always look at the result of an instruction and see if it makes sense or not, regardless of whether an error has been raised. This is a general rule of thumb: it never suffices to look at the console for errors, you should look at the actual result and judge its correctness.

Let's see an example by reading dataset *IBM HR Analytics Employee Attrition & Performance* with a wrong separator, semicolon rather than comma. First with R's read_csv2().

There is no error raised, but look at the result. The first row is *Rows: 1470 Columns: 1*, saying that the dataset apparently has 1470 rows but just one column. Below it reminds that the semicolon has been specified as the separator. This should be immediately recognized as very suspicious; it is very unlikely that a dataset has a single column, much more likely is that we have mistaken the separator. But, read the name of that seemingly unique column:

Age,Attrition,BusinessTravel,DailyRate,Department,DistanceFromHome,Education,Education Field,EmployeeCount...

Again, it should be immediately evident that something is odd, that cannot be the name of a column; instead, it is several column names glued together. By looking at how data are visualized, we don't see a tabular representation but something strange with values, again pasted together. This is why with a little practice you should be able to immediately recognize that the separator was wrong and fix it.

```
library(tidyverse)
read_csv2('datasets/IBM_Kaggle/WA_Fn-UseC_-HR-Employee-Attrition.csv')

Rows: 1470 Columns: 1
Delimiter: ";"
(1):Age,Attrition,BusinessTravel,DailyRate,Department,DistanceFromHome,
Education,EducationField,EmployeeCount,EmployeeNumber, ...

# A tibble: 1,470 × 1
Age,Attrition,BusinessTravel,DailyRate,Department,DistanceFromHome,
Education,EducationField,EmployeeCount,EmployeeNumber,...
   <chr>
1 41,Yes,Travel_Rarely,1102,Sales,1,2,Life Sciences,1,1,2,Female,94,3,2,
Sales Executive,4,Single,5993,19479,8,Y,Yes,11,3,1,8...
2 49,No,Travel_Frequently,279,R & D,8,1,Life Sciences,1,2,3,Male,61,2,2,
Research Scientist,2,Married,5130,2...
...
# ... with 1468 more rows,
```

With Python, it is the same. If we run the same example by using pd.read_csv() with sep=';', once again, no syntax error is raised, but looking at the result, it is evident that something is wrong because what we see is very different from what we expected, titles and values are glued together without a clear tabular organization.

```
import pandas as pd
pd.read_csv("datasets/IBM_Kaggle/WA_Fn-UseC_-HR-Employee-Attrition.csv", sep=';')
```

> **Tip**
>
> In R, a package called *vroom* has been developed providing advanced functionalities for reading tabular data. We will use it, for example, to read a CSV dataset directly from a zip-compressed file. The function is just `vroom()` and, as a feature, automatically guesses the separator among a predefined list (i.e. `c(",", "\t", " ", "|", ":", ";")`); therefore, it is truly exceptional the necessity to explicitly specify the separator by using vroom. Very handy, indeed.
>
> *But* if you are a beginner and are tempted to conclude that by using vroom you can just forget everything said about the correct choice of the separator presented so far, you are making a mistake because, as a beginner, it is much more valuable to learn the basics than figuring out a shortcut. Don't take the shortcut, practice with the more traditional reading functions, make errors, fix them, and learn the logic. Then you may decide to use vroom or anything like it for whatever functionality. This is the best path to learn the fundamentals of data science.

3.1.2 Selection by Column Name

Data frame *df* of our example has 35 columns, and we do not want to work with a data frame with so many columns if we are interested in just some of them for our analysis. The reason is practical, for better visualization of the results of our data wrangling operations and reduced chances of mistakes or confusion, all enhanced in the presence of excessive redundant information.

For example, let us assume to be interested in just *Attrition*, *Department*, *Gender*, and *MonthlyIncome*. We want to select this subset of columns from the *df* data frame and make it our new working data frame. For this, the easiest way to do is to use one of the most useful functions offered to us by loading the *tidyverse* library: `select()`, defined in the ***dplyr*** library, part of *tidyverse*.

Basic usage of function `select()` is easy: the data frame to use as data is specified, followed by the list of column names to select, comma-separated. If required, a column name could be specified enclosed in *single* or *double quotes*, with *backticks* when it contains reserved or illegal characters (e.g. a column name starting with a digit). Let us see an example.

```
select(df, Attrition, Department, Gender, MonthlyIncome)
```

Attrition	Department	Gender	MonthlyIncome
Yes	Sales	Female	5993
No	Research & Development	Male	5130
Yes	Research & Development	Male	2090
No	Research & Development	Female	2909
No	Research & Development	Male	3468
No	Research & Development	Male	3068
No	Research & Development	Female	2670
No	Research & Development	Male	2693
No	Research & Development	Male	9526
No	Research & Development	Male	5237

Using single or double quotes around column names would have produced the same result.

This way, however, we simply visualize the result of the selection; we still do not have a new working data frame with just these four columns. Forget to save into an object. The result of an instruction's execution is one of the most frequent errors. You will probably do it several time at the beginning, and there is nothing to worry about; it is just part of the way to work with a programming language that you are learning. With a little practice, it will become natural to first visualize the result, in order to check its correctness, then to save it as an object to use later.

```
df1= select(df, Attrition, Department, Gender, MonthlyIncome)
head(df1)
# A tibble: 6 × 4
  Attrition Department                Gender MonthlyIncome
  <chr>     <chr>                     <chr>          <dbl>
1 Yes       Sales                     Female          5993
2 No        Research & Development    Male            5130
3 Yes       Research & Development    Male            2090
4 No        Research & Development    Female          2909
5 No        Research & Development    Male            3468
6 No        Research & Development    Male            3068
```

Now we have the new object *df1*, of data frame type, containing our selection.

Tip

Question: Is it possible to save the selection into object *df* itself instead of a new one?

Answer: Yes, it is. That way, the content of *df* is simply rewritten with the new content, four columns instead of 35. But is it a good idea? In general, it is not because *df* is the result of reading the original dataset, and by overwriting *df* it may happen that we are forced to read the dataset again, for example, if we want to produce a different selection of columns. Reading datasets is a computationally intensive operation, in general, that we do not want to repeat, unless strictly necessary.

    Therefore, in theory, all R objects could be reused for storing new content; whether or not it is convenient should be decided case-by-case by trading off between two conflicting requirements: On the one hand, we want to avoid an excessive proliferation of objects for all sorts of intermediate results (i.e. to reduce the possibility of errors by confusion and memory allocation), but on the other hand we do not want to be forced to rerun previous operations just because we have lost the needed intermediate results.

3.1.3 Selection by Column Index Position

In addition to the basic usage of function `select()`, some alternatives are available, starting with the selection by *column index position*, instead of by name. A column order is assumed from left to right, starting from index 1. With this convention, column selection could be specified with index position in place of names. We want to reproduce the same selection as in the previous example, and to help us identify column positions, we use the **names()** function, and from its result, we just count.

```
names(df)
 [1] "Age"                "Attrition"
 [3] "BusinessTravel"     "DailyRate"
 [5] "Department"         "DistanceFromHome"
```

```
 [7] "Education"                "EducationField"
 [9] "EmployeeCount"            "EmployeeNumber"
[11] "EnvironmentSatisfaction"  "Gender"
[13] "HourlyRate"               "JobInvolvement"
[15] "JobLevel"                 "JobRole"
[17] "JobSatisfaction"          "MaritalStatus"
[19] "MonthlyIncome"            "MonthlyRate"
[21] "NumCompaniesWorked"       "Over18"
[23] "OverTime"                 "PercentSalaryHike"
[25] "PerformanceRating"        "RelationshipSatisfaction"
[27] "StandardHours"            "StockOptionLevel"
[29] "TotalWorkingYears"        "TrainingTimesLastYear"
[31] "WorkLifeBalance"          "YearsAtCompany"
[33] "YearsInCurrentRole"       "YearsSinceLastPromotion"
[35] "YearsWithCurrManager"
```

From this, we easily figure out the index positions corresponding to columns *Attrition*, *Department*, *Gender*, and *MonthlyIncome*; they are 2, 5, 12, and 19. With this information, the selection is equivalent to the previous case.

```
select(df, 2, 5, 12, 19)
# A tibble: 1,470 × 4
   Attrition Department              Gender MonthlyIncome
   <chr>     <chr>                   <chr>          <dbl>
 1 Yes       Sales                   Female          5993
 2 No        Research & Development  Male            5130
 3 Yes       Research & Development  Male            2090
 4 No        Research & Development  Female          2909
 5 No        Research & Development  Male            3468
# ... with 1,465 more rows
```

It is also possible to mix selections by name and by index position.

```
select(df, Attrition, 5, Gender, 19)
```

3.1.4 Selection by Range

A useful alternative when columns to select are contiguous is *selection by range*, which could be specified either by names or by positions. A range of columns is specified with the first and the last one, included in the selection, separated by *colon* (:). Here, we select columns from *Attrition* to *Department*.

```
select(df, Attrition:Department)
# A tibble: 1,470 × 4
   Attrition BusinessTravel  DailyRate Department
   <chr>     <chr>               <dbl> <chr>
 1 Yes       Travel_Rarely        1102 Sales
```

```
2 No         Travel_Frequently     279 Research & Development
3 Yes        Travel_Rarely        1373 Research & Development
4 No         Travel_Frequently    1392 Research & Development
5 No         Travel_Rarely         591 Research & Development
 … with 1,465 more rows
```

Again, it is possible to mix the different selection methods; here, we use a selection by range specifying positions and two more columns, one selected by name and the other by position.

```
select(df, 2:5, Gender, 19)
# A tibble: 1,470 × 6
    Attrition BusinessTravel    DailyRate Department               Gender Monthly…¹
    <chr>     <chr>                 <dbl> <chr>                    <chr>      <dbl>
  1 Yes       Travel_Rarely          1102 Sales                    Female      5993
  2 No        Travel_Frequently       279 Research & Development Male        5130
  3 Yes       Travel_Rarely          1373 Research & Development Male        2090
  4 No        Travel_Frequently      1392 Research & Development Female      2909
  5 No        Travel_Rarely           591 Research & Development Male        3468
   … with 1,465 more rows, and abbreviated variable name ¹MonthlyIncome
```

3.1.5 Selection by Exclusion

A different useful possibility is to select columns by specifying those to be *excluded from selection*, implicitly including all the others. The syntax has the notation with *exclamation mark* (!), which formally implements a *logical negation* in the condition implicitly used for the selection. In this example, we exclude *Attrition*.

```
select(df, !Attrition)
# A tibble: 1,470 × 34
      Age Busin…¹ Daily…² Depar…³ Dista…⁴ Educa…⁵ Educa…⁶ Emplo…⁷ Emplo…⁸ Envir…⁹
    <dbl> <chr>    <dbl> <chr>    <dbl>   <dbl> <chr>     <dbl>   <dbl>   <dbl>
  1    41 Travel…   1102 Sales        1       2 Life S…       1       1       2
  2    49 Travel…    279 Resear…      8       1 Life S…       1       2       3
  3    37 Travel…   1373 Resear…      2       2 Other         1       4       4
  4    33 Travel…   1392 Resear…      3       4 Life S…       1       5       4
  5    27 Travel…    591 Resear…      2       1 Medical       1       7       1
   … with 1,465 more rows, 24 more variables: Gender <chr>, HourlyRate <dbl>,
#    JobInvolvement <dbl>, JobLevel <dbl>, JobRole <chr>, JobSatisfaction <dbl>,
#    MaritalStatus <chr>, MonthlyIncome <dbl>, MonthlyRate <dbl>,
#    NumCompaniesWorked <dbl>, Over18 <chr>, OverTime <chr>,
#    PercentSalaryHike <dbl>, PerformanceRating <dbl>,
#    RelationshipSatisfaction <dbl>, StandardHours <dbl>,
#    StockOptionLevel <dbl>, TotalWorkingYears <dbl>, …
```

The resulting data frame has 34 columns, *Attrition* is missing. Same with an index position instead of a name.

```
select(df, !2)
# A tibble: 1,470 × 34
      Age Busin…¹ Daily…² Depar…³ Dista…⁴ Educa…⁵ Educa…⁶ Emplo…⁷ Emplo…⁸ Envir…⁹
    <dbl> <chr>    <dbl> <chr>    <dbl>   <dbl> <chr>     <dbl>   <dbl>   <dbl>
```

```
1      41 Travel...   1102 Sales        1      2 Life S...   1      1      2
2      49 Travel...    279 Resear...     8      1 Life S...   1      2      3
3      37 Travel...   1373 Resear...     2      2 Other      1      4      4
4      33 Travel...   1392 Resear...     3      4 Life S...   1      5      4
5      27 Travel...    591 Resear...     2      1 Medical    1      7      1
... with 1,465 more rows, 24 more variables ...
```

Now we consider a little more complicated example: we want to select all columns *except those from Attrition to Department*, meaning that we wish to specify an *exclusion range*. Let us first try with the negation symbol before the range definition.

```
select(df, !Attrition:Department)
# A tibble: 1,470 × 31
      Age Distan...¹ Educa...² Educa...³ Emplo...⁴ Emplo...⁵ Envir...⁶ Gender Hourl...⁷ JobIn...⁸
    <dbl>    <dbl>    <dbl> <chr>    <dbl>    <dbl>    <dbl> <chr>    <dbl>    <dbl>
1      41        1        2 Life S...     1        1        2 Female      94        3
2      49        8        1 Life S...     1        2        3 Male        61        2
3      37        2        2 Other        1        4        4 Male        92        2
4      33        3        4 Life S...     1        5        4 Female      56        3
5      27        2        1 Medical      1        7        1 Male        40        3
... with 1,465 more rows, 21 more variables ...
```

The result has 31 columns and is correct; all consecutive columns from *Attrition* to *Department* have been excluded. Let us try with nonconsecutive columns; for example, we want to exclude just *Attrition* and *Department*. We try the usual way.

```
select(df, !Attrition, !Department)
# A tibble: 1,470 × 35
      Age Busin...¹ Daily...² Depar...³ Dista...⁴ Educa...⁵ Educa...⁶ Emplo...⁷ Emplo...⁸ Envir...⁹
    <dbl> <chr>    <dbl> <chr>    <dbl>    <dbl> <chr>    <dbl>    <dbl>    <dbl>
1      41 Travel...   1102 Sales        1        2 Life S...     1        1        2
2      49 Travel...    279 Resear...     8        1 Life S...     1        2        3
3      37 Travel...   1373 Resear...     2        2 Other        1        4        4
4      33 Travel...   1392 Resear...     3        4 Life S...     1        5        4
5      27 Travel...    591 Resear...     2        1 Medical      1        7        1
... with 1,465 more rows, 25 more variables ...
```

In this case, the result is *not correct*; the data frame still has 35 columns, and although the result seems different (columns *Attribution* does no longer appear after *Age*), the column order has just been reshuffled, with *Attrition* in the last position. Why is this? What did we do wrong?

As usual, there is a logical explanation for the behavior that will result perfectly clear when we discuss logical conditions. In the meantime, we could simply recognize that the syntax *select(df, !Attrition, !Department)* does not have the meaning that intuitively we would have assigned to it which is "we want to select all columns except *Attrition* **or** *Department*". The actual meaning is "we want to select all columns except *Attrition* **and** all columns except *Department*", which logically returns all columns.

To specify the correct exclusionary list of noncontiguous columns, the special **R syntax for lists** has to be used; it is simply the notation c () , with attributes a list of elements, comma separated. Let us try this way.

```
select(df, !c(Attrition, Department))
# A tibble: 1,470 × 33
     Age Busine…¹ Daily…² Dista…³ Educa…⁴ Educa…⁵ Emplo…⁶ Emplo…⁷ Envir…⁸ Gender
   <dbl> <chr>      <dbl>   <dbl>   <dbl> <chr>     <dbl>   <dbl>   <dbl> <chr>
 1    41 Travel_…    1102       1       2 Life S…       1       1       2 Female
 2    49 Travel_…     279       8       1 Life S…       1       2       3 Male
 3    37 Travel_…    1373       2       2 Other         1       4       4 Male
 4    33 Travel_…    1392       3       4 Life S…       1       5       4 Female
 5    27 Travel_…     591       2       1 Medical       1       7       1 Male
# … with 1,465 more rows, 23 more variables …
```

Now it is correct; the result has 33 columns; *Attrition* and *Department* have been excluded.

A variation of the same case is produced by using the *minus symbol* (−) instead of the exclamation mark (!). With the minus symbol, the logic proceeds by subtraction instead of negation; the difference is subtle but not negligible. A few examples will clarify the different behaviors.

First, we consider when the two notations produce the same result: with the exclusion of a single column.

```
select(df, -Attrition)
# A tibble: 1,470 × 34
     Age Busin…¹ Daily…² Depar…³ Dista…⁴ Educa…⁵ Educa…⁶ Emplo…⁷ Emplo…⁸ Envir…⁹
   <dbl> <chr>     <dbl> <chr>     <dbl>   <dbl> <chr>     <dbl>   <dbl>   <dbl>
 1    41 Travel…    1102 Sales         1       2 Life S…       1       1       2
 2    49 Travel…     279 Resear…       8       1 Life S…       1       2       3
 3    37 Travel…    1373 Resear…       2       2 Other         1       4       4
 4    33 Travel…    1392 Resear…       3       4 Life S…       1       5       4
 5    27 Travel…     591 Resear…       2       1 Medical       1       7       1
 … with 1,465 more rows, 24 more variables …
```

The result has 34 columns; *Attrition* has been excluded. Let us try with two columns, as seen before.

```
select(df, -Attrition, -Department)
# A tibble: 1,470 × 33
     Age Busine…¹ Daily…² Dista…³ Educa…⁴ Educa…⁵ Emplo…⁶ Emplo…⁷ Envir…⁸ Gender
   <dbl> <chr>      <dbl>   <dbl>   <dbl> <chr>     <dbl>   <dbl>   <dbl> <chr>
 1    41 Travel_…    1102       1       2 Life S…       1       1       2 Female
 2    49 Travel_…     279       8       1 Life S…       1       2       3 Male
 3    37 Travel_…    1373       2       2 Other         1       4       4 Male
 4    33 Travel_…    1392       3       4 Life S…       1       5       4 Female
 5    27 Travel_…     591       2       1 Medical       1       7       1 Male
# … with 1,465 more rows, 23 more variables …
```

In this case, the result is correct; with 33 columns left, *Attrition* and *Department* have been excluded with no need for the c () notation. Then, what is the logic of the selection in this case? The logic is by subtraction, as said; therefore, it equals to "we want to select all columns minus *Attrition* **and** minus *Department*".

Now we try the exclusion of a range, with the same syntax used before, with minus in place of exclamation mark.

```
select(df, -Attrition:Department)
Warning in x:y: numerical expression has 34 elements: only the first used
# A tibble: 1,470 × 5
      Age Attrition BusinessTravel    DailyRate Department
    <dbl> <chr>     <chr>                 <dbl> <chr>
1      41 Yes       Travel_Rarely          1102 Sales
2      49 No        Travel_Frequently       279 Research & Development
3      37 Yes       Travel_Rarely          1373 Research & Development
4      33 No        Travel_Frequently      1392 Research & Development
5      27 No        Travel_Rarely           591 Research & Development
  ... with 1,465 more rows
```

Again, the result is not what we expected; only the first five columns have been returned, and a warning message is produced, *"Warning: numerical expression has 34 elements: only the first used"*. What was the logic? The warning message, although a little cryptic, explains it literally: the expression defining the range of columns has 34 elements on its left side, which are all columns minus *Attrition*; therefore, only the first one, which is *Age*, has been considered in range definition. As a consequence, the expression `-Attrition:Department` has been evaluated as equal to `Age:Department`, exactly corresponding to the result.

To specify an exclusion range with the minus sign, we need *parentheses*.

```
select(df, -(Attrition:Department))
# A tibble: 1,470 × 31
      Age Distan...¹ Educa...² Educa...³ Emplo...⁴ Emplo...⁵ Envir...⁶ Gender Hourl...⁷ JobIn...⁸
    <dbl>    <dbl>    <dbl> <chr>      <dbl>    <dbl>    <dbl> <chr>     <dbl>    <dbl>
1      41        1        2 Life S...      1        1        2 Female       94        3
2      49        8        1 Life S...      1        2        3 Male         61        2
3      37        2        2 Other          1        4        4 Male         92        2
4      33        3        4 Life S...      1        5        4 Female       56        3
5      27        2        1 Medical        1        7        1 Male         40        3
  ... with 1,465 more rows, 21 more variables ...
```

3.1.6 Selection with Selection Helper

A *selection helper* is a utility function useful in column selection because it permits specifying a property, either of the name syntax or of the data organization. The main ones are:

- `everything()`: it selects *all columns*, clearly not particularly useful in selection operations, but often handy in other important contexts when we actually need to specify "all columns";
- `last_col()`: it selects *the last column*, regardless of the dimension of the data frame, which is particularly useful when the dimension has changed after some data wrangling operations, such as the creation of new columns;
- `starts_with()`, `ends_with()`, and `contains()`: these selection helpers depend on the syntax of column names and select, respectively, columns beginning with, ending with, or containing a certain pattern, expressed as a string or a regular expression. This is often useful with column names with prefixes or suffixes, or with a regular syntactic structure, as is often the case with code names.

See some examples. First, we want to exclude the last column (in this case, the negation or the minus sign produces the same result).

```
select(df, !last_col())
# A tibble: 1,470 × 34
     Age Attri...¹ Busin...² Daily...³ Depar...⁴ Dista...⁵ Educa...⁶ Educa...⁷ Emplo...⁸ Emplo...⁹
   <dbl> <chr>    <chr>       <dbl> <chr>       <dbl>   <dbl> <chr>      <dbl>    <dbl>
1     41 Yes      Travel...    1102 Sales           1       2 Life S...      1        1
2     49 No       Travel...     279 Resear...       8       1 Life S...      1        2
3     37 Yes      Travel...    1373 Resear...       2       2 Other          1        4
4     33 No       Travel...    1392 Resear...       3       4 Life S...      1        5
5     27 No       Travel...     591 Resear...       2       1 Medical        1        7
# ... with 1,465 more rows, 24 more variables ...
```

Now we want to select all columns starting with "Job" and all columns ending with "Rate".

```
select(df, starts_with("Job"), ends_with('Rate'))
```

Job Involvement	JobLevel	JobRole	Job Satisfaction	Daily Rate	Hourly Rate	Monthly Rate
3	2	Sales Executive	4	1102	94	19479
2	2	Research Scientist	2	279	61	24907
2	1	Laboratory Technician	3	1373	92	2396
3	1	Research Scientist	3	1392	56	23159
3	1	Laboratory Technician	2	591	40	16632
3	1	Laboratory Technician	4	1005	79	11864
4	1	Laboratory Technician	1	1324	81	9964
3	1	Laboratory Technician	3	1358	67	13335
2	3	Manufacturing Director	3	216	44	8787
3	2	Healthcare Representative	3	1299	94	16577

In this case, single or double quotes are needed because *Job* and *Rate* are strings; otherwise, they would have been interpreted as variable names. We will see some more examples with selection helpers when we introduce logical conditions.

3.2 R: Rename and Relocate Columns

In this section, we introduce two basic and simple operations, respectively, for changing column names and changing their position in a data frame.

Tip

Both operations are never necessary; everything could be done without renaming or relocating columns, and for this reason, they might be overlooked. Why bother with writing new column names if that is not required? It is a legit question; the answer is that it is often useful to save time and reduce errors.

Descriptive column names are perfect for presentations because they are self-explanatory, but unfortunate for data wrangling because we need to focus our attention on the correct spelling, possibly complicated by accented characters, spaces, symbols, and quotation marks. That will take time, and even more time, to fix the inevitable spelling errors we will make.

Therefore, the time spent rewriting column names to make them easy to work with is almost always largely compensated by future gains. Same, but less relevant because of the possibility to subset data frame columns, is the possibility to change column positions.

As data, we use the dataset *Youth Behavior Risk Survey (High School)* from the *New York City Open Data*, which provides a good example for renaming column names.

```
ybrs= read_csv("datasets/NYC_OpenData/
               Youth_Behavior_Risk_Survey__High_School_April2023.csv")
```

We look at the column names with function `names()`.

```
names(ybrs)
 [1] "Survey"
 [2] "Prevalence"
 [3] "Year"
 [4] "Smoked at least once past 30 days"
 [5] "Binge drinking ‡ in past 30 days"
 [6] "Drank five or more alcoholic drinks in a row in past 30 days"
 [7] "Got help from a counselor in past 12 months"
 [8] "Drinks 1 or more sodas per day in past 7 days"
 [9] "Adolescent obesity"
[10] "Physically active 60 minutes per day"
```

These names are clearly self-explanatory and perfect for a publication, but definitely not well-suited for data wrangling and scripting.

R has two simple functions for changing column names and positions: **rename()** and **relocate()** both defined in package *dplyr*, included in *tidyverse*. The syntax is as follows:

- `rename()`: use syntax *new_name = old_name* to rename selected columns, only column names are changed, neither column order nor data frame attributes are affected;
- `relocate()`: alternatively use attributes **.before** or **.after** to specify the new position of a column; if neither is specified, the column is moved to first position.

Note

As discussed before, it is not recommended to adopt a mnemonic approach to learning the fundamentals of data wrangling and, in general, programming languages. Trying to memorize all the details of functions is worthless and ineffective. With practice, you will naturally memorize several functions and their attributes, but just the most frequently used. For all other cases, the technical documentation should be consulted, being the standard R library help pages, available in RStudio, or online sources.

(Continued)

> **(Continued)**
>
> In the case of these two functions, it is not important to memorize that the correct syntax for renaming columns is *new_name = old_name* rather than the other way around or that attributes *.before* and *.after* have the initial point. These are details to check when needed, important is to learn the possibility to rename and relocate and the logic behind those operations.

We can proceed with the example of renaming and relocating columns by using the *ybrs* data frame.

> **Tip**
>
> *Good practice*: prefer short and simple names, avoid spaces, accented letters, symbols, and punctuation. The character best suited to replace spaces and other symbols is the underscore (_), which typically is not a reserved symbol and does not require quotation marks.

```
ybrs<- rename(ybrs, Smoke = "Smoked at least once past 30 days",
        bingeDrink = "Binge drinking ‡ in past 30 days",
        alcholDrink = "Drank five or more alcoholic drinks in a row in past 30 days",
        counselor = "Got help from a counselor in past 12 months",
        sodaDrink = "Drinks 1 or more sodas per day in past 7 days",
        obesity = "Adolescent obesity",
        physActiv = "Physically active 60 minutes per day")
```

Now we change some column positions. We move columns related to drinking together, counselling first of categories, before smoking.

```
ybrs= relocate(ybrs, sodaDrink, .after = alcholDrink)
ybrs= relocate(ybrs, counselor, .before = Smoke)
```

Survey	Prevalence	Year	counselor	Smoke	binge Drink	alchol Drink	soda Drink	obesity	phys Activ
YBRS	Prevalence 2019	2019	n/a	3.3	8.9	n/a	12.4	13.8	14.5
YBRS	Lower 95% CI 2019	2019	n/a	2.7	7.8	n/a	11.2	12.7	13.0
YBRS	Upper 95% CI 2019	2019	n/a	4.0	10.1	n/a	13.7	15.1	16.2
…	…	…	…	…	…	…	…	…	…
YRBS	Prevalence 2021	2021	n/a	2.2	5.3	n/a	12.5	19.2	14.1
YRBS	Lower 95% CI 2021	2021	n/a	1.3	4.2	n/a	10.5	17.4	11.9
YRBS	Upper 95% CI 2021	2021	n/a	3.7	6.9	n/a	14.7	21.2	16.7

3.3 R: Slicing, Column Creation, and Deletion

We return to the example from dataset *IBM HR Analytics Employee Attrition & Performance*, for some of the most fundamental operations, first on data frame, then on columns.

Our data frame is *df* and we operate a selection of columns.

```
df1<- select(df, Age, Department, EducationField, Gender, MonthlyIncome)
```

3.3.1 Subsetting and Slicing

The first feature we consider is so-called *slicing*, which represents a technique for subsetting a data frame by specifying a subset of rows and/or of columns. Let us start with the simplest case, how to subset a data frame by a single column. The **standard syntax** uses the *dollar symbol* ($) to separate the data frame name from the column name.

```
df1$EducationField
   [1] "Life Sciences"    "Life Sciences"    "Other"
   [4] "Life Sciences"    "Medical"          "Life Sciences"
   [7] "Medical"          "Life Sciences"    "Life Sciences"
  [10] "Medical"          "Medical"          "Life Sciences"
  ...
```

This way, we have obtained the list of all 1470 values of column *EducationField*. Alternatively, we could use *brackets* instead of the dollar sign, and in this case, numerical indexes could be specified. Let us try with index 3, again corresponding to column *EducationField*.

```
df1[3]
# A tibble: 1,470 × 1
   EducationField
   <chr>
 1 Life Sciences
 2 Life Sciences
 3 Other
 4 Life Sciences
 5 Medical
 6 Life Sciences
 7 Medical
 8 Life Sciences
 9 Life Sciences
10 Medical
# ... with 1,460 more rows
```

It returns values of column *EducationField* as in the first example, but the result is not the same. This is a data frame with 1470 rows and one column; the previous one was a list of values. We can see the difference by checking the data type of the two results with function `class()`.

```
class(df1$EducationField)
[1] "character"
class(df1[3])
[1] "tbl_df"     "tbl"        "data.frame"
```

We have confirmation that the two results are not the same. Is this difference important? Yes, as always, there is a difference in data types, which means they are different objects, although logically with same values. Moreover, the difference between a data frame and a list type is relevant in the usage of several functions that might require one or the other type of data.

Alternatively, we can use brackets and specify *the column name between quotation marks*, single or double. If we want to specify more than one column, that is a list and takes the c() notation.

```
df1['EducationField']
# A tibble: 1,470 × 1
   EducationField
   <chr>
 1 Life Sciences
 2 Life Sciences
 3 Other
 4 Life Sciences
 5 Medical
 … with 1,465 more rows
df1[c("Gender",'EducationField')]
# A tibble: 1,470 × 2
   Gender EducationField
   <chr>  <chr>
 1 Female Life Sciences
 2 Male   Life Sciences
 3 Male   Other
 4 Female Life Sciences
 5 Male   Medical
# … with 1,465 more rows
```

This syntax is logically equivalent to the select() function.

What about *obtaining a list, instead of a data frame, but using column positions instead of names*? The syntax using the dollar sign does not accept a number in place of the column name. With *double brackets,* we achieve it.

```
df1[[3]]
    [1] "Life Sciences"  "Life Sciences"  "Other"
    [4] "Life Sciences"  "Medical"        "Life Sciences"
    [7] "Medical"        "Life Sciences"  "Life Sciences"
   [10] "Medical"        "Medical"        "Life Sciences"
 …
```

The result is a list.

So far, we have seen some basic mechanisms; now we want to *subset a data frame by rows and columns.* We already know how to do it by column names; we can do the same with positions.

```
df1[c(2,4)]
# A tibble: 1,470 × 2
   Department    Gender
   <chr>         <chr>
 1 Sales         Female
```

```
  2 Research & Development Male
  3 Research & Development Male
  4 Research & Development Female
  5 Research & Development Male
# ... with 1,465 more rows
```

However, the slicing operation is usually meant for contiguous rows and columns. We have seen the syntax for ranges; it takes the colon symbol, and we can also use it for slicing.

```
df1[2:4]
# A tibble: 1,470 × 3
   Department              EducationField Gender
   <chr>                   <chr>          <chr>
 1 Sales                   Life Sciences  Female
 2 Research & Development  Life Sciences  Male
 3 Research & Development  Other          Male
 4 Research & Development  Life Sciences  Female
 5 Research & Development  Medical        Male
# ... with 1,465 more rows
```

This way, we have sliced by columns. How can we do the same by rows? To select rows, we need a second attribute. Let us start with the simplest case.

```
df1[1,2]
# A tibble: 1 × 1
  Department
  <chr>
1 Sales
```

The result is the element *Sales*, corresponding to the *first row and second column*. Therefore, with two parameters, comma separated, the first one refers to rows and the second to columns. Let us add the slicing by columns.

```
df1[1,2:4]
# A tibble: 1 × 3
  Department EducationField Gender
  <chr>      <chr>          <chr>
1 Sales      Life Sciences  Female
```

We have obtained the same subsetting as previous example, but limited to the first row. Adding the slicing by rows is now immediate.

```
df1[10:15,2:4]
# A tibble: 6 × 3
   Department              EducationField Gender
   <chr>                   <chr>          <chr>
 1 Research & Development  Medical        Male
 2 Research & Development  Medical        Male
```

```
3 Research & Development Life Sciences  Female
4 Research & Development Life Sciences  Male
5 Research & Development Medical        Male
6 Research & Development Life Sciences  Male
```

What if we want a slicing by rows only? We have to specify both parameters, with the second about columns left undefined.

```
df1[10:15, ]
# A tibble: 6 × 5
    Age Department              EducationField Gender MonthlyIncome
  <dbl> <chr>                   <chr>          <chr>          <dbl>
1    36 Research & Development Medical         Male            5237
2    35 Research & Development Medical         Male            2426
3    29 Research & Development Life Sciences   Female          4193
4    31 Research & Development Life Sciences   Male            2911
5    34 Research & Development Medical         Male            2661
6    28 Research & Development Life Sciences   Male            2028
```

Practicing with subsetting and slicing using indexes is important because they are extremely common and useful operations that we can encounter in all kinds of data science projects.

3.3.2 Column Creation

To add a new column to a data frame, we consider here the standard mechanism that directly derives from what we have just seen about subsetting and slicing. It should also be anticipated that there exists an important function `mutate()`, of the *dplyr* package, that also creates new columns and will be one of the most relevant in following chapters.

The most basic syntax for adding a column to a data frame makes use of the same dollar symbol we have seen for subsetting a column and returning it as a list. Here we see it with an assignment.

```
df1$newCol1 = 0
```

In the same vein, the bracket notation with column position could also be used for adding a column.

```
df1[7]= "ABC"
```

Or, equivalently, using the name with quotation marks and brackets.

```
df1["newCol2"] = "xyz"
```

As we see, the syntax with the position has the limit of setting a default name, "...7" in the example, which is a better rename. Except for this detail, the three methods are equivalent. Below is the result of the creation of these columns.

Age	Department	Education Field	Gender	Monthly Income	new Col1	...7	new Col2
41	Sales	Life Sciences	Female	5993	0	ABC	xyz
49	Research & Development	Life Sciences	Male	5130	0	ABC	xyz
37	Research & Development	Other	Male	2090	0	ABC	xyz
33	Research & Development	Life Sciences	Female	2909	0	ABC	xyz
27	Research & Development	Medical	Male	3468	0	ABC	xyz
32	Research & Development	Life Sciences	Male	3068	0	ABC	xyz

The notation with the position has another subtlety to take into account. If the position corresponds to a column already existing, the former column is overwritten by the new one.

```
df1[8] = 1
```

Age	Department	Education Field	Gender	Monthly Income	new Col1	...7	new Col2
41	Sales	Life Sciences	Female	5993	0	ABC	1
49	Research & Development	Life Sciences	Male	5130	0	ABC	1
37	Research & Development	Other	Male	2090	0	ABC	1
33	Research & Development	Life Sciences	Female	2909	0	ABC	1
27	Research & Development	Medical	Male	3468	0	ABC	1
32	Research & Development	Life Sciences	Male	3068	0	ABC	1

This way, the former *newCol2* has been overwritten, and its data type has also changed, from character to double.

Tip

This behavior suggests exercising particular caution when a column is added by position because it is easy to mislead the expected result for the insertion at a certain position, rather than the overwriting, or to confuse the total number of columns and overwrite the last one. Better add a column by specifying the name, unless a very specific reason suggests using the position.

3.3.3 Column Deletion

To delete a column in a data frame is easy; it suffices to assign it to the **NULL** keyword.

```
df1$newCol1 = NULL
df1["newCol2"] = NULL
df1$...7 = NULL
```

3.3.4 Calculated Columns

Up to now, we have seen how to add a new column by assigning a constant value. While this could be sometimes useful, the typical case is when we add a new column with values calculated from other columns and therefore possibly different for each element. Possibilities are endless; common is the case of mathematical computations such as proportions and percent values, differences, descriptive statistics, and so forth.

In our example, we add a new column by computing its values as *the difference between the monthly income and the mean of monthly incomes among all employees*. Let us start with the mean. This is the *arithmetic mean* and is calculated by function **mean()** of base R, which is different from most of basic statistics that are defined in the **stats** package.

Tip

Function `mean()` has the important option **na.rm** useful to manage the presence of missing values. The default is *FALSE*, meaning that missing values are included in the calculation and, if present, the result of the mean is no value, represented by the keyword *NA*. In order to exclude missing values from the computation, **na.rm=TRUE** is needed.
  Missing values are particularly important; we will return on this in future chapters.

First, we calculate the average monthly income using column *MonthlyIncome*.

```
mean(df1$MonthlyIncome, na.rm=TRUE)
[1] 6502.931
```

Now, we can use it for the newly calculated column, which is defined as the difference between values of column *MontlyIncome* and the arithmetic mean.

```
df1$Diff_incomeMean= df1$MonthlyIncome - mean(df1$MonthlyIncome, na.rm=TRUE)
```

Age	Department	Education Field	Gender	Monthly Income	Diff_income Mean
41	Sales	Life Sciences	Female	5993	−509.9313
49	Research & Development	Life Sciences	Male	5130	−1,372.9313
37	Research & Development	Other	Male	2090	−4,412.9313
33	Research & Development	Life Sciences	Female	2909	−3,593.9313
27	Research & Development	Medical	Male	3468	−3,034.9313
32	Research & Development	Life Sciences	Male	3068	−3,434.9313

This way, a data frame could be enriched with new information derived from the existing ones. We will use calculated columns very often.

3.3.5 Function `mutate()` and Data Masking

The second important method to create a new column is through function **mutate()** of the *dplyr* package. As anticipated, this function will become fundamental in more advanced data wrangling operations when the standard method is not applicable. For now, it is simply an alternative method to the standard one.

Function `mutate()` has a particular attribute `.keep` that let to define how to handle columns used for the new calculated column. The options are the following:

- `.keep="all"` : keeps all previous columns (*default*);
- `.keep="used"` : just keep columns used to calculate the new one and discard the others;
- `.keep="unused"` : it is the dual of the previous one; it discards the columns used for calculating the new one and keeps all the others;
- `.keep="none"` : all previous columns are discarded and the result will be just the new column.

It should be evident that these options are no more than different combinations of column deletion, that we could easily perform setting columns to NULL, or of a subsetting produced by selecting the columns of interest.

About the syntax, it should be noted how *columns are specified only with name, without specifying the data frame, which only appears as the first parameter*. This is an important property of some functions of the *dplyr* package called ***data masking***.

```
mutate(df1, Diff_incomeMean= MonthlyIncome - mean(MonthlyIncome, na.rm=TRUE))
# A tibble: 1,470 × 6
      Age Department               EducationField Gender MonthlyIncome Diff_incom…¹
    <dbl> <chr>                    <chr>          <chr>          <dbl>        <dbl>
  1    41 Sales                    Life Sciences  Female          5993        -510.
  2    49 Research & Development   Life Sciences  Male            5130       -1373.
  3    37 Research & Development   Other          Male            2090       -4413.
  4    33 Research & Development   Life Sciences  Female          2909       -3594.
  5    27 Research & Development   Medical        Male            3468       -3035.
# … with 1,465 more rows, and abbreviated variable name ¹Diff_incomeMean
```

The result is the same as in the previous example, with the new column added.

3.4 R: Separate and Unite Columns

It is not uncommon to work with values that combine several information, sometimes in a codified format. We have mentioned that date and time are literally the combination of several information, but for their special relevance they are treated and managed as specific data types. However, it is sometimes the case with datasets with date and, less frequently, time information separated, for example, year, month, and day as distinct columns. In that case, it would be useful to reunite the parts into a data format in order to exploit the dedicated functions for the *datetime* format. An example of combined information is that of many codes, like product codes, we will see an example of this in a moment, or fiscal codes. For example, the US Social Security Number (SSN) used to have a structure combining different information, with the first three digits referring to the US state, but that changed in 2011 with full randomization of the SSNs. Other countries issue fiscal codes to their citizens by combining information that could be separated and often at least partially decoded.

3.4.1 Separation

The function most useful to separate column values into distinct columns is `separate()`, defined in package *tidyr*, part of the *tidyverse*. It has three main attributes:

- `col` : the column name whose values should be separated;
- `into` : the new columns resulting from separation; it is a list, therefore it takes the usual notation `c()`;
- `sep` : the rule for the separation, which may have two forms:
  - **a number**: it represents the number of characters before the cut (i.e. an offset, in practice) and it is useful for so-called *positional codes*, those codes that have constituent parts of fixed lengths. For example, *sep=3* means that values of the columns are separated in two new columns, where in the first one will go the first three characters of original values and in the second the others;
  - **an alphanumeric pattern**: with a pattern, we define the string to be recognized as the separator of the two parts that will go in distinct columns. It could be a *single character*, which is the typical case of dates (e.g. in 2023/04/25, the symbol / is the pattern to use, first to separate year from the rest then month from day). The pattern could also be a string of several characters if the format of values presents such a case. Particularly important is the more general case of a pattern defined as a ***regular expression*** (also indicated as *regexp* or *regex*). The language of regular expressions is a logical language to represent formal grammars; we do not delve into its details, but we will encounter regexp on other occasions, and we will learn how efficient they could be for operating on strings even with their basic semantic. To show just few elementary examples, `-{3}` matches `---`; `-{3}|*{3}` matches either `---` or `***`; `x{2,4}` matches `xx`, `xxx`, or `xxxx`, `[0-9a-zA-Z]*` matches all strings of any length composed of digits or letters, lower or upper case. The possibilities offered by regular expressions are almost unlimited, as the complexity they may reach.

Let us consider the example of *product codes* from the *Food & Drugs Administration (FDA)* (https://www.fda.gov/industry/import-program-tools/product-codes-and-product-code-builder). As described in the referred online page, an *FDA product code* is an alphanumeric positional code representing five components: *Industry Code* (two digits, from 02 to 98), *Class* (one letter), *Subclass* (one letter or a hyphen), *Process Indicator Code (PIC)* (one letter or hyphen), and the *Product (Group)* (two characters). With this information, we could separate FDA product codes into distinct columns.

We use the same three product codes on the FDA web page, corresponding to *Canned Tomato Soup (Concentrated)*, *Ibuprofen*, and *First Aid Kit including drugs*.

```
productCodes = c("38BEE27","62GBA41","79L-RR")
df <- tibble(productCodes)
df
# A tibble: 3 × 1
  productCodes
  <chr>
1 38BEE27
2 62GBA41
3 79L-RR
```

With this simple data frame, we can proceed to separate code parts into distinct columns.

```
df1= separate(df, into=c("Industry Code","other"), col="productCodes",sep = 2)
df1= separate(df1, into=c("Class","other"), col="other", sep=1)
df1= separate(df1, into=c("Subclass","other"), col="other", sep=1)
df1= separate(df1, into=c("Process Indicator Code (PIC)",
```

Industry Code	Class	Subclass	Process Indicator Code (PIC)	Product (Group)
38	B	E	E	27
62	G	B	A	41
79	L	–	–	RR

It is possible to produce the same result in a single operation by defining a list of positions for the cuts.

```
separate(df, into = c("Industry Code","Class","Subclass",
                      "Process Indicator Code (PIC)","Product (Group)"),
         col='productCodes', sep = c(2,3,4,5))
```

Date and time are another typical composed value well-suited to practice with separation operations, although, as already mentioned, *separating date's components is not the better way to handle dates*, rather they should be defined as *datetime* data type and functions specific for working on dates should be used.

Here, we show some operations with different date formats.

```
es_date = c("12/25/2022", "03/17/2021", "10/29/2020")
dt <- tibble(es_date)
dt
# A tibble: 3 × 1
  es_date
  <chr>
1 12/25/2022
2 03/17/2021
3 10/29/2020
```

With these dates, the separator is always the same (/), so a single operation is sufficient.

```
dt1=separate(dt, into = c("Month","Day","Year"), col="es_date",sep = "/")
dt1
# A tibble: 3 × 3
  Month Day   Year
  <chr> <chr> <chr>
1 12    25    2022
2 03    17    2021
3 10    29    2020
```

It should be noted that the data type of the new columns is still the same as the original one, that is *character*, there is no automatic type transformation with the `separate()` function.

Let us try with a more complicated example.

```
es_date2 = c("12October2022", "03July2021", "18December2020")
dt2 <- tibble(es_date2)
dt2
# A tibble: 3 × 1
  es_date2
  <chr>
1 12October2022
2 03July2021
3 18December2020
```

Clearly, the example is purely didactic, dates are never written this way but there always are spaces (e.g. 12 October 2022). In that case the example would have been the same of the previous one, with space as the separator. Now is different, there is no separator, and the positions of the components are not fixed. We start with days that can be separated by using the position.

```
dt3 = separate(dt2, into = c("Day","other"), col="es_date2",sep = 2)
```

Months and years cannot be separated as we have seen before, being the month names of different lengths. Year instead is of fixed length. We can count *backward* from the end of the value by using the minus sign.

```
dt3=separate(dt3, into = c("Month","Year"), col="other",sep = -4)
dt3
# A tibble: 3 × 3
  Day   Month    Year
  <chr> <chr>    <chr>
1 12    October  2022
2 03    July     2021
3 18    December 2020
```

3.4.2 Union

With `unite()`, we obtain the opposite of `separate()`, distinct columns are transformed into a single one and corresponding values are joined with or without a separator character or string (the underscore symbol _ is the default). Parameters are:

- `col` : the name of the new column;
- `remove` : if *TRUE* (default), original columns are deleted, otherwise if *FALSE*;
- `na.rm` : missing values are removed before joining values (default *FALSE*).

We show some examples by uniting columns we have previously separated, starting with product codes.

```
unite(df1, col= productCodes, everything(), sep = "", remove = FALSE)
# A tibble: 3 × 6
  productCodes 'Industry Code' Class Subclass Process Indicator Code (...¹
Produ...²
  <chr>        <chr>           <chr> <chr>    <chr>                    <chr>
1 38BEE27      38              B     E        E                        27
2 62GBA41      62              G     B        A                        41
3 79L-RR       79              L     -        -                        RR
# ... with abbreviated variable names ¹'Process Indicator Code (PIC)',
#    ²'Product (Group)'
```

Now with dates.

```
unite(dt1, col=Date, c(Year, Month, Day), sep = "-")
# A tibble: 3 × 1
  Date
  <chr>
1 2022-12-25
2 2021-03-17
3 2020-10-29
unite(dt3, col=Date, c(Day, Month, Year), sep = " ")
# A tibble: 3 × 1
  Date
  <chr>
1 12 October 2022
2 03 July 2021
3 18 December 2020
```

3.5 R: Sorting Data Frames

Sorting data frames by one or more columns is a fundamental operation, doing that in numeric or lexicographic order is easy, less so with other types of ordering criteria. Let us start with numeric or lexicographic order. We use again the *IBM HR Analytics Employee Attrition & Performance* dataset we read in a previous section, with a selection of columns in data frame *df*.

```
df<- select(df, Age, Department, EducationField, Gender, MonthlyIncome)
df
# A tibble: 1,470 × 5
    Age Department             EducationField Gender MonthlyIncome
  <dbl> <chr>                  <chr>          <chr>          <dbl>
1    41 Sales                  Life Sciences  Female          5993
2    49 Research & Development Life Sciences  Male            5130
3    37 Research & Development Other          Male            2090
4    33 Research & Development Life Sciences  Female          2909
5    27 Research & Development Medical        Male            3468
# ... with 1,465 more rows
```

First, we want to *sort by increasing age* (*ascending* and *descending* are the terms used by R).

The function is **arrange()**, of the *dplyr* package, included in *tidyverse*, the basic syntax is intuitive.

```
df1= arrange(df, Age)
head(df1,10)
```

Age	Department	EducationField	Gender	MonthlyIncome
18	Research & Development	Life Sciences	Male	1420
18	Sales	Medical	Female	1200
18	Sales	Marketing	Male	1878
18	Research & Development	Life Sciences	Male	1051
18	Research & Development	Medical	Male	1904
18	Research & Development	Life Sciences	Female	1611
18	Sales	Medical	Female	1569
18	Research & Development	Medical	Female	1514
19	Sales	Marketing	Male	1675
19	Research & Development	Medical	Female	1483

Now, we arrange *by monthly income, but decreasing this time.* We need the additional function **desc()** applied to the column whose values need to be in descending order.

```
df1= arrange(df, desc(MonthlyIncome))
head(df1)
```

Age	Department	EducationField	Gender	MonthlyIncome
52	Research & Development	Life Sciences	Male	19999
41	Research & Development	Life Sciences	Female	19973
56	Research & Development	Technical Degree	Female	19943
50	Research & Development	Life Sciences	Female	19926
55	Research & Development	Medical	Male	19859
51	Sales	Life Sciences	Male	19847

3.5.1 Sorting by Multiple Columns

It is often useful to sort by multiple columns instead of just one. That means the data frame is sorted by the first specified column, then rows with same values for the first column are ordered by the second specified column, and so forth for all columns specified for sorting. This also means that *the order in which columns selected for sorting are listed is important*. Changing the order of the selected columns changes the result.

See first an example ordering by *department*, then *age*, then *monthly income*, the last two in descending order.

```
arrange(df, Department, desc(Age), desc(MonthlyIncome))
```

Age	Department	EducationField	Gender	MonthlyIncome
59	Human Resources	Human Resources	Female	18844
59	Human Resources	Medical	Male	2267
56	Human Resources	Life Sciences	Male	19717
55	Human Resources	Human Resources	Male	19636
54	Human Resources	Human Resources	Female	17328
54	Human Resources	Medical	Male	10725

Let us try to change the order of the specified columns.

```
arrange(df, desc(Age), Department, desc(MonthlyIncome))
```

Age	Department	EducationField	Gender	MonthlyIncome
60	Research & Development	Life Sciences	Female	19566
60	Research & Development	Medical	Male	10883
60	Sales	Marketing	Female	10266
60	Sales	Marketing	Male	5405
60	Sales	Marketing	Male	5220
59	Human Resources	Human Resources	Female	18844
59	Human Resources	Medical	Male	2267
59	Research & Development	Life Sciences	Female	13726
59	Research & Development	Medical	Male	10512
59	Research & Development	Medical	Female	2670

In addition to these basic features, function `arrange()` has attribute **`.by_group`**, which will be relevant in grouping and aggregation operations.

3.5.2 Sorting by an External List

We encounter a different sorting criterion when we need *a data frame column ordered according to an external list of items*, which could represent names, categories, and ranks, various sorting criteria different from a lexicographic or a numerical order. Examples of this kind are many and very common, like the names of days of the week or the months, military ranks, and roles in an organization's hierarchy.

We see an example with *month names,* likely the most common with Open Data. To explain the logic and procedure, we need to anticipate some operations that will be discussed in future chapters. Here, we focus on this important sorting criteria.

For this example, we introduce a new dataset *Particulates – PM2.5 Speciation 2022,* from the *Air Data: Air Quality Data Collected at Outdoor Monitors Across the US,* of the United States Environmental Protection Agency (EPA). This dataset presents data about the *PM2.5 particulate,* a dangerous particulate for human health, as collected by EPA in 2022. It is a large dataset (Rows: 361 721, Columns: 29) that we read (here by means of function **vroom()**, from package **vroom**) and then take a random sample of 10 000 rows and a selection of columns.

```
library(vroom)
df= vroom('~/DS_Wiley/datasets/EPA/daily_88101_2022.zip')
```

The column *Arithmetic Mean* represents the average value for the day. With function **sample_n()** we take a sample of 10 000 rows.

```
df1= sample_n(df, 10000)
df1= select(df1,'Date Local', 'State Name', 'County Name',
              'City Name', 'Arithmetic Mean')
```

Date Local	State Name	County Name	City Name	Arithmetic Mean
2022-01-19	California	San Bernardino	Ontario	28.900000
2022-06-09	Vermont	Chittenden	Burlington	6.433333
2022-01-08	Utah	Salt Lake	Salt Lake City	2.500000
2022-02-26	Florida	Pinellas	Saint Petersburg	6.979167
2022-03-22	Mississippi	Hinds	Jackson	5.766667
2022-02-16	Utah	Cache	Smithfield	3.900000

Column *Date Local* is already of *datetime* type (type *date* is a subset of type *datetime* with only the date part); therefore, we can extract the month name and put it in a new column we name *Month.*

Tip

The example is done with the local system configuration set to *en_US* (*en_US.UTF-8* on MacOS), and as a result month names are in English. Local system configuration could be verified with command `Sys.getlocale()`. To set a regional local datetime configuration and obtain month names in national languages, the instruction is `Sys.setlocale("LC_TIME", "language/country name")`, where *language/country name* is composed of two parts, one is the **language name,** as for the standard *ISO 639.2* (https://www.loc.gov/standards/iso639-2/php/code_list.php), the second is the **country code,** as for the standard *ISO 3166* (https://www.iso.org/iso-3166-country-codes.html). Formally, it seems complicated, in practice it is not. Both are 2-letter codes, the first lowercase and the second uppercase, joined by underscore. They are usually quite intuitive: **fr_FR** for French of France, **es_ES** for Spanish

Now we create a new column by extracting the month name from the date. First, we rename column names more conveniently. Then, with function **format()**, of base R, we can format a date based on its components. Date format specifications will be introduced in a future chapter, here it suffices to know that codes like *%d*, *%m*, *%Y* represent the day, the month and the year part of a date, in different formats, *%Y*, for example, is the year with 4-digit. In our case, we want full month names, then: *%B*.

```
df1= rename(df1, Date='Date Local', State='State Name', County='County Name',
        City='City Name', PM25='Arithmetic Mean')

df1$Month <- format(df1$Date, "%B")
```

Date	State	County	City	PM25	Month
2022-01-19	California	San Bernardino	Ontario	28.900000	January
2022-06-09	Vermont	Chittenden	Burlington	6.433333	June
2022-01-08	Utah	Salt Lake	Salt Lake City	2.500000	January
2022-02-26	Florida	Pinellas	Saint Petersburg	6.979167	February
2022-03-22	Mississippi	Hinds	Jackson	5.766667	March
2022-02-16	Utah	Cache	Smithfield	3.900000	February

If we sort data frame *df1* by column *Date*, we obtain the correct order. Not so if we sort by *Month*.

```
arrange(df1, Date)
```

Date	State	County	City	PM25	Month
2022-01-01	Mississippi	Forrest	Hattiesburg	8.058333	January
2022-01-01	Tennessee	Davidson	Nashville-Davidson	5.700000	January
2022-01-01	Minnesota	Ramsey	St. Paul	2.250000	January
2022-01-01	California	Placer	Auburn	6.400000	January
2022-01-01	Missouri	St. Louis City	St. Louis	5.700000	January
...	...	...	...	...	...

```
arrange(df1, Month)
```

Date	State	County	City	PM25	Month
2022-04-05	New Jersey	Morris	Chester	6.000000	April
2022-04-25	New York	Monroe	Rochester	10.570833	April
2022-04-09	North Carolina	Davidson	Lexington	1.708333	April
2022-04-11	New Mexico	Dona Ana	Not in a city	6.300000	April
2022-04-23	California	Inyo	Not in a city	2.000000	April
…	…	…	…	…	…

The difference is that column *Date* is of type *datetime*; therefore, it is handled as a special type of value that should be sorted based on the Gregorian calendar. Values of column *Month*, instead, are just strings; the sorting is lexicographic, with April first and September last, not the correct one.

Let us see how we can proceed in a case like this in order to obtain the correct order of the month names:

1. Create a separate list with the unique values in the correct order. In our case, it will be the list of months.
2. Transform in *categorical elements* the column of the data frame to be sorted, which R calls *factors*. *Factors are names associated to levels*, and levels could be sorted based on the separate list of names.
3. *Sort* the column, which now has levels associated to the external ordered list.

STEP 1. We create the list with ordered month names.

```
monthOrder= c('January', 'February', 'March', 'April', 'May', 'June', 'July',
              'August', 'September', 'October', 'November', 'December')
```

STEP 2. We transform the *Month* column into **factors**, with level order given by the list *monthOrder*. If we look at data frame *df1* at this step, month names are still ordered incorrectly.

```
df1$Month<- factor(df1$Month, levels= monthOrder)
head(df1)
```

Date	State	County	City	PM25	Month
2022-01-19	California	San Bernardino	Ontario	28.900000	January
2022-06-09	Vermont	Chittenden	Burlington	6.433333	June
2022-01-08	Utah	Salt Lake	Salt Lake City	2.500000	January
2022-02-26	Florida	Pinellas	Saint Petersburg	6.979167	February
2022-03-22	Mississippi	Hinds	Jackson	5.766667	March
2022-02-16	Utah	Cache	Smithfield	3.900000	February

STEP 3. We just need to sort the data frame by the *Month* column. Now the order will be January->December.

```
arrange(df1, Month) -> df2
```

We can check by looking at the head and tail of the sorted data frame *df2*. To show both head and tail rows, we may combine them with the **rbind()** function.

```
rbind(head(df2, n = 4), tail(df2, n = 4))
```

Date	State	County	City	PM25	Month
2022-01-19	California	San Bernardino	Ontario	28.900000	January
2022-01-08	Utah	Salt Lake	Salt Lake City	2.500000	January
2022-01-12	Ohio	Hamilton	Cincinnati	8.700000	January
2022-01-04	California	San Luis Obispo	San Luis Obispo	2.400000	January
2022-10-09	Utah	Utah	Spanish Fork	5.170833	October
2022-10-27	Utah	Utah	Spanish Fork	4.600000	October
2022-10-24	Iowa	Linn	Cedar Rapids	6.800000	October
2022-10-06	Iowa	Linn	Cedar Rapids	11.608696	October

In the specific dataset of the example, the last month is actually October. This way of sorting is particularly important.

3.6   R: Pipe

So far, we have learned some basic functions for operating on data, and now we are able to define some logical flows by executing operations in a sequence. It is time to introduce a particularly efficient mechanism that R has called *pipe* that permits to smoothly combine sequences of operations.

3.6.1   Forward Pipe

The pipe mechanism and syntax have been introduced by package *magrittr*, part of *tidyverse*, and more specifically, it implements a *forward pipe*, meaning that the logic is that the output of an instruction becomes the input data of the following instruction and so on in a chain of unlimited length, in theory. Visually, it proceeds from left to right; the left-hand side of the pipe is the preceding instruction, and the right-hand side is the successor instruction. The syntax uses the combination %>%, indicating the flow from left to right.

```
data frame %>%
  instruction_1, data are the data frame content %>%
  instruction_2, data are instruction_1 result %>%
  ... %>%
  instruction_N, data are instruction_N-1 result -> resulting data frame
```

We will often use the pipe notation in the following chapters. As an example, we could rewrite the example seen before with several *rename* and *relocate* functions as a single piped instruction. We made use of the dataset *Youth Behavior Risk Survey (High School)* from the *New York City Open Data*, and wrote the following sequence of different instructions:

```
ybrs<- rename(ybrs, Smoke= "Smoked at least once past 30 days",
       bingeDrink= "Binge drinking I in past 30 days",
       alcholDrink= "Drank five or more alcoholic drinks in a row in past
       30 days",
       counselor= "Got help from a counselor in past 12 months",
       sodaDrink= "Drinks 1 or more sodas per day in past 7 days",
       obesity= "Adolescent obesity",
       physActiv= "Physically active 60 minutes per day")

ybrs= relocate(ybrs, sodaDrink, .after = alcholDrink)
ybrs= relocate(ybrs, counselor, .before = Smoke)
```

The same sequence of operations could be written as a single-piped instruction. Pay attention to the following aspects:

- The data frame is specified only in the first operation; all the following ones implicitly get data from the pipe mechanism.
- The logical order of operations does not change between a non-piped and a piped version.

```
ybrs %>%
  rename(Smoke="Smoked at least once past 30 days",
         bingeDrink="Binge drinking I in past 30 days",
         alcholDrink="Drank five or more alcoholic drinks in a row in past
         30 days",
         counselor="Got help from a counselor in past 12 months",
         sodaDrink="Drinks 1 or more sodas per day in past 7 days",
         obesity="Adolescent obesity",
         physActiv="Physically active 60 minutes per day") %>%
    relocate(sodaDrink, .after = alcholDrink) %>%
    relocate(counselor, .before = Smoke) -> ybrs1
```

Survey	Prevalence	Year	counselor	Smoke	binge Drink	alchol Drink	soda Drink	obesity	phys Activ
YBRS	Prevalence 2019	2019	n/a	3.3	8.9	n/a	12.4	13.8	14.5
YBRS	Lower 95% CI 2019	2019	n/a	2.7	7.8	n/a	11.2	12.7	13.0
YBRS	Upper 95% CI 2019	2019	n/a	4.0	10.1	n/a	13.7	15.1	16.2
YBRS	Prevalence 2017	2017	18.0	5.0	5.0	n/a	14.9	13.5	20.8
YBRS	Lower 95% CI 2017	2017	16.8	4.1	4.2	n/a	13.7	12.4	19.3
YBRS	Upper 95% CI 2017	2017	19.1	6.1	5.9	n/a	16.3	14.6	22.4

Note

Reading from the dataset is not included in the pipe. Technically, it could have been, it is however not suggested. As already noted, the data import operation is computationally intensive and should not be repeated as long as data are unchanged. This is the reason for not including it in a pipe.

Tip

The main advantage of the piped version is a more compact and smooth style of programming, which is particularly convenient for some combinations of instructions. It avoids the explicit creation of intermediate results decoupling one execution from the following one.

This advantage comes with one relevant disadvantage, though. The piped version is more difficult to debug when errors are raised, because it is logically considered a single instruction and then executed as a whole. It is not possible to execute it step-by-step, one piped instruction at time. Debugging a piped instruction means, in practice, to separate single instructions and verify them individually (actually, there exist custom packages supporting step-by-step executions of piped instructions, but if we exclude fancy visualizations, their actual utility is dubious with respect to a manual debugging).

As a good practice, it is recommended not to exaggerate with the pipe mechanism; as a general criterion, when 10 instructions at most are piped, it is time to break the pipe.

3.6.2 Pipe in Base R

A new pipe mechanism has been recently introduced in base R, in case one does not want to load *magrittr* package (or *tidyverse*). It has a simplified syntax (| >) and same semantic and usage of the *magrittr* forward pipe. See the same example we have run written with the new pipe. The result is identical.

```
ybrs |>
  rename(Smoke="Smoked at least once past 30 days",
         bingeDrink="Binge drinking ‡ in past 30 days",
         alcholDrink="Drank five or more alcoholic drinks in a row in past
         30 days",
         counselor="Got help from a counselor in past 12 months",
         sodaDrink="Drinks 1 or more sodas per day in past 7 days",
         obesity="Adolescent obesity",
         physActiv="Physically active 60 minutes per day") |>
  relocate(sodaDrink, .after = alcholDrink) |>
  relocate(counselor, .before = Smoke) -> ybrs1
```

It is not, however, a complete replacement of the *magrittr* pipe, because it lacks additional features that we introduce in the following: variants for special cases that would fail with the standard pipe and the important property of parameter placeholder.

3.6.2.1 Variant

Package *magrittr* offers some *variants* to the basic pipe mechanism that are useful in some special cases. The most relevant has the syntax %$% and is helpful in situations where we want to *pipe functions that do not have a data parameter, for which the basic pipe mechanism would fail.*

One typical case is the function mean() for calculating the arithmetic mean. In this case, to obtain the mean of the values of a column, we have to specify the column as the parameter with the standard syntax mean (df$column). However, if we have to do the same in a piped instruction, we run into troubles. If we try some alternatives, they all fail.

```
mean(ybrs1$Smoke, na.rm= TRUE)
[1] 5.572222
```

This is the mean of column *Smoke*. Let us try with standard pipe syntax.

```
ybrs1 %>% mean(Smoke, na.rm= TRUE)
Warning: argument is not numeric or logical: returning NA
[1] NA
```

It returns no value. We can try with the new pipe form of base R, but the result is still wrong.

```
ybrs1 |> mean(Smoke, na.rm= TRUE)
```

If we input just the column, it works.

```
ybrs1$Smoke %>% mean(na.rm= TRUE)
[1] 5.572222
```

The problem is that a piped sequence typically operates on a data frame, not on a single column; therefore, we usually are in the situation represented by the first case, the one that failed.

An identical situation happens with string manipulation functions, for example, when we want to replace a pattern, because like statistical functions as mean(), they operate on lists, meaning columns.

Variant %$% helps precisely in these cases, because it permits having the data frame as the input and specifying just the column.

```
library(magrittr)
ybrs1 %$% mean(Smoke, na.rm= TRUE)
[1] 5.572222
```

3.6.3 Parameter Placeholder

An important feature associated to the *magrittr* pipe mechanism is the ***parameter placeholder***. It is a special syntax for explicitly stating where, in an instruction following a pipe, input data should be used. The parameter placeholder has different forms depending on the number of parameters of the piped input. The standard case of one parameter is represented by the point symbol (**.**). With two parameters, the syntax has **.x** and **.y**, with more parameters, the syntax has numbers (**..1, ..2**, etc.).

The general form is x %>% f(y, .) that equals to f(y, x).

Let us see an example with function **sub** () that permits replacing a substring with another in a value. Continuing with data frame *ybrs1*, we replace in column *counselor* the string "n/a" with "Unknown".

```
sub("n/a", "Unknown", ybrs1$counselor)
 [1] "Unknown" "Unknown" "Unknown" "18.0"    "16.8"    "19.1"    "18.3"
 [8] "16.9"    "19.7"    "17.9"    "16.5"    "19.4"    "Unknown" "Unknown"
[15] "Unknown" "Unknown" "Unknown" "Unknown"
```

It works as expected. But, if we try different combinations to make the same with a piped instruction, we fail, as in all following cases:

```
ybrs1 %>% sub("n/a", "Unknown", counselor)
ybrs1 |> sub("n/a", "Unknown", counselor)

ybrs1$counselor %>% sub("n/a", "Unknown", counselor)
ybrs1$counselor %>% sub("n/a", "Unknown")
ybrs1$counselor %>% sub("n/a", "Unknown", ybrs1$counselor)
```

It is in these important cases and others that we will encounter in following chapters that we need the *parameter placeholder* to specify where the parameter containing piped data should be evaluated.

```
ybrs1$counselor %>% sub("n/a", "Unknown", .)
 [1] "Unknown" "Unknown" "Unknown" "18.0"    "16.8"    "19.1"    "18.3"
 [8] "16.9"    "19.7"    "17.9"    "16.5"    "19.4"    "Unknown" "Unknown"
[15] "Unknown" "Unknown" "Unknown" "Unknown"
```

Now it works as expected. This example with function sub () is also a case for the alternative *magrittr* pipe using syntax %$% because that is a function without an explicit data parameter.

```
ybrs1 %$% sub("n/a", "Unknown", counselor)
 [1] "Unknown" "Unknown" "Unknown" "18.0"    "16.8"    "19.1"    "18.3"
 [8] "16.9"    "19.7"    "17.9"    "16.5"    "19.4"    "Unknown" "Unknown"
[15] "Unknown" "Unknown" "Unknown" "Unknown"
```

3.7 Python: Column Selection

We proceed in parallel with what we have seen in previous sections using R to learn Python syntax and analyze similarities and differences between the two environments. As before, the first operation is to read dataset *IBM HR Analytics Employee Attrition & Performance*. First, we import the two basic libraries for Python data science, **NumPy** and **pandas**, as we always assume to do in this book. Then we read the dataset into data frame *df* and look at some properties and descriptive statistics.

```
import numpy as np
import pandas as pd
df= pd.read_csv("datasets/IBM_Kaggle/WA_Fn-UseC_-HR-Employee-Attrition.csv")
df.head()
```

	Age	Attrition	BusinessTravel	Daily Rate	Department	Distance From Home	Education Field
0	41	Yes	Travel_Rarely	1102	Sales	1	Life Sciences
1	49	No	Travel_Frequently	279	Research & Development	8	Life Sciences
2	37	Yes	Travel_Rarely	1373	Research & Development	2	Other
3	33	No	Travel_Frequently	1392	Research & Development	3	Life Sciences
4	27	No	Travel_Rarely	591	Research & Development	2	Medical

Attribute **shape** of a pandas data frame returns the size as number of rows and columns.

```
df.shape
(1470, 35)
```

With attribute **columns,** the list of column names is shown, expressed as values of the column index. This is a particularly useful attribute because we will often need to verify the list of column names or their exact spelling, which could be misleading from a standard visualization of the data frame (e.g. the presence of trailing spaces at the beginning or at the end of a column name).

```
df.columns
Index(['Age', 'Attrition', 'BusinessTravel', 'DailyRate', 'Department',
       'DistanceFromHome', 'Education', 'EducationField', 'EmployeeCount',
       'EmployeeNumber', 'EnvironmentSatisfaction', 'Gender', 'HourlyRate',
       'JobInvolvement', 'JobLevel', 'JobRole', 'JobSatisfaction',
       'MaritalStatus', 'MonthlyIncome', 'MonthlyRate', 'NumCompaniesWorked',
       'Over18', 'OverTime', 'PercentSalaryHike', 'PerformanceRating',
       'RelationshipSatisfaction', 'StandardHours', 'StockOptionLevel',
       'TotalWorkingYears', 'TrainingTimesLastYear', 'WorkLifeBalance',
       'YearsAtCompany', 'YearsInCurrentRole', 'YearsSinceLastPromotion',
       'YearsWithCurrManager'],
      dtype='object')
```

Function **info()** provides more detailed information about the data frame, such as: the *size* of the data frame, same as with **shape,** the *data type* for each column (*object* is the data type for alphanumeric values, *int64* for integer numbers, *float64* for floating point numbers, etc.), and the presence of *missing values* for each column expressed indirectly as the number of non-null values. In this example, there is no missing value in any column of the data frame. Finally, by specifying "*RangeIndex: 1470 entries, 0 to 1469*", it reminds us of the important detail that indexes of Python vectors start from 0.

```
df.info()
<class 'pandas.core.frame.DataFrame'>
RangeIndex: 1470 entries, 0 to 1469
Data columns (total 35 columns):
 #   Column                  Non-Null Count  Dtype
---  ------                  --------------  -----
 0   Age                     1470 non-null   int64
 1   Attrition               1470 non-null   object
 2   BusinessTravel          1470 non-null   object
 3   DailyRate               1470 non-null   int64
 4   Department              1470 non-null   object
 5   DistanceFromHome        1470 non-null   int64
 6   Education               1470 non-null   int64
 7   EducationField          1470 non-null   object
 8   EmployeeCount           1470 non-null   int64
 9   EmployeeNumber          1470 non-null   int64
 10  EnvironmentSatisfaction 1470 non-null   int64
 11  Gender                  1470 non-null   object
...
```

With function **describe()**, we obtain the descriptive statistics of numeric columns.

```
df.describe()
```

	Age	DailyRate	Distance FromHome	Education	Employee Count	Employee Number	...
count	1470.000000	1470.000000	1470.000000	1470.000000	1470.0	1470.000000	...
mean	36.923810	802.485714	9.192517	2.912925	1.0	1024.865306	...
std	9.135373	403.509100	8.106864	1.024165	0.0	602.024335	...
min	18.000000	102.000000	1.000000	1.000000	1.0	1.000000	...
25%	30.000000	465.000000	2.000000	2.000000	1.0	491.250000	...
50%	36.000000	802.000000	7.000000	3.000000	1.0	1020.500000	...
75%	43.000000	1157.000000	14.000000	4.000000	1.0	1555.750000	...
max	60.000000	1499.000000	29.000000	5.000000	1.0	2068.000000	...

To select a subset of data frame columns, we consider the two main options, that is either to select them while reading the dataset or, more generally, after having read it, from the resulting data frame with a slicing operation.

3.7.1 Selecting Columns from Dataset Read

Among the several parameters of function **pd.read_csv()** there is **usecols** that lets to specify the list of columns to be included in the result. Columns could be expressed either by name or by positional index.

In the following examples, we want to include only columns *Attrition, Department, Gender,* and *MonthlyIncome*. First, we select them by name, then by index.

```
pd.read_csv("datasets/IBM_Kaggle/WA_Fn-UseC_-HR-Employee-Attrition.csv",
            usecols = ['Attrition', 'Department', 'Gender', 'MonthlyIncome'])
```

	Attrition	Department	Gender	MonthlyIncome
0	Yes	Sales	Female	5993
1	No	Research & Development	Male	5130
2	Yes	Research & Development	Male	2090
3	No	Research & Development	Female	2909
4	No	Research & Development	Male	3468
...	...	...	...	...
1465	No	Research & Development	Male	2571
1466	No	Research & Development	Male	9991
1467	No	Research & Development	Male	6142
1468	No	Sales	Male	5390
1469	No	Research & Development	Male	4404

```
pd.read_csv("datasets/IBM_Kaggle/WA_Fn-UseC_-HR-Employee-Attrition.csv",
            usecols = [1, 4, 11, 18])
```

Selecting columns this way is handy but has the obvious drawback that if we want to change the selection, we need to read the dataset again, which, as we know, is an operation that should not be repeated if not strictly necessary.

3.7.2   Selecting Columns from a Data Frame

We now consider the second general case, when we have read the dataset and we want to select columns from the data frame. It is a slicing technique, similar to what we have seen with R, and it represents the *standard selection method* with Python data frames.

Let us start with the simplest case of *selecting a single column*. Two forms exist: either as slicing by the column name or as a data frame attribute. Pay attention to the type of result; it is a series, not a data frame.

```
df['Age']
0       41
1       49
2       37
3       33
4       27
        ..
1465    36
1466    39
1467    27
1468    49
1469    34
Name: Age, Length: 1470, dtype: int64
```

Now as data frame attribute. The result is the same.

```
df.Age
```

We now move on to the more general case of *selection of multiple columns*. We have to specify a list of columns. The Python syntax for expressing lists requires us to enclose values into brackets; therefore, we will have two pairs of brackets:

- one is for defining the list of selected columns, for example ['Attrition', 'Department', 'Gender', 'MonthlyIncome']
- another is for slicing, in order to apply the selection to a specific data frame, such as df [...]

```
df1 = df[['Attrition', 'Department', 'Gender', 'MonthlyIncome']] df1
```

	Attrition	Department	Gender	MonthlyIncome
0	Yes	Sales	Female	5993
1	No	Research & Development	Male	5130
2	Yes	Research & Development	Male	2090
3	No	Research & Development	Female	2909
4	No	Research & Development	Male	3468
...	...	...	...	...
1465	No	Research & Development	Male	2571
1466	No	Research & Development	Male	9991
1467	No	Research & Development	Male	6142
1468	No	Sales	Male	5390
1469	No	Research & Development	Male	4404

3.7.3 Selection by Positional Index, Range, or with Selection Helper

The column selection by positional index cannot be performed simply by replacing column names with indexes in the standard form. For example, the following instruction, logically equivalent to the previous selection, generates an error because index numbers are interpreted as names.

```
df[[1, 4, 11, 18]]
```

To execute it correctly, there are other ways that we will consider in the following chapters. They will make use of special attributes or adopt the syntax of *NumPy vectors and matrices*, rather than of pandas data frames.

Same considerations apply for selection by range or with selection helper, which need different syntax than standard selection on pandas data frames. They will also be presented in the following chapter.

3.7.4 Selection by Exclusion

With respect to the possibility of selecting columns by excluding one or more columns, pandas does not offer a solution as simple as the negation operator or the minus sign in R. The consequence of this is that there are several alternative ways to achieve the same, with no one to consider as the one to clearly prefer. They just work equally well.

Here we do not try to present all of them, just two: the most basic one and one with a specific function. The first solution is smart and makes use of the special meaning of the result of the attribute `columns`, which is more than just the list of column names.

```
df.columns
Index(['Age', 'Attrition', 'BusinessTravel', 'DailyRate', 'Department',
       'DistanceFromHome', 'Education', 'EducationField', 'EmployeeCount',
       'EmployeeNumber', 'EnvironmentSatisfaction', 'Gender', 'HourlyRate',
       'JobInvolvement', 'JobLevel', 'JobRole', 'JobSatisfaction',
       'MaritalStatus', 'MonthlyIncome', 'MonthlyRate', 'NumCompaniesWorked',

       'Over18', 'OverTime', 'PercentSalaryHike', 'PerformanceRating',
       'RelationshipSatisfaction', 'StandardHours', 'StockOptionLevel',
       'TotalWorkingYears', 'TrainingTimesLastYear', 'WorkLifeBalance',
       'YearsAtCompany', 'YearsInCurrentRole', 'YearsSinceLastPromotion',
       'YearsWithCurrManager'],
      dtype='object')
```

If we look at the details of this result, we see that it is an index expressed as a Python list. The idea is that we could use the same list for subsetting the data frame. Let us see the steps. First, we use the whole column index to view the data frame.

```
df[['Age', 'Attrition', 'BusinessTravel', 'DailyRate', 'Department',
    'DistanceFromHome', 'Education', 'EducationField', 'EmployeeCount',
    'EmployeeNumber', 'EnvironmentSatisfaction', 'Gender', 'HourlyRate',
    'JobInvolvement', 'JobLevel', 'JobRole', 'JobSatisfaction',
    'MaritalStatus', 'MonthlyIncome', 'MonthlyRate', 'NumCompaniesWorked',
    'Over18', 'OverTime', 'PercentSalaryHike', 'PerformanceRating',
    'RelationshipSatisfaction', 'StandardHours', 'StockOptionLevel',
    'TotalWorkingYears', 'TrainingTimesLastYear', 'WorkLifeBalance',
    'YearsAtCompany', 'YearsInCurrentRole', 'YearsSinceLastPromotion',
    'YearsWithCurrManager']]
```

	Age	Attrition	BusinessTravel	DailyRate	Department	...
0	41	Yes	Travel_Rarely	1102	Sales	...
1	49	No	Travel_Frequently	279	Research & Development	...
2	37	Yes	Travel_Rarely	1373	Research & Development	...
3	33	No	Travel_Frequently	1392	Research & Development	...
4	27	No	Travel_Rarely	591	Research & Development	...
...	...	...	...	...	...	...

Now we can simply slice the data frame by selecting only some columns. In this case, we want to implement a form of selection by negation, so we could just exclude one or more columns to obtain the corresponding subset. We try by excluding column *Attrition*.

```
df[['Age','BusinessTravel', 'DailyRate', 'Department',
    'DistanceFromHome', 'Education', 'EducationField', 'EmployeeCount',
    'EmployeeNumber', 'EnvironmentSatisfaction', 'Gender', 'HourlyRate',
    'JobInvolvement', 'JobLevel', 'JobRole', 'JobSatisfaction',
    'MaritalStatus', 'MonthlyIncome', 'MonthlyRate', 'NumCompaniesWorked',
    'Over18', 'OverTime', 'PercentSalaryHike', 'PerformanceRating',
    'RelationshipSatisfaction', 'StandardHours', 'StockOptionLevel',
    'TotalWorkingYears', 'TrainingTimesLastYear', 'WorkLifeBalance',
    'YearsAtCompany', 'YearsInCurrentRole', 'YearsSinceLastPromotion',
    'YearsWithCurrManager']]
```

	Age	BusinessTravel	DailyRate	Department	...
0	41	Travel_Rarely	1102	Sales	...
1	49	Travel_Frequently	279	Research & Development	...
2	37	Travel_Rarely	1373	Research & Development	...
3	33	Travel_Frequently	1392	Research & Development	...
4	27	Travel_Rarely	591	Research & Development	...
...	...	...	...	...	...

The solution could be dubbed inelegant, but it is effective and practical in many cases. It may present some difficulties when the number of columns is high.

A different, simple solution is offered by pandas function **difference()**, which takes two indices and *returns the elements of the first index that do not appear in the second one*. The general syntax is index1.difference(index2).

In our case, we have:

- *index1*: the index resulting from attribute columns;
- *index2*: the list of columns that should be *excluded* from selection.

Function difference() also has parameter **sort** to specify if the resulting column selection should be sorted; the default is *True*, with *False* the order of columns will remain unchanged. To show this feature, we operate a little modification to the data frame *df* by exchanging the position of column *Age* with *BusinessTravel*, so to have an unordered list of column names. To do that, we use the same technique adopted for subsetting; here, we just rewrite the order of the two columns.

```
df= df[['BusinessTravel', 'Attrition', 'Age', 'DailyRate', 'Department',
    'DistanceFromHome', 'Education', 'EducationField', 'EmployeeCount',
    'EmployeeNumber', 'EnvironmentSatisfaction', 'Gender', 'HourlyRate',
    'JobInvolvement', 'JobLevel', 'JobRole', 'JobSatisfaction',
    'MaritalStatus', 'MonthlyIncome', 'MonthlyRate', 'NumCompaniesWorked',

    'Over18', 'OverTime', 'PercentSalaryHike', 'PerformanceRating',
    'RelationshipSatisfaction', 'StandardHours', 'StockOptionLevel',
    'TotalWorkingYears', 'TrainingTimesLastYear', 'WorkLifeBalance',
    'YearsAtCompany', 'YearsInCurrentRole', 'YearsSinceLastPromotion',
    'YearsWithCurrManager']]
df.head()
```

	BusinessTravel	Attrition	Age	DailyRate	Department	...
0	Travel_Rarely	Yes	41	1102	Sales	...
1	Travel_Frequently	No	49	279	Research & Development	...
2	Travel_Rarely	Yes	37	1373	Research & Development	...
3	Travel_Frequently	No	33	1392	Research & Development	...
4	Travel_Rarely	No	27	591	Research & Development	...

We see here an example by excluding columns *Attrition* and *Department*, with the default for attribute `sort`.

```
df[df.columns.difference(['Attrition','Department'])]
```

	Age	BusinessTravel	DailyRate	DistanceFromHome	Education	EducationField	...
0	41	Travel_Rarely	1102	1	2	Life Sciences	...
1	49	Travel_Frequently	279	8	1	Life Sciences	...
2	37	Travel_Rarely	1373	2	2	Other	...
3	33	Travel_Frequently	1392	3	4	Life Sciences	...
4	27	Travel_Rarely	591	2	1	Medical	...
...	...	...	...	...	...	...	...

The resulting data frame does not have the two columns, and the column order has been rewritten. When we specify `sort=False`. The order remains like the initial one.

```
df[df.columns.difference(['Attrition','Department'], sort=False)]
```

	BusinessTravel	Age	DailyRate	DistanceFromHome	Education	EducationField	...
0	Travel_Rarely	41	1102	1	2	Life Sciences	...
1	Travel_Frequently	49	279	8	1	Life Sciences	...
2	Travel_Rarely	37	1373	2	2	Other	...
3	Travel_Frequently	33	1392	3	4	Life Sciences	...
4	Travel_Rarely	27	591	2	1	Medical	...
...	...	...	...	...	...	...	...

Alternative methods for selection by exclusion will make use of selection by positional indexes, range, and *selection helper* cited before, which will be discussed in the following chapter.

3.8   Python: Rename and Relocate Columns

We continue using data frame *df* of the previous section and extract a subset of columns

```
df= df[['Age','Department','EmployeeNumber','Gender','JobRole','MonthlyIncome']]
```

3.8.1   Standard Method

From what we have already seen in the selection of columns, attribute `columns` permit several usages, including renaming and relocating columns. For both, it is intuitive how to proceed (an example of changing column position has been already introduced in the previous section). Let us see an example with the subset of columns.

```
df.columns
Index(['Age', 'Department', 'EmployeeNumber', 'Gender', 'JobRole',
       'MonthlyIncome'],
     dtype='object')
```

We show renaming and relocating in two steps. First, we rename, technically by changing index columns' names.

```
df.columns= ['age','dept','employeeNum','gender','role','incomeMonth']
df.columns
Index(['age', 'dept', 'employeeNum', 'gender', 'role', 'incomeMonth'],
dtype='object')
```

Now we change the order of some columns.

```
df= df[['dept', 'employeeNum', 'role', 'incomeMonth', 'gender', 'age']]
```

	dept	employeeNum	role	incomeMonth	gender	age
0	Sales	1	Sales Executive	5993	Female	41
1	Research & Development	2	Research Scientist	5130	Male	49
2	Research & Development	4	Laboratory Technician	2090	Male	37
3	Research & Development	5	Research Scientist	2909	Female	33
4	Research & Development	7	Laboratory Technician	3468	Male	27

3.8.2   Functions `rename()` and `reindex()`

Beside the standard method, two pandas functions provide the same features. One is function **`rename()`** that renames columns specified with parameter **`columns`** as a ***dict*** (a *dict*, or *dictionary*, is a specific data type that will be introduced in the last chapter). The *dict* format uses *curly brackets* and pairs *key:value*, where the *key* is the name of the existing column and the *value* is the new name.

> **Tip**
>
> It is worth to repeat what was observed in the corresponding R section: the mnemonic approach to learning this material is definitely not recommended. For syntax details such as the *dict* format, the meaning of *key* and *value*, and the exact spelling of parameters (is it a *column* or *columns*?) the official pandas documentation should always be at hand and provide all such details.

We repeat the example seen before.

```
df= df.rename( columns={'Age':'age', 'Department':'dept',
                  'EmployeeNumber':'employeeNum', 'Gender':'gender',
                  'JobRole':'role', 'MonthlyIncome':'incomeMonth'})
```

	dept	employeeNum	role	incomeMonth	gender	age
0	Sales	1	Sales Executive	5993	Female	41
1	Research & Development	2	Research Scientist	5130	Male	49
2	Research & Development	4	Laboratory Technician	2090	Male	37
3	Research & Development	5	Research Scientist	2909	Female	33
4	Research & Development	7	Laboratory Technician	3468	Male	27
...	...	...	...	...	...	...

To change the order of columns, pandas function **reindex()** takes an index and permits to change it, either for modifying the order or to exclude some index values. Parameter **columns** specify that the index to change is associated to columns, it would have been the same with **axis=1** and without using columns. Function reindex() works also with a row index by specifying parameter **rows** or **axis=0**.

```
df.reindex(columns=['employeeNum','dept','role','incomeMonth','age','gender'])
```

	employeeNum	dept	role	incomeMonth	age	gender
0	1	Sales	Sales Executive	5993	41	Female
1	2	Research & Development	Research Scientist	5130	49	Male
2	4	Research & Development	Laboratory Technician	2090	37	Male
3	5	Research & Development	Research Scientist	2909	33	Female
4	7	Research & Development	Laboratory Technician	3468	27	Male
...	...	...	...	...	...	...

3.9   Python: NumPy Slicing, Selection with Index, Column Creation and Deletion

We introduce here some of the selection methods we have cited but not explained before, followed by column creation and deletion methods. The data frame is still *df* already used in the previous sections.

```
df= df[['Age','Department','EmployeeNumber','Gender','JobRole','MonthlyIncome']]
```

3.9.1   NumPy Array Slicing

Slicing of NumPy arrays is the most basic mechanism, useful in several situations when objects to manipulate are NumPy objects, rather than pandas data frames or series. Let us see a first simple example with a custom NumPy array.

```
a1= np.array([[1, 2, 3],
              [4, 5, 6],
              [7, 8, 9]])
```

Single vector elements can be selected simply with positional indexes.

```
print(a1[0,0])
print(a1[2,2])
1
9
```

Index 3 is out of matrix's bounds.

```
a1[3,3]
IndexError: index 3 is out of bounds for axis 0 with size 3
```

If we want to select a whole row or column, the syntax with colon should be used. This selects the first row. In this case, the colon could have been omitted.

```
a1[0, :]
array([1, 2, 3])
```

Differently, to select a column, the colon is necessary.

```
a1[:,2]
array([3, 6, 9])
```

The notation with colon, seen already with R, could be used to specify ranges. We increase the size of the matrix to observe the mechanism better.

```
a2= np.array([[1, 2, 3, 4, 5],
              [6, 7, 8, 9, 10],
              [11, 12, 13, 14, 15],
              [16, 17, 18, 19, 20]])
```

When we specify ranges, it is important to note that the first index value is *included* and the second is *excluded*. See some examples.

```
# First two rows, all columns
a2[0:2,:]
# Last three columns, all rows
a2[:, 2:]
# Third and fourth rows, second, third, and fourth columns
a2[2:4, 1:4]
array([[12, 13, 14],
       [17, 18, 19]])
```

3.9.2 Slicing of Pandas Data Frames

With the examples from NumPy slicing of vectors, we would like to apply similar techniques to pandas data frames. We have already encountered one technique for subsetting data frame columns by specifying the list of their names; now we consider other options.

The first option relies again on the flexibility of the `columns` attribute, which, by returning an index object, could be sliced by index values. For example, to select the second column index value:

```
df.columns[1]
'Department'
```

To specify ranges is straightforward with the use of the colon character. With the following, we select the third, fourth, and fifth columns.

```
df.columns[2:5]
Index(['EmployeeNumber', 'Gender', 'JobRole'], dtype='object')
```

To obtain a subset of data frame columns by using positional indexes is an easy extension.

```
df[df.columns[2:5]]
```

	EmployeeNumber	Gender	JobRole
0	1	Female	Sales Executive
1	2	Male	Research Scientist
2	4	Male	Laboratory Technician
3	5	Female	Research Scientist
4	7	Male	Laboratory Technician
...	...	...	...

Similarly, we can slice a pandas data frame by rows. For example, the first three rows.

```
df[0:3]
```

	Age	Department	Employee Number	Gender	JobRole	Monthly Income
0	41	Sales	1	Female	Sales Executive	5993
1	49	Research & Development	2	Male	Research Scientist	5130
2	37	Research & Development	4	Male	Laboratory Technician	2090

Another example is selecting 10 rows, starting from row of index 100.

```
df[100:110]
```

	Age	Department	Employee Number	Gender	JobRole	Monthly Income
100	37	Human Resources	133	Male	Human Resources	2073
101	32	Research & Development	134	Male	Research Scientist	2956
102	20	Research & Development	137	Female	Laboratory Technician	2926
103	34	Research & Development	138	Female	Research Scientist	4809
104	37	Research & Development	139	Male	Healthcare Representative	5163
105	59	Human Resources	140	Female	Manager	18844
106	50	Research & Development	141	Female	Research Director	18172
107	25	Sales	142	Male	Sales Executive	5744
108	25	Research & Development	143	Male	Research Scientist	2889
109	22	Research & Development	144	Female	Laboratory Technician	2871

It is now easy to slice a pandas data frame by rows and columns by putting together the two methods. We select ten rows starting from row of index 100 and columns *JobRole*, *Age*, and *Gender*. First by using column names. The two pairs of brackets are for the Python list and for the index.

```
df[100:110][['JobRole', 'Age', 'Gender']]
```

	JobRole	Age	Gender
100	Human Resources	37	Male
101	Research Scientist	32	Male
102	Laboratory Technician	20	Female
103	Research Scientist	34	Female
104	Healthcare Representative	37	Male
105	Manager	59	Female
106	Research Director	50	Female
107	Sales Executive	25	Male
108	Research Scientist	25	Male
109	Laboratory Technician	22	Female

Then with column indexes and a range for the first three columns.

```
df[100:110][df.columns[0:3]]
```

	Age	Department	EmployeeNumber
100	37	Human Resources	133
101	32	Research & Development	134
102	20	Research & Development	137
103	34	Research & Development	138
104	37	Research & Development	139
105	59	Human Resources	140
106	50	Research & Development	141
107	25	Sales	142
108	25	Research & Development	143
109	22	Research & Development	144

Another possibility is to transform the pandas data frame into a NumPy array and then slicing with the NumPy method.

```
a1= df.to_numpy()[100:110,3:6]
a1
array([['Male', 'Human Resources', 2073],
       ['Male', 'Research Scientist', 2956],
       ['Female', 'Laboratory Technician', 2926],
```

```
['Female', 'Research Scientist', 4809],
['Male', 'Healthcare Representative', 5163],
['Female', 'Manager', 18844],
['Female', 'Research Director', 18172],
['Male', 'Sales Executive', 5744],
['Male', 'Research Scientist', 2889],
['Female', 'Laboratory Technician', 2871]], dtype=object)
```

The drawback is that the result is not a data frame, obviously, it has missed column names (column index) and, if existed, the row index. We have to transform back into a pandas data frame with function **DataFrame()** and add again column names. It works, but it requires additional operations that we prefer to avoid.

```
pd.DataFrame(a1, columns= ['Gender','JobRole', 'MonthlyIncome'])
```

	Gender	JobRole	MonthlyIncome
0	Male	Human Resources	2073
1	Male	Research Scientist	2956
2	Female	Laboratory Technician	2926
3	Female	Research Scientist	4809
4	Male	Healthcare Representative	5163
5	Female	Manager	18844
6	Female	Research Director	18172
7	Male	Sales Executive	5744
8	Male	Research Scientist	2889
9	Female	Laboratory Technician	2871

3.9.3 Methods .loc and .iloc

The more specific method with pandas functionalities to slice a data frame is through two special methods, .loc and .iloc, which operates similarly on a row index but with different elements:

- .loc makes use of labels of row index values;
- .iloc makes use of the numeric row index, also said *implicit index*, starting from 0.

With these two methods, we can easily replicate the slicing techniques seen for NumPy and with R. Let us consider a first example with data frame *df*, which does not have a row index, other than the row numbers. We execute the same slicing operation on rows and columns by using first method .loc, then .iloc. Pay attention to the different results.

```
df.loc[100:110][['Age','Gender']]
```

	Age	Gender
100	37	Male
101	32	Male
102	20	Female
103	34	Female
104	37	Male
105	59	Female
106	50	Female
107	25	Male
108	25	Male
109	22	Female
110	51	Female

```
df.iloc[100:110][['Age','Gender']]
```

	Age	Gender
100	37	Male
101	32	Male
102	20	Female
103	34	Female
104	37	Male
105	59	Female
106	50	Female
107	25	Male
108	25	Male
109	22	Female

The difference is clear. Method `.loc` treats row index values as labels, and the range extremes are included. Differently for method `.iloc` that works with positional index values, similar to NumPy and follows the same rule, first value of the range is included, the second is excluded.

This behavior could perhaps raise a question about the actual difference between slicing using just the range numbers (NumPy style) and slicing through method `.iloc`. The question is completely legit; let us look at the difference. First, we subset by specifying just the range.

```
df[100:110]
```

	Age	Department	Employee Number	Gender	JobRole	Monthly Income
100	37	Human Resources	133	Male	Human Resources	2073
101	32	Research & Development	134	Male	Research Scientist	2956
102	20	Research & Development	137	Female	Laboratory Technician	2926
103	34	Research & Development	138	Female	Research Scientist	4809
104	37	Research & Development	139	Male	Healthcare Representative	5163
105	59	Human Resources	140	Female	Manager	18844
106	50	Research & Development	141	Female	Research Director	18172
107	25	Sales	142	Male	Sales Executive	5744
108	25	Research & Development	143	Male	Research Scientist	2889
109	22	Research & Development	144	Female	Laboratory Technician	2871

Then `.iloc` slicing.

```
df.iloc[100:110]
```

	Age	Department	Employee Number	Gender	JobRole	Monthly Income
100	37	Human Resources	133	Male	Human Resources	2073
101	32	Research & Development	134	Male	Research Scientist	2956
102	20	Research & Development	137	Female	Laboratory Technician	2926
103	34	Research & Development	138	Female	Research Scientist	4809
104	37	Research & Development	139	Male	Healthcare Representative	5163
105	59	Human Resources	140	Female	Manager	18844
106	50	Research & Development	141	Female	Research Director	18172
107	25	Sales	142	Male	Sales Executive	5744
108	25	Research & Development	143	Male	Research Scientist	2889
109	22	Research & Development	144	Female	Laboratory Technician	2871

The results are identical, so the answer to the question is that there is no difference between the two methods. However, *pandas documentation for better clarity suggests using methods* `.loc` *and* `.iloc` *for subsetting rows and leaving the syntax with just brackets for subsetting over columns.* It is a suggestion; therefore, everybody's free to choose differently, but it is the best practice to write code in the clearest way possible, because that has evident advantages when the code needs to be debugged, reused, or modified.

We consider another example, this time with an explicit index. To have it, we use pandas function **set_index()** that transforms a column into an index. We use column *Department*.

```
df2= df.set_index('Department')
df2
```

Department	Age	Employee Number	Gender	JobRole	Monthly Income
Sales	41	1	Female	Sales Executive	5993
Research & Development	49	2	Male	Research Scientist	5130
Research & Development	37	4	Male	Laboratory Technician	2090
Research & Development	33	5	Female	Research Scientist	2909
Research & Development	27	7	Male	Laboratory Technician	3468
...	...	...	...	...	...
Research & Development	36	2061	Male	Laboratory Technician	2571
Research & Development	39	2062	Male	Healthcare Representative	9991
Research & Development	27	2064	Male	Manufacturing Director	6142
Sales	49	2065	Male	Sales Executive	5390
Research & Development	34	2068	Male	Laboratory Technician	4404

Now *Department* is no longer a column, but an index level. We can verify it with attribute `columns`, where *Department* does not appear, and **index**, showing values of *Department*.

```
df2.columns
Index(['Age', 'EmployeeNumber', 'Gender', 'JobRole', 'MonthlyIncome'],
dtype='object')
df2.index
Index(['Sales', 'Research & Development', 'Research & Development',
       'Research & Development', 'Research & Development',
       'Research & Development', 'Research & Development',
       'Research & Development', 'Research & Development',
       'Research & Development',
       ...
       'Research & Development', 'Sales', 'Sales', 'Research & Development',
       'Sales', 'Research & Development', 'Research & Development',
       'Research & Development', 'Sales', 'Research & Development'],
     dtype='object', name='Department', length=1470)
```

Now we can use `.loc` with index labels. First with a single value.

```
df2.loc['Sales']
```

Department	Age	EmployeeNumber	Gender	JobRole	MonthlyIncome
Sales	41	1	Female	Sales Executive	5993
Sales	53	23	Female	Manager	15427
Sales	36	27	Male	Sales Representative	3407

Department	Age	EmployeeNumber	Gender	JobRole	MonthlyIncome
Sales	42	35	Male	Sales Executive	6825
Sales	46	38	Female	Manager	18947
…	…	…	…	…	…
Sales	45	2046	Female	Sales Executive	4850
Sales	50	2055	Male	Sales Executive	10854
Sales	39	2056	Female	Sales Executive	12031
Sales	26	2060	Female	Sales Representative	2966
Sales	49	2065	Male	Sales Executive	5390

With more values, we need the brackets for the list.

```
df2.loc[['Sales','Human Resources']]
```

Department	Age	EmployeeNumber	Gender	JobRole	MonthlyIncome
Sales	41	1	Female	Sales Executive	5993
Sales	53	23	Female	Manager	15427
Sales	36	27	Male	Sales Representative	3407
Sales	42	35	Male	Sales Executive	6825
Sales	46	38	Female	Manager	18947
…	…	…	…	…	…
Human Resources	27	1944	Female	Human Resources	2863
Human Resources	38	1972	Male	Human Resources	2991
Human Resources	55	1973	Male	Manager	19636
Human Resources	25	1987	Female	Human Resources	2187
Human Resources	35	2040	Female	Human Resources	8837

3.9.4 Selection with Selection Helper

With methods `.loc` and `.iloc` we have the full set of possibilities for subsetting a data frame by rows and columns. Now we add some *selection helpers*, which are utility functions providing features to select based on patterns of column names.

We read the dataset again to have the full list of columns and from data frame *df*, we select columns starting with string "Job" or string "Monthly" by means of pandas function `str.startswith()`. Since we are using index names, `.loc` is the right method. Pay attention to a detail of the function usage: we are using a list of values (i.e. 'Job', 'Monthly'), but the list syntax should not be used with brackets; otherwise, it raises an error.

```
df = pd.read_csv("datasets/IBM_Kaggle/WA_Fn-UseC_-HR-Employee-Attrition.csv")
df.loc[:,df.columns.str.startswith('Job','Monthly')]
```

	JobInvolvement	JobLevel	JobRole	JobSatisfaction
0	3	2	Sales Executive	4
1	2	2	Research Scientist	2
2	2	1	Laboratory Technician	3
3	3	1	Research Scientist	3
4	3	1	Laboratory Technician	2
...	...	...	...	...

In the same way, it could be used with the function `str.endswith()`.

```
df.loc[:,df.columns.str.endswith('Rate')]
```

	DailyRate	HourlyRate	MonthlyRate
0	1102	94	19479
1	279	61	24907
2	1373	92	2396
3	1392	56	23159
4	591	40	16632
...	...	...	...

Finally, columns could be selected through a pattern found generically in the name with function `str.contains()`.

```
df.loc[:,df.columns.str.contains('Year')]
```

	TotalWorking Years	TrainingTimes LastYear	YearsAt Company	YearsIn CurrentRole	YearsSinceLast Promotion	YearsWith CurrManager
0	8	0	6	4	0	5
1	10	3	10	7	1	7
2	7	3	0	0	0	0
3	8	3	8	7	3	0
4	6	3	2	2	2	2
...	...	...	...	...	...	...

3.9.5 Creating and Deleting Columns

The standard method for creating a column in a pandas data frame is the same we have seen with R: the new column is created by assigning a value. For simplicity, we take a subset of columns to work with.

```
df1= df[['Age','Department','EmployeeNumber','Gender','JobRole',
'MonthlyIncome']]
df1['New1']= 0
df1['New2']= "ABC"
df1
SettingWithCopyWarning:

A value is trying to be set on a copy of a slice from a DataFrame.
Try using .loc[row_indexer,col_indexer] = value instead

See the caveats in the documentation: https://pandas.pydata.org/pandas-docs/
stable/user_guide/indexing.html#returning-a-view-versus-a-copy
```

	Age	Department	Employee Number	Gender	JobRole	Monthly Income	New1	New2
0	41	Sales	1	Female	Sales Executive	5993	0	ABC
1	49	Research & Development	2	Male	Research Scientist	5130	0	ABC
2	37	Research & Development	4	Male	Laboratory Technician	2090	0	ABC
3	33	Research & Development	5	Female	Research Scientist	2909	0	ABC
4	27	Research & Development	7	Male	Laboratory Technician	3468	0	ABC
...	...	...	...	...	...	...	...	...

You may have noticed that the operation has raised a *warning message* telling us that we are trying to assign a value "on a copy of a slice from a DataFrame" and that instead we should use a different syntax ("Try using .loc[row_indexer,col_indexer] = value").

Warning messages, although not communicating a strict error condition, should always be read carefully, and although they might not always be crystal clear in their meaning, it is worth making efforts to interpret them because often they are communicating something we may have overlooked, not blocking the execution, but nevertheless a possible source of logical errors or behaviors different from what we are expecting.

This message is in fact telling us to pay attention to an important difference between what is known as **working on a view of data** or **working on a copy of data**. We will discuss it in following chapters because it becomes relevant when we modify values. In that case, we have to be sure to have modified the actual data, not a copy of them, if the modifications have to be persistent. In this case of column creation, the data frame *df1* has been actually modified with the addition of the two new columns, as we have verified.

To delete a column, there exists function **drop()** with attribute **columns** to specify columns to delete. Alternatively, there is attribute **axis=1** to specify that the operation will be applied on columns, **axis=0** tells the function to work on rows. It also exists attribute **inplace**, shared by several other functions, which if *True* directly saves the result to the data frame.

```
df1.drop(['New1','New2'], axis=1)
```

This shows data frame *df1* without columns *New1* and *New2*; it has to be saved to be a persistent modification. Otherwise, parameter `inplace` saves implicitly.

```
df1.drop(columns=['New1','New2'], inplace=True)
```

	Age	Department	Employee Number	Gender	JobRole	Monthly Income
0	41	Sales	1	Female	Sales Executive	5993
1	49	Research & Development	2	Male	Research Scientist	5130
2	37	Research & Development	4	Male	Laboratory Technician	2090
3	33	Research & Development	5	Female	Research Scientist	2909
4	27	Research & Development	7	Male	Laboratory Technician	3468
...	...	...	...	...	...	...

3.9.6 Functions `insert()` and `assign()`

There also exist two useful functions for column creation: `insert()` and `assign()`, offering some additional features with respect to the standard methods just seen.

With `insert()`, the position of the new column should be specified, whereas with standard creation, the new column is added at the end and should be subsequently relocated if a certain order is desired. Here we insert the new column in the second position.

```
df1.insert(1, "New1", "ABC")
```

	Age	New1	Department	Employee Number	Gender	JobRole	Monthly Income
0	41	ABC	Sales	1	Female	Sales Executive	5993
1	49	ABC	Research & Development	2	Male	Research Scientist	5130
2	37	ABC	Research & Development	4	Male	Laboratory Technician	2090
3	33	ABC	Research & Development	5	Female	Research Scientist	2909
4	27	ABC	Research & Development	7	Male	Laboratory Technician	3468
...	...	...	...	...	...	...	...

Function `assign()` could be particularly useful with calculated columns, because it offers a simple and clear method to create them, similar to the `mutate()` function of R. Here, we create three new columns by calculating the difference of element values with some statistics: the mean, maximum, and minimum monthly incomes.

```
df1= df.assign(Diff_monthInc_Mean= df.MonthlyIncome - df.MonthlyIncome.mean(),
               Diff_monthInc_Max= df.MonthlyIncome - df.MonthlyIncome.max(),
               Diff_monthInc_Min= df.MonthlyIncome - df.MonthlyIncome.min()
               )

df1[['Diff_monthInc_Mean','Diff_monthInc_Max','Diff_monthInc_Min']]
```

	Diff_monthInc_Mean	Diff_monthInc_Max	Diff_monthInc_Min
0	−509.931293	−14006	4984
1	−1372.931293	−14869	4121
2	−4412.931293	−17909	1081
3	−3593.931293	−17090	1900
4	−3034.931293	−16531	2459
...	...	...	...

3.10 Python: Separate and Unite Columns

3.10.1 Separate

For separating values of a column into several new columns, pandas has two useful utility functions, `str.split()` and `str.slice()`, respectively, based on *patterns or regular expressions* and on *positions*.

Function `str.split()` has the following main parameters:

- `pat` : a pattern or a regular expression could be specified as separator for splitting the string (default: *blank space*);
- `n` : the number of separations to operate (default: *all*);
- `expand` : if *True,* it produces a new data frame with the additional columns resulting from splitting the old one; if *False,* it produces independent series for each one of the new parts (default: *False*).

With function `str.slice()`, the important parameters are:

- `start`: the position (included) where to start the cut;
- `stop`: the final position (excluded) of the cut;
- `step`: the number of characters to move ahead for each character included in the result (default: 1, meaning each character is included in the result).

We replicate the examples seen in the corresponding R section with samples of *product codes* from the *FDA* (https://www.fda.gov/industry/import-program-tools/product-codes-and-product-code-builder).

```
productCodes= ["38BEE27","62GBA41","79L-RR"]
pc= pd.DataFrame(data=productCodes, columns=["prodCode"])
```

	prodCode
0	38BEE27
1	62GBA41
2	79L--RR

Those codes are positional; hence, we separate them by means of `str.slice()`, setting *start* and *stop* parameters.

```
pc["Industry Code"]= pc["prodCode"].str.slice(start=0, stop=2)
pc["Class"]= pc["prodCode"].str.slice(start=2, stop=3)
pc["Subclass"]= pc["prodCode"].str.slice(start=3, stop=4)
pc["Process Indicator Code (PIC)"]= pc["prodCode"].str.slice(start=4, stop=5)
pc["Product (Group)"]= pc["prodCode"].str.slice(start=5)
```

	prodCode	Industry Code	Class	Subclass	Process Indicator Code (PIC)	Product (Group)
0	38BEE27	38	B	E	E	27
1	62GBA41	62	G	B	A	41
2	79L--RR	79	L	—	—	RR

Checking column data type, we see that they keep the type of the original one.

```
pc.dtypes
prodCode                         object
Industry Code                    object
Class                            object
Subclass                         object
Process Indicator Code (PIC)     object
Product (Group)                  object
dtype: object
```

Now, let us consider dates for practicing with `str.split()`. As specified before, these examples of separation of dates are purely demonstrative of the features; separating dates into their components is not useful, in general, much better to treat them as *datatime* objects with specific functions.

```
es_date= ["12/10/2022", "03/07/2021", "18/09/2020"]
dt1= pd.DataFrame(data=es_date, columns=["Date"]
```

	Date
0	12/10/2022
1	03/07/2021
2	18/09/2020

We separate column *Date* with `str.split()` using option **expand=True** to obtain a new data frame. There is no parameter for specifying a list of names for the new columns, nor is there the possibility to keep all original columns of the data frame. The result is a data frame with just the new columns with conventional names. If we want them together with the original data frame, that is an operation to be executed separately, for example, with pandas function `concat()`.

```
split_df= dt1["Date"].str.split(pat="/", expand=True )
```

	0	1	2
0	12	10	2022
1	03	07	2021
2	18	09	2020

```
pd.concat([dt1, split_df], axis=1)
```

	Date	0	1	2
0	12/10/2022	12	10	2022
1	03/07/2021	03	07	2021
2	18/09/2020	18	09	2020

If we try with **expand=False**, the result is composed of three independent series.

```
dt1["Date"].str.split(pat="/", expand=False )
0    [12, 10, 2022]
1    [03, 07, 2021]
2    [18, 09, 2020]
Name: Date, dtype: object
```

We add some complications to date formats.

```
es_date2= ["12October2022", "03July2021", "18August2020"]
dt2= pd.DataFrame(data=es_date2, columns=["Date"])
```

	Date
0	12October2022
1	03July2021
2	18August2020

The day and year can be separated using `str.slice()`, and the year can be counted backward from the end of the string.

```
dt2["Day"]=dt2["Date"].str.slice(start=0, stop=2)
dt2["Year"]=dt2["Date"].str.slice(start=-4)
```

	Date	Day	Year
0	12October2022	12	2022
1	03July2021	03	2021
2	18August2020	18	2020

To obtain the month, we can combine the two previous examples.

```
dt2["Month"]=dt2["Date"].str.slice(start=2, stop=-4)
```

	Date	Day	Year	Month
0	12October2022	12	2022	October
1	03July2021	03	2021	July
2	18August2020	18	2020	August

3.10.2 Unite

To unite values from different columns into a single one, possibly adding a separator between the parts, several possibilities exist, either with base Python or with pandas functions. Here we see just one solution, not the most efficient if execution time is important, but simple enough to be useful in most of practical cases.

We use pandas function **`str.cat()`** and as common with string manipulation functions, it works on series (i.e. single columns). A caveat is that it requires that columns to unite are of *character* data type. To be sure, we add the type transformation by using function **`astype(str)`**. We see the example with dates just split.

```
dt2["Day"].astype(str).str.cat(dt2[["Month", "Year"]].astype(str), sep="/")
0    12/October/2022
1       03/July/2021
2     18/August/2020
Name: Day, dtype: object
```

The result is a series, not a data frame. If we try with a seemingly more intuitive form, by specifying all columns to unite as parameters of the `str.cat()` function, an error is generated because `str.cat()` works on series, not a data frame.

```
dt2.str.cat(dt2[["Day","Month", "Year"]].astype(str), sep="/")
AttributeError: 'DataFrame' object has no attribute 'str'
```

3.11 Python: Sorting Data Frame

Similar to the corresponding section on sorting with R, we use dataset *IBM HR Analytics Employee Attrition & Performance* to show the main features.

The main difference of sorting data frames in Python, with respect to the case of R, beside pure syntax, is the relevance that indexes have when we work with pandas data frames, possibly composed by multiple layers (in this case called ***multi-index***). The main functions for sorting pandas data frames are `sort_values()`, using columns, and `sort_index()` for index levels. The logic is the same for the two functions.

3.11.1 Sorting Columns

The usage of function `sort_values()` is intuitive and has the following parameters:

- `by` : to specify one or more columns (or possibly index levels) to use for sorting;
- `axis` : with `axis=0` (*default*) that means values are sorted by rows (index), whereas `axis=1` means the sorting is with respect to columns;
- `ascending` : if *True* (*default*) the sorting is from low to high values, if *False,* the order will be decreasing;
- `inplace`: it saves automatically the resulting data frame.

We see some simple examples.

```
df.head()
```

	Age	Attrition	Business Travel	Daily Rate	Department	Distance FromHome	Education	Education Field	...
0	41	Yes	Travel_Rarely	1102	Sales	1	2	Life Sciences	...
1	49	No	Travel_Frequently	279	Research & Development	8	1	Life Sciences	...
2	37	Yes	Travel_Rarely	1373	Research & Development	2	2	Other	...
3	33	No	Travel_Frequently	1392	Research & Development	3	4	Life Sciences	...
4	27	No	Travel_Rarely	591	Research & Development	2	1	Medical	...

First, we sort on single column *Age*, using all defaults.

```
df.sort_values(by="Age")
```

	Age	Attrition	BusinessTravel	DailyRate	Department	...
1311	18	No	Non-Travel	1431	Research & Development	...
457	18	Yes	Travel_Frequently	1306	Sales	...
972	18	No	Non-Travel	1124	Research & Development	...
301	18	No	Travel_Rarely	812	Sales	...
296	18	Yes	Travel_Rarely	230	Research & Development	...
...	...	...	...	...	...	...
536	60	No	Travel_Rarely	1179	Sales	...
427	60	No	Travel_Frequently	1499	Sales	...
411	60	No	Travel_Rarely	422	Research & Development	...
879	60	No	Travel_Rarely	696	Sales	...
1209	60	No	Travel_Rarely	370	Research & Development	...

Now we sort on more columns by specifying different sorting options.

```
df.sort_values(by=["JobRole","Age"], ascending=[True, False])[['Age','JobRole']]
```

	Age	JobRole
1209	60	Healthcare Representative
126	58	Healthcare Representative
308	58	Healthcare Representative
674	58	Healthcare Representative
163	57	Healthcare Representative
...	...	...
171	19	Sales Representative
688	19	Sales Representative
301	18	Sales Representative
457	18	Sales Representative
1153	18	Sales Representative

3.11.2 Sorting Index Levels

To show examples with sorting on index levels, first we have to create an index on rows. Here we use pandas function `set_index()` that transforms a list of columns into index levels. We will see in following chapters that typically it is with grouping and aggregation operations that we produce data frames with indexes. For example, we transform columns *Department* and *JobRole* into index levels. With attributes `columns` and `index,` we verify the result.

```
df1= df.set_index(['Department','JobRole'])
df1.head()
```

Department	JobRole	Age	Attrition	BusinessTravel	DailyRate	...
Sales	Sales Executive	41	Yes	Travel_Rarely	1102	...
Research & Development	Research Scientist	49	No	Travel_Frequently	279	...
	Laboratory Technician	37	Yes	Travel_Rarely	1373	...
	Research Scientist	33	No	Travel_Frequently	1392	...
	Laboratory Technician	27	No	Travel_Rarely	591	...

```
df1.index
MultiIndex([(                   'Sales',              'Sales Executive'),
            ('Research & Development',             'Research Scientist'),
            ('Research & Development',          'Laboratory Technician'),
            ('Research & Development',             'Research Scientist'),
            ('Research & Development',          'Laboratory Technician'),
            ('Research & Development',          'Laboratory Technician'),
            ('Research & Development',          'Laboratory Technician'),
            ('Research & Development',          'Laboratory Technician'),
            ('Research & Development',         'Manufacturing Director'),
            ('Research & Development', 'Healthcare Representative'),
            ...
            ('Research & Development',             'Research Scientist'),
            (                 'Sales',              'Sales Executive'),
            (                 'Sales',              'Sales Executive'),
            ('Research & Development',         'Manufacturing Director'),
            (                 'Sales',           'Sales Representative'),
            ('Research & Development',          'Laboratory Technician'),
            ('Research & Development', 'Healthcare Representative'),
            ('Research & Development',         'Manufacturing Director'),
            (                 'Sales',              'Sales Executive'),
            ('Research & Development',          'Laboratory Technician')],
           names=['Department', 'JobRole'], length=1470)
```

Data frame *df1* has a multi-index on rows with two levels: *Department* and *JobRole*. We sort it by means of the index levels with `sort_index()` and parameter **level**. *Index levels could be specified by name or by number.*

```
df1.sort_index(level='JobRole', ascending=False)
```

Department	JobRole	Age	Attrition	BusinessTravel	DailyRate	...
Sales	Sales Representative	26	No	Travel_Rarely	1167	...
	Sales Representative	23	Yes	Travel_Frequently	638	...
	Sales Representative	21	No	Travel_Rarely	501	...
	Sales Representative	52	No	Non-Travel	585	...

Department	JobRole	Age	Attrition	BusinessTravel	DailyRate	...
	Sales Representative	32	No	Travel_Rarely	234	...
...	...	...	...	...	...	...
Research & Development	Healthcare Representative	36	No	Travel_Rarely	1223	...
	Healthcare Representative	35	No	Non-Travel	1097	...
	Healthcare Representative	44	No	Travel_Rarely	1459	...
	Healthcare Representative	44	No	Travel_Rarely	477	...
	Healthcare Representative	36	No	Travel_Rarely	1299	...

Now we try with index levels expressed by numbers.

```
df1.sort_index(level=[0,1], ascending=[True, False])
```

Department	JobRole	Age	Attrition	BusinessTravel	DailyRate	...
Human Resources	Manager	59	No	Non-Travel	1420	...
	Manager	54	No	Non-Travel	142	...
	Manager	50	No	Travel_Frequently	1246	...
	Manager	41	No	Travel_Rarely	427	...
	Manager	41	No	Travel_Rarely	314	...
...	...	...	...	...	...	...
Sales	Manager	46	No	Travel_Rarely	563	...
	Manager	47	No	Travel_Rarely	1225	...
	Manager	40	No	Travel_Rarely	611	...
	Manager	58	No	Non-Travel	350	...
	Manager	58	No	Travel_Rarely	605	...

From this example, we also recognize an important detail: how index levels are ordered and should be counted. Here we have *level 0* in increasing order and *level 1* in decreasing order; therefore, *Department* is level 0 and *JobRole* is level 1. *Index levels are set starting from the most external (level 0).*

3.11.3 From Indexed to Non-indexed Data Frame

Having a data frame with an index on rows, it is often useful to convert it back to a non-indexed form, with index levels transformed into columns. There is a handy pandas function for this operation: `reset_index()` with some useful parameters:

- `level`: only index levels specified are transformed into columns, rather than all of them;
- `col_level` and `col_fill`: in case there exist a multi-index on columns, these two parameters permit to specify how row index levels transformed into columns should be inserted into the multi-index on columns. This is an uncommon case.

We could use data frame *df1* for some examples. First with the generic operation, then transforming a single level only.

```
df1.reset_index().head()
df1.reset_index(level='JobRole').head()
```

	JobRole	Age	Attrition	BusinessTravel	...
Department					
Sales	Sales Executive	41	Yes	Travel_Rarely	...
Research & Development	Research Scientist	49	No	Travel_Frequently	...
Research & Development	Laboratory Technician	37	Yes	Travel_Rarely	...
Research & Development	Research Scientist	33	No	Travel_Frequently	...
Research & Development	Laboratory Technician	27	No	Travel_Rarely	...

3.11.4 Sorting by an External List

To conclude the chapter, we replicate what we have discussed in the corresponding section with R regarding the case of sorting with respect to an external list. This is an important case that we could encounter on many occasions; one of the most frequent is with month names or weekdays.

The logic is identical to what we have seen for R and has the following steps:

1. *Create the external list* with the specific order of categories/values to be used as sorting criteria for the data frame.
2. Transform the data frame column to be sorted according to the external into *categorical data type*, with categories associated to the external list.
3. *Sort* the data frame column as usual.

We use dataset *Particulates – PM2.5 Speciation 2022,* from the *Air Data: Air Quality Data Collected at Outdoor Monitors Across the US*, of the United States Environmental Protection Agency (EPA). This dataset has data about the **PM2.5 particulate** collected by EPA in 2022. Being a large dataset (Rows: 565397, Columns: 29), we read it and take a random sample of 10 000 rows and a selection of columns.

```
df=pd.read_csv("~/DS_Wiley/datasets/EPA/daily_88101_2022.zip",
            usecols= ['Date Local', 'State Name', 'County Name',
                    'City Name', 'Arithmetic Mean'])
df1= df.sample(n=10000, replace=False, random_state=1)
df1.head()
```

	Date Local	Arithmetic Mean	State Name	County Name	City Name
313564	2022-07-20	10.800000	Utah	Iron	Enoch
346390	2022-08-03	7.000000	Wisconsin	Grant	Potosi
251278	2022-06-26	15.500000	Pennsylvania	Allegheny	North Braddock
251067	2022-04-29	8.091667	Pennsylvania	Allegheny	North Braddock
42660	2022-01-20	15.227273	California	Santa Clara	San Jose

Column *Date Local* first needs to be converted in *datetime* type. Then, we create a new column **Month** by extracting the month name from column *Date Local* with function `dt.month_name()`, then we sort it. The resulting order is alphabetical, hence incorrect.

```
df1['Date Local']= pd.to_datetime(df1['Date Local'])
df1['Month']= df1["Date Local"].dt.month_name()
df1.sort_values(by='Month')
```

	Date Local	Arithmetic Mean	State Name	County Name	City Name	Month
63092	2022-04-25	8.583333	District Of Columbia	District of Columbia	Washington	April
305565	2022-04-30	3.000000	Texas	Tarrant	Fort Worth	April
357422	2022-04-01	2.583333	Wyoming	Sheridan	Sheridan	April
146271	2022-04-29	6.991667	Michigan	Ingham	Lansing	April
46778	2022-04-13	6.565217	California	Tulare	Not in a city	April
...	...	...	...	...	...	...
344840	2022-09-27	1.900000	Wisconsin	Dodge	Kekoskee	September
319031	2022-09-10	32.200000	Utah	Salt Lake	Salt Lake City	September
351679	2022-09-05	3.787500	Wisconsin	Taylor	Not in a city	September
93574	2022-09-07	8.000000	Illinois	McLean	Normal	September
111828	2022-09-19	8.800000	Iowa	Clinton	Clinton	September

We consider the steps for the correct sorting of month names.
STEP 1. Create the external ordered list.

```
monthOrder= ['January', 'February', 'March', 'April', 'May', 'June', 'July',
             'August', 'September', 'October', 'November', 'December']
```

STEP 2. Pandas function `Categorical()` transforms column *Month* into categorical data type, and with parameter `categories,` we associate the external list. Parameter `ordered` specifies that categories are ordered.

```
df1.Month= pd.Categorical(
    df1.Month,
    categories= monthOrder,
    ordered= True)
```

Checking the data type of column *Month*, we see the result of the transformation.

```
df1.Month.dtype
CategoricalDtype(categories=['January', 'February', 'March', 'April', 'May',
                  'June', 'July', 'August', 'September', 'October',
                  'November', 'December'],
, ordered=True)
```

STEP 3. Now that we have the custom order associated to column *Month*, we just need to sort the data frame.

```
df1.sort_values(by='Month')
```

	Date Local	Arithmetic Mean	State Name	County Name	City Name	Month
48976	2022-01-05	3.100000	California	Ventura	Simi Valley	January
81850	2022-01-22	6.500000	Georgia	Washington	Sandersville	January
182713	2022-01-28	4.200000	Nevada	Clark	Spring Valley	January
205496	2022-01-06	0.916667	New Mexico	Santa Fe	Not in a city	January
96874	2022-01-03	9.800000	Illinois	Saint Clair	East Saint Louis	January
...	...	...	...	...	...	...
180583	2022-10-26	8.300000	Nebraska	Hall	Grand Island	October
115366	2022-10-13	12.300000	Iowa	Linn	Cedar Rapids	October
181478	2022-10-30	4.666667	Nebraska	Scotts Bluff	Scottsbluff	October
114763	2022-10-09	12.300000	Iowa	Linn	Cedar Rapids	October
113170	2022-10-10	15.800000	Iowa	Johnson	Iowa City	October

Questions

3.1 **(R/Python)**

A *tidy* dataset has:

A Rows representing single observations

B Columns representing values (e.g. years, weekdays, product codes, etc.)

C Columns representing observations

D Elements containing variables

(R: A)

3.2 (R/Python)

A *tidy* dataset does not have:

A Dates as element values

B Times as element values

C Columns as variables

D Years as column names

(R: D)

3.3 (R/Python)

With respect to a *tidy* dataset, an *untidy* dataset is:

A Better

B Worse

C It depends

D Equivalent

(R: C)

3.4 (R)

Considering data frame *df* of Section 3.1, what is the result produced by the following instruction?

```
df1= select(df, 2:4, Age)
```

A data frame *df1* with columns *Age, Attrition, BusinessTravel, DailyRate*, in this order

B data frame *df1* with columns *Attrition, BusinessTravel, DailyRate, Age*, in this order

C data frame *df1* with columns *Age, Attrition, BusinessTravel*, in this order

D data frame *df1* with columns *Attrition, BusinessTravel, Age*, in this order

(R: B)

3.5 (R)

Considering data frame *df* of Section 3.1, how many columns has the result produced by the following instruction?

```
df1= select(df, 1:4, Age, Attrition)
```

A 5

B 6

C 4

D it returns an error

(R: C)

3.6 (R)

Considering data frame *df* of Section 3.1, what is the result produced by the following instruction?

```
df1= select(df, 1:4, JobRole, !Attrition)
```

A 4
B 35
C 34
D it returns an error
(R: B)

3.7 **(R)**
Considering data frame *df* of Section 3.1, what is the result produced by the following instruction?

```
df1= select(df, 1:4, JobRole, -Attrition)
```

A 4
B 35
C 5
D it returns an error
(R: A)

3.8 **(R)**
Considering data frame *df* of Section 3.1, what is the result produced by the following instruction?

```
df1= select(df, !1:4)
```

A 3
B 35
C 31
D 4
(R: C)

3.9 **(R)**
Considering data frame *df* of Section 3.1, what is the result produced by the following instruction?

```
df1= select(df, -1:4)
```

A 3
B 35
C 31
D 4
(R: A)

3.10 **(R)**
Considering data frame *df* of Section 3.1, what is the result produced by the following instruction?

```
df1= select(df, -(1:4))
```

A 3
B 35
C 31
D 4
(R: A)

3.11 **(R)**

Considering data frame *df* of Section 3.1, what is the difference of results produced by the two following instructions?

```
df1= select(df, 6:10)
df1= df[6:10]
```

A the first produces a data frame 1,470 × 5, the second a data frame 6 × 10
B none, a data frame 1,470 × 5 with same columns
C the second produces an error
D the first produces a data frame, and the second a list of values
(R: B)

3.12 **(R)**

Considering data frame *df* of Section 3.1, what is the result produced by the following instruction?

```
df1= df[6:10,c(6,10)]
```

A an error
B a data frame with 2 columns and 5 rows
C a data frame with 5 columns and 5 rows
D a data frame with 5 rows and 2 columns
(R: D)

3.13 **(R)**

Considering data frame *df* of Section 3.1, what is the result produced by the following instruction?

```
df %>% select(1, 5, 7, 12) %>%
       mutate(Col1= Age - median(Age, na.rm=TRUE)) %>%
       arrange(desc(Col1))
```

A a data frame of 5 columns with values of column *Col1* all positive
B a data frame with 4 columns sorted by column *Col1* in descending order

    C a data frame with 5 columns with column *Col1* sorted in increasing order

    D a data frame with 5 columns and values of column *Age* in decreasing order

(R: D)

3.14   **(R)**

Considering data frame *df* of Section 3.1, what are the results produced by the following instructions? (assume to have run `library(magrittr)`)

```
df %$% (max(Age, na.rm=TRUE) - min(Age, na.rm=TRUE))
df %>% (max(Age, na.rm=TRUE) - min(Age, na.rm=TRUE))
```

  A both give 42 as result

  B both give an error

  C first one gives 42, and the second an error

  D first one gives an error, and the second 42

(R: C)

3.15   **(Python)**

Considering data frame *df* of Section 3.7, what is the result produced by the following instruction?

```
df1= df['Age', 'Department', 'Gender']
```

  A data frame *df1* with columns *Age, Attrition, Gender*, in this order

  B an error

  C three lists corresponding to the values of columns *Age, Attrition, Gender*

  D an empty data frame

(R: B)

3.16   **(Python)**

Considering data frame *df* of Section 3.7, what is the result produced by the following sequence of two instructions?

```
df1= df[['Age', 'Attrition', 'BusinessTravel', 'DailyRate',
'Department',
        'DistanceFromHome', 'Education', 'EducationField',
        'EmployeeCount','EmployeeNumber', 'EnvironmentSatisfaction',
        'Gender']] df1[df1.columns.difference(['BusinessTravel',
        'DailyRate', 'Department', 'DistanceFromHome', 'Education',
        'EducationField', 'EmployeeCount', 'EmployeeNumber',
        'EnvironmentSatisfaction'])]
```

  A a data frame with columns *Age, Attrition, Gender*

  B a data frame with columns *BusinessTravel, DailyRate, Department, DistanceFrom Home, Education, EducationField, EmployeeCount, EmployeeNumber, Environment Satisfaction*

    C an error

    D a list of column names

(*R: A*)

3.17 **(Python)**

Which is the result produced by the following sequence of instructions?

```
a= np.array([[1, 2, 3, 4, 5],
            ['A', 'B', 'C', 'D', 'E'],
            [6, 7, 8, 9, 10],
            ['F', 'G', 'H', 'I', 'J']])
a[[1,3],]
```

    A a matrix with one row and three columns

    B a matrix with all numbers as values

    C a matrix with all letters as values

    D an error

(*R: C*)

3.18 **(Python)**

Which is the result produced by the following sequence of instructions?

```
a= np.array([[1, 2, 3, 4, 5],
            ['A', 'B', 'C', 'D', 'E'],
            [6, 7, 8, 9, 10],
            ['F', 'G', 'H', 'I', 'J']])
a[2,1:3]
```

    A ['7', '8']

    B ['A', 'B','C']

    C ['A', 'B']

    D ['2', 'A']

(*R: A*)

3.19 **(Python)**

Which is the result produced by the following sequence of instructions?

```
a= np.array([[1, 2, 3, 4, 5],
            ['A', 'B', 'C', 'D', 'E'],
            [6, 7, 8, 9, 10],
            ['F', 'G', 'H', 'I', 'J']])
a[4,1]
```

    A F

    B an error

C 4

D nothing

(R: B)

3.20 **(Python)**

Considering data frame *df* of Section 3.7, what is the result produced by the following instruction?

```
df[20:25][df.columns[0:3]]
```

A a data frame with 4 rows and 3 columns

B a data frame with 4 rows and 2 columns

C an error

D a data frame with 5 rows and 3 columns

(R: D)

3.21 **(Python)**

Considering data frame *df* of Section 3.7, what is the result produced by the following instruction?

```
df.loc[20:25][df.columns[0:3]]
```

A a data frame with 6 rows and 3 columns

B a data frame with 5 rows and 3 columns

C same as `df[20:25][df.columns[0:3]]`

D an error

(R: A)

3.22 **(Python)**

Considering data frame *df* of Section 3.7, what is the result produced by the following instruction?

```
df.iloc[20:25][df.columns[0:3]]
```

A a data frame with 6 rows and 3 columns

B a data frame with 5 rows and 2 columns

C same as `df[20:25][df.columns[0:3]]`

D an error

(R: C)

C. ...
D. nothing
(A, B)

3.20 (Python)
Considering data frame df of Section 3.?, what is the result produced by the following instruction?

>>> df[df.reg == 'east']

A. a data frame with 4 rows and 3 columns
B. a data frame with 4 rows and 2 columns
C. an error
D. a data frame with 5 rows and 3 columns
(B, D)

3.21 (Python)
Considering data frame df of Section 3.?, what is the result produced by the following instruction?

>>> df[...][...]

A. a data frame with 6 rows and 3 columns
B. a data frame with 5 rows and 3 columns
C. same as df['col'][df.reg == 'west']
D. an error
(B, A)

3.22 (Python)
Considering data frame df of Section 3.?, what is the result produced by the following instruction?

>>> df[...][...]

A. ...
B. ...
C. ...
D. ...

4

Subsetting with Logical Conditions

In this chapter, we introduce ***logical conditions*** and the main ***logical operators***. These represent the key elements for selection operations based on logical criteria, not just a simple list of items or selection helpers. But most of all, we turn our attention *from columns to rows of a data frame,* and we have to assume that we may need to extract a subset of rows from thousands (still small datasets) or easily even from hundred thousand or millions of rows (already large datasets); therefore, as a general rule of thumb, no manual approach based on scrolling through data and listing rows is suitable. It is through the definition of logical conditions and their combination that we could express elaborated criteria to extract subsets of rows from real datasets.

To be more specific, turning our attention from columns to rows is not meant to say that logical conditions only apply to row selection. Selection based on logical conditions applies equally to rows and columns; however, speaking of open data and real data in general, there is typically a difference of many orders of magnitude in scale between rows and columns, and the scale of dataset sizes is not just a technicality; it is a characteristic deeply ingrained in data science, a pillar of both R and Python environments, which have been developed and present continuous innovations and improvements to deal with content and meaning of data and also with their ever-increasing scale. Therefore, working with datasets of few dozens of rows happens only in didactic examples and in few real cases, often of not great relevance and for which R and Python technologies are very likely unnecessary. You do not need to learn a programming language to script operations on a bunch of data; there are easier solutions available directly off the shelf for this. You need R and Python with their computational logic and features to handle the large datasets produced in corporate environments, public institutions, or available as open data. Of course, we may find exceptions to the scenario I have just depicted but scaling to large and very large dataset sizes should be considered as the natural development of everything presented in this book. Learning how to manage logical operators is an important part of this context.

4.1 Logical Operators

Logical operators we are interested in are just three, with a fourth that is often mentioned, so it is useful to know about them but is not necessary. Table 4.1 shows descriptions with symbols.

Data Science Fundamentals with R, Python, and Open Data, First Edition. Marco Cremonini.
© 2024 John Wiley & Sons, Inc. Published 2024 by John Wiley & Sons, Inc.
Companion website: www.wiley.com/go/DSFRPythonOpenData

Table 4.1 Main logical operators.

Operator	Symbol	Description
AND	&	**Logical conjunction**: A binary operator, the logical condition *A & B* is true (formally, TRUE or 1) when both conditions A and B are at the same time true. In other cases, *A & B* are false (FALSE or 0).
OR	|	**Logical disjunction**: A binary operator, the logical condition *A | B* is false (FALSE, 0) only when both conditions A and B are at the same time false. In other cases, *A | B* is true (TRUE, 1).
NOT	! (R) ~ (Py)	**Negation**: Unary operator that flips the logical value resulting from evaluating a condition, e.g. if condition *A* is true, *!A* returns false, and vice versa.
XOR	xor()	Binary operator, also called *exclusive OR*, the condition *xor(A,B)* is true if either condition *A* is true or condition *B* is true, but not if both of them are true or none of them is true. In these latter cases, it returns false. This is the unnecessary operator, because derived from a combination of AND and OR.

Tip

A logical operator producing True or False is also called **Boolean operator**, from George Boole, an English mathematician of mid-1800 who introduced an algebra for logical analysis, subsequently named after him as Boolean Algebra.

Logical operators are often presented by means of ***truth tables*** and graphically by means of ***set theory***. A detailed knowledge of these representations is not strictly necessary to understand and become familiar with logical conditions; here we present both of them shortly.

The truth tables for AND, OR, and XOR operators are presented in Table 4.2:

Table 4.2 Truth tables for binary operators AND, OR, and XOR.

Condition 1	Condition 2	AND (&)	OR (|)	XOR
TRUE	TRUE	TRUE	TRUE	FALSE
TRUE	FALSE	FALSE	TRUE	TRUE
FALSE	TRUE	FALSE	TRUE	TRUE
FALSE	FALSE	FALSE	FALSE	FALSE

By means of set theory, a simple and intuitive visual representation of binary operators is easily provided, as in Figure 4.1.

More elaborate representations with set theory are possible by adding the negation operator and variously combining it with the binary operators.

From truth tables or the set theory representation, it is almost immediate to understand the reason why the XOR operator is not a fundamental one: it is directly derived from combining AND and OR with basic algebra:

```
Cond.A XOR Cond.B = (Cond.A OR Cond.B) - (Cond.A AND Cond.B)
```

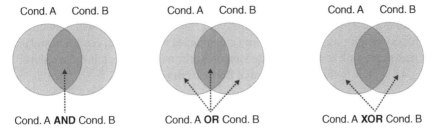

Figure 4.1 Binary logical operators AND, OR, and XOR: set theory.

However, even with just three basic logical operators (and, or, and the negation), the expressiveness of their combinations should not be underestimated; in fact, they permit to express elaborate logical conditions, possibly extremely elaborate conditions, which require great care in the definition and test because they easily defy the scrutiny even of expert programmers.

Important

Order of precedence: Operator NOT is executed before operator AND, with operator OR executed as last one.

Direct consequence of this order of precedence is that the use of parenthesis could be strictly needed to define the correct logic and order of evaluation of logical operators in a composite condition.

The overall logic is the same of arithmetic operations, multiplication and division take the precedence over addition and subtraction.

Datasets

Air Data: Air Quality Data Collected at Outdoor Monitors Across the US, EPA – United States Environmental Protection Agency https://aqs.epa.gov/aqsweb/airdata/download_files.html. Data are referred to *Particulates – PM2.5 FRM/FEM Mass (88101), Year 2022,* https://aqs.epa.gov/aqsweb/airdata/daily_88101_2022.zip. Accessed May 5, 2023. *Copyright*: Public domain (https://edg.epa.gov/epa_data_license.html)

State Population Totals: 2010-2019, US Census Bureau, https://www2.census.gov/programs-surveys/popest/datasets/2020-2022/state/totals/. Accessed May 5, 2023. *Copyright*: Public domain, Open Data Policy (https://www.cio.gov/handbook/it-laws/ogda/#:~:text=The%20OPEN%20Government%20Data%20Act,in%20the%20Data.gov%20catalog.)

4.2 R: Row Selection

In the previous chapter, we considered methods to select columns through their name or position (index value), with row selection limited to the base slicing technique. Now we focus on rows, and we want to select them according to logical conditions.

The main function to consider is `filter()`, defined in package *dplyr*, part of *tidyverse*.

Warning

If package *dplyr* or package *tidyverse* are not loaded, a function *filter()* would be still available, but defined by package *stats* (*stats::filter()*), the standard statistical R package. That function *stats::filter()* is completely different from the one used for row selection, *dplyr::filter()*.

Function `filter()`, as we will see in a moment, is very simple in its logic and usage, since it only requires a *data frame* and a *logical condition*, which could be simple or composed. Therefore, all the possible complexity of defining selection criteria is demanded to the logical condition and its evaluation. For this reason, we look at it closely by decomposing the working mechanism employed by the function `filter()`. Key to this is the notion of **Boolean mask**.

```
library(tidyverse)
library(vroom)
library(magrittr)
```

Let us start by using data from *Air Data: Air Quality Data Collected at Outdoor Monitors Across the United States*, by the United States Environmental Protection Agency (EPA), in particular data about the *PM2.5 FRM/FEM Mass* particulate. As done in the previous chapter, for convenience we select some columns and rename them.

```
df= vroom('~/DS_Wiley/datasets/EPA/daily_88101_2022.zip')

df %>%
  select('Date Local', 'State Name', 'County Name',
         'City Name', 'Arithmetic Mean') %>%
  rename(Date='Date Local', State='State Name', County='County Name',
      City='City Name', PM25='Arithmetic Mean') -> df1

head(df1)
```

Date	State	County	City	PM25
2022-01-02	Alabama	Baldwin	Fairhope	5.3
2022-01-05	Alabama	Baldwin	Fairhope	8.6
2022-01-08	Alabama	Baldwin	Fairhope	8.5
2022-01-11	Alabama	Baldwin	Fairhope	3.7
2022-01-14	Alabama	Baldwin	Fairhope	11.6
2022-01-17	Alabama	Baldwin	Fairhope	5.5

If we want to check whether all states are included, we could do it in different ways, the most basic one is to extract the list of unique names from column State with function `unique()` and either look at the result or count them with function `length()`.

```
length(unique(df1$State))

[1] 53
```

They are 53, not 50. Let us check the list of names.

```
unique(df1$State)
```

```
 [1] "Alabama"          "Alaska"              "Arizona"
 [4] "Arkansas"         "California"          "Colorado"
 [7] "Connecticut"      "Delaware"            "District Of Columbia"
[10] "Florida"          "Georgia"             "Hawaii"
[13] "Idaho"            "Illinois"            "Indiana"
[16] "Iowa"             "Kansas"              "Kentucky"
[19] "Louisiana"        "Maine"               "Maryland"
[22] "Massachusetts"    "Michigan"            "Minnesota"
[25] "Mississippi"      "Missouri"            "Montana"
[28] "Nebraska"         "Nevada"              "New Hampshire"
[31] "New Jersey"       "New Mexico"          "New York"
[34] "North Carolina"   "North Dakota"        "Ohio"
[37] "Oklahoma"         "Oregon"              "Pennsylvania"
[40] "Rhode Island"     "South Carolina"      "South Dakota"
[43] "Tennessee"        "Texas"               "Utah"
[46] "Vermont"          "Virginia"            "Washington"
[49] "West Virginia"    "Wisconsin"           "Wyoming"
[52] "Puerto Rico"      "Country Of Mexico"
```

Looking at the list, we can spot the *Country Of Mexico*, clearly not a US state, and also the *District Of Columbia* and *Puerto Rico*, which are typically included in lists of US states, although formally they are not. To find this difference, other means than a visual inspection are available. The main one will be presented in a future chapter dedicated to join operations between data frames. Here we consider a particularly useful operator.

The logic is that we have to first find the official list of the US states, easily available online. We chose an official source, the *United States Census Bureau*, which provides statistics about the population in US states and regions.

```
states= vroom('~/DS_Wiley/datasets/US_CensusBureau/NST-EST2022-POPCHG2020_2022.csv')
```

```
head(states)
```

```
# A tibble: 6 × 25
  SUMLEV REGION DIVISION STATE NAME      ESTIM...¹ POPES...² POPES...³ POPES...⁴ NPOPC...⁵
  <chr>  <chr>  <chr>    <chr> <chr>       <dbl>    <dbl>    <dbl>    <dbl>    <dbl>
1 010    0      0        00    United S... 3.31e8   3.32e8   3.32e8   3.33e8    61992
2 020    1      0        00    Northeas... 5.76e7   5.74e7   5.73e7   5.70e7  -160258
3 030    1      1        00    New Engl... 1.51e7   1.51e7   1.51e7   1.51e7   -41733
4 030    1      2        00    Middle A... 4.25e7   4.24e7   4.21e7   4.19e7  -118525
5 020    2      0        00    Midwest ... 6.90e7   6.90e7   6.88e7   6.88e7   -24494
6 030    2      3        00    East Nor... 4.74e7   4.73e7   4.72e7   4.71e7   -29893
# ... with 15 more variables: ...
```

The dataset contains different territorial entities, not just states, which are however easy to retrieve with value '040' of the *SUMLEV* column (pay attention to the data types; column *SUMLEV* is of character type, not numbers, therefore '040' with quotes or double quotes).

The comparison symbols are the usual ones:

- greater than and greater or equal (> and >=);
- less than and less or equal (< and <=);
- equal (==) and different (! =).

> **Note**
>
> The syntax to specify a **logical equivalence** is a **double equal sign** ==, being the single equal sign = reserved for assigning a value to a variable.

```
states= filter(states, SUMLEV=='040')
```

SUMLEV	REGION	DIVISION	STATE	NAME	ESTIMATES BASE2020
040	3	6	01	Alabama	5024356
040	4	9	02	Alaska	733378
040	4	8	04	Arizona	7151507
040	3	7	05	Arkansas	3011555
040	4	9	06	California	39538245
040	4	8	08	Colorado	5773733

```
nrow(states)

[1] 52
```

There are 52 rows, meaning that these are not strictly only the US states, in fact, the *District of Columbia* and *Puerto Rico* are included, as they were in the EPA dataset too.

4.2.1 Operator `%in%`

Now we need a convenient way to find the differences between two series, the list of unique states' names from the EPA dataset and the corresponding ones from the Census Bureau dataset. Base R has the binary operator `%in%` that serves exactly that purpose: with syntax x `%in%` y, it takes the series x of *values to be matched* and the series y of *values to be matched against* and returns a series of Boolean values with same length of x, where value *True* means that the match has been successful, and *False* means a failed match.

Said differently, *operator* `%in%` *implements a **logical condition**, whose truth table has TRUE if the x's value appears among y's values, FALSE otherwise. Being a logical condition, it could be employed in a filter() instruction, to select rows.*

This last observation is important and leads us to the notion of *Boolean mask*. But first, let us look at the example, starting with the basic usage of operator `%in%`. What we want to know is *which US States of the Census Bureau dataset do not appear among states listed in the EPA dataset.* In terms of data frame columns and their values, we are looking for the values of column *NAME* of data frame *states* that do *not match* unique values of column *State* of data frame *df1*. We can write the instruction; operator `%in%` gives us the positive matches, with negation operator ! we find the unsuccessful ones.

```
!(unique(df1$State) %in% states$NAME)

 [1] FALSE FALSE FALSE FALSE FALSE FALSE FALSE FALSE  TRUE FALSE FALSE FALSE
[13] FALSE FALSE FALSE FALSE FALSE FALSE FALSE FALSE FALSE FALSE FALSE FALSE
[25] FALSE FALSE FALSE FALSE FALSE FALSE FALSE FALSE FALSE FALSE FALSE FALSE
[37] FALSE FALSE FALSE FALSE FALSE FALSE FALSE FALSE FALSE FALSE FALSE FALSE
[49] FALSE FALSE FALSE FALSE  TRUE
```

The result is a list of 53 Boolean values, with 53 being the length of column *State* of data frame *df1*). Each *TRUE* value represents an unsuccessful match, there are two. How can we find which names they correspond to? As anticipated, operator `%in%` implements a logical condition and what we are looking at with the list of Boolean values is the truth table of that operator combined with negation. Therefore, we can just select the rows of data frame *df1*.

```
mask= !(unique(df1$State) %in% states$NAME)
unique(df1$State)[mask]

[1] "District Of Columbia" "Country Of Mexico"
```

Here are our missing states. The first one, *District Of Columbia* is simply an orthographic mismatch with *District of Columbia* from the Census Bureau (matching conditions between strings is typically case-sensitive), and the other one is the name we were looking at: *Country Of Mexico*.

4.2.2 Boolean Mask

Let us proceed with the example based on the EPA data of PM 2.5 particulate. The World Health Organization (WHO) stated that the safe threshold for PM 2.5 particulate is 15 micrograms per cubic meter per day (https://www.who.int/news-room/feature-stories/detail/what-are-the-who-air-quality-guidelines#:~:text=The%20WHO%20Air%20quality%20guidelines%20are%20a%20set%20of%20evidence,the%20guidelines%20was%20in%201987). The EPA dataset has values expressed in micrograms for cubic meter per day, so we can find which rows show a level of PM 2.5 over the threshold prescribed by the WHO.

```
filter(df1, PM25 > 15) %>% nrow()

[1] 23040
```

The resulting number of rows is about 6% of all observations. Better analyses of these data should be performed, and we will use this dataset again. For the moment, we are mostly interested in understanding how the filtering logic proceeds. We could replicate what we have seen before with operator `%in%` when we executed the logical condition out of the `filter()` function and obtained the truth table. In this case, the logical condition is whether values of column *PM25* of data frame *df1* are greater than 15. We can write it.

```
df1$PM25 > 15

 [1] FALSE FALSE FALSE FALSE FALSE FALSE FALSE FALSE FALSE ...
[16] FALSE FALSE FALSE FALSE FALSE FALSE FALSE FALSE FALSE ...
[31] FALSE FALSE FALSE FALSE FALSE FALSE FALSE FALSE FALSE ...
[46] FALSE FALSE FALSE FALSE FALSE FALSE  TRUE  TRUE FALSE ...
...
```

Let us look closely at this result:

- It is made of 371 721 rows, same length as column *PM25* and has Boolean values.
- *TRUE* when the value of *PM25* is greater than 15, *FALSE* otherwise.
- In this example, there are no missing values, but if there were any, then the result of the logical condition would have been a missing value, indicated by *NA*.

When this result is used inside a *filter* operation, as we did before, the results are the rows satisfying the logical condition. Therefore, *the filter operation works simply by taking the result of the logical condition, simple or composed, and returning the rows corresponding to TRUE. Logically, it is like a mask: FALSE values hide rows, and TRUE values let them into the result.*

This is the reason why the result of a logical condition used for selection operations is called **Boolean mask**, because it actually acts like a mask. It is a very general logic and mechanism applied almost in every selection function with logical conditions; we will see it identical in Python too.

Now that the logic and mechanism are clear, we can try some examples of row selection with logical conditions.

4.2.3 Examples

Example 4.1

All observations related to Kansas City or St. Louis. See the logical steps.

1. Which conditions? Two are the logical conditions to combine, the first is `City=="Kansas City"`, the second `City=="St. Louis"`.
2. What is the logical operation we should use for combining the two? Could it be an AND (*conjunction*)? With an AND, we would logically be asking for observations having **at the same time** Kansas City and St. Louis as values for the column *City*. That is not possible, each observation refers to one specific city. What we actually want are all observations referred to Kansas City and all those referred to St. Louis. Therefore, it is an OR (*disjunction*) the logical condition to employ.

We start checking the Boolean mask. The data frame *df1* is too big to allow for a visual inspection; hence, we turn to a programmatic method to check how many *TRUE* values are in the mask. We recall that *Boolean values are by convention associated to numerical values 0 corresponding to FALSE and 1 corresponding to TRUE*. Then, to count how many *True* are in a series of Boolean values, it suffices to sum the values.

```
sum(df1$City=="Kansas City" | df1$City=="St. Louis")

[1] 3673
```

There are 3673 observations matching the logical condition. We can now subset the data frame with `filter()`.

```
filter(df1, City=="Kansas City" | City=="St. Louis")
```

Date	State	County	City	PM25
2022-01-02	Kansas	Wyandotte	Kansas City	7.4
2022-01-05	Kansas	Wyandotte	Kansas City	6.5
2022-01-08	Kansas	Wyandotte	Kansas City	9.5
2022-01-11	Kansas	Wyandotte	Kansas City	5.2
2022-01-14	Kansas	Wyandotte	Kansas City	15.0
2022-01-17	Kansas	Wyandotte	Kansas City	5.7

Same result is obtained by enclosing single conditions in parentheses.

```
filter(df1, (City=="Kansas City") | (City=="St. Louis"))
```

In this case, parentheses are not necessary, but also do no harm. It is important, with logical conditions, to keep in mind the importance that parentheses have in many instances for a correct evaluation.

If we want to save the result of the selection in a new data frame, we perform the assignment.

```
df1_1= filter(df1, (City=="Kansas City") | (City=="St. Louis"))
```

4.2.3.1 Wrong Disjoint Condition

Special attention should be paid to a possibility that, at first sight, may appear more convenient for specifying logical OR. The idea could be this: Why do not we just use a list of terms with the `c()` syntax, instead of repeating the conditions? When we have multiple OR conditions, it could easily seem like a good idea. Something like the following example.

```
filter(df1, City==c("St. Louis","Kansas City")) -> test

head(test)
```

Date	State	County	City	PM25
2022-01-02	Kansas	Wyandotte	Kansas City	7.4
2022-01-08	Kansas	Wyandotte	Kansas City	9.5
2022-01-14	Kansas	Wyandotte	Kansas City	15.0
2022-01-20	Kansas	Wyandotte	Kansas City	2.9
2022-01-29	Kansas	Wyandotte	Kansas City	5.6
2022-02-04	Kansas	Wyandotte	Kansas City	7.4

The execution has been performed, but the result is not what we think it is, although it is easy to be misled. A hint that something is off is the *warning message* that is raised.

```
Warning: There was 1 warning in filter(). In argument: City == c("Kansas City",
"St. Louis"). Caused by warning in City == c("Kansas City", "St. Louis"): !
longer object length is not a multiple of shorter object length
```

Admittedly, the meaning of this message is quite cryptic, but it should make us suspicious of something to check more carefully. If we verify whether rows with both "Kansas City" and "St. Louis" have been selected, the result is positive. This increases the odds to be misled.

```
unique(test$City)

[1] "Kansas City" "St. Louis"
```

The problem becomes evident if we compare the number of rows returned with the correct syntax using separate conditions combined with OR and this abbreviated form. In the first case, the result has 3673 rows; in the second 1838, half of the rows are the correct result. Clearly, the second form is executing a logic that is completely different from the first, correct one.

To clarify even more, we try with a small custom data frame.

```
ID= c(1,2,3,4,5,6,7,8,9,10)
State= c('Kansas','Kansas','Kansas','Kansas','Kansas',
         'New York','New York','New York','Missouri','Missouri')
City= c('Kansas City','Kansas City','Kansas City','Kansas City','Kansas City',
        'New York City','New York City','New York City',
        'St. Louis','St. Louis')

test= tibble(ID,State,City)
test

# A tibble: 10 × 3
      ID State    City
   <dbl> <chr>    <chr>
 1     1 Kansas   Kansas City
 2     2 Kansas   Kansas City
 3     3 Kansas   Kansas City
 4     4 Kansas   Kansas City
 5     5 Kansas   Kansas City
 6     6 New York New York City
 7     7 New York New York City
 8     8 New York New York City
 9     9 Missouri St. Louis
10    10 Missouri St. Louis
```

With this small data frame, we could see exactly what happens with the compact form. Let us try some combinations.

```
filter(test, City==c("St. Louis","Kansas City"))

# A tibble: 3 × 3
     ID State    City
  <dbl> <chr>    <chr>
1     2 Kansas   Kansas City
2     4 Kansas   Kansas City
3     9 Missouri St. Louis

filter(test, City==c("New York City","St. Louis"))

# A tibble: 2 × 3
     ID State    City
  <dbl> <chr>    <chr>
1     7 New York New York City
2    10 Missouri St. Louis

filter(test, City==c("St. Louis","New York City","Kansas City" ))

# A tibble: 3 × 3
     ID State    City
  <dbl> <chr>    <chr>
1     3 Kansas   Kansas City
2     8 New York New York City
3    10 Missouri St. Louis
```

Now it should be clear that the compact form with a list of terms **is not equivalent** to the list of disjoint conditions combined by OR and should not be used.

Example 4.2

As is well known, two major towns named Kansas City exist, one in Kansas and the other in Missouri, and the previous condition does not make any difference between them. We want to be more precise and decouple the previous condition into two distinct ones:

1. All observations related to Kansas City, Kansas or St. Louis, Missouri.
2. All observations related to Kansas City, Missouri or St. Louis, Missouri.

   Now the logical steps have become more complicated.

1. We still have two main disjointed logical conditions, considering the first case: either we want observations from Kansas City, Kansas or from St. Louis Missouri. Similar for the second case. As in the previous example, we need an OR to combine these conditions.
2. However, now even the two conditions are by themselves composite ones, because, for the first one, we are asking to find observations regarding the city of Kansas City of state Kansas, in the first case, and the city of Kansas City of state Missouri, in the second. How should we have to specify that we look for Kansas City of Kansas? Could it be an OR, same as for the two main conditions? With an OR we would logically ask for *all observations from a city named Kansas City or all observations from a state named Kansas*, which clearly will not be correct because we would turn out having all observations from Kansas City of Kansas and of Missouri plus all observations from every Kansas towns. What we want, instead, are *observation having **at the same time** Kansas City as value of column City and Kansas as value of State*. Therefore, we need an AND for these conditions.

We start checking that with the previous case we retrieve Kansas City of both Kansas and Missouri. This is a perfect case for the special pipe operator `%$%` because function `unique()` has no data parameter.

```
filter(df1, City=="Kansas City") %$% unique(State)

[1] "Kansas"   "Missouri"
```

We have confirmation that we were finding Kansas City from both states. Now, for the first case, we want observations related to Kansas City, Kansas, or St. Louis, Missouri. We write the conditions as they appear in the sentence.

```
df1_1= filter(df1, City=="Kansas City" & State=='Kansas' |
                   City=="St. Louis" & State=='Missouri')
```

Let us check the result. We have to be sure that all observations with Kansas City have Kansas as State, and all those with St. Louis have Missouri. We use the pipe operator this time.

```
df1_1 %>% filter(City=='Kansas City' & State!="Kansas")

# A tibble: 0 × 5
# … with 5 variables: Date <date>, State <chr>, County <chr>, City <chr>,
#   PM25 <dbl>

df1_1 %>% filter(City=='St. Louis' & State!="Missouri")

# A tibble: 0 × 5
# … with 5 variables: Date <date>, State <chr>, County <chr>, City <chr>,
#   PM25 <dbl>
```

Both produce empty results, which is correct.

Now we can select the second subset, that one corresponding to all observations related to Kansas City, Missouri or St. Louis, Missouri. Being both in Missouri, we can simplify the condition as: all observations related to Kansas City or St. Louis, both from Missouri. Try writing it as it was spelled. The expression seems fine at first glance.

```
filter(df1, City=="Kansas City" | City=="St. Louis" & State=='Missouri')

# A tibble: 3,673 × 5
   Date       State  County    City         PM25
   <date>     <chr>  <chr>     <chr>        <dbl>
 1 2022-01-02 Kansas Wyandotte Kansas City    7.4
 2 2022-01-05 Kansas Wyandotte Kansas City    6.5
 3 2022-01-08 Kansas Wyandotte Kansas City    9.5
 4 2022-01-11 Kansas Wyandotte Kansas City    5.2
 5 2022-01-14 Kansas Wyandotte Kansas City   15
 6 2022-01-17 Kansas Wyandotte Kansas City    5.7
 7 2022-01-20 Kansas Wyandotte Kansas City    2.9
 8 2022-01-23 Kansas Wyandotte Kansas City    5.3
```

```
 9 2022-01-29 Kansas Wyandotte Kansas City   5.6
10 2022-02-01 Kansas Wyandotte Kansas City   6.9
# … with 3,663 more rows
```

But looking at the result, we recognize it is wrong; the first rows all show Kansas City, Kansas, not Missouri. Something is wrong with the condition we have written.

We have to keep in mind the order rule of logical operators, *AND is evaluated before OR*, therefore, the condition we have written is executed as: first `City=="St. Louis"` AND `State=='Missouri'`, the result OR `City=="Kansas City"`. That is why we see Kansas City, Kansas.

In other terms, the condition:

```
City=="Kansas City" | City=="St. Louis" & State=='Missouri'
```

equals to:

```
City=="Kansas City" | (City=="St. Louis" & State=='Missouri')
```

This second form with parentheses shows clearly that the logic is not what we intended to obtain. **Parentheses matter** in this case. The correct formulation is then the following:

```
filter(df1, (City=="Kansas City" | City=="St. Louis") & State=='Missouri')
```

Date	State	County	City	PM25
2022-01-01	Missouri	Jackson	Kansas City	6.579167
2022-01-02	Missouri	Jackson	Kansas City	6.220833
2022-01-03	Missouri	Jackson	Kansas City	6.850000
2022-01-04	Missouri	Jackson	Kansas City	4.142857
2022-01-05	Missouri	Jackson	Kansas City	4.945833
2022-01-06	Missouri	Jackson	Kansas City	4.212500

Example 4.3

Find all observations regarding California with PM 2.5 greater than 15 taken before March 01, 2022.

The logical steps are easy:

1. We have three conditions on different columns, *State*, *PM25*, and *Date*.
2. Observations should satisfy at the same time all three conditions, hence AND is the logical operator.

Being column *Date* defined as type *date*, we can use comparison operators on dates.

```
filter(df1, (State=="California") & (PM25 > 15) & (Date < "2022-03-01"))
```

Date	State	County	City	PM25
2022-01-12	California	Alameda	Livermore	16.08333
2022-01-13	California	Alameda	Livermore	19.50000
2022-01-16	California	Alameda	Livermore	24.00000
2022-01-17	California	Alameda	Livermore	18.41667
2022-01-26	California	Alameda	Livermore	18.04167
2022-01-28	California	Alameda	Livermore	17.29167

Similar to a previous case, we could find the list of cities included in the result by exploiting special pipe operator %$%.

```
filter(df1, (State=="California") & (PM25 > 15) &
            (Date < "2022-03-01")) %$% unique(City)

 [1] "Livermore"           "Oakland"
 [3] "Pleasanton"          "Chico"
 [5] "San Andreas"         "Cortina Indian Rancheria"
 [7] "Colusa"              "Concord"
 [9] "San Pablo"           "Fresno"
...

[63] "Sebastopol"          "Modesto"
[65] "Turlock"             "Yuba City"
[67] "Red Bluff"           "Visalia"
[69] "Thousand Oaks"       "Simi Valley"
[71] "Woodland"
```

Example 4.4

We change the previous example a little, we still want to find all observations regarding California with PM 2.5 greater than 15, but this time taken *before* January 6 and *after* August 15, 2022.

We proceed like before, but this time the condition on dates changes because it is a disjunction, therefore an OR.

Warning

It is worth noting a tiny detail of the way the condition on dates has been formulated: *before* January 6 and *after* August 15, 2022. For sure, no one reading the sentence froze because they detected the logical ambiguity that arises if we interpret the sentence literally as asking for dates that are **both** *before* January 6 **and** *after* August 15, 2022. Everybody put context in reading the sentence and did not interpret it literally, but in the way it makes sense, that is *before* January 6 **or** *after* August 15, 2022.

This is a simple example of a fundamental difference that always exists between human logic and computational logic. We put context and give interpretations to speeches, typically in the way that makes more sense to us. This way of doing very often is effective, but sometimes it fails us and we misinterpret. However, computational logic has none of this, it does not put context nor interpret; it understands literally what we specify by means of a programming language.

It happens that this difference defies us when we write logical conditions, especially when we are beginners trying to help ourselves by spelling a logical condition through natural language. It is a good and useful way to proceed, and it very often helps to clarify the logic that should be written, but you must be careful when translating literally the natural language into computational logic because it happens that insignificant details in verbal expressions become significant in an instruction.

We can now write the composite condition being already well-aware that the order rule between AND and OR is critical, so we put parentheses where they are necessary.

```
filter(df1, (State=="California") & (PM25 > 15) &
       ((Date < "2022-01-06") | (Date > "2022-08-15"))
       )
```

Date	State	County	City	PM25
2022-08-30	California	Alameda	Oakland	16.12500
2022-08-30	California	Alameda	Oakland	16.10000
2022-01-01	California	Butte	Chico	24.91667
2022-01-02	California	Butte	Chico	16.08333
2022-01-01	California	Butte	Chico	24.90000
2022-01-02	California	Butte	Chico	16.00000

Example 4.5

We change again the conditions on dates. This time we want observations regarding Fresno, California, with PM 2.5 greater than 15, taken in January 2022, but not during the week between January 16 and 22 included.

Different from previous cases, we may proceed in several ways. We could either specify two disjunct periods, between January 1 and 3 or between January 23 and 31, or we could proceed by negation, specifying the whole month of January except days between 16 and 22. The first option is like the previous example, so here we write the second one.

```
filter(df1, (State=="California") & (City=="Fresno") & (PM25 > 15) &
       (Date < "2022-01-31") &
       !((Date <= "2022-01-22") & (Date >= "2022-01-16"))
       )
```

Date	State	County	City	PM25
2022-01-06	California	Fresno	Fresno	22.1
2022-01-07	California	Fresno	Fresno	28.3
2022-01-11	California	Fresno	Fresno	33.5
2022-01-14	California	Fresno	Fresno	53.3
2022-01-23	California	Fresno	Fresno	38.6
2022-01-26	California	Fresno	Fresno	26.7

We can check the dates of the result.

```
filter(df1, (State=="California") & (PM25 > 15) &
       (Date < "2022-01-31") &
       !((Date <= "2022-01-22") & (Date >= "2022-01-16"))
       ) %$% unique(Date)

 [1] "2022-01-12" "2022-01-13" "2022-01-26" "2022-01-28"
     "2022-01-29" "2022-01-23" "2022-01-24"
 [8] "2022-01-27" "2022-01-01" "2022-01-02" "2022-01-10"
     "2022-01-11" "2022-01-30" "2022-01-14"
[15] "2022-01-06" "2022-01-07" "2022-01-03" "2022-01-04"
     "2022-01-05" "2022-01-09" "2022-01-25"
[22] "2022-01-15" "2022-01-08"
```

Dates of selected rows are correct. We could have written the last condition differently by remembering the equivalent forms when using negation: AND and OR.

```
Cond.A | Cond.B equals to !Cond.A & !Cond.B
Cond.A & Cond.B equals to !Cond.A | !Cond.B
```

```
filter(df1, (State=="California") & (PM25 > 15) &
       (Date < "2022-01-31") &
       ((Date > "2022-01-22") | (Date < "2022-01-16"))
       )
```

The result is the same as before.

4.2.4 Python: Row Selection

We use dataset *Particulates – PM2.5 Speciation 2022*, from the *Air Data: Air Quality Data Collected at Outdoor Monitors Across the US*, of the United States Environmental Protection Agency (EPA). This dataset has data about the *PM2.5 FRM/FEM Mass* particulate collected by EPA in 2022. Being a large dataset, we read it and take a selection of columns.

The main difference with R is that using function `filter()` is the standard way of selecting rows, while in Python and pandas more than one method is to be considered as standard. In this section, we consider these different methods.

```
import numpy as np
import pandas as pd
df=pd.read_csv("/Users/teddy/DS_Wiley/datasets/EPA/daily_88101_2022.zip",
          usecols= ['Date Local', 'State Name', 'County Name',
              'City Name', 'Arithmetic Mean'])
```

	Date Local	Arithmetic Mean	State Name	County Name	City Name
0	2022-01-02	5.3	Alabama	Baldwin	Fairhope
1	2022-01-05	8.6	Alabama	Baldwin	Fairhope
2	2022-01-08	8.5	Alabama	Baldwin	Fairhope
3	2022-01-11	3.7	Alabama	Baldwin	Fairhope
4	2022-01-14	11.6	Alabama	Baldwin	Fairhope
...	...	...	...	...	...
361716	2022-09-26	9.4	Country Of Mexico	SONORA	Not in a city
361717	2022-09-27	5.6	Country Of Mexico	SONORA	Not in a city
361718	2022-09-28	7.4	Country Of Mexico	SONORA	Not in a city
361719	2022-09-29	7.0	Country Of Mexico	SONORA	Not in a city
361720	2022-09-30	7.8	Country Of Mexico	SONORA	Not in a city

Column *Date Local* has to be converted in *datetime* type.

```
df['Date Local']=pd.to_datetime(df['Date Local'])
df.dtypes

Date Local        datetime64[ns]
Arithmetic Mean          float64
State Name                object
County Name               object
City Name                 object
dtype: object
```

The notion of Boolean mask and its use in row selection with logical conditions is exactly the same as we have discussed for R, only the syntax and the functions change.

4.2.5 Boolean Mask, Base Selection Method

The base method in Python to select a column, as already introduced, has two equivalent syntaxes.

```
dataframe["col_name"]
dataframe.col_name
```

Consequently, a single logical condition on a column values could be expressed in one of the following forms, with operators applying respectively to alphanumeric (string) or numeric values.

```
dataframe["col_name"] == "string"    | dataframe.col_name == "string"
dataframe["col_name"] != "string"    | dataframe.col_name != "string"
dataframe["col_name"] > number (or >=, <, <=) | dataframe.col_name > number
```

Single logical conditions could then be composed by means of logical operators (*and*, *or*, or *not*; having symbols &, | , and ~).

In the base selection method, Python syntax to select rows based on a logical condition, single or composed, is simple and does not make use of any function, but only of *square brackets*. It is very similar to the most basic R syntax for selection, typically superseded by the use of `filter()`. For example:

```
dataframe[logical condition]
```

Therefore, putting together the syntax to express a logical condition with that for selecting rows, the resulting base method is a little redundant in its syntax, but clear in the logic. For example:

```
dataframe[dataframe["col_name"] == "string"]
dataframe[dataframe.col_name != "string"]
dataframe[dataframe["col_name"] >= number]
dataframe[dataframe.col_name == number]
...
```

Let us see an example. We want to select rows related to Maine. First, we execute just the condition and obtain the Boolean mask.

```
df["State Name"]=='Maine'
0         False
1         False
2         False
3         False
4         False
          ...
361716    False
361717    False
361718    False
361719    False
361720    False
Name: State Name, Length: 361721, dtype: bool
```

It is a Boolean mask because it has same number of rows of the data frame and has Boolean values. We can retrieve the corresponding rows.

```
df[df["State Name"]=='Maine']
```

	Date Local	Arithmetic Mean	State Name	County Name	City Name
129855	2022-01-03	5.857143	Maine	Androscoggin	Lewiston
129856	2022-01-04	5.083333	Maine	Androscoggin	Lewiston
129857	2022-01-05	6.791667	Maine	Androscoggin	Lewiston
129858	2022-01-06	6.666667	Maine	Androscoggin	Lewiston
129859	2022-01-07	6.791667	Maine	Androscoggin	Lewiston
...	...	...	...	...	...
133995	2022-09-26	5.100000	Maine	Penobscot	Bangor
133996	2022-09-27	5.000000	Maine	Penobscot	Bangor
133997	2022-09-28	3.300000	Maine	Penobscot	Bangor
133998	2022-09-29	3.100000	Maine	Penobscot	Bangor
133999	2022-09-30	4.000000	Maine	Penobscot	Bangor

Now we compose the previous condition with a second one, that the month has to be April. We use pandas method **dt.month** to extract the month from the date. Also, we already know that particular care on the usage of parenthesis has to be taken. Python is somehow stricter than R; it requires parentheses even in cases where R does not. Like this one, for example. If we write it without enclosing single conditions into parentheses, we receive an error.

```
df["State Name"]=='Maine' & df['Date Local'].dt.month==4

TypeError: Cannot perform 'rand_' with a dtyped [int64] array and scalar of
type [bool]
```

With parentheses, everything's fine.

```
(df["State Name"]=='Maine') & (df['Date Local'].dt.month==4)
0          False
1          False
2          False
3          False
4          False
           ...
361716     False
361717     False
361718     False
361719     False
361720     False
Length: 361721, dtype: bool
```

As before, we produced a Boolean mask. To obtain the rows is straightforward; here presented are two steps.

```
mask= (df["State Name"]=='Maine') & (df['Date Local'].dt.month==4)
df[mask]
```

	Date Local	Arithmetic Mean	State Name	County Name	City Name
129943	2022-04-01	2.666667	Maine	Androscoggin	Lewiston
129944	2022-04-02	2.333333	Maine	Androscoggin	Lewiston
129945	2022-04-03	1.750000	Maine	Androscoggin	Lewiston
129946	2022-04-04	2.375000	Maine	Androscoggin	Lewiston
129947	2022-04-05	4.166667	Maine	Androscoggin	Lewiston
…	…	…	…	…	…

Let us complicate the logical conditions a little.

Example 4.6

We want rows from April, May, and June and only from Kennebec and Cumberland counties of Maine.

```
df[ ((df['Date Local'].dt.month == 4) |
     (df['Date Local'].dt.month == 5) |
     (df['Date Local'].dt.month == 6)) &
    ((df["County Name"]== 'Kennebec') |
     (df["County Name"]== 'Cumberland'))]
```

	Date Local	Arithmetic Mean	State Name	County Name	City Name
131588	2022-04-05	4.8	Maine	Cumberland	Portland
131589	2022-04-11	3.1	Maine	Cumberland	Portland
131590	2022-04-17	2.2	Maine	Cumberland	Portland
131591	2022-04-23	3.8	Maine	Cumberland	Portland
131592	2022-04-29	2.7	Maine	Cumberland	Portland
…	…	…	…	…	…

Being months consecutive, we could simplify by means of method `between()`.

```
df[ (df['Date Local'].dt.month.between(4,6)) &
    ((df["County Name"]== 'Kennebec') |
     (df["County Name"]== 'Cumberland'))]
```

Example 4.7

We want rows from all Maine counties except Cumberland and Kennebec and from February or any date past June 15.

```
df[((df["State Name"]== 'Maine') &
    (df["County Name"]!= 'Kennebec') &
    (df["County Name"]!= 'Cumberland')) &
   ( (df['Date Local'].dt.month == 2) | (df['Date Local'] > '2022-06-15') )
   ]
```

	Date Local	Arithmetic Mean	State Name	County Name	City Name
129884	2022-02-01	10.958333	Maine	Androscoggin	Lewiston
129885	2022-02-02	4.500000	Maine	Androscoggin	Lewiston
129886	2022-02-03	6.083333	Maine	Androscoggin	Lewiston
129887	2022-02-04	3.250000	Maine	Androscoggin	Lewiston
129888	2022-02-05	4.916667	Maine	Androscoggin	Lewiston
...	...	...	...	...	...
133995	2022-09-26	5.100000	Maine	Penobscot	Bangor
133996	2022-09-27	5.000000	Maine	Penobscot	Bangor
133997	2022-09-28	3.300000	Maine	Penobscot	Bangor
133998	2022-09-29	3.100000	Maine	Penobscot	Bangor
133999	2022-09-30	4.000000	Maine	Penobscot	Bangor

4.2.6 Row Selection with `query()`

Pandas function **`query()`** is what resembles most to R `filter()`. With function `query()`, column names are specified without data frame names; however, it is required to enclose the whole logical condition into quotes, single or double. In addition, these quotes cannot be the same quotes used, for example, to specify string values, in one case they should be single quotes, in the other double quotes. Also, column names with spaces, hence requiring quotes, take *backticks*. We re-run previous examples.

```
df.query(" `State Name`== 'Maine' & `Date Local`.dt.month== 2")
```

	Date Local	Arithmetic Mean	State Name	County Name	City Name
129884	2022-02-01	10.958333	Maine	Androscoggin	Lewiston
129885	2022-02-02	4.500000	Maine	Androscoggin	Lewiston
129886	2022-02-03	6.083333	Maine	Androscoggin	Lewiston
129887	2022-02-04	3.250000	Maine	Androscoggin	Lewiston
129888	2022-02-05	4.916667	Maine	Androscoggin	Lewiston
...	...	...	...	...	...

Let us see a longer composite condition. *To write conditions on new lines* and align them, character **backslash** (\ ) should be used to signal that code on different lines has to be evaluated as a unique operation.

```
df.query(" ('Date Local'.dt.month== 4 | \
           'Date Local'.dt.month== 5 | \
           'Date Local'.dt.month== 6) & \
           ('County Name'== 'Kennebec' | \
           'County Name'== 'Cumberland') ")
```

	Date Local	Arithmetic Mean	State Name	County Name	City Name
131588	2022-04-05	4.8	Maine	Cumberland	Portland
131589	2022-04-11	3.1	Maine	Cumberland	Portland
131590	2022-04-17	2.2	Maine	Cumberland	Portland
131591	2022-04-23	3.8	Maine	Cumberland	Portland
131592	2022-04-29	2.7	Maine	Cumberland	Portland
...	...	...	...	...	...
256542	2022-06-26	10.5	Pennsylvania	Cumberland	Carlisle
256543	2022-06-27	6.5	Pennsylvania	Cumberland	Carlisle
256544	2022-06-28	3.7	Pennsylvania	Cumberland	Carlisle
256545	2022-06-29	6.1	Pennsylvania	Cumberland	Carlisle
256546	2022-06-30	9.1	Pennsylvania	Cumberland	Carlisle

Careful here, county Cumberland exists in New Jersey, North Carolina, and Pennsylvania too. Remember that it is always too easy to forget a condition when several are combined and then repeated, or to make implicit assumptions on data that turn out to be false. In this instruction, `'State Name'=='Maine'` is needed.

Function `query()` sometimes requires that directive **engine="python"** be explicitly specified; otherwise, an error is raised. This happens when attributes of pandas methods are used, for example, with string manipulation methods (e.g. **str.startswith()**) and others. In this case, the syntax has to be like:

```
df.query(" col_names.str.startswith('ABC') ", engine="python").
```

We can see an example by rewriting the shorter form of the previous one using attribute `between()` of method `dt.month`. In this case, without directive `engine="python"` it returns an error, with the directive, instead, it produces the correct result.

```
df.query("'Date Local'.dt.month.between(4,6) & \
          'State Name'== 'Maine' & \
          ('County Name'== 'Kennebec' | 'County Name'== 'Cumberland')",
engine='python')
```

	Date Local	Arithmetic Mean	State Name	County Name	City Name
131588	2022-04-05	4.8	Maine	Cumberland	Portland
131589	2022-04-11	3.1	Maine	Cumberland	Portland
131590	2022-04-17	2.2	Maine	Cumberland	Portland
131591	2022-04-23	3.8	Maine	Cumberland	Portland
131592	2022-04-29	2.7	Maine	Cumberland	Portland
...	...	...	...	...	...

Questions

4.1 (R)

Considering data frame *df* of Section 4.2, which is the result of the sequence of the following two instructions:

```
mask= df$'State Name' %in% c('Vermont','Ohio')
sum(mask)
```

A The subset of *df* rows having Vermont or Ohio as state name

B An error

C The number of *df* rows having Vermont or Ohio as state name

D Zero

(R: C)

4.2 (R)

Considering data frame *df* of Section 4.2, which is the result of the sequence of the following two instructions:

```
mask= df$'City Name' %in% c('Vermont','Ohio')
sum(mask)
```

A The subset of *df* rows having Vermont or Ohio as state name

B An error

C The number of *df* rows having Vermont or Ohio as state name

D Zero

(R: D)

4.3 (R)

Considering data frame *df* of Section 4.2, which is the result of the sequence of the following two instructions:

```
mask= df$'State Name' %in% c('Vermont','Ohio')
df %>% filter(mask)
```

A The subset of *df* rows having Vermont or Ohio as state name
B An error
C The number of *df* rows having Vermont or Ohio as state name
D Zero
(R: A)

4.4 (R)
Considering data frame *df* of Section 4.2, which is the result of the following instruction:

```
df %>% filter('State Name'=='Vermont' | 'State Name'=='Ohio')
```

A The subset of *df* rows having Vermont and Ohio as state name
B Same as previous Q4.3
C The number of *df* rows having Vermont or Ohio as state name
D Zero
(R: B)

4.5 (R)
Considering data frame *df* of Section 4.2, which is the result of the following instruction:

```
df %>% filter('State Name' %in% c('Vermont','Ohio'))
```

A The subset of *df* rows having Vermont and Ohio as state name
B Same as previous Q4.4
C The number of *df* rows having Vermont or Ohio as state name
D An error
(R: B)

4.6 (R)
Considering data frame *df* of Section 4.2, which is the result of the following instruction:

```
df %>% filter('State Name'=='Vermont' & 'City Name'=='Burlington')
```

A The subset of *df* rows having Vermont as state name or Burlington as city name
B An empty data frame
C The number of *df* rows having Vermont as state name and Burlington as city name
D The subset of *df* rows having Vermont as state name and Burlington as city name
(R: D)

4.7 (R)
Considering data frame *df* of Section 4.2, which is the result of the following instruction:

```
df %>% filter('State Name'== c('Vermont','Ohio'))
```

A Same as Q4.6
B An empty data frame
C Same as Q4.4
D Wrong logical condition
(R: D)

4.8 (R)
Considering data frame *df* of Section 4.2, which is the result of the following instruction:

```
df %>% filter(c('State Name','City Name') %in%
              c('Vermont','Burlington'))
```

A The subset of *df* rows having Vermont as state name or Burlington as city name
B An error
C The number of *df* rows having Vermont as state name and Burlington as city name
D The subset of *df* rows having Vermont as state name and Burlington as city name
(R: B)

4.9 (R)
Considering data frame *df* of Section 4.2, which is the result of the following instruction:

```
df %>% filter('City Name'=='Vermont' & 'State Name'=='Burlington')
```

A The subset of *df* rows having Vermont as state name or Burlington as city name
B An empty data frame
C The number of *df* rows having Vermont as state name and Burlington as city name
D The subset of *df* rows having Vermont as state name and Burlington as city name
(R: B)

4.10 (R)
Considering data frame *df* of Section 4.2, which is the result of the following instruction:

```
df %>% filter('State Name'== c('Vermont','Ohio'))
```

A The subset of *df* rows having Vermont as state name or Burlington as city name
B An empty data frame
C The number of *df* rows having Vermont as state name and Burlington as city name
D The subset of *df* rows having Vermont as state name and Burlington as city name
(R: B)

4.11 (R)
Considering data frame *df* of Section 4.2, which of the following instructions likely returns more rows:

```
df %>% filter( 'Date Local'=='2022-01-02' &
```

```
                    ('State Name'=='Vermont' | 'State Name'=='Ohio'))
df %>% filter( 'Date Local'=='2022-01-02' &
                    'State Name'=='Vermont' | 'State Name'=='Ohio')
```

A The first one
B The second one
C They are the same
D Unknown
(R: B)

4.12 **(Python)**
Assuming *Col1* and *Col2* two columns of data frame *df*, what is the difference between the two following instructions?

```
(df['Col1'] =='ABC') & (df["Col2"] == 'XYZ')
(df.Col1 =='ABC') & (df.Col2 == 'XYZ')
```

A The first one is a logical condition; the second an assignment
B The second one produces an error
C They are both wrong
D They are correct and equivalent
(R: D)

4.13 **(Python)**
Assuming *Col1* and *Col2* two columns of data frame *df*, what is the difference between the two following instructions?

```
df['Col1'] =='ABC' & df["Col2"] == 'XYZ'
df.Col1 =='ABC' & df.Col2 == 'XYZ'
```

A The first one is a logical condition; the second an assignment
B The second one produces an error
C They are both wrong
D They are correct and equivalent
(R: C)

4.14 **(Python)**
Considering data frame *df* of Section 4.2, what is the difference between the two following instructions?

```
df['State Name'] =='California' & df["City Name"] == 'San Francisco'
df.'State Name' =='California' & df."City Name" == 'San Francisco'
```

A The first one is a logical condition; the second an assignment

B The second one produces an error

C They are both wrong

D They are correct and equivalent

(R: B)

4.15 **(Python)**

Considering data frame *df* of Section 4.2, what results are likely to return the two following instructions?

```
df[(df['State Name'] =='California') &
    df["City Name"] == 'San Francisco']
df[(df['State Name'] =='California') |
    df["City Name"] == 'Boston']
```

A Both are likely to return some rows

B The first one is likely to return some rows; the second will return no rows

C They are both logically wrong and return no rows

D They are both logically wrong and return an error

(R: C)

4.16 **(Python)**

Considering data frame *df* of Section 4.2, the following logical condition selects:

```
df[ ((df['Date Local'].dt.month == 4) |
     (df['Date Local'].dt.month == 5)) |
     (df['Date Local'].dt.month == 6) &
     (df["County Name"]== 'Kennebec') |
     (df["County Name"]== 'Cumberland')]
```

A Both are likely to return some rows

B All observations in April, May, or June

C They are both logically wrong and return no rows

D They are both logically wrong and return an error

(R: C)

4.17 **(Python)**

Considering data frame *df* of Section 4.2, the following logical condition selects:

```
df[ ((df['Date Local'].dt.month > 1) |
     (df['Date Local'].dt.month < 3)) |
     (df["State Name"]== 'California') |
     (df["State Name"]== 'Ohio')]
```

A The whole data frame

B Observations of February and observations from California or Ohio

    C No rows

    D It is logically wrong and returns an error

  (R: A)

4.18 **(Python)**

Considering data frame *df* of Section 4.2, the following logical condition selects:

```
df[ ((df['Date Local'].dt.month > 1) &
    (df['Date Local'].dt.month < 3)) |
    (df["State Name"]== 'California') |
    (df["State Name"]== 'Ohio')]
```

    A The whole data frame

    B Observations of February or observations from California or Ohio

    C No rows

    D Only observations of February

  (R: B)

4.19 **(Python)**

Considering data frame *df* of Section 4.2, the following logical condition selects:

```
df[ ((df['Date Local'].dt.month > 1) &
    (df['Date Local'].dt.month < 3)) |
    (df["State Name"]== 'California') &
    (df["State Name"]== 'Ohio')]
```

    A The whole data frame

    B Observations of February or observations from California or Ohio

    C No rows

    D All observations of February

  (R: D)

4.20 **(Python)**

Considering data frame *df* of Section 4.2, the following logical condition selects:

```
df[ ((df['Date Local'].dt.month > 1) &
    (df['Date Local'].dt.month < 3)) &
    (df["State Name"]== 'California') |
    (df["State Name"]== 'Ohio')]
```

    A The whole data frame

    B Observations of February from California or observations from Ohio

    C No rows

    D Only observations of February

  (R: B)

5

Operations on Dates, Strings, and Missing Values

Dates, with both the date and the time component, and alphanumeric strings are data types that, for their peculiar natures, are better handled by specific functions, tailored to their characteristics. Also, missing values, despite not being a data type, are literally the absence of data and represent a special case whose characteristics require a specific treatment and, sometimes, specific functions.

Regarding *date* and *time*, they both are special in their measurement units: base 60 for minutes and seconds, base 12 or 24 for hours, and more complicated for dates, even if we consider just the Gregorian calendar. At least, measurement units of time are regular; hours, minutes, and seconds always have the same duration; not so for dates, which are measured based on an irregular scale; months have different durations; and years too are not always of the same length. These complications have become so familiar to us that we consider it perfectly normal to count a different number of days for different months and to adjust February every four years, but for computational logic, such irregularities represent the difference between a trivial algebra and an irrational way of counting. For example, calculating the difference in days between two dates is in practice overly complicated, with respect to the triviality of the operation, because the calendar is needed, meaning that every operation is a special case. For this reason, date and time are almost always supported by a specific data type, e.g. *datetime*, and specific functions hide the complications of executing even elementary algebraic operations on dates.

Note

Usage of non-Gregorian calendars is common worldwide, although in Western countries and cultures, we tend to forget about that fact and consider the Gregorian calendar, which is a solar calendar, as the universal standard on which everybody has agreed. As a matter of fact, many other calendars exist and are currently adopted. There exist *lunar calendars* (e.g. the *Islamic Hijri calendar*), *lunisolar calendars*, partially lunar and solar (for example the *Jewish calendar*, the *Traditional Chinese calendar*, and the many variants of *Hindu calendars*), or *solar calendars* of different traditions than the Gregorian calendar (e.g. the *Iranian calendar* or the *Solar Hijri calendar*, the most ancient of all calendars still in use). All non-Gregorian calendar users face a lot of difficulties in handling dates with computational tools because the support is typically poor and often partial, if not absent. Open source tools we use, largely adopted worldwide from academia to corporations, typically present features only for the Gregorian calendar; for the others, with luck, custom implementations are available. Proprietary tools are no better, in general.

Alphanumeric strings represent one of the fundamental data types and do not pose particular problems. Specific functions are almost always available helping in the several operations that we may routinely want to perform on strings, such as finding patterns as substrings or as regular

Data Science Fundamentals with R, Python, and Open Data, First Edition. Marco Cremonini.
© 2024 John Wiley & Sons, Inc. Published 2024 by John Wiley & Sons, Inc.
Companion website: www.wiley.com/go/DSFRPythonOpenData

expressions and possibly replacing them with others, transforming the case, dividing, joining, and so forth. Strings are objects that are often manipulated like numbers are with algebraic operations. We have already seen some examples of column selection through selection helpers.

Differently from strings, *missing values*, already introduced in Chapter 2 and seen in some examples, are a constant source of problems, if left unaccounted or not handled properly. They do represent a truly special case because they literally are the absence of values, but conventionally they may have both *a value and a type*, so typically we can *sum missing values* (with the convention that *True* accounts for 0 and *False* accounts for 1) and we can define a *missing value of numeric or character type*, which logically makes no sense but in practice turns out to be quite useful. Being so peculiar and so easily a source of problems, several specific functions and methods are available for handling them efficiently. In no case should missing values be overlooked or treated lightly; instead, their presence should be checked carefully because, as we will see in some examples, they could be introduced as a result of the execution of data-wrangling operations, possibly unnoticed.

With missing values, it is also important to learn how to navigate among their subtleties. For example, they are typically shown in data frame visualizations with conventional forms like *NA*, *NaN*, *<NA>*, *None*, or *NULL*. There are small differences among all of these forms; they are not perfect synonyms, but what creates true difficulties for beginners, and not only for them, is the fact that sometimes those are just textual representations for void or absent values, and other times they are keywords possibly used to represent missing values. A typical error is to try to select rows with missing values in a column with a logical condition trying to match string "NA" or "NaN", which instead succeeds only if element values are the actual strings "NA" or "NaN", not missing values. However, on the other hand, common functions for reading data have the default behavior that if they find strings "NA" or "NaN" as element values, they interpret them as missing values rather than strings, which is in plain contradiction with how logical conditions work, or they sometimes recognize missing values as void strings (e.g. "") or with keyword *NA* or *None*. In other cases, missing values are introduced in place of values that, for some reason, cannot be interpreted or transformed. Therefore, the important message to always keep in mind is that missing values are sneaky; they look like the most uninteresting elements, but instead, they turn out to be the most insidious ones. Never forget about them.

Datasets

Air Data: Air Quality Data Collected at Outdoor Monitors Across the US, EPA – United States Environmental Protection Agency https://aqs.epa.gov/aqsweb/airdata/download_files.html. Data are referred to *Particulates – PM2.5 FRM/FEM Mass (88101), Year 2022,* https://aqs.epa.gov/aqsweb/airdata/daily_88101_2022.zip. Accessed May 6, 2023. *Copyright*: Public domain (https://edg.epa.gov/epa_data_license.html).

Better Life Index, OCSE – Organization for Economic Co-Operation and Development, OECD. Stat, https://stats.oecd.org/Index.aspx?DataSetCode=BLI (BLI_08052023.xls, BLI_08052023.csv). Accessed May 8, 2023. *Copyright*: Public domain with citation. (https://www.oecd.org/termsand-conditions/).

Final energy consumption from the Eurostat *Data Browser, All data – Tables on EU policy – Sustainable development indicators – Goal 7 – Affordable and clean energy*, (https://ec.europa.eu/eurostat/databrowser/view/sdg_07_11/default/table?lang=en). This dataset has data on final user energy consumption, with the exception of energy transformation and distribution (*sdg_07_11.tsv*). Accessed September 7, 2022. *Copyright*: Creative Commons Attribution 4.0 International

Fahrraddiebstahl in Berlin (en. Bicycle thefts in Berlin) is a dataset from *Berlin Open Data* (https://daten.berlin.de/datensaetze/fahrraddiebstahl-berlin) with data from police reports regarding bicycle thefts. The original dataset (Fahrraddiebstahl_12_2022.xlsx) has been automatically translated into English with Google Translate for convenience. This operation will be specifically discussed in this example. Accessed December 10, 2022. *Copyright*: Common Criteria Namensnennung 3.0 Deutschland (CC BY 3.0 DE) (https://creativecommons.org/licenses/by/3.0/de/).

5.1 R: Operations on Dates and Strings

5.1.1 Date and Time

To manipulate dates and time data, the best tool R makes available is package *lubridate*, included in *tidyverse* but not automatically loaded. RStudio has also created a useful *cheatsheet* for *lubridate* functions (https://posit.co/resources/cheatsheets/).

5.1.1.1 Datetime Data Type

Data type *datetime* (also indicated as *POSIXct* or *POSIXt*, with a tiny difference between the two, irrelevant in our case) expresses the format that includes both the data and the time components. When time is absent, by convention it is shown as 00:00:00; when it is the date to be unspecified, also by convention it is indicated in R as 1/1/1970, a special date representing the origin of the ***UNIX EPOCH TIME***. The UNIX EPOCH TIME is important because it is the number that, for all Unix-based systems and tools, represents ***the number of seconds that passed from 00:00:00 Coordinated Universal Time (UTC) on 1/1/1970*** and serves as the basis for all date and time representations in system internals. Dates before 1/1/1970 are represented with a negative sign.

Tip

For those interested in a beautiful piece of history of computing, the Web Archive stores a copy of the original *first edition Unix Programmer's Manual* of 1971 by Bell Labs. On page 13, function *time* is said to return the time in sixtieth of seconds (because an oscillator with a 60 Hz frequency was used at the time) from 00:00:00 on 1/1/1971, not 1970. In 1973, the Unix epoch was 1/1/1972. So, at first, it was not 1/1/1970 the origin of Unix time, unless the problem of counting based on the sixtieth of seconds arose because it would have consumed the 32-bit counter in few years. The solution was to reduce the frequency to seconds and to conventionally assume 1/1/1970 as the origin, a convention that is still valid nowadays (https://web.archive.org/web/20220305094724/https://www.bell-labs.com/usr/dmr/www/pdfs/man22.pdf).

Unix Epoch Time is not the only epoch in use, it is just the most famous. For example, some Microsoft Windows systems use 1 January 1601 00:00:00 UTC, GPS systems use 6 January 1980, and the Ingenuity helicopter, part of NASA's rover Perseverance on Mars, has 1 January 2020 as the epoch time. Therefore, it is important to know that also for digital systems, like for human societies, time has to be counted starting from a conventional moment in the past. At what point in time was set? The beginning of official time is a matter of debate and possibly harsh controversies, but it has to be set somehow; otherwise, dates and calendars have no meaning.

For example, we could obtain the Unix Epoch Time of a date and time value with two data type conversions: first, it is converted into a *datetime* object, with base R function `as.POSIXct()` or *lubridate* function `as_datetime()`; then it is transformed into a numeric value with `as.numeric()`. Parameter `tz` specifies the time zone, which is often necessary to avoid errors due to inconsistencies in time zones.

```
library(tidyverse)
library(lubridate)
as.POSIXct("2023-12-25 00:00:00", tz='CET')
[1] "2023-12-25 CET"
as.numeric(as.POSIXct("2023-12-25 00:00:00", tz='CET'))
[1] 1703458800
```

We have obtained the Unix Epoch Time of Christmas 2023 at midnight in the Central European Timezone (CET): 1703458800. We can do the opposite, from the Unix Epoch Time, to obtain the date. Again, care should be taken with time zones.

```
as.POSIXct(1703458800, origin="1970-01-01")
[1] "2023-12-25 CET"
as_datetime(1703458800)
[1] "2023-12-24 23:00:00 UTC"
as_datetime(1703458800, tz='CET')
[1] "2023-12-25 CET"
```

With `as.POSIXct()`, we need to specify the origin with parameter **origin**, and if the time zone is not specified, it takes the one defined in the local system. In this example, the result is correct because the local system is set on the CET, the same of the time zone specified for the transformation. With `as_datetime()` the behavior is different. By default, it takes the origin of the Unix Epoch Time without synchronizing the time zone with the local system, instead, it takes the standard UTC (Coordinated Universal Time or Universal Time Coordinated), which, at the time of writing this book, is one hour off with respect to CET (standard time and daylight saving time are correctly considered). The result shows that, being one hour earlier. By specifying the time zone, everything works fine.

From data type *datetime*, two subtypes are derived: **Date** and **Time**, for data having only one of the two components. However, types *datetime*, *Date*, and *Time* are fully compatible with each other, there is no need for conversions between them.

5.1.2 Parsing Dates

We start by considering how to convert alphanumeric values into type *datetime* by specifying the *data format*. For simplicity, we will consider the *data* part only, for *time* there is no difference.

First, the logic should be made clear. The functions we introduce in a moment, from the *lubridate* package, are all based on the same principle: we have an alphanumeric representation of dates like "1/5/2023," "5 January 2023," or "1 May 2023," and we should tell R how to parse those values: which part is the day, which one is the month and which one is the year. With 5 January 2023 or 1 May 2023 there is no ambiguity, so we are safe using a generic transformation function without specifying the data format. Differently with 1/5/2023, whose interpretation depends on a social norm. For example, most Europeans will read it as 1 May 2023, on the contrary, many American readers will likely read it as January 5, 2023. In cases like this, we should tell R how that string should be interpreted to produce the correct date. Time has no such differences and it is unanimously interpreted as hours, minutes, and seconds.

Package *lubridate* has a collection of *date and time parsing functions*, whose task is precisely to specify how to interpret strings as date and time. For example, there are functions called **mdy()**, **mdy_hm()**, and **mdy_hms()** that take as data a series (a column) and interpret values as follows:

- mdy(): it interprets values as composed by *month*, *day*, and *year*, from the letters forming the function name, possibly divided by a separator character (es. 01-25-2020 or 7/8/2022), and, for the month, either expressed with a number or a name, shortened (es. 20 Jan 2021) or full (es. 20 January 2021). If the parsing succeeds, the values are converted in a conventional form, which is typically *year-month-day*. So, for example, 01-25-2020 becomes 2020-01-25, 7/8/2022 becomes 2022-07-08, and 20 January 2021 becomes 2021-01-20.
- mdy_hm(): same as before, but in addition, there is also the time component expressed as hour and minute (es. 2020-12-01 12:35).
- mdy_h(), mdy_hms(): same as before but with the time component formed differently, just the hour in the first case, with hour, minute, and second in the second case.

All other functions are variations of this scheme, so we have, for example, **dmy()**, which is the common European format *day/month/year* (with variants **dmy_hms()**, **dmy_hm()**), and **dmy_h()**). Let us see some examples.

We start with one function, in this case, dmy(), and various forms of the same date.

```
dmy("05 June 2022")
dmy("05 Jun 2022")
dmy("05-06-2022")
dmy("05-06-22")
dmy("05/06/2022")
dmy("05 06 2022")
```

They are all correctly parsed as 2022-06-05. Now we try with the generic transformation function as_datetime().

```
as_datetime("05 June 22")
[1] "2005-06-22 UTC"
as_datetime("05-06-2022")
Warning: All formats failed to parse. No formats found.
[1] NA
as_datetime("05-06-22")
[1] "2005-06-22 UTC"
as_datetime("June 05, 22")
Warning: All formats failed to parse. No formats found.
[1] NA
as_datetime("05 06 22")
[1] "2005-06-22 UTC"
```

In this case, none is correctly parsed. Two have raised an error, the first because it failed to parse 2022, by default it just parses years with two digits, and the second because it did not recognize the elements. The others have been converted, but in the wrong way, because the format *year/month/day* was assumed, so 05 became the year 2005 and 22 day 22. The errors came from the fact that function as_datetime() has a parameter **format** to use for specifying a date format, otherwise it just applies the default. So why we would need function as_datetime()? Because it is the more general datetime transformation function and parameter `format` permits a great deal of flexibility. All specific functions like `dmy()`, `mdy_hms()`, and the like are simply front-ends of the `as_datetime()` each with a certain configuration of parameter `format`.

With `as_date()` only the date is obtained. We can see the difference, for the same parsed date.

```
as_datetime("2023-12-25 12:35:52")
[1] "2023-12-25 12:35:52 UTC"
as_datetime("2023-12-25")
[1] "2023-12-25 UTC"
as_date("2023-12-25")
[1] "2023-12-25"
```

Another detail should be noted, which will be important in a particularly elaborated example we will consider shortly: the two dates for which the parsing failed did not provoke a blocking error, but just a warning message. Those dates have been actually transformed, but not into dates, they were transformed into missing values, we can see that with the output **[1] NA**. This is important, **by default failing to parse a date introduces a missing value**. We need to be extra-careful with dates and missing values.

Let us consider another detail. We have seen that *lubridate* functions recognize the month name, both shortened (three letters) or full. What about languages different than English? They can be managed first by having the dictionary installed in the local system, then by specifying a different local configuration through parameter **locale** and command **Sys.setlocale("LC_TIME", "<language>")**.

```
dmy("5 March 2023")
[1] "2023-03-05"
dmy("5 Mars 2023", locale = Sys.setlocale("LC_TIME", "fr_FR"))
[1] "2023-03-05"
dmy("5 Marzo 2023", locale = Sys.setlocale("LC_TIME", "es_ES"))
[1] "2023-03-05"
```

5.1.3 Using Dates

The aim of converting dates into *datetime* data type is to calculate differences between dates and functions to access the components of a date.

Differences in dates are executed as usual and we obtain the time difference in days.

```
a1=dmy("05 06 2022")
a2=dmy("01/01/2022")
a3=a1-a2
print(a3)
Time difference of 155 days
```

The answer is correct, but not usable in a computation because the particular type of data produced by making a time difference, *difftime*, is not compatible. We can try with a simple operation.

```
a3+days(10)
```

It results in an error: *Error: Incompatible classes: <difftime> + <Period>*.

We have to proceed differently, by using functions **days()**, **months()**, and **years()**. For example:

```
a4=days(a1-a2)
a4
[1] "155d 0H 0M 0S"
```

Now we can use this this result in other operations.

```
a4+days(10)
[1] "165d 0H 0M 0S"
```

Some other examples.

```
date(a1+30)
[1] "2022-07-05"
a1+months(2)
[1] "2022-08-05"
a1+days(15)
[1] "2022-06-20"
a1-years(5)
[1] "2017-06-05"
```

5.1.4 Selection with Logical Conditions on Dates

The biggest advantage of having *datetime* values is the possibility to use dates or elements from dates in logical conditions, which is an extremely common case when we need to select rows based on values of *datetime* columns.

Let us consider again data from *Air Data: Air Quality Data Collected at Outdoor Monitors Across the United States*, by the United States Environmental Protection Agency (EPA), the *PM2.5 FRM/FEM Mass* particulate, which has dates.

```
library(vroom)

df= vroom('datasets/EPA/daily_88101_2022.zip')
df %>%
  select('Date Local', 'State Name', 'County Name',
        'City Name', 'Arithmetic Mean') %>%
  rename(Date='Date Local', State='State Name', County='County Name',
      City='City Name', PM25='Arithmetic Mean') -> df1
```

In the previous chapter, we already showed some examples with conditions on dates, when we asked rows with value of column *Date* before (*smaller than*) or after (*greater than*) a certain day.

The possibility of employing relational operators on dates is one of the benefits of having the column set as *datetime*. Here, we expand on these possibilities of using information from dates for the definition of logical conditions. Package *lubridate* offers a range of functions, the main ones are those for extracting the day, month, or year component, respectively, functions `day()`, `month()`, and `year()`.

Warning

Pay attention to the syntax, these functions for extracting date components, `day()`, `month()`, and `year()` look very similar to those used in arithmetic operations with dates, `days()`, `months()`, and `years()`. They perform different operations, but it is easy to mistake one for the other. In this case, it is particularly useful to have the *lubridate* cheatsheet at hand and check which syntax does what.

As a first example, we select rows by months. We want the observations taken in New York City from December to March.

```
filter(df1, (City=="New York") &
            (month(Date) == 12 | month(Date) <= 03)
       )
```

Date	State	County	City	PM25
2022-01-05	New York	Bronx	New York	7.7
2022-01-08	New York	Bronx	New York	4.8
2022-01-11	New York	Bronx	New York	4.9
2022-01-14	New York	Bronx	New York	10.9
2022-01-17	New York	Bronx	New York	4.5
2022-01-20	New York	Bronx	New York	7.2
2022-01-23	New York	Bronx	New York	12.2
2022-01-26	New York	Bronx	New York	3.8
2022-02-04	New York	Bronx	New York	3.8
...	...	...	...	...

We want to be more specific and select exactly the winter season, from December 21 to March 21, for any year. The condition could be a little tricky at first because we need to put together a condition on days and on months for the two days defining the winter season. One could be tempted to extend the previous case by specifying just the two days as follows: The result seems correct, at first glance.

```
filter(df1, (City=="New York") &
            ((month(Date) == 12 & day(Date) >= 21) |
            (month(Date) <= 03 & day(Date) <= 21) )
       )
```

Date	State	County	City	PM25
2022-01-05	New York	Bronx	New York	7.7
2022-01-08	New York	Bronx	New York	4.8
2022-01-11	New York	Bronx	New York	4.9
2022-01-14	New York	Bronx	New York	10.9
2022-01-17	New York	Bronx	New York	4.5
2022-01-20	New York	Bronx	New York	7.2
2022-02-04	New York	Bronx	New York	3.8
2022-02-07	New York	Bronx	New York	10.1
2022-02-10	New York	Bronx	New York	10.4
2022-02-13	New York	Bronx	New York	4.7

But let us check more closely which days are included in the result.

```
filter(df1, (City=="New York") &
             ((month(Date) == 12 & day(Date) >= 21) |
              (month(Date) <= 03 & day(Date) <= 21) )
       ) %$% unique(Date)
 [1] "2022-01-05" "2022-01-08" "2022-01-11" "2022-01-14" "2022-01-17"
 [6] "2022-01-20" "2022-02-04" "2022-02-07" "2022-02-10" "2022-02-13"
[11] "2022-02-16" "2022-02-19" "2022-03-03" "2022-03-12" "2022-03-15"
[16] "2022-03-18" "2022-03-21" "2022-01-01" "2022-01-02" "2022-01-03"
[21] "2022-01-04" "2022-01-06" "2022-01-07" "2022-01-09" "2022-01-10"
[26] "2022-01-12" "2022-01-13" "2022-01-15" "2022-01-16" "2022-01-18"
[31] "2022-01-19" "2022-01-21" "2022-02-01" "2022-02-02" "2022-02-03"
[36] "2022-02-05" "2022-02-06" "2022-02-08" "2022-02-09" "2022-02-11"
[41] "2022-02-12" "2022-02-14" "2022-02-15" "2022-02-17" "2022-02-18"
[46] "2022-02-20" "2022-02-21" "2022-03-01" "2022-03-02" "2022-03-04"
[51] "2022-03-05" "2022-03-07" "2022-03-08" "2022-03-09" "2022-03-10"
[56] "2022-03-11" "2022-03-13" "2022-03-06" "2022-03-14" "2022-03-16"
[61] "2022-03-17" "2022-03-19" "2022-03-20"
```

Is it not odd that there is no day past 21 in the whole period? It is, in fact, the third condition is wrong because it excludes all days past 21 for all months from January to March. We need two conditions, one for March and another for January and February. We fix it and check the dates of the results. There is no date in December, but that is correct; there is not any in the data.

```
filter(df1, (City=="New York") &
             ( (month(Date) == 12 & day(Date) >= 21) |
               (month(Date) == 03 & day(Date) <= 21) |
               (month(Date) < 03) )
       ) %$% unique(Date)
[1] "2022-01-05" "2022-01-08" "2022-01-11" "2022-01-14"
    "2022-01-17" "2022-01-20" "2022-01-23"
[8] "2022-01-26" "2022-02-04" "2022-02-07" "2022-02-10"
    "2022-02-13" "2022-02-16" "2022-02-19"
...
```

This is again an example of how easily we could define the wrong logical condition with a mistake that could go unnoticed if both the conditions and the result are not checked carefully.

Important

At this point, you may think that it is of paramount importance to always write the correct logical condition, and hence the goal is to learn how to never make a mistake.

That would be the wrong conclusion for a correct premise. It is true that, ***ultimately***, we should always write correct logical conditions because they are such a critical element of a computational logic that an error in a logical selection might result in completely wrong results and hence analyses. However, that does not mean that we have to write them correctly every time on first attempt. On the contrary, we all make errors in writing logical conditions, no matter how many years of experience you may have. Experience may teach you to avoid the most trivial ones, but even that is not granted. What experience actually teaches is that you will make errors, logical errors, and syntactical errors. It will happen, for sure; it is not a possibility. Therefore, instead of trying to find a nonexistent way to never make errors, always assume that the logical condition you have just written has an error and prove that it is not the case by double-checking the logic and the results.

Experienced data scientists are those that are good at finding and fixing their errors, not those that boast that they do not need to check because they do not make mistakes. This is a good piece of advice that will serve you well in many circumstances.

An alternative option for filtering with respect to an interval of dates is to define an interval with function `interval()` (or the analogous syntax `%--%`) and then use operator `%within%` in a logical condition. Here is an example, we want to find observations made in Summer 2022.

```
Summer22 <- interval(ymd("2022-06-21"), ymd("2022-09-21"))
Summer22
[1] 2022-06-21 UTC--2022-09-21 UTC
```

Now we filter *df1* using `%within%` and check the *max* and *min* date of the result.

```
df1 %>% filter(Date %within% Summer22) -> test
max(test$Date)
[1] "2022-09-21"
min(test$Date)
[1] "2022-06-21"
```

5.1.5 Strings

To manipulate strings, package ***stringr*** is the main reference. It is part of *tidyverse* and automatically loaded with it. Also, *stringr* has a useful RStudio cheatsheet. The main functions offered by package *stringr* are listed in Table 5.1. They all work on series/columns, not on the whole data frame. Often, we will have the need to repeat string manipulation operations on multiple columns, as well as other operations like data type conversion. With these functions, it is not possible to directly instruct them to repeat the execution on multiple series/columns, it has to be done manually or by means of special constructs for multicolumn execution, which we will introduce in Chapter 9.

Table 5.1 Main functions of package stringr.

Usage	Functions	Description
Pattern matching	`str_view()` `str_detect()` `str_count()` `str_starts()` `str_ends()` `str.length()`	Find strings that include, start with, end with a certain alphanumeric pattern, or match a given *regexp*. Calculate string length, etc.
Transformation	`str_replace()` `str_replace_all()` `str_c()` `str_sub()` `str_trim()` `str_to_lower()` `str_to_upper()` `str_to_title()`	Find a pattern and replace it with a new one, join multiple strings in one, extract a substring, delete spaces at the beginning and at the end of a string, etc.

This time, we employ a small custom data frame to show the initial examples. It represents a few personal records where we use either the notation "??", "unknown", or "Unknown" to indicate an unknown value.

Tip
Clearly, this is an artificial case study, but it should not be considered unrealistic. Using custom formulations for indicating missing or unspecified values is very common and should not be considered a bad practice, on the contrary we will see examples from international institutions adopting that method. On the contrary, using different custom formulations for representing unavailable data in the same dataset is definitely a bad practice because it unreasonably complicates things, but when data are manually inserted, possibly by different persons, that could happen.

```
Name = c("Polycarp Arthmail", "Lada Damon", "Stribog Castor")
Age = c(23, "??", 42)
City = c("Des Moines", "Hanover", "unknown")
State = c("Iowa", "??", "Unknown")
Job = c("full_time", "part_time", "full_time")
df <- data.frame(Name, Age, City, State, Job)
df
```

Name	Age	City	State	Job
Polycarp Arthmail	23	Des Moines	Iowa	full_time
Lada Damon	??	Hanover	??	part_time
Stribog Castor	42	unknown	Unknown	full_time

We can use `str_detect()` to find a certain substring in column values (e.g. we look for "full" in column *Job*). It should be noted that the result is composed of Boolean values; we use it as a Boolean mask in the following logical selection.

```
str_detect(df$Job,'full')
[1]  TRUE FALSE  TRUE
filter(df, str_detect(Job,'full'))
```

Name	Age	City	State	Job
Polycarp Arthmail	23	Des Moines	Iowa	full_time
Stribog Castor	42	unknown	Unknown	full_time

We want to replace "Unknown" in column *State* with "NA".

```
df$State %>% str_replace_all("Unknown", "NA")
[1] "Iowa" "??"   "NA"
```

However, this does not actually replace values in the data frame; it just shows the result. To make it permanent, we have to save the column.

```
df$State %>% str_replace_all("Unknown", "NA") -> df$State
df
```

Name	Age	City	State	Job
Polycarp Arthmail	23	Des Moines	Iowa	full_time
Lada Damon	??	Hanover	??	part_time
Stribog Castor	42	unknown	NA	full_time

Warning

Careful, here we have replaced a string with another string, which happens to be "NA", it is not a missing value.

Now we want the rows with "??" in at least one column. We do first with one column. It produces an error.

```
filter(df, str_detect(Age,'??' ))
Error in filter(df, str_detect(Age, "??")) :
Caused by error in `stri_detect_regex()`:
! Syntax error in regex pattern. (U_REGEX_RULE_SYNTAX, context='?¿)
```

Try to interpret the message. As usual, it is not really crystal clear, but it makes some sense because it mentions a syntax error in the regex pattern and ??. Does it mean it has been interpreted ?? as a regex? Yes, regex special symbol **?** matches 1 or 0 character preceding the question mark, for example, regex *dogs?* matches *dog* or *dogs*. Clearly, regex ?? makes no sense, hence the error. We need the escaping with double backslash \\.

```
filter(df, str_detect(Age, "\\?\\?"))
```

Name	Age	City	State	Job
Lada Damon	??	Hanover	??	part_time

Now that it is correct, we can write the condition for all columns.

```
pat= '\\?\\?'
filter(df, str_detect(Age,pat ) |
           str_detect(City,pat) |
           str_detect(State,pat) |
           str_detect(Job,pat))
```

We now move from the initial didactic example to a real one, by considering OECD's dataset *Better Life Index*, based on 24 indicators aimed at measuring the well-being of societies. From the OECD, we can choose different formats to download, for example, CSV or Excel. The organization of data is not the same between the two datasets, the first being in *long form*, with both countries and indicators in single columns, and the second in *wide form*, with indicators as distinct columns (we will present these different data organizations in the next chapter). There is another difference in values that interest us, for example.

We read the Excel version with function **read_excel()**, for this, we need to load library ***readxl***. Unfortunately, it is a little bit tricky to read because the Excel sheet has several headers with merged cells. For simplicity, we have duplicated the data in a second sheet and minimally modified it by hand, separating some merged cells and deleting useless rows and columns. We read the cells by range, using parameters **sheet** and **range**. We also removed the *first row* (it has the units, not a country), and the *last one* (it carries an automatic note from OECD.Stats with the timestamp of the download). We could do that in several ways; here, we just use basic slicing. Similarly, we remove the last two columns that have no data (we could have just adjusted the range, but this way, how to remove the last two columns is shown). Below is an excerpt.

```
library(readxl)
bli <- read_excel('datasets/OECD/BLI_08052023.xls', sheet=2, range= "A6:AA50")
New names:
• "" -> `...26`
• "" -> `...27`
head(bli)
```

Country	Dwellings without basic facilities	Housing expenditure	Rooms per person	Household net-adjusted disposable income	Household net wealth
Unit	Percentage	Percentage	Ratio	US Dollar	US Dollar
Australia	..	19.40	..	37433	528768
Austria	0.80	20.80	1.60	37001	309637
Belgium	0.70	20.00	2.10	34884	447607
Canada	0.20	22.90	2.60	34421	478240
Chile	9.40	18.40	1.90	..	135787

The first and the last lines and the last two columns are removed.

```
bli[-1,] -> bli
bli[-43,] -> bli
select(bli, -last_col(offset=1), -last_col()) -> bli
```

We can glimpse at the 24 *Better Life Index* indicators and the 41 countries plus the OECD total.

```
names(bli)
 [1] "Country"
 [2] "Dwellings without basic facilities"
 [3] "Housing expenditure"
 [4] "Rooms per person"
 [5] "Household net adjusted disposable income"
 [6] "Household net wealth"
 [7] "Labour market insecurity"
 [8] "Employment rate"
 [9] "Long-term unemployment rate"
...
unique(bli$Country)
 [1] "Australia"      "Austria"       "Belgium"       "Canada"
 [5] "Chile"          "Colombia"      "Costa Rica"    "Czech Republic"
 [9] "Denmark"        "Estonia"       "Finland"       "France"
...
```

This long preparation of the data frame is useful to practice with data that needs to be cleaned up and adjusted before being usable. Now the reason for having selected this dataset: as you can see from the excerpt, values that are not available are indicated with a double point (..). This made by the OECD is not an unusual choice. Using a codified value to indicate an absent value (e.g. "..", "n/a", "NA" and the like) helps avoid some ambiguity with empty cells and, at the same time, is easy to manage computationally. Here, we want to replace those double points with missing values. It is a string substitution; we should parse values of all columns, find the double points, and replace them with a missing value.

Let us try with one column first. The function we use is **str_replace_all()**. The point is like the question mark of a previous example, a special symbol in regex, so the escape is needed. The second issue is how to specify a missing value, which presents some subtleties to learn. First, we can try to replace ".." with another generic value like "n/a".

```
bli$'Dwellings without basic facilities' %>%
                str_replace_all("\\.\\.","n/a")
 [1] "n/a"                "0.80000000000000004" "0.69999999999999996"
 [4] "0.20000000000000001" "9.4000000000000004"  "12.300000000000001"
 [7] "2.2999999999999998" "0.5"                 "0.5"
 ...
```

It works, having checked this, we could save the modified column and repeat it for all of them, although a convenient way to do that will be presented in Chapter 9 with multicolumn operations.

However, replacing ".." with "n/a" has some purpose only if we are normalizing the way missing values are reported and our norm is to use "n/a" as the standard value. Instead, much more relevant is to replace custom representations of missing values—"..", "n/a", "unknown", "NA" and the like—with actual missing values, which need a special code to be recognized as such, because then we can exploit all specialized functions and methods to handle missing values. This will be the subject of the next section.

5.2   R: Handling Missing Values and Data Type Transformations

The fact that missing values are relevant is well established at this point. Here we see how to handle them with some specific functions. It is worth recalling that three are the main strategies for handling missing values: replace them with certain values, remove rows or columns exhibiting missing values, and do nothing but consider them case by case when operations are performed. All these strategies have pros and cons that need to be evaluated; none could be considered right or wrong by default.

The first two strategies have the advantage of eliminating missing values, one way or the other, so that for subsequent operations none of the problems they could cause can arise. However, they both artificially modify the data, which is always an extremely critical operation, to perform with maximum care. Replacing missing values with actual values is completely legit only when we know that the replacement values are true. Typically, it is zero, and it happens when the absence of value means that there was no observation of a certain property. For instance, this happens when values are the result of measuring how a certain quantity differs from the initial state. In that case, no value equals zero difference, except in case of failure of the measuring tool. In all other cases, replacing missing values with a certain value, for example, with the arithmetic mean of the other values, is a choice that is frequently made and inevitably represents a unilateral alteration of data. This may be done in a reasonable way, but nevertheless, it is a subjective decision that cannot be proved to be completely correct. Similarly, when rows or columns containing missing values are deleted, those operations inevitably delete also legitimate values contained in the same rows or columns. This, again, implies a unilateral alteration of data.

Important

Altering data requires strong motivations and extraordinary prudence, and if done, must be disclosed. Doing that in a sloppy and careless way is probably the second worst thing one can do with data, being the absolute worst mistake losing them in an irremediable way.

If neither replacement nor deletion is chosen, then missing data should be taken care of in each operation we execute, and, as already mentioned, they are tricky sometimes. Let us start with the basic functions to handle missing data.

5.2.1 Missing Values as Replacement

We continue with the example of the last section, where we finished by replacing a custom representation of missing values with another one. Here we want to replace it with actual missing values, and to do that we have to consider some of their subtleties. Data frame *bli* is the one we were using at the end of the previous section, that with ".." to signal a missing value.

Now we need to find a way to specify a missing value as the replacement. We first try simply using "", it will not do what we want. Then we try with the keyword **NA** (without quotes; otherwise, it is a string, not a keyword), which will fail too, and finally with the correct way. First, let us check what happens by replacing with the void value "".

```
bli$`Dwellings without basic facilities` %>% str_replace_all("\\.\\.","")
 [1] ""                    "0.80000000000000004" "0.69999999999999996"
 [4] "0.20000000000000001" "9.4000000000000004"  "12.300000000000001"
 ...
```

This result does not correspond to having set missing values; those we have replaced are recognized as a different kind of data, although in practice there is no value. We will prove it shortly. Missing values are a special case that needs specific solutions.

5.2.1.1 Keywords for Missing Values
Let us try with the keyword **NA**.

```
bli$`Dwellings without basic facilities` %>% str_replace_all("\\.\\.", NA)
Error in `str_replace_all()`:
! `replacement` must be a character vector, not `NA`.
```

Here we receive an error that tells us something: the replacement must be of character type, and keyword **NA**, apparently is not. But what does it mean that a missing value should be of a certain data type? This is a typical idiosyncrasy of computational logic that does not care if a missing value, according to common sense, has no type; the priority is to maintain coherence in data types; otherwise, everything goes awry. For this reason, there are keywords for ***typed missing values***: **NA_integer_**, **NA_real_**, **NA_complex_**, and **NA_character_**, all of them correspond to keyword **NA**, but with a type, for cases where it is needed. In this case, the error message tells us we need a character type for replacement, so we use NA_character_.

```
bli$`Dwellings without basic facilities` %>%
  str_replace_all("\\.\\.", NA_character_)
 [1] NA                    "0.80000000000000004" "0.69999999999999996"
 ...
[16] "0"                   "0.20000000000000001" NA
 ...
[25] "25.899999999999999"  "0.10000000000000001" NA
 ...
```

This is correct; the NAs we see in the result are not strings "NA," they are special keywords representing an empty element. With this, we could save the modified column.

```
bli$`Dwellings without basic facilities` %>%
               str_replace_all("\\.\\.", NA_character_) ->
  bli$`Dwellings without basic facilities`
```

Country	Dwellings without basic facilities	Housing expenditure	Rooms per person	Household net-adjusted disposable income	Household net wealth
Australia	<NA>	19.400	…	37433	528768
Austria	0.800	20.800	1.600	37001	309637
Belgium	0.700	20.000	2.100	34884	447607
Canada	0.200	22.900	2.600	34421	478240
Chile	9.400	18.400	1.900	…	135787
Colombia	12.300	…	1.00	…	…

The operation should be repeated for all columns, which is where multicolumn operations show their efficacy, as we will see in Chapter 9.

5.2.2 Introducing Missing Values in Dataset Reads

There is another way to obtain a data frame *bli* with missing values in place of the custom representation with "..". It will look like a bit as a trick, but actually it is an important detail to know because it might save you from obtaining apparently incoherent data from a dataset read. The fact to know is that functions we can use to read a dataset, such as the `read_excel()` used in this example, as well as base `read.csv()` (and variants), *readr*'s `read_csv()` (and variants), and also `vroom()`, all have a parameter that specifies which values are to be interpreted as missing values. The parameter name may change; it is **na.strings** for `read.csv()`, just **na** for the others, but in all cases, it has one or more values recognized as missing values, which is **only blank values ("") for** `read.csv()` **and either a blank value ("") or the string "NA" for the others**.

This is the truly important point: string "NA" is by default interpreted as representing missing values for most of read functions in R. While that could be useful because there are good reasons for preferring to have a string value like "NA" in dataset to represent absent values, rather than a blank field, it also inevitably introduces errors when strings "NA" have a legitimate meaning different than the assumed "Not Available". *The Free Dictionary* (https://acronyms .thefreedictionary.com/NA) presents a nice list of 101 possible meanings of the acronym "NA", including "North America", the Sodium symbol, the country of Namibia, or the province of Naples in Italy. So, there exist many instances that produce an incoherent dataset read due to the default values of that **na** parameter. This is why it is a detail you should be aware of.

In our example, though, we could use it in our favor by setting it to ".." and having them automatically converted to missing values.

```
read_excel('datasets/OECD/BLI_08052023.xls', sheet=2,
           range = "A6:AA50", na= "..") -> bli
bli[-1,] -> bli
bli[-43,] -> bli
select(bli, -last_col(offset=1), -last_col()) -> bli
head(select(bli,1:6))
```

Country	Dwellings without basic facilities	Housing expenditure	Rooms per person	Household net-adjusted disposable income	Household net wealth
Australia	<NA>	19.400		37433	528768
Austria	0.800	20.800	1.600	37001	309637
Belgium	0.700	20.000	2.100	34884	447607
Canada	0.200	22.900	2.600	34421	478240
Chile	9.400	18.400	1.900	<NA>	135787
Colombia	12.300	<NA>	1.00	<NA>	<NA>

5.2.3 Verifying the Presence of Missing Values

Function **is.na()** is simple and important because it permits verifying whether or not a data frame or a column contains missing values. If the result is positive, then we wish to know where they are and how many there are in order to decide how to handle them.

Function is.na() implements a logical condition, meaning that it returns a Boolean mask and can be used in selections. Let us see some examples with the *bli* data frame with all missing values in place of the "..". We start asking if there are missing values in the whole data frame; the result is an excerpt of the result and shows the Boolean values.

```
is.na(bli)
       Country Dwellings without basic facilities Housing expenditure Rooms
per person
 [1,]    FALSE                               TRUE               FALSE    TRUE
 [2,]    FALSE                              FALSE               FALSE   FALSE
 [3,]    FALSE                              FALSE               FALSE   FALSE
 [4,]    FALSE                              FALSE               FALSE   FALSE
 [5,]    FALSE                              FALSE               FALSE   FALSE
 [6,]    FALSE                              FALSE                TRUE   FALSE
 ...
```

If we recall that Boolean values by default also have a numeric interpretation, with TRUE equals to 1 and FALSE equal to 0, we could just sum them. There are 73 missing values in *bli* data frame.

```
sum(is.na(bli))
[1] 73
```

We could also use a single column as data, for example, *Housing expenditure*.

```
is.na(bli$'Housing expenditure')
 [1] FALSE FALSE FALSE FALSE FALSE  TRUE FALSE FALSE FALSE FALSE FALSE FALSE
[13] FALSE FALSE FALSE  TRUE FALSE  TRUE FALSE FALSE FALSE FALSE FALSE FALSE
[25] FALSE FALSE FALSE FALSE FALSE FALSE FALSE FALSE FALSE FALSE FALSE FALSE
[37] FALSE FALSE FALSE  TRUE FALSE FALSE
```

Again, we could sum the Boolean values in order to find how many missing values are present. There are four in column *Housing expenditure*.

```
sum(is.na(bli$'Housing expenditure'))
[1] 4
```

A single series of Boolean values can be used as a Boolean mask for selection. We can select the 4 rows corresponding to a missing value in column *Housing expenditure*.

```
filter(bli, is.na('Housing expenditure'))
```

Country	Dwellings without basic facilities	Housing expenditure	Rooms per person	...
Colombia	12.300	<NA>	1	...
Iceland	0	<NA>	1.600	...
Israel	<NA>	<NA>	1.2	...
Brazil	6.700	<NA>	<NA>	...

What if we want the rows *NOT* corresponding to missing values in column *Housing expenditure*, as is usually the case? It is a normal logical condition, and we already know how to use the negation operator.

```
filter(bli, !is.na('Housing expenditure'))
```

Can we replace function is.na() with a traditional logical condition using == or !=? Not really. The following alternatives all return an empty result.

```
filter(bli, 'Housing expenditure'== '')
filter(bli, 'Housing expenditure'== 'NA')
filter(bli, 'Housing expenditure'== NA)
filter(bli, 'Housing expenditure'== NA_character_)
```

5.2.3.1 Functions `any()`, `all()`, and `colSums()`

We have seen so far how to count missing values in a data frame or a column and how to select rows based on missing values. We now add other useful functions that help in handling the missing values: `any()`, `all()`, and `colSums()`.

Let us start with `any()` and `all()`, both functions of base R, that answer two basic questions. Given a vector of Boolean values, array, or matrix:

`any()`: Is there at least one TRUE value?
`all()`: Are they all TRUE values?

They could be applied to all logical results, including `is.na()`, evidently.

Some examples. Is there at least one missing value in data frame *bli*? Yes. Are all values missing? No.

```
any(is.na(bli))
[1]  TRUE
all(is.na(bli))
[1]  FALSE
```

Same for a single column. Is there at least one missing value in column *Country*? No. And in column on *Housing expenditure*? Yes.

```
any(is.na(bli$Country))
[1]  FALSE
any(is.na(bli$'Housing expenditure'))
[1]  TRUE
```

It also exists a short form for the combination `any(is.na())`: **anyNA()**.

```
anyNA(bli$'Housing expenditure')
[1]  TRUE
```

The third function we consider, **`colSums()`** is also a function of base R and returns a result that is often particularly useful: *for each columns it computes the sum of the values*. It has the important parameter, **`na.rm`** that if *TRUE* ignores missing values in the calculation, if *FALSE* and missing values are present, the result is *NA*. *FALSE* is the default. There are *variants* of the `colSums()`, respectively, for calculating the *sum by row* and for calculating the *arithmetic mean*, by column or by row: **`rowSums()`**, **`colMeans()`**, and **`rowMeans()`**.

The combination between `colSums()` *and* `is.na()` *is particularly important because it gives us the answer to an important question: How many missing values each column has?*

Note

The information provided by `colSums(is.na())` should be used regularly with all datasets as part of the preliminary analysis aimed at gathering basic information and simple descriptive statistics. It is a simple method that offers a key information.

With data frame *bli*.

```
colSums(is.na(bli))
                                           Country
                                                 0
                   Dwellings without basic facilities
                                                 3
                              Housing expenditure
                                                 4
                               Rooms per person
                                                 3
            Household net adjusted disposable income
                                                 6
                                               ...
```

With the combination **rowSums(is.na())** we find which rows contain missing values and its number.

```
rowSums(is.na(bli))
 [1] 2 0 0 0 3 6 5 2 1 0 0 0 0 0 0 4 0 5 0
     2 1 1 2 1 2 0 1 0 0 1 1 1 1 2 3 3 0 0
[39] 0 9 5 9
```

5.2.4 Replacing Missing Values

We now see how to implement one of the possible strategies for handling missing values: replacing them with a value. We see first the base method using slicing, then with specific functions.

We recall that with square brackets (**[]**) it is possible to select values from a column based on a Boolean mask. In order to replace missing values with an actual value, we should first select them.

```
# For convenience we use a copy of data frame bli
test= bli

# First we count missing values in column 'Housing expenditure'
sum(is.na(test$'Housing expenditure')) # there are 4
[1] 4
# Then we select them, with slicing or with filter()
test$'Housing expenditure'[is.na(test$'Housing expenditure')]
[1] NA NA NA NA
```

Now we can use an assignment to set a value. We use column *Housing expenditure,* and we want to assign to missing values the arithmetic mean of the same column. The column is of character data type, so first it needs to be transformed into numeric type with function **as_numeric()** (we anticipate this type transformation that we will see in a future section). Then the mean can be assigned to elements with a missing value. The result has no *NA* and instead has a mean value of 20.35.

```
# First the column is converted to numeric type
test$'Housing expenditure'= as.numeric(test$'Housing expenditure')

# The arithmetic mean of the column is calculated
meanA= mean(test$'Housing expenditure', na.rm = TRUE)

# Print the value
cat("meanA: ", meanA, "\n")
meanA:  20.35
# Finally, we assign the value of the mean to the empty elements
test$'Housing expenditure'[is.na(test$'Housing expenditure')] = meanA

print(test$'Housing expenditure')
 [1] 19.40 20.80 20.00 22.90 18.40 20.35 17.00 23.40 23.30 17.00 23.10 20.70
[13] 20.00 21.80 19.90 20.35 20.60 20.35 22.50 21.80 14.70 20.80 18.40 20.70
[25] 17.80 19.60 25.00 17.70 21.20 19.60 27.40 18.20 21.70 20.10 21.40 18.90
[37] 23.20 18.30 20.50 20.35 17.40 18.10
```

Alternatives to the base slicing method exist, in particular with replacing functions. One is function **replace_na()**, of package *tidyr*, included in *tidyverse*. The usage is easy; it works on a column and only needs the replacement value. We again use the arithmetic mean.

```
replace_na(test$'Housing expenditure', meanA)
```

We can write it in a pipe using the special pipe operator **%$%**, being replace_na() another function without an explicit data parameter.

```
test %$% replace_na('Housing expenditure', meanA)
```

The generic function **replace()** of base R also serves the same purpose, but it is more complicated because it takes two parameters: one is an index vector, whose indexes correspond to elements to be replaced, and the second is a corresponding vector of replacement values. Hence, we need to obtain the index of elements with missing values. Function **which()** gives us this information.

```
indexA= which(is.na(test$'Housing expenditure'))

cat("indexA: ", indexA, "\n\n")
indexA:  6 16 18 40
test$'Housing expenditure' %>% replace(indexA, meanA)
```

When values are of character type, we could also use functions for string manipulation, like **str_replace_na()** of package *stringr*. By default, it turns missing values into the string "NA", otherwise, with parameter **replacement,** a specific string could be provided. We try with column *Housing expenditure* without turning it into numeric type.

```
test= bli

test$'Housing expenditure' %>% str_replace_na()
  [1] "19.400" "20.800" "20"     "22.900"
  [5] "18.400" "NA"     "17"     "23.400"
  [9] "23.300" "17"     "23.100" "20.700"
 [13] "20"     "21.800" "19.900" "NA"
 [17] "20.600" "NA"     "22.5"
```

This way we have string "NA" where missing values occurred. If the replacement string is "..", we return to the original form.

```
test$'Housing expenditure' %>% str_replace_na(replacement="..")
```

5.2.5   Omit Rows with Missing Values

Another option for handling missing data is to omit rows or columns containing them. How to achieve is easy; at this point, we have already done it when we have seen the following example:

```
filter(bli, !is.na('Housing expenditure'))
```

With this, we select rows that do not have missing values in the specific column (38 columns over 42). *This is how we omit missing values by subsetting the data frame.* The logical condition could involve more columns, of course. For example:

```
filter(bli, !(is.na('Housing expenditure') |
               is.na('Household net wealth') |
               is.na('Personal earnings') |
               is.na('Time devoted to leisure and personal care') )
)
```

The result now has just 22 rows, over 42 of the original data frame. Remember that if you negate single conditions, it takes the AND (&), not the OR (|), the previous equals to

```
filter(bli, !is.na('Housing expenditure') &
               !is.na('Household net wealth') &
               !is.na('Personal earnings') &
               !is.na('Time devoted to leisure and personal care')
)
```

Finally, if the aim is to *omit all rows containing missing values*, regardless of the column, the base package **stats** offers the handy **na.omit()** function that does exactly that; it returns only the rows with no missing values. For our *bli* data frame, there are just 17 rows with no missing values.

```
stats::na.omit(bli)
```

Table 5.2 Data type verification and transformation functions.

Type	Description	Verification	Transformation
Logical	Boolean values TRUE and FALSE, corresponding to 1 and 0	`is.logical()`	`as.logical()`
Numeric	Numeric data, general	`is.numeric()`	`as.numeric()`
Double	Numeric data, real	`is.double()`	`as.double()`
Integer	Numeric data, integer	`is.integer()`	`as.integer()`
Character	Alphanumeric data (alphabetic characters, digits, symbols, and punctuation)	`is.character()`	`as.character()`
List	Lists	`is.list()`	`as.list()`
Factor	Categorical values, assigned to levels	`is.factor()`	`as.factor()`

5.2.6 Data Type Transformations

We already encountered some instances where a data type transformation was necessary, the last one in the previous section to convert a column from character to numeric. Table 5.2 shows the main ones. Every ***transformation function*** has a corresponding ***verification function***. With the former type we convert data type, with the latter we verify if data are of a certain type. These are the ones defined in base R, variations may exist implemented in custom packages.

For example, we consider dataset *Final energy consumption* from Eurostat. It is similar in the organization to the OCSE's *Better Life Index* dataset we considered previously, but with an additional complication that helps us practicing with data type transformations. The dataset has extension *.tsv*, we guess that tab is the separator (\t), so we use `read_tsv()` for reading it.

```
fec= read_tsv("datasets/Eurostat/sdg_07_11.tsv")
```

unit,geo\time	2000	2001	2002	2003	2004	2005	...
I05,AL	80.6	82.6	94.6	92.6	103.8	100.0	...
I05,AT	85.2	90.3	91.1	95.7	97.1	100.0	...
I05,BE	103.1	105.5	99.4	102.9	103.4	100.0	...
I05,BG	89.5	89.6	89.5	96.2	95.2	100.0	...
I05,CY	90.0	93.2	93.9	99.4	100.0	100.0	...
I05,CZ	95.8	97.5	95.6	100.3	101.4	100.0	...

Let us check if any missing value is present. There are none.

```
anyNA(fec)
[1] FALSE
```

We are mostly interested in column data types; we use function `str()` to look at that information. All columns are of character data type, although their values logically are numbers.

We will find that we are in a situation similar to what we have encountered with the *Better Life Index* dataset, but for now, let us assume we do not know why all columns are of type character and we just try to transform them into numeric type.

```
str(fec)
spc_tbl_ [116 × 22] (S3: spec_tbl_df/tbl_df/tbl/data.frame)
 $ unit,geo\time : chr [1:116] "I05,AL" "I05,AT" "I05,BE" "I05,BG" ...
 $ 2000         : chr [1:116] "80.6" "85.2" "103.1" "89.5" ...
 $ 2001         : chr [1:116] "82.6" "90.3" "105.5" "89.6" ...
 $ 2002         : chr [1:116] "94.6" "91.1" "99.4" "89.5" ...
 $ 2003         : chr [1:116] "92.6" "95.7" "102.9" "96.2" ...
 $ 2004         : chr [1:116] "103.8" "97.1" "103.4" "95.2" ...
```

We try the transformation with one column with function `as.numeric()`.

```
as.numeric(fec$'2000')
```

The conversion succeeds, but a *warning message* has been raised, and, as we already know, it is better to read and try to make sense of it, because often warnings tell us something we should be aware of. This one says: *NAs introduced by coercion*, what does it mean? This time it is not cryptic; on the contrary, it could be read literally: the operation has introduced missing values into the data, and we know that there were none before the transformation. Why did that happen?

The reason is the *standard behavior of R data type transformation functions* that, when they encounter a value that cannot be converted to the destination data type, they replace the original value with an empty cell, therefore the warning that missing values have been introduced.

This behavior could sometimes be useful, for instance, to transform custom representations of missing values into actual missing values but could also delete values that could have been converted with a little bit of work. This example is exactly of this kind; we will save some legitimate values from being overwritten with NAs. We start by counting how many NAs have been introduced.

```
sum(is.na(as.numeric(fec$'2000')))
Warning: NAs introduced by coercion
[1] 9
```

They are 9, and none of them existed before the transformation. We have to find them and for each one, figure out what the original value was and why it failed to be transformed into the numeric data type. Reasons why a value cannot be transformed into numeric data type usually revolve around the fact that the value has some non-numeric characters, either alphabetic, symbols, or punctuation characters. For example, like in the previous section, missing values have been represented with some custom code like "..". Therefore, we start looking for punctuation symbols. How can we do that, except by trying to manually list all of them (an approach definitely not recommended)?

There are special operators and constructs supporting such needs. For example, RStudio cheatsheet of library *stringr* has a section titled Regular Expressions that lists some of them, called **character classes**: **[:digit:]** for digits, **[:alpha:]** for alphabetic characters, **[:punct:]** for punctuation, **[:symbol:]** for symbols, and so on. The *[:punct:]* looks promising, let us try that with function `str_detect()` that permits finding a pattern or a regular expression in strings. We want to find all elements having punctuation characters in column 2000. We pipe the command with `sum()` to see how many elements are matched.

```
fec$'2000' %>% str_detect('[:punct:]') %>% sum()
[1] 116
```

This does not help; it matches all elements because all of them have the decimal point, which is indeed a punctuation character. To improve it, we should omit the point from the list of punctuation characters, but given that requirement, it is worth considering a more general way of writing regular expressions. We use a more canonical form for regex:

- to match *punctuation*, it can be used the regex `\p{P}` and `\p{S}` for matching *symbols*. These special operators are defined in *Unicode regular expressions*, a notation that R fully supports. We use both, therefore we will use the following regex, `[\\p{P}\\p{S}]` , with the second backslash as the escape character;
- to match alphabetic characters, lower and upper case, it can be used `[a-zA-Z]`.

This way, we have a finer control of what is matched. First, we try with punctuation and symbols.

```
fec$'2000' %>% str_detect('[\\p{P}\\p{S}]') %>% sum()
[1] 116
```

The result is again all 116 rows, which is correct because we are still matching the decimal points. To omit the point from the character matched, we have two general methods, and for the subtleties of the different grammars of regular expressions (we do not delve into these details), it is possible that in some systems they both work or only one of them is supported:

1. to exclude some matches from a regex, the syntax `--[ ]` could be used, where what is specified into the square brackets is prevented from matching in the main expression. In our case, it is only the point that we want to omit; therefore, our regex becomes `[\\p{P}\\p{S}--[.]]` ;
2. alternatively, we can use a notation called ***forward looking***, more general, that is specified placing notation `(?! )` *before* the main regex. Inside the `(?! )` we can write a regex, and its result will be *excluded* from the result of the main regex . Again, in our case, we want to exclude just the point; therefore the final regex will be `(?![.]) [\\p{P}\\p{S}]` .

Let us try both ways.

```
fec$'2000' %>% str_detect('[\\p{P}\\p{S}--[.]]') %>% sum()
[1] 6
fec$'2000' %>% str_detect('(?![.]) [\\p{P}\\p{S}]') %>% sum()
[1] 6
```

They both work and find six rows. Let us look at them.

```
filter(fec, str_detect('2000', '(?![.]) [\\p{P}\\p{S}]')) %>%
  select(1,2) -> t1
```

unit,geo\time	2000
I05,ME	:
MTOE,BA	:
MTOE,ME	:
TOE_HAB,BA	:
TOE_HAB,ME	:
TOE_HAB,XK	:

They have colons as symbols representing missing values, very similar to what we have seen with the OCSE dataset. However, three of the nine elements that the conversion in numeric data type replaced with NAs are still unknown. We have checked punctuation and symbols; we can try with letters.

```
filter(fec, str_detect('2000', '[a-zA-Z]')) %>%
  select(1,2) -> t1
```

unit,geo\time	2000
TOE_HAB,EU27_2020	2.28 b
TOE_HAB,HR	1.34 e
TOE_HAB,PL	1.44 b

Here they are, these elements do actually have a legitimate numerical value, but they also have letters, the remains of a reference to a footnote in the original dataset. These values could (and should) be prevented from becoming missing values, they are valuable data, we just need to clean them from the spurious characters and convert into numerical type.

Function `str_replace_all()` specifies that more substitutions could be done with a single operation by using a peculiar notation: `c(pattern1 = replacement1, pattern2 = replacement2 ...)`. Alternatively, we could repeat twice the operation. In addition to the replacement, we also remove trailing white spaces from beginning and end of the value with **str_trim()**, of package *stringr*, or **trimws()** of base R, they are equivalent.

```
str_replace_all(fec$'2000', c('b' = '', 'e' = '')) %>% str_trim()
  [89] "1.74"  "1.97"  "2.28"  "4.71"  "2.55"  "1.34"  "1.58"  "2.84"  ...
 [100] "8.04"  "1.37"  ":"     "0.78"  "1.15"  "3.27"  "4.03"  "1.44"  ...
 [111] "3.94"  "2.30"  "2.03"  "0.86"  "2.60"  ":"
```

Replacements and trimming of white spaces have been executed correctly (values are showed in bold, corresponding to indexes 91, 94, and 107), we can save the column.

```
fec$'2000'= str_replace_all(fec$'2000', c('b' = '', 'e' = '')) %>% str_trim()
```

We can check the result by counting again how many NAs would be inserted with the conversion in numerical type. It should be six, corresponding to the elements with colon as value.

```
sum(is.na(as.numeric(fec$'2000')))
Warning: NAs introduced by coercion
[1] 6
```

It is correct, we can finally save the column.

```
fec$'2000'= as.numeric(fec$'2000')
Warning: NAs introduced by coercion
```

With this, we have just converted one column; other 20 remain and doing it manually is clearly a cumbersome task. Again, how useful are multicolumn operations that repeat the task for us, appears evident.

5.3 R: Example with Dates, Strings, and Missing Values

In this section, we consider an example more complex than the ones presented so far. What we are going to see is aimed at practicing with operations on dates, strings, and missing values, but it will show us more than that. We will see how apparently innocuous operations and assumptions that at first appear completely safe may change data with unforeseen consequences and in ways that easily mislead us. We will use real data and a real online service, the case study, although fictitious, is realistic and should be considered as an example of problems that could be encountered in the field and of evaluations that might look sound but instead turn out to be wrong during the development of a real data science project.

We use the dataset *Fahrraddiebstahl in Berlin* (translated, *Bicycle thefts in Berlin*) from the Open Data of the city of Berlin, Germany. The original dataset is in Excel format, which we have already used, and requires function read_excel() of package *readxl*, included in *tidyverse*. We read the dataset.

```
df= read_excel("datasets/Berlin_OpenData/Fahrraddiebstahl_12_2022.xlsx")
names(df)
 [1] "ANGELEGT_AM"          "TATZEIT_ANFANG_DATUM"  "TATZEIT_ANFANG_STUNDE"
 [4] "TATZEIT_ENDE_DATUM"   "TATZEIT_ENDE_STUNDE"   "LOR"
 [7] "SCHADENSHOEHE"        "VERSUCH"               "ART_DES_FAHRRADS"
[10] "DELIKT"               "ERFASSUNGSGRUND"
```

Unsurprisingly, it is in German, which would be fine for German-speakers but incomprehensible for everybody else. We need a translation, if we want to use it, and… hey, we are in year 2024; it is not a big deal to have one readily available! Online translation services have enormously improved in recent years. They might still have some rough edges dealing with literary texts, or they may provide translations that sound a little artificial when a prose is translated, but in this case, we have neither prose nor grammatical structures, just words and names, so it is perfectly reasonable to expect an acceptable result. We go with the most famous among the online free translation services: *Google Translate*, which accepts documents in Excel format. We upload the original German dataset, and, in a snap, we obtain the translated one, that we read.

```
df= read_excel("datasets/Berlin_OpenData/Fahrraddiebstahl_12_2022_EN.xlsx")
names(df)
 [1]  "CREATED_AM"          "DEED TIME_START_DATE" "TIME_START_HOUR"
 [4]  "DEED TIME_END_DATE"  "TIME_END_HOUR"        "LOR"
 [7]  "DAMAGES"             "EXPERIMENT"           "TYPE_OF_BICYCLE"
[10]  "OFFENSE"             "REASON FOR DETECTION"
```

Much better, at least for non-German speakers. The description of columns is provided in Table 5.3.

Some columns contain dates (*CREATED_AM*, *DEED TIME_START_DATE* e *DEED TIME_END_DATE*), but they are not defined as *datetime* types, so we want to transform them. First, we need some information about their values.

```
any(is.na(df))
[1] FALSE
```

There is no missing value in the data frame. Now we need to check the format of the date. We start with the first column, *CREATED_AM*.

```
unique(df$CREATED_AM)
[1]  "09.12.2022" "08.12.2022" "07.12.2022" "06.12.2022" "05.12.2022" ...
[8]  "02.12.2022" "12/01/2022" "11/30/2022" "11/29/2022" "11/28/2022" ...
...
```

We see, for instance, 11/30/2022, so we guess that the format is *month/day/year*. However, we also note something a little weird, some dates have the point as a separator, others have the forward

Table 5.3 Dataset Fahrraddiebstahl in Berlin (translated), column description.

Column	Description
CREATED_AM	date of entry's creation
DEED TIME_START_DATE DEED TIME_END-DATE	time period (dates) when the theft is supposed to be perpetrated
TIME_START_HOUR TIME_END-HOUR	time period (hours) when the theft has been perpetrated
LOR	geographic reference to Berlin's zone system
DAMAGES	value of the stolen bicycle
TYPE_OF_BYCICLE	type of bicycle
OFFENSE	type of offense
REASON FOR DETECTION	reason for the call to the police

slash. Could it be because the data entry happened manually and a standard for date was not enforced? Yes, it could be, with manual data entry all sorts of odd things may happen (*Note*: this assumption will turn out to be wrong, but think about it, would not it be reasonable and realistic, given the information we have?).

Note

This line of reasoning is fictitious; we will see shortly that something unexpected happened, but it is also realistic, so let us stick with it. We obtain interesting insights even from errors, often especially from errors.

We need to decide if we want to normalize dates by transforming points in slashes or vice versa. It seems a good idea having the same format (*Note*: pay attention to this assumption), but which transformation is best? Using slashes is probably more common (not if you are German, but we are assuming not to be), but let us decide according to the majority of cases. We select rows with slash in dates and with points, and then we see which case is more frequent. We know how to do, with function `str_detect()`. The point is a special symbol in regex; we need to escape it to use it as a punctuation character. The slash, instead, has no special meaning.

```
filter(df,str_detect(CREATED_AM,'\\.')) %>% nrow()
[1] 6913
filter(df,str_detect(CREATED_AM,'/')) %>% nrow()
[1] 34256
```

Dates with slashes are the large majority, then we transform points into slashes with `str_replace_all()`.

```
df$CREATED_AM= str_replace_all(df$CREATED_AM, "\\.","/")
df$'DEED TIME_START_DATE'= str_replace_all(df$'DEED TIME_START_DATE', "\\.","/")
df$'DEED TIME_END_DATE'= str_replace_all(df$'DEED TIME_END_DATE', "\\.","/")
```

We have normalized dates, and now we can transform the data type of the three columns into *datetime*. We have guessed the format, *month/day/year*, then we can use function `mdy()` of *lubridate* package. Let us try with the first column.

```
mdy(df$CREATED_AM)
Warning:  776 failed to parse.
[1] "2022-09-12" "2022-09-12" "2022-09-12" "2022-09-12" "2022-09-12" ...
[8] "2022-09-12" "2022-09-12" "2022-09-12" "2022-09-12" "2022-09-12" ...
```

It works, but there is a warning message, 776 dates cannot be parsed. How's that? May be there are some custom symbols to represent missing values, as we have seen in two examples before? Or other spurious characters? We need to check; this warning message cannot be ignored, and let 776 dates be overwritten by NAs. To check, we can exploit the fact that data type transformation functions force missing values when they fail to parse values. We can transform the column, find elements forced to NA, and then retrieve the corresponding values in the original column.

We use a copy of data frame *df* for not re-reading the dataset later, then we covert the first column and filter all rows with a missing value in column *CREATED_AM*.

```
temp= df
temp$CREATED_AM= mdy(temp$CREATED_AM)
Warning: 776 failed to parse.
filter(temp, is.na(CREATED_AM))
```

CREATED_AM	DEED TIME_START_DATE	TIME_START_HOUR	DEED TIME_END_DATE
<NA>	11/11/2022	9	11/12/2022
<NA>	14/11/2022	8	14/11/2022
<NA>	14/11/2022	7	14/11/2022
<NA>	14/11/2022	18	14/11/2022
<NA>	14/11/2022	12	14/11/2022
<NA>	11/10/2022	18	11/11/2022

Now we have to find the corresponding rows in the original data frame and check what values of column *CREATED_AM* make the transformation fail. We can just sample few rows, starting with the first. In the original data frame *df* we look for a column with value of column *DEED TIME_START_DATE* equals to 11/11/2022, value of *TIME_START_HOUR* equals to 9, and value of *DAMAGES* equals to 530, likely we will find a single match.

```
filter(df, `DEED TIME_START_DATE`=="11/11/2022" &
           TIME_START_HOUR==9 &
           DAMAGES==530)
```

CREATED_AM	DEED TIME_START_DATE	TIME_START_HOUR	DEED TIME_END_DATE	TIME_END_HOUR	DAMAGES
14/11/2022	11/11/2022	9	11/12/2022	18	530

The value of *CREATED_AM* is 14/11/2022, which is definitely unexpected because it is a date with *day/month/year* format, not *month/day/year* as we have assumed. That's the reason for the function mdy() to fail. This data frame is getting complicated to handle, and these dates are increasingly looking like a mess. Now we have even a bigger problem, because if both formats exist, *day/month/year* and *month/day/year*, how can we figure out which one is correct for dates that satisfy both of them, like 10/05/2021, for example?

In theory, the answer is that we cannot, but we do not despair and try an empirical approach. As done before, we check the format of the majority of dates. We know that function mdy() cannot parse 776 dates; how many functions dmy() cannot parse ?

```
temp= dmy(df$CREATED_AM)
Warning: 24565 failed to parse.
sum(is.na(temp))
[1] 24565
```

With function `dmy()`, 24565 dates cannot be parsed, which reassures us about the fact that *month/day/year* is the main format for these dates, with some exceptions formatted as *day/month/year* (Note: A gentle reminder that this is a fictitious case). But is it really possible to find such a confusion in a real dataset? It could be, real datasets could be messy, especially when data are entered manually, and since we know nothing about the way this dataset has been produced, everything's possible. Never forget that behind data often there are persons, workers, citizens, researchers. The data we enjoy using are available thanks to the work of some people, but not all data are produced by automatic system. And people often make mistakes, use common sense or use personal judgement, that is how inconsistencies often arise. We should not blame those providing us with open data because they are not perfectly tidy and free from errors. Instead, we should learn how to wrangle with data and prepare them for analysis.

This is a good piece of advice that I recommend readers to always keep in mind. However, this is not what caused such a mess in these dates. Another, even better, good piece of advice is that perhaps it is us those making wrong assumptions, possibly because there is something important that we have overlooked.

5.3.1 When an Invisible Hand Mess with Your Data

The previous description of events is not real but realistic indeed. It may have happened as described and it should not have surprised us. That is why it tells us something useful and why we will proceed with that fictional scenario, but now is time to disclose what was the real cause for those messy dates with different separators and different formats.

Let us go back to the beginning, to the German dataset, and have a closer look at it (previously, on purpose I did not show the content, it was a little trick to corroborate the fictional story).

```
dfDE= read_excel("datasets/Berlin_OpenData/Fahrraddiebstahl_12_2022.xlsx")
```

Let us look at the first column, *ANGELEGT_AM*, corresponding to *CREATED_AM* in the translated version.

```
unique(dfDE$ANGELEGT_AM)
[1] "09.12.2022" "08.12.2022" "07.12.2022" "06.12.2022" "05.12.2022" ...
[8] "02.12.2022" "01.12.2022" "30.11.2022" "29.11.2022" "28.11.2022" ...
```

All dates have points, not slashes, as separators (*Note*: with better information about German standards, we would have known that the point is the typical separator for dates in Germany). We check for it.

```
filter(dfDE,str_detect(ANGELEGT_AM,'/')) %>% nrow()
[1] 0
```

There is no date with slash separator in the original column. We also see dates clearly in *day/month/year* format, three in two rows (i.e. 30.11.2022, 29.11.2022, 28.11.2022), hardly an exception. At this point, your inner data scientist's voice should have started screaming as hell that very likely you have made some totally wrong assumptions. A test is needed: try to convert the column as *day/month/year,* with dmy().

```
dmy (dfDE$ANGELEGT_AM)
```

No warning message, all dates have been converted correctly, zero missing values inserted, everything is completely fine with the original dataset, no inconsistencies from manual data entry, no lack of standard whatsoever. These are the things that make a data scientist bangs his or her head onto the wall.

The culprit is now clear: the online translation service has tried to translate also the dates into English and made a mess, because converting dates needs context and meaning, the things that an automatic translation tool has the most problems to deal with. But, if the cause is now known, who's the responsibility? Is Google Translate responsible for having tried to translate dates which should have left untouched? May be, perhaps partially, translating date formats is probably not a good idea and should be avoided, but on the other hand Google has never said that its translation service is perfect, we all know it makes mistakes. So, the responsibility is ours? Again, may be partially it is, we know that modifying data is always a critical operation that, if something goes wrong, may end up with dire consequences for our data science project. But did we really do something wrong or careless? Not really, having considered the online translation of the dataset as a safe operation was not wrong. We just forget about the dates, but it was quite difficult to imagine beforehand. So, nobody's really responsible? Probably this is the correct conclusion, it is not a matter of who's responsible of having done a mistake or something careless, it is a matter of exercising extra-care with data and check, double-check, and be suspicious of everything apparently weird when wrangling with data. Those different separators should have rung alarm bells that may be there was another explanation in addition to the messy data entry. We should have asked ourselves: who or what has touched the data? It was completely possible that the weirdness was actually in the data, but it was also possible that an "invisible hand" (relatively speaking, because that hand is typically ours) messed with data.

Having revealed the true cause for the inconsistent dates, however, does not make the example less interesting. It is a good one for practicing with an unusual scenario. We continue assuming that all inconsistencies were in the data, not introduced artificially.

We were at the point that we discovered two different date formats in the data frame and have to convert the values into *datetime* format. We have basically two approaches to possibly follow:

- One that we call *Base method,* which make use of base functionalities and proceeds manually.
- Another using high-level functions that let us manage at the same time more than one date format.

We will see both, starting with the first.

5.3.2 Base Method

A logic we could follow could be this: for each column with dates, we select rows with format *month/day/year*, the one we guessed was correct, and convert with *lubridate* function mdy(). Then we take the other rows, those with format *day/month/year*, and convert with function dmy().

Makes sense, but how can we tell which rows have dates with one format and which with the other one? The criterion for this fictional example is the one we have devised before: we assume format *month/day/year* is the correct one because it finds way fewer dates that is unable to parse than with the other format. So, one column at time, we transform dates with mdy(), those that are parsed without errors are fine and the corresponding rows can be selected. This is the first partial data frame. The other rows, those corresponding to dates with NAs inserted by mdy(), can be selected and represent the second partial data frame, the one whose dates needs to be transformed with function dmy().

There is a caveat: by exploiting the NAs introduced with function mdy(), we can easily select rows with missing values in dates, but this way we have also lost the original dates, which instead we have to transform with dmy(). We need to keep a copy of them, so we should start by making a duplicate of the columns with dates, before the first transformation with mdy().

Duplicated columns are useless for the first partial data frame with dates correctly parsed and could be ignored, at the end we will delete them. But they are necessary for the second data frame, the one with NAs in dates, because we could copy the original dates from the duplicate column and overwrite the NAs introduced, so to restore the values. Then we transform them with dmy(). The second partial data frame has now the column with all dates transformed in datetime type. The two parts can be reassembled, and the procedure repeated for the other columns.

We can write the instruction following the steps we have just described. We consider just column *CREATED_AM*. First, we duplicate it, transform with mdy(), and select the rows for the two partial data frames, *df_mdy* and *df_dmy*.

```
# Duplication of column CREATED_AM
df$CREATED_AM_copy= df$CREATED_AM
# Transform the column with mdy()
# This introduces 776 NAs, as we already know
df$CREATED_AM= mdy(df$CREATED_AM)
# Select rows without NAs in CREATED_AM
# This is the first partial data frame
df_mdy = filter(df, !(is.na(CREATED_AM)))
# Select rows with NAs in CREATED_AM
# This is the second partial data frame that needs
# to be further transformed
df_dmy = filter((df, is.na(CREATED_AM))
```

With data frame *df_dmy*, we overwrite the NAs introduced in *CREATED_AM* with the original values kept in the duplicated *CREATED_AM_copy*, then transform with dmy(). All dates are parsed correctly.

```
# With the second data frame, we copy the values of
# CREATED_AM_copy over CREATED_AM (having all NAs)
df_dmy$CREATED_AM= df_dmy$CREATED_AM_copy
# Transform the column with dmy()
# All dates are parsed correctly
df_dmy$CREATED_AM= dmy(df_dmy$CREATED_AM)
```

Finally, we reassemble the two partial data frame in a single one using base R function `bind_rows()` and delete the duplicated column.

```
df_final=bind_rows(df_mdy, df_dmy)
df_final$CREATED_AM_copy= NULL
```

At this point we should repeat the same steps for the other columns with dates if the result of the transformation would not have turned out to be wrong. Let us check what is the latest date for the transformed column *CREATED_AM* and compare it with the corresponding latest date of the original column *ANGELEGT_AM* in the German dataset.

```
arrange(df_final, desc(CREATED_AM))
```

CREATED_AM	DEED TIME_START_DATE	TIME_START_HOUR	DEED TIME_END_DATE
2022-12-01	11/29/2022	17	11/30/2022
2022-12-01	11/30/2022	16	12/01/2022
2022-12-01	11/01/2022	23	11/02/2022

As a matter of fact, the result turns out to be not correct, if compared with the original dataset before the translation. We can verify it by transforming the original column and finding the latest date.

```
dfDE$ANGELEGT_AM= dmy(dfDE$ANGELEGT_AM)
arrange(dfDE, desc(ANGELEGT_AM))
```

ANGELEGT_AM	TATZEIT_ANFANG_DATUM	TATZEIT_ANFANG_STUNDE	TATZEIT_ENDE_DATUM
2022-12-09	09.12.2022	9	09.12.2022
2022-12-09	09.12.2022	14	09.12.2022
2022-12-09	08.12.2022	20	08.12.2022

They are not the same. The result from the German dataset is obviously the correct one. The origin of our mistake is the wrong assumption we made at the very beginning. When we had to devise a solution, we opted for *month/day/year* as the reference format for all rows because compatible with the large majority of rows, and *day/month/year* only for the few dates that failed the transformation. This wrong assumption forced a date like 09.12.2022, the true latest date of the dataset, to become 2022-09-12, that is 12 September 2022, and so for many others. We chose the wrong heuristic, which is an error sometimes difficult to avoid, but possible to discover with careful checking the correctness of the logic.

5.3.3 A Better Heuristic

It turns out that there was a better heuristic, relatively easy to find afterward, less so to know beforehand. The two separators in dates were not just a glitch of something unexpected that happened, they were an actual signal of the different adopted criterion: dates with **points** were to be interpreted as *day/month/year* because they are the original values with the German standard notation, while dates with **slashes** are in *month/day/year* because translated by Google Translation into the typical American format and with slashes, common in USA. We can check it quickly with the following simple steps:

1. For column *CREATED_AM*, extract rows with points as separator and save in *a1*, then extract rows with slashes as separator and save in *a2*.
2. Convert column *CREATED_AM* of *a1* as *day/month/year* and save, then convert column *CREATED_AM* of *a2* as *month/day/year* and save. Notice that these two conversions produce no warning message, all dates are converted correctly.
3. Put together the rows in *a3*. The latest value is correct: 9 December 2022 (2022-12-09).

```
df= read_excel("datasets/Berlin_OpenData/Fahrraddiebstahl_12_2022_EN.xlsx")

filter(df,str_detect(CREATED_AM,'\\.')) -> a1
filter(df,str_detect(CREATED_AM,'/')) -> a2

a1$CREATED_AM= dmy(a1$CREATED_AM)
a2$CREATED_AM= mdy(a2$CREATED_AM)

rbind(a1,a2) -> a3
max(a3$CREATED_AM)
[1] "2022-12-09"
```

We stop here without completing the example for the other two columns, it would be just a repetition of what seen so far and as said, with functionality we will see in next chapters, it could be approached much more efficiently.

Note

You may wonder why some dates were transformed into the American form and other were left untouched. It was not because the former could have been interpreted as *month/day/year* and the latter could not, in fact you may find *07.05.2021* and *05/06/2021*, for example. The answer is that we do not know exactly what criterion Google Translate has applied, may be someone at Google knows, but may be neither there they know the answer.

5.3.4 Specialized Functions

5.3.4.1 Function `parse_date_time()`

In *lubridate* package, a seemingly minor function is actually a powerful tool to handle complicated scenarios with dates, like the one we have created on purpose with the translated version of the *Fahrraddiebstahl in Berlin* dataset. The function is `parse_date_time()` with parameter `orders` that permits to specify a list of date formats to try when parsing the values, which is exactly what is needed in our case.

Table 5.4 Symbols for date formats.

Symbols	Description	Example
%a	Day of the week (abbreviated)	Sun, Thu
%A	Day of the week (full)	Sunday, Thursday
%b or %h	Month name (abbreviated)	May, Jul
%B	Month name (full)	May, July
%d	Day of the month 01–31	27, 07
%j	Day of the year 001–366	148, 188
%m	Month (number) 01–12	05, 07
%U	Week (number) 01–53	22, 27
%u	Day of the week (number, Mon is 1) 1–7	7, 4
%w	Day of the week (number, Sun is 0) 0–6	0, 4
%W	Week (number) 00–53	21, 27
%x	Date in a local format	
%y	Year (2 digits) 00–99	84, 05
%Y	Year (4 digits)	1984, 2005
%C	Century	19, 20
%D	Date with format %m/%d/%y	05/27/84, 07/07/05

Formats could be expressed in the simplified form with just the initials (like the corresponding functions), for example ***mdy*** or ***dmy***, or more precisely using symbols for date formats and the separators. Table 5.4 shows the list of the main symbols for date formats. In our case study formats are **%m/%d/%Y** or **%d/%m/%Y** (with the forward slash as the separator, similar if the point is used).

To test function `parse_date_time()`, we try different configurations of the order parameter and test the data frame translated without replacing points with slashes, so to have two formats and two separators. We want to see whether the function shows some limitations. The comparison is made checking the latest date

```
df= read_excel("datasets/Berlin_OpenData/Fahrraddiebstahl_12_2022_EN.xlsx")
dfDE= read_excel("datasets/Berlin_OpenData/Fahrraddiebstahl_12_2022.xlsx")
```

We parse the first column *CREATED_AM* using different configurations: with only the short format, with symbols but separators not existing in the data, with only slash as the separator, and with both point and slash as separators. We also test with respect to the original German dataset. We want to see the differences.

```
# 1
parse_date_time(df$CREATED_AM, c("mdy", "dmy"),
                          tz="CET") -> test1
# 2
parse_date_time(df$CREATED_AM, c("%m-%d-%Y","%d-%m-%Y"),
                          tz="CET") -> test2
```

```
# 3
parse_date_time(df$CREATED_AM, c("%m/%d/%Y","%d/%m/%Y"),
                                tz="CET") -> test3
# 4
parse_date_time(df$CREATED_AM, c("%m/%d/%Y","%d/%m/%Y",
                                 "%m.%d.%Y","%d.%m.%Y"),
                                tz="CET") -> test4
#5
parse_date_time(dfDE$ANGELEGT_AM, c("dmy"),
                                tz="CET") -> test5
```

There is no conversion error, now let us check the latest date resulting from each test.

```
print("Test1 - Latest date: "); print(max(test1))
[1] "Test1 - Latest date: "
[1] "2022-12-09 CET"
print("Test2 - Latest date: "); print(max(test2))
[1] "Test2 - Latest date: "
[1] "2022-12-09 CET"
print("Test3 - Latest date: "); print(max(test3))
[1] "Test3 - Latest date: "
[1] "2022-12-09 CET"
print("Test4 - Latest date: "); print(max(test4))
[1] "Test4 - Latest date: "
[1] "2022-12-09 CET"
print("Original dataset - Latest date: "); print(max(test5))
[1] "Original dataset - Latest date: "
[1] "2022-12-09 CET"
```

For all variants the latest date is correct, the function implements the right heuristic. To check this conclusion, we could replace all points with slashes and re-run the conversion with function `parse_date_time()`. This time the heuristic based on the different separator is no longer available.

```
temp = str_replace_all(df$CREATED_AM, "\\.","/")
parse_date_time(temp, c("mdy", "dmy"),
                      tz="CET") -> test6

print("Test6 - Normalized separator, Latest date: "); print(max(test6))
[1] "Test6 - Normalized separator, Latest date: "
[1] "2022-12-01 CET"
```

Now the latest date is no longer 9 December 2022, but 1 December 2022, same as with our fallacious base method and normalized separators. Same results are also produced with all variations tested before. Function `parse_date_time()` is an excellent solution, and the case with translated dates by Google Translate is confirmed to be particularly tricky.

5.3.5 Result Comparison

So far, we have verified that results obtained with the base method and with function `parse_date_time()` match by only checking the latest dates. It would be possible to require a more thorough verification by checking that the two transformed columns are the same. There is a simple way to do that: with the logical equality (==). It compares the corresponding elements one by one, so the two series *must be ordered the same way*, and it returns a series of Boolean values: TRUE for pairs of elements that match, FALSE for pairs that do not match. As usual with Boolean values, to verify the number of positive matches, we can just sum them. With series, `sort()` is the base R function for sorting. We compare column *CREATED_AM* of *a3*, the working data frame we have produced with the base method and the correct heuristic, and *test1*, produced with *lubridate* function `parse_date_time()`.

```
sum(sort(a3$CREATED_AM) == sort(test1))
[1] 41169
```

All elements are TRUE and the two results are the same.

In general, for comparing several columns of large data frames, an operation that is typically computational-intensive, a simple logical comparison with the == operator might not be the best solution. Package **arsenal** is worth a try. It implements a known comparison mechanism derived from SAS, the leading commercial system for so-called business intelligence. The function to use is `comparedf()`, with `summary(comparedf())` a detailed result is obtained.

5.4 Pyhton: Operations on Dates and Strings

5.4.1 Date and Time

The discussion regarding *datetime* data type in Python is not different from what we have presented in the corresponding section for R. The characteristics and features are general and common to the large majority of programming languages. Python and, specifically, pandas offer functionalities that coincide with those seen for R and *lubridate*. In the following, we replicate most of the examples seen before and discuss the differences between the two environments.

5.4.1.1 Function `pd.to_datetime()`
Pandas supports advanced parsing functions for date and time formats in data frame columns or series. The general transformation function is `to_datetime()`, which is able to parse several formats. Let us see some examples.

```
pd.to_datetime("15 Sep 2022")
pd.to_datetime("15 September 2022")
pd.to_datetime("15-09-2022")
pd.to_datetime("15-09-22")
pd.to_datetime("15/09/2022")
```

All formats have been parsed correctly as *day/month/year* returning *Timestamp('2022-09-15 00:00:00')*. We can check the data type.

```
type(pd.to_datetime("15/09/2022"))
pandas._libs.tslibs.timestamps.Timestamp
```

The result, as it can be seen, is of a special type *Timestamp*, which is the pandas equivalent of the general *datetime* type defined by Python. For everything that concerns to us, we can consider them as the same.

However, from our previous experience with the Berlin Open Data example, we should be wary of the apparent simplicity in handling dates because subtleties and inconsistencies are quick to appear. Let us try one more test.

```
pd.to_datetime("15/09/2022")
Timestamp('2022-09-15 00:00:00')
pd.to_datetime("05/09/2022")
Timestamp('2022-05-09 00:00:00')
```

The two results have been interpreted with different date formats. The first case has been transformed assuming the format *day/month/year*, because that was the only compatible, but the second one, has been transformed with the US standard *month/day/year*. Here again making the wrong assumption could result in serious problems, you have to be extra-careful when dealing with dates.

The safe way of using function `to_datetime()` is by specifying a format with parameter **format** that accepts the same notations we have seen in Table 5.4 of the previous section.

```
pd.to_datetime("15/09/2022", format='%d/%m/%Y')
pd.to_datetime("05/09/2022", format='%d/%m/%Y')
```

Now both are interpreted correctly. But what if we have mixed formats, for example, with year expressed with two or four digits and different separators? We try with an array of values.

```
test=["15/09/2022", "05/09/2022", "15/09/22", "05/09/22",
    "15.09.2022", "05.09.2022", "15.09.2022", "05.09.2022"]
pd.to_datetime(test, format='%d/%m/%Y')
ValueError: time data '15/09/22' does not match format '%d/%m/%Y' (match)
```

It does not work with mixed formats (in this case, it is the year, with 2 or 4 digits). For a case like this, two other parameters exist, **dayfirst** and **yearfirst**, which, when set to *True*, instruct the parser to consider, respectively, the first value as the day or the year.

```
pd.to_datetime(test, dayfirst=True)
DatetimeIndex(['2022-09-15', '2022-09-05', '2022-09-15', '2022-09-05',
                '2022-09-15', '2022-09-05', '2022-09-15', '2022-09-05'],
              dtype='datetime64[ns]', freq=None)
```

However, as for version 2.0.1 of pandas, both `dayfirst` and `yearfirst` are not strict; in fact, with the next example, it does not consider the first value as the day and convert the date without raising a warning or an error, which could be fine in most cases, but there could be situations in which instead it would have been better if the anomaly were signaled.

```
pd.to_datetime("10/23/22", dayfirst=True)
Timestamp('2022-10-23 00:00:00')
```

Another important parameter of function `to_datetime()` is **errors** that control the behavior when a value cannot be transformed into a *datetime* type. The options are:

- `errors='raise'` : in this case the execution is blocked and an error is generated;
- `errors='coerce'` : the invalid value is replaced by a missing value (formally a ***NaT***, *Not a Time*, a missing value of type *datetime*);
- `errors='ignore'` : do nothing and return the input unmodified.

An example follows.

```
pd.to_datetime(test, errors='coerce', format="%d/%m/%Y")
DatetimeIndex(['2022-09-15', '2022-09-05', 'NaT', 'NaT',
               'NaT', 'NaT', 'NaT', 'NaT'],
```

5.4.1.2 Function `datetime.datetime.strptime()`

As an alternative to pandas function `to_datetime()`, module **datetime**, which comes pre-installed in Python, has function **`datetime.datetime.strptime()`** that converts values in ***object*** type (character) into *datetime* type. Module *datetime* should be loaded, and the standard alias is **dt**.

Note

It is easy to get confused by the syntax, `datetime.datetime.strptime()` is correct; the first `datetime` is the module name, which could be replaced by alias `dt`; the second `datetime` is the attribute name within the module; then the function name. Using the alias, it can be written as `dt.datetime.strptime()`.

We see an example with also the ***locale*** configuration, which we use to change the system settings, for example, the language (the corresponding dictionary should be installed in Python, in order to switch to a language different from the default one).

```
import datetime as dt
import locale
```

We set the pre-defined locale configuration; in case we had previously modified it for any reason.

```
locale.setlocale(locale.LC_ALL, '')
locale.getlocale()
('en_US', 'UTF-8')
```

Now, we run again the previous examples with dates, using function `strptime()`. It necessarily requires specifying the format, without any parameter name.

```
dt.datetime.strptime("05 Nov 2022", '%d %b %Y')
dt.datetime.strptime("05/November/2022", '%d/%B/%Y')
dt.datetime.strptime("05-11-2022 10:15", '%d-%m-%Y %H:%M')
dt.datetime.strptime("05-11-22", '%d-%m-%y')
dt.datetime.strptime("05.11.22", '%d.%m.%y')
```

They are all correctly transformed into *datetime.datetime(2022, 11, 5, 0, 0)*. Checking the type, it is *datetime*, rather than the pandas *Timestamp*. In this case, the equivalent of R's types *Date* and *Time* can be obtained with methods **date()** and **time()**.

```
dt.datetime.strptime("05-06-2022 10:15:30", '%d-%m-%Y %H:%M:%S').date()
dt.datetime.strptime("05-06-2022 10:15:30", '%d-%m-%Y %H:%M:%S').time()
```

The results are, respectively, `datetime.date(2022, 6, 5)` and `datetime.time(10, 15, 30)`.

5.4.1.3 Locale Configuration

If we change the locale language, we can use non-English month names. You should be careful with these locale configurations because they work at system level and are persistent, affecting all system functions, not just the single execution. So, if you test different locale settings, remember to restore the default configuration once you have finished. We try with German. First, we change the local configuration.

```
locale.setlocale(locale.LC_TIME, 'de_DE')
'de_DE'
```

Now we can use German month names, abbreviated and in full.

```
dt.datetime.strptime("10/Oktober/2022", "%d/%B/%Y").date()
dt.datetime.strptime("10 Okt 2022", "%d %b %Y")
datetime.datetime(2022, 10, 10)
datetime.datetime(2022, 10, 10, 0, 0)
```

Then we reset the default configuration.

```
locale.setlocale(locale.LC_ALL, '')
'en_US.UTF-8'
```

5.4.1.4 Function `datetime.datetime.strftime()`

The difference between function **`datetime.datetime.strftime()`** with respect to the previous `datetime.datetime.strptime()` is that it reverses the data type of input and output. Previously, we had strings as input and *datetime* values as output, now it is the opposite, *function* `strftime()` *takes datetime values and returns strings*.

Let us see a simple example. First, we create a *datetime* object with `pd.to_datetime()` (alternatively, function `datetime.datetime()` could be used). As we have seen, function `pd.to_datetime()` produces an object of type *Timestamp*, which is practically equivalent to type *datetime*.

```
XMas= pd.to_datetime("2023/12/25", format='%Y/%m/%d')
XMas
type(XMas)
Timestamp('2023-12-25 00:00:00')
<class 'pandas._libs.tslibs.timestamps.Timestamp'>
```

Now, we use object *XMas* as the input for function `strftime()`, and we specify which information we want to show about that date, for example, day, month name (full), year, name of the day, and week number.

```
XMas_str= dt.datetime.strftime(XMas,'%d %B %Y %A %U')
XMas_str
type(XMas_str)
'25 December 2023 Monday 52'
<class 'str'>
```

5.4.1.5 Pandas Timestamp Functions

Pandas offers its own set of functions for handling dates and time, under the attribute *dt*. Among them it has **`dt.strftime()`** (but not a `strptime()`) equivalent to the one just seen for package *datetime*. The only difference is that the pandas version is easily applied to data frames elements, like single elements of type *Timestamp*.

Other useful functions for data frame elements specific components of dates or time, such as **`year()`**, **`month()`**, **`day()`**, and **`weekday()`**. They are very similar to *lubridate* functions for R. The usage, given what we already know about the subtleties of dates, is straightforward.

We can use again dataset *Air Data: Air Quality Data Collected at Outdoor Monitors Across the US*, by the United States Environmental Protection Agency (EPA), the *PM2.5 FRM/FEM Mass* particulate, to practice with pandas functions for dates. Column *Date Local* has type *object*, so we convert in *datetime*.

```
df= pd.read_csv("datasets/EPA/daily_88101_2022.zip",
                usecols=["Date Local", "State Name", "County Name",
                "City Name", "Arithmetic Mean"])

df["Date Local"] = pd.to_datetime(df["Date Local"], format='%Y-%m-%d')
```

We can use pandas **`dt.strftime()`** to extract components of dates from data frame *df*.

Important

Careful here because it is easy to get confused. This *dt* of pandas function is the attribute name, not the same *dt* as with the alias of `import datetime as dt`. We are looking at almost identical functionalities and names: previously they were from package *datetime* and there was no need for *pandas*; now they are from *pandas* and there is no need for package *datetime*.

Tip

Function `copy()` with parameter `deep=True` is the correct way of duplicating a pandas data frame. If you just write a simple assignment, like *test=df*, you will find that what was assumed to be a copy is actually something different. We will talk about this in the next section.

```
# We use a copy of the data frame for convenience
temp= df.copy(deep=True)

temp['Year']= temp["Date Local"].dt.strftime("%Y")
temp['MonthName']= temp["Date Local"].dt.strftime("%B")
temp['Day']= temp["Date Local"].dt.strftime("%d")
temp['WeekDay']= temp["Date Local"].dt.strftime("%A")

temp[['Date Local','Year','MonthName','Day','WeekDay']].head()
```

	Date Local	Year	MonthName	Day	WeekDay
0	2022-01-02	2022	January	02	Sunday
1	2022-01-05	2022	January	05	Wednesday
2	2022-01-08	2022	January	08	Saturday
3	2022-01-11	2022	January	11	Tuesday
4	2022-01-14	2022	January	14	Friday

Analogously, we can obtain the same result using specific functions for date components. In this case, similar to *lubridate* function for R, *the locale configuration for the language could be specified as a parameter, which makes changing the system configuration unnecessary, and the locale configuration is valid only for the execution of the function.*

```
temp=df.copy(deep=True)

temp["Year"]= temp["Date Local"].dt.year
temp["Month"]= temp["Date Local"].dt.month
temp["MonthName"]= temp["Date Local"].dt.month_name()
temp["Day"]= temp["Date Local"].dt.day
temp["DayWeek"]= temp["Date Local"].dt.day_name()
temp["MonthName_ES"]= temp["Date Local"].dt.month_name("es_ES")
temp["DayWeek_ES"]= temp["Date Local"].dt.day_name("es_ES")

temp[['Date Local','Year','Month','MonthName',
'Day','DayWeek','MonthName_ES','DayWeek_ES']].head()
```

	Date Local	Year	Month	MonthName	Day	DayWeek	MonthName_ES	DayWeek_ES
0	2022-01-02	2022	1	January	2	Sunday	Enero	Domingo
1	2022-01-05	2022	1	January	5	Wednesday	Enero	Miércoles
2	2022-01-08	2022	1	January	8	Saturday	Enero	Sábado
3	2022-01-11	2022	1	January	11	Tuesday	Enero	Martes
4	2022-01-14	2022	1	January	14	Friday	Enero	Viernes

5.4.2 Selection with Logical Conditions on Dates

Specifying logical conditions on date with the functions just seen presents no problem. We can use relational operators applied to dates and usual rules for combining conditions with logical operators. For example, we want observations from January 11.

```
df[(df["Date Local"].dt.month==1) & (df["Date Local"].dt.day==11)]
```

	Date Local	Arithmetic Mean	State Name	County Name	City Name
3	2022-01-11	3.700000	Alabama	Baldwin	Fairhope
60	2022-01-11	1.900000	Alabama	Clay	Ashland
118	2022-01-11	3.300000	Alabama	DeKalb	Crossville
...	...	...	...	...	...
360945	2022-01-11	39.300000	Country Of Mexico	BAJA CALIFORNIA NORTE	Mexicali
361218	2022-01-11	7.812500	Country Of Mexico	SONORA	Not in a city
361479	2022-01-11	7.800000	Country Of Mexico	SONORA	Not in a city

Again, the observations from August and September (in Spanish).

```
df[(df["Date Local"].dt.month_name() == 'August') |
   (df["Date Local"].dt.month_name('es_ES') == 'Septiembre')]
```

	Date Local	Arithmetic Mean	State Name	County Name	City Name
3267	2022-08-01	1.041667	Alaska	Anchorage	Anchorage
3268	2022-08-02	1.916667	Alaska	Anchorage	Anchorage
3269	2022-08-03	2.666667	Alaska	Anchorage	Anchorage
...	...	...	...	...	...
361718	2022-09-28	7.400000	Country Of Mexico	SONORA	Not in a city
361719	2022-09-29	7.000000	Country Of Mexico	SONORA	Not in a city
361720	2022-09-30	7.800000	Country Of Mexico	SONORA	Not in a city

Lastly, the observations between February, 15 and April, 9, written using `pd.query()`, which is a little tricky in this case because it necessarily needs *backticks* for column name *Date Local*, which may look not intuitive.

```
df.query(' (`Date Local`.dt.month == 2 & `Date Local`.dt.day >= 15) | \
          `Date Local`.dt.month == 3 | \
          (`Date Local`.dt.month == 4 & `Date Local`.dt.day <= 9) ')
```

	Date Local	Arithmetic Mean	State Name	County Name	City Name
14	2022-02-16	9.3	Alabama	Baldwin	Fairhope
15	2022-02-19	6.2	Alabama	Baldwin	Fairhope
16	2022-02-22	7.7	Alabama	Baldwin	Fairhope
...	...	...	...	...	...
361559	2022-04-07	7.4	Country Of Mexico	SONORA	Not in a city
361560	2022-04-08	6.9	Country Of Mexico	SONORA	Not in a city
361561	2022-04-09	6.8	Country Of Mexico	SONORA	Not in a city

5.4.3 Strings

For operations on strings, pandas offer attribute **str** and several functions to perform the kind of operations that we already have learnt as typical of string manipulation. Table 5.5 shows the main ones, which always operates on series/columns, not on the whole data frame.

Table 5.5 Pandas functions for string manipulation.

Usage	Function	Description
Pattern matching	`str.contains()` `str.match()` `str.startswith(` `str.endswith()` `str.len()`	Find strings that include, start with, end with a certain alphanumeric pattern, or match a given *regexp*. Calculate string length, etc.
Transformation	`replace()` `str.replace()` `str.removeprefix()` `str.removesuffix()` `str.lower()` `str.upper()` `str.join()` `str.cat()` `str.strip()`	Find a pattern and replace it with a new one, change case, remove prefix or suffix, join multiple strings, extract a substring, delete spaces at the beginning and at the end of a string, etc.

5.5 Python: Handling Missing Values and Data Type Transformations

Handling missing values with Python and supporting functionalities are almost identical to what we have seen for R, even the syntax has minimal differences.

We replicate the examples seen before with R. Even with Python, setting missing values should be treated with care because there are different ways to express them, with subtle differences. The main ones are ***None***, mostly for pandas data frames and ***np.nan***, which is the definition given by NumPy.

A first difference that might be the reason for misunderstandings is that *None* and *np.nan* behave differently in logical expressions; in particular, *None* is logically equal to itself, while *np.nan* is not.

```
import numpy as np
import pandas as pd
None==None
True
np.nan==np.nan
False
```

5.5.1 Missing Values as Replacement

We use OECD dataset *Better Life Index*, based on 24 indicators aimed at measuring well-being of societies. To read an Excel spreadsheet, pandas has function **pd.read_excel()** with several options specific to Excel files, like **sheet_name** to select a sheet by name or by index, **skiprows** to skip initial rows and **skipfooter** to skip rows from the bottom, and many others, including the well-known usecols.

Tip
There have been recent changes in the internal mechanism used by pd.read_excel(), in particular, it included features from an external package **xlrd**. It is possible that when an Excel file is read, an error is raised, asking to install a version of *xlrd > 2.0.0*. At the time of writing, the latest version of *xlrd* is 2.0.1, so you may need to manually install or upgrade the package. There is also an excellent alternative package for reading Excel files, **openpyxl**. To use it, pd.read_excel() should be instructed with parameter **engine** (pd.read_excel('path', engine='openpyxl')).

We read the dataset by skipping the first five rows and the last one and selecting columns using the Excel format (i.e. *A:Y*). The first row after the header is spurious; we omit it using function **drop()** and specifying the *row index* (0) and *axis=0*.

```
import xlrd

bli= pd.read_excel('datasets/OECD/BLI_08052023.xlsx',
                   sheet_name=1,
                   skiprows=range(0,5),
                   skipfooter=1,
                   usecols='A:Y').drop(0, axis=0)

bli.iloc[1:6, 0:4].head()
```

	Country	Dwellings without basic facilities	Housing expenditure	Rooms per person
2	Austria	0.8	20.8	1.6
3	Belgium	0.7	20	2.1
4	Canada	0.2	22.9	2.6
5	Chile	9.4	18.4	1.9
6	Colombia	12.3		1

As we know, in this dataset, missing values are represented with two points.

```
bli.columns
Index(['Country', '  Dwellings without basic facilities',
       '  Housing expenditure', '  Rooms per person',
       '  Household net adjusted disposable income', '  Household net wealth',
       '  Labour market insecurity', '  Employment rate',
       '  Long-term unemployment rate', '  Personal earnings',
       '  Quality of support network', '  Educational attainment',
       '  Student skills', '  Years in education', '  Air pollution',
       '  Water quality',
       '  Stakeholder engagement for developing regulations',
       '  Voter turnout', '  Life expectancy', '  Self-reported health',
       '  Life satisfaction', '  Feeling safe walking alone at night',
       '  Homicide rate', '  Employees working very long hours',
       '  Time devoted to leisure and personal care'],
      dtype='object')
```

A detail to be noted is that column names have many trailing spaces at the beginning of the name. That is inconvenient, it would be better to fix all of them. Function **pd.str.strip()** does the job.

```
bli.columns= bli.columns.str.strip()
bli.columns
Index(['Country', 'Dwellings without basic facilities', 'Housing expenditure',
       'Rooms per person', 'Household net adjusted disposable income',
       'Household net wealth', 'Labour market insecurity', 'Employment rate',
       'Long-term unemployment rate', 'Personal earnings',
       'Quality of support network', 'Educational attainment',
       'Student skills', 'Years in education', 'Air pollution',
       'Water quality', 'Stakeholder engagement for developing regulations',
       'Voter turnout', 'Life expectancy', 'Self-reported health',
       'Life satisfaction', 'Feeling safe walking alone at night',
       'Homicide rate', 'Employees working very long hours',
       'Time devoted to leisure and personal care'],
      dtype='object')
```

We have read the spreadsheet correctly, now we want to replace elements with double points (. .) with Python missing values.

5.5.1.1 Function `pd.replace()`

There are at least two main methods to replace values with other values, including missing values. The first is the NumPy way of replacing values in an array; the second is pandas function `pd.replace()`. To set the missing values, we use **np.nan**. You must be careful here, using *None* instead of *np.nan* does not raise any error, but the replaced values are likely wrong. Let us start with the NumPy way, which is the most basic. The general form is as follows:

```
array[array == old_value] = new_value
```

Basically, what NumPy lets us do is slice the array with the logical condition (*array[array == old_value]*) and assign a new value to the slice (= *new_value*). NumPy directly permits modifying *by view*; we are accessing the original data, instead of *by copy* (we will discuss this distinction in a moment). In our case, the array is a single column, and the new value is *np.nan*.

```
# We use a copy for convenience
temp= bli.copy(deep=True)

temp['Rooms per person'][temp['Rooms per person'] == '..'] = np.nan

temp['Rooms per person']
1     NaN
2     1.6
3     2.1
...
38    2.4
39    1.7
40    NaN
41      1
42    NaN
Name: Rooms per person, dtype: object
```

Now with pandas **pd.replace()**, which is easier. The result is the same as the previous one.

```
bli['Rooms per person'].replace('..', np.nan)
```

You should be aware that using ' ' instead of *np.nan* looks like as setting missing values, but they are not really missing values. We will verify it in the next section.

5.5.2 Introducing Missing Values in Dataset Reads

There is an alternative way to replace the custom representation, for instance, the two points, for missing values with actual missing values in a data frame and is exactly the same as we presented with R: functions for reading datasets, either as plain text (CSV, TSV), as spreadsheets, or in other formats, have a parameter to specify which string pattern should be interpreted as a missing value, hence transformed into keywords *NA* (R) or *NaN* (Python).

With R, we have seen that different functions from different packages have different standard patterns recognized as missing values, not just blank spaces but also the string "NA", which may cause problems with a legitimate "NA" value, if not carefully considered.

With Python and pandas, in particular, we have the same mechanism, with the difference that the list of string patterns recognized as missing values is much longer (as for pandas v. 2.0.1): '','#N/A', '#N/A N/A', '#NA', '-1.#IND', '-1.#QNAN', '-NaN', '-nan', '1.#IND', '1.#QNAN', '<NA>', 'N/A', 'NA', 'NULL', 'NaN', 'None', 'n/a', 'nan', 'null'.

On the one side, this long list makes the introduction of missing values easier for some of the most common custom representations, but on the other, the odds of misleading a legitimate value for a missing value increase. In our example, the transformation of all double points into *NaN* is immediate using parameter **na_values**. The same parameter is available when using pd.read_csv().

Here we read again dataset *Better Life Index* of OECD considering the double points as missing values.

```
pd.read_excel('datasets/OECD/BLI_08052023.xlsx',
              sheet_name=1,
              skiprows=range(0,5),
              skipfooter=1,
              usecols='A:Y',
              na_values='..').drop(0, axis=0)
```

5.5.3 Verifying the Presence of Missing Values

Again, the way Python and pandas verify the presence of missing values in a series or data frame is almost identical to R. Two functions are particularly useful: **isna()** and **any()**, the first representing a logical condition to check whether elements of a series or data frame correspond to missing values, and the second returning *True* when at least one *True* value is present in its argument.

As seen for R, missing values cannot be selected with a normal logical condition, for instance *df.column == "NaN"*, *df.column == NaN*, or *df.column == np.nan*.

To show an example, we use the previous case, reading the dataset *Better Life Index* with missing values introduced in place of the double points and column names stripped of trailing spaces.

```
df1=pd.read_excel('datasets/OECD/BLI_08052023.xlsx',
                  sheet_name=1,
                  skiprows=range(0,5),
                  skipfooter=1,
                  usecols='A:Y',
                  na_values='..').drop(0, axis=0)
df1.columns= df1.columns.str.strip()
```

If we try the wrong way, with normal logical condition, we obtain a result that is all *False* for the first three cases (no missing value is recognized) and an error for the last one.

```
df1['Dwellings without basic facilities'] == 'NaN'
df1['Dwellings without basic facilities'] == np.nan
df1['Dwellings without basic facilities'] == None
df1['Dwellings without basic facilities'] == NaN
```

Instead, we need to use the specific isna() function, possibly combined with any(axis=0) or used as a Boolean mask for a selection. Used with the whole data frame, it returns the result for each column.

```
df1.isna().any(axis=0)
Country                                     False
Dwellings without basic facilities           True
Housing expenditure                          True
Rooms per person                             True
Household net adjusted disposable income     True
Household net wealth                          True
Labour market insecurity                     True
Employment rate                             False
Long-term unemployment rate                  True
...
```

Vice versa, with any(axis=1), we obtain the same information by rows.

```
df1.isna().any(axis=1)
1        True
2       False
3       False
4       False
5        True
6        True
7        True
8        True
9        True
10      False
...
```

To replicate the functionality of R's colSums() and have for each column the number of missing values, we just need the normal **sum()** function, again specifying the axis parameter. Here for columns.

```
df1.isna().sum(axis=0)
Country                                      0
Dwellings without basic facilities           3
Housing expenditure                          4
Rooms per person                             3
Household net adjusted disposable income     6
Household net wealth                         12
Labour market insecurity                     7
Employment rate                              0
Long-term unemployment rate                  2
...
```

Same for rows.

```
df1.isna().sum(axis=1)
1     2
2     0
3     0
4     0
5     3
6     6
7     5
8     2
9     1
10    0
...
```

There is one last check to make: what if we set void values (`''`, with no space between the quotes) instead of `np.nan` for missing values, are they recognized by `isna()`?

```
df1['Rooms per person'].replace(np.nan, '').isna().any()
False
```

No, they are not, void values set as `''` are not recognized as missing values. This is a tiny detail you should be aware of because it could produce unexpected results, for example, in selections looking for missing values, as described in the next section.

5.5.4 Selection with Missing Values

Finally, if we want to select rows with or without missing values in one or more columns, we compose logical conditions using `isna()`. For example, we want rows *with* missing values in columns *Rooms per person* or *Personal earnings*.

```
df1[ (df1['Rooms per person'].isna()) | \
     (df1['Personal earnings'].isna()) ]\
     [['Country','Rooms per person','Personal earnings']]
```

	Country	Rooms per person	Personal earnings
1	Australia	NaN	55206
6	Colombia	1	NaN
7	Costa Rica	1.2	NaN
36	Türkiye	1	NaN
40	Brazil	NaN	NaN
41	Russia	1	NaN
42	South Africa	NaN	NaN

On the contrary, we want to select rows *without* missing values in columns *Rooms per person* or *Personal earnings*. Pay attention to the negations and the logical operator.

```
df1[ (~df1['Rooms per person'].isna()) & \
     (~df1['Personal earnings'].isna()) ]\
     [['Country','Rooms per person','Personal earnings']]
```

	Country	Rooms per person	Personal earnings
2	Austria	1.6	53132
3	Belgium	2.1	54327
4	Canada	2.6	55342
...	...	...	...
37	United Kingdom	2	47147
38	United States	2.4	69392
39	OECD - Total	1.7	49165

Using pd.query() we need to add the directive engine='python' otherwise, a particularly cryptic error is raised.

```
df1.query(" ~('Rooms per person'.isna() | \
           'Personal earnings'.isna() ) ", \
           engine='python')
```

5.5.5 Replacing Missing Values with Actual Values

To replace missing values with some actual values, basically the opposite of the operation seen before, we have at least three methods. One is exactly the same we have used to replace actual values with missing values, by using pandas **replace()** function. Here we replicate the same example simply by exchanging the parameters of the function.

```
df1['Rooms per person'].replace(np.nan, 'Unknown')
1     Unknown
2         1.6
3         2.1
4         2.6
...
38        2.4
39        1.7
40    Unknown
41          1
42    Unknown
Name: Rooms per person, dtype: object
```

Another possibility is with the pandas-specific function **fillna()**, which requires only the replacement value. The result is identical.

```
df1['Rooms per person'].fillna('Unknown')
```

The third way is with base slicing, and it is the most general method, which, however, hides some subtleties that we are discussing with the next few examples. It is important to understand very clearly how Python operates when we are trying to assign values to a subset of rows or columns.

5.5.6 Modifying Values *by View* or *by Copy*

Let us start by finding the rows with missing values in column *Rooms per person*.

```
# For convenience we make a copy
a1= df1.copy(deep=True)
a1[a1["Rooms per person"].isna()]
```

	Country	Dwellings without basic facilities	Housing expenditure	Rooms per person	Household net-adjusted disposable income
1	Australia	NaN	19.4	NaN	37433
40	Brazil	6.7	NaN	NaN	NaN
42	South Africa	35.9	18.1	NaN	9338

With this subset of rows, we select the column *Rooms per person* and assign "Unknown" to the elements.

```
a1[a1["Rooms per person"].isna()][["Rooms per person"]]= 'Unknown'

A value is trying to be set on a copy of a slice from a DataFrame.
Try using .loc[row_indexer,col_indexer] = value instead

See the caveats in the documentation: https://pandas.pydata.org/pandas-docs/
stable/user_guide/indexing.html#returning-a-view-versus-a-copy
```

The operation is executed, but we receive a warning message telling us that "A value is trying to be set on a copy of a slice from a DataFrame." What does it mean? Is it relevant? Let us look at column *Rooms per person* of data frame *a1*, which we have just tried to modify.

```
a1["Rooms per person"]
1     NaN
2     1.6
3     2.1
4     2.6
...
38    2.4
39    1.7
40    NaN
41      1
42    NaN
Name: Rooms per person, dtype: object
```

Missing values are still there, none of our assignments with value *Unknown* have been done. Why? What did we do wrong? The warning message told us what just happened, *we modified **a** copy of the content of the data frame a1, not the original data frame a1.* We never modified the original data. So, when did it happen that we made a copy of data frame *a1*? We never made such a copy! No, we did not explicitly, at least, but that is how the slicing mechanism works. When we slice a data frame and obtain a subset, for example, with:

```
a1[a1["Rooms per person"].isna()][["Rooms per person"]]
```

what we are actually doing is to make a copy of the content of the original data frame. Therefore, if we assign a value (e.g. 'Unknown'), we are working on the copy. To make the modifications permanent, we need to access the original data.

When we work on a whole column, to save the modifications is easier because we are not subsetting some rows, so we can overwrite the whole column with the new values. As an example, suppose that we want to transform all country names of data frame *a1* to upper cases. For this, we have to change the whole column *Country*. We would execute three logical steps:

1. Slice column *Country* (make a copy): `a1.Country` or `a1['Country']`;
2. Modify the values on the copy: `a1['Country'].str.upper()`;
3. Make it permanent by overwriting the original column: `a1['Country']= a1['Country'].str.upper()`.

In practice, we just write the last one, but logically, there are three different steps.

```
a1.Country= a1.Country.str.upper()
```

	Country	Dwellings without basic facilities	Housing expenditure	Rooms per person
1	AUSTRALIA	NaN	19.4	NaN
2	AUSTRIA	0.8	20.8	1.6
3	BELGIUM	0.7	20	2.1
...	...	...	...	...
40	BRAZIL	6.7	NaN	NaN
41	RUSSIA	13.8	17.4	1
42	SOUTH AFRICA	35.9	18.1	NaN

Modifying a whole column is easy, but not so if we modify only a subset of elements of a column. What we need to do is work **by view**, not *by copy*, meaning that we have to modify the original values, not a copy of them, and to do that, it is again the warning message that gives us the right suggestion with "Try using *.loc[row_indexer,col_indexer]* = *value* instead".

We need the features of attribute `.loc()` that permits us to select the subset of values and then assign the new value to that selection. In this case there is no copy involved. Let us do the assignment again to the subset of values following this syntax.

```
a1.loc[a1["Rooms per person"].isna(), "Rooms per person"]= 'Unknown'
```

Now, check data frame *a1*.

```
a1["Rooms per person"]
1       Unknown
2           1.6
3           2.1
4           2.6
...
38          2.4
39          1.7
40      Unknown
41            1
42      Unknown
Name: Rooms per person, dtype: object
```

The result is correct; *we have modified* ***the view***, *meaning the actual values, not a copy.*

This just seen is the correct and general way to modify values in a pandas data frame, which we should always use to assign values to a subset of elements of a column or row.

The solution *by copy* is acceptable only when new values are assigned to a whole column/row; in that case, the modified copy could be used to overwrite the original column/row. Understanding the difference between assigning values *by copy* or *by view* is very important. It is recommended to practice with examples until the mechanism is completely clear.

5.5.7   Data Type Transformations

We already encountered several examples that required a data type transformation. Following Table 5.6 shows the main ones. Like in R, every ***transformation function*** has a corresponding ***verification function***. With the former type, we convert data type, with the latter, we verify if data are of a certain type.

In addition to the functions specific to the different data types, there exists a general one `astype()`, whose first parameter is the data type of the result (e.g. `df.col1.astype("Int64")` transforms column *col1* of *df* into the integer data type). It is possible to express the transformation of more than one column by means of the dict syntax `{col1:dtype, col2:dtype, ...}`.

5.6   Python: Examples with Dates, Strings, and Missing Values

In this last chapter's section, we show two examples replicating what we already have presented for corresponding R functionality.

5.6.1   Example 1: Eurostat

We start with dataset *Final energy consumption* from Eurostat. In this case, we need to convert the column values into numeric type, but there are some string values to take care of . We practice with string manipulation functions.

Table 5.6 Data type verification and transformation functions.

Type	Description	Verification	Transformation
Boolean `boolean`	Boolean values TRUE and FALSE, corresponding to 1 and 0	`is_bool()`	`astype("boolean")`
Numeric `Int64` `Float64`	Numeric data	`is_numeric_dtype()`	`to_numeric()`
Lists `list tuple range`	Lists, intervals	`is_list_like()`	`to_list()`
Dictionary `dict`	Dict format *{key : value, …}*	`is_dict_like()`	`to_dict()`
Categories `category`	Categorical values, possibly ordered	`is_categorical()`	`astype("category")`
Date/Time `datetime`	Date and time	`is_datetime64_dtype()`	`to_datetime()`
Strings `string` `object`	Letters, digits, punctuation, and symbols	`is_string_dtype()`	`to_string()`

```
import numpy as np
import pandas as pd
fec= pd.read_csv("datasets/Eurostat/sdg_07_11.tsv", sep='\t')
fec.head()
```

	unit,geo\time	2000	2001	2002	...	2018	2019	2020
0	I05,AL	80.6	82.6	94.6	…	112.6	109.1	103.4
1	I05,AT	85.2	90.3	91.1	…	100.0	101.7	93.6
2	I05,BE	103.1	105.5	99.4	…	99.4	97.8	91.0
3	I05,BG	89.5	89.6	89.5	…	97.8	97.1	94.1
4	I05,CY	90.0	93.2	93.9	…	101.3	102.9	85.8

Columns from *2000* to *2020* are defined as *object* type (string) when instead they should be numeric. We try with the transformation function `pd.to_numeric()` using just column *2000*.

```
pd.to_numeric(fec['2000'])
```

We receive an error: *KeyError: '2000'*. It looks like we used the wrong column name, it seems strange; we used exactly the same name in R and everything was fine. We should look closer to the column names.

```
fec.columns
Index(['unit,geo\time', '2000 ', '2001 ', '2002 ', '2003 ', '2004 ', '2005 ',
       '2006 ', '2007 ', '2008 ', '2009 ', '2010 ', '2011 ', '2012 ', '2013 ',
       '2014 ', '2015 ', '2016 ', '2017 ', '2018 ', '2019 ', '2020 '],
      dtype='object')
```

There are blank spaces at the end of each name. Clearly, R reading function automatically trims trailing spaces, whereas pandas' does not. We already dealt with this inconvenience; it is easy to solve.

```
fec.columns= fec.columns.str.strip()
```

We try again the transformation into numeric type.

```
pd.to_numeric(fec['2000'])
```

As expected, since we already know this dataset, there are some values with non-numeric values. In this case, the error message is more detailed than in R; it explicitly tells us the reason: *ValueError: Unable to parse string ":" at position 23.* Now we know there are elements with colon as value, used to represent missing values. However, we still do not know how many values failed to be transformed into numeric values and among them how many are colons. We should find this information.

First, we count how many missing values are present in column *2000*, then we run the transformation again, this time instructing the function to insert missing values where elements cannot be transformed and count the missing values again. Finally, we want to know how many colons as values are present in the original column. We use function **pd.str.contains()**.

```
# For convenience, we work on a copy
temp= fec.copy(deep=True)

temp['2000'].isna().sum()
0
pd.to_numeric(temp['2000'], errors='coerce').isna().sum()
9
temp['2000'].str.contains(':').sum()
6
```

There is no missing value in original column 2000, instead nine would be inserted with the transformation, and six are the elements with colon as value. There are three left that fail to transform into a numeric type.

We can find out using the regex, but unfortunately, Unicode string patterns used in R regex, i.e. \p{P} and \p{S} used to match punctuation and symbols, are not commonly supported in Python. For an extended support of regex in Python, we forward the interested reader to the package **regex**. For our example, we need to find simple alternatives. For example, there is the special symbol

\w matching *any Unicode word character*. We could select the rows not containing word characters in column *2000*, for example.

```
temp[~temp['2000'].str.contains('[\w]', regex=True)][['2000']]
```

	2000
23	:
40	:
62	:
79	:
101	:
115	:

Here are the elements with just colon. We could have done it in another way, using the negation character (^) inside the regex (`temp['2000'].str.contains('[^\w]', regex=True)`). However, that would have matched all values except letters, digits, and the underscore symbol. This means we would have matched the six elements with just colon, plus all those containing the decimal point, meaning all elements. We need to exclude the point, if we use this form, as we did with R. There is also another little detail to consider: All values have a blank space at the end; we could strip it or add \s that matches all blank spaces (of any type) (`temp['2000'].str.contains('(?![.])[^\w\s]', regex=True)`). A nice outcome of these more elaborate regex is that we would find all the values we were looking for.

```
temp[temp['2000'].str.strip().str.contains('(?![.])[^\w\s]', regex=True)]
[['2000']]
```

	2000
23	:
40	:
62	:
79	:
90	2.28 b
93	1.34 e
101	:
106	1.44 b
115	:

Otherwise, we can specifically look for elements with letters.

```
temp[temp['2000'].str.contains('[a-zA-A]', regex=True)][['2000']]
```

	2000
90	2.28 b
93	1.34 e
106	1.44 b

These ones could be modified by deleting the letters and blank spaces, and then we can transform the column into numeric data type by coercing missing values.

```
temp['2000'].replace('[\sa-zA-Z]','', regex=True, inplace=True)
temp['2000']= pd.to_numeric(temp['2000'], errors= 'coerce')
```

We finally check the number of missing values inserted. They are six, corresponding to the elements with colon.

```
temp['2000'].isna().sum()
6
```

The first column *2000* has now the correct numerical data type; we should repeat the operations for all of the remaining, but for this, we wait for multicolumn operations.

5.6.2   Example 2: Open Data Berlin

We use the dataset *Fahrraddiebstahl in Berlin* from the Berlin Open Data that we have extensively exploited for a particularly elaborated case study in the R corresponding section. We do not replicate the whole fictional case with the different alternative interpretations, often wrong but not unreasonable, that we have considered. We want instead to check how pandas functions handle the subtleties of *datetime* transformations.

As we already know, we have two datasets, the original German one and the English one, translated with Google Translate. We read them.

```
dfDE= pd.read_excel("datasets/Berlin_OpenData/Fahrraddiebstahl_12_2022.xlsx")
df= pd.read_excel("datasets/Berlin_OpenData/Fahrraddiebstahl_12_2022_EN.xlsx")
```

As we know, the translation resulted in mixed formats, *month/day/year* dates with slashes as separator, *day/month/year* dates in the original form with points. 9 December 2022 is the latest date.

```
df.CREATED_AM.unique()
array([' 09.12.2022', ' 08.12.2022', ' 07.12.2022', ' 06.12.2022',
       ' 05.12.2022', ' 04.12.2022', ' 03.12.2022', ' 02.12.2022',
       ' 12/01/2022', ' 11/30/2022', ' 11/29/2022', ' 11/28/2022',
       ' 11/27/2022', ' 11/26/2022', ' 11/25/2022', ' 11/24/2022',
       ...
```

You may notice that all values have a blank space at the beginning. We have already encountered this case, and we know it could create problems. It is better to strip them off.

```
df.CREATED_AM= df.CREATED_AM.str.strip()
```

The description of all columns can be found in Section 5.4. For our purpose, we are interested in just the first one, *ANGELEGT_AM* (original), *CREATED_AM* (translated). Neither data frames have missing values. We start transforming into *Timestamp* type the column *ANGELEGT_AM*.

```
dfDE["ANGELEGT_AM"]= pd.to_datetime(dfDE["ANGELEGT_AM"],
                                    format='%d.%m.%Y', errors='raise')

dfDE["ANGELEGT_AM"]
0          2022-12-09
1          2022-12-09
2          2022-12-09
3          2022-12-09
4          2022-12-09
              ...
41164      2021-01-02
41165      2021-01-01
41166      2021-01-01
41167      2021-01-01
41168      2021-01-01
Name: ANGELEGT_AM, Length: 41169, dtype: datetime64[ns]
```

No error, as expected, all original dates have the same format *%d.%m.%Y*.

With column *CREATED_AM* there are two formats, resulting from the translation with Google Translate; therefore, we cannot use the `format` parameter because it does not support multiple formats, nor can we use the `dayfirst` parameter because one format has the month first. We try with the default.

```
pd.to_datetime(df["CREATED_AM"], errors='coerce')
0          2022-09-12
1          2022-09-12
2          2022-09-12
3          2022-09-12
4          2022-09-12
              ...
41164      2021-01-02
41165      2021-01-01
41166      2021-01-01
41167      2021-01-01
41168      2021-01-01
Name: CREATED_AM, Length: 41169, dtype: datetime64[ns]
```

Again, no errors, meaning that it has transformed all dates with both formats, but are they correct? Let us check which is the latest date.

```
pd.to_datetime(df["CREATED_AM"]).sort_values(ascending=False)
369     2022-12-01
359     2022-12-01
346     2022-12-01
347     2022-12-01
348     2022-12-01
...
```

The latest date is 01 December, and it is wrong; it has misinterpreted the original format. We need to proceed manually, separating the two subsets of rows with different date formats, transforming them, and then putting them together again. It is the same logic we followed in R for the base method. We start with the subset of dates with the original format of *day/month/year* and points as separator. First, we select them, then we transform with format *%d.%m.%Y*.

```
mask= df['CREATED_AM'].str.contains('.', regex=False)
df_dmy= df[mask]
df_dmy
```

	CREATED_AM	DEED TIME_START_DATE	TIME_START_ HOUR	DEED TIME_END_DATE	TIME_END_HOUR
0	09.12.2022	09.12.2022	9	09.12.2022	10
1	09.12.2022	09.12.2022	14	09.12.2022	22
2	09.12.2022	08.12.2022	20	08.12.2022	21
3	09.12.2022	08.12.2022	17	08.12.2022	19
4	09.12.2022	02.12.2022	15	03.12.2022	9
...	...	...	...	...	...
41150	04.01.2021	01/02/2021	16	01/03/2021	11
41151	04.01.2021	01/01/2021	14	04.01.2021	10
41152	04.01.2021	04.01.2021	7	04.01.2021	18
41153	04.01.2021	01/03/2021	17	04.01.2021	14
41154	04.01.2021	04.01.2021	8	04.01.2021	14

```
df_dmy['CREATED_AM']= pd.to_datetime(df_dmy['CREATED_AM'],
                      format='%d.%m.%Y', errors='raise').dt.date
df_dmy['CREATED_AM']
0       2022-12-09
1       2022-12-09
2       2022-12-09
3       2022-12-09
4       2022-12-09
           ...
41150   2021-01-04
41151   2021-01-04
41152   2021-01-04
41153   2021-01-04
41154   2021-01-04
```

Now the same operations with the second format.

```
mask= df['CREATED_AM'].str.contains('/', regex=False)
df_mdy= df[mask]

df_mdy['CREATED_AM']= pd.to_datetime(df_mdy['CREATED_AM'],
                    format='%m/%d/%Y', errors='raise').dt.date
df_mdy['CREATED_AM']
316        2022-12-01
317        2022-12-01
318        2022-12-01
319        2022-12-01
320        2022-12-01
            ...
41164      2021-01-02
41165      2021-01-01
41166      2021-01-01
41167      2021-01-01
41168      2021-01-01
```

We have converted the two subsets separately; they could be reassembled with pandas function `concat()`. We save the data frame for the final check.

```
dfEN= pd.concat([df_mdy,df_dmy]).sort_values('CREATED_AM',ascending=False)
dfEN
```

	CREATED_AM	DEED TIME_START_DATE	TIME_START_ HOUR	DEED TIME_END_DATE	TIME_END_ HOUR
1	2022-12-09	09.12.2022	14	09.12.2022	22
26	2022-12-09	07.12.2022	19	07.12.2022	19
20	2022-12-09	03.12.2022	20	04.12.2022	8
21	2022-12-09	09.12.2022	21	09.12.2022	21
22	2022-12-09	02.12.2022	11	03.12.2022	11
...	...	...	...	...	...
41158	2021-01-02	01/01/2021	1	01/02/2021	10
41167	2021-01-01	01/01/2021	5	01/01/2021	8
41165	2021-01-01	01/01/2021	9	01/01/2021	11
41166	2021-01-01	01/01/2021	20	01/01/2021	20
41168	2021-01-01	01/01/2021	17	01/01/2021	18

Now it looks correct. For a final verification, we compare column *ANGELEGT_AM* of the German dataset *dfDE*, after conversion to *datetime*, with column *CREATED_AM* of *dfEN*, just created. Pandas function `compare()` makes a comparison between pairs of elements. It has a couple of requirements: the two columns must be sorted the same way, and both must have *the same index labels*. To comply with the latter, we reset the index of the two data frames.

```
# Data frame dfEN has already been sorted.
dfEN= dfEN.reset_index()
dfDE= dfDE.sort_values('ANGELEGT_AM', ascending=False).reset_index()

dfEN['CREATED_AM'].compare(dfDE['ANGELEGT_AM'])
```

The `compare()` function returns the differences; since we obtain an empty result, it means they are identical.

Questions

5.1 (R)

What are the results of the following two instructions?

```
mdy('01-10-2023')
dmy('01-10-2023')
```

A Both January 10th, 2023
B The first is January 10th, 2023, the second is October 1st, 2023
C The first is October 1st, 2023, the second is January 10th, 2023
D One of the two produces an error, depending on the local settings
(R: B)

5.2 (R)

Given column *Month* of hypothetical data frame *df* containing month names (in English, full names), which months are matched by the following instruction?

```
df$Month %>% str_detect('ber')
```

A None
B One among September, October, November, or December
C Both September, October, November, and December
D September
(R: C)

5.3 (R)

Given the following instruction, how do we need to specify the pattern of the str_detect() function in order to match the element with *double semicolon but not the one with single semicolon*?

```
c('A;B', 'C.D', 'E;;F', 'G\\H') %>% str_detect(...)
```

A str_detect(';',';',';')

B str_detect('\\;\\;') or str_detect(';;')
C only str_detect('\\;\\;')
D only str_detect(';;')
(R: B)

5.4 (R)

Given the following instruction, how do we need to specify the pattern of the str_detect() function in order to match the element with *dot*?

```
c('A;B', 'C.D', 'E;;F', 'G\\H') %>% str_detect(...)
```

A str_detect('.')
B str_detect('\\.')
C str_detect('\.')
D str_detect('..')
(R: B)

5.5 (R)

Given the following instruction, how do we need to specify the pattern of the str_detect() function in order to match the element with *backslash* (the second backslash of G\\H is needed to escape the first one)?

```
c('A;B', 'C.D', 'E;;F', 'G\\H') %>% str_detect(...)
```

A str_detect('\')
B str_detect('\\')
C str_detect('\\\')
D str_detect('\\\\')
(R: D)

5.6 (R)

Do the following instructions match elements of *Col1* with missing values?

```
df %>% filter(Col1 == 'NA')
df %>% filter(Col1 == NA)
```

A No
B Only the first one
C Only the second one
D Yes, both
(R: A)

5.7 (R)

Do the following instructions tell whether or not there are missing values in *Col1*?

```
any(is.na(df$Col1))
any(is.na(df$Col1))
```

A No
B Only the first one
C Only the second one
D Yes, both
(R: B)

5.8 (R)

What does the following instruction return?

```
sum(is.na(df$Col1))
```

A An error
B The number of missing values in *Col1*
C TRUE/FALSE
D Zero
(R: B)

5.9 (R)

What does the following instruction return?

```
colSums(is.na(df))
```

A An error
B TRUE/FALSE
C The number of missing values for each column of data frame *df*
D The total number of missing values in data frame *df*
(R: C)

5.10 (Python)

Do one of the following instructions match missing values?

```
df['Col1'] == 'NaN' df['Col1'] == np.nan df['Col1'] == None
```

A All of them
B Only the second and the third
C Only the second
D None
(R: D)

5.11 **(Python)**

Does the following instruction return whether missing values are present for each column of *df*?

```
df.isna().any(axis=0)
```

A Yes
B No, but it does with axis=1
C No, but it does with all(axis=0)
D No, but it does with all(axis=1)

(R: A)

5.12 **(Python)**

Does the following instruction return the number of missing values for each column of *df*?

```
df.isna().sum(axis=1)
```

A Yes
B No, but it does with axis=0
C It returns an error
D It returns the total number of missing values in *df*

(R: A)

5.13 **(Python)**

Is the following instruction correct for replacing missing values with 0 in Col1?

```
df[df["Col1"].isna()]= 0
```

A No, the replacement requires special functions
B No, it operates on a copy
C It returns an error
D Yes

(R: B)

5.14 **(Python)**

Is the following instruction correct for replacing missing values with 0 in Col1?

```
df.loc[df["Col1"].isna(), "Col1"]= 0
```

A No, the replacement requires special functions
B No, it operates on a copy
C It returns an error
D Yes

(R: D)

6

Pivoting and Wide-long Transformations

We consider an *untidy* organization of data that is commonly encountered because it eases readability when the dataset is visually inspected. It can be observed almost every time data are presented in tabular form. Examples are endless, from *Eurostat* (https://ec.europa.eu/eurostat/databrowser/explore/all/all_themes) to *Our World in Data* (https://ourworldindata.org/), just to mention two cases. That is the so-called **wide form** (or *horizontal* or *rectangular*), with the alternative one called **long form** (or *vertical*), which is typical of *tidy* organizations of data.

Wide and *long* refers to the *meaning* of columns in a dataset, not just their number; even two columns could be either in wide or long form, because it depends on what information they represent. In the long form, a column represents one or more general features of the observed system, while in the wide form, a column represents a value of a certain feature. It is the same difference we have presented to distinguish tidy from untidy organizations. Therefore, with just two columns, the most basic example, we may have columns *Republican* and *Democrat*, each with the number of votes for each state on rows. This is a wide form because *Republican* and *Democrat* are values of a more general feature than is *Party*. Therefore, still two columns, *Party* and *Votes*, are the equivalent long form. Is it really equivalent? Not exactly. We can count the number of values in the two cases. In the first case, we have 50 states (rows) and the two columns, then 100 values. In the second case, for each state, we have two rows and again two columns, then four values, in total 200 values. If the election had three parties (*Independent*, too), then the wide form would have 150 values, while the long form would have 300, the difference increases with the number of values of the general feature.

A particularly clear example of the wide form could be observed in the *GDP Forecast* (Gross Domestic Product) presented by the OECD (Organization for Economic Co-operation and Development) (https://data.oecd.org/gdp/real-gdp-forecast.htm#indicator-chart). Its tabular form (visible with *Show: Table*) is clearly in wide form, with columns for each one of the 48 quarters and just two rows.

Similar to data from the *United Nations World Population Prospects* presented by Our World in Data – *The global population is projected to peak at around 10.4 billion in 2086* (https://ourworldindata.org/world-population-update-2022#the-global-population-is-projected-to-peak-at-around-10-4-billion-in-2086). By selecting *Table*, columns are shown through a slider, each one associated with a year, again a wide form representation. However, if tab *Chart* is selected, a dynamic data visualization is presented. Data shown by the two tabs are clearly the same; however, to produce the visual representation, they are very likely in long form because they are much better suited for that task. The long form can be seen by downloading the dataset (*Download*),

Data Science Fundamentals with R, Python, and Open Data, First Edition. Marco Cremonini.
© 2024 John Wiley & Sons, Inc. Published 2024 by John Wiley & Sons, Inc.
Companion website: www.wiley.com/go/DSFRPythonOpenData

Figure 6.1 Example of long-form dataset.

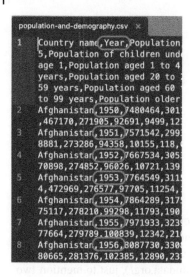

```
population-and-demography.csv  ×
1   Country name,Year,Population
    5,Population of children und
    age 1,Population aged 1 to 4
    years,Population aged 20 to
    59 years,Population aged 60
    to 99 years,Population older
2   Afghanistan,1950,7480464,301
    ,467170,271905,92691,9499,12
3   Afghanistan,1951,7571542,299
    8881,273286,94358,10155,118,
4   Afghanistan,1952,7667534,305
    70898,274852,96026,10721,139
5   Afghanistan,1953,7764549,311
    4,472969,276577,97705,11254,
6   Afghanistan,1954,7864289,317
    75117,278210,99298,11793,190
7   Afghanistan,1955,7971933,323
    77664,279789.100839,12342,21
8   Afghanistan,1956,8087730,330
    80665,281376,102385,12890,23
```

which presents a single column Year and a column Population for values. Each country has as many rows as the years of the dataset (in total, there are 38354 rows). Figure 6.1 shows a detail of the dataset.

From this introduction to wide and long forms, two important points arise: The first is that it is not always true that a wide form has many columns and a long form has a few. It tends to be that way, but not necessarily. Also, a dataset could have some columns in wide form and some others in long form. Wide and long forms depend on columns' meaning; it is a property of columns, not of the dataset. The second point is that there is no form better than the other. It depends on the purpose of the data representation. For visual inspection, but also for certain data wrangling operations and graphic types, the wide form is better than the long one. On the contrary, for computational purposes and most graphic types, the long form is usually better.

Figure 6.2 shows the logical schema of the wide-long transformation. In the example depicted, arrows indicate a transformation from wide to long form, with years as columns that become a pair of columns, usually called *key:value pair*, one with the keys, the years in this case, and the other with corresponding values, country's population in this case.

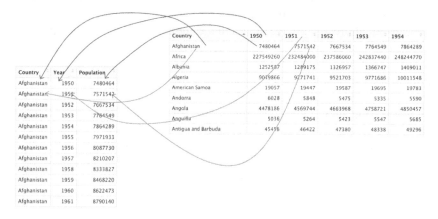

Figure 6.2 Wide-long transformation schema.

Reversing the arrow direction, the schema for the long to wide transformation is obtained: unique values of the key column (*Year*) become the new column names, and elements of the value column (*Population*) become elements of the new columns.

This chapter shows how to efficiently transform long to wide form, and the other way around, the operation is called *pivoting*.

Datasets

World Population Prospects 2022, the 27th edition of population estimation and forecasting from the United Nations Department of Economic and Social Affairs, Population Division (https://population.un.org/wpp/Download/Standard/CSV/). *Copyright*: Attribution 3.0 IGO (CC BY 3.0 IGO) (https://creativecommons.org/licenses/by/3.0/igo/).

Gender pay gap, from the United Kingdom Open Data – GOV.UK (https://gender-pay-gap.service .gov.uk/), presents updated data on gender pay gap from employers with more than 250 employees. *Copyright*: Open Government License v3.0 (https://www.nationalarchives.gov.uk/doc/open-government-licence/version/3/).

Youth Behavior Risk Survey (YBRS) (High School) from New York City Open Data (NYC Open Data) (https://data.cityofnewyork.us/Health/Youth-Behavior-Risk-Survey-High-School-/3qty-g4aq), aggregated results from a survey on youth risk behaviors. *Copyright*: NYC Open Data, Open Data Law (https://opendata.cityofnewyork.us/open-data-law/).

Tourist/visitor arrivals and tourism expenditure, United Nations Open Data (http://data.un.org/), contains data about tourist arrivals and expenditures for a sample of countries. *Copyright*: "All data and metadata provided on UNdata's website are available free of charge and may be copied freely, duplicated, and further distributed provided that UNdata is cited as the reference." (Terms and Conditions of Use, http://data.un.org/Host.aspx?Content=UNdataUse).

6.1   R: Pivoting

For pivoting operations in R, two particularly efficient functions exist, `pivot_wider()` for transforming *from long to wide form*, and `pivot_longer()` for *wide-to-long* transformations. Both are defined in the *tidyr* package, which is included in *tidyverse*.

6.1.1   From Long to Wide

Important attributes of function `pivot_wider()` are:

- `id_cols`: the list of columns whose values will uniquely identify each row, therefore excluded from those to be transformed from long to wide form. The default is that all columns except those specified for the transformation are considered as identifiers. Usually, the default corresponds to what is meant to be executed.
- `names_from`: the name of the column in long form (or names, multiple columns could be specified) whose unique values should become names of the new columns in wide form. This is the column(s) acting as *key*, in the *key:value* pairs.
- `values_from`: the name of the column(s) in long form whose elements should become the elements of the new columns in wide form. This is the column(s) acting as *value*, in the *key:value* pairs.

- other attributes provide utility functions, such as `names_prefix` that adds a prefix to the names of the new columns in wide form. This is useful, for example, when names are composed only of digits and we want to avoid the consequent required usage of quotes. For example, with column *Year*, if we use `names_prefix="Y"`, the new names will become `Y1950`, `Y1951`, etc.

Let us start with the United Nation's dataset *The global population is projected to peak at around 10.4 billion in 2086*, for a transformation from long to wide form.

```
popLong= read_csv("datasets/United Nations/population-and-demography.csv")
```

Country name	Year	Population	Population of children under the age of 1	...
Afghanistan	1950	7480464	301735	...
Afghanistan	1951	7571542	299368	...
Afghanistan	1952	7667534	305393	...
Afghanistan	1953	7764549	311574	...
Afghanistan	1954	7864289	317584	...
Afghanistan	1955	7971933	323910	...

```
names(popLong)

 [1] "Country name"
 [2] "Year"
 [3] "Population"
 [4] "Population of children under the age of 1"
 [5] "Population of children under the age of 5"
 [6] "Population of children under the age of 15"
 [7] "Population under the age of 25"
 [8] "Population aged 15 to 64 years"
 [9] "Population at age 1"
[10] "Population aged 1 to 4 years"
[11] "Population aged 5 to 9 years"
[12] "Population aged 10 to 14 years"
[13] "Population aged 15 to 19 years"
[14] "Population aged 20 to 29 years"
[15] "Population aged 30 to 39 years"
[16] "Population aged 40 to 49 years"
[17] "Population aged 50 to 59 years"
[18] "Population aged 60 to 69 years"
[19] "Population aged 70 to 79 years"
[20] "Population aged 80 to 89 years"
[21] "Population aged 90 to 99 years"
[22] "Population older than 100 years"
```

Columns referring to different population age intervals are already in wide form. For long to wide transformations, we have two options: transforming column *Year* or column *Country name*, as the key. As the value, several possibilities exist, all columns with population values could be selected. We choose the one with total population values (column *Population*).

We specify all main attributes, starting with `id_cols`. We choose to transform years; therefore, *Country name* column should be the identifier. Names of the new columns should be the unique values of the *Year* column, and as elements of the new columns, we decided to pick column *Population*. All the remaining columns will be omitted.

```
popWide= pivot_wider(popLong, id_cols= "Country name",
            names_from= "Year", values_from= "Population")
```

Country name	1950	1951	1952	...	2099	2100
Afghanistan	7480464	7571542	7667534	...	110621220	110854790
Africa (UN)	227549260	232484000	237586060	...	3909421300	3924420600
Albania	1252587	1289175	1326957	...	1123710	1097163
Algeria	9019866	9271741	9521703	...	67845530	67792980
American Samoa	19057	19447	19587	...	13242	12704
Andorra	6028	5848	5475	...	60477	60264

The result is a data frame of 254 rows and 152 columns. If we want to transform into wide form the country names, the operation is similar.

```
popWide= pivot_wider(popLong, id_cols= "Year",
            names_from= "Country name", values_from= "Population")
```

Year	Afghanistan	Africa (UN)	Albania	...	Zambia	Zimbabwe
1950	7480464	227549260	1252587	...	2318453	2791336
1951	7571542	232484000	1289175	...	2384835	2881722
1952	7667534	237586060	1326957	...	2453523	2973720
1953	7764549	242837440	1366747	...	2525032	3067904
1954	7864289	248244770	1409011	...	2599545	3164515
1955	7971933	253847730	1453732	...	2677214	3263631

6.1.2 From Wide to Long

Now it is the turn of wide-to-long transformations with function `pivot_longer()`, whose main attributes are:

- `cols`: the list of columns to transform into a *key:value* pair with one column with elements from the original column names and the other with elements from the original column values.
- `names_to`: the name of the new column with keys; if not specified, a default name is assigned.

- `values_to`: similarly, the name of the new column with values; if not specified, a default name is assigned.
- Other attributes provide utility functions, none of which are particularly relevant.

For example, we use data frame *popWide* just created and transform it into a long format. We use country names.

```
popLong= pivot_longer(popWide, cols= Afghanistan:last_col(),
                names_to= "Country name", values_to= "Population")
```

Year	Country name	Population
1950	Afghanistan	7480464
1950	Africa (UN)	227549260
1950	Albania	1252587
1950	Algeria	9019866
1950	American Samoa	19057
1950	Andorra	6028

We have obtained the original data frame again; the only differences are the position of the first two columns and the sorting criteria.

> **Tip**
>
> Functions `pivot_longer()` and `pivot_wider()` have been introduced in recent years, replacing previous `gather()` and `spread()`, which are still available but deprecated (meaning that they can be used, but it is suggested to move to the newer ones). The features, in practice, are the same between the two pairs of functions, with some improvements for the newer and more intuitive naming.

6.1.3 GOV.UK: Gender Pay Gap

We now use the second dataset, *Gender pay gap,* from GOV.UK for some additional examples.

```
df= read_csv("datasets/GOV_UK/UK Gender Pay Gap Data - 2022 to 2023.csv")
```

EmployerName	...	MaleTopQuartile	FemaleTopQuartile
1509 GROUP	...	65.62	34.38
A P P WHOLESALE LIMITED	...	78.50	21.50
A.J.N. STEELSTOCK LTD.	...	87.10	12.90
AB AGRI LIMITED	...	63.80	36.20
AB WORLD FOODS LIMITED	...	44.60	55.40
ABACUS EMPLOYMENT SERVICES LIMITED	...	80.90	19.10

```
names(df)

 [1] "EmployerName"                 "EmployerId"
 [3] "Address"                      "PostCode"
 [5] "CompanyNumber"                "SicCodes"
 [7] "DiffMeanHourlyPercent"        "DiffMedianHourlyPercent"
 [9] "DiffMeanBonusPercent"         "DiffMedianBonusPercent"
[11] "MaleBonusPercent"             "FemaleBonusPercent"
[13] "MaleLowerQuartile"            "FemaleLowerQuartile"
[15] "MaleLowerMiddleQuartile"      "FemaleLowerMiddleQuartile"
[17] "MaleUpperMiddleQuartile"      "FemaleUpperMiddleQuartile"
[19] "MaleTopQuartile"              "FemaleTopQuartile"
[21] "CompanyLinkToGPGInfo"         "ResponsiblePerson"
[23] "EmployerSize"                 "CurrentName"
[25] "SubmittedAfterTheDeadline"    "DueDate"
[27] "DateSubmitted"
```

The dataset contains data from 619 employers and has 27 variables with self-explanatory names. We notice several cases of wide-form paired columns, all those prefixed by *Male* or *Female*. Those pairs could be transformed into long-form pairs with column Sex for keys Male/Female and a second column for values. For example, *MaleTopQuartile* and *FemaleTopQuartile* could be transformed into *Sex* and *TopQuartile*. There is no apparent benefit in transformations like this, but, as mentioned in the introduction, it depends on the purpose and what form is more convenient. We could also transform more columns, like *MaleTopQuartile*, *FemaleTopQuartile*, *MaleUpperMiddleQuartile*, *FemaleUpperMiddleQuartile*, *MaleLowerMiddleQuartile*, *FemaleLowerMiddleQuartile*, *MaleLowerQuartile*, and *FemaleLowerQuartile*. All of them could be transformed into a pair *Sex/Quartile*. Similar for columns starting with *DiffMean* and *DiffMedian*.

Let us see an example. We want to transform into long form all columns ending with "Quartile". The *selection helper* **ends_with()** comes at hand in this case.

```
df %>% pivot_longer(cols= ends_with('Quartile'),
                    names_to= "Sex", values_to= "Quartile") %>%
  select('EmployerName', 'Sex','Quartile') -> df1
```

EmployerName	...	Sex	Quartile
1509 GROUP	...	MaleLowerQuartile	38.46
1509 GROUP	...	FemaleLowerQuartile	61.54
1509 GROUP	...	MaleLowerMiddleQuartile	35.94
1509 GROUP	...	FemaleLowerMiddleQuartile	64.06
1509 GROUP	...	MaleUpperMiddleQuartile	56.25
1509 GROUP	...	FemaleUpperMiddleQuartile	43.75

Now we can transform into long-form two-column groups, those ending with 'Quartile' and those starting with "Diff". It is an easy addition by means of the selection helper **starts_with()**.

```
df %>% pivot_longer(cols= ends_with('Quartile'),
                names_to= "Sex", values_to= "Quartile") %>%
  pivot_longer(cols= starts_with('Diff'),
                names_to= "Diff", values_to= "Percent") -> dfLong
select(dfLong, 'Sex','Quartile','Diff','Percent')
```

EmployerName	...	Sex	Quartile	Diff	Percent
1509 GROUP	...	MaleLowerQuartile	38.46	DiffMeanHourlyPercent	16.13
1509 GROUP	...	MaleLowerQuartile	38.46	DiffMedianHourlyPercent	19.99
1509 GROUP	...	MaleLowerQuartile	38.46	DiffMeanBonusPercent	NA
1509 GROUP	...	MaleLowerQuartile	38.46	DiffMedianBonusPercent	NA
1509 GROUP	...	FemaleLowerQuartile	61.54	DiffMeanHourlyPercent	16.13
1509 GROUP	...	FemaleLowerQuartile	61.54	DiffMedianHourlyPercent	19.99

Finally, we can reverse the transformations by restoring the original wide forms by piping two `pivot_wider()` operations; for the second, we exploit the default for the `id_cols` attribute.

```
dfLong %>% pivot_wider(id_cols= "EmployerName":"Quartile",
                   names_from= "Diff", values_from= "Percent") %>%
  pivot_wider(names_from= "Sex", values_from= "Quartile")
```

6.2 Python: Pivoting

Pandas offers functions similar to R's for pivoting operations on data frame columns. The logic of wide-long transformations is the same, with just few differences in the syntax, which is a little less intuitive, and the additional role of indexes, which as usual have a much relevant role in Python than in R.

We start with the dataset from the NYC Open Data regarding risk behaviors among youths.

```
df_ny= pd.read_csv("datasets/NYC_OpenData/
                   Youth_Behavior_Risk_Survey__High_School_April2023.csv")
```

It is a small dataset with aggregated data. Column names are impractical for data wrangling; it is better to rename them. We select a subset of rows using the selection helper **str.startswith()** and function query(), which in this case requires attribute engine="python".

```
df_ny.columns

Index(['Survey', 'Prevalence', 'Year', 'Smoked at least once past 30 days',
       'Binge drinking ‡ in past 30 days ',
       'Drank five or more alcoholic drinks in a row in past 30 days',
       'Got help from a counselor in past 12 months',
       'Drinks 1 or more sodas per day in past 7 days', 'Adolescent obesity',
```

```
        'Physically active 60 minutes per day'],
      dtype='object')

df_ny.columns= ['survey', 'prevalence', 'year', 'smoke','binge_drink',
            'alcoholic','counselor','sodas', 'obesity','phys_active']

df_ny= df_ny.query("prevalence.str.startswith('Prevalence')", engine="python")
df_ny
```

	survey	prevalence	year	smoke	binge_ drink	alco- holic	counselor	sodas	obesity	phys_ active
0	YBRS	Prevalence 2019	2019	3.3	8.9	NaN	NaN	12.4	13.8	14.5
3	YBRS	Prevalence 2017	2017	5.0	5.0	NaN	18.0	14.9	13.5	20.8
6	YBRS	Prevalence 2015	2015	5.8	NaN	8.5	18.3	15.8	12.4	20.9
9	YBRS	Prevalence 2013	2013	8.2	NaN	10.8	17.9	15.7	11.8	18.7
12	YBRS	Prevalence 2011	2011	8.5	NaN	12.7	NaN	20.9	11.6	20.3
15	YRBS	Prevalence 2021	2021	2.2	5.3	NaN	NaN	12.5	19.2	14.1

The result is a data frame with size 6 × 10 and columns in wide form, useful to practice with pandas pivoting operations on columns.

6.2.1 From Wide to Long with Columns

Function **pd.melt()** is logically equivalent to R's pivot_longer() with a less intuitive name. It performs a wide-to-long transformation on some columns, using one or more columns as *unique identifiers* of rows. The result, as expected, is a pair of new columns in the form *key:value* with names of the original columns as values of the *key* column and elements of the original columns as values of the *value* column. The main attributes are:

- id_vars: List of columns acting as unique identifiers of observations (rows) (default: none).
- value_vars: List of columns to be transformed from wide to long (default: all columns except those specified as identifiers).
- var_name: Name of the new key column (default: *variable*).
- value_name: Name of the new value column (default: *value*).
- col_level: If a column multi-index is present, it specifies the level to be transformed from wide to long.

In our example, columns *survey*, *prevalence*, and *year* will be the identifiers; therefore, reproduced as is in the new long-form data frame, all the others, from *smoke* to *phys_active* will be transformed. We specify all attributes without using the defaults.

```
df_long= df_ny.melt(id_vars= ['survey', 'prevalence', 'year'],
            value_vars= ['smoke','binge_drink','alcoholic','counselor',
                    'sodas','obesity','phys_active'],
            var_name= 'risk', value_name= 'percent')

df_long.head(10)
```

	survey	prevalence	year	risk	percent
0	YBRS	Prevalence 2019	2019	smoke	3.3
1	YBRS	Prevalence 2017	2017	smoke	5.0
2	YBRS	Prevalence 2015	2015	smoke	5.8
3	YBRS	Prevalence 2013	2013	smoke	8.2
4	YBRS	Prevalence 2011	2011	smoke	8.5
5	YRBS	Prevalence 2021	2021	smoke	2.2
6	YBRS	Prevalence 2019	2019	binge_drink	8.9
7	YBRS	Prevalence 2017	2017	binge_drink	5.0
8	YBRS	Prevalence 2015	2015	binge_drink	NaN
9	YBRS	Prevalence 2013	2013	binge_drink	NaN

```
df_long.shape

(42, 5)
```

From the original size of 6×10, the long-form data frame has become 42×5, as we already know, the wide-to-long transformation introduces repetitions, increasing the size.

The same operation, by exploiting the defaults, could be rewritten in a shorter form.

```
df_ny.melt(id_vars= ['survey','prevalence','year'])
```

6.2.2 From Long to Wide with Columns

The opposite transformation, from long to wide, could be performed with pandas function `pd.pivot()`. With respect to R's `pivot_wider()`, it includes an additional attribute for the definition of one or more index levels. Important attributes are:

- `index`: List of columns to be transformed into index levels (default: none).
- `columns`: The *key* column(s) of the long form whose unique values will become the names of the new columns (default: none).
- `values`: The *value* column(s) of the long form whose elements will become the values of the new columns (default: none).

We can see an example by using data frame *df_long* just created. Unique values of column *risk* will be the names of the columns in wide form, and elements of column *percent* will be their values. Columns *prevalence* and *year* will become index levels, and then columns if we reset the index. Column *survey* is omitted.

```
df_long.pivot(index= ['prevalence','year'], \
          columns= "risk", \
          values= "percent")
```

prevalence	year	risk	alcoholic	binge_drink	counselor	obesity	phys_active	smoke	sodas
Prevalence 2011	2011	12.7	NaN	NaN	11.6	20.3	8.5	20.9
Prevalence 2013	2013	10.8	NaN	17.9	11.8	18.7	8.2	15.7
Prevalence 2015	2015	8.5	NaN	18.3	12.4	20.9	5.8	15.8
Prevalence 2017	2017	NaN	5.0	18.0	13.5	20.8	5.0	14.9
Prevalence 2019	2019	NaN	8.9	NaN	13.8	14.5	3.3	12.4
Prevalence 2021	2021	NaN	5.3	NaN	19.2	14.1	2.2	12.5

By resetting the index, we obtain the original data frame, except for the *survey* column.

```
df_long.pivot(index= ['prevalence','year'], \
              columns= "risk", \
              values= "percent").reset_index()
```

risk	prevalence	year	alcoholic	binge_drink	counselor	obesity	phys_active	smoke	sodas
0	Prevalence 2011	2011	12.7	NaN	NaN	11.6	20.3	8.5	20.9
1	Prevalence 2013	2013	10.8	NaN	17.9	11.8	18.7	8.2	15.7
2	Prevalence 2015	2015	8.5	NaN	18.3	12.4	20.9	5.8	15.8
3	Prevalence 2017	2017	NaN	5.0	18.0	13.5	20.8	5.0	14.9
4	Prevalence 2019	2019	NaN	8.9	NaN	13.8	14.5	3.3	12.4
5	Prevalence 2021	2021	NaN	5.3	NaN	19.2	14.1	2.2	12.5

Now, let us produce some variations, in order to fully understand the features of function `pivot()`. We try with just column *year* for the index.

```
a1= df_long.pivot(index= 'year', columns= "risk", values= "percent")
a1
```

year	risk	alcoholic	binge_drink	counselor	obesity	phys_active	smoke	sodas
2011		12.7	NaN	NaN	11.6	20.3	8.5	20.9
2013		10.8	NaN	17.9	11.8	18.7	8.2	15.7
2015		8.5	NaN	18.3	12.4	20.9	5.8	15.8
2017		NaN	5.0	18.0	13.5	20.8	5.0	14.9
2019		NaN	8.9	NaN	13.8	14.5	3.3	12.4
2021		NaN	5.3	NaN	19.2	14.1	2.2	12.5

Looking at columns, we see that they are from *alcoholic* to *sodas*, while *survey* and *prevalence* have been omitted.

```
a1.columns

Index(['alcoholic', 'binge_drink', 'counselor', 'obesity', 'phys_active',
       'smoke', 'sodas'],
     dtype='object', name='risk')
```

In general, the pairs `melt()` and `pivot()` allows performing all pivoting operations we may need. However, by exploiting pandas data frame indexes, some wide-long transformations might be produced more efficiently, as we will see in the next section.

6.2.3 Wide-long Transformation with Index Levels

Pandas offers the pair of functions **pd.stack()** and **pd.unstack()**, particularly handy in presence of **multi-indexes**. The logic for both functions is to perform pivoting operations by exploiting index levels instead of columns.

Function `stack()` has two important attributes:

- `level`: Index levels to be kept as-is; the others will be transformed to columns (default: the most inner level).
- `dropna`: If *True*, it removes rows with missing values from the result (default: *True*).

Similarly, for function `unstack()` attributes are:

- `level`: Index levels to be transformed into columns (default: none).
- `fill_value`: Value to fill in to replace missing values (default: none).

In order to practice with `pd.stack()` and `pd.unstack()` functions, we need a data frame with index levels. We use the last dataset listed for this chapter, *Tourist/visitor arrivals and tourism expenditure*, from the United Nations Open Data.

```
df= pd.read_csv("datasets/United Nations/
SYB65_176_202209_Tourist-Visitors Arrival and Expenditure.csv", decimal=',')
```

```
df.info()

<class 'pandas.core.frame.DataFrame'>
RangeIndex: 2235 entries, 0 to 2234
Data columns (total 9 columns):
 #   Column                                Non-Null Count   Dtype
---  ------                                --------------   -----
 0   Region/Country/Area                   2235 non-null    int64
 1   Country                               2235 non-null    object
 2   Year                                  2235 non-null    int64
 3   Series                                2235 non-null    object
 4   Tourism arrivals series type          1154 non-null    object
 5   Tourism arrivals series type footnote 0 non-null       float64
```

```
6    Value                              2235 non-null    float64
7    Footnotes                           873 non-null    object
8    Source                             2235 non-null    object
dtypes: float64(2), int64(2), object(5)
memory usage: 157.3+ KB
```

6.2.4 Indexed Data Frame

From this data frame, we need to produce an indexed version. To this end, we anticipate an important operation that we will discuss in the next chapter, groupby(); for the purpose of this example, it suffices to know that it produces an indexed and aggregated version of the data frame.

```
df1= df.groupby(['Series','Country','Year']).agg({'Value': 'sum'})
df1
```

Series	Country	Year	Value
Tourism expenditure (millions of US dollars)	Afghanistan	2010	147.000
		2018	50.000
		2019	85.000
		2020	75.000
	Albania	1995	70.000
...	...	...	...
Tourist/visitor arrivals (thousands)	Zimbabwe	2005	1.559
		2010	2.239
		2018	2.580
		2019	2.294
		2020	639.000

Let us see which are columns and which are index levels. First, the columns, it is just *Value*, with elements corresponding either to tourism expenditure or tourist arrivals.

```
df1.columns
Index(['Value'], dtype='object')
```

Next, the index levels, *Series*, *Country*, and *Year* are index levels.

```
df1.index
MultiIndex([('Tourism expenditure (millions of US dollars)', ...),
            ('Tourism expenditure (millions of US dollars)', ...),
            ('Tourism expenditure (millions of US dollars)', ...),
            ('Tourism expenditure (millions of US dollars)', ...),
            ...
```

```
(          'Tourist/visitor arrivals (thousands)', ...),
(          'Tourist/visitor arrivals (thousands)', ...),
(          'Tourist/visitor arrivals (thousands)', ...),
(          'Tourist/visitor arrivals (thousands)', ...)],
     names=['Series', 'Country', 'Year'], length=2235)
```

So, we have a row multi-index with three levels and just one column.

6.2.4.1 Function `unstack()`

We start with **`unstack()`** and see what it produces without specifying any attribute.

```
df1.unstack()
```

		Value					
	Year	**1995**	**2005**	**2010**	**2018**	**2019**	**2020**
Series	**Country**						
Tourism expenditure (millions of US dollars)	Afghanistan	NaN	NaN	147.000	50.000	85.000	75.000
	Albania	70.000	880.000	1.778	2.306	2.458	1.243
	Algeria	NaN	477.000	324.000	197.000	140.000	50.000
	Andorra	NaN	NaN	NaN	NaN	1.910	NaN
	Angola	27.000	103.000	726.000	557.000	395.000	19.000
...	...	...	...	...	...	...	...
Tourist/visitor arrivals (thousands)	Venezuela (Boliv. Rep. of)	700.000	706.000	526.000	NaN	NaN	NaN
	Viet Nam	1.351	3.477	5.050	15.498	18.009	3.687
	Yemen	61.000	336.000	1.025	NaN	NaN	NaN
	Zambia	163.000	669.000	815.000	1.072	1.266	502.000
	Zimbabwe	1.416	1.559	2.239	2.580	2.294	639.000

To make sense of the result, it is better to look at columns and index levels.

```
df1.unstack().columns

MultiIndex([('Value', 1995),
            ('Value', 2005),
            ('Value', 2010),
            ('Value', 2018),
            ('Value', 2019),
            ('Value', 2020)],
           names=[None, 'Year'])
```

```
df1.unstack().index

MultiIndex([('Tourism expenditure (millions of US dollars)', ...),
            ('Tourism expenditure (millions of US dollars)', ...),
            ('Tourism expenditure (millions of US dollars)', ...),
            ('Tourism expenditure (millions of US dollars)', ...),
            ...
            (          'Tourist/visitor arrivals (thousands)', ...),
            (          'Tourist/visitor arrivals (thousands)', ...),
            (          'Tourist/visitor arrivals (thousands)', ...)],
           names=['Series', 'Country'], length=426)
```

Columns have become a multi-index *(Value, Year)*, while index levels are just *Series* and *Country*. Therefore, unstack() *has produced a long-to-wide transformation of an index level into a column multi-index*. Values of *Years* have become columns, in wide form. Let us try specifying a level.

```
df1.unstack(level=0)
```

		Value	
	Series	**Tourism expenditure (millions of US dollars)**	**Tourist/visitor arrivals (thousands)**
Country	**Year**		
Afghanistan	2010	147.0	NaN
	2018	50.0	NaN
	2019	85.0	NaN
	2020	75.0	NaN
Albania	1995	70.0	NaN
...	...	...	...
Zimbabwe	2005	99.0	1.559
	2010	135.0	2.239
	2018	191.0	2.580
	2019	285.0	2.294
	2020	66.0	639.000

```
df1.unstack(level=0).columns

MultiIndex([('Value', 'Tourism expenditure (millions of US dollars)'),
            ('Value',           'Tourist/visitor arrivals (thousands)')],
           names=[None, 'Series'])
```

With **level=0**, we have transformed index level *Series* into a column multi-index. This tells us that index levels are numbered from the outer to the inner. If we specify **level=2,** we obtain the same result of the case without any attribute.

What if we list more index levels to be unstacked?

```
df1.unstack(level=[1,2])
```

	Value										
Country	**Afghanistan**				**Albania**						...
Year	2010	2018	2019	2020	1995	2005	2010	2018	2019	2020	...
Series											
Tourism expenditure (millions of US dollars)	147.0	50.0	85.0	75.0	70.0	880.0	1.778	2.306	2.458	1.243	...
Tourist/visitor arrivals (thousands)	NaN	NaN	NaN	NaN	NaN	NaN	2.191	5.340	6.128	2.604	...

```
df1.unstack(level=[1,2]).columns

MultiIndex([('Value',                      'Afghanistan', 2010),
            ('Value',                      'Afghanistan', 2018),
            ('Value',                      'Afghanistan', 2019),
            ('Value',                      'Afghanistan', 2020),
            ('Value',                          'Albania', 1995),
            ('Value',                          'Albania', 2005),
            ('Value',                          'Albania', 2010),
            ('Value',                          'Albania', 2018),
            ('Value',                          'Albania', 2019),
            ('Value',                          'Albania', 2020),
            ...
            ('Value',                          'Türkiye', 1995),
            ('Value',                           'Uganda', 1995),
            ('Value',                          'Ukraine', 1995),
            ('Value', 'United Rep. of Tanzania', 1995),
            ('Value',                       'Uzbekistan', 1995),
            ('Value',                          'Vanuatu', 1995),
            ('Value',                         'Viet Nam', 1995),
            ('Value',                            'Yemen', 1995),
            ('Value',                            'Yemen', 2005),
            ('Value',                           'Zambia', 1995)],
           names=[None, 'Country', 'Year'], length=1234)
```

Similarly, the two index levels are transformed into wide form, and we produce a column multi-index with three levels. Columns are now 1234, one for each combination of country and year.

6.2.4.2 Function `stack()`

With `stack()`, the opposite operation is executed, from a column multi-index representing a wide form, we transform column names into index levels on rows (long form). In the example, we use the data frame with column multi-index just produced.

```
df2= df1.unstack(level=[1,2])
```

We start by stacking a single level of the column multi-index, for example, the *Country* level. We can use `level=1` or `level="Country"`.

```
df2.stack(level="Country")
```

		Value					
	Year	1995	2005	2010	2018	2019	2020
Series	Country						
Tourism expenditure (millions of US dollars)	Afghanistan	NaN	NaN	147.000	50.000	85.000	75.000
	Albania	70.000	880.000	1.778	2.306	2.458	1.243
	Algeria	NaN	477.000	324.000	197.000	140.000	50.000
	Andorra	NaN	NaN	NaN	NaN	1.910	NaN
	Angola	27.000	103.000	726.000	557.000	395.000	19.000
...	...	...	...	...	...	...	...
Tourist/visitor arrivals (thousands)	Venezuela (Boliv. Rep. of)	700.000	706.000	526.000	NaN	NaN	NaN
	Viet Nam	1.351	3.477	5.050	15.498	18.009	3.687
	Yemen	61.000	336.000	1.025	NaN	NaN	NaN
	Zambia	163.000	669.000	815.000	1.072	1.266	502.000
	Zimbabwe	1.416	1.559	2.239	2.580	2.294	639.000

We have reproduced the data frame with two index levels on rows. We could also notice that the stacked column becomes the most inner index level.

We can try stacking both Country and Year from column to row index levels.

```
df2.stack(level=[1,2])
```

			Value
Series	**Country**	**Year**	
Tourism expenditure (millions of US dollars)	Afghanistan	2010	147.000
		2018	50.000
		2019	85.000
		2020	75.000
	Albania	1995	70.000
...	...	...	...
Tourist/visitor arrivals (thousands)	Zimbabwe	2005	1.559
		2010	2.239
		2018	2.580
		2019	2.294
		2020	639.000

This way, we have reproduced the original data frame. What if we stack the outer level of the column multi-index, the one with all values "Value"?

```
df2.stack(level=0)
```

	Country	Afghanistan				Albania						...
	Year	2010	2018	2019	2020	1995	2005	2010	2018	2019	2020	...
Series												
Tourism expenditure (millions of US dollars)	Value	147.0	50.0	85.0	75.0	70.0	880.0	1.778	2.306	2.458	1.243	...
Tourist/visitor arrivals (thousands)	Value	NaN	NaN	NaN	NaN	NaN	NaN	2.191	5.340	6.128	2.604	...

```
df2.stack(level=0).index
MultiIndex([('Tourism expenditure (millions of US dollars)', 'Value'),
            (        'Tourist/visitor arrivals (thousands)', 'Value')],
          names=['Series', None])
```

The inner index level has all values "Value," useless as an index level. We can delete it with pandas function **droplevel()**, which deletes index levels on rows or on columns by specifying the usual attribute `axis`.

```
df2.stack(level=0).droplevel(level=1, axis=0)
```

Country	Afghanistan				Albania						...
Year	2010	2018	2019	2020	1995	2005	2010	2018	2019	2020	...
Series											
Tourism expenditure (millions of US dollars)	147.0	50.0	85.0	75.0	70.0	880.0	1.778	2.306	2.458	1.243	...
Tourist/visitor arrivals (thousands)	NaN	NaN	NaN	NaN	NaN	NaN	2.191	5.340	6.128	2.604	...

```
df2.stack(level=0).droplevel(level=1, axis=0).index
Index(['Tourism expenditure (millions of US dollars)', 'Tourist/visitor
arrivals (thousands)'], dtype='object', name='Series')
```

We could have done the same by removing the index level when it was in the column multi-index. In that case, it was the outer level.

```
df1.unstack(level=[1,2]).droplevel(level=0, axis=1)
```

Country	Afghanistan				Albania						...
Year	2010	2018	2019	2020	1995	2005	2010	2018	2019	2020	...
Series											
Tourism expenditure (millions of US dollars)	147.0	50.0	85.0	75.0	70.0	880.0	1.778	2.306	2.458	1.243	...
Tourist/visitor arrivals (thousands)	NaN	NaN	NaN	NaN	NaN	NaN	2.191	5.340	6.128	2.604	...

6.2.5 From Long to Wide with Elements of Numeric Type

A variant of the `pd.pivot()` is represented by function **`pd.pivot_table()`**, which is very similar except for an additional feature that could be useful when we work with *numerical values* and need to *aggregate* them with a certain statistical function. It produces a long-to-wide transformation with columns, like the `pd.pivot()`. Important attributes are the same already seen before — index, columns, and values — plus the one related to the aggregation function: **agg-func**, which could specify one of the NumPy statistics, (e.g. 'max', 'min', 'mean', 'median', 'sum', 'count', etc., or the equivalent form np.max, np.min, np.mean, etc.). The default is the arithmetic mean.

Let us look at an example using the previous *df1* data frame having three row index levels.

```
df1
```

Series	Country	Year	Value
Tourism expenditure (millions of US dollars)	Afghanistan	2010	147.000
		2018	50.000
		2019	85.000
		2020	75.000
	Albania	1995	70.000
...	...	...	...
Tourist/visitor arrivals (thousands)	Zimbabwe	2005	1.559
		2010	2.239
		2018	2.580
		2019	2.294
		2020	639.000

First two examples do not specify the aggfunc attribute. Here, values have been aggregated for years, and the arithmetic mean has been calculated.

```
df1.pivot_table(
    values=["Value"],
    index=["Series"],
    columns=["Country"])
```

	Value					
Country	Afghanistan	Albania	Algeria	...	Yemen	Zambia
Series						
Tourism expenditure (millions of US dollars)	89.25	159.630	237.600	...	1.291	582.400
Tourist/visitor arrivals (thousands)	NaN	4.065	186.590	...	132.675	358.556

We aggregate for countries and again calculate the mean.

```
df1.pivot_table(
    values=["Value"],
    index=["Series"],
    columns=["Year"])
```

	Value					
Year	1995	2005	2010	2018	2019	2020
Series						
Tourism expenditure (millions of US dollars)	163.110364	170.289147	171.512881	169.913968	158.799066	157.529161
Tourist/visitor arrivals (thousands)	157.886882	170.203490	175.007761	126.154177	116.919091	176.128623

Now we specify an aggregate function (median).

```
df1.pivot_table(
    values=["Value"],
    index=["Series"],
    columns=["Year"],
    aggfunc=np.median)
```

	Value					
Year	1995	2005	2010	2018	2019	2020
Series						
Tourism expenditure (millions of US dollars)	48.5	51.959	27.208	21.5940	20.0755	33.5
Tourist/visitor arrivals (thousands)	44.0	43.500	24.577	15.4225	15.1190	30.0

The median is considerably smaller than the mean; there should be values much larger than the median. We could check the maximum values.

```
df1.pivot_table(
    values=["Value"],
    index=["Series"],
    columns=["Year"],
    aggfunc='max')
```

	Value					
Year	**1995**	**2005**	**2010**	**2018**	**2019**	**2020**
Series						
Tourism expenditure (millions of US dollars)	995.0	969.0	998.0	996.0	992.0	955.0
Tourist/visitor arrivals (thousands)	918.0	933.0	984.0	997.0	894.0	952.0

Indeed, maximum values are much larger than the median.

Questions

6.1 (R/Python)

What is a pair of columns representing *keys* and *values* in a wide-form data frame?

A An index

B A data representation in which the meaning of values can be derived from the corresponding keys, rather than from the column name

C A data representation in which the meaning of keys can be derived from the corresponding values, rather than from the column name

D An untidy and inefficient data representation

(R: B)

6.2 (R/Python)

Why do we need to transform one or more data frame columns into the corresponding wide form?

A Because it is a more convenient data organization for the operation that we want to execute

B To have an indexed data frame

C To tidy the data organization

D Because it is a better data organization

(R: A)

6.3 (R/Python)

Does a data frame in long form and in wide form has the same shape (equal number of columns and number of rows)?

A Yes

B No, the wide form has always more columns

C No, the wide form has always more rows

D No, the long form has typically more rows

(R: D)

6.4 (R/Python)

Is it always possible to easily transform a data frame from long form to wide form and vice versa?

A Yes
B Only if the number of columns is the same
C Only if the number of rows is the same
D Not easily; it takes several operations
(R: A)

6.5 **(R/Python)**
If we have a data frame with two columns for *Male* and *Female* with information corresponding to the two categories (let us consider it as just an example, any other binary categorization is equivalent) and we transform them into two columns for *Sex* and *Value*, have we performed a long-form transformation?
A No, because the columns are still the same number
B No, because the number of rows changes
C Technically, yes, but the transformation is meaningless
D Yes
(R: D)

6.6 **(R)**
Considering the following instruction, what is the expected result?

```
pivot_wider(df, id_cols= "Col1",
            names_from= "Col2", values_from= "Col3")
```

A Values of column *Col1* become column names
B Values of column *Col2* become column names, values from Col3 become values of the new columns, and *Col1* remains unchanged
C Values of column *Col2* become column names, values from Col3 become values of the new columns, and *Col1* is omitted from the result
D Values of column *Col2* become column names, values from Col3 become values of the new columns, and *Col1* becomes the index of the data frame
(R: B)

6.7 **(R)**
Considering the following instruction, what is the expected result?

```
pivot_longer(df, cols= "Col1:Col3",
             names_to= "Variable", values_to= "Value")
```

A Values of columns *Col1*, *Col2*, and *Col3* become values of the new column *Value*, names of *Col1*, *Col2*, and *Col3* become the corresponding keys of column *Variable*
B Columns *Col1*, *Col2*, and *Col3* are omitted from the result; all the others are transformed into the corresponding long form
C *Col1*, *Col2*, and *Col3* become three new columns of the long-form data frame
D Values of columns *Col1*, *Col2*, and *Col3* become values of the new column *Variable*, names of *Col1*, *Col2*, and *Col3* become the corresponding keys of column *Value*
(R: A)

6.8 (Python)

Considering the following instruction, what is the expected result?

```
df.melt(id_vars= ['Col1', 'Col2'], \
        value_vars= ['Col3','Col4','Col5'], \
        var_name= 'Variable', value_name= 'Value')
```

A Values of columns *Col1, Col2,* and *Col3* become values of the new column *Value,* names of *Col1, Col2,* and *Col3* become the corresponding keys of column *Variable*

B Columns *Col1* and *Col2* remain the same, and columns *Col3, Col4,* and *Col5* are transformed in long form with their names as keys of the new *Value* column and their elements as values of the new *Variable* column

C *Col1* and *Col2* are omitted from the result, columns *Col3, Col4,* and *Col5* are transformed in long form with their names as keys of the new *Variable* column and their elements as values of the new *Value* column

D Columns *Col1* and *Col2* remain the same, columns *Col3, Col4,* and *Col5* are transformed in long form with their names as keys of the new *Variable* column and their elements as values of the new *Value* column

(R: D)

6.9 (Python)

Considering the following instruction, what is the expected result?

```
df.pivot(index= ['Col1','Col2'], \
         columns= "Variable", \
         values= "Value")
```

A Values of columns *Col1* and *Col2* become a row multi-index; all other columns are transformed into long form with keys in column *Variable* and values in column *Value*

B Values of columns *Col1* and *Col2* become a column multi-index, all other columns are transformed into long form with keys in column *Variable* and values in column *Value*

C Values of columns *Col1* and *Col2* become a row multi-index, values of column *Variable* become the names of the new columns and elements of column *Values* the corresponding values of the new columns

D Values of columns *Col1* and *Col2* become a row multi-index, values of column *Value* become the names of the new columns and elements of column *Variable* the corresponding values of the new columns

(R: C)

6.10 (Python)

Considering the following instruction, what is the expected result?

```
df.pivot(index= ['Col1','Col2'], \
         columns= "Variable", \
         values= "Value").reset_index()
```

A Same as Question 6.9, but row numbers become a column
B Same as Question 6.9, but the index level corresponding to *Col2* is restored as a column
C Same as Question 6.9, but the index level corresponding to *Col1* is restored as a column
D Same as Question 6.9, but both index levels corresponding to *Col1* and *Col2* are restored as columns

(R: D)

6.11 **(Python)**
Considering the following instruction, what is the expected result?

```
df.unstack(level=1)
```

A The first index level on rows is transformed into wide form becoming new columns
B The second index level on rows is transformed into wide form becoming new columns
C All columns are transformed into wide form
D It is a wrong instruction

(R: B)

6.12 **(Python)**
Considering the following instruction, what is the expected result?

```
df.stack(level="Col1")
```

A Wide-form column *Col1* is transformed into index level *Col1*
B Index *Col1* is transformed into wide-form column *Col1*
C All columns are transformed into index level *Col1*
D It is a wrong instruction

(R: A)

6.13 **(Python)**
Considering the following instruction, what is the expected result?

```
df.stack(level=[0,2])
```

A Levels 0 and 2 of the row multi-index are transformed into two columns
B The instruction is wrong
C Levels 0 and 2 of the row multi-index are transformed long form as key and value columns
D Levels 0 and 2 of the column multi-index are transformed into two row index levels

(R: D)

6.14 **(Python)**
Considering the following instruction, what is the expected result?

```
df1.pivot_table( values=["Col1"],
                 index=["Col2"],
                 columns=["Col3"],
                 aggfunc=np.median)
```

A A wide-form transformation of values of *Col3* as names of new columns, *Col1* as values of the new columns, and *Col1* as the row index level, values are aggregated using the median

B A long-form transformation of column index level *Col2* into as a column with keys *Col2* and values as *Col1*, values are aggregated using the median

C Calculates the median of values of *Col1* having the same index as *Col2* and puts the result in the new column *Col3*

D It is a wrong instruction

(R: A)

7

Groups and Operations on Groups

Up to now, we have seen data wrangling operations on a full data frame or on subsets of rows and columns. Often, we also need to calculate statistics on groups of rows sharing common properties. For instance, based on population data, we may want to obtain statistics on gender, age, place of residence, education level, and so forth. This means that we need a way, first, to identify rows with the common feature (e.g. same gender, same education level), then to compute statistics for each subset of observations.

With the knowledge we have gained so far, we already know how to achieve this kind of results, but it is highly inefficient. To obtain subsets of rows sharing common properties, we could use logical conditions and filtering functions, one for each group of rows we are interested in, and create a new data frame for each group. Then, for each data frame, we could calculate the desired statistics, like the mean, max/min, etc. This solution works, indeed, but at what cost? Well... it depends. If we have a dataset with US census data and we just want general statistics for women and men, that requires obtaining two data frames and calculating the statistics for each data frame. It may not look like a tremendous effort or a waste of time. What about if we want those statistics at regional level? In the US Census data, at level 3, regions are nine ("New England," "Middle Atlantic," "East North Central," "West North Central," "South Atlantic," "East South Central," "West South Central," "Mountain," "Pacific"), which means that simply to have statistics about men and women, we need to extract 18 subsets and calculate statistics for each of them. It is still doable, but it starts looking like a waste of time. What if we want the statistics at state level? States are 50 (or 52, if DC and Puerto Rico are included, as commonly is), which means creating 100 (or 104) data frames and for each one to calculate the statistics. Of course, it could be done, but now it definitely looks like a waste of time and an inefficient solution. And, if we want them for US counties? There are around 3100 counties, meaning that more than 6000 data frames should be created and the statistics calculated for each one. Also, maybe we do not want to stop to men and women statistics; maybe we want statistics for other dimensions, like age or ethnic groups, voter registrations, education levels, and so forth. It definitely sounds like pure nonsense to do it manually. Therefore, the manual solution works, but it is *not scalable*, meaning that when the size of data increases, the cost/effort to achieve the solution grows, either linearly or more than linearly. In short, in theory, it works, but in practice, it does not. All manual solutions are not scalable, that is the human nature and physiology.

We need a scalable and efficient solution to obtain results like those ones, and both R and Python provide one, almost identical in the two cases.

Data Science Fundamentals with R, Python, and Open Data, First Edition. Marco Cremonini.
© 2024 John Wiley & Sons, Inc. Published 2024 by John Wiley & Sons, Inc.
Companion website: www.wiley.com/go/DSFRPythonOpenData

Dataset

On-Time : Reporting Carrier On-Time Performance (1987–present) from the *Bureau of Transportation Statistics*, United States Department of Transportation. The dataset contains data about US domestic flights operated in March 2023. (https://transtats.bts.gov/Fields.asp?gnoyr_VQ=FGJ)

7.1 R: Groups

Operations on groups of rows comply with a logic that repeats with only a few variations. The first step is always the definition of logical groups, meaning that rows are indexed according to a grouping criterion. Rows with common specified features are *logically grouped together*. After this initial step, operations on groups follow. Typical are aggregation operations that calculate statistics or new columns with calculated values based on the group structure, rather than the whole flat data frame.

The R function for creating indexed groups is `group_by()`, the one for the definition of aggregation operations is `summarize()`, and `mutate()`, already met before, is for the creation of new columns. All these functions are defined in package *dplyr*. Others are common, like function `arrange()` for sorting or the family of functions `slice_*()` for slicing rows from groups. It is typical to pipe the sequence of operations on groups.

We use the dataset *On-Time: Reporting Carrier On-Time Performance (1987–present)* of the *Bureau of Transportation Statistics* and select a subset of columns. The dataset is stored in a compressed ZIP file together with another file of information about the data. The regular function `read_csv()` could read ZIP files by automatically decompressing them, but with the constraint that only the CSV dataset must be included in the ZIP, no other file of any format is allowed; otherwise, an error is generated. In our case, there is an HTML file together with the CSV dataset in the ZIP file that would make the read fail. A solution is, obviously, to extract the content of the ZIP file and then read the CSV dataset. An alternative is function `vroom()`, which has advanced features and better flexibility than the ordinary `read_csv()`. In this case, it is able to read the CSV dataset from the ZIP file, even if it is not the only file included.

```
library(tidyverse)
library(vroom)

flightsMarch2023= vroom("datasets/Bureau_Trans_Stats/Flights_March2023.zip")

flightsMarch2023 %>%
  select(5,6,7,10,15,16,17,19,24,25,26,28,
         31,32,37,38,39,40,42,43,48,50,53,55)  -> df
```

DayOf Week	Flight Date	Reporting _Airline	Tail_ Number	Origin	Origin City Name	Origin State Name	Dest	Dest City Name	Dest State Name	Dep Time	Dep Delay	...
1	2023-03-13	OH	N609NN	TRI	Bristol/ Johnson City/ Kingsport, TN	Tennessee	CLT	Charlotte, NC	North Carolina	1421	−12	...

DayOf Week	Flight Date	Reporting _Airline	Tail _Number	Origin	Origin City Name	Origin State Name	Dest	Dest City Name	Dest State Name	Dep Time	Dep Delay	...
3	2023-03-15	OH	N561NN	TRI	Bristol/ Johnson City/ Kingsport, TN	Tennessee	CLT	Charlotte, NC	North Carolina	1428	−5	...
4	2023-03-16	OH	N615NN	TRI	Bristol/ Johnson City/ Kingsport, TN	Tennessee	CLT	Charlotte, NC	North Carolina	1420	−13	...
5	2023-03-17	OH	N547NN	TRI	Bristol/ Johnson City/ Kingsport, TN	Tennessee	CLT	Charlotte, NC	North Carolina	1427	−6	...
7	2023-03-19	OH	N572NN	TRI	Bristol/ Johnson City/ Kingsport, TN	Tennessee	CLT	Charlotte, NC	North Carolina	1424	−9	...
1	2023-03-20	OH	N572NN	TRI	Bristol/ Johnson City/ Kingsport, TN	Tennessee	CLT	Charlotte, NC	North Carolina	1423	−10	...

From the data frame, we can check the column names and missing values.

```
names(df)

 [1] "DayOfWeek"        "FlightDate"        "Reporting_Airline"
 [4] "Tail_Number"      "Origin"            "OriginCityName"
 [7] "OriginState"      "OriginStateName"   "Dest"
[10] "DestCityName"     "DestState"         "DestStateName"
[13] "DepTime"          "DepDelay"          "TaxiOut"
[16] "WheelsOff"        "WheelsOn"          "TaxiIn"
[19] "ArrTime"          "ArrDelay"          "Cancelled"
[22] "Diverted"         "AirTime"           "Distance"


colSums(is.na(df))

       DayOfWeek        FlightDate  Reporting_Airline       Tail_Number
               0                 0                  0               761
          Origin    OriginCityName        OriginState    OriginStateName
               0                 0                  0                 0
            Dest      DestCityName          DestState      DestStateName
               0                 0                  0                 0
         DepTime          DepDelay            TaxiOut          WheelsOff
            7150              7152               7319               7319
        WheelsOn            TaxiIn            ArrTime           ArrDelay
            7579              7579               7579               8789
       Cancelled          Diverted            AirTime           Distance
               0                 0               8789                 0
```

7.1.1 Groups and Group Indexes

7.1.1.1 Function `group_by()`

Function `group_by()` requires a list of columns to be used for defining groups of rows. Each combination of values of the specified columns will become a logical group of rows, all sharing that specific combination of values. For example, if we choose *OriginStateName* and *DestStateName* as grouping columns, all pairs of US states will identify a group of flights departing from a certain state and arriving to another one. Also, pairs with same state for origin and destination are valid. Similar if instead of the state we choose cities (i.e. *OriginCityName*, *DestCityName*), the number of combinations increases widely, and so do the logical groups, but the logic is exactly the same and all the work is done computationally, not manually. Even more will be the combinations if we choose the airports (*Origin*, *Dest*), cities may have more than one airport. Here we have always mentioned example with two columns and the combinations of values between those two, but everything is the same if we have just one column for grouping; in that case, the number of groups corresponds to the unique values of the column, or more than two columns; again, combinations among column values define the groups. We can verify what we have just stated. First, with two columns.

```
dfState= group_by(df, OriginStateName, DestStateName)

dfCity= group_by(df, OriginCityName, DestCityName)

dfAirport= group_by(df, Origin, Dest)
```

Apparently, nothing changed with respect to the original data frame; the result in all three cases looks the same: same number of rows and columns, same order, same values, no visible group. Everything's the same, except for some tiny details that make a great difference.

First, for all grouped data frame, a new information appeared on top of the table that was not there in the original ungrouped data frame, **Groups:** followed by the columns that have been chosen and a number, the number of groups logically created.

```
# Groups:   OriginStateName, DestStateName [1,233]

# Groups:   OriginCityName, DestCityName [5,243]

# Groups:   Origin, Dest [5,679]
```

As we anticipated, the number of groups corresponds to the combinations between column values, and it was expected to grow for the three examples; the results confirm that. Something actually happened.

The second difference emerges when we check the data types of the original data frame and of a grouped data frame.

```
class(df)

[1] "tbl_df"     "tbl"        "data.frame"
```

```
class(dfState)

[1] "grouped_df" "tbl_df"      "tbl"           "data.frame"
```

Both are of type *data.frame* and *tibble*, but the second is also of type *"grouped_df."* It is not the same kind of data frame; the grouped data frame has something more; it has an *associated index*.

The third difference is physical and could be observed by checking the amount of memory allocated to a data frame. Function **object.size()** of base package ***utils*** can be used; **format()** is needed just to have the results expressed in Mb instead of bytes.

```
format(object.size(df), units = "auto")
format(object.size(dfState), units = "auto")
format(object.size(dfCity), units = "auto")
format(object.size(dfAirport), units = "auto")

[1] "106.9 Mb"
[1] "109.3 Mb"
[1] "109.6 Mb"
[1] "109.6 Mb"
```

The four data frames have exactly the same data, but they are not of same size in memory. The difference is the index, which is absent in the ungrouped *df*, and becomes increasingly larger the more the groups. Therefore, again, what grouping produces may not be immediately visible, but the effects are relevant.

Let us try two more examples, one with a single column and the other with three grouping columns.

```
dfDestState= group_by(df, DestStateName)
format(object.size(dfDestState), units = "auto")

# Groups:   DestStateName [52]
[1] "109.2 Mb"
```

As expected, groups are 52, the number of US States plus the District of Columbia and Puerto Rico, and the allocation in memory is smaller than the case with origin and destination states.

```
df3Cols= group_by(df, DayOfWeek, Reporting_Airline, DestStateName)
format(object.size(df3Cols), units = "auto")

# Groups:   DayOfWeek, Reporting_Airline, DestStateName [3,767]
[1] "109.5 Mb"
```

We have 3767 combinations of day of week, airline, and destination state, and hence groups.

7.1.1.2 Index Details

Despite the group index is managed behind the scene, it is not inaccessible. We can look at details with some specific functions, the first of which is `tally()`.

```
tally(dfState)
```

Origin StateName	Dest StateName	*n*
Alabama	Colorado	146
Alabama	Florida	140
Alabama	Georgia	710
Alabama	Illinois	151
Alabama	Maryland	26
Alabama	Michigan	60
…	…	…

The result shows combinations of values, here *OriginStateName* and *DestStateName,* and the number of rows corresponding to each one. For example, from Alabama to Florida, 140 flights have been operated in March 2023, 60 from Alabama to Michigan, and so on.

Other information about an index could be obtained with `group_keys()`, `group_indices()`, `group_rows()`, and `group_vars()`.

Function `group_keys()` shows the values (*keys*) of the index. We look here to index keys for groups of *df3Cols.*

```
group_keys(df3Cols)
```

DayOfWeek	Reporting_ Airline	DestStateName
1	9E	Alabama
1	9E	Arkansas
1	9E	Connecticut
1	9E	Florida
1	9E	Georgia
1	9E	Illinois
…	…	…

These are the combinations among the three column values corresponding at least to one row in the data frame.

Function `group_indices()` shows to what group each row belongs.

```
group_indices(dfState)

   [1]  1012 1012 1012 1012 1012 1012 1012 1012 1012 1012 ...
  [24]  1055 1055 1055 1055 1055 1055 1055 1055 1055 1055 ...
  ...
```

The meaning of this result is that the first row of the data frame *dfState* belongs to group 1012, the 25th to group 1055, and so on. Why is that? Because the first row has an origin state equal to Tennessee and a destination state equal to North Carolina, which evidently is the 1021st index key, whereas the 25th row has Texas and Ohio as origin and destination states, the 1055th key of the index.

Function `group_rows()` does the opposite, namely for each group shows which rows are associated to it. Try looking at the 1021st group; we should see the first rows of the data frame listed.

```
group_rows(dfState)[[1012]]

  [1]     1      2      3      4      5      6      7      8    ...
 [17]   265    266    267    268    269    270    271    272   ...
```

Exactly, as expected. Finally, function `group_vars()` just returns the list of columns used to create the group index.

```
group_vars(dfState)

[1] "OriginStateName" "DestStateName"
```

To summarize, these are utility functions specific for gathering information about a group index; they are rarely necessary, but it is worth to know that they exist and that a group index is not an inaccessible black box; on the contrary, it could be inspected in order to verify any doubts concerning the logic followed to group a data frame.

7.1.2 Aggregation Operations

7.1.2.1 Functions `group_by()` and `summarize()`

So far, we have only defined logical groups with different criteria but not used them for anything. The most typical reason for grouping a data frame is to calculate statistics on groups and produce a result that is no longer the original data frame (e.g. all 500 000+ flights), but a shorter version with aggregated values, i.e. the statistics on groups. For example, we want to know the number of flights for each pair of cities, or the average departure delay for each airport, or the maximum arrival delay for each day of week and airline, and so on. In all these cases, we have to execute aggregation operations on a grouped data frame. The function to execute aggregation operations is **`summarize()`** (or the equivalent `summarise()`). This function is a sort of wrapper for specific functions, it does not produce any result by itself, but it is needed to specify that a certain statistic should be calculated for groups. In the following, we consider the main aggregation operations.

7.1.2.2 Counting Rows: function `n()`

The most basic statistic we may want to obtain is to know *how many rows belong to groups*, like how many flights are operated between two states or two airports, how many flights have been cancelled for any day of the month or day of the week, and so on. To this end, the function to use is `n()` with no attribute because counting the number of rows for each group does not depend on any specific column; it depends on the index, which has already been created. It is not a coincidence that this resembles to what we have said for function `tally()` and that in its result there was a column named *n*. Function `tally()` implicitly uses this same function `n()`. Let us see some examples. First, the number of flights between two states.

```
df %>% group_by(OriginStateName, DestStateName) %>%
        summarize(NumFlights= n())
```

OriginStateName	DestStateName	NumFlights
Alabama	Colorado	146
Alabama	Florida	140
Alabama	Georgia	710
Alabama	Illinois	151
Alabama	Maryland	26
Alabama	Michigan	60
...	...	...

Now, the number of cancelled flights for each day of week. The meaning of *Cancelled* values is: 0 for not cancelled, 1 for cancelled.

```
df %>% group_by(DayOfWeek, Cancelled) %>%
        summarize(NumFlights= n())
```

DayOfWeek	Cancelled	NumFlights
1	0	77251
1	1	510
2	0	71488
2	1	1420
3	0	91614
3	1	594
...	...	...

7.1.2.3 Arithmetic Mean: function `mean()`

The arithmetic mean is another fundamental statistic; the function is **mean()**. Previous function `n()` is an exception in not requiring any attribute; all other aggregating functions need to know, at least, the column whose values should be used. Often, something else should be specified. For `mean()`, as well as for most statistical and arithmetic operations, another information to specify is *how to handle missing values*. The default is to not handle them, meaning that they are included in the computation, which may have the consequence of invalidating the result, for example, producing a missing value, as is the case with the mean. This is why the attribute **na.rm** is so important (*na.rm* stands for *NA remove*). If not specified, the default is na.rm=FALSE, meaning that the missing values are included in the calculation. Otherwise, we should specify **na.rm=TRUE** and the mean is calculated only on valid values. We should almost always specify that we omit missing values from calculation.

We run some examples, starting with the *percentage of cancelled flights for each state*. The percentage is 100 multiplied by the mean of cancelled flights. The result could be sorted by percentage of cancelled flights.

```
df %>% group_by(OriginStateName) %>%
  summarize(NumFlights= n(),
          PercentCancel= round(100*mean(Cancelled, na.rm=TRUE),2)) %>%
  arrange(desc(PercentCancel))
```

OriginStateName	NumFlights	PercentCancel
New Hampshire	548	5.66
West Virginia	300	4.67
Maine	1001	4.49
Vermont	660	4.24
Alaska	2730	3.74
North Dakota	1460	3.63
Massachusetts	12490	2.49
Connecticut	2094	2.48
Michigan	13519	2.35
South Dakota	998	2.20
...	...	...

As was easy to imagine, northern states with harsher weather conditions have proportionally more cancelled flights, West Virginia being the exception. A typical mistake in this case is to include *Cancelled* in the grouping columns. If we do that, the result we obtain is meaningless, as the result shows clearly. It should always be remembered that aggregation operations are performed on the groups defined by the index.

```
df %>% group_by(OriginStateName, Cancelled) %>%
      summarize(NumFlights= n(),
              PercentCancel= 100*mean(Cancelled, na.rm=TRUE))
```

OriginStateName	Cancelled	NumFlights	PercentCancel
Alabama	0	2360	0
Alabama	1	27	100
Alaska	0	2628	0
Alaska	1	102	100
Arizona	0	17883	0
Arizona	1	178	100
…	…	…	…

Now, we calculate the average departure and arrival delay for flights between Los Angeles Airport (LAX) and New York JFK (JFK) for each day of week. Since we want a specific pair of airports, we need to select them from origin and destination airports first.

```
df %>% filter(Origin=="LAX" & Dest=="JFK") %>%
  group_by(DayOfWeek) %>%
     summarize(
        NumFlights= n(),
        MeanDepDelay= round(mean(DepDelay, na.rm=TRUE),2),
        MeanArrDelay= round(mean(ArrDelay, na.rm=TRUE),2))
```

DayOfWeek	NumFlights	MeanDepDelay	MeanArrDelay
1	112	26.17	2.72
2	108	26.55	5.46
3	134	22.80	−6.98
4	140	15.32	−4.21
5	140	15.20	1.28
6	88	22.69	0.69
7	110	17.83	−7.04

7.1.2.4 Maximum and Minimum Values: Functions `max()` and `min()`

To retrieve maximum and minimum values is analogous to what we have just seen with the arithmetic mean, in this case using `max()` and `min()` functions. We can add max and min delays to the previous example.

```
df %>% filter(Origin=="LAX" & Dest=="JFK") %>%
  group_by(DayOfWeek) %>%
     summarize(
        NumFlights= n(),
        MeanDepDelay= round(mean(DepDelay, na.rm=TRUE),2),
        MeanArrDelay= round(mean(ArrDelay, na.rm=TRUE),2),
        MinDepDelay= round(min(DepDelay, na.rm=TRUE),2),
```

```
MinArrDelay= round(min(ArrDelay, na.rm=TRUE),2),
MaxDepDelay= round(max(DepDelay, na.rm=TRUE),2),
MaxArrDelay= round(max(ArrDelay, na.rm=TRUE),2))
```

DayOfWeek	Num Flights	Mean DepDelay	Mean ArrDelay	MinDep Delay	MinArr Delay	MaxDep Delay	MaxArr Delay
1	112	26.17	2.72	−12	−73	400	409
2	108	26.55	5.46	−15	−52	475	447
3	134	22.80	−6.98	−17	−67	335	287
4	140	15.32	−4.21	−14	−49	729	704
5	140	15.20	1.28	−11	−50	251	245
6	88	22.69	0.69	−15	−62	677	640
7	110	17.83	−7.04	−16	−52	302	256

7.1.2.5 Summing Values: function sum()

The sum is perhaps the most basic arithmetic operation, and it is also a useful aggregation operation with function sum(). The usage is intuitive, but strangely, it is sometimes confused with n(). The difference between the two should be clear: n() counts the number of rows for each group; implicitly, it executes an addition of course, but its scope is limited to just counting rows and nothing else. Function sum() is the generic sum applied to a certain column of numeric values; therefore, the column has to be of numeric type, and it suffers the same problem with missing values of mean(); they have to be handled with na.rm=TRUE. To clarify, let us return to the previous example with the number of cancelled flights. We wrote the following code:

```
df %>% group_by(DayOfWeek, Cancelled) %>%
    summarize(NumFlights= n())
```

DayOfWeek	Cancelled	NumFlights
1	0	77251
1	1	510
2	0	71488
2	1	1420
3	0	91614
3	1	594
…	…	…

If we look at this more closely, it is true that we have obtained the information required, but not just that; we have grouped flights based on the cancelled status, together with day of week, and then counted the rows. A better, more direct solution is to group for day of week only and sum up the values of column Cancelled, exploiting the fact that values are 1 and 0.

```
df %>% group_by(DayOfWeek) %>%
       summarize(NumCancelled= sum(Cancelled, na.rm=TRUE))
```

DayOfWeek	NumCancelled
1	510
2	1420
3	594
4	1279
5	1890
6	973
7	740

7.1.2.6 List of Aggregation Functions

Other aggregation functions exist, all with the same logic, as seen in previous examples. The following list is from the documentation of function `summarize()`; several of these are defined in package *base*, others in *stats*.

- Arithmetic mean and median: `mean()`, `median()`
- Standard deviation, interquartile range, median absolute deviation: `sd()`, `IQR()`, `mad()`
- Max, min, and quantiles: `min()`, `max()`, `quantile()`
- First, last, or *n*th value: `first()`, `last()`, `nth()`
- Counting rows: `n()`, `n_distinct()`
- Logical: `any()`, `all()`

7.1.3 Sorting Within Groups

Sorting data frames is one of the fundamental operations; it is easy and useful. With aggregated results, however, we need to consider a special case when we want to *sort rows within groups*, not on the whole data frame. Previously, we have seen an example where we sorted states by percentage of cancelled flights. That was a traditional sorting, all rows were sorted according to the values of a column.

But what if we add airports to the grouping variables and, for each state, we want to sort airports for cancelled flights? Let us try this. First, we add *Origin* to the grouping variables.

```
df %>% group_by(OriginStateName, Origin) %>%
  summarize(NumFlights= n(),
            PercentCancel= round(100*mean(Cancelled, na.rm=TRUE), 3))
```

OriginStateName	Origin	NumFlights	PercentCancel
Alabama	BHM	1267	1.342
Alabama	DHN	62	0.000

OriginStateName	Origin	NumFlights	PercentCancel
Alabama	HSV	664	0.904
Alabama	MGM	177	0.000
Alabama	MOB	217	1.843
Alaska	ADK	9	0.000
...	...	...	...

We have 338 groups, as many airports are in the data. Now we want to sort airports based on percent of cancelled flights, *for each state*. We can try adding the normal sorting.

```
df %>% group_by(OriginStateName, Origin) %>%
  summarize(NumFlights= n(),
            PercentCancel= round(100*mean(Cancelled, na.rm=TRUE),3)) %>%
  arrange(desc(PercentCancel))
```

OriginStateName	Origin	NumFlights	PercentCancel
Alaska	OTZ	62	22.581
Alaska	OME	62	19.355
Utah	VEL	54	16.667
Pennsylvania	LBE	31	12.903
Alaska	ADQ	58	12.069
Arizona	FLG	183	12.022
...	...	...	...

We have the whole data frame sorted for *PercentCancel*, but this is not what we asked. This way, we have lost the group organization in state names. Instead, we specified that we want airports sorted *for each state*, meaning that we want to keep the groups based on states, we do not want a flat list of airports. How can we do that? R makes things easy in this case, because it is just the attribute **.by_group** of function arrange() to be specified with a logical TRUE of FALSE (default).

```
df %>% group_by(OriginStateName, Origin) %>%
  summarize(NumFlights= n(),
            PercentCancel= round(100*mean(Cancelled, na.rm=TRUE),3)) %>%
  arrange(desc(PercentCancel), .by_group= TRUE)
```

OriginStateName	Origin	NumFlights	PercentCancel
Alabama	MOB	217	1.843
Alabama	BHM	1267	1.342
Alabama	HSV	664	0.904

(Continued)

OriginStateName	Origin	NumFlights	PercentCancel
Alabama	DHN	62	0.000
Alabama	MGM	177	0.000
Alaska	OTZ	62	22.581
...	...	...	...

This is correct, now we have sorted by percent of cancelled flights, for each state, not flatly over the whole data frame.

Let us look at another example. We want to calculate the average *TaxiOut* time of each departure airport, grouped by state. Next, we want to sort average taxi time for each state.

```
df %>% group_by(OriginStateName, Origin) %>%
  summarize(AvgTaxiOut= round(mean(TaxiOut, na.rm=TRUE),2)) %>%
  arrange(desc(AvgTaxiOut), .by_group= TRUE)
```

OriginStateName	Origin	AvgTaxiOut
Alabama	MGM	17.11
Alabama	DHN	16.37
Alabama	HSV	16.00
Alabama	MOB	15.64
Alabama	BHM	15.12
Alaska	FAI	16.54
...	...	...

7.1.4 Creation of Columns in Grouped Data Frames

An operation often required is to create new columns following grouping and aggregation. This is reasonable, with grouping and aggregation we produce new information that could be used for new calculated columns. In this case, the standard column creation method, the one directly assigning a value to the new column (e.g. *df$newCol= value*), is not well-suited. Much better using function `mutate()` in a pipe.

For example, we want to group the flights for airline, calculate mean airtime and distance and create a new column with mean speed as miles/hour and km/hour. The result should be sorted by mean speed.

```
df %>% group_by(Reporting_Airline) %>%
  summarize('AvgAirtime (minutes)'= round(mean(AirTime, na.rm=TRUE),2),
            'AvgDistance (miles)'= round(mean(Distance, na.rm=TRUE),2)) %>%
  mutate('AvgSpeed (mph)'= round('AvgDistance (miles)'/
                                ('AvgAirtime (minutes)'/60),2),
         'AvgSpeed (km/h)'= round(('AvgDistance (miles)'*1.60934)/
                                ('AvgAirtime (minutes)'/60),2)) %>%
  arrange(desc('AvgSpeed (mph)'))
```

Reporting_Airline	AvgAirtime (minutes)	AvgDistance (miles)	AvgSpeed (mph)	AvgSpeed (km/h)
AS	183.68	1401.39	457.77	736.71
HA	113.05	858.12	455.44	732.95
UA	149.87	1127.34	451.33	726.34
DL	128.00	941.00	441.09	709.87
F9	141.42	1039.27	440.93	709.60
B6	153.91	1126.08	438.99	706.48
AA	132.01	963.52	437.93	704.78
G4	127.24	926.31	436.80	702.96
NK	132.78	966.44	436.71	702.82
WN	101.47	716.87	423.89	682.18
…	…	…	…	…

We can enrich the example by adding the state as a grouping variable. We have two options: either specify (*OriginStateName, Reporting_Airline*) or (*Reporting_Airline, OriginStateName*), and order within groups. The presentation of results changes, it depends on context which one is better.

```
df %>% group_by(OriginStateName, Reporting_Airline) %>%
  summarize('AvgAirtime (minutes)'= round(mean(AirTime, na.rm=TRUE),2),
            'AvgDistance (miles)'= round(mean(Distance, na.rm=TRUE),2)) %>%
  mutate('AvgSpeed (mph)'= round('AvgDistance (miles)'/
                              ('AvgAirtime (minutes)'/60),2),
         'AvgSpeed (km/h)'= round(('AvgDistance (miles)'*1.60934)/
                              ('AvgAirtime (minutes)'/60),2)) %>%
  arrange(desc('AvgSpeed (mph)'), .by_group= TRUE) %>%
  select(1,2,5,6)
```

OriginStateName	Reporting_Airline	AvgSpeed (mph)	AvgSpeed (km/h)
Alabama	YX	436.87	703.07
Alabama	OH	392.95	632.39
Alabama	WN	392.45	631.58
Alabama	9E	369.10	594.01
Alabama	OO	364.22	586.16
Alabama	MQ	357.42	575.21
Alabama	AA	356.56	573.83
Alabama	DL	274.08	441.09
Alaska	UA	508.76	818.77
Alaska	DL	484.25	779.33
Alaska	AS	440.83	709.45
Arizona	B6	544.94	877.00
Arizona	DL	512.83	825.31

(Continued)

OriginStateName	Reporting_Airline	AvgSpeed (mph)	AvgSpeed (km/h)
Arizona	NK	505.28	813.16
Arizona	F9	503.99	811.09
...	...	...	...

```
df %>% group_by(Reporting_Airline,OriginStateName) %>%
  summarize('AvgAirtime (minutes)'= round(mean(AirTime, na.rm=TRUE),2),
            'AvgDistance (miles)'= round(mean(Distance, na.rm=TRUE),2)) %>%
  mutate('AvgSpeed (mph)'= round('AvgDistance (miles)'/
                          ('AvgAirtime (minutes)'/60),2),
         'AvgSpeed (km/h)'= round(('AvgDistance (miles)'*1.60934)/
                          ('AvgAirtime (minutes)'/60),2)) %>%
  arrange(desc('AvgSpeed (mph)'), .by_group= TRUE) %>%
  select(1,2,5,6)
```

Reporting_Airline	OriginStateName	AvgSpeed (mph)	AvgSpeed (km/h)
9E	Nebraska	538.12	866.03
9E	Oklahoma	505.40	813.36
9E	Texas	503.80	810.78
9E	Missouri	486.50	782.94
9E	Arkansas	446.46	718.50
9E	Florida	443.24	713.33
...	...	...	...

The combination *group_by()+summarize()+mutate()* is particularly flexible and adaptable to several cases. We will see it again, for example, with conditional operations, when we need to create a categorical variable from a continuous one, and in multicolumn operations.

7.1.5 Slicing Rows on Groups

Another very common requirement, when we have a grouped and aggregated data frame, is to somehow simplify the result by selecting only a few rows for each group. Typically, the criterion is based on column values, for example we want for each group the row with the highest value in a column or the lowest, or the *n* rows with the highest/lowest values for each group. This is often necessary in presentations and reports where it cannot be presented a table with hundreds of rows or more, a compact version is needed instead. Another criterion is to show just a sample of rows for each group. In all these cases, what we should do is slice rows *from each group*, not from the whole flat data frame, and for this we need some specialized functions.

7.1.5.1 Functions slice_*()
A family of functions for slicing from groups is provided by package *dplyr*, here generically referred to as slice_*(), where the symbol * indicates one of the existing variants: **slice_head()**, **slice_tail()**, **slice_min()**, **slice_max()**. Important arguments for these functions are:

- `n`: the number of rows to select.
- `prop`: the proportion of selected rows with respect to the number of rows of the group.
- `order_by`: the column whose values should be considered for selecting rows.

The first two attributes are mutually exclusive, either we specify the number of rows per group to return (e.g. "three rows," n=3) or the proportion (e.g. "30% of the rows," `prop=0.3`).

For the examples, we consider `slice_max()` and `slice_min()` that answer the common requirement of extracting for each group the n rows with the highest/lowest values for the given column. We want for each airline the three states with the highest average speed. It should be noticed that sorting with `arrange()` is no longer needed because the result of `slice_max()` is automatically sorted.

```
df %>% group_by(Reporting_Airline,OriginStateName) %>%
  summarize('AvgAirtime (minutes)'= round(mean(AirTime, na.rm=TRUE),2),
            'AvgDistance (miles)'= round(mean(Distance, na.rm=TRUE),2)) %>%
  mutate('AvgSpeed (mph)'= round('AvgDistance (miles)'/
                                 ('AvgAirtime (minutes)'/60),2),
         'AvgSpeed (km/h)'= round(('AvgDistance (miles)'*1.60934)/
                                  ('AvgAirtime (minutes)'/60),2)) %>%
  slice_max(n=3, order_by= 'AvgSpeed (km/h)') %>%
  select(1,2,5,6)
```

Reporting_Airline	OriginStateName	AvgSpeed (mph)	AvgSpeed (km/h)
9E	Nebraska	538.12	866.03
9E	Oklahoma	505.40	813.36
9E	Texas	503.80	810.78
AA	Hawaii	563.51	906.88
AA	California	520.86	838.25
AA	Nevada	517.92	833.51
AS	Hawaii	525.88	846.32
AS	Washington	477.34	768.21
AS	California	467.40	752.20

Now, we want for each origin state, the two airlines with a shorter average distance of their flights.

```
df %>% group_by(OriginStateName,Reporting_Airline) %>%
  summarize('AvgAirtime (minutes)'= round(mean(AirTime, na.rm=TRUE),2),
            'AvgDistance (miles)'= round(mean(Distance, na.rm=TRUE),2)) %>%
  mutate('AvgSpeed (mph)'= round('AvgDistance (miles)'/
                                 ('AvgAirtime (minutes)'/60),2),
         'AvgSpeed (km/h)'= round(('AvgDistance (miles)'*1.60934)/
                                  ('AvgAirtime (minutes)'/60),2)) %>%
  slice_min(n=2, order_by= 'AvgDistance (miles)') %>%
  select(1,2,4)
```

OriginStateName	Reporting_Airline	AvgDistance (miles)
Alabama	DL	152.80
Alabama	9E	318.72
Alaska	AS	772.63
Alaska	DL	1,599.33
Arizona	OO	512.63
Arizona	MQ	590.34
Arkansas	WN	408.09
Arkansas	OO	465.84
California	OO	469.15
California	WN	612.81
…	…	…

For the other variants of `slice_*()`, the usage is the same.

7.1.5.2 Combination of Functions `filter()` and `rank()`

There is an alternative to `slice_min()` and `slice_max()` that makes use of more basic functions `filter()`, the traditional function for selecting rows based on a logical condition, and a particular one, **`rank()`** that produces the Boolean mask needed by the `filter()`. The logic is that `rank()` implicitly orders group rows. It is implicit because it does not actually sort the rows, but for each element, it calculates its rank, whether it is the first, the second, the *n*th, etc. Let us look at a simple didactic example to understand what `rank()` does.

```
items= c("Mary","John","Ulf","Aaron","Zelda")

rank(items)

[1] 3 2 4 1 5
```

So, rank produces a series with the same size of the data, and for each element, it shows the position (the rank) of the element if the data were ordered increasingly (ascending), either numerically or lexicographically. The second step is that we can specify a logical condition on the result of `rank()` based on the position. The result of this is a series of Boolean values. For example, we ask for the positions lesser than three, meaning the first and the second element (we could have specified <= 2).

```
rank(items) < 3

[1] FALSE  TRUE FALSE  TRUE FALSE
```

This is the answer: a series of Boolean values with TRUE for elements that satisfy the condition and FALSE for the others. It also looks very much like a Boolean mask, making it useful for `filter()`. What if we want to extract the rows with rank lesser than three? We just need a simple transformation of the series into a data frame, and for convenience, we also set the column name to *Name*. Then we just use `filter()` with the result of `rank()` as a Boolean mask.

```
# transform series items into dataframe test
test= as_tibble(items)

# give name 'Name' to the column
colnames(test)[1] <- "Name"

test %>% filter(rank(Name) < 3)
# A tibble: 2 × 1
  Name
  <chr>
1 John
2 Aaron
```

The result is not sorted, but correct, John and Aaron are actually the second and the first elements of the ordered series. What if instead we want the last two elements, those with higher rank? The trivial solution is to adjust the logical condition, rather than *lesser than three*, we use *greater or equal to four*, meaning the 4th and the 5th elements, Ulf and Zelda.

```
rank(items) >= 4

[1] FALSE FALSE  TRUE FALSE  TRUE
```

However, this way is inconvenient because we have to consider the actual size of the series and make the calculation. If the length is five, then we should specify >= 4, if the length is 18860, we should specify >= 18859, and if it is 362252378292927734646, we should specify >= 362252378292927734645. Truly awkward. There is a much better way: If we want the elements with higher ranks, it suffices to sort the items in descending order, and the highest-ranked elements are on top. Then we can express the logical condition as lesser than, instead of greater than.

```
test %>% filter(rank(desc(Name)) <= 2)

# A tibble: 2 × 1
  Name
  <chr>
1 Ulf
2 Zelda
```

This way is easy, and we use the same logic in the two cases. If this mechanism is clear, then applying it to our real example with flights is straightforward.

Functions `slice_min()` and `slice_max()` are easier, more intuitive, and produce an ordered result, then they are preferred in most cases, but the combination *filter()+rank()* is a lower-level implementation of the same feature that could be adapted to unconventional situations. First, we replicate the two examples with `slice_min()` and `slice_max()` to analyze the details of the combination *filter()+rank()*, then we consider an unusual case.

First, the two airlines with shorter average distance of their flights for each origin state.

```
df %>% group_by(OriginStateName,Reporting_Airline) %>%
  summarize('AvgAirtime (minutes)'= round(mean(AirTime, na.rm=TRUE),2),
            'AvgDistance (miles)'= round(mean(Distance, na.rm=TRUE),2)) %>%
  mutate('AvgSpeed (mph)'= round('AvgDistance (miles)'/
                              ('AvgAirtime (minutes)'/60),2),
         'AvgSpeed (km/h)'= round(('AvgDistance (miles)'*1.60934)/
                              ('AvgAirtime (minutes)'/60),2)) %>%
  filter(rank('AvgDistance (miles)') < 3) %>%
  select(1,2,4)
```

OriginStateName	Reporting_Airline	AvgDistance (miles)
Alabama	9E	318.72
Alabama	DL	152.80
Alaska	AS	772.63
Alaska	DL	1,599.33
Arizona	MQ	590.34
Arizona	OO	512.63
Arkansas	OO	465.84
Arkansas	WN	408.09
California	OO	469.15
California	WN	612.81
...	...	...

Then the three states with the highest average speed for each airline.

```
df %>% group_by(Reporting_Airline,OriginStateName) %>%
  summarize('AvgAirtime (minutes)'= round(mean(AirTime, na.rm=TRUE),2),
            'AvgDistance (miles)'= round(mean(Distance, na.rm=TRUE),2)) %>%
  mutate('AvgSpeed (mph)'= round('AvgDistance (miles)'/
                              ('AvgAirtime (minutes)'/60),2),
         'AvgSpeed (km/h)'= round(('AvgDistance (miles)'*1.60934)/
                              ('AvgAirtime (minutes)'/60),2)) %>%
  filter(rank(desc('AvgSpeed (km/h)')) <=3 ) %>%
  select(1,2,5,6)
```

Reporting_Airline	OriginStateName	AvgSpeed (mph)	AvgSpeed (km/h)
9E	Nebraska	538.12	866.03
9E	Oklahoma	505.40	813.36
9E	Texas	503.80	810.78
AA	California	520.86	838.25
AA	Hawaii	563.51	906.88

Reporting_Airline	OriginStateName	AvgSpeed (mph)	AvgSpeed (km/h)
AA	Hawaii	563.51	906.88
AA	Nevada	517.92	833.51
AS	California	467.40	752.20
AS	Hawaii	525.88	846.32
AS	Washington	477.34	768.21
...	...	...	...

These were easy, but there is no advantage in using *filter()+rank()* over *slice_max()* and *slice_min()*, on the contrary, the latter case is better, more intuitive, and returns the result already sorted, which instead should be done separately using *filter()+rank()*. However, as said, base solutions often have the virtue of being particularly adaptable to uncommon cases, so let us consider one. We still want to slice over groups of rows, but we want some rows with the highest values and some other rows with the lowest values. In other terms, we want to show the head and the tail for each group, which is not a case that uncommon. How can we do that? Of course, it is easy to do it separately, but that is not what we have asked.

For example, for each airline and state, we want *the highest and the lowest average speed*. Clearly, it is some kind of logical condition, but how can we implement it with `slice_max()` and `slice_min()`? There is no evident way to do it; we should probably figure out something ad-hoc. The difference is that with *filter()+rank()*, which are already expressed as a logical condition, it suffices to compose the two conditions the usual way with the OR operator. We can sort the results for each group so that min and max average speed are always in the same order.

```
df %>% group_by(Reporting_Airline, OriginStateName) %>%
  summarize('AvgAirtime (minutes)'= round(mean(AirTime, na.rm=TRUE),2),
            'AvgDistance (miles)'= round(mean(Distance, na.rm=TRUE),2)) %>%
  mutate('AvgSpeed (mph)'= round('AvgDistance (miles)'/
                        ('AvgAirtime (minutes)'/60),2),
         'AvgSpeed (km/h)'= round(('AvgDistance (miles)'*1.60934)/
                        ('AvgAirtime (minutes)'/60),2)) %>%
  filter( (rank(desc('AvgSpeed (km/h)')) < 2) |
          (rank('AvgSpeed (km/h)') < 2)
        ) %>%
  arrange('AvgSpeed (km/h)', .by_group=TRUE) %>%
  select(1,2,5,6)
```

Reporting_Airline	OriginStateName	AvgSpeed (mph)	AvgSpeed (km/h)
9E	Connecticut	171.91	276.67
9E	Nebraska	538.12	866.03
AA	Kansas	342.56	551.29
AA	Hawaii	563.51	906.88
AS	Wyoming	385.43	620.30
AS	Hawaii	525.88	846.32

(Continued)

Reporting_Airline	OriginStateName	AvgSpeed (mph)	AvgSpeed (km/h)
B6	U.S. Virgin Islands	197.87	318.43
B6	New Mexico	546.90	880.14
DL	Alabama	274.08	441.09
DL	Hawaii	557.39	897.02
...	...	...	...

This is an example of why studying base methods is not worthless, even when there are higher-level functions better suited for (almost) all cases.

7.1.6 Calculated Columns with Group Values

Lastly, we consider a common case that might be tricky for figuring out the best way to proceed. The problem is when we have a data frame, neither grouped nor aggregated, and we want to create a new column with calculated values, but these values have to depend on columns of the data frame *and on aggregated values referred to groups*.

For example, we may consider taxi times of the flights (columns *TaxiIn* and *TaxiOut*), which might provide a relevant knowledge regarding situations of air traffic congestion. An information we may find interesting to have is the ratio between taxi times of single flights and *the average taxi time of the specific airport* of departure or arrival. That would be a more precise and valuable information than referring the taxi time to the national average time, which aggregates so many different situations that it probably has little value as an information. However, to calculate that ratio, we need to do what we have described at the beginning, to use values obtained from the grouped and aggregated data frame, for a column of the non-grouped and non-aggregated original data frame.

One could think about first creating a grouped and aggregated data frame with average taxi times for each airport. That is the easy part. Secondly, he/she should devise an ad-hoc procedure, that for each flight, retrieves the origin or destination airports, goes to the aggregated data frame, selects the airports, retrieves the average taxi time, goes back to the non-aggregated data frame, calculates the ratio for the single flight, then moves to the next flight and repeats. A lot more complicated than what is needed. There is a smarter way to proceed.

The key is to not aggregate data; *therefore, avoid using* `summarize()`. We do not need it in this case, because we need the aggregated statistics (the mean taxi time for each airport), but not the aggregated form of the data frame. So, do not use `summarize()` to create a second data frame and instead create a new column in the original, not aggregated data frame with the statistic. Let us look at an example with origin airports and taxi times before takeoff.

We start by selecting few columns for better readability, then we group by airport and create a new column with the statistic we need (mean taxi out time). The value is the average taxi out time for the airport, and correctly, it is the same for all flights with same origin airport. The data frame is still non-aggregated, 580 000+ rows.

```
df %>% select(FlightDate, Reporting_Airline, Tail_Number,
              Origin, TaxiOut) %>%
  group_by(Origin) %>%
  mutate(AvgTaxiOut= round(mean(TaxiOut, na.rm= TRUE), 1))
```

FlightDate	Reporting_Airline	Tail_Number	Origin	TaxiOut	AvgTaxiOut
2023-03-13	OH	N609NN	TRI	9	15.2
2023-03-15	OH	N561NN	TRI	15	15.2
2023-03-16	OH	N615NN	TRI	11	15.2
2023-03-17	OH	N547NN	TRI	10	15.2
2023-03-19	OH	N572NN	TRI	21	15.2
2023-03-20	OH	N572NN	TRI	27	15.2
2023-03-22	OH	N549NN	TRI	14	15.2
2023-03-23	OH	N589NN	TRI	15	15.2
2023-03-24	OH	N597NN	TRI	14	15.2
2023-03-26	OH	N565NN	TRI	NA	15.2
...	...	...	...	...	...

At this point, creating the new column *TaxiIndex* with the ratio between taxi time of a flight and the average taxi time of the corresponding airport is trivial; we have the required information. We can even remove the *AvgTaxiOut* column from the final result.

```
df %>% select(FlightDate, Reporting_Airline, Tail_Number,
              Origin, TaxiOut) %>%
  group_by(Origin) %>%
  mutate(
    AvgTaxiOut= round(mean(TaxiOut, na.rm= TRUE),1),
    TaxiIndex= round(TaxiOut/AvgTaxiOut, 2)) %>%
  select(-AvgTaxiOut)
```

FlightDate	Reporting_Airline	Tail_Number	Origin	TaxiOut	TaxiIndex
2023-03-13	OH	N609NN	TRI	9	0.59
2023-03-15	OH	N561NN	TRI	15	0.99
2023-03-16	OH	N615NN	TRI	11	0.72
2023-03-17	OH	N547NN	TRI	10	0.66
2023-03-19	OH	N572NN	TRI	21	1.38
2023-03-20	OH	N572NN	TRI	27	1.78
2023-03-22	OH	N549NN	TRI	14	0.92
2023-03-23	OH	N589NN	TRI	15	0.99
2023-03-24	OH	N597NN	TRI	14	0.92
2023-03-26	OH	N565NN	TRI	NA	NA
...	...	...	...	...	...

For a more compact version, we could avoid creating the intermediate *AvgTaxiOut* column and directly calculate average taxi times in the formula of the new column.

```
df %>% select(FlightDate, Reporting_Airline, Tail_Number,
              Origin, TaxiOut) %>%
  group_by(Origin) %>%
  mutate(TaxiIndex= round(TaxiOut/mean(TaxiOut, na.rm= TRUE),2))
```

The result is the same of the previous case; however, the addition of a new intermediate column calculated with *group_by()+mutate()* is not in general useful only to demonstrate the logic; there are cases where it is more convenient to have it, then use the column name for following computations, and at last remove it from the final result.

Once explained, the solution is simple, but it requires to have understood the logic of aggregation operations, it is one thing to compute statistics, which are by definition aggregated results, and another one to present the data frame in an aggregated form. Statistical and arithmetic functions like mean(), median(), sum(), n(), sd(), etc. calculate aggregated results; summarize() transforms the grouped data frame in the aggregated form. It is recommended to practice with these combinations of functions to grasp all the details and possible variants.

7.2 Python: Groups

In this section, we reproduce the examples seen in the previous one, again using the dataset of the US domestic flights of March 2023, which is particularly useful for practicing with groups. Pandas offers functionalities very similar to those discussed for R; the logic is the same and also the syntax is alike. As usual, the main difference lies in the role of indexes, which are relevant in pandas data frames.

The main pandas function to define indexed groups on a data frame is **groupby()** (the difference with R is just the underscore, here missing); the one for aggregation operations is **aggregate()**, with the shortened alias **agg()**.

We read the dataset and select a subset of columns. Differently than R function vroom() that could read the CSV dataset compressed in the ZIP file even if it is not the only file included, the regular pd.read_csv() cannot (same for the corresponding read_csv() of R). It exists a specific *zipfile* module (https://docs.python.org/3/library/zipfile.html) that could be imported (from zipfile import ZipFile) and allows opening the included CSV file even when it is not the only file of the ZIP. In most cases it is not really necessary, but we try it to show the usage.

First, the specific CSV file included in the ZIP should be opened with the base Python **open** function. This operation does not read the content of the file or create a data frame object immediately usable. To open the file means to physically access the content and store it in a variable (*data*).

```
import numpy as np
import pandas as pd

from zipfile import ZipFile

with ZipFile("datasets/Bureau_Trans_Stats/Flights_March2023.zip") as myzip:
    with myzip.open("On_Time_Reporting_Carrier_On_Time_
                     Performance_(1987_present)_2023_3.csv") as myfile:
data= myfile.read()
```

Now *data* has the content of the CSV, but there is one additional problem, *data* is of type *bytes*, it is not a file path or a file-like object that the `pd.read_csv()` can read. This is why we need a further conversion provided by module ***ByteIO***.

```
from io import BytesIO

df= pd.read_csv(BytesIO(data),
                usecols=[4,5,6,9,14,15,16,18,23,24,25,27,30,
                        31,36,37,38,39,41,42,47,49,52,54])
```

Alternatively, if the hassle of going through this procedure is not worth it, the ZIP file could simply be manually decompressed, and the CSV could be read as usual:

```
df= pd.read_csv("datasets/Bureau_Trans_Stats/Flights_March2023/
    On_Time_Reporting_Carrier_On_Time_Performance_(1987_present)_2023_3.csv",
    usecols=[4,5,6,9,14,15,16,18,23,24,25,27,30,
            31,36,37,38,39,41,42,47,49,52,54])
```

One way or the other, we have read the dataset.

These are the US domestic flights for March 2023. It is a large dataset of more than 580 000 observations and 110 variables, of which 24 we have selected. The description of columns has been shown in Table 7.1 of the previous section, and it is available on the Bureau of Public Transportation's web site (https://transtats.bts.gov/Fields.asp?gnoyr_VQ=FGJ).

Column *FlightDate* is of type *object*; it should be converted into *datetime* with format *yyyy-mm-dd*.

```
df.FlightDate= pd.to_datetime(df.FlightDate, format='%Y-%m-%d')
```

We can observe some information about these data.

```
df.info()

<class 'pandas.core.frame.DataFrame'>
RangeIndex: 580322 entries, 0 to 580321
Data columns (total 24 columns):
 #   Column            Non-Null Count    Dtype
---  ------            --------------    -----
 0   DayOfWeek         580322 non-null   int64
 1   FlightDate        580322 non-null   datetime64[ns]
 2   Reporting_Airline 580322 non-null   object
 3   Tail_Number       579561 non-null   object
 4   Origin            580322 non-null   object
 5   OriginCityName    580322 non-null   object
 6   OriginState       580322 non-null   object
 7   OriginStateName   580322 non-null   object
 8   Dest              580322 non-null   object
 9   DestCityName      580322 non-null   object
 10  DestState         580322 non-null   object
```

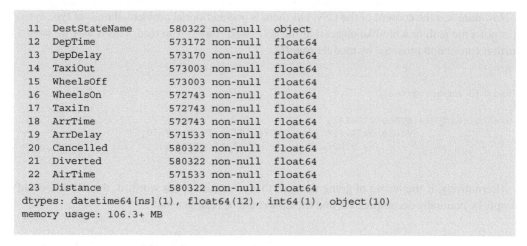

```
   11   DestStateName      580322 non-null   object
   12   DepTime            573172 non-null   float64
   13   DepDelay           573170 non-null   float64
   14   TaxiOut            573003 non-null   float64
   15   WheelsOff          573003 non-null   float64
   16   WheelsOn           572743 non-null   float64
   17   TaxiIn             572743 non-null   float64
   18   ArrTime            572743 non-null   float64
   19   ArrDelay           571533 non-null   float64
   20   Cancelled          580322 non-null   float64
   21   Diverted           580322 non-null   float64
   22   AirTime            571533 non-null   float64
   23   Distance           580322 non-null   float64
dtypes: datetime64[ns](1), float64(12), int64(1), object(10)
memory usage: 106.3+ MB
```

Table 7.1 Columns selected from the US domestic flight dataset.

Column	Description
DayOfWeek	Day of week (number)
FlightDate	Flight Date (yyyy-mm-dd)
Reporting_Airline	Carrier Code
Tail_Number	Tail Number
Origin	Origin Airport
OriginCityName	Origin Airport, City Name
OriginState	Origin Airport, State Code
OriginStateName	Origin Airport, State Name
Dest	Destination Airport
DestCityName	Destination Airport, City Name
DestState	Destination Airport, State Code
DestStateName	Destination Airport, State Name
DepTime	Actual Departure Time (local time: hhmm)
DepDelay	Difference in minutes between scheduled and actual departure time. Early departures are in negative numbers
TaxiOut	Taxi Out Time (minutes)
WheelsOff	Wheels Off Time (local time: hhmm)
WheelsOn	Wheels On Time (local time: hhmm)
TaxiIn	Taxi In Time (minutes)
ArrTime	Actual Arrival Time (local time: hhmm)
ArrDelay	Difference in minutes between scheduled and actual arrival time. Early arrivals are in negative numbers.
Cancelled	Cancelled Flight Indicator (1=Yes)
Diverted	Diverted Flight Indicator (1=Yes)
AirTime	Flight Time (minutes)
Distance	Distance between airports (miles)

Several missing values are present in different columns, for example, in departure and arrival time (*DepTime* and *ArrTime*). Particular attention should be paid to the fact that values of columns *DepDelay* and *ArrDelay* could be positive or negative, with negative values meaning early departures or arrivals and positive values meaning late departures and arrivals.

```
df[['FlightDate','Reporting_Airline','DepDelay','ArrDelay']].sample(10)
```

	FlightDate	Reporting_Airline	DepDelay	ArrDelay
424148	2023-03-29	YX	−3.0	−5.0
141038	2023-03-15	DL	23.0	−6.0
144224	2023-03-01	DL	−2.0	−17.0
166235	2023-03-26	DL	6.0	−17.0
126657	2023-03-06	UA	5.0	−6.0
406153	2023-03-13	YX	−7.0	−1.0
169039	2023-03-22	DL	−6.0	−12.0
2327	2023-03-19	OH	−1.0	−16.0
345250	2023-03-26	WN	46.0	89.0
93032	2023-03-26	UA	−1.0	−8.0

7.2.1 Group Index and Aggregation Operations

7.2.1.1 Functions `groupby()` and `aggregate()`

We start with some simple examples. First, we want to group rows by the origin state of the flight and the destination state. This way, we expect to be able to manage all flights connecting airports of a certain state with airports of another state and produce statistics accordingly, like all flights from Pennsylvania to Florida, or from California to Texas, and so forth.

```
df1= df.groupby(["OriginState","DestState"])

<pandas.core.groupby.generic.DataFrameGroupBy object at 0x7fce36a24250>
```

The result is an indexed data frame of type *DataFrameGroupBy*, ready for further operations on the defined groups, such as aggregation, selection, or transformation operations.

7.2.1.2 Counting Rows, Computing Arithmetic Means, and Sum for Each Group

We start with some of the most common statistics on groups. First, we find the average flight duration for each group. One column is *AirTime*, with the duration of each flight. We want the arithmetic mean for each group of *(Origin State, Destination State)*. Since it is a single operation, the `aggregate()` function is not needed; we can just use `mean()`.

```
df1[["AirTime"]].mean().round(1)
```

		AirTime
OriginState	**DestState**	
AK	**AK**	53.0
	AZ	304.4
	CA	283.3
	CO	283.6
	HI	346.5
...	...	...
WY	**NJ**	216.2
	NY	212.2
	TX	139.9
	UT	44.7
	WA	96.7

The result has 1233 rows, corresponding to the pairs *(Origin State, Destination State)*, and on rows, the multi-index has two levels, corresponding to the two columns specified in the pd.groupby(). The first observation related to the definition of groups is that the columns become index levels, with levels corresponding to the order of writing in the pd.groupby() function.

Now we also add the number of flights for each pair of states; this means we need to count the number of rows for each group. We use function **count()**, and this time we also need function aggregate() to specify both operations.

```
df.groupby(["OriginState","DestState"])[["AirTime"]].\
agg(['mean','count']).round(1)
```

		AirTime	
		mean	**count**
OriginState	**DestState**		
AK	AK	53.0	1486
	AZ	304.4	28
	CA	283.3	31
	CO	283.6	30
	HI	346.5	72
...	...	...	...
WY	NJ	216.2	25
	NY	212.2	4
	TX	139.9	84
	UT	44.7	124
	WA	96.7	12

We may add other columns to use for aggregate results, for example, *Distance*, and we still want the average value, plus the maximum and the minimum. Adding the counting of rows is useless since it will be the same as the one already calculated for *AirTime*. The syntax changes a little because now we need to specify the association between a column and the operations. It takes a syntax typical of the *dictionary (dict)* data structure composed of *key:value* pairs between curly brackets.

```
df2= df.groupby(["OriginState","DestState"])[["AirTime","Distance"]].\
aggregate({"AirTime":['mean','count'],
          "Distance":['mean','max','min']}).round(1)
```

		AirTime		Distance		
		mean	count	mean	max	min
OriginState	DestState					
AK	AK	53.0	1486	337.3	1192.0	31.0
	AZ	304.4	28	2552.0	2552.0	2552.0
	CA	283.3	31	2345.0	2345.0	2345.0
	CO	283.6	30	2405.0	2405.0	2405.0
	HI	346.5	72	2813.3	2874.0	2777.0
...	...	...	...	...	...	...
WY	NJ	216.2	25	1874.0	1874.0	1874.0
	NY	212.2	4	1887.0	1887.0	1887.0
	TX	139.9	84	1109.6	1265.0	1047.0
	UT	44.7	124	233.8	320.0	205.0
	WA	96.7	12	621.0	621.0	621.0

Here we can also observe a clear example with multi-indexes, on rows and on columns, both with two levels. Let us look at the columns.

```
df2.columns

MultiIndex([( 'AirTime',    'mean'),
           ( 'AirTime',   'count'),
           ('Distance',    'mean'),
           ('Distance',     'max'),
           ('Distance',     'min')],
          )
```

We have five columns, each one with a two-level name. If we want to slice the data frame by columns, we need to use those composed names. Parentheses are needed in this case to indicate that it is a single column name.

```
df2[[('AirTime','mean'), ('Distance','mean')]]
```

OriginState	DestState	AirTime mean	Distance mean
AK	AK	53.0	337.3
	AZ	304.4	2552.0
	CA	283.3	2345.0
	CO	283.6	2405.0
	HI	346.5	2813.3
...	...	...	...
WY	NJ	216.2	1874.0
	NY	212.2	1887.0
	TX	139.9	1109.6
	UT	44.7	233.8
	WA	96.7	621.0

We can see an example with `sum()` and *datetime* functions. We want to obtain the total number of cancelled or diverted flights per day. Checking the documentation of this dataset, we know that value 0 in columns *Cancelled* and *Diverted* means that the flight has been operated regularly, and value 1 means that it was cancelled or diverted. Then, summing up the values of the two columns, we retrieve the number of cancelled or diverted flights.

```
df.groupby(df.FlightDate.dt.day)[['Cancelled','Diverted']].agg('sum')
```

FlightDate	Cancelled	Diverted
1	144.0	79.0
2	527.0	63.0
3	653.0	176.0
4	500.0	22.0
5	74.0	24.0
6	56.0	23.0
7	42.0	8.0
8	38.0	24.0
9	135.0	83.0
10	191.0	42.0
...	...	...

If we still want to know the detailed information for each pair of states, we have to group accordingly.

```
df.groupby(["OriginState", "DestState", df.FlightDate.dt.day])
    [['Cancelled','Diverted']].agg('sum')
```

			Cancelled	Diverted
OriginState	**DestState**	**FlightDate**		
AK	AK	**1**	20.0	4.0
		2	4.0	2.0
		3	3.0	0.0
		4	7.0	0.0
		5	7.0	0.0
...	...	...	...	...
WY	WA	**11**	0.0	0.0
		12	0.0	0.0
		13	0.0	0.0
		18	0.0	0.0
		25	0.0	0.0

7.2.2 Names on Columns with Aggregated Values

A multi-index on columns is often just an inconvenience; better would be to have flat names. There are different ways to transform the column multi-index into a list of flat column names, but one method is probably the best because it prevents the multi-index to be created. The syntax requires using function **NamedAgg()** with two attributes, `column` and `aggfunc`, whose specification could be omitted. With function NamedAgg(), it is no longer needed to explicitly slice the data frame columns with double square brackets because they are specified as function attributes. We replicate the previous example.

```
df1= df.groupby(["OriginState","DestState"]).aggregate(
    MeanAirTime= pd.NamedAgg(column= "AirTime", aggfunc= 'mean'),
    NumFlights= pd.NamedAgg(column= "AirTime", aggfunc= 'count'),
    MeanDist= pd.NamedAgg("Distance",'mean'),
    MaxDist= pd.NamedAgg("Distance",'max'),
    MinDist= pd.NamedAgg("Distance",'min')).round(1)
df1
```

		MeanAirTime	NumFlights	MeanDist	MaxDist	MinDist
OriginState	**DestState**					
AK	AK	53.0	1486	337.3	1192.0	31.0
	AZ	304.4	28	2552.0	2552.0	2552.0
	CA	283.3	31	2345.0	2345.0	2345.0

(Continued)

		MeanAirTime	NumFlights	MeanDist	MaxDist	MinDist
	CO	283.6	30	2405.0	2405.0	2405.0
	HI	346.5	72	2813.3	2874.0	2777.0
...	...	...	...	...	...	...
WY	NJ	216.2	25	1874.0	1874.0	1874.0
	NY	212.2	4	1887.0	1887.0	1887.0
	TX	139.9	84	1109.6	1265.0	1047.0
	UT	44.7	124	233.8	320.0	205.0
	WA	96.7	12	621.0	621.0	621.0

7.2.3 Sorting Columns

Sorting is one of the most basic operations on data frames. Pandas function for sorting column values is **sort_values()** with attribute **by** to specify the column(s) and ascending *True/False* for the criteria. Continuing with the previous example, we want to sort flights by mean airtime.

```
df1.sort_values(by= 'MeanAirTime', ascending= False)
```

OriginState	DestState	MeanAirTime	NumFlights	MeanDist	MaxDist	MinDist
MA	HI	666.2	17	5095.0	5095.0	5095.0
NY	HI	656.3	60	4983.0	4983.0	4983.0
NJ	HI	641.8	35	4955.4	4962.0	4904.0
VA	HI	627.0	18	4817.0	4817.0	4817.0
GA	HI	580.6	55	4471.0	4502.0	4431.0
...	...	...	...	...	...	...
KS	KS	22.6	114	81.5	88.0	74.0
VI	PR	20.6	34	68.0	68.0	68.0
MS	MS	20.2	28	69.0	69.0	69.0
IA	IA	19.5	54	61.0	61.0	61.0
PR	VI	18.2	29	68.0	68.0	68.0

Flights from the East Coast to Hawaii are the longest in time, more than 10 hours, while flights from Puerto Rico (PR) and U.S. Virgin Islands (VI) are the shortest, less than 20 minutes.

Sorting for number of flights shows that internal flights connecting California or Texas airports are by far the most numerous. Considering different states for origin and destination, New York and Florida are the most connected.

```
df1.sort_values(by= 'NumFlights', ascending= False)
```

		MeanAirTime	NumFlights	MeanDist	MaxDist	MinDist
OriginState	**DestState**					
CA	CA	59.4	16955	356.3	577.0	77.0
TX	TX	49.0	12513	280.4	677.0	89.0
HI	HI	27.9	6686	136.0	263.0	84.0
NY	FL	149.1	6112	1031.8	1334.0	828.0
FL	NY	136.9	6105	1031.9	1334.0	828.0
...	...	...	...	...	...	...
LA	OH	119.0	1	917.0	917.0	917.0
OR	MI	206.0	1	1833.0	1833.0	1833.0
MS	FL	82.0	1	588.0	588.0	588.0
NH	PA	66.0	1	289.0	289.0	289.0
PA	NH	52.0	1	289.0	289.0	289.0

We now use information about early or late departures and arrivals on flights from California to New York state.

```
df2= df.query(" OriginState=='CA' & DestState=='NY'").\
groupby(["OriginCityName","DestCityName"]).agg(
  MeanAirTime= pd.NamedAgg(column= "AirTime", aggfunc= 'mean'),
  NumFlights= pd.NamedAgg(column= "AirTime", aggfunc= 'count'),
  MeanDepDel= pd.NamedAgg(column= "DepDelay", aggfunc= "mean"),
  MeanArrDel= pd.NamedAgg(column= "ArrDelay", aggfunc= "mean"),
  ).round(1)
```

		MeanAirTime	NumFlights	MeanDepDel	MeanArrDel
OriginCityName	**DestCityName**				
Burbank, CA	New York, NY	267.1	26	52.7	31.3
Los Angeles, CA	Buffalo, NY	264.0	1	13.0	10.0
	New York, NY	273.1	827	20.5	−1.4
Ontario, CA	New York, NY	269.3	31	105.8	88.4
Palm Springs, CA	New York, NY	258.7	30	47.8	34.5
Sacramento, CA	New York, NY	277.5	30	12.2	1.8
San Diego, CA	New York, NY	268.9	227	15.5	−1.5
San Francisco, CA	New York, NY	282.9	642	20.0	3.6
San Jose, CA	New York, NY	283.3	6	28.2	21.2
Santa Ana, CA	New York, NY	272.3	31	12.6	−0.1

In sorting, we can specify more columns with different sorting criteria. The logic is that rows will be sorted on the first specified column, for equal values, they will be sorted on the second specified column and so on. Columns and sorting criteria are specified as lists. Index levels could be specified together with columns. Here we sort for destination city name (with *DestCityName* being an index level), in ascending order, and for average arrival delay (*MeanArrDel*, a column), descending.

```
df2.sort_values(by= ['DestCityName','MeanArrDel'], ascending= [True,False])
```

OriginCityName	DestCityName	MeanAirTime	NumFlights	MeanDepDel	MeanArrDel
Los Angeles, CA	Buffalo, NY	264.0	1	13.0	10.0
Ontario, CA	New York, NY	269.3	31	105.8	88.4
Palm Springs, CA	New York, NY	258.7	30	47.8	34.5
Burbank, CA	New York, NY	267.1	26	52.7	31.3
San Jose, CA	New York, NY	283.3	6	28.2	21.2
San Francisco, CA	New York, NY	282.9	642	20.0	3.6
Sacramento, CA	New York, NY	277.5	30	12.2	1.8
Santa Ana, CA	New York, NY	272.3	31	12.6	−0.1
Los Angeles, CA	New York, NY	273.1	827	20.5	−1.4
San Diego, CA	New York, NY	268.9	227	15.5	−1.5

7.2.4 Sorting on Index Levels

When sorting is done on index levels only, there is a different function, **sort_index()** that has attribute **level** to specify levels, rather than attribute by to specify columns. The logic is the same as before. We can sort for the two index levels, departure city (*OriginCityName*) and arrival city (*DestCityName*). As we have seen before, also sort_values() works with index levels, the difference between the two is that with the sort_index() either numerical index levels or index names could be used, while the sort_values() only accepts names.

```
# with numerical index levels
df2.sort_index(level= [0,1], ascending= True)

# these two forms work, too
# df2.sort_index(level= ['OriginCityName','DestCityName'], ascending= True)
# df2.sort_values(by= ['OriginCityName','DestCityName'], ascending= True)

# this one does not work
# df2.sort_values(by= [0,1], ascending= True)
```

OriginCityName	DestCityName	MeanAirTime	NumFlights	MeanDepDel	MeanArrDel
Burbank, CA	New York, NY	267.1	26	52.7	31.3
Los Angeles, CA	Buffalo, NY	264.0	1	13.0	10.0
	New York, NY	273.1	827	20.5	−1.4

OriginCityName	DestCityName	MeanAirTime	NumFlights	MeanDepDel	MeanArrDel
Ontario, CA	New York, NY	269.3	31	105.8	88.4
Palm Springs, CA	New York, NY	258.7	30	47.8	34.5
Sacramento, CA	New York, NY	277.5	30	12.2	1.8
San Diego, CA	New York, NY	268.9	227	15.5	−1.5
San Francisco, CA	New York, NY	282.9	642	20.0	3.6
San Jose, CA	New York, NY	283.3	6	28.2	21.2
Santa Ana, CA	New York, NY	272.3	31	12.6	−0.1

7.2.5 Slicing Rows on Groups

As seen in the corresponding R section, this is the case when, given groups, we want to select some rows from each group according to a certain criterion. The typical criteria are based on values of one or more columns such as: for each group the *n* rows with higher/lower values on column *x*. This situation is very common, for example for presentation purposes, when we have groups with possibly a large number of observations, but just the most relevant, according to a certain criterion, are worth considering.

For instance, for each airline (column *Reporting_Airline*), we want to obtain the average departure delay (column *DepDelay*) for each state (column *OriginState*).

```
df.groupby(['Reporting_Airline','OriginState']).agg({'DepDelay':'mean'})./
        round(2)
```

Reporting_Airline	OriginState	DepDelay
9E	AL	8.16
	AR	6.31
	CT	0.00
	FL	11.25
	GA	5.35
...	...	...
YX	TN	4.77
	TX	10.03
	VA	1.12
	VT	2.48
	WI	−1.46

The early or late departures are not ordered, we cannot identify easily the worst and best cases. Let us sorting the result by *DepDelay*, then.

```
df.groupby(['Reporting_Airline','OriginState']).\
agg({'DepDelay': 'mean'}).round(2).\
sort_values(by='DepDelay', ascending= False)
```

Reporting_Airline	OriginState	DepDelay
F9	SD	98.92
AA	WY	85.58
	ID	83.02
HA	TX	82.27
MQ	UT	78.00
…	…	...
UA	SD	−5.00
G4	NJ	−5.16
YX	SD	−6.40
MQ	NE	−7.00
YX	KS	−8.00

Here we have the data frame sorted and we can see that, in March 2023, Frontier Airline (F9) had the largest average departure delay for flights from South Dakota, it is an information but not what we've asked. The problem is that with sorting we have lost the organization by groups. Instead, we want to *keep the group organization* and *for each airline* find out the departure state with the largest delay.

In cases like this, which is **when we do not need to execute aggregation operations on sorted values**, there is a solution in two simple steps:

1. Sort the data frame according to the desired criterion so that rows are in order of relevance.
2. Group on the first variable used for sorting and select with `head()` the desired number of rows from each group.

The reason this simple solution works is that function `groupby()` *keeps the existing row order when it defines groups*. Let us see the example: for each airline, we want to select the three flights with the largest departure delay.

STEP 1: We sort by airline and by departure delay. The delay must be sorted in descending order, for the airline the direction is not relevant. For clarity, we omit rows without values in *DepDelay* and select just the two columns of interest.

```
df[~df.DepDelay.isna()][['Reporting_Airline','DepDelay']].\
sort_values(by= ['Reporting_Airline','DepDelay'], ascending= [True,False])
```

	Reporting_Airline	DepDelay
455281	9E	1177.0
445433	9E	1091.0
444199	9E	1048.0
449727	9E	1012.0
457050	9E	989.0
...	...	...
429432	YX	−20.0
423185	YX	−21.0
410092	YX	−22.0
427715	YX	−22.0
428446	YX	−22.0

STEP 2: Looking at the data frame, it appears how rows are in the correct order, for each airline and delay. Now we need to create groups by grouping on the first sorted column (*Reporting_Airline*) and select the desired number of rows from the top of each group with head() (conversely, from bottom if we use tail()). We want the three flights with largest delay, then head(3).

```
df[~df.DepDelay.isna()][['Reporting_Airline','DepDelay']].\
sort_values(by= ['Reporting_Airline','DepDelay'], ascending= [True,False]).\
groupby("Reporting_Airline").head(3)
```

	Reporting_Airline	DepDelay
455281	9E	1177.0
445433	9E	1091.0
444199	9E	1048.0
489418	AA	4413.0
520793	AA	3249.0
485265	AA	2810.0
539909	AS	602.0
557281	AS	464.0
557737	AS	439.0
557763	B6	1376.0
557764	B6	1327.0
557776	B6	1274.0
...	...	...

These are single flights, what if we want the largest *average* departure delay for each airline and destination state? We just need a few more preparation steps, but the logic is the same.

STEP 1: First, we need to produce the data frame with the average delays, sort it by airline and departure delay, and reset the index.

```
df3= df.groupby(['Reporting_Airline','OriginState']).\
agg({'DepDelay': 'mean'}).round(2).\
sort_values(by= ['Reporting_Airline','DepDelay'],
           ascending= [True,False]).reset_index()
df3
```

	Reporting_Airline	OriginState	DepDelay
0	9E	KS	57.74
1	9E	MA	40.19
2	9E	MO	16.87
3	9E	WV	11.75
4	9E	FL	11.25
...	...	...	...
550	YX	OH	−1.70
551	YX	LA	−2.21
552	YX	IA	−4.42
553	YX	SD	−6.40
554	YX	KS	−8.00

STEP 2: Same as before, group on the first column and select the desired number of rows from each group.

```
df3.groupby("Reporting_Airline").head(1)
```

	Reporting_Airline	OriginState	DepDelay
0	9E	KS	57.75
33	AA	WY	85.59
78	AS	HI	24.47
114	B6	NM	55.17
147	DL	ME	25.73
196	F9	SD	98.92
234	G4	LA	52.89
275	HA	TX	82.27
285	MQ	UT	78.00

	Reporting_Airline	OriginState	DepDelay
324	NK	WV	73.14
359	OH	AR	49.42
388	OO	NC	28.87
433	UA	RI	62.78
479	WN	NV	18.42
522	YX	FL	11.47

7.2.5.1 Functions `nlargest()` and `nsmallest()`

An alternative is provided by functions **`nlargest()`** and **`nsmallest()`**, which select the n rows with the highest/lowest values. In this case, sorting is not necessarys what is needed is grouping and selecting the column to be used. However, this method is not completely equivalent to the previous one because only a single column could be selected, and the result is an array/series not a data frame. To have the result as a data frame, the pandas function **`to_frame()`** makes the transformation.

```
df4= df.groupby(['Reporting_Airline','OriginState']).\
agg(''DepDelay': 'mean'').round(2).reset_index()
df4.groupby('Reporting_Airline')["DepDelay"].nlargest(1).to_frame()
```

7.2.6 Calculated Columns with Group Values

The new case we consider is when pandas function **`transform()`** should be used instead of `aggregate()`. Both work on a grouped data frame, but the results are different. Let us see an example. We want to obtain the average taxi time of airplanes after embarkment and before the takeoff (column *TaxiOut*) and the corresponding taxi time after landing and before reaching the terminal for disembarking passengers (column *TaxiIn*). These are useful data referred to airports to signal possible traffic congestion. We calculate the mean taxi time for airports, first using `aggregate()`, then using `transform()`, and compare the two results.

```
df.groupby(['Origin'])[['TaxiOut','TaxiIn']].aggregate('mean')
```

Origin	TaxiOut	TaxiIn
ABE	17.508951	9.884910
ABI	12.523810	8.750000
ABQ	14.620036	7.613879
ABR	18.716667	10.766667

(Continued)

	TaxiOut	**TaxiIn**
ABY	14.136364	9.147727
...	...	...
WRG	6.879310	4.192982
XNA	15.319104	10.773746
XWA	31.392857	8.050000
YAK	15.310345	3.824561
YUM	15.413223	10.157025

This result shows the 388 airports with average taxi times. Now with `transform()`.

```
df.groupby(['Origin'])[['TaxiOut','TaxiIn']].transform('mean')
```

	TaxiOut	**TaxiIn**
0	15.217082	11.231317
1	15.217082	11.231317
2	15.217082	11.231317
3	15.217082	11.231317
4	15.217082	11.231317
...	...	...
580317	17.258827	8.135058
580318	17.139525	8.983666
580319	17.139525	8.983666
580320	18.428437	8.971937
580321	15.677000	9.241500

The result of `transform()` may look bizarre at first sight. Function `aggregate()` calculates the aggregate function on groups (e.g. for each airport, the average taxi times) and *shows the result as aggregated*, with one row for each airport and 388 in total. Function `transform()` does exactly the same in calculating the aggregate function on groups; *the difference is the form of the result, which is not aggregated*, therefore not a single row for each airport but all flights with average taxi times values repeated. In short, the result of `transform()` has the same size as the original data frame (580 322 in this example), and this is the key for its usage.

When does this feature become useful? In the same cases we have discussed in previous section about R, namely when we create a new column in the original data frame and its elements are calculated using both values from other columns *and aggregated values referred to groups*. It is the second component to be key in this case. A typical case is *when we want a ratio or a percentage of values for single observations with respect to the average value of the group to which the observation belongs.* For example, for each flight, we want to calculate the ratio between taxi times of single flights and the average taxi times of the airport of origin or destination. Many other situations exist, for example, with population data, we want to calculate for each county the ratio between the average income with respect to the average state income, or for each employer the ratio between the satisfaction index with respect to the average satisfaction index of the unit or department where he/she works. In all these cases, we refer the calculated value to a logical group, not to the whole data frame because that makes the calculated value more meaningful or precise.

Without function `transform()` obtaining such results is not that easy. To do it manually, we should create the aggregated values (e.g. the average taxi times for each airport) separately with `aggregate()`. Then, in the original data frame, for each flight, we should look at the departure airport, find the corresponding row in the data frame with average airport taxi time, take the value of taxi out, go back to the original data frame, and calculate the ratio between the taxi out of the single flight and the taxi out of the airport. It could be done, of course, but it is cumbersome.

Function `transform()` makes all of this very easy because the result it produces are not aggregated and are in the same order as the original; therefore, for each flight, we already have all values we need to calculate the ratio. Let us look at an example.

First, we save the result of the `transform()` in a working data frame. Then, we just create the new columns *TaxiOut_percent* and *TaxiIn_percent* in the original data frame by referring to the columns in the two data frames.

```
df_transform= df.groupby(['Origin'])[['TaxiOut','TaxiIn']].transform('mean')
df["TaxiOut_percent"]= (100 * df.TaxiOut / df_transform.TaxiOut).round(2)
df["TaxiIn_percent"]= (100 * df.TaxiIn / df_transform.TaxiIn).round(2)
df[['FlightDate','Origin','TaxiOut',
    'TaxiOut_percent','TaxiIn','TaxiIn_percent']].sample(10)
```

	FlightDate	Origin	TaxiOut	TaxiOut_percent	TaxiIn	TaxiIn_percent
520882	2023-03-19	ORD	10.0	44.73	4.0	56.58
241344	2023-03-23	COU	15.0	84.12	10.0	94.15
539095	2023-03-02	SEA	28.0	142.44	4.0	55.23
435625	2023-03-19	OMA	8.0	51.47	5.0	56.95
200196	2023-03-29	RNO	11.0	64.28	10.0	137.09
118936	2023-03-20	TPA	11.0	75.08	8.0	95.07
264029	2023-03-27	EWR	14.0	56.77	21.0	271.62
466989	2023-03-10	STT	24.0	159.65	8.0	67.22
83459	2023-03-04	DEN	13.0	72.79	22.0	332.02
422181	2023-03-27	BOS	20.0	98.35	7.0	78.83

7.2.7 Sorting Within Groups

We have left this case at the end because, despite sorting rows by keeping the group structure intact is a common feature and should be easy to do (in R it is just an attribute of the sorting function), with pandas data frames it is unusually complicated.

To describe the way to proceed, we need to anticipate a syntactical construct a little complicate that associates function **apply()** to a ***lambda function***, both of them will be presented in the next chapter. For now, the aim is just to focus on the logic and the procedure for sorting within groups, while details about the `apply()` and the lambda functions will be skipped.

We proceed step-by-step. First, we consider a detail of pandas grouped data frames that we have already encountered; this time, it should be highlighted because it will turn out to be the key for what we want to achieve. Let us execute the groupby() again and look at the data type of the result.

```
df1= df.groupby(["OriginState","DestState"])
type(df1)

pandas.core.groupby.generic.DataFrameGroupBy
```

Function groupby() returns a result of type *DataFrameGroupBy*; we should keep in mind this detail. Now, we can add aggregation operations.

```
df1= df.groupby(["OriginState","DestState"]).agg(
  NumFlights= pd.NamedAgg(column= 'AirTime', aggfunc= 'count'),
  MeanAirTime= pd.NamedAgg("AirTime", "mean"),
  MeanDepDel= pd.NamedAgg("DepDelay", "mean"),
  MeanArrDel= pd.NamedAgg("ArrDelay", "mean")
  )

df1.round(1)
```

OriginState	DestState	NumFlights	MeanAirTime	MeanDepDel	MeanArrDel
AK	AK	1486	53.0	3.4	3.4
	AZ	28	304.4	3.6	10.2
	CA	31	283.3	−3.8	−9.8
	CO	30	283.6	7.6	−2.2
	HI	72	346.5	3.5	−0.3
...	...	...	...	...	...
WY	NJ	25	216.2	75.4	70.3
	NY	4	212.2	76.8	56.5
	TX	84	139.9	66.5	70.4
	UT	124	44.7	12.4	12.2
	WA	12	96.7	18.6	21.5

What we want to obtain is the ability to sort flights within groups. Now that each group defined by *OriginState* is sorted by default for *DestState*, we want a different order, for example, by number of flights. We already know from the section about sorting values that if we use function sort_values(), the group structure gets lost, like in the following example.

```
df1.sort_values(by= 'NumFlights', ascending= False).head()
```

		NumFlights	MeanAirTime	MeanDepDel	MeanArrDel
OriginState	**DestState**				
CA	CA	16955	59.360896	11.625720	8.961427
TX	TX	12513	48.964996	10.583540	7.238232
HI	HI	6686	27.908166	11.369767	14.796739
NY	FL	6112	149.076080	21.908185	14.095877
FL	NY	6105	136.948075	21.544327	17.886978

Differently from R, function `sort_values()` has no attribute to specify sorting within groups, and unfortunately, things get complicated. Let us look at the data type of the result after aggregation operations.

```
type(df1)

pandas.core.frame.DataFrame
```

The problem at the root of this annoying complication is that a data frame after grouping but before aggregation is of type *DataFrameGroupBy*, which is the data type for data ready to execute group-related operations; after aggregation, the type returns to the common *DataFrame*, which is not group-ready. This is the reason why when we sort with `sort_values()`, the result does not maintain the group structure; the data type just has no support for groups.

You may wonder whether the problem disappears if we sort immediately after grouping. It would not be a solution because we do not have the new columns, like *NumFlights*, which we want to sort. But probably we may figure something, only if it would work, which is not the case though, the type *DataFrameGroupBy* does not support `sort_values()` method.

```
df.groupby(["OriginState","DestState"]).\
sort_values(by= 'NumFlights', ascending= False)

AttributeError: 'DataFrameGroupBy' object has no attribute 'sort_values'
```

The next two instructions will appear somehow cryptic at first, but the previous observations and few explanations should clarify the overall logic and at least partially the syntax. The logic is the following: Since the problem lies in the data type and the one we need is *DataFrameGroupBy*, not *DataFrame*, how can we obtain the former from the latter? We know the answer; it is with `groupby()`. We just need to choose as grouping variable the outer index level (**level=0**) of the aggregated data frame (*df1*). That variable is the one for which we want to have the groups (*OriginState*, in our example). We rewrite all the instructions.

```
df1= df.groupby(["OriginState","DestState"]).agg(
  NumFlights= pd.NamedAgg(column= 'AirTime', aggfunc= 'count'),
  MeanAirTime= pd.NamedAgg("AirTime", "mean"),
```

```
    MeanDepDel= pd.NamedAgg("DepDelay", "mean"),
    MeanArrDel= pd.NamedAgg("ArrDelay", "mean")
    )

df2= df1.groupby(level=0)
```

Data frame *df2* has all the new columns and the right type *DataFrameGroupBy*.

```
type(df2)

pandas.core.groupby.generic.DataFrameGroupBy
```

Now it is the turn of the *lambda function*. In short, a *lambda function* (specified with **lambda x:**) has the goal of *executing a single operation with variable data*. The single operation is sorting a column; therefore, **lambda x: x.sort_values()**. What are the variable data? They are represented by the *x* in the lambda function and they should be the rows of each group, one group at time. So, the logic is: for each group, the rows are the variable of the lambda function, the function sorts and returns them, then the next group is considered, its rows are passed to the lambda function, and so on for all groups. The last detail to explain is how we can pass to the lambda function the rows of each group. This is the job of the apply() function that does just that: given a certain operation, it repeats it for each column, rows, or group. In our case, *df2* is of type *DataFrameGroupBy*; therefore, the apply() function repeats the operation, which is the lambda function sorting rows, for each group.

The result of this unintuitive and overly complicated combination of operations is the very common and basic feature of sorting rows within groups. Let us look the example.

```
df2.apply(lambda x: x.sort_values('NumFlights',ascending= False))

df2.round(2)
```

OriginState	OriginState	DestState	NumFlights	MeanAirTime	MeanDepDel	MeanArrDel
AK	AK	AK	1486	52.97	3.40	3.40
		WA	866	166.12	5.21	3.66
		HI	72	346.54	3.472	−0.31
		OR	56	190.70	2.12	1.32
		CA	31	283.26	−3.77	−9.84
...	...	...	...	...	...	...
WY	WY	GA	29	176.48	33.39	15.24
		FL	27	242.48	87.93	98.04
		NJ	25	216.24	75.36	70.32
		WA	12	96.67	18.58	21.50
		NY	4	212.25	76.75	56.50

Questions

7.1 **(R/Python)**

What does it mean that a manual solution to group operations is not scalable?

    A It is time consuming

    B It is error prone

    C The effort/time to complete grows more than linearly with the size of data

    D The effort/time to complete is unpredictable

(R: C)

7.2 **(R/Python)**

What does it mean to logically group data frame rows?

    A Physical objects with subset of rows are created

    B All columns of the data frame are indexed

    C Rows are reshuffled to form logical groups

    D Rows are indexed based on a logical criterion on some variables

(R: D)

7.3 **(R/Python)**

What is the main difference between a grouped and an ungrouped data frame?

    A An index on selected variables is created

    B Subsets of rows are created

    C The grouped data frame is sorted

    D The grouped data frame is searchable

(R: A)

7.4 **(R/Python)**

What is an *aggregation* operation?

    A A different way to refer to the sum operation

    B An operation that creates logical groups of rows

    C An operation to manage logical groups

    D An operation to compute aggregate results based on rows belonging to the same logical group

(R: D)

7.5 **(R/Python)**

The result of an *aggregation* operation, typically has...

    A The same number of rows of the original data frame

    B Less rows than the original data frame

    C More rows than the original data frame

    D It depends

(R: B)

7.6 **(R)**

Considering Section 7.1, why does the number of logical groups increase in the three examples? An excerpt is presented below.

```
# Groups:   OriginStateName, DestStateName [1,233]
```

```
# Groups:   OriginCityName, DestCityName [5,243]
# Groups:   Origin, Dest [5,679]
```

A Because groups are added from one example to the next
B Because the number of distinct values of the combination of selected variables increases
C Because the size of the variables is different
D By chance
(R: B)

7.7 (R)

Considering Section 7.1, what is the meaning of the following operation?

```
df %>% group_by(Origin) %>% summarize(Col1= n())
```

A It is wrong; function n() needs a column to be specified
B To create column *Col1* with the mean of all flights for each origin airport
C To create column *Col1* with the number of flights departing from each airport
D To create data frame *Col1* with the number of flights departing from each airport
(R: C)

7.8 (R)

Considering Section 7.1, what is the meaning of the following operation?

```
df %>% group_by(OriginStateName, Origin) %>%
  summarize(Col1= mean(na.rm=TRUE)) %>%
  arrange(desc(Col1))
```

A It is wrong; function mean() needs a column to be specified
B To sort column *Col1* in descending order
C To create column *Col1* with the mean number of flights departing from each state, then sort it
D To create data frame *Col1* with the mean number of flights departing from each state, then sort it
(R: A)

7.9 (R)

Considering Section 7.1, if we want to sort airports for the mean number of cancelled flights *within each group defined by the origin state*, is the following operation correct?

```
df %>% group_by(OriginStateName, Origin) %>%
  summarize(Col1= mean(Cancelled, na.rm=TRUE)) %>%
  arrange(desc(Col1))
```

A Yes

B No, option `.by_groups` of the `arrange()` function is needed

C No, we need to group only by *OriginStateName*

D No, that operation is impossible

(R: B)

7.10 (R)

Considering Section 7.1.6, what is the meaning of the following operation?

```
df %>% group_by(Reporting_Airline, OriginStateName) %>%
  summarize('AvgAirtime (minutes)'= mean(AirTime, na.rm=TRUE),
            'AvgDistance (miles)'= mean(Distance, na.rm=TRUE)) %>%
  mutate('AvgSpeed (mph)'= 'AvgDistance (miles)'/
                          ('AvgAirtime (minutes)'/60)) %>%
  slice_max(n=3, order_by= 'AvgSpeed (mph)')
```

A For each airline, calculate the average airtime and distance of flights departing from the same state, then create a column with average speed, and finally, for each group defined by airlines, take the three states with higher average speed

B For each state, calculate the average airtime and distance of flights operated by the same airline, then create a column with average speed, and finally, for each group defined by states, take the three states with higher average speed

C For each airline, calculate the average airtime and distance of flights operated by the same airline, then create a column with average speed, and finally, for each group defined by airlines, take the three states with higher average speed

D For each state, calculate the average airtime and distance of flights departing from the same state, then create a column with average speed, and finally, for each group defined by states, take the three states with higher average speed

(R: A)

7.11 (R)

Considering Section 7.1, what is the meaning of the following operation?

```
df %>% group_by(Origin) %>%
  mutate(Col1= TaxiOut/mean(TaxiOut, na.rm= TRUE))
```

A It is wrong; there is no aggregation operation with `summarize()`

B It creates a new column with the average taxi time for each airport

C It creates a new column with the ratio between the taxi time of each airport and the average taxi time of all airports

D It creates a new column with the ratio between the taxi time of each airport and the average taxi time of airports located in the same state

(R: D)

7.12 (Python)

Considering Section 7.2, what is the meaning of the following operation?

```
df.groupby(["OriginState","DestState"])[["Distance"]].\
aggregate(' "Distance":['count','mean','max','min']')
```

A Group on pairs origin and destination states, then for each group count the number of flights and compute the mean, min, and max distance

B Group on pairs of origin and destination states, then for each group create a new column *Distance* with the number of flights and the mean, min, and max distance

C It is wrong; counting the number of flights does not depend on a specific column

D Subsetting on column *Distance* is wrong

(R: A)

7.13 **(Python)**
Considering Section 7.2, is the following operation correct or wrong? Why?

```
df.groupby([df.FlightDate.dt.day])[['Cancelled','Diverted']].agg('sum')
```

A Wrong, we must count the number of cancelled and diverted flights, not sum them up

B Wrong, we must also group on origin or destination airports

C Correct because in this case cancelled and diverted flights are defined as logical values

D Correct because in this case cancelled and diverted flights are indicated with 1, and the others with 0

(R: D)

7.14 **(Python)**
Considering Section 7.2, are the two following operations equivalent?

```
df[~df.DepDelay.isna()][['Reporting_Airline','DepDelay']].\
sort_values(by= ['Reporting_Airline','DepDelay'],
            ascending= [True,False]).\
groupby("Reporting_Airline").head(3)
df[~df.DepDelay.isna()][['Reporting_Airline','DepDelay']].\
groupby("Reporting_Airline") \
sort_values(by= ['Reporting_Airline','DepDelay'],
            ascending= [True,False]).head(3)
```

A Yes, the order between sorting and grouping is irrelevant

B No, with the first, the result is not sorted

C No, with the second, the sorting is not within groups

D Yes, in both cases, the three flights with max delay are produced

(R: C)

7.15 **(Python)**
Considering Section 7.2, what is the usage case for pandas function `transform()`?

A When we need to keep the data frame not aggregated and calculate a new column based on existing column values and aggregated values

B When we need to calculate a new column based on aggregated values but `aggregate()` is not supported

C When we need to transform values of existing columns

D It is the same as `aggregate()`

(R: A)

8

Conditions and Iterations

It is common during data wrangling operations to encounter a situation where one of two different actions should be chosen depending on a certain *condition*. For example, if the value of a variable or an element is positive, we should do something; if it is negative, we should do something else; or if a string contains a certain pattern, we should assign a certain value to a variable; if not, we assign a different one; and so forth. The cases are infinite. These are just examples between two alternatives, there could be more, each one with its corresponding action, the logic does not change, though. We will see cases applied to column values to be transformed in different ways, or a calculated column, whose values will be assigned according to a condition on values of a different column.

Complementary to conditions and *conditional operations* are *iterations* and *cycle operations*. In this case, the logic is to repeat the same set of operations on the elements of a series, often a column, iterating on all of them. For each element of the series/column, we could, for example, evaluate a condition, if the value satisfies the condition, we execute a certain action; otherwise, we execute another action. As conditions could be expressed on more than two alternatives, similar iterations could be *nested*, so that if we need to iterate on a matrix/data frame, rather than a series/column, the logic repeats itself, when all elements of the first column have been selected by iterating on rows, we move to the second column and repeat, and so on until the last column. The logic is the same for data structures with more than two dimensions, iterations could be nested for all dimensions.

Conditional instructions and cycles are fundamental syntactical constructs for every programming language; they could be employed on countless occasions. However, we will also see that they have some drawbacks, especially iterations, when it comes to performances. Iterations could take a long time to complete when the dataset is not small.

Datasets

On-Time : Reporting Carrier On-Time Performance (1987–present) from the *Bureau of Transportation Statistics*, United States Department of Transportation. The dataset contains data about US domestic flights operated in March 2023. (https://transtats.bts.gov/Fields.asp?gnoyr_VQ=FGJ)
The global population is projected to peak at around 10.4 billion in 2086, *World Population Prospects 2022*, United Nations, Department of Economic and Social Affairs, Population Division. *Copyright*: Attribution 3.0 IGO (CC BY 3.0 IGO) (https://creativecommons.org/licenses/by/3.0/igo/).

Data Science Fundamentals with R, Python, and Open Data, First Edition. Marco Cremonini.
© 2024 John Wiley & Sons, Inc. Published 2024 by John Wiley & Sons, Inc.
Companion website: www.wiley.com/go/DSFRPythonOpenData

Note: In this chapter, we use a modified version of the second dataset. The modification, for didactic purposes, consisted of having transformed numerical values with the indication of the measurement unit.

8.1 R: Conditions and Iterations

The conditional operation in R has two main forms, respectively, provided by function `ifelse()`, with variants `if_else()` and `case_when()`, and function `if()` with the constructs *if-else* and *if-else-if-else*. It is easy to get confused among these seemingly almost identical forms and variants, but with some practice, the differences will emerge clearly.

We use again dataset *On-Time: Reporting Carrier On-Time Performance (1987–present)* of the *Bureau of Transportation Statistics*, as we did in the previous chapter.

8.1.1 Conditions

Function `ifelse()` Function `ifelse()` belongs to base R and has a simple semantic with three attributes: a logical condition, the value returned when the condition is true, and the value returned when the condition is false. It is important to note that *the action is always to return just a value, not to execute an instruction or else*. Let us look at the first example.

```
library(tidyverse)
library(vroom)

df= vroom("datasets/Bureau_Trans_Stats/Flights_March2023.zip") %>%
   select(5,6,7,10,15,16,17,19,24,25,26,28,31,32,37,38,39,40,42,43,48,50,53,55)

Multiple files in zip: reading 'On_Time_Reporting_Carrier_On_Time_Performance
_(1987_present)_2023_3.csv'
```

```
names(df)

 [1] "DayOfWeek"         "FlightDate"        "Reporting_Airline"
 [4] "Tail_Number"       "Origin"            "OriginCityName"
 [7] "OriginState"       "OriginStateName"   "Dest"
[10] "DestCityName"      "DestState"         "DestStateName"
[13] "DepTime"           "DepDelay"          "TaxiOut"
[16] "WheelsOff"         "WheelsOn"          "TaxiIn"
[19] "ArrTime"           "ArrDelay"          "Cancelled"
[22] "Diverted"          "AirTime"           "Distance"
```

What we want now is to create a new column *AirTimeClass* to categorize flights based on their duration into three classes with the following criteria:

- *Short*: airtime less than or equal to 1h.
- *Medium*: airtime greater than 1h and less than 4h.
- *Long*: airtime greater or equal to 4h.

The logic will be the following: we create the new column *AirTimeClass* and for each element of column *AirTime*, we evaluate *if AirTime <= 60* we write *Short* into *AirTimeClass*, *else if Airtime > 60 and <= 240* we write *Medium*; *otherwise,* we write *Long*.

Tip

This is also the typical way of creating a categorical variable from a continuous one by defining categories corresponding to intervals.

To create the new column, we use the already-well-known function `mutate()` and base function `ifelse()` to choose the value to write in the elements of the new column.

We start with a simpler version by choosing only between two alternatives, *Short* and *Medium-Long*, then extend the example to the three alternatives. The result showed a random sample of the flights.

```
mutate(df, AirTimeClass= ifelse( AirTime <= 60, "Short",
                                             "MediumLong")) %>%
  select(2,3,5,9,AirTime,AirTimeClass) %>%
  slice_sample(n=20)
```

FlightDate	Reporting_Airline	Origin	Dest	AirTime	AirTimeClass
2023-03-10	G4	PIE	ABE	131	MediumLong
2023-03-08	WN	STL	ICT	71	MediumLong
2023-03-20	OH	CLT	PNS	79	MediumLong
2023-03-25	WN	ECP	DAL	106	MediumLong
2023-03-05	OO	OTH	SFO	64	MediumLong
…	…	…	…	…	…
2023-03-22	OO	ATL	ASE	*NA*	*NA*
2023-03-21	OO	DFW	LCH	47	Short
2023-03-02	AS	SEA	GEG	39	Short
2023-03-23	WN	MDW	SLC	202	MediumLong
2023-03-25	DL	ATL	SNA	290	MediumLong

With two alternatives, it is straightforward; we just specify the condition and fill in the two alternative values. Now we want three alternatives and three values. Function `ifelse()` does not support more than two values, corresponding to the two possible logical results of the condition. How can we proceed, then? By nesting the conditions, typically using the FALSE alternative. In particular, we specify the first condition (*AirTime <= 60*), and if true, we can write *Short*, but if it is false, we have two other alternatives left. Then we can write a second condition (*AirTime > 60 AND AirTime < 240*) and if true we can write *Medium*, if false we can write *Long*. This way, we can support as many alternatives as we want by nesting an equivalent (minus 1) number of `ifelse()` operations. We can write an example.

```
mutate(df, AirTimeClass= ifelse( AirTime <= 60,
                                 "Short",
                                 ifelse((AirTime > 60 &
                                         AirTime < 240),
                                        "Medium",
                                        "Long"))) %>%
    select(2,3,5,9,AirTime,AirTimeClass) %>% slice_sample(n=20)
```

FlightDate	Reporting_Airline	Origin	Dest	AirTime	AirTimeClass
2023-03-17	OO	DEN	GTF	98	Medium
2023-03-13	DL	BZN	SLC	52	Short
2023-03-14	B6	PBI	LGA	*NA*	*NA*
2023-03-10	WN	BUR	PHX	64	Medium
2023-03-18	UA	SFO	BNA	222	Medium
...	...	...	...	...	...
2023-03-13	DL	ATL	BOI	248	Long
2023-03-26	WN	SEA	DEN	130	Medium
2023-03-09	NK	MCO	MYR	63	Medium
2023-03-19	AA	DEN	DFW	85	Medium
2023-03-02	WN	SLC	LAS	52	Short

We could simplify by specifying the condition for *Long*, rather than for *Medium*. The result is the same.

```
mutate(df, AirTimeClass= ifelse( AirTime <= 60,
                                 "Short",
                                 ifelse(AirTime > 240,
                                        "Long",
                                        "Medium")
                                 )
      )
```

Now we can complicate the example a little. We use *Distance* and the categories should be:

- *VeryShort*: less or equal to 50 mi.
- *Short*: greater than 50 and less than or equal to 200 mi.
- *Medium*: greater than 200 and less than or equal to 1000 mi.
- *Long*: greater than 1000 less or equal to 3000 mi.
- *VeryLong*: greater than 3000 mi.

We know how to proceed; we just need to be careful with the syntax because it is easy to get confused with parentheses and commas. It is good practice to indent with care.

```
df %>%
  mutate(DistanceClass= ifelse(Distance<=50,
                               "VeryShort",
```

```
                          ifelse(Distance>50 &
                                 Distance<=200,
                                 "Short",
                                 ifelse(Distance>200 &
                                        Distance<=1000,
                                        "Medium",
                                        ifelse(Distance>=1000 &
                                               Distance<=3000,
                                               "Long",
                                               "VeryLong"))))) %>%
  select(2,3,5,9,Distance,DistanceClass) %>% slice_sample(n=20)
```

FlightDate	Reporting_Airline	Origin	Dest	Distance	Distance Class
2023-03-23	OO	PHX	OMA	1,037	Long
2023-03-22	UA	ORD	BUF	474	Medium
2023-03-22	DL	DTW	GRR	120	Short
2023-03-15	B6	SLC	JFK	1,990	Long
2023-03-30	UA	DEN	OGG	3,302	VeryLong
...	...	...	...	...	...
2023-03-29	UA	IAH	MIA	964	Medium
2023-03-03	DL	MKE	ATL	669	Medium
2023-03-29	UA	DEN	MSY	1,062	Long
2023-03-10	WN	MKE	RSW	1,183	Long
2023-03-13	AA	SAN	DFW	1,171	Long

8.1.1.1 Function `if_else()`

A variant of function `ifelse()` is **`if_else()`**, defined in package *dplyr*, that handles the case of *missing values*. With `ifelse()` missing values are neither true nor false, with respect to the condition, and remain as such in the result; therefore, if needed, they should be treated separately, for example, by replacing them with a certain value. Function `if_else()` adds a new attribute for the value to assign to missing values. Since there are missing values in columns *AirTime* and *Distance*, we can rewrite previous examples with function `if_else()`. Note that we need to use it just for the first condition, not in the following ones where we have only two alternatives.

```
mutate(df, AirTimeClass= if_else(AirTime <= 60,
                                 "Short",
                                 ifelse(AirTime > 240,
                                        "Long",
                                        "Medium"),
                                 "Unknown")) %>%
  select(2,3,5,9,AirTime,AirTimeClass) %>% slice_sample(n=20)
```

FlightDate	Reporting_Airline	Origin	Dest	AirTime	AirTimeClass
2023-03-20	WN	LAS	BNA	171	Medium
2023-03-18	WN	RSW	MCI	169	Medium
2023-03-15	OO	PSP	SFO	*NA*	Unknown
2023-03-26	OO	MSP	FAR	40	Short
2023-03-07	UA	ORF	ORD	119	Medium
…	…	…	…	…	…
2023-03-04	HA	OGG	HNL	25	Short
2023-03-12	AS	SEA	SMF	85	Medium
2023-03-24	AA	AUS	DFW	37	Short
2023-03-13	WN	RIC	ATL	81	Medium
2023-03-14	UA	MSY	SFO	290	Long

8.1.1.2 Function `case_when()`

Another variant of function `ifelse()` is **`case_when()`**, also defined in package *dplyr*, which simplifies how to specify more alternatives, avoiding nested `ifelse()`. With `case_when()`, alternatives are simply listed, each one associated with the corresponding value to return by using the tilde symbol (~). Attribute **`.default`** returns the associated value when all other conditions match a false or missing value. For missing values, they could be explicitly handled by using as a condition the traditional `is.na()`, with the variable. We repeat the previous examples once again to show the differences.

```
df %>% mutate(AirTimeClass = case_when(
  AirTime<=60 ~ "Short",
  AirTime >60 & AirTime <= 240 ~ "Medium",
  AirTime>240 ~ "Long",
  is.na(AirTime) ~ "Unknown",
  .default = "Error")) %>%
  select(2,3,5,9,AirTime,AirTimeClass) %>% slice_sample(n=20)
```

FlightDate	Reporting_Airline	Origin	Dest	AirTime	AirTimeClass
2023-03-14	MQ	PSP	AUS	135	Medium
2023-03-03	AA	DFW	IAD	153	Medium
2023-03-21	UA	DEN	RNO		Unknown
2023-03-13	F9	ISP	MCO		Unknown
2023-03-29	NK	MIA	IAH	146	Medium
…	…	…	…	…	…
2023-03-14	AS	PHL	SEA	330	Long
2023-03-13	MQ	IND	ORD	40	Short
2023-03-08	DL	IAH	MSP	147	Medium
2023-03-03	OO	MOT	MSP	66	Medium
2023-03-30	WN	ATL	RIC	68	Medium

```
df %>% mutate(DistanceClass = case_when(
    Distance<=50 ~ "VeryShort",
    Distance >50 & Distance <= 200 ~ "Short",
    Distance >200 & Distance <= 1000 ~ "Medium",
    Distance >1000 & Distance <= 3000 ~ "Long",
    Distance>3000 ~ "VeryLong")) %>%
  select(2,3,5,9,Distance,DistanceClass) %>% slice_sample(n=20)
```

FlightDate	Reporting_Airline	Origin	Dest	Distance	DistanceClass
2023-03-18	AA	ELP	DFW	551	Medium
2023-03-30	DL	PIT	ATL	526	Medium
2023-03-04	B6	SJU	JFK	1,598	Long
2023-03-14	AA	EWR	ORD	719	Medium
2023-03-11	UA	DEN	HDN	141	Short
…	…	…	…	…	…
2023-03-10	OO	SEA	RNO	564	Medium
2023-03-18	F9	PHX	DTW	1,671	Long
2023-03-04	B6	BOS	EYW	1,373	Long
2023-03-04	F9	LAS	DEN	628	Medium
2023-03-29	WN	GEG	SMF	649	Medium

8.1.1.3 Function `if()` and Constructs If-else and If-else If-else

The evident limitation of previous functions is to not let specifying instructions to execute as alternatives. This is the reason for function `if()` of base R that *associates true and false values to expressions, which could be composed by one or more instructions.* There are two forms available, construct *if-else:*

```
if (condition) {
    expression
} else {
    expression
}
```

And construct *if-else if-else:*

```
if (condition) {
    expression
} else if {
    expression
} else {
    expression}
```

Similar to previous cases, several **else if{}** conditions could be nested to match all the alternatives. Before presenting an example, we introduce *iterations* so we discuss a case that combines both.

8.1.2 Iterations

An iteration, or cycle, is to a certain extent the complementary operation of conditional instructions because it is common to combine both: we iterate on a list of values like a column or a data frame, check a condition, and execute different actions.

8.1.2.1 Function `for()`

Function **for()**, of base R, is the typical function for iterations and exists in almost all programming languages. The syntax changes among different languages, but the logic is always the same: an *iterator* selects one element of a list or matrix at a time, while an expression is executed. The iteration stops when all elements have been selected or, exceptionally, when the cycle is explicitly stopped. It is common to use the expression *for cycle* to refer to an iteration realized with a for() function. The syntax could be summarized as follows: for(iterator) { expression }.

The *iterator* is typically realized with a variable and a range of values representing the indexes of the list of elements. It is a common choice to use for the iterator variable names like *i, j, k,* etc. The for() instruction automatically initializes the iterator variable with the first value of the range, increases it (possibly with a step different than 1), and terminates the iteration after the last element.

In R, the syntax of the iteration is the following:

```
for(i in 1st_value:last_value) { expression }
```

with *i* the name of the *iterator variable* (the choice of the name is free), **in** a keyword of the syntax, and *1st_value:last_value* the form to express the interval, with the *colon* as the separator between the two values. For instance, we may have the following iterators:

```
for(i in 1:100) { expression }

for(j in 3:10) { expression }

for(k in c(2,5,13,25,33)) { expression }

for(i in 1:length(ListA)) { expression }
```

Particularly useful are the functions **length()**, **nrow()**, and **ncol()** to specify the end of the interval, respectively, for a list, data frame rows, and data frame columns.

First, we consider a simple didactic example, using as the expression just function **cat()**, of package *purrr*, similar to print(). We define a list and iterate over it with for().

```
ListA= c("If", "you", "really", "want", "to", "hear", "about", "it")

for(i in 1:length(ListA)) {
  cat("Element", i, ": ", ListA[i], "\n")
}
```

```
Element 1 :   If
Element 2 :   you
Element 3 :   really
Element 4 :   want
Element 5 :   to
Element 6 :   hear
Element 7 :   about
Element 8 :   it
```

From this simple example, we should note that elements of the list (or column) are read using the iterator variable *i* as the index, and that the value of *i* is automatically incremented each time the expression has been executed.

We can now replicate a little more complicate example we previously described with functions `mutate()` and `ifelse()`, this time using `for()` instead of `mutate()`. The example uses the dataset of US domestic flights in March 2023, which has more than 580 000 rows. An observation that was done in the introduction of the chapter should be recalled now: iterations are extremely adaptable but slow. Some care is needed here because the dataset is large, so instead of iterating over the whole *AirTime* column, we limit the number of elements to 5000 and record the execution time of the iteration with the standard function *Sys.time*.

```
df$AirTimeClass= NULL
df$AirTimeClass= ":"

start_time <- Sys.time()

for(i in 1:5000){
  df$AirTimeClass[i] <- ifelse(df$AirTime[i] <60,"Short","MediumLong")
  }

end_time <- Sys.time()

df %>% select(2,3,5,9,AirTime,AirTimeClass) %>% head(10)

print(end_time - start_time)
Time difference of 11.25224 secs
```

FlightDate	Reporting_Airline	Origin	Dest	AirTime	AirTimeClass
2023-03-13	OH	TRI	CLT	36	Short
2023-03-15	OH	TRI	CLT	36	Short
2023-03-16	OH	TRI	CLT	26	Short
2023-03-17	OH	TRI	CLT	34	Short
2023-03-19	OH	TRI	CLT	32	Short
2023-03-20	OH	TRI	CLT	33	Short
2023-03-22	OH	TRI	CLT	31	Short
2023-03-23	OH	TRI	CLT	26	Short
2023-03-24	OH	TRI	CLT	28	Short
2023-03-26	OH	TRI	CLT	*NA*	*NA*

The time to complete the iteration over 5000 rows has been approximately 11 seconds; a back of the envelope estimate for the whole column would be over 1000 seconds, close to 20 minutes, possibly considerably more than that. Clearly, this is not an acceptable performance, even less so if compared with alternative much faster methods.

This is one of the reasons why base iterations do not substitute higher-level specialized functions like `mutate()` or, as we will see, multicolumn operations. Iterations are useful when their adaptability to a variety of situations is the functionality we need.

8.1.2.2 Function Foreach()

Package *foreach* offers function **foreach()**, an alternative version of base `for()`, and is specialized for parallel computations (of course, the hardware architecture should support it). The syntax is simple with special operator `%do%`.

```
library(foreach)

df$AirTimeClass= NULL
df$AirTimeClass= ":"

start <- Sys.time()

foreach(i=1:5000) %do% {
  df$AirTimeClass[i] = ifelse(df$AirTime[i] <60,"Short","MediumLong")
}
end <- Sys.time()
print(end - start)
```

The time to complete the iteration over 5000 elements is still around 10 seconds; function `foreach()` does not improve over function `for()` in a traditional mode of operation. It is really dedicated only to parallel computations.

8.1.3 Nested Iterations

Up to now, we have iterated only over a list or a single column, but it is often needed to iterate over a matrix or a data frame, therefore over a 2-dimensional data structure and possibly more than two dimensions. The technique is to nest several *for cycles*, each one for each dimension of the data structure. The schema for two dimensions will be as follows:

```
for(i in 1st_value:last_value) {
   for(j in 1st_value:last_value) {
    expression }
```

with *i* and *j* the names of the iterator variables for rows and columns of a data frame. For example, we use a dataset *The global population is projected to peak at around 10.4 billion in 2086*, from the United Nations and already used in previous chapters, but this time modified to practice with nested iterations. The modification regards the population values that have been rewritten with the unit of measurement's symbol, as described in Table 8.1. For example, a population of 10 530 000 has been rewritten as 10.53M; one of 856 000 has become 856K.

Table 8.1 Unit of measurement and symbols.

Metric unit	Numeric unit	Value (extended)	Value (short)
Kilo (K)	Thousand (K)	×1000	e + 03
Mega (M)	Million (M)	×1000000	e + 06
Giga (G)	Billion (B)	×1000000000	e + 09
Tera (T)	Trillion (T)	×1000000000000	e + 12

The modification is interesting for us because rewritten values are now alphanumeric and cannot be directly converted into a numeric data type. We need to replace the unit symbols with the extended or shortened numerical forms. We chose the latter, so what we want to do is replace the **K** with **e + 03**, **M** with **e + 06**, and **B** with **e + 09**. This should be done for all columns with population data. Then they could be transformed into numerical types. We see how to proceed by using nested iterations.

> **Note**
>
> This presented is not a common case; actually, it is quite unlikely to find a dataset with values recorded in that way, especially from established organizations offering Open Data. However, the more general case of data frame elements that need to be individually checked and possibly transformed in different ways or used to select a certain action based on their value is not unusual.

```
df1= read_csv("datasets/United Nations/population-and-demography_MOD.csv")
```

Country name	2000	2001	2002	2003	...
Afghanistan	19.542986M	19.688634M	21.000258M	22.645136M	...
Africa (UN)	818.95206M	839.4639M	860.61146M	882.34925M	...
Albania	3.182027M	3.153615M	3.123554M	3.092993M	...
Algeria	30.774624M	31.200984M	31.6247M	32.055882M	...
American Samoa	58.251K	58.342K	58.2K	57.962K	...
Andorra	66.116K	67.841K	70.868K	73.929K	...
...	...	...	...	...	...

```
cat("Size of the data frame. Rows:", nrow(df1), " Columns:", ncol(df1))

Size of the data frame. Rows: 254  Columns: 102
```

We proceed step-by-step, first by finding how to produce a single replacement.

8.1.3.1 Replacing a Single-Element Value

In order to replace the value of a single element, we need three steps: selecting the element, checking which replacement should be executed, and replacing the value. For the selection, we use row and column indexes, starting from the second column of the data frame, because the first is for country names.

```
cat("Element 1,2: ", df1[[1,2]], "\n")

Element 1,2:  19.542986M

cat("Element 1,3: ", df1[[1,3]], "\n")

Element 1,3:  19.688634M

cat("Element 2,2: ", df1[[2,2]], "\n")

Element 2,2:  818.95206M
```

The notation with double brackets is what we need. For discovering the replacement to perform and doing it, we look at string manipulation functions provided by package *stringr*, and in particular to functions `str_detect()` and `str_replace()`. With the first, we can check whether a pattern is contained in the string, with a Boolean true/false as the result. This way, we can check if the element value contains *K*, *M*, or *B*. With the second function, we replace the symbol with the corresponding numeric form. We use function `if()` and the construct *if-else if-else*.

```
library(stringr)

if(str_detect(df1[[1,2]],"K") ) {
  str_replace(df1[[1,2]],"K","e+03")
} else if (str_detect(df1[[1,2]],"M")) {
  str_replace(df1[[1,2]],"M","e+06")
} else {str_replace(df1[[1,2]],"B","e+09")}
[1] "19.542986e+06"
```

The same could be done also with `case_when()`.

```
case_when(
    str_detect(df1[[1,2]],"K") ~ "K",
    str_detect(df1[[1,2]],"M") ~ "M",
    str_detect(df1[[1,2]],"B") ~ "B",
) -> unit

if(unit=="K") {str_replace(df1[[1,2]],"K","e+03")
} else if(unit=="M") {str_replace(df1[[1,2]],"M","e+06")
    } else str_replace(df1[[1,2]],"B","e+09")
[1] "19.542986e+06"
```

8.1.3.2 Iterate on the First Column

Now that we know how to perform conditional replacements, we need to iterate on the elements. We start with the first column of population data, which is the second column of the data frame, with name 2000. We define a *for cycle*, the iterator starts from row 1 until the last row (`nrow(df1)`).

```
test= df1

for(i in 1:nrow(df1)){
  if( str_detect(test[[i,2]],"K") ) {
  test[[i,2]]= str_replace(test[[i,2]],"K","e+03")
  } else if (str_detect(test[[i,2]],"M")) {
  test[[i,2]]= str_replace(test[[1,2]],"M","e+06")
  } else {
  test[[i,2]]= str_replace(test[[i,2]],"B","e+09")
  }
}

test
```

Country name	2000	2001	2002	2003	...
Afghanistan	19.542986e + 06	19.688634M	21.000258M	22.645136M	...
Africa (UN)	19.542986e + 06	839.4639M	860.61146M	882.34925M	...
Albania	19.542986e + 06	3.153615M	3.123554M	3.092993M	...
Algeria	19.542986e + 06	31.200984M	31.6247M	32.055882M	...
American Samoa	58.251e + 03	58.342K	58.2K	57.962K	...
Andorra	66.116e + 03	67.841K	70.868K	73.929K	...
...	...	...	...	...	...

8.1.3.3 Iterate on all Columns

Given the iteration over one column, we need to nest it into a second *for cycle* that will iterate over all columns. It is easy, provided that one is careful and uses indexes and brackets correctly. We measure the time it takes to complete the whole iteration.

```
test= df1
start_time<- Sys.time()

for(j in 2:ncol(df1)) {
  for(i in 1:nrow(df1)){    if( str_detect(df1[[i,j]],"K") ) {
      test[[i,j]]=str_replace(df1[[i,j]],"K","e+03")
      } else if (str_detect(df1[[i,j]],"M")) {
      test[[i,j]]=str_replace(df1[[i,j]],"M","e+06")
      } else {
      test[[i,j]]=str_replace(df1[[i,j]],"B","e+09")
      }
  }
}
```

```
end_time<- Sys.time()
test

print(end_time-start_time)

Time difference of 22.64831 secs
```

Country name	2000	2001	2002	2003	...
Afghanistan	19.542986e + 06	19.688634e + 06	21.000258e + 06	22.645136e + 06	...
Africa (UN)	818.95206e + 06	839.4639e + 06	860.61146e + 06	882.34925e + 06	...
Albania	3.182027e + 06	3.153615e + 06	3.123554e + 06	3.092993e + 06	...
Algeria	30.774624e + 06	31.200984e + 06	31.6247e + 06	32.055882e + 06	...
American Samoa	58.251e + 03	58.342e + 03	58.2e + 03	57.962e + 03	...
Andorra	66.116e + 03	67.841e + 03	70.868e + 03	73.929e + 03	...
...	...	...	...	...	...

Again, the execution is slow; there were around 250 000 substitutions (254×101), and it took more than 20 seconds.

Tip

In the example, we have iterated on rows (inner *for cycle*) and then moved to the next column (outer *for cycle*). The opposite would have been equally correct, iterating on columns (inner *for cycle*) and then moving to the next row (outer *for cycle*).

8.2 Python: Conditions and Iterations

8.2.1 Conditions

The logic of conditional operations in Python is the same as in R's and in most programming languages. The syntax, too, is similar, except for a peculiar feature of Python that we encounter here for the first time: the ***indentation***. Writing code with clear indentation, *meaning using tabulation or spaces*, is a general good practice because, with few efforts, it helps reading the code, checking the logic, correctly writing parentheses, troubleshooting errors, and finding bugs. A good indentation has undoubtedly a lot of benefits and is warmly suggested every time code is written, even for a simple script. But for most programming languages, that is all a good practice.

Some others, and Python among them, make a step further by transforming the indentation good practice into a syntax rule of the language, therefore subjected to the control of the interpreter and generating an error if not managed correctly.

Opinions about this syntactic rule are divergent; for some, it is a good thing to force coders to adopt correct indentation; for others, it is annoying as a formal requirement. In our context, it would produce a little discomfort at first, but with some practice, it is easy and effortless.

8.2.1.1 Function `if()`

The syntactic rule about indentation could be immediately tested with the traditional conditional function `if()`, of base Python, which has the following form. To be noted that the operations of *case TRUE must be indented.*

```
if (condition):
  operation (case TRUE)
  ...
  operation (case TRUE)
operation (case FALSE or after all operations of case TRUE)
```

We check with a simple example that uses a random integer number between 1 and 10 and sets a condition on the value.

```
import random

a= random.randint(1, 10)
if (a >= 5):
  print('Greater or equal than 5: ', a)
print('Other operations')
Greater or equal than 5:  10
Other operations
```

Let us see what happens if we do not indent the operation for case TRUE.

```
import random

a= random.randint(1, 10)
if (a >= 5):
print('Greater or equal than 5: ', a)
print('Other operations')

SyntaxError: unexpected EOF while parsing (<string>, line 1)
Greater or equal than 5:  2
Other operations
```

An error has been generated, and the logic of the condition has been skipped because the first operation is executed regardless of the condition.

The basic form of the `if()` function has evident limitations in expressing conditional clauses; for example, we cannot define an alternative, more elaborate forms are needed.

8.2.1.2 Constructs If-else and If-elif-else

Constructs ***if-else*** and ***if-elif-else*** are aimed at a better expressiveness of conditional clauses. With *if-else*, we can express the simple alternative between two operations, whereas with *if-elif-else* several conditional clauses could be nested to express more than two alternatives. Let us see again a simple example with random integers. First, with only two alternatives.

```
import random

a=random.randint(1, 10)

if (a >= 5):
  print('Greater or equal than 5: ', a)
else:
  print('Less than 5: ', a)

Greater or equal than 5:  9
```

Now, with more than just two alternatives, pay attention to the parenthesis.

```
b= random.randint(1, 10)

if (b <= 3):
  print('Less or equal than 3: ', b)
elif ( (b > 3) & (b <= 5) ):
  print('Greater than 3 but less or equal than 5: ', b)
elif ( (b > 5) & (b <= 8) ):
  print('Greater than 5 but less or equal than 8: ', b)
else: print('Greater than 8:', b)

Less or equal than 3:  2
```

8.2.1.3 Function `np.where()`

In package NumPy, function **`np.where()`** is available and represents a conditional operation with two alternatives, associated with case true and case false. Logically, it is like an *if-else* construct, but it works on series.

For a use case, we replicate examples seen in the previous R section with data from *On-Time: Reporting Carrier On-Time Performance (1987–present)* of the *Bureau of Transportation Statistics*.

```
import numpy as np
import pandas as pd

df= pd.read_csv("datasets/Bureau_Trans_Stats/Flights_March2023/
On_Time_Reporting_Carrier_On_Time_Performance_(1987_present)_2023_3.csv",
usecols=[4,5,6,9,14,15,16,18,23,24,25,27,30,31,36,37,38,39,41,42,47,49,52,54])
```

We want to create a new column *ArrOntime* based on late or early arrivals with the following criterion:

- *Late arrival*: Late arrivals of more than 15 minutes.
- *On time*: Arrivals included in −15 and +15 minutes with respect to the scheduled time.
- *Early arrival*: Early arrivals of more than 15 minutes.

```
test=df.copy(deep=True)

test["ArrOntime"]= np.where(
```

```
      (test.ArrDelay <= 15) & (test.ArrDelay >= -15),
      "On time",
      np.where((test.ArrDelay > 15),
      "Late arrival",
      "Early arrival")
      )

test[["ArrDelay", "ArrOntime"]]
```

	ArrDelay	ArrOntime
0	−35.0	Early arrival
1	−11.0	On time
2	−32.0	Early arrival
3	−24.0	Early arrival
4	−10.0	On time
...	...	...
580317	−24.0	Early arrival
580318	−24.0	Early arrival
580319	−24.0	Early arrival
580320	−24.0	Early arrival
580321	−24.0	Early arrival

8.2.1.4 Function `np.select()`

NumPy function **np.select()** allows for a more schematic definition of alternatives with corresponding values. It might be particularly useful when there are many alternatives and writing nested conditions could easily lead to confusion.

We replicate the example just seen by defining two lists, one for the conditions and the other for the corresponding values. Function np.select() associates them in pairs.

```
test=df.copy(deep=True)

conditions= [
  (test.ArrDelay < 15) & (test.ArrDelay > -15),
  (test.ArrDelay > 15),
  (test.ArrDelay <= -15)]

values= ['On time','Late arrival','Early arrival']


test['ArrOntime']= np.select(conditions, values)

test[["ArrDelay", "ArrOntime"]][0:10]
```

	ArrDelay	ArrOntime
0	−35.0	Early arrival
1	−11.0	On time
2	−32.0	Early arrival
3	−24.0	Early arrival
4	−10.0	On time
5	−11.0	On time
6	−22.0	Early arrival
7	−15.0	Early arrival
8	−15.0	Early arrival
9	NaN	0

We can notice that row 9 has a missing value in column ArrDelay; therefore, the corresponding value of the new column *ArrOntime* is set by default to 0. It is possible to explicitly specify which value to assign as a default, meaning when no condition is matched, with attribute `default`. We can set it to "Not available."

```
test=df.copy(deep=True)

conditions= [
  (test.ArrDelay < 15) & (test.ArrDelay > -15),
  (test.ArrDelay > 15),
  (test.ArrDelay <= -15)]

values= ['On time','Late arrival','Early arrival']

test['ArrOntime']= np.select(conditions,values,
                          default= "Not available")

test[["ArrDelay","ArrOntime"]][0:10]
```

	ArrDelay	ArrOntime
0	−35.0	Early arrival
1	−11.0	On time
2	−32.0	Early arrival
3	−24.0	Early arrival
4	−10.0	On time
5	−11.0	On time
6	−22.0	Early arrival
7	−15.0	Early arrival
8	−15.0	Early arrival
9	NaN	Not available

With `np.select()`, we can also easily replicate the second example seen in previous R section when we used column *Distance* to create categories. The result shows a random sample of 10 rows.

```
import random
test2= df.copy(deep=True)

conditions= [
  (test2.Distance <= 50),
  (test2.Distance > 50) & (test.Distance <= 200),
  (test2.Distance > 200) & (test.Distance <= 1000),
  (test2.Distance > 1000) & (test.Distance <= 3000),
  (test2.Distance > 3000) ]

values= ['Very short','Short','Medium','Long','Very long']

test2['DistanceClass']= np.select(conditions,values,
                        default="Not available")

test2[["Distance","DistanceClass"]].sample(10)
```

	Distance	DistanceClass
309413	888.0	Medium
154936	432.0	Medium
237629	102.0	Short
153626	321.0	Medium
313197	255.0	Medium
324784	1514.0	Long
187339	1892.0	Long
540149	867.0	Medium
441662	594.0	Medium
578989	632.0	Medium

8.2.1.5 Functions `pd.where()` and `pd.mask()`

Turning to pandas, two useful functions, **`pd.where()`** and **`pd.mask()`**, are available. They both represent a conditional operation, but of specific forms. In practice, they implement a simplified version of the `if()` with a replacement associated. Between the two, the difference is in the replacement:

`pd.where()`: Replaces values for which the condition is *False*, leaving untouched those corresponding to the condition *True*.

`pd.mask()`: Replaces values for which the condition is *True* and leaves untouched those corresponding to the condition *False*.

First, we test the mechanism with a simple didactic data frame.

```
a1= pd.DataFrame(np.array(
  [[1, 2, 3, 4, 5],
   [6, 7, 8, 9, 10],
```

```
          [11, 12, 13, 14, 15],
          [16, 17, 18, 19, 20]]),
          columns= ['A', 'B', 'C', 'D', 'E'])
```

With `where()`, we replace values less than 10 with 0 and leave the others unmodified.

```
a1.where((a1 > 10), 0)
```

	A	B	C	D	E
0	0	0	0	0	0
1	0	0	0	0	0
2	11	12	13	14	15
3	16	17	18	19	20

Conversely, with `mask()`, we replace values greater than 10 with 0 and leave the others unmodified.

```
a1.mask((a1 > 10), 0)
```

	A	B	C	D	E
0	1	2	3	4	5
1	6	7	8	9	10
2	0	0	0	0	0
3	0	0	0	0	0

This way, the usefulness of the two functions looks very limited and equivalent to other basic functions. However, there is a use case when the two functions become handy: *when of a data frame we want to hide the values of some rows based on the values of one or more column*. This is easily done by subsetting a data frame, therefore presenting only a subset of rows, but the information about which rows have been masked is missed. With `pd.where()` and `pd.mask()`, we can show all rows.

For example, using data frame *test* with the new column *ArrOntime*, we want to make visible only the rows related to *On time* flights and masking without removing the others.

```
test.where(test.ArrOntime == "On time").head(10)
```

	DayOfWeek	FlightDate	Reporting_ Airline	Origin	OriginState	Dest	...	ArrTime	ArrDelay	ArrOntime
0	NaN	NaN	NaN	NaN	NaN	NaN	...	NaN	NaN	NaN
1	3.0	2023-03-15	OH	TRI	TN	CLT	...	1534.0	−11.0	On time
2	NaN	NaN	NaN	NaN	NaN	NaN	...	NaN	NaN	NaN
3	NaN	NaN	NaN	NaN	NaN	NaN	...	NaN	NaN	NaN
4	7.0	2023-03-19	OH	TRI	TN	CLT	...	1535.0	−10.0	On time
5	1.0	2023-03-20	OH	TRI	TN	CLT	...	1534.0	−11.0	On time
6	NaN	NaN	NaN	NaN	NaN	NaN	...	NaN	NaN	NaN
7	NaN	NaN	NaN	NaN	NaN	NaN	...	NaN	NaN	NaN
8	NaN	NaN	NaN	NaN	NaN	NaN	...	NaN	NaN	NaN
9	NaN	NaN	NaN	NaN	NaN	NaN	...	NaN	NaN	NaN

Only rows with value *On time* have all values visible; the others have values masked by *NaN*. Similarly, from data frame *test2*, we want to hide flights with *Long* or *VeryLong* in *DistanceClass* column.

```
test2.mask( (test2.DistanceClass == "Very Long") |
            (test2.DistanceClass == "Long") ).sample(10)
```

	DayOf Week	Flight Date	Reporting_ Airline	Origin	Origin State	Dest	...	ArrTime	ArrDelay	Distance Class
63507	5.0	2023-03-10	OO	SLC	UT	BOI	...	956.0	6.0	Medium
39441	NaN	NaN	NaN	NaN	NaN	NaN	...	NaN	NaN	NaN
521935	NaN	NaN	NaN	NaN	NaN	NaN	...	NaN	NaN	NaN
493869	4.0	2023-03-30	AA	ORF	VA	CLT	...	1801.0	−19.0	Medium
399943	4.0	2023-03-30	WN	COS	CO	PHX	...	1146.0	1.0	Medium
577710	NaN	NaN	NaN	NaN	NaN	NaN	...	NaN	NaN	NaN
435805	1.0	2023-03-13	G4	RIC	VA	PIE	...	2255.0	60.0	Medium
383505	2.0	2023-03-14	WN	BUR	CA	DEN	...	1552.0	−8.0	Medium
563495	NaN	NaN	NaN	NaN	NaN	NaN	...	NaN	NaN	NaN
360542	4.0	2023-03-16	WN	ATL	GA	FLL	...	16.0	11.0	Medium

8.2.2 Iterations

8.2.2.1 Functions `for()` and `while()`

Iterations in Python adopt traditional logic and forms. Function `for()` provides the general functionality, with function `while()` as the main variant. The schema of the *for cycle* is the following:

```
for iterator in range:
    operations
```

with **in**, the colon symbol, and the indentation as elements of the syntax. The iterator is a variable that acts as an index to select an element (e.g. a column's element), and the range is the interval of iterator values, often expressed using function **range()** or as values of a predefined list, for example, the column names returned by df.columns or index values returned by df.index. Another utility function often useful in iterations is **len()**, which returns the number of elements in a list, or **df.shape[0]** and **df.shape[1]**, respectively, returning the number of rows and columns of a data frame *df*. Useful keywords to control the iteration are **break**, to stop the whole iteration, and **continue** to move to the next element. For both keywords, the typical use case is when a certain condition is verified, and consequently the iteration is stopped or the current element is not processed any more.

The *for cycle* has a shortened form when it involves a single operation.

```
[operation for iterator in range]
```

Function while() is a variant of for() with the following form:

```
initialization of iterator

while (condition on iterator):
    iterator update
    expression
```

with parentheses, colon symbol, and indentation as part of the syntax. The *while cycle* is a little more complicated to handle than the *for cycle*, basically because it needs a manual management of the iterator that has to be explicitly updated (e.g. incremented by 1) for the iteration to match the *stop condition*, which is when the condition on the iterator becomes *False*. Otherwise, the *while cycle* may continue indefinitely.

Let us start with a simple didactic example to practice with both the *for* and the *while cycle*. We use variable *i* as an iterator and the range goes from *0* (included) to len(a1) (excluded), with *a1* being a NumPy array of values.

```
a1= np.array(['A', 'B', 'C', 'D', 'E'])

for i in range(0, len(a1)):
  print(a1[i])

A
B
C
D
E
```

In the shortened form:

```
[print(a1[i]) for i in range(0, len(a1))]

A
B
C
D
E

[None, None, None, None, None]
```

Now with function `while()`, we need to write a condition on the iterator to let executing the operations on data unless the condition becomes *False*. Here we have a list of length *len*(a1), which means we want to iterate on elements of index 0, 1, ..., *len*(a1) – 1. Therefore, the stop condition should be $i < len(a1)$. Iterator i has to be initialized at value 0 and incremented by 1 at each iteration with $i = i + 1$ or the equivalent form $i + = 1$.

```
a1 = np.array(['A', 'B', 'C', 'D', 'E'])

i=0
while (i<len(a1)):
   print(a1[i])
   i=i+1

A
B
C
D
E
```

Consider now the two *typical errors* of the *while cycle*: failing to initialize the iterator and failing to update it correctly. We try with the first one; here the iterator is *j* and is not initialized.

```
a1 = np.array(['A', 'B', 'C', 'D', 'E'])

while (j<len(a1)):
   print(a1[j])
   j+=1

NameError: name 'j' is not defined
```

The error is easy to solve; object *j* is undefined. Now the second error is when we fail to update the iterator, for example, because the instruction is not indented correctly.

```
a1 = np.array(['A', 'B', 'C', 'D', 'E'])

j=0
while (j<len(a1)):
  print(a1[j])
j=j+1
A
A
A
A
A
A
A
A
A
A
A
A
...
```

The cycle never ends and keeps processing the first element; in this case, the exit from the cycle should be forced by terminating the program. It is a common error; there is nothing to worry about if it happens when we are practicing, but it might be dangerous in a production system because it inevitably causes a malfunction. Therefore, be careful with *while cycles* and check carefully that the stop condition will actually be met at some point.

8.2.3 Nested Iterations

We now consider the case of nested iterations, for example, when we want to handle elements of a matrix/data frame, or higher-dimensional data structures. *For* or *while cycles* should be nested, one for each dimension of data.

```
a2= np.matrix(
  [[1, 2, 3, 4, 5],
  [6, 7, 8, 9, 10],
  [11, 12, 13, 14, 15],
  [16, 17, 18, 19, 20]])
```

First, we use function `for()`. The number of rows and columns are given by attribute `shape`, with `shape[0]` for the rows and `shape[1]` for the columns.

```
nrow= a2.shape[0]
ncol= a2.shape[1]

for i in range(0, nrow):
print("Row:", i)
  for j in range(0, ncol):
    print("(Element:", i, j, ") Value: ", a2[i,j])

Row: 0
(Element: 0 0 ) Value:  1
(Element: 0 1 ) Value:  2
```

```
(Element:  0 2 ) Value:   3
(Element:  0 3 ) Value:   4
(Element:  0 4 ) Value:   5
Row: 1
(Element:  1 0 ) Value:   6
(Element:  1 1 ) Value:   7
(Element:  1 2 ) Value:   8
(Element:  1 3 ) Value:   9
(Element:  1 4 ) Value:  10
Row: 2
(Element:  2 0 ) Value:  11
(Element:  2 1 ) Value:  12
(Element:  2 2 ) Value:  13
(Element:  2 3 ) Value:  14
(Element:  2 4 ) Value:  15
Row: 3
(Element:  3 0 ) Value:  16
(Element:  3 1 ) Value:  17
(Element:  3 2 ) Value:  18
(Element:  3 3 ) Value:  19
(Element:  3 4 ) Value:  20
```

Now the equivalent version with function `while()`. More care is needed to increase the iterators correctly. The result is the same as the *for cycle*.

```
nrow= a2.shape[0]
ncol= a2.shape[1]

i=0
while (i<nrow):
  print("Row:", i)
  j=0
  while (j<ncol):
    print("(Element:", i, j, ") Value: ", a2[i,j])
    j +=1
  i +=1
```

Again, a simple wrong indentation is sufficient to generate errors.

```
nrow= a2.shape[0]
ncol= a2.shape[1]

i=0
while (i<nrow):
  print("Row:", i)
  j=0
  while (j<ncol):
    print("(Element:", i, j, ") Value: ", a2[i,j])
    j +=1
    i +=1

Row: 0
(Element:  0 0 ) Value:  1
```

```
(Element: 1 1 ) Value:    7
(Element: 2 2 ) Value:   13
(Element: 3 3 ) Value:   19
IndexError: index 4 is out of bounds for axis 0 with size 4
```

8.2.3.1 Execution Time

We test execution time with Python-nested iterations. As for the corresponding R section, we use the modified version of dataset *The global population is projected to peak at around 10.4 billion in 2086*, from the United Nations. What we want to do is replace all the symbols for the measurement units: **K** with **e + 03**, **M** with **e + 06**, and **B** with **e + 09**. This has to be done for all columns with population data. After that, columns could be transformed into numerical types. Execution time could be measured by importing module *time* and using function `time()`.

```
df1= pd.read_csv("datasets/United Nations/population-and-demography_MOD.csv")

df1.head()
```

	Country name	2000	2001	2002	...	2098	2099	2100
0	Afghanistan	19.542986M	19.688634M	21.000258M	...	110.36693M	110.62122M	110.85479M
1	Africa (UN)	818.95206M	839.4639M	860.61146M	...	3.8937976B	3.9094213B	3.9244206B
2	Albania	3.182027M	3.153615M	3.123554M	...	1.150654M	1.12371M	1.097163M
3	Algeria	30.774624M	31.200984M	31.6247M	...	67.88455M	67.84553M	67.79298M
4	American Samoa	58.251K	58.342K	58.2K	...	13.769K	13.242K	12.704K
...	...		...	...	...	...	...	...

We proceed step-by-step. First, we test the replacement of just one element. If we have three alternatives, then the construct *if-elif-else* is the correct one.

```
if ('K' in df1.iloc[0,1]):
  print('replacing K')
  df1.iloc[0,1].replace("K","e+03")
elif ('M' in df1.iloc[0,1]):
  print('replacing M')
  df1.iloc[0,1].replace("M","e+06")
else:
  print('replacing B')
  df1.iloc[0,1].replace("B","e+09")
```

The replacement logic is clear; we can test with the iteration on a single column.

```
test= df1.copy(deep=True)
nrow= test.shape[0]
```

```
for i in range(0, nrow):   if ('K' in test.iloc[i,1]):
     test.iloc[i,1].replace("K","e+03")
   elif ('M' in test.iloc[i,1]):
     test.iloc[i,1].replace("M","e+06")
   else:
     test.iloc[i,1].replace("B","e+09")

'19.542986e+06'
'818.95206e+06'
'3.182027e+06'
'30.774624e+06'
'58.251e+03'
'66.116e+03'
'16.394067e+06'
'11.071e+03'
...
```

It is correct. Finally, we add the second cycle to move through columns, starting from the second column. We can save the replacements and measure the execution time.

```
import time

test= df1.copy(deep=True)
nrow= test.shape[0]
ncol= test.shape[1]

start= time.time()

for j in range(1, ncol):
   for i in range(0, nrow):     if ('K' in test.iloc[i,j]):
       test.iloc[i,j]= test.iloc[i,j].replace("K","e+03")
     elif ('M' in test.iloc[i,j]):
       test.iloc[i,j]= test.iloc[i,j].replace("M","e+06")
     else:
       test.iloc[i,j]= test.iloc[i,j].replace("B","e+09")

end= time.time()
print('Execution time (sec.): ', end-start)

Execution time (sec.):   6.070853233337402
```

The execution of the two nested cycles with Python is faster than with R, but still slow in general terms and not scalable to large datasets.

8.2.4   Iterating on Multi-index

Iterations could be usefully employed on index levels. We consider an example with a column multi-index. First, we create it with aggregation operations. The dataset is *On-Time: Reporting Carrier On-Time Performance (1987–present)* from the *Bureau of Transportation Statistics*, which we already know well.

```
df= pd.read_csv("datasets/Bureau_Trans_Stats/Flights_March2023/
On_Time_Reporting_Carrier_On_Time_Performance_(1987_present)_2023_3.csv",
usecols= [4,5,6,9,14,15,16,18,23,24,25,27,30,31,36,37,38,39,41,42,47,49,52,54])
```

```
df.columns

Index(['DayOfWeek', 'FlightDate', 'Reporting_Airline', 'Tail_Number', 'Orig-
in',
       'OriginCityName', 'OriginState', 'OriginStateName', 'Dest',
       'DestCityName', 'DestState', 'DestStateName', 'DepTime', 'DepDelay',
       'TaxiOut', 'WheelsOff', 'WheelsOn', 'TaxiIn', 'ArrTime', 'ArrDelay',
       'Cancelled', 'Diverted', 'AirTime', 'Distance'],
      dtype='object')
```

We aggregate data so to have a column multi-index.

```
df1= df.groupby(["Reporting_Airline"]).\
      agg({"DepDelay":['mean','median','max','min'],
           "ArrDelay":['mean','median','max','min'],
           "AirTime":['min','max','mean']}).round(2)
df1
```

	DepDelay				ArrDelay				AirTime		
	mean	median	max	min	mean	median	max	min	min	max	mean
Reporting_ Airline											
9E	6.13	−4.0	1177.0	−32.0	0.17	−10.0	1159.0	−51.0	17.0	237.0	68.51
AA	18.68	−2.0	4413.0	−25.0	15.65	−2.0	4405.0	−73.0	16.0	525.0	132.01
AS	7.42	−2.0	602.0	−42.0	5.21	−2.0	611.0	−59.0	8.0	420.0	183.68
B6	23.13	0.0	1376.0	−31.0	17.57	0.0	1354.0	−67.0	15.0	425.0	153.91
DL	13.12	−1.0	1256.0	−27.0	6.54	−6.0	1277.0	−75.0	16.0	695.0	128.00
F9	23.09	1.0	1229.0	−28.0	19.89	2.0	1237.0	−51.0	34.0	556.0	141.42
G4	21.35	−1.0	1931.0	−34.0	22.72	2.0	1928.0	−53.0	35.0	300.0	127.24
HA	14.39	5.0	1351.0	−23.0	17.06	9.0	1360.0	−48.0	16.0	724.0	113.05
MQ	9.55	−2.0	1294.0	−33.0	7.87	−3.0	1270.0	−49.0	21.0	268.0	81.68
NK	23.59	1.0	1272.0	−29.0	20.36	2.0	1298.0	−80.0	31.0	387.0	132.78
OH	4.96	−5.0	1996.0	−20.0	1.98	−8.0	2016.0	−53.0	17.0	202.0	67.14
OO	9.94	−3.0	1575.0	−39.0	7.24	−5.0	1578.0	−69.0	12.0	251.0	74.31
UA	11.25	−2.0	1552.0	−23.0	6.93	−4.0	1557.0	−66.0	21.0	671.0	149.87
WN	12.44	1.0	681.0	−20.0	7.24	−2.0	667.0	−59.0	14.0	434.0	101.47
YX	1.81	−5.0	1345.0	−22.0	−2.59	−10.0	1389.0	−57.0	18.0	264.0	79.89

We have a 2-level column multi-index, which is often impractical for subsequent data wrangling operations, like selections, subsetting, and so forth. It is much better having a single-level column index.

Function **droplevel()** permits to drop an index level, the same way function drop() lets drop a column or a row. If this is sufficient for returning a useful flat index, then this is the simplest solution. Unfortunately, it is often not the case, like in our example, because if we drop one level of the column multi-index, we are left with identical column names, which represents an even bigger problem.

```
test= df1.copy(deep=True)

test.droplevel(level=0, axis=1).columns

Index(['mean', 'median', 'max', 'min', 'mean', 'median', 'max', 'min', 'min',
       'max', 'mean'],
      dtype='object')
```

A second option is to manually rename all columns, like in the following example.

```
test= df1.copy(deep=True)
test.columns= ['DepDel_mean','DepDel_median','DepDel_max', 'DepDel_min',
               'ArrDel_mean','ArrDel_median','ArrDel_max', 'ArrDel_min',
               'AirT_mean','AirT_max', 'AirT_min']
test.head()
```

Reporting_ Airline	DepDel_ mean	DepDel_ median	DepDel_ max	DepDel_ min	ArrDel_ mean	ArrDel_ median	ArrDel_ max	ArrDel_ min	AirT_ mean	AirT_ max	AirT_ min
9E	6.13	−4.0	1177.0	−32.0	0.17	−10.0	1159.0	−51.0	17.0	237.0	68
AA	18.68	−2.0	4413.0	−25.0	15.65	−2.0	4405.0	−73.0	16.0	525.0	132
AS	7.42	−2.0	602.0	−42.0	5.21	−2.0	611.0	−59.0	8.0	420.0	183
B6	23.13	0.0	1376.0	−31.0	17.57	0.0	1354.0	−67.0	15.0	425.0	153
DL	13.12	−1.0	1256.0	−27.0	6.54	−6.0	1277.0	−75.0	16.0	695.0	128

This solution is simple but only practical when the columns are not many; otherwise, we need a solution that automatically renames all columns. Let us consider the logic:

1. We have to iterate on column names (column multi-index values).
2. For each name, we need a transformation from the multiple-level form to a flat format, which has to be unique. There could be various ways to achieve that, the main two are:
   1. A fixed name with appended the iterator value (e.g. *col1*, *col2*, *col3*…).
   2. A name is composed by appending the different components of the multilevel name possibly with a separator (e.g. "*DepDelay_mean*").

Let us see the first option, which is simpler. We use function **append()** to add new names to the list *name_list*.

```
test= df1.copy(deep=True)

i=0
name_list=[]
for col in test.columns:
  name = "Col"+str(i)
```

```
    name_list.append(name)
    i+=1

test.columns= name_list
test.head()
```

	Col0	Col1	Col2	Col3	Col4	Col5	Col6	Col7	Col8	Col9	Col10
Reporting_Airline											
9E	6.13	−4.0	1177.0	−32.0	0.17	−10.0	1159.0	−51.0	17.0	237.0	68
AA	18.68	−2.0	4413.0	−25.0	15.65	−2.0	4405.0	−73.0	16.0	525.0	132
AS	7.42	−2.0	602.0	−42.0	5.21	−2.0	611.0	−59.0	8.0	420.0	183
B6	23.13	0.0	1376.0	−31.0	17.57	0.0	1354.0	−67.0	15.0	425.0	153
DL	13.12	−1.0	1256.0	−27.0	6.54	−6.0	1277.0	−75.0	16.0	695.0	128

It works but has the evident flaw that column names are no longer self-explanatory. We consider the second option, for which we have two solutions.

8.2.4.1 Function `join()`

Python function `join()` appends the values of a list to form a unique string. A separator could be placed among values in the resulting string.

> **Warning**
>
> This function `join()` is from base Python and provides a basic paste mechanisms for strings. It has nothing to do with *pandas join operations on data frames*, which are much more sophisticated functions to concatenate data frames and maintain the logical correspondence between the rows by means of logical keys. Data frame join is the subject of the next chapter.

The function `join()` has a particular syntax, which may easily confuse:

```
'separator'.join(list of elements to paste in a unique string)
```

For example:

```
col=['DepDelay', 'mean']
"_".join(col)


'DepDelay_mean'
```

This is the basic mechanism; we use it in the iteration over the column names, as we have seen in the previous example.

```
test= df1.copy(deep=True)

name_list=[]

for col in test.columns:
  name = '_'.join(col)
  name_list.append(name)

test.columns=name_list

test.head()
```

	DepDelay_ mean	DepDelay_ median	DepDelay_ max	DepDelay_ min	ArrDelay_ mean	ArrDelay_ median	ArrDelay_ max	...
Reporting_Airline								
9E	6.13	−4.0	1177.0	−32.0	0.17	−10.0	1159.0	...
AA	18.68	−2.0	4413.0	−25.0	15.65	−2.0	4405.0	...
AS	7.42	−2.0	602.0	−42.0	5.21	−2.0	611.0	...
B6	23.13	0.0	1376.0	−31.0	17.57	0.0	1354.0	...
DL	13.12	−1.0	1256.0	−27.0	6.54	−6.0	1277.0	...

```
test.columns

Index(['DepDelay_mean', 'DepDelay_median', 'DepDelay_max', 'DepDelay_min',
       'ArrDelay_mean', 'ArrDelay_median', 'ArrDelay_max', 'ArrDelay_min',
       'AirTime_min', 'AirTime_max', 'AirTime_mean'],
      dtype='object')
```

The compact form of the `for()` function could also be used, although it looks less intuitive.

```
test= df1.copy(deep=True)

test.columns= ['_'.join(col) for col in test.columns]
```

8.2.4.2 Function `items()`

Pandas function `items()` returns the name of column and row values, index included. We can see the basic feature of `items()` in the following example:

```
test= df1.copy(deep=True)

colname_list=[]
item_list=[]

for column_name, item in test.items():
    colname_list.append(column_name)
    item_list.append(item)
```

```
print("Name first column:", colname_list[0])

Name first column: ('DepDelay', 'mean')

print("First item:\n", item_list[0])


First item:
 Reporting_Airline
9E      6.13
AA     18.68
AS      7.42
B6     23.13
DL     13.12
F9     23.09
G4     21.35
HA     14.39
MQ      9.55
NK     23.59
OH      4.96
OO      9.94
UA     11.25
WN     12.44
YX      1.81
Name: (DepDelay, mean), dtype: float64
```

For our example, we may just use the column name returned by `items()` and proceed as in the previous solution. Clearly, in this particular example there is no advantage to using `items()` rather than attribute `columns`, but it is worth knowing this possibility, in case we would need to iterate on column and use not just the name but the items too.

```
test= df1.copy(deep=True)
test.columns=['_'.join(col_name) for col_name, item in test.items()]
```

Questions

8.1 **(R/Python)**
   What is a conditional operation?
      A It is an operation that succeeds depending on a logical condition
      B It is an operation that is executed only if a certain condition is met
      C It is an operation that produces a result if a certain condition is met and another one if the condition is not met
      D It just means that first we define a logical condition, then we execute an operation
      (R: C)

8.2 **(R/Python)**
   What is an iteration?
      A It is a construct to repeat certain operations on the elements of a series

B It is an operation that iteratively checks a logical condition and then executes different operations

C It is a conditional operation repeated recursively

D It just means that we repeat the same set of operations on different data

(R: A)

8.3 (R)

Could we execute different operations based on a logical condition with an `ifelse()` instruction?

A No, but we could with the alternative `if_else()`

B No, it just returns different values; it does not execute operations

C We could, but only two alternative operations could be executed

D Yes, we could

(R: B)

8.4 (R)

Does the `ifelse()` instruction handle missing values specifically?

A No, but the alternative `if_else()` does

B Yes, there is a specific attribute for them

C No, missing values must be always omitted before using `ifelse()`

D No, missing values produce an error

(R: A)

8.5 (R)

What the `case_when()` is useful for?

A Same usage case of the `ifelse()`

B Same usage case of the `if_else()` but it avoids writing nested conditional operations

C Same usage case of the `if_else()` but it better handles missing values

D When we need to define a default value

(R: B)

8.6 (R)

Could we execute different operations based on a logical condition with an *if-else* construct?

A No, but we could use the alternative *if-elseif-else* construct

B No, it just returns different values; it does not execute operations

C We could, but only two alternative operations could be executed

D Yes, we could use for any number of alternatives

(R: C)

8.7 (R)

What is the main difference between the *if-else* construct and the *if-elseif-else* one?

A They are equivalent

B The first one just has two alternatives, and the second only has three

C The second one has the default alternative

D With the second one, we could define any number of alternatives

(R: D)

8.8 (R)

What is the meaning of the following operation?

```
for(i in 1:nrow(df)){

  df$Col1[i] <- ifelse(df$Col2[i] >=0,"Zero or Positive","Negative")
  }
```

A It iterates on columns, and if the value of the element of *Col2* is zero or positive, it writes "Zero or Positive" in the corresponding element of *Col1*; otherwise, it writes "Negative"

B It iterates on the whole data frame, and if the value of the element of *Col2* is zero or positive, it writes "Zero or Positive" in the corresponding element of *Col1*; otherwise, it writes "Negative"

C It iterates on rows, and if the value of the element of *Col2* is zero or positive, it writes "Zero or Positive" in the corresponding element of *Col1*; otherwise, it writes "Negative"

D For each row, if there is an element with value zero or positive, it writes "Zero or Positive" in the corresponding element of *Col1*; otherwise, it writes "Negative"

(R: C)

8.9 (R)

What is the meaning of the following operation?

```
for(j in 3:ncol(df)) {
   for(i in 3:nrow(df)){
      df1[i,j] <- ifelse(df[i,j] >=0,"Zero or Positive","Negative")
   }

}
```

A It iterates on the whole data frame, ignoring the first two rows and columns, and if the value of the element of *df* is zero or positive, it writes "Zero or Positive" in the corresponding element of *df1*; otherwise, it writes "Negative"

B It iterates on the whole data frame, and if the value of the element of *df* is zero or positive, it writes "Zero or Positive" in the corresponding element of *df1*; otherwise, it writes "Negative"

C It iterates on the first two rows and columns, and if the value of the element of *df* is zero or positive, it writes "Zero or Positive" in the corresponding element of *df1*; otherwise, it writes "Negative"

D It changes numerical values of *df* with textual values "Zero or Positive" or "Negative"

(R: A)

8.10 (Python)

Is the indentation relevant in Python conditional operations and iterations?

A Not at all

B No, but it is a good practice

C Only when more than three alternatives are defined

D Yes, it is a requirement of the syntax

(R: D)

8.11 (Python)

Does the `if()` function define two alternative operations?

A Yes, but just two

B No, it just defines one or more operations to be executed if the condition is met

C No, it defines one single operation to be executed if the condition is met

D Yes, any number of alternative operations

(R: B)

8.12 (Python)

What is the result of the following operations when variable *test* is equal to 0?

```
if (test == 0):
    result= "Zero"
    result= "Non zero"

if (test == 0):
    result= "Zero"
result= "Non zero"

if (test == 0):
result= "Zero"
result= "Non zero"
```

A First one returns an error for bad indentation, second one sets *result* to "Zero," and third one sets *result* to "Non zero"

B First one sets *result* to "Zero," second one sets *result* to "Non zero," and third one returns an error for bad indentation

C First one sets *result* to "Non zero," second one sets *result* to "Zero," and third one returns an error for bad indentation

D They are all the same and set result to "Non zero"

(R: C)

8.13 (Python)

How many alternatives does the *if-elif-else* construct support?

A Any number

B Two plus the default action

C Two plus the one specific for missing values

D Only three

(R: A)

8.14 (Python)

Is the following iteration syntactically correct?

```
for j in range(1, ncol):
  for i in range(0, nrow):
```

```
if ('ABC' in test.iloc[i,j]):
   test.iloc[i,j]= test.iloc[i,j].replace("ABC","CBA")
elif ('XYZ' in test.iloc[i,j]):
   test.iloc[i,j]= test.iloc[i,j].replace("XYZ","ZYX")
else:
   test.iloc[i,j]= test.iloc[i,j].replace("0","zero")
```

A No, bad indentation

B No, an `if()` function cannot be included in a *for cycle*

C No, you must either use *elif* or *else*, but not both in the same iteration

D Yes

(R: D)

9

Functions and Multicolumn Operations

The possibility that users have to define ***custom functions*** is common in programming languages. It serves the purpose of letting users specify their own set of operations to be executed repeatedly with different data and parameters. Custom functions may implement new functionalities; it is typical to offer them built into independent packages or could be defined to have a more modular structure of the code and for convenience, in order not to rewrite the same sequence of operations simply with different data and parameters. We will see a few basic examples of general user-defined functions.

A particular case is of ***anonymous functions*** or ***lambda functions***; the two definitions are synonyms. These ones represent a simplified version of the general user-defined function that turns out to be useful in specific situations when normal constructs or predefined functions are unable to efficiently support a certain kind of operation. This is the case, for example, of some types of column creation or special sorting criteria.

Multicolumn operations are useful to repeat operations on data frame columns, a common requirement in many situations. As usual in data science, size matters, and the scalability of a solution could be the single most important feature. Repeating a single operation on a few columns would not be a hassle in terms of time and efforts, but columns might be dozens, even hundreds, and operations could be more than a single one, so time and efforts could increase fast. We have already encountered a solution for automatically repeating operations on columns with iterations, but we have also verified how performance could be particularly poor with them. There are other solutions that are more specific and efficient.

Datasets

NYC Dog Licensing. NYC Open Data (https://opendata.cityofnewyork.us/). (https://data.cityofnewyork.us/Health/NYC-Dog-Licensing-Dataset/nu7n-tubp). The dataset contains information on dog registration in New York City. *Copyright*: Public domain (https://www.nyc.gov/home/terms-of-use.page).

Final energy consumption. All data – Tables on EU policy – Sustainable development indicators – Goal 7 – Affordable and clean energy, from Eurostat – Data Browser (https://ec.europa.eu/eurostat/databrowser/view/sdg&uscore;07&uscore;11/default/table?lang=en). The dataset presents the energy consumption of final users in different countries, except for energy consumption for transformation and distribution. *Copyright*: Creative Commons Attribution 4.0 International (CC BY 4.0). (https://commission.europa.eu/legal-notice&uscore;en#copyright-notice, http://creativecommons.org/licenses/by/4.0/).

Data Science Fundamentals with R, Python, and Open Data, First Edition. Marco Cremonini.
© 2024 John Wiley & Sons, Inc. Published 2024 by John Wiley & Sons, Inc.
Companion website: www.wiley.com/go/DSFRPythonOpenData

9.1 R: User-defined Functions

The general syntax for an R user-defined function is the following:

```
function_name <- function( attributes ) {
  expression
  return result
}
```

Attributes could be data and parameters, whereas the result may or may not be explicitly returned with keyword **return**. For example, if the goal of the function is to calculate a certain result that should be used in the main script, that result should be returned to the instruction that has called the function. Otherwise, if the goal of the function is different, like modifying a data frame, a result to be explicitly returned to the caller is not needed. This is a very broad explanation, not a rule; returning or not a result is handled case-by-case.

As a simple example, we want to calculate the difference between maximum and minimum values of a series, together with their mean and median. Imagine that we have to run this sequence of operations repeatedly with several series, and for this reason, we prefer to define it as a function.

```
# Function maxmin

maxmin <- function(values) {
    a1= max(values)-min(values)
    a2= mean(values)
    a3= median(values)
    return(c(a1,a2,a3))
}

# Data
seriesA = c(23, 3, 45, 89, 56, 2)
seriesB = c(55, -8, 32, -15, 3, 77, 2, 0, -1, 19, 100, 23)
seriesC = c(-9, -87, -45, -2, -21, -3, -6, -80)

# Calling maxmin function in different ways
resA <- maxmin(seriesA)
resB <- seriesB %>% maxmin()
resC <- seriesC |> maxmin()
```

We can now print the results.

```
cat("Max-Min: ", resA[1], " Mean:", resA[2], " Median:", resA[3],"\n")
Max-Min:  87  Mean: 36.33333  Median: 34
cat("Max-Min: ", resB[1], " Mean:", resB[2], " Median:", resB[3],"\n")
Max-Min:  115  Mean: 23.91667  Median: 11
cat("Max-Min: ", resC[1], " Mean:", resC[2], " Median:", resC[3],"\n")
Max-Min:  85  Mean: -31.625  Median: -15
```

<table>
<tr><td>Tip</td></tr>
<tr><td>The requirement is that the function must be defined before its usage; otherwise, an error is raised.</td></tr>
</table>

This presented is only a simple demonstration of the concept, infinite variations are possible, and the complexity of user-defined functions could be increased almost limitless.

9.1.1 Using Functions

To practice with functions and learn about a peculiarity of R, we use dataset *NYC Dog Licensing*, from the NYC Open Data.

```
df= read_csv("datasets/NYC_OpenData/NYC_Dog_Licensing_Dataset.csv")
```

Animal Name	Animal Gender	Animal BirthYear	Breed Name	Zip Code	License IssuedDate	License Expireddate
PAIGE	F	2014	American Pit Bull Mix/Pit Bull Mix	10035	09/12/2014	09/12/2017
YOGI	M	2010	Boxer	10465	09/12/2014	10/02/2017
ALI	M	2014	Basenji	10013	09/12/2014	09/12/2019
QUEEN	F	2013	Akita Crossbreed	10013	09/12/2014	09/12/2017
LOLA	F	2009	Maltese	10028	09/12/2014	10/09/2017
IAN	M	2006	Unknown	10013	09/12/2014	10/30/2019
...	...	...	...	...	...	...

We obtained some information about the dataset.

```
dim(df)
[1] 508196       8
str(df)
spc_tbl_ [508,196 × 8] (S3: spec_tbl_df/tbl_df/tbl/data.frame)
 $ AnimalName       : chr [1:508196] "PAIGE" "YOGI" "ALI" "QUEEN" ...
 $ AnimalGender     : chr [1:508196] "F" "M" "M" "F" ...
 $ AnimalBirthYear  : num [1:508196] 2014 2010 2014 2013 2009 ...
 $ BreedName        : chr [1:508196] "American Pit Bull Mix / Pit Bull Mix"
"Boxer" "Basenji" "Akita Crossbreed" ...
 $ ZipCode          : num [1:508196] 10035 10465 10013 10013 10028 ...
 $ LicenseIssuedDate : chr [1:508196] "09/12/2014" "09/12/2014" "09/12/2014"
"09/12/2014" ...
 $ LicenseExpiredDate: chr [1:508196] "09/12/2017" "10/02/2017" "09/12/2019"
"09/12/2017" ...
 $ Extract Year     : num [1:508196] 2016 2016 2016 2016 2016 ...
```

Columns *LicenseIssueDate* and *LicenseExpiredDate* could be converted into datetime format.

```
df$LicenseIssuedDate= mdy(df$LicenseIssuedDate)

df$LicenseExpiredDate= mdy(df$LicenseExpiredDate)
```

The dataset is substantial, with more than 500 000 rows and 8 columns describing some characteristics of registered dogs (i.e. name, gender, age, and breed) and few information about the registration, the zip code of the owner's residence, and license issuing and expiring dates.

To start, we simply want to calculate the current age of each dog in a new column.

```
df %>%
  mutate(Age= years(year(Sys.time()) - AnimalBirthYear)) %>%
  select(1,2,3,last_col())
```

AnimalName	AnimalGender	AnimalBirthYear	Age
PAIGE	F	2014	9y 0m 0d 0H 0M 0S
YOGI	M	2010	13y 0m 0d 0H 0M 0S
ALI	M	2014	9y 0m 0d 0H 0M 0S
QUEEN	F	2013	10y 0m 0d 0H 0M 0S
LOLA	F	2009	14y 0m 0d 0H 0M 0S
IAN	M	2006	17y 0m 0d 0H 0M 0S
…	…	…	…

This way, *Age* is of type *Period* and shows the age in years. Now, we simply want to rewrite the example with a user-defined function *age* that calculates the current dog's age.

```
age <- function(par1) {
  years(year(Sys.time()) - par1)
}

df %>% mutate(Age= age(AnimalBirthYear))
```

The result is the same as in the previous example. In this case, the solution with the function does not add any benefit, but it is useful for practice. In a general case, user-defined functions could be considerably more complex.

Let us try with a little more complicated example. We want to group and aggregate the data frame in order to calculate a new column with the proportion, for each breed, between the dog's gender and the total of the same breed. First, we write the operations without user-defined functions.

```
df %>%
  group_by(BreedName, AnimalGender) %>%
  summarize(Num = n()) %>% arrange(desc(Num)) -> df1
df1 %>%
```

```
group_by(BreedName) %>%
mutate(BreedTot= sum(Num, na.rm= TRUE),
       GenderRatio= round(Num / BreedTot, 2)) %>%
relocate(GenderRatio, .before= Num)
```

BreedName	AnimalGender	GenderRatio	Num	BreedTot
Unknown	M	0.51	23,994	46,973
Unknown	F	0.49	22,976	46,973
Yorkshire Terrier	M	0.57	17,301	30,212
Shih Tzu	M	0.57	15,840	27,623
Yorkshire Terrier	F	0.43	12,908	30,212
Shih Tzu	F	0.43	11,780	27,623
Chihuahua	M	0.52	10,975	21,035
Chihuahua	F	0.48	10,060	21,035
Maltese	M	0.57	8,966	15,672
Labrador Retriever	M	0.51	7,951	15,693
...	...	...	...	...

Now, we want to calculate the new column with proportions using a custom function. What parameters should we pass to this function? The data for the `mutate()` function, which is data frame *df1* in this case , and the name of the column to use for grouping, *BreedName*.

```
calcRatio <- function(data, tot) {
  data %>% mutate(BreedTot= sum(tot, na.rm= TRUE),
       GenderRatio= round(tot / BreedTot, 2))
}
```

Then we can replace the whole `mutate()` function with a call to our `calcRatio()`. Do we need to specify the data frame in the call to `calcRatio()`? No, because we are piping the instructions.

```
df %>%
  group_by(BreedName, AnimalGender) %>%
  summarize(Num = n()) %>% arrange(desc(Num)) -> df1

df1 %>%
  group_by(BreedName) %>%
  calcRatio(Num) %>%
  relocate(GenderRatio, .before= Num)
In argument: `BreedTot = sum(tot, na.rm = TRUE)`.
In group 1: `BreedName = "AFFENPINSCHER"`.
Caused by error:
! object 'Num' not found
```

Something is wrong, we received an error. It is a strange error, though, because it seems we have misspelled the name of the column *Num* or that the column is not present in the data, but neither of them is true. The data frame *df1* was read correctly; otherwise, it could not have found column *BreedName* and its first value, also checking *df1*, column *Num* is there. What did we do wrong?

Note

As a general rule, we may assume that function parameters (variables) are **local to the function**, meaning they are **copies of the original objects** (data frames, variables). This mechanism is called **parameters passing by value**, in short, as copies. Being copies, every change made to them does not affect the original objects, which should be handled explicitly, if what we want is to modify the original objects.

However, R management of function parameters is more complicated than that because function parameters are not always copies. On the contrary, when an R function is called, what is passed are not copies of the original objects but pointers to the actual original objects through their memory locations. This method is called **parameters passing by reference**, meaning through the reference to the original objects. This way, memory space is saved because it duplicates all objects passed as parameters. The peculiarity of R is that function parameters remain references to original objects until an operation modifying their content is executed. At that point, they are automatically duplicated, and the operation is executed on copies, not on the original objects.

This management of data passing is efficient because it only executes copy operations (slow and memory consuming) if needed.

From a practical point of view, this sophisticated management is transparent for the user; therefore, it is correct, logically, to assume that function parameters in R are passed by value and we operate on copies.

9.1.2 Data Masking

The previous, strange error arises from a special mechanism called *tidy evaluation* that library *dplyr* uses to manage some of its functions, in particular `arrange()`, `count()`, `filter()`, `group_by()`, `mutate()`, and `summarise()`. All these functions implement a feature called **data masking**, which is the much-appreciated possibility of not repeating the name of the data frame when we specify a column. For example, we do not write *arrange(df, df$Year)* to sort column *Year* of data frame *df*, but simply *arrange(df, Year)*. Similarly, we write *df %>% group_by(Col1, Col2)* instead of *df %>% group_by(df$Col1, df$Col2)*, same with `filter()`, `mutate()`, and `summarise()`. This is *data masking*.

It is a very convenient feature, but in a few cases, it creates some problems, in particular in cases of *indirection*, for example, when variables are passed as function parameters. In these cases, the data masking feature fails, and the function cannot find the columns just by name. This is the reason for that strange error, column *Num* is neither misspelled nor missing; it is the `mutate()` function that cannot find the column in the data because it is a function parameter.

Once the source of the error is clear, there is a simple solution called **variable embracing**, which is the *special notation with double curly brackets* (`{{variable}}`). We need to specify this special notation for all variables/columns that require the data masking. In our example, it is just the variable **tot** of the `ratio_gender()` function.

```
ratio_gender <- function(data, tot) {
  data %>% mutate(BreedTot= sum({{tot}}, na.rm= TRUE),
          GenderRatio= round({{tot}} / BreedTot, 2))
}
```

Now, we can execute the operations again, and the result is produced correctly.

```
df %>%
  group_by(BreedName, AnimalGender) %>%
  summarize(Num = n()) %>% arrange(desc(Num)) -> df1
'summarise()' has grouped output by 'BreedName'. You can override using the
'.groups' argument.
df1 %>%
  group_by(BreedName) %>%
  ratio_gender(Num) %>%
  relocate(GenderRatio, .before= Num)
```

BreedName	AnimalGender	GenderRatio	Num	BreedTot
Unknown	M	0.51	23994	46973
Unknown	F	0.49	22976	46973
Yorkshire Terrier	M	0.57	17301	30212
Shih Tzu	M	0.57	15840	27623
Yorkshire Terrier	F	0.43	12908	30212
Shih Tzu	F	0.43	11780	27623
Chihuahua	M	0.52	10975	21035
Chihuahua	F	0.48	10060	21035
Maltese	M	0.57	8966	15672
Labrador Retriever	M	0.51	7951	15693
...	...	...	...	...

To practice a little more with this special case, we could include in the function the grouping too, and specify the names of the new columns as parameters. Now *four variables require the special notation with embracing*:

- Those referencing data frame columns for the `group()` and the `mutate()` functions (i.e. `{{colGrp}}`, `{{tot}}`);
- Those referencing the name of new columns created by the `mutate()` (i.e. `{{newCol1}}`, `{{newCol2}}`).

But there is more, *the syntax for assigning the name to a new column is different*, the usual symbol = produces an error because it is incompatible with the special notation with embracing. It must be replaced by the special notation :=.

The correct syntax for this case is the following:

```
ratio2 <- function(data, colGrp, tot, newCol1, newCol2) {
  data %>% group_by({{colGrp}}) %>%
    mutate({{newCol1}} := sum({{tot}}, na.rm= TRUE),
           {{newCol2}} := round({{tot}} / {{newCol1}}, 2))
}
df %>%
  group_by(BreedName, AnimalGender) %>%
  summarize(Num = n()) %>% arrange(desc(Num)) -> df1
df1 %>%
  ratio2(BreedName, Num, BreedTot, GenderRatio) %>%
  relocate(GenderRatio, .before= Num) %
```

BreedName	AnimalGender	GenderRatio	Num	BreedTot
Unknown	M	0.51	23994	46973
Unknown	F	0.49	22976	46973
Yorkshire Terrier	M	0.57	17301	30212
Shih Tzu	M	0.57	15840	27623
Yorkshire Terrier	F	0.43	12908	30212
Shih Tzu	F	0.43	11780	27623
Chihuahua	M	0.52	10975	21035
Chihuahua	F	0.48	10060	21035
Maltese	M	0.57	8966	15672
Labrador Retriever	M	0.51	7951	15693
...	...	...	...	...

It looks a little complicated at first, but this way we have defined a truly general custom function that could be reused in several instances where we have to calculate an equivalent result, regardless of the names of the columns involved.

For example, let us assume we wish to obtain for all zip codes, the ratio of each breed with respect to the total number of dogs in the same zip code. We can use `ratio2()` again, simply specifying different arguments as parameters.

```
df %>%
  group_by(ZipCode, BreedName) %>%
  summarize(Num = n()) %>% arrange(desc(Num)) -> df1
'summarise()' has grouped output by 'ZipCode'. You can override using the
'.groups' argument.
df1 %>%
  ratio2(ZipCode, Num, BreedTot, BreedRatio) %>%
  relocate(BreedRatio, .before= Num) %>%
  arrange(ZipCode)
```

ZipCode	BreedName	BreedRatio	Num	BreedTot
0	Terrier Crossbreed	1.0	1	1
121	Schnauzer, Miniature	1.0	1	1
687	Bichon Frise	1.0	1	1
923	Poodle Crossbreed	1.0	1	1
1001	Maltese	1.0	1	1
1002	Poodle, Miniature	0.4	2	5
1002	Shih Tzu	0.4	2	5
1002	Poodle Crossbreed	0.2	1	5
1006	Dachshund	1.0	2	2
1009	American Pit Bull Mix / Pit Bull Mix	0.4	2	5
...	...	...	...	...

Note

We recall the observation made in the introduction of this chapter. User-defined functions are a general feature that could be applied in an infinite number of circumstances. However, whether to use it or not should be evaluated based on the trade-off with rewriting part of the code. In some cases, it would be clearly extremely beneficial; in others, it would be evidently useless, and in most cases, it would need the subjective judgment of the programmer.

9.1.3 Anonymous Functions

Derived from the general definition of a user-defined function, a simplified form has been introduced with the name of ***anonymous functions***. These ones follow the same logic as general user-defined functions, but with some constraints and a special syntax.

Anonymous functions do not have a name and can execute a single operation only. Therefore, they cannot be executed by specifying their name like general user-defined functions and cannot implement a logic composed by several operations. A caveat should be noted, however: *a sequence of piped instructions is considered as a single operation.*

Their utility is to be included in other standard functions when certain results cannot be obtained easily with normal attributes. We will see some typical examples of such cases.

Anonymous functions have two equivalent syntaxes, the second introduced from R v.4.0.1. With **x** we indicate the name of the function's attribute, and with **data** the object passed as a parameter. A third form, specific to package ***purrr***, will be introduced in the next section for multicolumn operations.

```
(function(x) operation(x) )(data)

(\(x) operation(x) )(data)
```

For now, we just consider few simple examples only to practice with the syntax and the basic logic. Using anonymous functions as stand-alone functions is practically useless. They became useful in combination with high-level functions, like multicolumn operations or special grouping and sorting cases.

```
# Data
seriesA = c(23, 3, 45, 89, 56, 2)
seriesB = c(55, -8, 32, -15, 3, 77, 2, 0, -1, 19, 100, 23)
seriesC = c(-9, -87, -45, -2, -21, -3, -6, -80)

# Anonymous functions
(function(x) max(x)-min(x) )(seriesA)
[1] 87
(\(x) x-mean(x) )(seriesB)
 [1]  31.0833333 -31.9166667   8.0833333 -38.9166667 -20.9166667  53.0833333
 [7] -21.9166667 -23.9166667 -24.9166667  -4.9166667  76.0833333  -0.9166667
(function(x) x-mean(x) )(seriesC)
[1]  22.625 -55.375 -13.375  29.625  10.625  28.625  25.625 -48.375
```

9.2 R: Multicolumn Operations

Multicolumn operations make it possible to efficiently repeat operations on several columns, a common requirement in many situations. As often observed throughout the book, in data science, scale matters, so repeating a few operations on a few columns is not a problem. There is not a great advantage in writing a multicolumn operation with respect to rewriting the transformation operation for each column. However, if the columns are dozens or hundreds, things are different, as well as if instead of a simple data type transformation, a more complicated set of operations should be executed on columns.

As a second note to introduce multicolumn operations, we have already encountered the most general of the multicolumn operations, the iteration with a *for cycle*. The iteration construct is always available as a potential solution, but it is a low-level functionality that may require a substantial amount of work in complex cases, a complexity that specialized multicolumn operations might have solved. It also has poor performances, which may heavily affect the usage even for medium-sized datasets.

9.2.1 Base Method

9.2.1.1 Functions `apply()`, `lapply()`, and `sapply()`

To introduce the first examples, we use again the little didactic dataset employed in Chapter 5.

```
Name = c("Polycarp Arthmail", "Lada Damon", "Stribog Castor")
Age = c(23, "??", 42)
City = c("Des Moines", "Hanover", "unknown")
State = c("Iowa", "??", "Unknown")
Job = c("full_time", "part_time", "full_time")

df <- data.frame(Name, Age, City, State, Job)
df
```

Name	Age	City	State	Job
Polycarp Arthmail	23	Des Moines	Iowa	full_time
Lada Damon	??	Hanover	??	part_time
Stribog Castor	42	Unknown	Unknown	full_time

The goal is to substitute the different forms used to indicate an unspecified value with a common one. As a replacement, we choose string "NA" and start with a simple user-defined function.

```
uniformNA <- function(x,y) {
  str_replace_all(string= x, pattern= y, replacement= "NA")
}
```

We execute the transformations on column *State*.

```
a="unknown"
b="Unknown"
c="\\?\\?"

uniformNA(df$State,a) %>% uniformNA(b) %>% uniformNA(c)
```

Name	Age	City	State	Job
Polycarp Arthmail	23	Des Moines	Iowa	full_time
Lada Damon	??	Hanover	NA	part_time
Stribog Castor	42	Unknown	NA	full_time

It works, but everything should be done manually, for all columns.

We consider function **apply()**, of base R, and its variants **lapply()** and **sapply()**. Function apply() works on array/matrices and its important arguments are:

- X: the data as array or matrices, in our case columns.
- MARGIN: how to apply the function, MARGIN=1 means to apply it on rows, MARGIN=2 means on columns.
- FUN: the function to execute.

We test it on our little data frame. The first problem to solve is how to specify the columns to function str.replace_all(). If we just write the function, the data for the str.replace_all() is unspecified, and an error is generated. Here, the anonymous function comes to help. We just need to write the str.replace_all() in an anonymous function, and columns are handled correctly. First, we try with just one replacement.

```
pattern1= c("\\?\\?")
string1= "NA"

apply(X= df,
      MARGIN= 2,
      FUN= function(x) str_replace_all(x, pattern = pattern1,
                                          replacement = string1))
```

Name	Age	City	State	Job
Polycarp Arthmail	23	Des Moines	Iowa	full_time
Lada Damon	NA	Hanover	NA	part_time
Stribog Castor	42	unknown	Unknown	full_time

It is correct, it has replaced all "??". For multiple substitutions, function str.replace_all() accepts the pattern as a named vector, like c(pattern1 = replacement1, pattern2 = replacement2, ...), attribute *replacement* in this case is no longer needed.

```
pattern1= c("\\?\\?"=string1, "unknown"=string1, "Unknown"=string1)
string1= "NA"

apply(X= df,
      MARGIN= 2,
      FUN= function(x) str_replace_all( x, pattern= pattern1)) -> df1
```

Let us check the data type of the result.

```
class(df1)

[1] "matrix" "array"
```

It is a matrix; we should transform it into a data frame.

```
data.frame(df1)
```

Name	Age	City	State	Job
Polycarp Arthmail	23	Des Moines	Iowa	full_time
Lada Damon	NA	Hanover	NA	part_time
Stribog Castor	42	NA	NA	full_time

Variant **lapply()** works on lists; therefore, columns by default do not need an argument to specify it. It also returns a list.

```
pattern1= c("\\?\\?"=string1, "unknown"=string1, "Unknown"=string1)
string1= "NA"

lapply(df,
       function(x) str_replace_all( x, pattern= pattern1)) -> df1
df1
$Name
[1] "Polycarp Arthmail" "Lada Damon"        "Stribog Castor"

$Age
[1] "23" "NA" "42"

$City
[1] "Des Moines" "Hanover"    "NA"

$State
[1] "Iowa" "NA"   "NA"

$Job
[1] "full_time" "part_time" "full_time"
```

The result is a list that we can convert into data frame.

```
class(df1)
[1] "list"
as_tibble(df1)
```

Function **sapply()** is another variant, similar to `lapply()`, but it returns a vector/matrix rather than a list.

```
pattern1= c("\\?\\?"=string1, "unknown"=string1, "Unknown"=string1)
string1= "NA"

sapply(df,
     function(x) str_replace_all( x, pattern = pattern1)) -> df1
df1
     Name                Age   City          State    Job
[1,] "Polycarp Arthmail" "23"  "Des Moines"  "Iowa"   "full_time"
[2,] "Lada Damon"        "NA"  "Hanover"     "NA"     "part_time"
[3,] "Stribog Castor"    "42"  "NA"          "NA"     "full_time"
```

The result is a matrix that, again, we can transform into a data frame.

```
class(df1)
[1] "matrix" "array"
as_tibble(df1)
```

9.2.1.2 Mapping

Function map() and Variants Function `apply()` and its variants are general multicolumn (or multirow) functions with the advantage of being defined in base R. More specialized functions exist, though.

Function **map()** is defined in package **purrr** and is often used to work on lists. It has several variants for specific cases. We start from `map()` that repeats the execution of an operation and returns a list to be transformed into a data frame, as already seen with `apply()`. Data are associated to attribute **.x** and, same as before, through an anonymous function, the columns are passed to a function working on series, like all string manipulation or *datetime* functions.

```
pattern1= c("\\?\\?"=string1, "unknown"=string1, "Unknown"=string1)
string1= "NA"

df_map= map(.x= df,
          function(x) str_replace_all(string= x, pattern= pattern1)
     )
df_map
$Name
[1] "Polycarp Arthmail" "Lada Damon"       "Stribog Castor"

$Age
[1] "23" "NA" "42"
```

```
$City
[1] "Des Moines" "Hanover"     "NA"

$State
[1] "Iowa" "NA"    "NA"

$Job
[1] "full_time" "part_time" "full_time"
class(df_map)
[1] "list"
```

Other variants of the general `map()` function are those producing a result of a certain type:

- **`map_lgl()`,`map_int()`,`map_dbl()`,`map_chr()`**: these variants return a vector of type corresponding to the name suffix, *logical*, *integer*, *double*, or *character*. They are appropriate when columns are all of the same type, and so will be the result.
- **`map_dfr()`** and **`map_dfc()`** : these ones return a *data frame* created by repeating the function specified as attribute *by rows* (*map_dfr*) or *by columns* (*map_dfc*).

In our case, we have different data types and expect a data frame as a result. Replacements could be executed either by rows or by column; the result does not change. We can use both `map_dfr()` or `map_dfc()`.

```
pattern1= c("\\?\\?"=string1, "unknown"=string1, "Unknown"=string1)
string1= "NA"

df_map= map_dfc(df,
          function(x) str_replace_all(string= x, pattern= pattern1))
```

The result is already a data frame.

```
class(df_map)
```

```
[1] "tbl_df" "tbl" "data.frame"
```

Warning

The use of functions `map_dfr()` and `map_dfc()` is currently *superseded* (from package *purrr* v.1.0.0). The status of *superseded* is different from *deprecated* for a function. When a function is *deprecated*, it means that there is already a better alternative, and the function is scheduled for removal in next versions of the package. On the contrary, a function is *superseded* when there is a better alternative, but the function will not be removed. In other words, with a deprecated function, you should stop using it, with a superseded one, you may give a try to the alternative and then choose the one you prefer.

The alternative to functions `map_dfr()` and `map_dfc()` that are suggested is to use general `map()` function and then manage the list result, either by immediately transforming it into data frame (`as.data.frame()` or `as_tibble()`), possibly with a more complex procedure if list elements should be transformed into data frame singularly and then combined, by rows (`list_rbind()`) or by columns (`list_cbind()`).

9.2.2 Mapping and Anonymous Functions: *purrr-style* Syntax

With function map(), but also with filter() and reduce(), a *third syntax exists to define an anonymous function* in addition to the canonical two (i.e. function(x) and \ (x)). It simply uses the **tilde symbol** (~), which in R is meant to indicate a formula, but most of all it allows a more flexible data handling by means of *dot notations* (.), .x and .y, or ..1, ..2, ..3 etc.

> **Tip**
>
> *purrr-style* is an informal way to refer to this particular syntax that is often found in comments and examples, and it derives from the fact that the first examples of its usage were presented in the documentation of function map(), which is defined in package *purrr*.

Let us see the example with purrr-style anonymous functions and the dot notation to indicate the position where data should be evaluated. Without the dot notation, an error is generated (*argument "string" is missing*, where argument *string* in function str_replace_all() is the first one associated to the data).

```
pattern1= c("\\?\\?"=string1, "unknown"=string1, "Unknown"=string1)
string1= "NA"

df_map= map_dfc(df, ~ str_replace_all(., pattern= pattern1))
```

The result is the substitution of all patterns with the string.

To have a glimpse about the different forms of dot notations, function **as_mapper()** could be executed right after having run the previous example. This is a service function that shows the logic behind *purrr* functions.

```
as_mapper(~ str_replace_all(., pattern = pattern1))
<lambda>
function (..., .x = ..1, .y = ..2, . = ..1)
str_replace_all(., pattern = pattern1)
attr(,"class")
[1] "rlang_lambda_function" "function"
```

From the result, it could be noted the correspondence between different dot notations for data and also the origin of the name **lambda function** as a synonym of *anonymous function*; it is the standard name used to specify this particular class of functions.

9.2.3 Conditional Mapping

We now consider a more complex case than the simple replacement of string patterns in data frame columns. What we want to do is execute different operations based on a logic condition, again repeated for all columns. This is the use case for function **map_if()**, another variant of map(), that returns a list.

To show an example, we modify the previous didactic data frame by adding more columns of different types and transforming *Job* into *factors* (Categories).

```
Name= c("Polycarp Arthmail", "Lada Damon", "Stribog Castor")
Age= c(23, "??", 42)
City= c("Des Moines", "Hanover", "unknown")
State= c("Iowa", "??", "Unknown")
Job= c("full_time", "part_time", "full_time")
Salary= c(50000, 20000, 80000 )
Seniority= c(3, 1, 10)

df1 <- data.frame(Name, Age, City, State, Job, Salary, Seniority)
df1$Job= as.factor(df1$Job)
df1
```

Name	Age	City	State	Job	Salary	Seniority
Polycarp Arthmail	23	Des Moines	Iowa	full_time	50000	3
Lada Damon	??	Hanover	??	part_time	20000	1
Stribog Castor	42	unknown	Unknown	full_time	80000	10

Function `map_if()` is particularly handy for selecting columns based on their data type and then applying different operations to the different columns. Attributes of `map_if()` are the following:

- `.x`: the data, e.g. a data frame.
- `.p`: a logical condition or a vector of Boolean elements of the same size of the data.
- `.f`: a function specified either with name (e.g. *mean*), an anonymous function, or a formula.
- `.else`: to define an alternative function.

Let us try to transform *numeric column elements* into the difference between the single value and the mean of column values, and *character column elements* into upper case. Since function `map_if()` returns a list, we have to convert the result to data frame.

```
map_if(.x= df1, .p= is.numeric,
       .f= ~ .x-mean(.x), .else= toupper) %>% as_tibble()
```

Name	Age	City	State	Job	Salary	Seniority
POLYCARP ARTHMAIL	23	DES MOINES	IOWA	FULL_TIME	0	−1.666667
LADA DAMON	??	HANOVER	??	PART_TIME	−30000	−3.666667
STRIBOG CASTOR	42	UNKNOWN	UNKNOWN	FULL_TIME	30000	5.333333

The result is correct, except for a detail: column *Job* was of data type *factor*, but after the operation, the type *factor* got lost and *Job* is back to *character*. What if we try to exclude factor columns from the transformation to upper case? How can we handle more conditions than just two? It is not simple, `map_if()` does not have much flexibility. We may wonder if a second `map_if()` checking for factors and returning them to lower case could work.

```
df1 %>%
  map_if(.p= is.numeric, .f= ~ .x-mean(.x), .else= toupper) %>%
  map_if(.p= is.factor, .f= tolower) %>% as_tibble()
```

It does not work, *Job* elements are still upper case, and this is because in the transformation to upper case the *factor* type gets lost and the *Job* column is again a generic *character* type, therefore the second `map_if()` does not match any column of type *factor*. There is a trick, though, which consists in not using the `.else` attribute but first transforming all numeric columns, then all character ones. This way, factor type columns are left untouched.

```
df1 %>%
  map_if(.p= is.numeric, .f= ~ .x-mean(.x)) %>%
  map_if(.p= is.character, .f= toupper) %>% as_tibble()
```

Name	Age	City	State	Job	Salary	Seniority
POLYCARP ARTHMAIL	23	DES MOINES	IOWA	full_time	0	−1.666667
LADA DAMON	??	HANOVER	??	part_time	−30000	−3.666667
STRIBOG CASTOR	42	UNKNOWN	UNKNOWN	full_time	30000	5.333333

A different solution would have been to use **map_at()**, another variant that selects columns based on an array of ***positions*** or by ***name***.

```
df1 %>%
  map_if(is.numeric, ~ .x-mean(.x)) %>%
  map_at(c(1,3,4), toupper) %>% as_tibble()
```

The analogous form with column names:

```
df1 %>%
  map_if(is.numeric, ~ .x-mean(.x)) %>%
  map_at(c("Name","City","State"), toupper) %>% as_tibble()
```

9.2.4 Subsetting Rows with Multicolumn Logical Condition

9.2.4.1 Combination of Functions `filter()` and `if_any()`
Another particularly interesting case is when we want to subset rows with a logical condition using a traditional `filter()`, but the condition should be checked on multiple or all columns of the data frame. This is the use case for the combination between functions `filter()` and `if_any()`, of package *dplyr* that returns TRUE if the logical condition is verified on at least one column of those selected. The companion function `if_all()` returns TRUE if the logical condition is verified on all selected columns.

The important parameter of function `if_any()` is `.cols`, which specifies the columns to transform. It accepts all usual forms for selecting columns, by name, position, or range, and with selection helpers, for example, **`everything()`** to select all columns. The other parameter is the logical condition. As a result, `if_any()` produces a Boolean mask, handled by `filter()`.

Again, using our small didactic data frame, we want to select rows with string "known" or symbol "?" in a column, it does not matter which one. Here we use function **`str_detect()`** of package *stringr*, which executes pattern matching and returns TRUE for positive matches and FALSE otherwise.

```
df %>% filter(if_any(.cols=everything(),
                     ~ (str_detect(., "known") | str_detect(., "\\?"))
                     )
             )
```

Name	Age	City	State	Job
Lada Damon	??	Hanover	??	part_time
Stribog Castor	42	unknown	Unknown	full_time

We can see a variant with a different column selection. We exclude columns *Age* and *State*. The result, correctly, includes just one row.

```
df %>% filter(if_any(!c("Age","State"),
                     ~ (str_detect(., "known") | str_detect(., "\\?"))) )
```

Name	Age	City	State	Job
Stribog Castor	42	unknown	Unknown	full_time

9.2.5 Multicolumn Transformations

9.2.5.1 Combination of Functions `mutate()` and `across()`

Another particularly useful function for multicolumn operations is **`across()`**, of *dplyr* package, which combined with **`mutate()`**, offers an efficient method for repeating transformation operations over multiple columns. In theory, function `across()` can be used together with `filter()` too, providing the same functionality we discussed in the previous section. However, the combination of `filter()` and `across()` is deprecated, in favor of `filter()` and `if_any()` or `if_all()`.

Attributes of `across()` are mostly the same of `if_any()`, with `.cols` as the selection of columns, followed by the operation to execute. The combination with `mutate()` implies the creation or the transformation of columns, an operation often needed.

With this combination of functions, we can modify the previous example with string replacements, finally arriving at the most efficient solution.

```
pattern1= c("\\?\\?"=string1, "unknown"=string1, "Unknown"=string1)
string1= "NA"

df %>% mutate(across(.cols= everything(),
                ~ str_replace_all( ., pattern= pattern1)))
```

Name	Age	City	State	Job
Polycarp Arthmail	23	Des Moines	Iowa	full_time
Lada Damon	NA	Hanover	NA	part_time
Stribog Castor	42	NA	NA	full_time

Alternatively, we can be more precise in column selection.

```
df %>% mutate(across(.cols= 2:last_col(),
                ~ str_replace_all( ., pattern= pattern1)))
```

9.2.6 Introducing Missing Values

A further step would be to replace patterns with actual *missing values*, rather than with the string "NA," in order to exploit specialized functions to retrieve or filter missing values. There are some details to consider, though, because there is not just one type of missing value. First, we try with some naive methods, like replacing a pattern with ″ (two single quotes without space) or with keyword *NULL*.

```
df %>% mutate(across(.cols= 2:last_col(),
                ~ str_replace_all( ., "Unknown", ""))) -> df1
```

Name	Age	City	State	Job
Polycarp Arthmail	23	Des Moines	Iowa	full_time
Lada Damon	??	Hanover	??	part_time
Stribog Castor	42	unknown		full_time

If we check the number of missing values, there are none. The two quotes without space are not a missing value.

```
colSums(is.na(df1))
  Name  Age City State  Job
    0    0    0    0    0
```

With keyword *NULL*, we obtain an error; it cannot be used as a value.

Missing values are a very specific type of value. There are several forms to specify them:

- keyword **NA**: it is the most general form, and usually it correctly sets a missing value. In some cases, however, it is possible that errors based on conflicting data types are raised. In that cases, we need to choose a more specific version of the keyword.
- keyword **NA_character_**: represents a typed missing value, in this case of type character, and solves problems in assigning a missing value in a character column.
- keywords **NA_integer_**, **NA_real_**, and **NA_complex_**: similarly, they are typed missing values for assignments in columns of corresponding numeric types.

We try the example, first with **keyword NA**.

```
pattern1= c("\\?\\?"=string1, "unknown"=string1, "Unknown"=string1)
string1= NA

df %>% mutate(across(.cols= 2:last_col(),
                 ~ str_replace_all( ., pattern1)))
```

It does not work and raises an error saying that "'replacement' must be a character vector, not a logical vector". There is something with the type of NA that is not correct.

Let us try with the typed **NA_character_**.

```
pattern1= c("\\?\\?"=string1, "unknown"=string1, "Unknown"=string1)
string1= NA_character_

df %>% mutate(across(.cols= 2:last_col(),
                 ~ str_replace_all( ., pattern1)))
```

Name	Age	City	State	Job
Polycarp Arthmail	23	Des Moines	Iowa	full_time
Lada Damon	*NA*	Hanover	*NA*	part_time
Stribog Castor	42	*NA*	*NA*	full_time

The specific keyword NA_character_ worked correctly. Let us check if the conversion in numeric data type of column *Age* works too. It works.

```
as.integer(df1$Age)
Warning: NAs introduced by coercion
[1] 23 NA 42
```

9.2.7 Use Cases and Execution Time Measurement

We present here two use cases for the application of multicolumn operations. Both were considered before to show data wrangling operations on strings and involved multiple columns. In the second case, we also tackle with a problem we discovered in the previous chapter related to the poor performance of iterations, easily in the order of several minutes and more with medium-sized data frames. We have to verify with specialized multicolumn functions if the problem still persists or is mitigated.

9.2.7.1 Case 1

We consider again the dataset *Final energy consumption* from Eurostat that presents an interesting use case. In this dataset, missing values are reported using the colon symbol (:) and some elements have a numerical value plus a character, referred to as footnotes in the original dataset. We showed how to perform the pattern matching with regex, but only demonstrated it on one column. Now we can efficiently repeat it on all columns.

```
eurostat= read_tsv("datasets/Eurostat/sdg_07_11.tsv")
```

For one column, the substitutions and the data type transformation are as follows:

```
str_replace_all(eurostat$'2000', c('[a-zA-Z\\s]'= ",
                       '(?![.])[\\p{P}\\p{S}]'= ")) %>%
  as.numeric()
```

To repeat them on all columns from *2000* to *2020*, we use the combination `mutate(across())`. The operations to perform are actually two: the pattern matching and replacement, and the transformation to numeric type. An anonymous function can only execute one operation, but using the pipe, the two separate instructions become logically a single operation.

```
eurostat %>%
  mutate(across(.cols = '2000':'2020',
           ~ str_replace_all(.,c('[a-zA-Z\\s]'=",
                       '(?![.])[\\p{P}\\p{S}]'=")) %>%
             as.numeric()))
```

unit,geo\time	2000	2001	2002	2003	2004	2005	2006	...
I05,AL	80.6	82.6	94.6	92.6	103.8	100	91.1	...
I05,AT	85.2	90.3	91.1	95.7	97.1	100	100.1	...
I05,BE	103.1	105.5	99.4	102.9	103.4	100	100.3	...
I05,BG	89.5	89.6	89.5	96.2	95.2	100	103.7	...
I05,CY	90.0	93.2	93.9	99.4	100.0	100	101.7	...
I05,CZ	95.8	97.5	95.6	100.3	101.4	100	101.5	...
I05,DE	100.2	101.9	100.2	102.2	101.5	100	102.6	...
I05,DK	95.0	97.6	95.5	97.6	99.1	100	101.1	...
I05,EA19	94.0	96.5	95.8	98.7	99.6	100	100.2	...
I05,EE	84.6	92.8	91.4	96.0	98.3	100	100.7	...
...	...	...	...	...	...	...	...	...

The same could be done with `map_dfc()` or `map()` plus the transformation into data frame. But first, we need to omit the first column, to avoid replacements on that one too.

```
select(eurostat, !1) %>%
  map( ~ str_replace_all(.,c('[a-zA-Z\\s]'='',
                             '(?![.])[\\p{P}\\p{S}]'='')) %>%
  as.numeric()) %>% as_tibble()
```

2000	2001	2002	2003	2004	2005	2006	...
80.6	82.6	94.6	92.6	103.8	100	91.1	...
85.2	90.3	91.1	95.7	97.1	100	100.1	...
103.1	105.5	99.4	102.9	103.4	100	100.3	...
89.5	89.6	89.5	96.2	95.2	100	103.7	...
90.0	93.2	93.9	99.4	100.0	100	101.7	...
95.8	97.5	95.6	100.3	101.4	100	101.5	...
100.2	101.9	100.2	102.2	101.5	100	102.6	...
95.0	97.6	95.5	97.6	99.1	100	101.1	...
94.0	96.5	95.8	98.7	99.6	100	100.2	...
84.6	92.8	91.4	96.0	98.3	100	100.7	...
...	...	...	...	...	...	...	...

The result is correct, but now the first column is missing. We should reunite it with the others by using **bind_cols()**.

```
bind_cols(
  select(eurostat, 1),
  select(eurostat, !1) %>%
  map_dfc( ~ str_replace_all(.,c('[a-zA-Z\\s]'='',
                                 '(?![.])[\\p{P}\\p{S}]'='')) %>%
                   as.numeric())
)
```

9.2.7.2 Case 2

We consider again the case we have discussed for nested iterations that lets us conclude about the good adaptability of iterations but poor performance. Here, we rewrite the solution by using multicolumn operations and measure the execution time again. For the example, we made use of the modified dataset of population forecasts by the United Nations.

```
df= read_csv("datasets/United Nations/population-and-demography_MOD.csv")
```

The goal is to replace units of measurement (i.e. *K*, *M*, and *B*) with values in the compact form ($e+03$, $e+06$, and $e+09$). To execute the replacements, we first define a custom function `replaceUnit()` that, given a column as parameter, iterates over all elements and replaces values.

```
replaceUnit <- function(x) {
  for(i in 1:length(x)) {
      if( str_detect(x[i],"K") ) {
        x[i]=str_replace(x[i],"K","e+03")
        } else if (str_detect(x[i],"M")) {
          x[i]=str_replace(x[i],"M","e+06")
        } else if (str_detect(x[i],"B")) {
            x[i]=str_replace(x[i],"B","e+09")
            } else x[i]=x[i]
  }
  return(x)
  }
```

Now we execute the two multicolumn operations, first calling our custom function `replace Unit()`, then converting to numeric type all columns. We also measure the execution time.

```
start_time<- Sys.time()

df %>%
  mutate(across(.cols= "2000":last_col(),
                ~ replaceUnit(.x) )) %>%
  mutate(across(.cols= "2000":last_col(),
                ~ as.numeric(.x) )) -> a1

end_time<- Sys.time()

print(end_time-start_time)
Time difference of 5.477391 secs
```

Country name	2000	2001	2002	2003	2004	2005	2006	...
Afghanistan	19542986	19688634	21000258	22645136	23553554	24411196	25442946	...
Africa (UN)	81895206	83946390	86061146	88234925	90478130	92789810	95174030	...
Albania	3182027	3153615	3123554	3092993	3062629	3032636	3003391	...
Algeria	30774624	31200984	31624700	32055882	32510184	32956690	33435082	...
American Samoa	58251	58342	58200	57962	57653	57277	56857	...
Andorra	66116	67841	70868	73929	76950	79845	80241	...
...	...	...	...	...	...	...	...	...

The result is correct. To complete all replacements and type conversions, the execution time is of few seconds. With this solution, instead of having two nested *for cycles*, we have just one, and the performance improves, broadly, by an order of magnitude.

We can further simplify by removing the remaining iteration and replacing it with a fully piped version of the operations. In this case, the custom function `replaceUnit()` is no longer necessary.

```
start_time<- Sys.time()

df %>%
  mutate(across(.cols= "2000":last_col(),
                ~ str_replace_all(.,'K', "e+03"))) %>%
  mutate(across(.cols= "2000":last_col(),
                ~ str_replace_all(.,'M', "e+06"))) %>%
  mutate(across(.cols= "2000":last_col(),
                ~ str_replace_all(.,'B', "e+09"))) %>%
  mutate(across(.cols= "2000":last_col(),
                ~ as.numeric(.x) )) -> a1

end_time<- Sys.time()

print(end_time-start_time)
Time difference of 0.2112682 secs
```

The result is correct and with no iterations the execution time improves by another order of magnitude (tenths of a second, rather than seconds).

Once again, these simple performance tests make clear that iterations are extremely useful for their flexibility, but their usage should be limited to small data frames or series; otherwise, the cost in terms of performance might become unbearable.

9.3 Python: User-defined and Lambda Functions

9.3.1 User-defined Functions

The general syntax for a user-defined function in Python follows a conventional schema and adopts the peculiar Python syntactic rule about indentation. **def** is a keyword, and together with the colon and the indentation, they are mandatory elements.

```
def name(x, y, ...):
  operations(x,y,...)
  variable= operations(x,y,...)
  return(variable)
```

Let us see the same simple case presented for R.

```
def maxmin(values):
  a1= max(values) - min(values)
  a2= np.mean(values)
  a3= np.median(values)
  return([a1,a2,a3])
seriesA = [23, 3, 45, 89, 56, 2]
seriesB = [55, -8, 32, -15, 3, 77, 2, 0, -1, 19, 100, 23]
seriesC = [-9, -87, -45, -2, -21, -3, -6, -80]
```

```
print("test1: ", maxmin(seriesA))
print("test2: ", maxmin(seriesB))
print("test3: ", maxmin(seriesC))
test1:  [87, 36.333333333333336, 34.0]
test2:  [115, 23.916666666666668, 11.0]
test3:  [85, -31.625, -15.0]
```

The basic usage is simple, and user-defined functions, as already mentioned, could be used in countless cases, from simple to extremely complex ones; it only depends on the choices of the coder.

We consider here an example with a pandas data frame, using the dataset of US domestic flights of March 2023.

```
df= pd.read_csv("datasets/Bureau_Trans_Stats/Flights_March2023/
On_Time_Reporting_Carrier_On_Time_Performance_(1987_present)_2023_3.csv",
usecols=[4,5,6,9,14,15,16,18,23,24,25,27,30,31,36,37,38,39,41,42,47,49,52,54])
```

We want to add a new column with the ratio between the delay for late arrivals of each flight with respect to the mean delay for late arrivals of the destination airport. This is a typical use case for function **transform()**.

```
df1= df.query(" ArrDelay < 0 ")

df_MeanAD= df1.groupby(['Dest'])[['ArrDelay']].transform('mean')

df_MeanAD
```

	ArrDelay
0	−13.822881
1	−13.822881
2	−13.822881
3	−13.822881
4	−13.822881
...	...
580317	−16.315974
580318	−13.978417
580319	−13.978417
580320	−14.218419
580321	−13.978417

Now we add the new column *arrdelayRatio* in data frame *df1*.

```
df1['arrdelayRatio']= (df1.ArrDelay / df_MeanAD.ArrDelay).round(2)

df1[['Dest','ArrDelay','arrdelayRatio']]
```

	Dest	ArrDelay	arrdelayRatio
0	CLT	−35.0	2.53
1	CLT	−11.0	0.80
2	CLT	−32.0	2.32
3	CLT	−24.0	1.74
4	CLT	−10.0	0.72
…	…	…	…
580317	JFK	−24.0	1.47
580318	FLL	−24.0	1.72
580319	FLL	−24.0	1.72
580320	CHS	−24.0	1.69
580321	FLL	−24.0	1.72

Now, we want to rewrite this solution with a user-defined function **delayRatio()**. The name of the new column is created using function **join()** of base Python that unites the column name passed as a parameter to the function and the fixed string "Ratio". No separator is added.

```
def delayRatio(col_name, df, df_transform):
  new_col_name= "".join([col_name,"Ratio"])
  df[new_col_name]= (df[col_name] / df_transform[col_name]).round(2)
```

Then we select flights with late arrivals and call the custom function for creating the new column.

```
df1= df.query(" ArrDelay < 0 ")

delayRatio('ArrDelay', df1, df_MeanAD)
```

The result is the same of the previous example.

We can easily calculate other similar columns, for example, the corresponding one for departure delays.

```
df_MeanDD= df1.groupby(['Origin'])[['DepDelay']].transform('mean')

delayRatio('DepDelay', df1, df_MeanDD)

df1[['Dest','ArrDelay','ArrDelayRatio', 'DepDelay','DepDelayRatio']]
```

	Dest	ArrDelay	ArrDelayRatio	DepDelay	DepDelayRatio
0	CLT	−35.0	2.53	−12.0	1.88
1	CLT	−11.0	0.80	−5.0	0.79
2	CLT	−32.0	2.32	−13.0	2.04
3	CLT	−24.0	1.74	−6.0	0.94
4	CLT	−10.0	0.72	−9.0	1.41
...	...	...	...	...	...
580317	JFK	−24.0	1.47	13.0	−6.91
580318	FLL	−24.0	1.72	−3.0	0.74
580319	FLL	−24.0	1.72	−4.0	0.99
580320	CHS	−24.0	1.69	−12.0	5.75
580321	FLL	−24.0	1.72	−14.0	3.11

9.3.1.1 Lambda Functions

Python's *lambda functions* are equivalent to R's anonymous functions and serve the same purpose: they can only execute a single operation and have no name. A concatenation of instructions is considered a single operation, like a piped instruction in R.

Let us consider a simple example with the data frame of US flights. We want to aggregate for airlines and create a new column with the difference between the maximum early arrival and the minimum late arrival (which is the largest late arrival, being the negative number).

Logically, we would have to execute something like the following operation:

```
df.groupby(["Dest"]).agg(
    EarlyArr_max= pd.NamedAgg(column="ArrDelay", aggfunc="max"),
    LateArr_max= pd.NamedAgg(column="ArrDelay", aggfunc="min"),
    diff= EarlyArr_max - LateArr_max)
```

But obviously, it does not work this way; columns *EarlyArr_max* and *LateArr_max* are not referred to any data frame in the third operation and this produces an error:

```
NameError: name 'EarlyArr_max' is not defined
```

We should do it in two steps.

```
temp= df.groupby(["Dest"]).agg(
  EarlyArr_max= pd.NamedAgg(column="ArrDelay", aggfunc="max"),
  LateArr_max= pd.NamedAgg(column="ArrDelay", aggfunc="min"))

temp['diff']= temp.EarlyArr_max - temp.LateArr_max

temp
```

	EarlyArr_max	LateArr_max	diff
Dest			
ABE	333.0	−34.0	367.0
ABI	214.0	−18.0	232.0
ABQ	990.0	−31.0	1021.0
ABR	34.0	−42.0	76.0
ABY	153.0	−23.0	176.0
...	...	...	...
WRG	69.0	−24.0	93.0
XNA	864.0	−37.0	901.0
XWA	218.0	−29.0	247.0
YAK	114.0	−30.0	144.0
YUM	837.0	−23.0	860.0

With a *lambda function*, we are able to calculate the third column in the same expression. We just need to explicitly use NumPy functions `np.nanmax()` and `np.nanmin()` to ignore missing values or the corresponding pandas `x.max()` and `x.min()`, which by default ignore missing values.

```
df.groupby(["Dest"]).agg(
    EarlyArr_max= pd.NamedAgg("ArrDelay", aggfunc="max"),
    LateArr_max= pd.NamedAgg("ArrDelay", aggfunc="min"),
    diff= pd.NamedAgg("ArrDelay", aggfunc= lambda x: np.nanmax(x)-np.nanmin(x)))
df.groupby(["Dest"]).agg(
    EarlyArr_max= pd.NamedAgg("ArrDelay", aggfunc="max"),
    LateArr_max= pd.NamedAgg("ArrDelay", aggfunc="min"),
    diff= pd.NamedAgg("ArrDelay", aggfunc= lambda x: x.max()-x.min()))
```

9.3.2 Python: Multicolumn Operations

Python, too, has functions that permit executing multicolumn operations and avoid writing nested iterations, which may cause a hefty penalty in terms of execution time. With pandas' functions, they often natively support the multicolumn execution if a data frame is passed as a parameter. However, it exists the general function `apply()` able to automatically repeat the execution on columns, rows, or groups, as we have seen in Chapter 7 when we anticipated the method to sort rows within groups.

We use again our previous tiny didactic data frame for the first examples.

```
df = pd.DataFrame(np.array(
  [["Polycarp Arthmail", "23", "Des Moines","Iowa","full_time"],
  ["Lada Damon", "??", "Hanover","??","part_time"],
  ["Stribog Castor","42","unknown","Unknown","full_time"]]),
  columns=['Name', 'Age', 'City', 'State', 'Job'])
df
```

	Name	Age	City	State	Job
0	Polycarp Arthmail	23	Des Moines	Iowa	full_time
1	Lada Damon	??	Hanover	??	part_time
2	Stribog Castor	42	unknown	Unknown	full_time

We want to replace the different versions used to express that a value is unspecified with a unique one, the string "NA". With pandas **replace()** is very easy because it accepts either a series (a column) or a data frame. We can concatenate single replacements.

```
string1= "Unknown"
string2= "unknown"
string3= "??"

repl= "NA"

df.replace(string1, repl).replace(string2, repl).replace(string3, repl)
```

	Name	Age	City	State	Job
0	Polycarp Arthmail	23	Des Moines	Iowa	full_time
1	Lada Damon	NA	Hanover	NA	part_time
2	Stribog Castor	42	NA	NA	full_time

Or we can specify a list of replacements. To save the result, we could use the `inplace` argument.

```
temp= df.copy(deep=True)

temp.replace([string1, string2, string3], repl, inplace=True)
```

In both cases, it has executed a multicolumn replacement on the whole data frame. We could have specified a *subset of columns*. Special care should be exercised in this case because we are assigning values to a subset, and we should be aware that this operation is *executed by copy, not by value*. We can easily test it.

```
temp= df.copy(deep=True)

temp[['Age','State']].replace([string1, string2, string3], repl, inplace=True)
temp
```

	Name	Age	City	State	Job
0	Polycarp Arthmail	23	Des Moines	Iowa	full_time
1	Lada Damon	??	Hanover	??	part_time
2	Stribog Castor	42	unknown	Unknown	full_time

The result shows no replacements because they have been done on a copy of the data frame's columns. It should be handled correctly.

```
temp= df.copy(deep=True)

temp.loc[:, ['Age','State']]= temp.loc[:, ['Age','State']].\
                               replace([string1, string2, string3], repl)
temp
```

	Name	Age	City	State	Job
0	Polycarp Arthmail	23	Des Moines	Iowa	full_time
1	Lada Damon	NA	Hanover	NA	part_time
2	Stribog Castor	42	unknown	NA	full_time

9.3.2.1 Execution Time

We test the execution time of the multicolumn `replace()` function with the modified version of dataset *The global population is projected to peak at around 10.4 billion in 2086*, according to the United Nations, as already used to this end in previous sections.

```
df= pd.read_csv("datasets/United Nations/population-and-demography_MOD.csv")
```

With the `replace()` function, it is possible to define a list for both the patterns and the replacements. The function associates the values of the two lists in pairs. In this case, if we run the replacements on the whole data frame, the first column of country names is included, and replacements might mistakenly happen on names too. We could specify a *regex to instruct the function to find the patterns only at the end of values* (i.e. [$K], [$M], [$B]). *Otherwise, we need to omit the first column from the selection*. We measure the execution time.

```
import time
start1= time.time()

df.replace(['[$K]','[$M]','[$B]'],['e+03','e+06','e+09'], regex=True)

end1= time.time()
print('Execution time (sec.):', end1 - start1)
Execution time (sec.): 0.22796392440795898
```

The execution time drops by an order of magnitude with respect to the case with nested iterations and is similar to R. A tiny penalty is likely introduced by regular expressions. We can try a version without regex by slicing the columns to omit the first. Then we have to unite again the first column to the others, we can use pandas `join()` function, that we anticipate from the next chapter.

```
import time
start2 = time.time()

df[df.columns.difference(['Country name'], sort=False)].\
replace(['K','M','B'],['e+03','e+06','e+09']).join(df[['Country name']])

end2 = time.time()
print('Execution time (sec.):', end2 - start2)
Execution time (sec.): 0.01689291000366211
```

A tiny difference in favor of the version without regex exists, but column *Country name* has become the last one. Rearranging the position makes the gain disappear. However, this test is useful to verify the fact that regex could also affect the performance.

9.3.3 General Case

9.3.3.1 Function `apply()`
We now consider the general case when there is no function natively performing multicolumn computation. The generic function **`apply()`** helps in such cases to repeat on multiple rows, columns, or groups a certain operation, which could be defined by existing functions, user-defined functions, or lambda functions.

For example, we use again dataset *Final energy consumption* from Eurostat that we have already employed in date and string operations.

```
es= pd.read_csv("datasets/Eurostat/sdg_07_11.tsv", sep='\t')
```

	unit,geo\time	2000	2001	2002	2003	2004	...	2016	2017	2018	2019	2020
0	I05,AL	80.6	82.6	94.6	92.6	103.8	...	100.2	109.7	112.6	109.1	103.4
1	I05,AT	85.2	90.3	91.1	95.7	97.1	...	100.8	102.4	100.0	101.7	93.6
2	I05,BE	103.1	105.5	99.4	102.9	103.4	...	99.5	98.6	99.4	97.8	91.0
3	I05,BG	89.5	89.6	89.5	96.2	95.2	...	95.2	97.6	97.8	97.1	94.1
4	I05,CY	90.0	93.2	93.9	99.4	100.0	...	96.3	101.6	101.3	102.9	85.8
...	...	...	...	...	...	...	...	...	...	...	...	...
111	TOE_HAB,SI	2.30	2.41	2.36	2.44	2.48	...	2.36	2.40	2.39	2.32	2.09
112	TOE_HAB,SK	2.03	2.13	2.16	2.09	2.06	...	1.92	2.05	2.04	2.05	1.89
113	TOE_HAB,TR	0.86	0.78	0.84	0.89	0.91	...	1.22	1.33	1.30 be	1.29 be	1.27
114	TOE_HAB,UK	2.60	2.61	2.53	2.55	2.56	...	2.04	2.02	2.03	2.01	:
115	TOE_HAB,XK	:	:	:	0.46	0.46	...	0.81 e	0.85 e	0.82	0.85	:

This dataset has colon (:) in place of missing values and has letters and spaces together with some numeric values. We need to remove all of them in order to convert the column to a numerical data type.

First, we consider the simplest solution, concatenating the replacement of values and the conversion to numeric type. We first strip all spaces from column names.

```
es.columns
Index(['unit,geo\time', '2000 ', '2001 ', '2002 ', '2003 ', '2004 ', '2005 ',
       '2006 ', '2007 ', '2008 ', '2009 ', '2010 ', '2011 ', '2012 ', '2013 ',
       '2014 ', '2015 ', '2016 ', '2017 ', '2018 ', '2019 ', '2020 '],
      dtype='object')
es.columns= es.columns.str.strip()
```

We use function `drop()` to omit the first column from the selection. It is a variant of the solution seen in the previous example.

```
temp=es.copy(deep=True)

# Drop the first column from the list
cols = temp.columns.drop('unit,geo\\time')

temp[cols]=temp[cols].\
replace("[\s:a-zA-Z]","", regex=True).\
apply(pd.to_numeric)
temp
```

	unit,geo\time	2000	2001	2002	2003	2004	...	2017	2018	2019	2020
0	I05,AL	80.60	82.60	94.60	92.60	103.80	...	109.70	112.60	109.10	103.40
1	I05,AT	85.20	90.30	91.10	95.70	97.10	...	102.40	100.00	101.70	93.60
2	I05,BE	103.10	105.50	99.40	102.90	103.40	...	98.60	99.40	97.80	91.00
3	I05,BG	89.50	89.60	89.50	96.20	95.20	...	97.60	97.80	97.10	94.10
4	I05,CY	90.00	93.20	93.90	99.40	100.00	...	101.60	101.30	102.90	85.80
...	...	...	...	...	...	...	...	...	...	...	...
111	TOE_HAB,SI	2.30	2.41	2.36	2.44	2.48	...	2.40	2.39	2.32	2.09
112	TOE_HAB,SK	2.03	2.13	2.16	2.09	2.06	...	2.05	2.04	2.05	1.89
113	TOE_HAB,TR	0.86	0.78	0.84	0.89	0.91	...	1.33	1.30	1.29	1.27
114	TOE_HAB,UK	2.60	2.61	2.53	2.55	2.56	...	2.02	2.03	2.01	NaN
115	TOE_HAB,XK	NaN	NaN	NaN	0.46	0.46	...	0.85	0.82	0.85	NaN

Checking the columns data type, they are correct, years are numerical.

```
temp.dtypes
unit,geo\time      object
2000              float64
2001              float64
2002              float64
2003              float64
```

```
2004              float64
2005              float64
...               ...
2017              float64
2018              float64
2019              float64
2020              float64
dtype: object
```

A variant is with a *for cycle* on the column names starting from the second one.

```
temp=es.copy(deep=True)

for i in temp.columns[1:] :
    temp.loc[:, i]= temp.loc[:, i].\
    replace("[\s:a-zA-Z]","", regex=True).\
    apply(pd.to_numeric)
```

In the third variant, we wish to remove the *for cycle*, because we know it is bad for performance, but still want to use .loc[] for the slicing. The idea is to specify in .loc[] the range of columns ('*2000':).

```
temp1= es.copy(deep=True)

temp1.loc[:,'2000':]= temp.loc[:,'2000':].\
replace("[\s:a-zA-Z]","", regex=True).\
apply(pd.to_numeric)

temp1
```

	unit,geo\time	2000	2001	2002	2003	2004	...	2017	2018	2019	2020
0	I05,AL	80.6	82.6	94.6	92.6	103.8	...	109.7	112.6	109.1	103.4
1	I05,AT	85.2	90.3	91.1	95.7	97.1	...	102.4	100.0	101.7	93.6
2	I05,BE	103.1	105.5	99.4	102.9	103.4	...	98.6	99.4	97.8	91.0
...	...	...	...	...	...	...	...	...	...	...	...
113	TOE_HAB,TR	0.86	0.78	0.84	0.89	0.91	...	1.33	1.3	1.29	1.27
114	TOE_HAB,UK	2.6	2.61	2.53	2.55	2.56	...	2.02	2.03	2.01	NaN
115	TOE_HAB,XK	NaN	NaN	NaN	0.46	0.46	...	0.85	0.82	0.85	NaN

It looks correct, until we check the column types.

```
temp1.dtypes
unit,geo\time      object
2000               object
```

```
2001            object
2002            object
2003            object
2004            object
2005            object
...             ...
2017            object
2018            object
2019            object
2020            object
dtype: object
```

All columns are still of type *object*, meaning their values are strings. Apparently, the conversion to numeric failed for unknown reasons. But there is more weirdness in this case. Let us try to execute an arithmetic operation on a year column; if the values are strings, we should obtain an error.

```
temp1['2010'].sum()
7054.980000000002
```

It works as for numeric values. This is an error of Python/pandas that gets somehow confused with slicing, function `apply()`, and type conversion.

To avoid the problem, the easiest way is avoiding the slicing with `.loc[]` and `apply()`, but subsetting the columns with a mask, as done before.

```
temp= es.copy(deep=True)

temp.loc[:,'2000':]= temp.loc[:,'2000':].replace("[\s:a-zA-Z]","", regex=True)

cols= temp.columns.drop('unit,geo\\time')
temp[cols]= temp[cols].apply(pd.to_numeric)

temp.dtypes
unit,geo\time       object
2000              float64
2001              float64
2002              float64
2003              float64
2004              float64
2005              float64
...                 ...
2017              float64
2018              float64
2019              float64
2020              float64
dtype: object
```

Now it is correct. A more complex solution is to decouple replacements from multicolumn type conversion as before. After that, function **assign()** that creates calculated columns could be used.

This way, year columns are recreated of the numeric type, and they overwrite the corresponding ones of object type. The syntax is unintuitive, though, because it needs a special notation with double star symbols (**), referring to a special attribute of some pandas function called **kwargs** (*keyword arguments*). This attribute makes column names keywords for the new columns created with function assign(). Definitely not intuitive. To try to clarify the logic, it is as if we would write the following:

```
temp.assign( '2000'= temp['2000'].apply(pd.to_numeric),
             '2001'= temp['2001'].apply(pd.to_numeric),
             '2002'= temp['2002'].apply(pd.to_numeric),
             '2003'= temp['2003'].apply(pd.to_numeric),
             ...
```

With function assign(), we are creating new columns with the same names of the existing ones, thus overwriting them with the correct version. This is the idea. Let us try it.

```
temp= es.copy(deep=True)

temp.loc[:,'2000':]= temp.loc[:,'2000':].replace("[\s:a-zA-Z]","", regex=True)

temp= temp.assign(**temp.loc[:,'2000':].apply(pd.to_numeric))
```

The transformations and column types are correct. Obviously, there is no need to choose such a complicated method when there are much simpler alternatives, but as usual, this is useful as an exercise for understanding an unintuitive logic.

As a last variant, we can explicitly make the replacements with missing values as NumPy *NaN*. Then we convert the subset of column (here selected in another different way) by using **astype()**, which works on multiple columns.

```
temp=es.copy(deep=True)

temp.loc[:,'2000':]=temp.loc[:,'2000':].replace("[:a-zA-Z]",np.NaN, regex=True)
temp[temp.columns[1:]]= temp[temp.columns[1:]].astype('float64')
```

This presentation of several variants to achieve the same result is mostly aimed at showing one particular feature of Python with which it would be worth familiarizing: as a tool, it is extremely flexible and allows for the definition of many alternative solutions to common practical problems. Knowing all the alternatives is not necessary. What is important is not to stick to just one solution because it might not work in certain conditions, and it is almost certain that there exists an alternative that lets bypassing the problem. Look for an alternative, try it, understand the different logic, and evaluate if it is unreasonably complicated. If it looks like that, there is probably a simpler solution, so find it.

Questions

9.1 (R/Python)

Are user-defined functions mostly useful for...

A Implementing previously unavailable functionalities

B Implementing operations to be re-executed with different data or parameters

C Improving performances

D Producing new packages

(R: B)

9.2 (R/Python)

Are multicolumn operations useful to...

A Repeat operations on data frame columns

B Compute operations on more columns at once

C Implement new functionalities

D Replicate conditional operations

(R: A)

9.3 (R)

Is it necessary in an R user-defined function to include a *return* instruction?

A Yes, it is

B Yes, when the expression produces some results

C Yes, when we want to change some R objects

D No, it depends on the computational logic

(R: D)

9.4 (R)

What is the logical difference between the alternative syntax presented below?

```
result <- func1(A)
result <- A %>% func1()
result <- A |> func1()
```

A None, they are equivalent

B The third one produces a syntax error

C The second and the third one produce a syntax error

D *result* is wrong, we should use *return*

(R: A)

9.5 (R)

Is the following fragment of code correct?

```
result <- func1(A)
func1 <- function(value) {
    a1= max(value)-min(value)
    return(a1)
}
```

A Yes, it is

B No, it should be *A* not *value* in the definition of the function

C No, the function definition should appear before its usage

D No, `return(a1)` is not needed

(R: C)

9.6 **(R)**

Is the following fragment of code correct?

```
func1 <- function(value) {
     100*(max(value)-min(value))/min(value)
}
df %>% mutate(Col2= func1(Col1))
```

A Yes, it is

B No, it should be *Col1* not *value* in the definition of the function

C No, the function definition could not appear in a `mutate()` function

D No, a return instruction is needed

(R: A)

9.7 **(R)**

Is the following fragment of code correct?

```
func1 <- function(data, value) {
     data %>% mutate(Col2= 100*(max(value)-min(value))/min(value))
}

df %>% group_by(Col2) %>%
     func1(Col1)
```

A Yes, it is

B No, it should be *df* and *Col2* not *data* and *value* in the definition of the function

C No, a data frame could not be a parameter of a function

D No, because the `mutate()` function adopts the data masking mechanism, and when used in a function, it does not work as usual

(R: D)

9.8 **(R)**

What does it mean that the *variable embracing* is needed in the following fragment of code?

```
func1 <- function(data, Col) {
     data %>% mutate(Col2= 100*(max(Col)-min(Col))/min(Col))
}
df %>% group_by(Col2) %>%
     func1(Col1)
```

A When we call the function, we should write `func1({{Col1}})`

B In the function, column names of data masking functions need the {{ }} syntax

C In the function, we must write

D `data %>% mutate(Col2= 100*(max({Col})-min({Col}))/min({Col}))`

E In the function, we must write

F `{{data}} %>% mutate(Col2= 100*(max(Col)-min(Col))/min(Col))`

(R: B)

9.9 (R)

What is the logical difference between the alternative syntax presented below?

```
(function(x) max(x)-min(x) )(A)
(\(x) max(x)-min(x) )(A)
```

A None, they are equivalent

B The second one produces a syntax error

C The first one is wrong, instead of *function* it needs a user-defined name

D In the second one, the escape symbol \ is wrong

(R: A)

9.10 (R)

What is the expected result of the following instructions?

```
pat1= c("\\.\\."=string1, "\\?\\?"=string1, "::"=string1)
string1= "undefined"
df1= map(.x= df,
         function(x) str_replace_all(string= x, pattern= pat1)
      )
```

A In the first three *df* columns, it replaces all element values corresponding to "undefined" with one of the three patterns

B In all *df* columns, it replaces all element values corresponding to one of the three patterns with "undefined"

C In the first *df* column, it replaces all element values corresponding to one of the three patterns with "undefined"

D In all *df* columns, it finds all element values corresponding to one of the three patterns or to "undefined"

(R: B)

9.11 (R)

With respect to Question 9.9.10, what is the logical difference between that example and the following instruction?

```
df1= map(df, ~ str_replace_all(., pattern= pat1))
```

A None, they are equivalent
B This one replaces patterns with "undefined" only in the first column
C This one is wrong; the point in the `str_replace_all()` function is meaningless
D This one is wrong; the tilde symbol does not represent an anonymous function
(R: A)

9.12 (R)
What is the expected result of the following instructions?

```
df %>% mutate(across(.cols= 5:last_col(),
                     ~ str_replace_all( ., "undefined", 'n/a')))
```

A In *df* fifth column and last one, it replaces the string "undefined" with "n/a"
B In all *df* columns, it replaces the string "undefined" with "n/a"
C In *df* columns from the fifth to the last one, it replaces the string "n/a" with "undefined"
D In *df* columns from the fifth to the last one, it replaces the string "undefined" with "n/a"
(R: D)

9.13 (Python)
What are the expected results of the two set of operations presented below?

```
df.groupby(["Col1"]).agg(
    Col3= pd.NamedAgg(column="Col2", aggfunc="max"),
    Col4= pd.NamedAgg(column="Col2", aggfunc="min"),
    diff= Col3 - Col4)

df.groupby(["Col1"]).agg(
    Col3= pd.NamedAgg(column="Col2", aggfunc="max"),
    Col4= pd.NamedAgg(column="Col2", aggfunc="min")
    diff= pd.NamedAgg("Col2", aggfunc= lambda x: x.max()-x.min()))
```

A None, they are equivalent
B The first one produces a syntax error
C The second one is wrong, x in the lambda function is undefined
D In the second one, the lambda function must be defined before the *groupby*
(R: B)

9.14 (Python)
What is the expected result of the operations presented below?

```
string1= "undefined"
string2= "not available"
string3= "unknown"
repl= "n/a"
df.replace([string1, string2, string3], repl)
```

    A A multicolumn replacement of the three strings with the replacement one

    B A syntax error, one or more columns should be specified

    C In the first column of *df*, replacement of the three strings with the replacement one

    D A multicolumn replacement of elements containing all the three strings with the replacement one

(R: A)

9.15   **(Python)**

What is the expected result of the operation presented below?

```
df[df.columns].replace("[\s:a-zA-Z]","", regex=True).\
apply(pd.to_numeric)
```

    A None, it is syntactically wrong

    B On all *df* columns, it replaces spaces and letters with nothing, then transforms all columns to numeric data type

    C On all *df* columns, it replaces all values containing spaces with nothing, then transforms all columns to numeric data type

    D On all *df* columns, it replaces spaces and letters with corresponding numeric representations

(R: B)

10

Join Data Frames

The *join operation* between data frames is among the most important operations on data because it is not just technically powerful; it is one of the pillars of the creativity and exploration intrinsic to data science. Looking at data science as just a set of technicalities and logical or statistical skills would largely mislead the whole sense and nature of the discipline, which is to discover knowledge buried deep into data. And the act of discovering knowledge is not just a mechanistic or stochastic process; it is a creative process that requires curiosity and imagination, desire to know more and better about unfamiliar phenomena, and the ability to observe the nuances of reality, which is seldom described with an easy categorization. The join operation is so fundamental because it allows to logically combine different data frames through shared characteristics, permitting to say that an observation in one data frame could be put together with an observation of another data frame because they are both parts of a more complete observation. Like watching a scene from two different perspectives, they are different because they describe what happens from different angles, but they nevertheless describe the same scene, so they could be joined to form a more comprehensive description. This is the invaluable role of join operations.

Several other operations let you combine data frames. Usually, it is said they *concatenate* or *bind* data frames, either by columns or by rows, and from this, the typical name of the functions is a variation of *concatenate()* or *bind()*. But those are not *join* operations because they just technically put together rows or columns coherently with the size of the data frames. They do not respect the logical associations between the content of the data frames, putting together only rows that are logically describing the same observation. This is, instead, the core of a join operation, and from this derives the fundamental concept of **keys of a join operation**, meaning those *variables whose values uniquely and unambiguously identify an observation*. It is by defining key columns to be joined that rows corresponding to the same observation could be recognized and *joined*, which is then combined to form a unique resulting data frame.

Datasets

Gini index, from the World Bank (https://data.worldbank.org/indicator/SI.POV.GINI), presents indicators measuring the distribution of income, wealth, or consumption across the population for a large set of countries. Value 0 of the Gini index means that there is perfect equality, whereas value 1 means maximum inequality. *Copyright*: Creative Commons Attribution 4.0 (CC-BY 4.0) (https://creativecommons.org/licenses/by/4.0/)

Data Science Fundamentals with R, Python, and Open Data, First Edition. Marco Cremonini.
© 2024 John Wiley & Sons, Inc. Published 2024 by John Wiley & Sons, Inc.
Companion website: www.wiley.com/go/DSFRPythonOpenData

Military spending as a share of GDP, from *Our World in Data* using data from the *Stockholm International Peace Research Institute (SIPRI)*, has data regarding military spending with respect to the GDP (Gross Domestic Production).

Source: SIPRI Military Expenditure Database, Stockholm International Peace Research Institute (SIPRI).

Copyright: Usage is free for publication in scientific journals, monographic publications, and book chapters (https://www.sipri.org/about/terms-and-conditions).

10.1 Basic Concepts

In this chapter, we use datasets *Gini index*, from the World Bank, and *Military spending as a share of GDP*, from Our World in Data/SIPRI, and assume we want to join their rows by respecting the logical associations between countries listed in the two datasets. For instance, the Gini index row of Finland should be joined with the corresponding row of Finland's military spending; the USA's Gini index row should be joined with the USA's military spending, and so on. Obviously, it should not happen that a Gini index row of one country is joined with the military spending of another, because that would produce incoherent data. Instead, it would be possible that some countries appear in the Gini index dataset but not in the military spending one, or vice versa, some would appear in the military spending dataset but not in the Gini index one. In those cases, no join would be possible for those rows, because there are no *logically* corresponding rows between the two datasets. Those missing correspondences should be managed, and, as we will see, there are some alternatives. At any rate, with join operations, the *logical correspondence* between rows is key; everything is done in order to make sure that the correspondence among rows is reliable, because joining data frames might remarkably increase the meaningfulness of our data, and we might be able to perform a whole new level of analysis, but we must not mess everything up by joining unrelated data.

One may wonder if having rows without correspondence between two data frames to join is an exceptional case. It is not, it is the norm, and we should always assume there will be some, even in cases when, logically, we might expect to find none. For example, the list of countries for which the World Bank estimates the Gini index is very likely different from the list of countries for which SIPRI evaluates military spending. There could be missing values, countries not providing official figures, and so forth; there is no solid motivation to assume that the two lists of countries would be the same. But there is another case, which is subtler and might induce errors. Let us consider cases when we may reasonably assume that the list of entities in two datasets is the same. For example, the European Union has 27 member countries. It would not be unreasonable to think that in official documents or communications, country names of EU members are official too, therefore uniquely spelled. We may look at the page *Country Profiles* on the European Union website (https://european-union.europa.eu/principles-countries-history/country-profiles_ en) and find the official names. For example, *Czechia*. Similarly, we may look at the page *Countries in the EU and EEA* on the official UK Government site (https://www.gov.uk/eu-eea) to find the list of EU member countries. There is no *Czechia*, there is the *Czech Republic*. The problem arises because if we are joining two data frames with information on the 27 EU country members, we may believe that country names are the official ones and uniquely defined. It would not be an unsound assumption, but unfortunately, it is also untrue. Let us assume that one dataset has taken the country names from the official EU site and the other from the official UK.GOV site. We know that *Czechia* and the *Czech Republic* are the same country, but for a computational tool,

Gini index

Country Name	Country Code	2019	2020
Afghanistan	AFG		
Africa Eastern and Southern	X AFE		
Africa Western and Central	X AFW		
Albania	ALB	30.8	
Algeria	DZA		
American Samoa	X ASM		
Andorra	X AND		
Angola	AGO		
Antigua and Barbuda	X ATG		
Arab World	X ARB		
Argentina	ARG	42.9	42.3
Armenia	ARM	29.9	25.2
Aruba	X ABW		
Australia	AUS		
Austria	AUT	30.2	
Azerbaijan	AZE		
Bahamas, The	X BHS		

Military spending - %GDP

Entity	Code	2019	2020
Afghanistan	AFG	1.12	1.37
Albania	ALB	1.29	1.54
Algeria	DZA	6.02	6.66
Angola	AGO	1.64	1.62
Argentina	ARG	0.71	0.76
Armenia	ARM	4.77	4.86
Australia	AUS	1.88	2.06
Austria	AUT	0.73	0.84
Azerbaijan	AZE	3.87	5.39
Bahrain	BHR	4.06	4.07
Bangladesh	BGD	1.35	1.30
Belarus	BLR	1.23	1.25
Belgium	BEL	0.89	1.08
Belize	BLZ	1.33	1.57
Benin	BEN	0.47	0.47
Bolivia	BOL	1.46	1.57
Bosnia and Herzegovina	BIH	0.82	0.88
Botswana	BWA	2.81	3.50

Figure 10.1 Example of join between data frames.

those are simply two different names, then two different countries, if we instructed it to use country names to create logical correspondences. This is just one example among countless other entities that are logically the same but are represented differently, even from the most reputable and official sources. For us, it is easy to recognize that, but nearly impossible for almost all join operation functions. These cases must be managed carefully, and they are extremely common. One mandatory check we will repeat in all examples is to find unmatched rows and analyze the reasons why that happened. If there is a logical correspondence but not a syntactic correspondence, like *Czechia* and the *Czech Republic*, then we need to fix it.

Figure 10.1 shows the general logic of a join operation between data frames. It shows some rows that match using country names or country codes between the *Gini index* and the *Military spending* data frames, and others that do not match, in the example because they appear in the first data frame but not in the second data frame.

10.1.1 Keys of a Join Operation

Variables used to logically match rows between data frames in a join operation are called *keys of the join operation*. They could be one or more for each data frame, and the requirement is that the values of the keys uniquely identify rows to join (actually, there could be less strict conditions than the exact, unique correspondence between keys, but it is just a variant of the basic rule, the logic does not change). This is the reason why there could be more than a single variable for each data frame: a single variable might not be enough to define a unique association. The classical example is with territorial entities, like city names, counties, states (or provinces, regions). We can imagine having two data frames with information about territorial entities. In one data frame, we may have population data; in the other, we may have income and educational data. We want to join the two data frames. We assume city, county and state names are present in both data frames. Would it be sufficient to use only the variable with city names to join the two data frames? No, it would not, except in very specific cases, because there are many cities with same name, it is not uncommon, so the city name would likely not uniquely identify a pair of rows in the two data frames. This case typically produces an error. But even worse than that, it could identify a unique pair of rows that actually corresponds to two different cities, because it happened that in the first data frame there was Hanover, New Hampshire, but not Hanover, Minnesota, and on the contrary, the second data frame had the opposite. By joining on city names only, the two would match, uniquely, resulting in incoherent data, the worst result. We need to add the state name (for the USA, this would be sufficient; there are no cities with same name in the same state; however, that could be untrue in other countries, so it is possible that a third variable is needed for an intermediate territorial entity like the county or the province).

Another possibility, often better than relying on names, is to rely on **official codes**, which have typically been created for uniquely identify entities independently from their descriptive names, which might be affected by a number of problems, like homonyms, misspelling, abbreviations, lack of standard, etc. Territorial entities have, almost always, some form of coding, at the very least the **zip code** defined by the postal service, which uniquely identifies an area. In many countries is present an official code for territorial entities defined by the central administration of the country, this code is typically used in **land registry** and is unique. Same problem exists if we move from territorial entities to populations, products, organizational divisions, etc., homonyms and uncertain spelling affect all name systems that are not codes, and in almost all cases, a standard coding has been defined; even more than one is not uncommon, like social security numbers, fiscal identification codes, identification codes of all sorts (e.g. the bar code for products or the ISBN code for publications).

By using codes instead of names, typically the number of unmatched rows in a join operation is lower. However, caution is still necessary; codes are helpful but not perfect, and you might find errors or inconsistencies in codes too, therefore *the result of a join operation must be carefully checked, regardless of the keys used.*

Note

Care is needed with codes because it is not uncommon to have several standards for coding official entities like countries. The most common are defined by ISO (International Standard Organization) with its ISO-3166 standard, which specifies two codes for countries, respectively, called **alpha-2** (2-letter codes) and **alpha-3** (3-letter codes). But others exist and are used, typically defined by international organizations like the European Union, the United States Geological Survey, or the International Olympic Committee. This is another instance of the traditional problem of competing standards. Therefore, which standard coding is used should be checked and verified.

In our example with the *Gini index* and *Military spending* data frames, in both we have the country name and a country code. In the former, columns are *Country Name* and *Country Code*; in the latter, columns are *Entity* and *Code*. The two alternatives for the choice of join keys are: *Country Name – Entity* or *Country Code – Code*. In the first case, the join operation will match on values of country names; in the second case, on values of country codes.

Note

One could wonder whether both country names and country codes should be used as keys, then matching between *(Country Name, Country Code) – (Entity, Code)*. It is possible, of course, but the benefit is not evident, while the cost in terms of additional computation time is certain. Could it be that a country is uniquely matched with the combination of both information but not with just one name or code? No, it could not.

10.1.2 Types of Join

It was left to establish what to do with rows with keys that do not match between the data frames. They could simply be ignored, returning only the rows that have matched and then joined between the two data frames. Or the result could return all of them, with rows that have matched keys showing information from both data frames and rows that have non-matched keys showing only the information of their original data frame and missing values for the columns from the other data frame. The join operation is technically always the same; what changes is how the result is presented.

This is the basis of the different types of join; they all have the same logic and matching keys, but the result differs in the presentation:

- **Inner join**: only rows with matching keys are presented, with values from both data frames joined.
- **Outer or full join**: all rows of both data frames are presented; rows with matching keys have values from both data frames; rows without matching keys have the values of their original data frame and missing values for columns of the other data frame.

The difference between *inner* and *outer/full join* is the most important to learn. There are two more variants that depend on the order in which data frames are specified in the join operation. Assuming a generic join operation with the form dfA join dfB, we call *dfA* the data frame on the **left**, and *dfB* the data frame on the **right** of the join. With this definition of *left* and *right data frames*, two additional variants are defined:

- **Left join**: a variant of the *outer/full join* where all rows of only the *left* data frame are presented in the result.
- **Right join**: same as the left join, but with all rows of only the *right* data frame presented in the result.

10.1.3   R: Join Operation

We start by reading the two datasets, *Gini index* and *Military spending*.

```
gini= read_csv("datasets/World_Bank/API_SI.POV.GINI_DS2_en_csv_v2_4651513.csv")
```

Country Name	Country Code	Indicator Name	Indicator Code	1960	1961	1962	1963	...
Aruba	ABW	Gini index	SI.POV.GINI	NA	NA	NA	NA	...
Africa Eastern and Southern	AFE	Gini index	SI.POV.GINI	NA	NA	NA	NA	...
Afghanistan	AFG	Gini index	SI.POV.GINI	NA	NA	NA	NA	...
Africa Western and Central	AFW	Gini index	SI.POV.GINI	NA	NA	NA	NA	...
Angola	AGO	Gini index	SI.POV.GINI	NA	NA	NA	NA	...
Albania	ALB	Gini index	SI.POV.GINI	NA	NA	NA	NA	...
...	...	...	...	...	...	...	...	...

We look at the size of *gini* and its column names.

```
cat("#rows:", nrow(gini), " #columns:", ncol(gini))
#rows: 266  #columns: 67
names(gini)
```

```
[1]  "Country Name"   "Country Code"   "Indicator Name" "Indicator Code"
[5]  "1960"           "1961"           "1962"           "1963"
[9]  "1964"           "1965"           "1966"           "1967"
...
[57] "2012"           "2013"           "2014"           "2015"
[61] "2016"           "2017"           "2018"           "2019"
[65] "2020"           "2021"           "...67"
```

```
military= read_csv("datasets/SIPRI/military-expenditure-share-gdp.csv")
```

Same for *military*, size, and column names.

```
cat("#rows:", nrow(military), " #columns:", ncol(military))
#rows: 7684   #columns: 4
names(military)
[1] "Entity"                  "Code"
[3] "Year"                    "military_expenditure_share_gdp"
```

The *gini* data frame is in *wide* form, with respect to years; the *military* one is in *long* form.

```
military
```

Entity	Code	Year	military_expenditure_share_gdp
Afghanistan	AFG	1970	1.63
Afghanistan	AFG	1973	1.87
Afghanistan	AFG	1974	1.61
Afghanistan	AFG	1975	1.72
Afghanistan	AFG	1976	2.05
Afghanistan	AFG	1977	2.01
...	...	...	...

We need a common form to join the data frames. To ease readability, we transform the *military* data frame in *wide* form.

```
military %>%
  pivot_wider(names_from= Year,
              values_from= military_expenditure_share_gdp) -> military
```

Now *military* has one country for each row, 166 in total, with years as columns.

```
cat("#rows:", nrow(military), " #columns:", ncol(military))
#rows: 166   #columns: 74
```

Both data frames show substantial historical series, from 1960 to 2021 for the *Gini index* and from 1949 to 2020 for the *Military spending*. For simplicity, we take a subset of the years from both data frames, just the last three years.

```
gini %>% select(1, 2, "2019":"2021") -> gini
```

Country Name	Country Code	2019	2020	2021
Aruba	ABW	*NA*	*NA*	*NA*
Africa Eastern and Southern	AFE	*NA*	*NA*	*NA*
Afghanistan	AFG	*NA*	*NA*	*NA*
Africa Western and Central	AFW	*NA*	*NA*	*NA*
Angola	AGO	*NA*	*NA*	*NA*
Albania	ALB	30.8	*NA*	*NA*
Andorra	AND	*NA*	*NA*	*NA*
Arab World	ARB	*NA*	*NA*	*NA*
United Arab Emirates	ARE	*NA*	*NA*	*NA*
Argentina	ARG	42.9	42.3	*NA*
…	…	…	…	…

```
military %>% select(1, 2, "2018", "2019","2020") -> military
```

Entity	Code	2018	2019	2020
Afghanistan	AFG	1.01	1.12	1.37
Albania	ALB	1.16	1.29	1.54
Algeria	DZA	5.47	6.02	6.66
Angola	AGO	1.87	1.64	1.62
Argentina	ARG	0.75	0.71	0.76
Armenia	ARM	4.12	4.77	4.86
Australia	AUS	1.89	1.88	2.06
Austria	AUT	0.74	0.73	0.84
Azerbaijan	AZE	3.56	3.87	5.39
Bahrain	BHR	4.07	4.06	4.07
…	…	…	…	…

From these initial transformations, we have learned that in the *Gini index* data frame, there are 266 countries, while in the *Military spending* is just 166. Also, they both have a 3-letter country code (ISO alpha-3) and country names are in the title case. We can run join operations between the two.

10.1.4   Join Functions

Four functions correspond to the four join types we have introduced, all defined in package *dplyr*: `inner_join()`, `full_join()`, `left_join()`, and `right_join()`. The basic syntax is the same for all of them:

```
*_join(left_df, right_df, by= )      # non piped
left_df %>% *_join(right_df, by= )    # piped
```

with attribute **by** defining the join keys that might be specified with two forms, where ***colLeft*** and ***colRight*** respectively refer to the key(s) of the *left* data frame and of the *right* data frame:

- by= `join_by(colLeft == colRight)`
- by= `c("colLeft" = "colRight")`

They both works. There are variants:

- by= `join_by(colName)`: when the key variables in the two data frames have the same name, just the name is enough (same with by= `c(colName)`).
- by= `join_by(col1Left == col1Right, col2Left == col2Right, ...)`: when the key is formed by multiple variables, the associations are specified in pairs (same with by= `c("col1Left" = "col1Right", "col2Left" = "col2Right", ...)`).

The join functions have other attributes, not fundamental but nevertheless important:

- `suffix`: when the two data frames to join have columns with same names, to disambiguate them in the result, a suffix is added. By default, they are `.x` and `.y` for the *left* and the *right* data frame columns, but custom prefixes could be specified with this attribute.
- `keep`: if FALSE (default), only key columns of the left data frame are kept in the result; if TRUE, key columns of both the left and the right data frames are kept.
- `na_matches`: this handles a nonintuitive feature that may cause unexpected results. *By default, two missing values are considered equal; therefore, they match as keys in a join.* From a strict logical perspective, this action is wrong, missing values are not actual values and the logic of a join operation is to associate rows with logically corresponding keys. It should be specified `na_matches= "never"` to avoid the default behavior. This default behavior would be much better if reversed.
- `multiple`: with this attribute, it is possible to handle nonunique matches between key values. If a value of the left data frame's key corresponds to multiple values of the right data frame's key, the default is to raise a warning and then return all multiple matches. Other options are `"all,"` `"any,"` `"first,"` `"last,"` respectively to return all matches or /one/the first/the last among the multiple matches, `"error"` throws a blocking error.

Let us look at some examples with data frames *gini* and *military*.

10.1.4.1   Function `inner_join()`

First, we use function `inner_join()` with keys column *Country Name* (from *gini*) and *Entity* (from *military*).

```
gini %>% inner_join(military,
                by= join_by('Country Name' == Entity)) %>% head(10)
```

Country Name	Country Code	2019.x	2020.x	2021	Code	2018	2019.y	2020.y
Afghanistan	AFG	*NA*	*NA*	*NA*	AFG	1.01	1.12	1.37
Angola	AGO	*NA*	*NA*	*NA*	AGO	1.87	1.64	1.62
Albania	ALB	30.8	*NA*	*NA*	ALB	1.16	1.29	1.54
United Arab Emirates	ARE	*NA*	*NA*	*NA*	ARE	*NA*	*NA*	*NA*
Argentina	ARG	42.9	42.3	*NA*	ARG	0.75	0.71	0.76
Armenia	ARM	29.9	25.2	*NA*	ARM	4.12	4.77	4.86
Australia	AUS	*NA*	*NA*	*NA*	AUS	1.89	1.88	2.06
Austria	AUT	30.2	*NA*	*NA*	AUT	0.74	0.73	0.84
Azerbaijan	AZE	*NA*	*NA*	*NA*	AZE	3.56	3.87	5.39
Burundi	BDI	*NA*	*NA*	*NA*	BDI	1.88	2.50	1.98

Let us look at the result:

- *Number of corresponding rows*: 148; therefore, not all 166 country names in *military* have a match in the 266 countries of *gini*.
- *Column names*: columns from the two data frames with same name now have a prefix .x if they come from the left data frame, or .y if they come from the right data frame.
- *Keys columns*: only key columns from the left data frame are kept (*Country Name*; in this case, *Entity* has been dropped).

We can try reversing the order of the two data frames, and see that the result is logically the same, the only change is the order of columns, first those from *military* then those from *gini*. We also specify a custom suffix, to see more clearly from which data frame columns come and keep both key columns, *Entity* and *Country names*.

```
military %>% inner_join(gini, by= join_by(Entity == 'Country Name'),
                        suffix= c('_mil','_gini'),
                        keep= TRUE) %>% head(10)
```

Entity	Code	2018	2019_mil	2020_mil	Country Name	Country Code	2019_gini	2020_gini	2021
Afghanistan	AFG	1.01	1.12	1.37	Afghanistan	AFG	*NA*	*NA*	*NA*
Albania	ALB	1.16	1.29	1.54	Albania	ALB	30.8	*NA*	*NA*
Algeria	DZA	5.47	6.02	6.66	Algeria	DZA	*NA*	*NA*	*NA*
Angola	AGO	1.87	1.64	1.62	Angola	AGO	*NA*	*NA*	*NA*
Argentina	ARG	0.75	0.71	0.76	Argentina	ARG	42.9	42.3	*NA*
Armenia	ARM	4.12	4.77	4.86	Armenia	ARM	29.9	25.2	*NA*
Australia	AUS	1.89	1.88	2.06	Australia	AUS	*NA*	*NA*	*NA*
Austria	AUT	0.74	0.73	0.84	Austria	AUT	30.2	*NA*	*NA*
Azerbaijan	AZE	3.56	3.87	5.39	Azerbaijan	AZE	*NA*	*NA*	*NA*
Bahrain	BHR	4.07	4.06	4.07	Bahrain	BHR	*NA*	*NA*	*NA*

Now we can try the second combination of keys, *Country Code* and *Code*.

```
gini %>% inner_join(military, by= c("Country Code" = "Code"),
                    suffix= c('_gini','_mil')) %>% head(10)
```

Country Name	Country Code	2019_gini	2020_gini	2021	Entity	2018	2019_mil	2020_mil
Afghanistan	AFG	*NA*	*NA*	*NA*	Afghanistan	1.01	1.12	1.37
Angola	AGO	*NA*	*NA*	*NA*	Angola	1.87	1.64	1.62
Albania	ALB	30.8	*NA*	*NA*	Albania	1.16	1.29	1.54
United Arab Emirates	ARE	*NA*	*NA*	*NA*	United Arab Emirates	*NA*	*NA*	*NA*
Argentina	ARG	42.9	42.3	*NA*	Argentina	0.75	0.71	0.76
Armenia	ARM	29.9	25.2	*NA*	Armenia	4.12	4.77	4.86
Australia	AUS	*NA*	*NA*	*NA*	Australia	1.89	1.88	2.06
Austria	AUT	30.2	*NA*	*NA*	Austria	0.74	0.73	0.84
Azerbaijan	AZE	*NA*	*NA*	*NA*	Azerbaijan	3.56	3.87	5.39
Burundi	BDI	*NA*	*NA*	*NA*	Burundi	1.88	2.50	1.98

The result is different, now we have 164 rows, 16 more than with country names. Still, they are not all 166 countries in *military* data frame, but just two, evidently, do not have a match with codes. We will check and verify the reason for unmatched rows in the two cases, but first let us look at the most common error. What if we match a country name with a country code?

```
military %>% inner_join(gini, by= join_by(Entity == 'Country Code'))
# A tibble: 0 × 9
# ... with 9 variables: Entity <chr>, Code <chr>, 2018 <dbl>, 2019.x <dbl>,
#   2020.x <dbl>, Country Name <chr>, 2019.y <dbl>, 2020.y <dbl>, 2021 <dbl>
```

The result is an empty data frame. No country name is equal to a country code, regardless of the fact that they might logically correspond to the same country. This is a common mistake for beginners, confusing the logical association with the computational mechanism that takes key values and checks for equality. Always check the result, it reveals most errors.

10.1.4.2 Function `full_join()`

With function `full_join()` the logic is the same, but the result changes. Here we count the number of rows of the resulting data frame.

```
gini %>% full_join(military, by= join_by("Country Name" == Entity)) %>% nrow()
[1] 284
```

With the *full join*, we always have more rows than with the *inner join*, if there are unmatched keys, or the same number if all keys match; in this case, the full join and the inner join are equivalent. Here we have 284 rows, which came from: rows with matching keys (148, as we have seen from the inner join) plus rows from *gini* with unmatched keys $(266 - 148 = 118)$ plus rows from *military* with unmatched keys $(166 - 148 = 18)$, corresponding to $148 + 118 + 18 = 284$.

If we execute the full join with codes as keys, the result is different, because the number of matching keys is different.

```
gini %>% full_join(military, by= join_by("Country Code" == Code)) %>% nrow()
[1] 268
```

Now the rows are 268, resulting from 164 (matched keys) + 102 (*gini*'s unmatched keys) + 2 (*military*'s unmatched keys).

10.1.4.3 Functions `left_join()` and `right_join()`
The last two types are variants of the full join, respectively, returning all rows of only the left or the right data frame.

```
gini %>% left_join(military, by = c("Country Code" = "Code")) %>% nrow()
[1] 266
```

With the left join, rows are 164 (matching keys) + 102 (*gini*'s unmatched keys). Analogously for the right join, rows are 164 (matching keys) + 2 (*military*'s unmatched keys).

```
gini %>% right_join(military, by = c("Country Code" = "Code")) %>% nrow()
[1] 166
```

10.1.4.4 Function `merge()`
There exists an alternative form to the four join function just discussed provided by function `merge()`, which is defined in base R and is able to execute all four join types by setting its parameters as follows:

- `all= FALSE` corresponds to an **inner join** and is the *default*.
- `all= TRUE` corresponds to a **full join**.
- `all.x= TRUE` corresponds to a **left join**.
- `all.y= TRUE` corresponds to a **right join**.

To specify the keys, the parameters are:

- `by` : the list of key columns having **same name** in the two data frames.
- `by.x` : the list of key columns of the **left** data frame.
- `by.y` : the list of key columns of the **right** data frame.

Here are the examples using the `merge()` function. Only the size of the resulting data frame is visualized.

```
gini %>% merge(military, by.x = "Country Code", by.y = "Code",
               all= FALSE) %>% dim()
[1] 164   9
gini %>% merge(military, by.x = "Country Code", by.y = "Code",
               all= TRUE) %>% dim()
[1] 268   9
```

```
gini %>% merge(military, by.x = "Country Code", by.y = "Code",
               all.x= TRUE) %>% dim()
[1] 266    9
gini %>% merge(military, by.x = "Country Code", by.y = "Code",
               all.y= TRUE) %>% dim()
[1] 166    9
```

10.1.5 Duplicated Keys

Up to now, we have seen examples without duplicated values in join keys or duplicated rows in data frames. It is not always this way; duplications often exist and should be dealt with. For this case, we define two custom didactic data frames with different types of duplication. We simulate data about some purchases in retail shops, which is extremely simplified and schematic.

```
df1 <- data.frame(
  Buyer = c('Polycarp', 'Lada', 'Strigbod', 'Mario'),
  Seller = c('Brand1', 'Brand2', 'Brand3', 'Brand4'),
  Product = c('shirt', 'shoes', 'hat', 'scarf'),
  buyCity = c('Des Moines', 'Hanover', 'Madison', 'Venice'),
  selCity = c('Boston', 'Milan','Paris', 'London'))
```

Buyer	Seller	Product	buyCity	selCity
Polycarp	Brand1	shirt	Des Moines	Boston
Lada	Brand2	shoes	Hanover	Milan
Strigbod	Brand3	hat	Madison	Paris
Mario	Brand4	scarf	Venice	London

```
df2 <- data.frame(
  City = c('Des Moines', 'Hanover', 'Madison', 'Venice',
           'Boston', 'Milan','Paris', 'London'),
  Country = c('USA', 'USA', 'USA', 'Italy',
              'USA', 'Italy', 'France', 'UK')
  )
```

City	Country
Des Moines	USA
Hanover	USA
Madison	USA
Venice	Italy
Boston	USA
Milan	Italy
Paris	France
London	UK

We want to join the two data frames to have two new columns of buyers' and sellers' countries corresponding to the cities. Here, we show it with two separate steps: first, the join based on keys *buyCity* and *City*, then the second join with keys *selCity* and *City*. In this case, either the *inner join* or the *left join* produces the same result.

```
df1 %>% left_join(df2, by = c("buyCity" = "City")) -> temp1
```

Buyer	Seller	Product	buyCity	selCity	Country
Polycarp	Brand1	shirt	Des Moines	Boston	USA
Lada	Brand2	shoes	Hanover	Milan	USA
Strigbod	Brand3	hat	Madison	Paris	USA
Mario	Brand4	scarf	Venice	London	Italy

```
temp1 %>% left_join(df2, by = c("selCity" = "City"))
```

Buyer	Seller	Product	buyCity	selCity	Country.x	Country.y
Polycarp	Brand1	shirt	Des Moines	Boston	USA	USA
Lada	Brand2	shoes	Hanover	Milan	USA	Italy
Strigbod	Brand3	hat	Madison	Paris	USA	France
Mario	Brand4	scarf	Venice	London	Italy	UK

The result is correct; we can improve it a little using a pipe and renaming the two *Country* columns in a more meaningful way.

```
df1 %>% left_join(df2, by = c("buyCity" = "City")) %>%
  rename(buyCountry = Country) %>%
  left_join(df2, by = c("selCity" = "City")) %>%
  rename(selCountry = Country)
```

Buyer	Seller	Product	buyCity	selCity	buyCountry	selCountry
Polycarp	Brand1	shirt	Des Moines	Boston	USA	USA
Lada	Brand2	shoes	Hanover	Milan	USA	Italy
Strigbod	Brand3	hat	Madison	Paris	USA	France
Mario	Brand4	scarf	Venice	London	Italy	UK

Now, we can start complicating the example by adding duplication.

Case 1 – *Duplicated keys in the left data frame (df1)*. Changes are:

- One buyer (Lada) is registered with two different purchases (*partial duplication*);
- Another buyer (Mario) is registered with two identical purchases (*complete duplication*).

```
df1 <- data.frame(
    Buyer = c('Polycarp', 'Lada', 'Lada', 'Strigbod', 'Mario', 'Mario'),
    Seller = c('Brand1', 'Brand2', 'Brand3', 'Brand3', 'Brand4', 'Brand4'),
    Product = c('shirt', 'shoes', 'hat', 'hat', 'scarf', 'scarf'),
    buyCity = c('Des Moines', 'Hanover', 'Hanover','Madison', 'Venice', 'Venice'),
    selCity = c('Boston', 'Milan', 'Paris','Paris', 'London', 'London'))
```

Buyer	Seller	Product	buyCity	selCity
Polycarp	Brand1	shirt	Des Moines	Boston
Lada	Brand2	shoes	Hanover	Milan
Lada	Brand3	hat	Hanover	Paris
Strigbod	Brand3	hat	Madison	Paris
Mario	Brand4	scarf	Venice	London
Mario	Brand4	scarf	Venice	London

We have 6 purchases, and the goal is to see what happens with join operations when we have partially or completely duplicated rows. Re-run the same join operation.

```
df1 %>% left_join(df2, by = c("buyCity" = "City")) %>%
    rename(buyCountry = Country) %>%
    left_join(df2, by = c("selCity" = "City")) %>%
    rename(selCountry = Country)
```

Buyer	Seller	Product	buyCity	selCity	buyCountry	selCountry
Polycarp	Brand1	shirt	Des Moines	Boston	USA	USA
Lada	Brand2	shoes	Hanover	Milan	USA	Italy
Lada	Brand3	hat	Hanover	Paris	USA	France
Strigbod	Brand3	hat	Madison	Paris	USA	France
Mario	Brand4	scarf	Venice	London	Italy	UK
Mario	Brand4	scarf	Venice	London	Italy	UK

The result is correct; we have joined the two data frames and the duplicated rows, partial or complete, have been preserved. We still have information about the 6 purchases.

Note

In order to remove duplicated rows in a data frame, either the function `duplicated()` of R base or the function `distinct()` of package *dplyr*, serve the same purpose.

Function `duplicated()` *returns FALSE for non-duplicated objects and TRUE for duplicated ones.* For example: `duplicated(df)`: `TRUE` for duplicated rows; `duplicated(df$col)`: `TRUE` for duplicated column values. It derives that *if we want to remove duplicated objects (rows, values), we have to negate the Boolean result of* `duplicated()`.

The semantic of function `distinct()` is the opposite and somehow more specific: it applies to data frames and *keeps only unique/distinct rows.* If applied to a grouped data frame, groups are maintained. A list of columns could be specified to be used to determine row uniqueness; otherwise, all columns are used.

Case 2 *– Add a duplication in the right data frame (df2).* In addition to the duplication introduced in the previous case, we want now to have duplication also in the second data frame. For simplicity, we just duplicate all values.

```
df2 <- data.frame(
  City = c('Des Moines', 'Hanover', 'Madison', 'Venice',
           'Boston', 'Milan','Paris', 'London',
           'Des Moines', 'Hanover', 'Madison', 'Venice',
           'Boston', 'Milan','Paris', 'London'),
  Country = c('USA', 'USA', 'USA', 'Italy', 'USA', 'Italy', 'France', 'UK',
              'USA', 'USA', 'USA', 'Italy', 'USA', 'Italy', 'France', 'UK') )
```

Again, we run the same join operation.

```
df1 %>% left_join(df2, by = c("buyCity" = "City")) %>%
  rename(buyCountry = Country) %>%
  left_join(df2, by = c("selCity" = "City")) %>%
  rename(selCountry = Country)
```

Buyer	Seller	Product	buyCity	selCity	buyCountry	selCountry
Polycarp	Brand1	shirt	Des Moines	Boston	USA	USA
Polycarp	Brand1	shirt	Des Moines	Boston	USA	USA
Polycarp	Brand1	shirt	Des Moines	Boston	USA	USA
Polycarp	Brand1	shirt	Des Moines	Boston	USA	USA
Lada	Brand2	shoes	Hanover	Milan	USA	Italy
Lada	Brand2	shoes	Hanover	Milan	USA	Italy
Lada	Brand2	shoes	Hanover	Milan	USA	Italy
Lada	Brand2	shoes	Hanover	Milan	USA	Italy
Lada	Brand3	hat	Hanover	Paris	USA	France
Lada	Brand3	hat	Hanover	Paris	USA	France
Lada	Brand3	hat	Hanover	Paris	USA	France
Lada	Brand3	hat	Hanover	Paris	USA	France
Strigbod	Brand3	hat	Madison	Paris	USA	France
Strigbod	Brand3	hat	Madison	Paris	USA	France
Strigbod	Brand3	hat	Madison	Paris	USA	France
Strigbod	Brand3	hat	Madison	Paris	USA	France
Mario	Brand4	scarf	Venice	London	Italy	UK
Mario	Brand4	scarf	Venice	London	Italy	UK
Mario	Brand4	scarf	Venice	London	Italy	UK
Mario	Brand4	scarf	Venice	London	Italy	UK
Mario	Brand4	scarf	Venice	London	Italy	UK
Mario	Brand4	scarf	Venice	London	Italy	UK
Mario	Brand4	scarf	Venice	London	Italy	UK
Mario	Brand4	scarf	Venice	London	Italy	UK

Now the result contains several redundant duplications; basically, every original row has been duplicated three times. It has to be fixed.

An idea could be to use functions `duplicated()` or `distinct()`, they produce the same result.

```
df1 %>% left_join(df2, by = c("buyCity" = "City")) %>%
  rename(buyCountry = Country) %>%
  left_join(df2, by = c("selCity" = "City")) %>%
  rename(selCountry = Country) %>%
  filter(!duplicated(.))
```

Buyer	Seller	Product	buyCity	selCity	buyCountry	selCountry
Polycarp	Brand1	shirt	Des Moines	Boston	USA	USA
Lada	Brand2	shoes	Hanover	Milan	USA	Italy
Lada	Brand3	hat	Hanover	Paris	USA	France
Strigbod	Brand3	hat	Madison	Paris	USA	France
Mario	Brand4	scarf	Venice	London	Italy	UK

Technically, the solution worked correctly; duplicated rows have been removed, but *logically, the result is wrong*, we had six purchases, now we have just five, and the two identical ones made by Mario have not been recognized as distinct.

A reasonable objection at this point would be that it never happens that identical but distinct purchases are recorded with identical rows in an archive of transactions. There could be a variable for quantity, if identical items are purchased contextually, or there will be the time of the purchase if they are timely distinct, or more generally, there will be some sort of *unique code* associated with each purchase.

The objection is obviously correct, but on one hand this is a custom didactic data frame, and they are almost always unrealistic, differently from Open Data, but on the other hand, it is definitely possible to have exactly identical rows in data frames, so in abstract, this represents a real scenario.

But ultimately, the objection would make a point, if observations/rows in a data frame represent logically distinct objects, they should be unique, and this is exactly what we are considering now. To obtain a correct result, we need to transform the data frame in order to make distinct rows unique. The usual way to do that is to add a column with a **unique code** for each distinct row. Unique codes may have countless forms, e.g. random values, incremental values, or unique values computed based on custom algorithms. Here we choose the simplest solution by adding the row number as values of a new *id* column of *df1*.

```
df1= mutate(df1, id= row_number()) %>% relocate(id, .before=1)
```

id	Buyer	Seller	Product	buyCity	selCity
1	Polycarp	Brand1	shirt	Des Moines	Boston
2	Lada	Brand2	shoes	Hanover	Milan
3	Lada	Brand3	hat	Hanover	Paris
4	Strigbod	Brand3	hat	Madison	Paris
5	Mario	Brand4	scarf	Venice	London
6	Mario	Brand4	scarf	Venice	London

Now we can execute the join and remove the duplicated rows.

```
df1 %>% left_join(df2, by = c("buyCity" = "City")) %>%
  rename(buyCountry = Country) %>%
  left_join(df2, by = c("selCity" = "City")) %>%
  rename(selCountry = Country) %>%
  distinct(.)
```

id	Buyer	Seller	Product	buyCity	selCity	buyCountry	selCountry
1	Polycarp	Brand1	shirt	Des Moines	Boston	USA	USA
2	Lada	Brand2	shoes	Hanover	Milan	USA	Italy
3	Lada	Brand3	hat	Hanover	Paris	USA	France
4	Strigbod	Brand3	hat	Madison	Paris	USA	France
5	Mario	Brand4	scarf	Venice	London	Italy	UK
6	Mario	Brand4	scarf	Venice	London	Italy	UK

> **Note**
>
> Before version 1.0.10 of library *dplyr* (August 2022), a specific argument `multiple` was available for function `duplicated()`, providing the nice feature of handling duplicated rows logically, meaning that it was able to recognize if duplication came from a single or distinct identical rows. In our case, it would have managed the removal of duplicated rows correctly even without the addition of the unique code, keeping the two identical rows of the original data frame. At the time of writing (July 2023), argument `multiple` only exists in the developer version of the *dplyr* library; it is unknown to this author if and when it would be made available again and with which functionality.

10.1.6 Special Join Functions

10.1.6.1 Semi Join

A special variant of the *inner join* is the **semi join**, with the following characteristics:

- *like the inner join*, it returns only rows with matching keys.
- *unlike the inner join,* it does not copy in the result columns from the *right* data frame and automatically removes duplicated rows.

To test this case, we further modify data frame *df2* of our example by:

- adding a new column *State_Region* with the state for US cities and the region for European cities.
- removing from *df2* one of the cities present in *df1* (Madison) so to have a value of key columns without a match in the join.
- duplicating one row (Venice, Italy, Veneto) so to have the incorrect duplication of rows in the join.

```
df2 <- data.frame(
   City= c('Des Moines', 'Hanover', 'Milan', 'Boston',
            'Paris', 'London','Venice','Venice'),
   Country= c('USA', 'USA', 'Italy', 'USA', 'France', 'UK', 'Italy', 'Italy'),
   State_Region= c('Iowa', 'New Hampshire', 'Lombardia', 'Massachusetts',
                   'Île de France', 'Greater London','Veneto','Veneto') )
```

City	Country	State_Region
Des Moines	USA	Iowa
Hanover	USA	New Hampshire
Milan	Italy	Lombardia
Boston	USA	Massachusetts
Paris	France	Île de France
London	UK	Greater London
Venice	Italy	Veneto
Venice	Italy	Veneto

We have again the *df1* with six purchases, to test how the semi join handles duplicates and non-matching key values. First, we run the *inner join* and the *left join* with keys *buyCity* and *City*.

```
df1 %>% inner_join(df2, by= c("buyCity" = "City"))
```

Buyer	Seller	Product	buyCity	selCity	Country	State_Region
Polycarp	Brand1	shirt	Des Moines	Boston	USA	Iowa
Lada	Brand2	shoes	Hanover	Milan	USA	New Hampshire
Lada	Brand3	hat	Hanover	Paris	USA	New Hampshire
Mario	Brand4	scarf	Venice	London	Italy	Veneto
Mario	Brand4	scarf	Venice	London	Italy	Veneto
Mario	Brand4	scarf	Venice	London	Italy	Veneto
Mario	Brand4	scarf	Venice	London	Italy	Veneto

As expected, with the *inner join,* the purchase of Strigbod is absent because the value of *Madison* in *buyCity* of *df1* does not have a match in *City* of *df2*. The two identical purchases by Mario have been duplicated due to the duplicated row in *df2* and to handle them correctly, we should add a new column with a unique row identifier, as seen previously.

Running the *left join*, we see Strigbod's purchase with missing values for *df2*'s columns. The duplication of Mario's rows is the same as for the inner join.

```
df1 %>% left_join(df2, by= c("buyCity" = "City"))
```

Buyer	Seller	Product	buyCity	selCity	Country	State_Region
Polycarp	Brand1	shirt	Des Moines	Boston	USA	Iowa
Lada	Brand2	shoes	Hanover	Milan	USA	New Hampshire
Lada	Brand3	hat	Hanover	Paris	USA	New Hampshire
Strigbod	Brand3	hat	Madison	Paris	*NA*	*NA*
Mario	Brand4	scarf	Venice	London	Italy	Veneto
Mario	Brand4	scarf	Venice	London	Italy	Veneto
Mario	Brand4	scarf	Venice	London	Italy	Veneto
Mario	Brand4	scarf	Venice	London	Italy	Veneto

Now, let us look at the *semi join*.

```
df1 %>% semi_join(df2, by = c("buyCity" = "City"))
```

Buyer	Seller	Product	buyCity	selCity
Polycarp	Brand1	shirt	Des Moines	Boston
Lada	Brand2	shoes	Hanover	Milan
Lada	Brand3	hat	Hanover	Paris
Mario	Brand4	scarf	Venice	London
Mario	Brand4	scarf	Venice	London

The result is like the *inner join*, with the Strigbod's row missing, but only columns from *df1* (left data frame) are presented. Interestingly, the duplicated rows have been handled correctly, preserving the two original identical rows.

To summarize, the *semi join* combines features of the *inner join* and some data-wrangling operations. It is interesting, but typically not particularly useful.

10.1.6.2 Anti Join

The *semi join* is functional to introduce the second variant called **anti join**, which essentially represents the dual of the *semi join*, meaning that:

- It matches keys values and *returns the rows with values of the keys in the left data frame **without a match** in the right data frame.*
- It does not copy columns from the right data frame and handle correctly the removal of duplicated rows.

The functionality of the *anti join* could often be useful because, as commented before, we almost always have to check for values of the keys without a match. It is however important to remark that the *anti join does not return all values of the keys without a match, but just those of the left data frame*. This means that *to find all unmatched key values of both data frames, we need to run the anti join twice, the second by switching the left and the right data frames and corresponding key columns*. Let us see an example.

```
df1 %>% anti_join(df2, by= c("buyCity" = "City"))
```

Buyer	Seller	Product	buyCity	selCity
Strigbod	Brand3	hat	Madison	Paris

This way, we have obtained the rows with the key values of the left data frame *df1* (*buyCity*) unmatched in *df2* (*City*), which is only Madison, corresponding to Strigbod's purchase.

If we switch left and right data frames, this time the left data frame is *df2,* and the result is *df2*'s rows with key values unmatched in *df1*.

```
df2 %>% anti_join(df1, by= c("City" = "buyCity"))
```

City	Country	State_Region
Milan	Italy	Lombardia
Boston	USA	Massachusetts
Paris	France	Île de France
London	UK	Greater London

The *anti join* is nice and easy, but it is worth considering how we can obtain the same result with base functions, in order to decide whether or not we want to use it. The goal is to find unmatched keys in the result of a join operation, which logic should we follow? First, how could we identify an unmatched key? Where do we have such information? Not in the result of an *inner join*, there we only know the matching keys. It is in the *full join* that we have all information about which keys have matched and which have not, for both data frames, and it is quite easy to find because, given the key columns:

- *rows with matching key values* have valid values in key columns.
- *rows with unmatched key values of the left data frame* have valid values in key columns of the left data frame and missing values in columns of the right data frame.
- *rows with unmatched key values of the right data frame* have valid values in key columns of the right data frame and missing values in columns of the left data frame.

Given this logic, it is easy to find rows with unmatched values by checking for the presence of missing values in key columns. Let us try first with the simple custom data frames and then with the *Gini index* and *Military spending* ones. First, the *full join* with keep=TRUE.

```
df1 %>% full_join(df2, by= c("buyCity" = "City"), keep= TRUE) -> fulldf
```

Buyer	Seller	Product	buyCity	selCity	City	Country	State_Region
Polycarp	Brand1	shirt	Des Moines	Boston	Des Moines	USA	Iowa
Lada	Brand2	shoes	Hanover	Milan	Hanover	USA	New Hampshire
Lada	Brand3	hat	Hanover	Paris	Hanover	USA	New Hampshire
Strigbod	Brand3	hat	Madison	Paris	*NA*	*NA*	*NA*
Mario	Brand4	scarf	Venice	London	Venice	Italy	Veneto
Mario	Brand4	scarf	Venice	London	Venice	Italy	Veneto
Mario	Brand4	scarf	Venice	London	Venice	Italy	Veneto
Mario	Brand4	scarf	Venice	London	Venice	Italy	Veneto
NA	*NA*	*NA*	*NA*	*NA*	Milan	Italy	Lombardia
NA	*NA*	*NA*	*NA*	*NA*	Boston	USA	Massachusetts
NA	*NA*	*NA*	*NA*	*NA*	Paris	France	Île de France
NA	*NA*	*NA*	*NA*	*NA*	London	UK	Greater London

Key columns are *buyCity* and *City*; we can easily see from the result which rows have unmatched key values: *those with NA in one of the key columns.*

```
fulldf %>% filter( is.na(buyCity) | is.na(City) ) %>% select(buyCity, City)
```

buyCity	City
Madison	NA
NA	Milan
NA	Boston
NA	Paris
NA	London

These are the unmatched keys. Now with *gini* and *military* data frames using *Country Code* and *Code* as keys.

```
military %>% full_join(gini, by = c("Code" = "Country Code"), keep=TRUE) %>%
   filter( is.na('Country Code') | is.na(Code) ) %>% select(Code, 'Country
Code')
```

Code	Country Code
OWID_KOS	*NA*
TWN	*NA*
NA	ABW
NA	AFE
NA	AFW
NA	AND
NA	ARB
NA	ASM
NA	ATG
NA	BHS
…	…

The two country codes that appear in the *Military spending* dataset but not in the *Gini* dataset are OWID_KOS, which is an unconventional code for Kosovo, a country with still an uncertain status, and TWN, which identifies Taiwan, which is officially recognized as a China province rather than an independent country. Many more (102) are the codes appearing in the *Gini* dataset but not in the *Military spending*.

Interestingly, there is Kosovo in the *Gini* dataset too, with code XKX; therefore, *the two codes should be normalized to one version*, meaning that in one of the two datasets (or data frames), the Kosovo's code should be replaced and the join re-executed to permit the correct association.

```
gini$'Country Name' %>% str_detect(., "Kosovo") -> mask
filter(gini, mask)
```

Country Name	Country Code	2019	2020	2021
Kosovo	XKX	*NA*	*NA*	*NA*

We assume to replace the code in *military* data frame with the one from *gini* and re-execute the inner join with codes. The rows with matching keys are now 165, from 164 that were before.

```
military$Code %>% str_replace(., 'OWID_KOS', 'XKX') -> military$Code
military %>% inner_join(gini, by= join_by(Code == 'Country Code')) %>% nrow()
[1] 165
```

We can repeat the verification of unmatched key values with keys *Country Name* and *Entity*.

```
military %>% full_join(gini, by = c("Entity" = "Country Name"), keep=TRUE) %>%
   filter( is.na('Country Name') | is.na(Entity) ) %>% select(Entity, 'Country
Name')
```

Entity	Country Name
Brunei	*NA*
Cape Verde	*NA*
Congo	*NA*
Democratic Republic of Congo	*NA*
Egypt	*NA*
…	…
Turkey	*NA*
Venezuela	*NA*
Yemen	*NA*
NA	Aruba
NA	Africa Eastern and Southern
NA	Africa Western and Central
NA	Andorra
…	…
NA	Congo, Dem. Rep.
…	…
NA	Egypt, Arab Rep.
…	…

As we already know, there are many more, with several instances of same country with two different denominations, like the *Democratic Republic of Congo* and *Congo, the Dem. Rep.*, *Egypt* and *Egypt, the Arab Rep.*, and so on. It is worth noting that there is not Kosovo in the list because by name it matches between the two datasets, not so by code instead. This is an interesting example to keep in mind. Codes are typically much more precise than names, but they are not guaranteed to be perfect in all cases. Therefore, the result of a join must be checked carefully and patiently.

10.2 Python: Join Operations

In this section, we again use the *Gini index* and the *Military spending* datasets. We will observe many similarities; the logic is identical, but there are some differences due to the role of indexes in Python and certain options specific to pandas functions. We start with the *Gini index* dataset.

```
gini= pd.read_csv("./datasets/World_Bank/API_SI.POV.GINI_DS2_en_csv_v2_4651513.csv")
```

	Country Name	Country Code	Indicator Name	Indicator Code	1960	1961	…	2017	2018	2019	2020	2021
0	Aruba	ABW	Gini index	SI.POV.GINI	NaN	NaN	…	NaN	NaN	NaN	NaN	NaN
1	Africa Eastern and Southern	AFE	Gini index	SI.POV.GINI	NaN	NaN	…	NaN	NaN	NaN	NaN	NaN

	Country Name	Country Code	Indicator Name	Indicator Code	1960	1961	...	2017	2018	2019	2020	2021
2	Afghanistan	AFG	Gini index	SI.POV.GINI	NaN	NaN	...	NaN	NaN	NaN	NaN	NaN
3	Africa Western and Central	AFW	Gini index	SI.POV.GINI	NaN	NaN	...	NaN	NaN	NaN	NaN	NaN
4	Angola	AGO	Gini index	SI.POV.GINI	NaN	NaN	...	NaN	51.3	NaN	NaN	NaN
...	...	...	...	...	...	...	...	...	...	...	...	...

For simplicity, we select just a few columns.

```
gini= gini.iloc[:,[0, 1, 62, 63, 64, 65]]
```

	Country Name	Country Code	2018	2019	2020	2021
0	Aruba	ABW	NaN	NaN	NaN	NaN
1	Africa Eastern and Southern	AFE	NaN	NaN	NaN	NaN
2	Afghanistan	AFG	NaN	NaN	NaN	NaN
3	Africa Western and Central	AFW	NaN	NaN	NaN	NaN
4	Angola	AGO	51.3	NaN	NaN	NaN
...	...	...	...	...	...	...
261	Kosovo	XKX	NaN	NaN	NaN	NaN
262	Yemen, Rep.	YEM	NaN	NaN	NaN	NaN
263	South Africa	ZAF	NaN	NaN	NaN	NaN
264	Zambia	ZMB	NaN	NaN	NaN	NaN
265	Zimbabwe	ZWE	NaN	50.3	NaN	NaN

Now the *Military spending* dataset.

```
military= pd.read_csv("./datasets/SIPRI/military-expenditure-share-gdp.csv")
```

	Entity	Code	Year	military_expenditure_share_gdp
0	Afghanistan	AFG	1970	1.63
1	Afghanistan	AFG	1973	1.87
2	Afghanistan	AFG	1974	1.61
3	Afghanistan	AFG	1975	1.72
4	Afghanistan	AFG	1976	2.05
...	...	...	...	...

The *gini* data frame is in *wide* form, the *military* one is in *long* form. For the join, we need to have a common format, and for better readability, we choose to transform *military* into a *wide* form so to have one country for each row.

```
military= military.pivot(index=['Entity','Code'],
        columns='Year',
        values='military_expenditure_share_gdp').reset_index()
```

Year	Entity	Code	1949	1950	...	2016	2017	2018	2019	2020
0	Afghanistan	AFG	NaN	NaN	...	0.96	0.95	1.01	1.12	1.37
1	Albania	ALB	NaN	NaN	...	1.10	1.11	1.16	1.29	1.54
2	Algeria	DZA	NaN	NaN	...	6.38	5.92	5.47	6.02	6.66
3	Angola	AGO	NaN	NaN	...	2.73	2.51	1.87	1.64	1.62
4	Argentina	ARG	NaN	2.91	...	0.81	0.86	0.75	0.71	0.76
...	...	...	...	...	...	...	...	...	...	...

Finally, as done before, for simplicity, we select just a few columns.

```
military= military .iloc[:,[0, 1, 71,72, 73]]
```

Year	Entity	Code	2018	2019	2020
0	Afghanistan	AFG	1.01	1.12	1.37
1	Albania	ALB	1.16	1.29	1.54
2	Algeria	DZA	5.47	6.02	6.66
3	Angola	AGO	1.87	1.64	1.62
4	Argentina	ARG	0.75	0.71	0.76
...	...	...	...	...	...
161	Venezuela	VEN	NaN	NaN	NaN
162	Vietnam	VNM	2.28	NaN	NaN
163	Yemen	YEM	NaN	NaN	NaN
164	Zambia	ZMB	1.41	1.22	1.15
165	Zimbabwe	ZWE	1.22	0.70	NaN

We can proceed with the join operations.

10.2.1.1 Function `merge()`

Function **merge()** defined by pandas is very similar to the corresponding merge() of base R because, with a single function, we manage all four main join types: *inner, outer/full, left,* and *right join*. The function takes the following typical form: left_df.merge(right_df, attributes).

The attribute choice defines the type of join and the key columns:

- `how` : defines the join type, values could be *'left'*, *'right'*, *'outer'*, or *'inner'* (default *'inner'*);
- `on` : the key column name(s) when the key columns have the same name (or names, if the key is composed by multiple columns for each data frame) in left and right data frames;
- `left_on` : the key column name(s) of the *left* data frame;
- `right_on` : the key column name(s) of the *right* data frame.

Let us see the examples.

10.2.1.2 Inner Join

We first produce the join by using country names; hence, columns *Country Name* and *Entity* are the keys.

```
gini.merge(military, how= 'inner',
           left_on= 'Country Name',
           right_on= 'Entity')
```

	Country Name	Country Code	2018	2019	2020	2021	Entity	Code	2018	2019	2020
0	Afghanistan	AFG	NaN	NaN	NaN	NaN	Afghanistan	AFG	1.01	1.12	1.37
1	Angola	AGO	51.3	NaN	NaN	NaN	Angola	AGO	1.87	1.64	1.62
2	Albania	ALB	30.1	30.8	NaN	NaN	Albania	ALB	1.16	1.29	1.54
3	United Arab Emirates	ARE	26.0	NaN	NaN	NaN	United Arab Emirates	ARE	NaN	NaN	NaN
4	Argentina	ARG	41.3	42.9	42.3	NaN	Argentina	ARG	0.75	0.71	0.76
...	...	...	...	...	...	...	...	...	...	...	...
143	Vietnam	VNM	35.7	NaN	NaN	NaN	Vietnam	VNM	2.28	NaN	NaN
144	Kosovo	XKX	NaN	NaN	NaN	NaN	Kosovo	OWID_KOS	0.80	0.83	1.06
145	South Africa	ZAF	NaN	NaN	NaN	NaN	South Africa	ZAF	0.98	0.98	1.07
146	Zambia	ZMB	NaN	NaN	NaN	NaN	Zambia	ZMB	1.41	1.22	1.15
147	Zimbabwe	ZWE	NaN	50.3	NaN	NaN	Zimbabwe	ZWE	1.22	0.70	NaN

From the result, we observe that:

- *Number of rows*: they are 148, corresponding to the matching keys of the two data frames. Obviously, it is the same number of rows we have seen using R.
- *Key columns*: all key columns are present in the result.

There is something strange; however, in this result, apparently the columns with identical names in the two data frames (i.e. *2018*, *2019*, and *2020*) still have identical names in the joined data frame, too, which would be very inconvenient for all sorts of operations. We need to investigate a little more about this unexpected result because the normal behavior when joined columns have identical names is to add suffixes to disambiguate them. Default suffixes are _*x*, *and* _*y*, which could be personalized by using attribute `suffixes`. Oddly, there is no suffix in the result we have obtained. We should check those column names.

```
print(gini.columns)
print(military.columns)
Index(['Country Name', 'Country Code', '2018', '2019', '2020', '2021'],
      dtype='object')

Index(['Entity', 'Code', 2018, 2019, 2020], dtype='object', name='Year')
```

Now the problem is clear: those columns do not actually have identical names, which is why suffixes have not been appended. However, in that form, those column names would cause us a lot of troubles, much better to rename them either with clearly different names or with equal names and let suffixes do their job. We choose the equal format and rename year columns in *military*.

```
military.columns=['Entity', 'Code', '2018', '2019', '2020']
```

We can re-run the join.

```
gini.merge(military, how= 'inner',
           left_on= 'Country Name', right_on= 'Entity')
```

	Country Name	Country Code	2018_x	2019_x	2020_x	2021	Entity	Code	2018_y	2019_y	2020_y
0	Afghanistan	AFG	NaN	NaN	NaN	NaN	Afghanistan	AFG	1.01	1.12	1.37
1	Angola	AGO	51.3	NaN	NaN	NaN	Angola	AGO	1.87	1.64	1.62
2	Albania	ALB	30.1	30.8	NaN	NaN	Albania	ALB	1.16	1.29	1.54
3	United Arab Emirates	ARE	26.0	NaN	NaN	NaN	United Arab Emirates	ARE	NaN	NaN	NaN
4	Argentina	ARG	41.3	42.9	42.3	NaN	Argentina	ARG	0.75	0.71	0.76
...	...	...	...	...	...	...	...	...	...	...	...

The standard suffixes have appeared. We can try with custom ones _*gini* and _*mil*.

```
gini.merge(military, how= 'inner',
           left_on= 'Country Name', right_on= 'Entity',
           suffixes=('_gini','_mil'))
```

	Country Name	Country Code	2018_ gini	2019_ gini	2020_ gini	2021	Entity	Code	2018_ mil	2019_ mil	2020_ mil
0	Afghanistan	AFG	NaN	NaN	NaN	NaN	Afghanistan	AFG	1.01	1.12	1.37
1	Angola	AGO	51.3	NaN	NaN	NaN	Angola	AGO	1.87	1.64	1.62
2	Albania	ALB	30.1	30.8	NaN	NaN	Albania	ALB	1.16	1.29	1.54
3	United Arab Emirates	ARE	26.0	NaN	NaN	NaN	United Arab Emirates	ARE	NaN	NaN	NaN
4	Argentina	ARG	41.3	42.9	42.3	NaN	Argentina	ARG	0.75	0.71	0.76
...	...	...	...	...	...	...	...	...	...	...	...

Now, we can test the *inner join* by using country codes as keys instead of names.

```
gini.merge(military, how= 'inner',
           left_on= 'Country Code', right_on= 'Code',
           suffixes=('_gini','_mil'))
```

The columns are the same of the previous case, but this time rows are 164 rather than 148 obtained using country names. Codes are typically more precise than names, although we know from the analysis done in the R section that country codes, in this case, are not always better than names, Kosovo is the exception, it matches by name but not by code.

10.2.1.3 Outer/Full Join

This time we run the example with an *outer join*, first by using country names as keys, then country codes. We want to check the size of the result in the two cases.

```
gini.merge(military, how= 'outer',
           left_on= 'Country Name', right_on= 'Entity').shape
(284, 11)
```

We have 284 rows, as in the R case obviously, given by: 148 rows with matching keys, 118 rows from *gini* with unmatched keys, and 18 rows from *military* with unmatched keys. If we re-run by using country codes as keys, the result changes.

```
gini.merge(military, how= 'outer',
           left_on= 'Country Code', right_on= 'Code').shape
(268, 11)
```

Rows are now 268, given by 164 matched keys, 102 *gini*'s unmatched keys, and 2 *military*'s unmatched keys).

Left Join and Right Join   To complete the overview of the main join types, the *left* and *right* joins are presented. Starting with the *left join*, we expect to obtain all 266 *gini*'s rows and all columns of the joined data frames. With the *right join*, instead, we expect to see all 166 *military*'s rows.

```
gini.merge(military, how= 'left',
           left_on= 'Country Code', right_on= 'Code').shape
(266, 11)
gini.merge(military, how= 'right',
           left_on= 'Country Code', right_on= 'Code').shape
(166, 11)
```

10.2.2   Join Operations with Indexed Data Frames

As usual with Python and pandas, indexes could be actively exploited in data wrangling operations. Here, we want to see how a join operation performs in case of indexed data frames. Obviously, an indexed data frame could be de-indexed with the `reset_index()` function, but let us assume to keep data frame indexed. We start by indexing the *gini* data frame, columns *Country Name* and *Country Code* are set as index levels, and the result is saved in a new data frame *gini_index*.

```
gini_index= gini.set_index(['Country Name','Country Code'])
```

Country Name	Country Code	2018	2019	2020	2021
Aruba	ABW	NaN	NaN	NaN	NaN
Africa Eastern and Southern	AFE	NaN	NaN	NaN	NaN
Afghanistan	AFG	NaN	NaN	NaN	NaN
Africa Western and Central	AFW	NaN	NaN	NaN	NaN
Angola	AGO	51.3	NaN	NaN	NaN
...	...	...	...	...	...
Kosovo	XKX	NaN	NaN	NaN	NaN
Yemen, Rep.	YEM	NaN	NaN	NaN	NaN
South Africa	ZAF	NaN	NaN	NaN	NaN
Zambia	ZMB	NaN	NaN	NaN	NaN
Zimbabwe	ZWE	NaN	50.3	NaN	NaN

We can re-run the *inner join* by using the new *gini_index* as the *left* data frame. *Country Code* is now an index level, while *Code* is still a column.

```
gini_index.merge(military, how='inner',
           left_on= 'Country Code', right_on= 'Code',
           suffixes=('_gini','_mil'))
```

	2018_gini	2019_gini	2020_gini	2021	Entity	Code	2018_mil	2019_mil	2020_mil
0	NaN	NaN	NaN	NaN	Afghanistan	AFG	1.01	1.12	1.37
1	51.3	NaN	NaN	NaN	Angola	AGO	1.87	1.64	1.62
2	30.1	30.8	NaN	NaN	Albania	ALB	1.16	1.29	1.54
3	26.0	NaN	NaN	NaN	United Arab Emirates	ARE	NaN	NaN	NaN
4	41.3	42.9	42.3	NaN	Argentina	ARG	0.75	0.71	0.76
...	...	...	...	...	...	...	...	...	...

The result is still the joining of the two data frames, 164 rows is the same result we have obtained before, so it works even with *an index level as the left key and a column as the right key*. The difference is that in the result, the original index levels have been deleted, so there is no longer neither *Country Name* nor *Country Code*.

We can try a variant; this time we set as index levels *Entity* and *Code* in *military* and save in the new *military_index* data frame. Then we re-run the *inner join,* and this time we have column *Country Code* from *gini* as the left key and index level *Code* from *military_index* as the right key.

```
military_index= military.set_index(['Entity','Code'])
```

Entity	Code	2018	2019	2020
Afghanistan	AFG	1.01	1.12	1.37
Albania	ALB	1.16	1.29	1.54
Algeria	DZA	5.47	6.02	6.66
Angola	AGO	1.87	1.64	1.62
Argentina	ARG	0.75	0.71	0.76
...	...	...	...	...
Venezuela	VEN	NaN	NaN	NaN
Vietnam	VNM	2.28	NaN	NaN
Yemen	YEM	NaN	NaN	NaN
Zambia	ZMB	1.41	1.22	1.15
Zimbabwe	ZWE	1.22	0.70	NaN

```
gini.merge(military_index, how= 'inner',
           left_on= 'Country Code', right_on= 'Code')
```

	Country Name	Country Code	2018_x	2019_x	2020_x	2021	2018_y	2019_y	2020_y
0	Afghanistan	AFG	NaN	NaN	NaN	NaN	1.01	1.12	1.37
1	Angola	AGO	51.3	NaN	NaN	NaN	1.87	1.64	1.62
2	Albania	ALB	30.1	30.8	NaN	NaN	1.16	1.29	1.54
3	United Arab Emirates	ARE	26.0	NaN	NaN	NaN	NaN	NaN	NaN
4	Argentina	ARG	41.3	42.9	42.3	NaN	0.75	0.71	0.76
...	...	...	...	...	...	...	...	...	...

Same logic of the previous case: we have obtained the joined data frame (164 rows), but index levels, *Entity* and *Code*, have been omitted from the result.

There is a third variant that could be tested, *the case with both left and right keys as index levels.*

```
gini_index.merge(military_index, how= 'inner',
         left_on= 'Country Code', right_on= 'Code')
KeyError: "None of ['Country Code'] are in the columns"
```

It does not work, attributes `left_on`, `right_on`, and `on` require at least one key for each pair to be a column.

For the case with indexes, there are attributes **left_index** and **right_index**, which take a Boolean value True/False, but these attributes exclude using `left_on` and `right_on`. This implies that they only work for index levels (or index levels/columns) with identical names. To test it, we change column name *Country Code* into *Code*, in a copy of *gini*, then we try the join with *Code* as an index in both data frames.

```
test= gini.copy(deep= True)
test.columns= ['Country Name', 'Code', '2018', '2019', '2020', '2021']
test_index= test.set_index(['Country Name','Code'])
test_index
```

Country Name	Code	2018	2019	2020	2021
Aruba	ABW	NaN	NaN	NaN	NaN
Africa Eastern and Southern	AFE	NaN	NaN	NaN	NaN
Afghanistan	AFG	NaN	NaN	NaN	NaN
Africa Western and Central	AFW	NaN	NaN	NaN	NaN
Angola	AGO	51.3	NaN	NaN	NaN
...	...	...	...	...	...
Kosovo	XKX	NaN	NaN	NaN	NaN
Yemen, Rep.	YEM	NaN	NaN	NaN	NaN
South Africa	ZAF	NaN	NaN	NaN	NaN
Zambia	ZMB	NaN	NaN	NaN	NaN
Zimbabwe	ZWE	NaN	50.3	NaN	NaN

Having now the same name for the index level in *test_index* and the column in *military*, we can first try argument **on**.

```
test_index.merge(military, how= 'inner', on= 'Code')
```

	Code	2018_x	2019_x	2020_x	2021	Entity	2018_y	2019_y	2020_y
0	AFG	NaN	NaN	NaN	NaN	Afghanistan	1.01	1.12	1.37
1	AGO	51.3	NaN	NaN	NaN	Angola	1.87	1.64	1.62
2	ALB	30.1	30.8	NaN	NaN	Albania	1.16	1.29	1.54
3	ARE	26.0	NaN	NaN	NaN	United Arab Emirates	NaN	NaN	NaN
4	ARG	41.3	42.9	42.3	NaN	Argentina	0.75	0.71	0.76
...	...	...	...	...	...	...	...	...	...

As expected, with one index level and one column, the classic join works, and the original index levels are omitted.

Now, with both index levels, we have to use `left_index` and `right_index` attributes.

```
test_index.merge(military_index, how= 'inner',
        left_index= True, right_index= True)
```

Code	Country Name	Entity	2018_x	2019_x	2020_x	2021	2018_y	2019_y	2020_y
AFG	Afghanistan	Afghanistan	NaN	NaN	NaN	NaN	1.01	1.12	1.37
AGO	Angola	Angola	51.3	NaN	NaN	NaN	1.87	1.64	1.62
ALB	Albania	Albania	30.1	30.8	NaN	NaN	1.16	1.29	1.54
ARE	United Arab Emirates	United Arab Emirates	26.0	NaN	NaN	NaN	NaN	NaN	NaN
ARG	Argentina	Argentina	41.3	42.9	42.3	NaN	0.75	0.71	0.76
...	...	...	...	...	...	...	...	...	...

This time, in the joined data frame, all index levels have been kept. However, this variant has the requirement of same name for index levels used as keys.

10.2.3 Duplicated Keys

We consider now some cases of duplicated key values to verify how pandas `merge()` handles them. The dataset for these examples is the same custom dataset employed in the R section that lets us easily reproduce different variants.

```
df1= pd.DataFrame(
   {'Buyer'   : ['Polycarp', 'Lada', 'Strigbod', 'Mario'],
    'Seller'  : ['Brand1', 'Brand2', 'Brand3', 'Brand4'],
    'Product' : ['shirt', 'shoes', 'hat', 'scarf'],
    'buyCity' : ['Des Moines', 'Hanover', 'Madison', 'Venice'],
    'selCity' : ['Boston', 'Milan','Paris', 'London']})

df2= pd.DataFrame(
   {'City'    : ['Des Moines', 'Hanover', 'Madison', 'Venice',
                 'Boston', 'Milan','Paris', 'London'],
    'Country' : ['USA', 'USA', 'USA', 'Italy', 'USA', 'Italy', 'France', 'UK']})
```

With join operations, we want to obtain a data frame with information about the country corresponding to each city of buyers (*buyCity*) and sellers (*sellCity*). We run the two join operations separately, first with respect to *buyCity*, then to *selCity*.

```
temp= df1.merge(df2, how= "inner",
            left_on= 'buyCity',
            right_on= 'City')
temp
```

	Buyer	Seller	Product	buyCity	selCity	City	Country
0	Polycarp	Brand1	shirt	Des Moines	Boston	Des Moines	USA
1	Lada	Brand2	shoes	Hanover	Milan	Hanover	USA
2	Strigbod	Brand3	hat	Madison	Paris	Madison	USA
3	Mario	Brand4	scarf	Venice	London	Venice	Italy

```
dfJoin= temp.merge(df2, how= "inner",
            left_on= 'selCity',right_on= 'City',
            suffixes=('_buy','_sel'))
dfJoin
```

	Buyer	Seller	Product	buyCity	selCity	City_buy	Country_buy	City_sel	Country_sel
0	Polycarp	Brand1	shirt	Des Moines	Boston	Des Moines	USA	Boston	USA
1	Lada	Brand2	shoes	Hanover	Milan	Hanover	USA	Milan	Italy
2	Strigbod	Brand3	hat	Madison	Paris	Madison	USA	Paris	France
3	Mario	Brand4	scarf	Venice	London	Venice	Italy	London	UK

There are duplicated columns, *buyCity* and *City_buy* are identical, same for *selCity* and *City_sel*. They should be handled separately, either by selecting a subset of columns or dropping the duplicates. Below is the compact version with duplicated columns dropped.

```
df1.merge(df2, how= "inner", left_on= 'buyCity', right_on= 'City').\
    merge(df2, how= "inner", left_on= 'selCity',right_on= 'City',
        suffixes=('_buy','_sel')).\
    drop(['City_buy','City_sel'], axis=1)
```

	Buyer	Seller	Product	buyCity	selCity	Country_buy	Country_sel
0	Polycarp	Brand1	shirt	Des Moines	Boston	USA	USA
1	Lada	Brand2	shoes	Hanover	Milan	USA	Italy
2	Strigbod	Brand3	hat	Madison	Paris	USA	France
3	Mario	Brand4	scarf	Venice	London	Italy	UK

Now we introduce duplicates in key values.

Case 1 *– Duplicated keys in the left data frame (df1).* Changes are:

- One buyer (Lada) is registered with two different purchases (*partial duplication*);
- Another buyer (Mario) is registered with two identical purchases (*complete duplication*).

```
df1= pd.DataFrame(
   {'Buyer' : ['Polycarp', 'Lada', 'Lada', 'Strigbod', 'Mario', 'Mario'],
    'Seller' : ['Brand1', 'Brand2', 'Brand3', 'Brand3', 'Brand4', 'Brand4'],
    'Product' : ['shirt', 'shoes', 'boots', 'hat', 'scarf', 'scarf'],
    'buyCity' : ['Des Moines', 'Hanover', 'Hanover', 'Madison', 'Venice',
'Venice'],
    'selCity' : ['Boston', 'Milan','Paris', 'Paris', 'London', 'London']})
df1
```

	Buyer	Seller	Product	buyCity	selCity
0	Polycarp	Brand1	shirt	Des Moines	Boston
1	Lada	Brand2	shoes	Hanover	Milan
2	Lada	Brand3	boots	Hanover	Paris
3	Strigbod	Brand3	hat	Madison	Paris
4	Mario	Brand4	scarf	Venice	London
5	Mario	Brand4	scarf	Venice	London

We re-run the join operation in the compact form.

```
df1.merge(df2, how= "inner", left_on= 'buyCity', right_on= 'City').\
    merge(df2, how= "inner", left_on= 'selCity',right_on= 'City',
        suffixes=('_buy','_sel')).\
    drop(['City_buy','City_sel'], axis=1)
```

	Buyer	Seller	Product	buyCity	selCity	Country_buy	Country_sel
0	Polycarp	Brand1	shirt	Des Moines	Boston	USA	USA
1	Lada	Brand2	shoes	Hanover	Milan	USA	Italy
2	Lada	Brand3	boots	Hanover	Paris	USA	France
3	Strigbod	Brand3	hat	Madison	Paris	USA	France
4	Mario	Brand4	scarf	Venice	London	Italy	UK
5	Mario	Brand4	scarf	Venice	London	Italy	UK

The joined data frame is correct; we had 6 purchases in the original data, and the same have been reproduced in the result.

Case 2 – *Add a duplication in the right data frame (df2).* In addition to the duplication introduced in the previous case, we want to have duplication in the second data frame as well. For simplicity, we just duplicate all values.

```
df2= pd.DataFrame(
    {'City' : ['Des Moines', 'Hanover', 'Madison', 'Venice',
               'Boston', 'Milan','Paris', 'London',
               'Des Moines', 'Hanover', 'Madison', 'Venice',
               'Boston', 'Milan','Paris', 'London'],
     'Country' : ['USA', 'USA', 'USA', 'Italy', 'USA', 'Italy', 'France', 'UK',
                  'USA', 'USA', 'USA', 'Italy', 'USA', 'Italy', 'France', 'UK']})
df2
```

	City	Country
0	Des Moines	USA
1	Hanover	USA
2	Madison	USA
3	Venice	Italy
4	Boston	USA
5	Milan	Italy
6	Paris	France
7	London	UK
8	Des Moines	USA
9	Hanover	USA
10	Madison	USA
11	Venice	Italy
12	Boston	USA
13	Milan	Italy
14	Paris	France
15	London	UK

Again, the same join operation is re-run.

```
df1.merge(df2, how= "inner", left_on= 'buyCity', right_on= 'City').\
   merge(df2, how= "inner", left_on= 'selCity',right_on= 'City',
        suffixes=('_buy','_sel')).\
   drop(['City_buy','City_sel'], axis=1)
```

	Buyer	Seller	Product	buyCity	selCity	Country_buy	Country_sel
0	Polycarp	Brand1	shirt	Des Moines	Boston	USA	USA
1	Polycarp	Brand1	shirt	Des Moines	Boston	USA	USA
2	Polycarp	Brand1	shirt	Des Moines	Boston	USA	USA
3	Polycarp	Brand1	shirt	Des Moines	Boston	USA	USA
4	Lada	Brand2	shoes	Hanover	Milan	USA	Italy
5	Lada	Brand2	shoes	Hanover	Milan	USA	Italy
6	Lada	Brand2	shoes	Hanover	Milan	USA	Italy
7	Lada	Brand2	shoes	Hanover	Milan	USA	Italy
8	Lada	Brand3	boots	Hanover	Paris	USA	France
9	Lada	Brand3	boots	Hanover	Paris	USA	France
10	Lada	Brand3	boots	Hanover	Paris	USA	France
11	Lada	Brand3	boots	Hanover	Paris	USA	France
12	Strigbod	Brand3	hat	Madison	Paris	USA	France
13	Strigbod	Brand3	hat	Madison	Paris	USA	France
14	Strigbod	Brand3	hat	Madison	Paris	USA	France
15	Strigbod	Brand3	hat	Madison	Paris	USA	France
16	Mario	Brand4	scarf	Venice	London	Italy	UK
17	Mario	Brand4	scarf	Venice	London	Italy	UK
18	Mario	Brand4	scarf	Venice	London	Italy	UK
19	Mario	Brand4	scarf	Venice	London	Italy	UK
20	Mario	Brand4	scarf	Venice	London	Italy	UK
21	Mario	Brand4	scarf	Venice	London	Italy	UK
22	Mario	Brand4	scarf	Venice	London	Italy	UK
23	Mario	Brand4	scarf	Venice	London	Italy	UK

The result is now incorrect; many duplicates have been created, three for each original purchase. Pandas has a function to remove duplicated rows in a data frame, **pd.drop_duplicates()**. We try it.

```
df1.merge(df2, how= "inner", left_on= 'buyCity', right_on= 'City').\
   merge(df2, how= "inner", left_on= 'selCity',right_on= 'City',
        suffixes=('_buy','_sel')).\
   drop(['City_buy','City_sel'], axis=1).\
   drop_duplicates()
```

	Buyer	Seller	Product	buyCity	selCity	Country_buy	Country_sel
0	Polycarp	Brand1	shirt	Des Moines	Boston	USA	USA
4	Lada	Brand2	shoes	Hanover	Milan	USA	Italy
8	Lada	Brand3	boots	Hanover	Paris	USA	France
12	Strigbod	Brand3	hat	Madison	Paris	USA	France
16	Mario	Brand4	scarf	Venice	London	Italy	UK

It works as expected, all duplicated rows have been dropped. Technically, it is correct, but logically, in this specific example, it is not, because we originally had six purchases and ended up with just five. The solution, like discussed in the R section, is to have unique identifiers for each distinct observation, so that the two identical purchases made by Mario are not represented as duplicated rows.

One easy way *to create in df1 a new column with a unique row identifier is to reset the index. This way, the implicit row index becomes a column with distinct values for each row.*

```
df11= df1.reset_index()
df11
```

	index	Buyer	Seller	Product	buyCity	selCity
0	0	Polycarp	Brand1	shirt	Des Moines	Boston
1	1	Lada	Brand2	shoes	Hanover	Milan
2	2	Lada	Brand3	boots	Hanover	Paris
3	3	Strigbod	Brand3	hat	Madison	Paris
4	4	Mario	Brand4	scarf	Venice	London
5	5	Mario	Brand4	scarf	Venice	London

Now *index* is a column. We can rename it as *ID*.

```
df11= df11.rename(columns={'index':'ID'})
df11
```

	ID	Buyer	Seller	Product	buyCity	selCity
0	0	Polycarp	Brand1	shirt	Des Moines	Boston
1	1	Lada	Brand2	shoes	Hanover	Milan
2	2	Lada	Brand3	boots	Hanover	Paris
3	3	Strigbod	Brand3	hat	Madison	Paris
4	4	Mario	Brand4	scarf	Venice	London
5	5	Mario	Brand4	scarf	Venice	London

Finally, the join operation removes duplicated rows.

```
df11.merge(df2, how= "inner", left_on= 'buyCity', right_on= 'City').\
    merge(df2, how= "inner", left_on= 'selCity',right_on= 'City',
            suffixes=('_buy','_sel')).\
    drop(['City_buy','City_sel'], axis=1).\
    drop_duplicates()
```

	ID	Buyer	Seller	Product	buyCity	selCity	Country_buy	Country_sel
0	0	Polycarp	Brand1	shirt	Des Moines	Boston	USA	USA
4	1	Lada	Brand2	shoes	Hanover	Milan	USA	Italy
8	2	Lada	Brand3	boots	Hanover	Paris	USA	France
12	3	Strigbod	Brand3	hat	Madison	Paris	USA	France
16	4	Mario	Brand4	scarf	Venice	London	Italy	UK
20	5	Mario	Brand4	scarf	Venice	London	Italy	UK

The result is correct; we have the original six purchases. It is interesting to note the implicit index, which identifies the first row for each series of duplicated rows.

10.2.4 Special Join Types

10.2.4.1 Semi Join: Function `isin()`

We have introduced the **semi join** in the corresponding R section as a variant of the inner join, which returns only rows with matching key values, but it does not copy in the result columns from the *right* data frame.

To test it in Python, we modify data frame *df2* to have a key value that does not match, duplication, and additional information. Specifically:

- add a new column *State_Region* with the state for US cities or the region of European cities.
- remove from *df2* one of the cities present in *df1* (Madison) so to have an unmatched key value.
- duplicate one row (Venice, Italy, Veneto) so to have the incorrect duplication of rows in the join.

```
df2= pd.DataFrame(
    {'City'  : ['Des Moines', 'Hanover', 'Venice',
                'Boston', 'Milan','Paris', 'London', 'Venice'],
     'Country'  : ['USA', 'USA', 'Italy', 'USA', 'Italy', 'France', 'UK', 'Italy'],
     'State_Region'  : ['Iowa', 'New Hampshire', 'Veneto','Massachusetts',
                'Lombardia','Île de France', 'Greater London', 'Veneto']})
df2
```

	City	Country	State_Region
0	Des Moines	USA	Iowa
1	Hanover	USA	New Hampshire
2	Venice	Italy	Veneto
3	Boston	USA	Massachusetts
4	Milan	Italy	Lombardia
5	Paris	France	Île de France
6	London	UK	Greater London
7	Venice	Italy	Veneto

A specific function for the semi join is not available in Python and pandas, but it could be realized with function `isin()`, which works either on series or on data frames and has the following general template: `df.isin(values)` or `series.isin(values)`. *It returns a Boolean result:* ***True*** *for each value of the data frame or series that appears in values;* ***False*** *for those not present.*

To obtain a *semi join*, the logic is that we want to check each value of the left key column(s) with respect to the list of values of the right key column(s) and, for those values that have a match, return the row of the left data frame. So, logically, it is the combination of two operations: create a Boolean mask based on the match between left and right key column(s) and filter the rows of the left data frame.

First, the Boolean mask.

```
df1['buyCity'].isin(df2['City'])
0      True
1      True
2      True
3      False
4      True
5      True
Name: buyCity, dtype: bool
```

Value corresponding to index 3 of *buyCity* does not appear in *City*; it is Madison that we have deleted from *df2*. With the mask, it is immediate to obtain the rows.

```
df1[df1['buyCity'].isin(df2['City'])]
```

	Buyer	Seller	Product	buyCity	selCity
0	Polycarp	Brand1	shirt	Des Moines	Boston
1	Lada	Brand2	shoes	Hanover	Milan
2	Lada	Brand3	boots	Hanover	Paris
4	Mario	Brand4	scarf	Venice	London
5	Mario	Brand4	scarf	Venice	London

As expected, the purchase done by Strigbod does not appear in the result, and only columns from the left data frame are included. The same result, obviously, could have been obtained from a normal *inner join* by selecting only rows from the left data frame.

10.2.4.2 Anti Join: Variants

The **anti join** is the more useful version of the *semi join* because it works analogously but with the dual logic: *it returns the rows of the left data frame whose key values **did not have a match***, which is particularly useful information for checking and managing the result of a join.

Being the dual operation of the semi join, computing it is immediate; it suffices to just add a *negation* to the *semi join*. Again, first the Boolean mask, then the row selection.

```
~(df1['buyCity'].isin(df2['City']))
0    False
1    False
2    False
3     True
4    False
5    False
Name: buyCity, dtype: bool
```

The only true value of *buyCity* now corresponds to Madison, and by filtering rows, we obtain the Strigbod's purchase.

```
df1[~(df1['buyCity'].isin(df2['City']))]
```

	Buyer	Seller	Product	buyCity	selCity
3	Strigbod	Brand3	hat	Madison	Paris

However, while using the `isin()` function to find unmatched key values is effective, the alternative, equally well-suited and perhaps more intuitive, is to work with missing values introduced by an *outer join*, or equally a *left* or *right join* if only columns of one data frame are requested.

We run the example using the *Gini index* and *Military spending* datasets, finding key values that did not match. By using *Country Name* and *Entity* as keys, we know that several key values go unmatched. We find them by using logical conditions on missing values in the key columns. We proceed schematically as before: first the mask, then the filter on rows.

```
dfOuter= gini.merge(military, how= 'outer',
                left_on= 'Country Name', right_on= 'Entity')

mask= dfOuter['Country Name'].isna() | dfOuter['Entity'].isna()

dfOuter[mask][['Country Name','Entity']]
```

	Country Name	Entity
0	Aruba	NaN
1	Africa Eastern and Southern	NaN
3	Africa Western and Central	NaN
6	Andorra	NaN
7	Arab World	NaN
...	...	...
279	NaN	Taiwan
280	NaN	Timor
281	NaN	Turkey
282	NaN	Venezuela
283	NaN	Yemen

Analogously, by using *Country Code* and *Code* as keys.

```
dfOuter= gini.merge(military, how= 'outer',
              left_on= 'Country Code', right_on= 'Code')

mask= dfOuter['Country Code'].isna() | dfOuter['Code'].isna()

dfOuter[mask][['Country Code','Code']]
```

	Country Code	Code
0	ABW	NaN
1	AFE	NaN
3	AFW	NaN
6	AND	NaN
7	ARB	NaN
...	...	...
259	WLD	NaN
260	WSM	NaN
261	XKX	NaN
266	NaN	OWID_KOS
267	NaN	TWN

Pandas makes the definition of the Boolean mask even more intuitive with a *special argument of the* merge() *function*. By specifying `indicator=True,` the result of the merge() will have a new column with default name *_merge*, whose elements may have three values: ***both***, ***left_only***, or ***right_only***, respectfully for rows whose keys matched, left key did not match, or right key did not match.

```
gini.merge(military, how= 'outer',
           left_on= 'Country Code', right_on= 'Code',
           indicator= True)
```

	Country Name	Country Code	2018_x	2019_x	...	Entity	Code	2018_y	2019_y	2020_y	_merge
0	Aruba	ABW	NaN	NaN	...	NaN	NaN	NaN	NaN	NaN	left_only
1	Africa Eastern and Southern	AFE	NaN	NaN	...	NaN	NaN	NaN	NaN	NaN	left_only
2	Afghanistan	AFG	NaN	NaN	...	Afghanistan	AFG	1.01	1.12	1.37	both
3	Africa Western and Central	AFW	NaN	NaN	...	NaN	NaN	NaN	NaN	NaN	left_only
4	Angola	AGO	51.3	NaN	...	Angola	AGO	1.87	1.64	1.62	both
...	...	...	...	...	...	...	...	...	...	...	...
263	South Africa	ZAF	NaN	NaN	...	South Africa	ZAF	0.98	0.98	1.07	both
264	Zambia	ZMB	NaN	NaN	...	Zambia	ZMB	1.41	1.22	1.15	both
265	Zimbabwe	ZWE	NaN	50.3	...	Zimbabwe	ZWE	1.22	0.70	NaN	both
266	NaN	NaN	NaN	NaN	...	Kosovo	OWID_KOS	0.80	0.83	1.06	right_only
267	NaN	NaN	NaN	NaN	...	Taiwan	TWN	1.74	1.82	1.92	right_only

This way, *rows corresponding to unmatched keys can be easily extracted with a condition on values of the _merge column*. This solution is equivalent to the previous one that checked missing values, only it checks column *_merge* values instead of using isna() on key columns.

```
dfOuter= gini.merge(military, how= 'outer',
           left_on= 'Country Name', right_on= 'Entity',
           indicator= True)

mask= dfOuter['_merge'] != 'both'

dfOuter[mask][['Country Name','Entity']]
```

	Country Name	Entity
0	Aruba	NaN
1	Africa Eastern and Southern	NaN
3	Africa Western and Central	NaN
6	Andorra	NaN
7	Arab World	NaN

	Country Name	Entity
...	...	...
279	NaN	Taiwan
280	NaN	Timor
281	NaN	Turkey
282	NaN	Venezuela
283	NaN	Yemen

To obtain the result of the *anti join*, it suffices to create the mask based only on the *left key column(s)* (e.g. `dfOuter['Country Name'].isna()`) or with value *left_only* (e.g. `dfOuter['_merge'] == 'left_only'`), then drop the columns from the right data frame or select those of the left one.

Questions

10.1 (R/Python)
Join operations between data frames...
  A Add rows of one data frame to the rows of the other
  B Combine rows with same position in two data frames
  C Combine logically related rows of different data frames
  D Combine columns of a data frame with columns of another one
  (R: C)

10.2 (R/Python)
Key columns in join operations between data frames...
  A Are the columns to be put together in the resulting joined data frame?
  B Contain elements whose values are matched for equality
  C Must contain only values that appear in all key columns
  D Select the rows to be returned in the joined data frame
  (R: B)

10.3 (R/Python)
Is it possible that in a join operation, the data frame with less rows has values in the key column(s) that do not appear in the corresponding key column(s) of the data frame with more rows?
  A No, it is not possible
  B No, otherwise an error is raised
  C No, otherwise the result is unpredictable
  D Yes, of course it is possible
  (R: D)

10.4 (R/Python)
Is it possible that in a join operation, two key values logically refer to the same information but are spelled differently?

    A No, it is not possible, if values are different the logical entities are also different

    B No, otherwise an error is raised

    C Yes, it is possible, and different values referred to the same logical entity should be normalized

    D Yes, of course it is possible, and it is not a problem

(R: C)

10.5 (R/Python)

With respect to Question 10.4, if two key values logically refer to the same information but are spelled differently, does it mean that one of the two values has been misspelled by mistake?

    A No, it is entirely possible that both values are legitimate names of the same entity

    B No, but one of the two is an abbreviation or an acronym of the other one

    C Yes, in that case, one of the two is a mistake

    D It is impossible to tell

(R: A)

10.6 (R/Python)

Let us consider two data frames with city names and other territorial information (e.g. county, region, state, etc.). Is it a good choice to use just city names as keys for the join operation?

    A Yes, they are fine

    B Yes, provided that city names are spelled correctly

    C No, city names could be too long

    D No, it is not, it is not unusual to have different cities with same name

(R: D)

10.7 (R/Python)

With respect to Question 10.6, which would be a reasonably good choice for join keys in order to correlate rows referring to the same city?

    A City Name, Country Name

    B City Name, State Name (or Region)

    C City Name, County (or Province)

    D County (or Province), State Name (or Region)

(R: C)

10.8 (R/Python)

If the choice is between City Name and a unique code for cities (e.g. City Code) in a join between two data frames, what would typically be a good choice for keys?

    A Data Frame 1: City Name; Data Frame 2: City Name

    B Data Frame 1: City Name; Data Frame 2: City Code

C Data Frame 1: City Code; Data Frame 2: City Name
D Data Frame 1: City Code; Data Frame 2: City Code
(R: D)

10.9 **(R/Python)**
When codes associated to entities are available, is it granted that in a join operation between two data frames we will not find mismatches between same entity with different codes?
A Yes, with codes mismatches cannot exist
B No, in fact, it is better selecting both names and codes as keys
C Yes, unless the data frames come from different countries
D No, it is not granted, the result should still be checked for mismatches between keys
(R: D)

10.10 **(R/Python)**
Does an outer/full join always have more rows than an inner join?
A Yes, of course
B Yes, unless missing values are present in keys
C No, they could have the same number of rows if there is no unmatched key
D No, they have the same number of rows
(R: C)

10.11 **(R/Python)**
What is the typical result of matching two missing values in key columns?
A They do not match
B They match only if they are in numerical columns
C They match unless the columns are of logical type
D They usually match
(R: D)

10.12 **(R/Python)**
What is the typical usage case for an anti-join?
A To reveal unmatched keys
B Same as left join
C Same as right join
D Same as inner join but only columns from the left data frame are in the result
(R: A)

10.13 **(R/Python)**
Is it possible to retrieve unmatched keys from the result of an inner join?
And from the result of an outer/full join?
A Yes, in both cases
B Yes, from the inner join; not from the outer/full join

     C Yes, from the outer/full join; not from the inner join

     D No, neither of them allows for that

  (R: C)

10.14 **(R/Python)**

With respect to Question 10.13, which information is mostly useful to retrieve unmatched keys?

     A When both keys in the joined data frame have actual values

     B When both keys are missing values

     C When one key has an actual value and the other has a missing value

     D The anti-join is needed

  (R: C)

11

List/Dictionary Data Format

The data format called **list** in R or **dictionary** in Python, usually shortened as **dict**, has a long history in the management of data, being one of the simpler but useful evolutions of basic data formats like arrays and matrices. Arrays and matrices by definition have data of the same type, and the most reasonable evolution is to have data formats that allow for data of different types. We have already seen this throughout the whole book with the *data frame* format, which basically extends the notion of a matrix with columns (variables) possibly of different types. The *list/dict* data format follows the same logic but is realized in an alternative way with respect to the data frame, with different pros and cons. The following is an example of a list/dict data structure describing personal information:

```
{ 1: { 'name': 'Polycarp',
       'surname': 'Arthmail',
       'city': 'Des Moines',
       'state': 'IA',
       'department': 'Divinity School',
       'address': { 'street': '45 Francis Avenue',
                    'zipcode': '02138',
                    'city': 'Cambridge',
                    'state': 'MA'}
                  },
  2: { 'name': 'Lada',
       'surname': 'Damon',
       'city': 'Hanover',
       'state': 'NH',
       'department': 'Chemistry',
       'address': { 'street': '12 OXFORD STREET',
                    'zipcode': '02138',
                    'city': 'Cambridge',
                    'state': 'MA'}},
...}
```

This is a typical form of a list/dict (technically, it uses Python syntax), with information expressed as pairs ***name:value*** (sometimes also called *key:value* or *label:value*) and organized in a highly structured organization composed of ***nested levels***. In the example, we see the *first level* composed of elements with names 1, 2, …, followed by a colon. Curly brackets embrace each complex element. In detail, how is composed the value part for each name 1, 2, …? It is a list/dict forming the *second*

Data Science Fundamentals with R, Python, and Open Data, First Edition. Marco Cremonini.
© 2024 John Wiley & Sons, Inc. Published 2024 by John Wiley & Sons, Inc.
Companion website: www.wiley.com/go/DSFRPythonOpenData

level of the data structure, with elements *name, surname, city, state, department,* and *address,* each one with a corresponding value, which is an actual value for all but *address* that instead has a list/dict as a value, representing the *third level* of the data structure, with each *address* element associated to a list/dict composed by elements *street, zipcode, city,* and *state.* It should be noted that elements *city* and *state* at the second level are logically different than *city* and *state* at third level. The path into the list structure uniquely defines the names.

Clearly, the list/dict data structure is a different way of organizing information than the tabular form adopted by data frames. Information might be the same, but the organization differs. In particular, with the list/dict it is easy to represent *hierarchical structures,* which are not easily reproduced in a data frame. There is no nesting expressed with the columns of a data frame, so it would be less straightforward to represent the fact that there is a city and state associated with the person's name and a city and state associated with the department where the person works or is affiliated with. To clarify this point, it could be useful to think of a possible join operation between a data frame with only personal information and the name of the department and another data frame with the department's information. The department's names would be the join keys. The result would have columns *city* and *state* from both data frames, and, as we have seen in the previous chapter, the solution is to add prefixes to disambiguate the identical names, such as *city_emp, state_emp,* and *city_dep, state_dep.* Elements of the list/dict and a corresponding data frame would be the same, but the nested organization of the list would be transformed into a flat, tabular organization of the data frame. On the other hand, a data frame makes it easy to execute a number of operations on data because of the tabular form, as we have seen in previous chapters. Operations that would be much more difficult with the list/dict structure, starting from the simple computation of descriptive statistics on variables' values.

Hence, as is usual in data science, there is no data structure that is definitely better than the others; they serve different purposes. The consequence, both logical and practical, as we have learned, is that we should be able to manage the different data structures and efficiently transform one into another. In this case, the key transformation is *from list/dict to data frame,* in order to have the possibility to use all data wrangling techniques we have seen so far.

In this chapter, we will learn the logic and technical tools to transform from list/dict to data frame with increasingly complex configurations.

In addition, we will consider the **JSON** (JavaScript Object Notation) data format, which has a list/dict organization and is widely diffused for online data exchange and data representation. The JSON format is the alternative to the CSV among open, nonproprietary formats; it is important to practice with it, which is another good reason to learn how to manage data as list/dict.

Datasets

Climate at a Glance: Global Time Series, NOAA National Centers for Environmental Information, a dataset on average temperature anomalies (retrieved on August 8, 2023, from https://www .ncei.noaa.gov/access/monitoring/climate-at-a-glance/global/time-series). *Copyright:* Open Data Policy.

Historical events is a JSON dataset extracted from Wikipedia pages through the Web API made available by *Vizgr.org.* It is a generic collection of historical events referring to a specified country. For the case study, England has been chosen (https://www.vizgr.org/historical-events/search.php? query=England&format=json). *Copyright:* Wikipedia Open Data Policy.

The Nobel Prize (https://www.nobelprize.org/), a dataset of Nobel laureates available through the Web API provided by The Nobel Prize Foundation (https://api.nobelprize.org/v1/prize.json). *Copyright*: Data in the public domain with CC0 license (https://creativecommons.org/share-your-work/public-domain/cc0/).

Everypolitician, an English charity collecting public information on MEPs from several countries. The data extracted are referred to MEPs of the 116th Congress of the United States of America. (https://cdn.rawgit.com/everypolitician/everypolitician-data/e0f0bbde5851a8c99ffe154a00a87d81 71b1bebf/data/United_States_of_America/House/ep-popolo-v1.0.json). *Copyright*: Wikipedia Open Data Policy.

11.1 R: List Data Format

As we explained in the introduction of the chapter, a list could have elements of different data types. In R, the base function `list()` creates a list. The simplest form is to omit names and have only values. In the example, we create a list data structure with elements as vectors of numeric, character, and Boolean values. The common utility function `str()` lets inspect the list content.

> **Note**
>
> With R, it is easy to have misunderstandings because of the terminology related to lists. In the example, the `list()` function creates a data object with the characteristics of R *lists* ("dict" is a Python term). However, also a collection of values is commonly called "a list," in common parlance, so it is easy to get confused: is it the specific R data structure or a colloquial generic collection? To try to avoid ambiguity, in this chapter, we will use "list" specifically to refer to the *list data structure* with the particular organization, equivalent to the Python *dictionary* or *dict*. Instead, we will use "vector" to refer to generic collection of values, for example, c(10,20,30,40).

```
a1 <- list(c(10,20,30,40,50), c('A','AB','ABC','ABCD'), TRUE)
a1

[[1]]
[1] 10 20 30 40 50

[[2]]
[1] "A"     "AB"    "ABC"   "ABCD"

[[3]]
[1] TRUE
str(a1)

List of 3
 $ : num [1:5] 10 20 30 40 50
 $ : chr [1:4] "A" "AB" "ABC" "ABCD"
 $ : logi TRUE
```

We have created list *a1* composed of three elements, two vectors, one numeric and the other of character type, and a Boolean value.

Lists, being an evolution of arrays and matrices, still have their elements accessible through the positional index.

```
a1[1]

[[1]]
[1] 10 20 30 40 50

a1[2]

[[1]]
[1] "A" "AB" "ABC" "ABCD"

a1[3]

[[1]]
[1] TRUE
```

Double brackets work too.

```
a1[[1]]

[1] 10 20 30 40 50

a1[[2]]

[1] "A" "AB" "ABC" "ABCD"

a1[[3]]

[1] TRUE
```

We introduce *names*, so we have list elements as pairs ***name:value***.

```
a2 <- list(NUMBERS= c(10,20,30,40,50),
           STRINGS= c('A','AB','ABC','ABCD'),
           LOGIC= TRUE)

a2

$NUMBERS
[1] 10 20 30 40 50

$STRINGS
[1] "A" "AB" "ABC" "ABCD"

$LOGIC
[1] TRUE

str(a2)

List of 3
 $ NUMBERS: num [1:5] 10 20 30 40 50
 $ STRINGS: chr [1:4] "A" "AB" "ABC" "ABCD"
 $ LOGIC  : logi TRUE
```

Names work as an explicit index in selections.

```
a2["NUMBERS"]

$NUMBERS
[1] 10 20 30 40 50

a2["STRINGS"]

$STRINGS
[1] "A" "AB" "ABC" "ABCD"

a2["LOGIC"]

$LOGIC
[1] TRUE
```

It is interesting to notice the perfect similarity of this R syntax with Python's syntax for selecting a data frame column. Languages have much more in common than it looks at first sight and share mechanisms at their core.

We could also use the more familiar R syntax with the *dollar sign $* for selecting variables in a data frame. In a list data, variables do not correspond to columns (there is no column in a list!), but still, the concept of *variable* persists and corresponds to *list elements identified by name.*

```
a2$NUMBERS

[1] 10 20 30 40 50

a2$STRINGS

[1] "A" "AB" "ABC" "ABCD"

a2$LOGIC

[1] TRUE
```

Lists are important to represent **nested data structures**, like **hierarchies**. Here we define a second level of lists for each element.

```
a3 <- list(NUMBERS= list(tens= c(10,20,30,40,50),
                         hundreds= c(100,200,300,400),
                         tenths= c(1.1, 3.2, 2.3, 6.4, 3.5, 7.6)
                        ),
           STRINGS= list( UPPER= c('A','AB','ABC','ABCD'),
                         lower= c('a','ab','abc','abcd'),
                         Title= c('A','Ab','Abc','Abcd')
                        ),
           PEOPLE= list( name= c('Polycarp','Lada','Stribog',"Cassandra"),
                        surname= c('Arthmail','Demon',"Castor",'Shpynx'),
                        sex= c('M','F','M','F'),
```

```
                    birthdate= c('2002/02/02','1998/12/12',
                                 '2005/10/30','1990/08/18'),
                    attending=c(TRUE,TRUE,FALSE,TRUE)
                    )
)
str(a3)
List of 3
 $ NUMBERS:List of 3
  ..$ tens    : num [1:5] 10 20 30 40 50
  ..$ hundreds: num [1:4] 100 200 300 400
  ..$ tenths  : num [1:6] 1.1 3.2 2.3 6.4 3.5 7.6
 $ STRINGS:List of 3
  ..$ UPPER: chr [1:4] "A" "AB" "ABC" "ABCD"
  ..$ lower: chr [1:4] "a" "ab" "abc" "abcd"
  ..$ Title: chr [1:4] "A" "Ab" "Abc" "Abcd"
 $ PEOPLE :List of 5
  ..$ name    : chr [1:4] "Polycarp" "Lada" "Stribog" "Cassandra"
  ..$ surname : chr [1:4] "Arthmail" "Demon" "Castor" "Shpynx"
  ..$ sex     : chr [1:4] "M" "F" "M" "F"
  ..$ birthdate: chr [1:4] "2002/02/02" "1998/12/12" "2005/10/30" "1990/08/18"
  ..$ attending: logi [1:4] TRUE TRUE FALSE TRUE
```

The RStudio viewer offers the possibility to inspect a list, as shown in Figure 11.1, it might be helpful to use sometimes.

```
View(a3)
```

Alternatively, a list could be inspected with command line functions. Function **names** () returns the names of the list elements for a specific list level. Again, it is worth noting that *it is the same function that returns column names in a data frame*. The concept of variable, as mentioned, is the same, but represented differently.

Name	Type	Value
⊙ a3	list [3]	List of length 3
⊙ NUMBERS	list [3]	List of length 3
tens	double [5]	10 20 30 40 50
hundreds	double [4]	100 200 300 400
tenths	double [6]	1.1 3.2 2.3 6.4 3.5 7.6
⊙ STRINGS	list [3]	List of length 3
UPPER	character [4]	'A' 'AB' 'ABC' 'ABCD'
lower	character [4]	'a' 'ab' 'abc' 'abcd'
Title	character [4]	'A' 'Ab' 'Abc' 'Abcd'
⊙ PEOPLE	list [5]	List of length 5
name	character [4]	'Polycarp' 'Lada' 'Stribog' 'Cassandra'
surname	character [4]	'Arthmail' 'Demon' 'Castor' 'Shpynx'
sex	character [4]	'M' 'F' 'M' 'F'
birthdate	character [4]	'2002/02/02' '1998/12/12' '2005/10/30' '1990/08/18'
attending	logical [4]	TRUE TRUE FALSE TRUE

Figure 11.1 The list structure of a3 with the native RStudio viewer.

```
names(a3)

[1] "NUMBERS"  "STRINGS"  "PEOPLE"
```

This shows variable names at the topmost level of the list structure. To inspect inner levels, the path should be specified using ***double brackets***. For example, if we want to retrieve variable names from element *PEOPLE*. This is the second level of the list structure.

```
names(a3[['PEOPLE']])

[1] "name"      "surname"   "sex"       "birthdate" "attending"
```

The typical R notation with the dollar sign works well too, accessing the second level.

```
names(a3$PEOPLE)

[1] "name"      "surname"   "sex"       "birthdate" "attending"
```

To proceed to deeper levels, the syntax with double brackets has to be repeated, until the value of a certain element is reached. For example, we want to access value *Lada*, we need to specify three levels of indexing.

```
a3[['PEOPLE']][['name']][[2]]

[1] "Lada"
```

In equivalent notation, implicit index values could be used. They all access value *Lada*.

```
a3[['PEOPLE']][[1]][[2]]
a3[[3]][[1]][[2]]
```

Now we complicate the data structure by *mixing data frames and lists*. What might happen, and it does sometimes, is that we have a data frame, and for one or more columns, the *column elements have lists as values*. Here is a simple example. We create a data frame with the `tibble()` function, and one column has lists as element values.

```
df <- tibble(
  A = 1:3,
  B = c("a", "b", "c"),
  C = list(NUMBERS=c(10,20,30,40,50),
           STRINGS=c('A','AB','ABC','ABCD'),
           LOGIC=TRUE))
```

A	B	C
1	a	[<dbl[5]>]
2	b	[<chr[4]>]
3	c	[<lgl[1]>]

The visualization clearly shows that column *C* has lists as values of three different data types and is by itself of type *list*. We can complicate even further with *nested lists as data frame column values*.

```
df1 <- tibble(
  A = 1:3,
  B = c("a", "b", "c"),
  C = list(
  NUMBERS= list(tens= c(10,20,30,40,50),
                hundreds= c(100,200,300,400),
                tenths= c(1.1, 3.2, 2.3, 6.4, 3.5, 7.6)
  ),
  STRINGS= list(UPPER= c('A','AB','ABC','ABCD'),
                lower= c('a','ab','abc','abcd'),
                Title= c('A','Ab','Abc','Abcd')
  ),
  PEOPLE= list(name= c('Polycarp','Lada','Stribog',"Cassandra"),
               surname= c('Arthmail','Demon',"Castor",'Shpynx'),
               sex= c('M','F','M','F'),
               birthdate= c('2002/02/02','1998/12/12',
                            '2005/10/30','1990/08/18'),
               attending=c(TRUE,TRUE,FALSE,TRUE))
  )
)
```

A	B	C
1	a	[<named list[3]>]
2	b	[<named list[3]>]
3	c	[<named list[5]>]

This time the visualization shows that elements of column *C* are named lists without specifying a data type because their elements do not have just one; they are complex data structures with elements of different data types.

To inspect a data frame column with lists as elements, two basic methods are available. With the first, we just pipe the column to str().

```
df1$C %>% str()
```

With the second, we use function **pull()**, which is specific to lists. The outcome is the same.

```
df1 %>% pull(C)
```

```
$NUMBERS
$NUMBERS$tens
[1] 10 20 30 40 50

$NUMBERS$hundreds
[1] 100 200 300 400

$NUMBERS$tenths
[1] 1.1 3.2 2.3 6.4 3.5 7.6


$STRINGS
$STRINGS$UPPER
[1] "A"     "AB"    "ABC"   "ABCD"

$STRINGS$lower
[1] "a"     "ab"    "abc"   "abcd"

$STRINGS$Title
[1] "A"     "Ab"    "Abc"   "Abcd"


$PEOPLE
$PEOPLE$name
[1] "Polycarp"  "Lada"      "Stribog"   "Cassandra"

$PEOPLE$surname
[1] "Arthmail" "Demon"     "Castor"    "Shpynx"

$PEOPLE$sex
[1] "M" "F" "M" "F"

$PEOPLE$birthdate
[1] "2002/02/02" "1998/12/12" "2005/10/30" "1990/08/18"

$PEOPLE$attending
[1]  TRUE  TRUE FALSE  TRUE
```

Tip

Package **repurrrsive** has some popular examples of lists, from the characters of the *Game of Thrones* saga to a sample of GitHub users.

11.1.1 Transformation of List Columns to Ordinary Rows and Columns

Having data frame columns of type list, like those in previous examples, is not uncommon, but it is an inconvenience because the usual data wrangling operations cannot be applied to those data, unless they are first transformed into ordinary rows and columns. Transforming columns from list types might require several operations and a certain degree of patience because the elements organized as lists could have a complicated structure that has to be *unnested level by level*. R has two main functions provided by package *tidyr* for this task: **unnest_wider()** and **unnest_longer()**. It is by combining these two functions, together with more traditional data wrangling ones, that the transformation of a list column could be completed. The names of the two functions remind of the two used for pivoting in long-wide transformations. It is not a coincidence; they actually share a logic that is similar in the two cases, although unnesting list columns could be more complicated than pivoting.

Function `unnest_wider()` When the elements of a list column in a data frame are lists *with same names and number of values*, the transformation in ordinary columns is very easy, and it actually reminds closely of a long-to-wide transformation, resulting in *more columns than the original data frame.* Let us consider a simple didactic example.

```
df2 <- tribble(
  ~N, ~Attendees,
  1, list(name="Polycarp",surname="Arthmail",sex="M",
          birthdate="2002/02/02",attending=TRUE),
  2, list(name="Lada",surname="Demon",sex="F",
          birthdate="1998/12/12",attending=TRUE),
  3, list(name="Stribog",surname="Castor",sex="M",
          birthdate="2005/10/30",attending=FALSE),
  4, list(name="Cassandra",surname="Shpynx",sex="F",
          birthdate="1990/08/18",attending=FALSE)
  )
view(df2)
```

Using the RStudio viewer to look at the data frame (Figure 11.2), it is evident that a transformation of the list element into ordinary columns with names as the list elements names is straightforward. We are transforming a single list column into five ordinary columns; it is a wide-type transformation, therefore `unnest_wider()`. There is a detail to consider: we are going to transform the single list column, so it has to be specified as the attribute of the function.

	N		Attendees	
1		1	list(name = "Polycarp", surname = "Arthmail", sex [...]	🔍
2		2	list(name = "Lada", surname = "Demon", sex = "F", [...]	🔍
3		3	list(name = "Stribog", surname = "Castor", sex = " [...]	🔍
4		4	list(name = "Cassandra", surname = "Shpynx", sex = [...	🔍

Figure 11.2 RStudio viewer visualization of data frame df2.

```
df2 %>% unnest_wider(Attendees)
```

N	name	surname	sex	birthdate	attending
1	Polycarp	Arthmail	M	2002/02/02	TRUE
2	Lada	Demon	F	1998/12/12	TRUE
3	Stribog	Castor	M	2005/10/30	FALSE
4	Cassandra	Shpynx	F	1990/08/18	FALSE

Function `unnest_longer()` On the contrary, function `unnest_longer()` *transforms column lists into ordinary rows*, meaning that *the resulting data frame has more rows than the original* one, and this motivates the suffix *longer*, reminding us of the corresponding wide to long transformation. Let us see the result again with list column *Attendees*. We may use the RStudio viewer again to have a better look at the result (see Figure 11.3).

```
df2 %>% unnest_longer(Attendees) %>% view()
```

Figure 11.3 Result of the `unnest_longer()` function.

	N	Attendees	Attendees_id
1	1	Polycarp	name
2	1	Arthmail	surname
3	1	M	sex
4	1	2002/02/02	birthdate
5	1	TRUE	attending
6	2	Lada	name
7	2	Demon	surname
8	2	F	sex
9	2	1998/12/12	birthdate
10	2	TRUE	attending
11	3	Stribog	name
12	3	Castor	surname
13	3	M	sex
14	3	2005/10/30	birthdate
15	3	FALSE	attending
16	4	Cassandra	name
17	4	Shpynx	surname
18	4	F	sex
19	4	1990/08/18	birthdate
20	4	FALSE	attending

The result looks very much like a wide-to-long transformation, indeed, with a new column (*Attendees_id*) acting as keys for the column with values (*Attendees*).

These are the two basic tools for transforming list columns into ordinary columns and rows.

11.1.1.1 Other Options

If we look again at the previous example, this time without the RStudio viewer, a detail that went unnoticed becomes evident: after the transformation, the column *Attendees* has *maintained the list data type*. Values are actually single values of type character or logical; this is the reason why the RStudio viewer shows them, but formally, they are still lists, *<chr[1]>* and *<lgl[1]>*. Being formally defined as list, that column cannot be used for usual data wrangling operations. It needs to be converted.

```
df2 %>% unnest_longer(Attendees)
```

N	Attendees	Attendees_id
1	[<chr[1]>]	name
1	[<chr[1]>]	surname
1	[<chr[1]>]	sex
1	[<chr[1]>]	birthdate
1	[<lgl[1]>]	attending
2	[<chr[1]>]	name
2	[<chr[1]>]	surname
2	[<chr[1]>]	sex
2	[<chr[1]>]	birthdate
2	[<lgl[1]>]	attending
…	…	…

A useful available option is attribute **transform,** which executes a type conversion. This option performs the standard type conversion, so the possibility that it raises errors depends on the value types. In general, it should be used only on values of same type, unless we are well aware of the results for different types.

Values of the attribute are the names of the common conversion functions. In our case, we have both characters and logical values but, for the aim of the example, we convert all of them into character types. The function to execute would be as.character(), and correspondingly, the attribute transfer is specified as **transform= as.charachter**.

```
df2 %>% unnest_longer(Attendees, transform= as.character)
```

N	Attendees	Attendees_id
1	Polycarp	name
1	Arthmail	surname
1	M	sex
1	2002/02/02	birthdate
1	TRUE	attending
2	Lada	name
2	Demon	surname
…	…	…

The result is an ordinary data frame in long form, with column *Attendees* of character type. This means that we have lost the logical typization of TRUE and FALSE; they are just strings now, not Boolean.

Another option is function **unnest_auto()**, which could be useful, especially for a first look at list columns and quick inspection, but should not be used as a standard solution, especially in scripts. For regular solutions, unnest_longer() and unnest_wider() have to be used, not this one.

Basically, what is the use case for unnest_auto()? As said, it is just the very first inspection, when we have not looked into the list column that needs attention and have not really thought about how to handle it. In this case, the unnest_auto() decides by itself if to execute unnest_wider() or unnest_longer() according to a *simple criterion*: if all elements of the list column are *unnamed* or they have at least *one name in common across all components*, then it executes unnest_wider(). Otherwise, it executes unnest_longer().

This criterion is not a general solution; it is just a simple heuristic to make a choice between the two possibilities. This is why it should not be used regularly and in scripts. *You have to figure out explicitly and case-by-case the correct way to unnest a list column; this is the standard solution.* However, on many occasions, its criterion makes sense, so it is useful to understand its logic.

We can see what it produces with the two previous examples of data frames, *df1* for column *C* and *df2* for column *Attendees*. Let us start with *df2*.

```
df2 %>% unnest_auto(Attendees)

Using `unnest_wider(Attendees)`; elements have 5 names in common
```

N	name	surname	sex	birthdate	attending
1	Polycarp	Arthmail	M	2002/02/02	TRUE
2	Lada	Demon	F	1998/12/12	TRUE
3	Stribog	Castor	M	2005/10/30	FALSE
4	Cassandra	Shpynx	F	1990/08/18	FALSE

It has executed unnest_wider() and the comment it produces explains the logic: elements are named and have at least one name in common (actually they have all names in common). It makes sense for this simple example. Now for *df1*.

```
df1 %>% unnest_auto(C)

Using `unnest_longer(C, indices_include = TRUE)`; elements are named, but have
no names in common
```

A	B	C	C_id
1	a	[<dbl[5]>]	tens
1	a	[<dbl[4]>]	hundreds
1	a	[<dbl[6]>]	tenths
2	b	[<chr[4]>]	UPPER

(Continued)

A	B	C	C_id
2	b	[<chr[4]>]	lower
2	b	[<chr[4]>]	Title
3	c	[<chr[4]>]	name
3	c	[<chr[4]>]	surname
3	c	[<chr[4]>]	sex
3	c	[<chr[4]>]	birthdate
3	c	[<lgl[4]>]	attending

This time it has executed unnest_longer() and, again, the message explains the reason: elements do not have any names in common, i.e. element 1 has no names in common with elements 2 and 3. As we can see, column *C* is a list column with elements of different types and sizes, some numeric (<dbl[]>), others characters (<chr[]>), and the last one logical (<lgl[]>). This case is more complex than the previous one, and we will see in the following how to proceed.

11.1.2 Function `map` in List Column Transformations

Function map() is often useful with list columns. The easiest case is to extract the values of a name shared by multiple elements, such as we have in *df2*, but not in *df1*. The logic underneath function map() is to repeat the execution of an operation; in this case, we just want to read the value corresponding to a certain name. In column *Attendees*, we may want to read all surnames, for example.

```
map(df2$Attendees, 'surname')

[[1]]
[1] "Arthmail"

[[2]]
[1] "Demon"

[[3]]
[1] "Castor"

[[4]]
[1] "Shpynx"
```

Alternatively, we can use the *element position*, rather than the name. Piping is also possible. We may want to read birthdays.

```
df2$Attendees %>% map(4)

[[1]]
[1] "2002/02/02"
```

```
[[2]]
[1] "1998/12/12"

[[3]]
[1] "2005/10/30"

[[4]]
[1] "1990/08/18"
```

We can consider again the example with *df1,* whose column C we have not yet transformed into ordinary rows and columns. First, we have to figure out if the best approach is to use `unnest_wider()` or `unnest_longer()`. With `unnest_auto()` we saw the execution of `unnest_longer()`, let us try the alternative.

```
df1 %>% unnest_wider(C)
```

A	B	tens	hundreds	tenths	UPPER	lower	Title	name	surname	...
1	a	[<dbl[5]>]	[<dbl[4]>]	[<dbl[6]>]	[[NULL]]	[[NULL]]	[[NULL]]	[[NULL]]	[[NULL]]	...
2	b	[[NULL]]	[[NULL]]	[[NULL]]	[<chr[4]>]	[<chr[4]>]	[<chr[4]>]	[[NULL]]	[[NULL]]	...
3	c	[[NULL]]	[[NULL]]	[[NULL]]	[[NULL]]	[[NULL]]	[[NULL]]	[<chr[4]>]	[<chr[4]>]	...

The `unnest_wider()` makes a new column for each name contained in list column *C*, but in this case, it is not a wise choice because there is no shared name between the lists, so the result has many columns with a lot of missing values. It is definitely very impractical. Function `unnest_longer()` is a better choice.

```
df1 %>% unnest_longer(C)
```

A	B	C	C_id
1	a	[<dbl[5]>]	tens
1	a	[<dbl[4]>]	hundreds
1	a	[<dbl[6]>]	tenths
2	b	[<chr[4]>]	UPPER
2	b	[<chr[4]>]	lower
...	...	...	...

The result is the same we have already seen with `unnest_auto(C)`, it is in long form and, although still not completely transformed, it is a good intermediate result, it is compact, has an order, and we can work on it. Column *C*, as resulting from the first unnesting, needs further consideration because it is still a list column, but elements are not immediately transformable into ordinary rows and columns because they are of different data types and have a true list structure. Forcing a type conversion will result in errors or missing values, so it is not the way to proceed.

Let us consider the logic of the operation. Now that column *C* is still a list column with nested lists even after the first unnesting operation, what should we do, *logically*? If it still has nested lists, we should unnest the next level. Logically, this is how we proceed, unnesting one level at time, so we need one more *unnest_longer* operation. Logically, it is correct, but if we execute it (df1 %>% unnest_longer(C) %>% unnest_longer(C)), we end up with an error. The problem is the different data types of the lists. Initially, the elements of column *C* were all of the generic type list (<list[]>), so the unnest_wider() worked fine. But now they have three different types: numeric, character, and logical. *We have to subset the data frame for list elements of same type, and, for each subset unnest column C.*

To subset the rows, we may use the common filter(), but how could we express a logical condition on the type of the elements? A convenient solution is provided by a variant of the map() function: **map_lgl()**. It works on a column and requires as attribute the name of one of the functions that checks the data type (e.g., is.numeric(), is.character(), is.logical()). The result is a vector of Boolean values, *True* is the corresponding element of the column if the data type is checked, and *False* if not. This represents the Boolean mask for the filter() function, and the combination **filter(map_lgl())** turns out to be particularly useful.

We can apply this solution to the example, starting with numeric lists of column *C* after the first unnesting.

STEP 1. Subset rows corresponding to different list types in column C after the first unnesting. Here for the numeric lists.

```
df1 %>% unnest_longer(C) %>%
  filter(map_lgl(C, is.numeric))
```

A	B	C	C_id
1	a	[<dbl[5]>]	tens
1	a	[<dbl[4]>]	hundreds
1	a	[<dbl[6]>]	tenths

STEP 2. With a subset of list elements of same type, unnest the second level of the structure again with unnest_longer().

```
df1 %>% unnest_longer(C) %>%
  filter(map_lgl(C, is.numeric)) %>%
  unnest_longer(C) -> df1_num

df1_num
```

A	B	C	C_id
1	a	10.0	tens
1	a	20.0	tens
1	a	30.0	tens
1	a	40.0	tens
1	a	50.0	tens
1	a	100.0	hundreds
1	a	200.0	hundreds
1	a	300.0	hundreds
1	a	400.0	hundreds
1	a	1.1	tenths
1	a	3.2	tenths
1	a	2.3	tenths
1	a	6.4	tenths
1	a	3.5	tenths
1	a	7.6	tenths

It is correct, the subset has been fully unnested and for this data frame *df1_num*, we have ordinary rows and columns. In the same way, we could repeat the operations for the other two data types and save them in separate data frames.

```
df1 %>% unnest_longer(C) %>%
   filter(map_lgl(C, is.character)) %>%
   unnest_longer(C) -> df1_char
```

A	B	C	C_id
2	b	A	UPPER
2	b	AB	UPPER
2	b	ABC	UPPER
2	b	ABCD	UPPER
2	b	a	lower
2	b	ab	lower
2	b	abc	lower
2	b	abcd	lower
2	b	A	Title
...	...	...	...

```
df1 %>% unnest_longer(C) %>%
  filter(map_lgl(C, is.logical)) %>%
  unnest_longer(C) -> df1_log
```

A	B	C	C_id
3	c	TRUE	attending
3	c	TRUE	attending
3	c	FALSE	attending
3	c	TRUE	attending

The result is composed of three separate data frames with same structure but different data types for column C.

11.2   R: JSON Data Format and Use Cases

The **JSON** (JavaScript Object Notation) data format is an open and human-readable format that is extremely common, in particular for data exchange between online services, and as data format for open datasets. Its syntax is logically equivalent to a list/dictionary data structure and is derived from the XML-based syntax of the JavaScript language, a very common and widely employed programming language for web applications. So, being highly structured, a JSON data file is particularly well-suited to be parsed by scripts and automatic services, but it is sufficiently user-friendly to be handled by humans as well, with the usual pros and cons of the list/dictionary data organization.

In addition to being able to work with traditional list/dictionary data, a good reason anyway is that familiarizing with the transformations of list columns to ordinary data frame rows and columns is indispensable for working with JSON datasets, a skill that is increasingly important. Not always we have the luxury of choosing our preferred data format when we download a dataset we need. Sometimes the data owner just makes a single format available, and increasingly often it could be JSON.

R functions to read and handle JSON datasets are offered by more than one package. The main one, now included in the R base distribution, is **jsonlite**. The basic function for reading is `read_json()`, similar to other R read functions. There also exists a function `fromJSON()` that converts a JSON string into an R object. Function `toJSON()` does the opposite; an R object is converted into JSON data.

In the following, we consider several real examples of JSON datasets. We will read the data and proceed to transform list columns until an ordinary data frame is obtained. In some cases, the procedure will be easy, almost immediate. In others, we will have to work more, unnesting several levels of data.

NOAA – National Centers for Environmental Information   For this case study, we use a dataset from *NOAA National Centers for Environmental Information* titled *Climate at a Glance: Global Time Series*. The data show the average temperature anomaly of June on a global scale. Data span from 1850 to 2023.

We start by reading the JSON dataset and first inspecting the structure with `str()`.

```
library(jsonlite)

nooa= read_json("datasets/NOOA/data.json")

str(nooa)

List of 2
 $ description:List of 4
  ..$ title       : chr "Global Land and Ocean June Temperature Anomalies"
  ..$ units       : chr "Degrees Celsius"
  ..$ base_period : chr "1901-2000"
  ..$ missing     : chr "-999"
 $ data       :List of 174
  ..$ 1850: chr "-0.12"
  ..$ 1851: chr "-0.16"
  ..$ 1852: chr "-0.08"
  ..$ 1853: chr "-0.08"
  ..$ 1854: chr "-0.08"
  ..$ 1855: chr "-0.22"
  ..$ 1856: chr "-0.16"
  ..$ 1857: chr "-0.31"
  ..$ 1858: chr "-0.20"
  ..$ 1859: chr "-0.12"
  ..$ 1860: chr "-0.20"
  ..$ 1861: chr "-0.29"
  ..$ 1862: chr "-0.33"
  ..$ 1863: chr "-0.25"
  ..$ 1864: chr "-0.10"
  ...
```

It contains two lists: *description* and *data*, the first with some metadata and the second with the actual data. We start the transformation first by converting it into a data frame.

```
nooa <- tibble(nooa)
```

---
nooa

<list[4]>
<list[174]>

Now it is a data frame with a single list column *nooa* and two elements corresponding to the two lists. From the output of the `str()` function, we know that all elements are of character type, even the temperature variations. Do we have to unnest longer or wider? Recalling the previous examples, unnesting wider is useful when the list elements have names in common that transform into new columns. But if there is no element in common, the wider unnesting is not useful. This is the case of these columns, so we choose to unnest longer.

```
nooa %>% unnest_longer(nooa) %>% head(10)
```

nooa	nooa_id
Global Land and Ocean June Temperature Anomalies	title
Degrees Celsius	units
1901–2000	base_period
−999	missing
−0.12	1850
−0.16	1851
−0.08	1852
−0.08	1853
−0.08	1854
−0.22	1855
...	...

We have obtained two ordinary columns in long format, with column *nooa_id* as keys for values of column *nooa*. For what concerns the conversion from JSON to an ordinary data frame, the job is done; now it is a matter of normal data wrangling. For example, we may want to transform this very compact data frame into wide form, for better readability.

```
nooa %>% unnest_longer(nooa) %>%
   pivot_wider(names_from= nooa_id, values_from= nooa) %>% select(1:10)
```

title	units	base_period	missing	1850	1851	1852	1853	1854	1855	...
Global Land and Ocean June Temperature Anomalies	Degrees Celsius	1901–2000	−999	−0.12	−0.16	−0.08	−0.08	−0.08	−0.22	...

It is in wide form, but not really very useful as a single row with 178 columns. We can easily improve it, for example, by transforming again into long form the columns referring to the years, which are too many for a wide representation.

```
nooa %>% unnest_longer(nooa) %>%
   pivot_wider(names_from= nooa_id, values_from= nooa) %>%
   pivot_longer(names_to= "Year", values_to= "Anomaly",
                cols= "1850":last_col()) %>%
   select(Year,Anomaly)
```

Year	Anomaly
1850	−0.12
1851	−0.16
1852	−0.08

Year	Anomaly
1853	−0.08
1854	−0.08
1855	−0.22
1856	−0.16
1857	−0.31
1858	−0.20
1859	−0.12
...	...

Now it is fine; we have obtained a data frame ready for statistics, visualization, etc.

Historical Events: England The second example is provided by using the Historical Events JSON dataset.

```
eng= read_json("datasets/Historical_Events/England_historical_events.json")
```

This is quite a large list, which is not easily inspected in a visual way, neither with str() nor with View(). We can use command line names() and find that the structure is pretty straightforward. Basically, it is a single list *result* with an element *count*, with the number of events as the value, followed by all *event* elements. Let us transform it into data frame and work on it.

```
eng<- tibble(eng)
```

eng

<list[1,239]>

As anticipated, it is a single list with 1239 elements. Unnesting wider, we will obtain a corresponding data frame with a single row and a huge number of columns. It is not a good choice. We go with unnesting longer.

```
eng %>% unnest_longer(eng)
```

eng	eng_id
<chr[1]>	count
<list[6]>	event
<list[6]>	event

(Continued)

eng	eng_id
<list[6]>	event
<list[6]>	event
<list[6]>	event
...	...

It is a two-column data frame, with column *eng_id* as keys and column *eng* as values. Differently from the previous case, column *eng* is still a list column, so we have to further unnest it. This time the list elements of column *eng* have several names in common that are well-suited to be exploded as new columns; therefore, `unnest_wider()` is the best choice.

```
eng %>%
  unnest_longer(eng) %>%
  unnest_wider(eng)

Error in `unnest_wider()`:
In column: `eng`.
In row: 1.
Caused by error:
! Can't unnest elements with missing names.
```

The result is an error, though. Why? It is easy solved; just look at column *eng* row 1, as for the error message. That element is not a real list; it is a value for the corresponding key *count*; there is nothing to unnest in that. We should omit that row. We can do that in several way. Let us use the solution with `map_lgl()` we have seen before and unnest again.

```
eng %>%
  unnest_longer(eng) %>%
  filter(!map_lgl(eng, is_character)) %>%
  unnest_wider(eng)
```

date	description	lang	category1	category2	granularity	eng_id
51	In Britain, Governor Publius Ostorius Scapula defeats Caratacus ...	en	By place	Roman Empire	year	event
79/08/24	Agricola found Mamucium, a frontier fort and settlement in the North West of England. ...	en	By place	Roman Empire	year	event
122	Vindolanda, a Roman auxiliary fort ("castrum") in northern England...	en	By place	Roman Empire	year	event
180/03/17	Northern Brits from beyond Hadrian's Wall invade the North...	en	By place	Roman Empire	year	event
220	Great frost in England is said to have lasted for five months...	en	By place	Roman Empire	year	event
...	...	...	...	...	...	...

Dates sometimes have spurious values, but they come from the dataset. Overall, the transformation is correct.

The Nobel Prize For this third case study, the JSON dataset is the collection of Nobel laureates from the *The Nobel Prize Foundation*. We proceed as usual.

```
nobelprize= read_json("datasets/Nobel/prize.json")
```

This time, the data structure could also be inspected with View(), and nested lists are clearly recognizable. There is a top-level list *nobelprize* that contains list *prizes* with 664 elements. Each element is again a list of three elements: *year*, *categories,* and *laureates*; the last one is again a list with information of each Nobel laureate: *id, firstname, surname, motivation,* and *share.* Four nested levels, in total.

```
nobel<- tibble(nobelprize)
```

---
nobelprize

<list[664]>

After the transformation into data frame, we obtain a single list column with a single element. We use unnest_longer() on list column *nobelprize* to explode the single list into its elements (see Figure 11.4).

```
nobel %>% unnest_longer(nobelprize)
```

nobelprize	list [1]	List of length 1
prizes	list [664]	List of length 664
[[1]]	list [3]	List of length 3
year	character [1]	'2022'
category	character [1]	'chemistry'
laureates	list [3]	List of length 3
[[1]]	list [5]	List of length 5
id	character [1]	'1015'
firstname	character [1]	'Carolyn'
surname	character [1]	'Bertozzi'
motivation	character [1]	"for the development of click chemistry and bioorthogonal chemistry"
share	character [1]	'3'
[[2]]	list [5]	List of length 5
id	character [1]	'1016'
firstname	character [1]	'Morten'
surname	character [1]	'Meldal'
motivation	character [1]	"for the development of click chemistry and bioorthogonal chemistry"
share	character [1]	'3'

Figure 11.4 The Nobel Prize JSON data format.

nobelprize
<list[3]>
<list[3]>
<list[3]>
<list[3]>
<list[3]>
...

The result is 664 lists, which is the number of Nobel Prizes of the dataset. These lists have all the same structure as common names. The unnest wider is the right one this time.

```
nobel %>%
  unnest_longer(nobelprize) %>%
  unnest_wider(nobelprize)
```

year	category	laureates	overallMotivation
2022	chemistry	<list[3]>	NA
2022	economics	<list[3]>	NA
2022	literature	<list[1]>	NA
2022	peace	<list[3]>	NA
2022	physics	<list[3]>	NA
2022	medicine	<list[1]>	NA
2021	chemistry	<list[2]>	NA
2021	economics	<list[3]>	NA
2021	literature	<list[1]>	NA
2021	peace	<list[2]>	NA
...	...	...	...

It is good result. We have four columns and 664 rows. Each row corresponds to a Nobel Prize, for a certain category and year, with *year* and *category* as ordinary columns. The third column *laureates* is still a list column to unnest. We repeat the steps with another pair of *unnest_longer-unnest_wider* applied to column *laureates*.

```
nobel %>%
  unnest_longer(nobelprize) %>%
  unnest_wider(nobelprize) %>%
  unnest_longer(laureates) %>%
  unnest_wider(laureates)
```

year	category	id	firstname	surname	motivation	share	overallMotivation
2022	chemistry	1015	Carolyn	Bertozzi	"for the development of click chemistry and bioorthogonal chemistry"	3	NA
2022	chemistry	1016	Morten	Meldal	"for the development of click chemistry and bioorthogonal chemistry"	3	NA
2022	chemistry	743	Barry	Sharpless	"for the development of click chemistry and bioorthogonal chemistry"	3	NA
2022	economics	1021	Ben	Bernanke	"for research on banks and financial crises"	3	NA
2022	economics	1022	Douglas	Diamond	"for research on banks and financial crises"	3	NA
2022	economics	1023	Philip	Dybvig	"for research on banks and financial crises"	3	NA
2022	literature	1017	Annie	Ernaux	"for the courage and clinical acuity with which she uncovers the roots, estrangements, and collective restraints of personal memory"	1	NA
...	...	...	...	...	...	...	...

The data frame has been completely transformed and is ready for analysis.

US Politicians   This JSON dataset is made available by *Everypolitician* and contains public information regarding MEPs of the 116th Congress of the United States of America.

```
pol= read_json("datasets/Everypoliticians/ep-popolo-v1.0.json")
names(pol)
[1] "posts"        "persons"       "organizations" "meta"

[5] "memberships"  "events"        "areas"
```

At top level, there are seven lists, but it is a large JSON, and visually inspecting it could not be easy; it would be better to work on the data frame.

```
pol <- tibble(pol)
```

pol

<list[0]>
<list[1,739]>

(*Continued*)

pol
<list[9]>
<list[1]>
<list[8,941]>
<list[136]>
<list[504]>

Here are the seven lists as elements of the list column *pol*. The second and the fifth are the largest, corresponding to *persons* and *memberships*. Even without a direct inspection, it is unlikely that such lists have common names; therefore, unnesting wider will certainly result in a very sparse data frame with many columns and missing values. Again, `unnest_longer()` is the best choice.

```
pol %>% unnest_longer(pol)
```

pol	pol_id
<list[13]>	
<list[13]>	
<list[13]>	
<list[13]>	
<list[13]>	
<list[13]>	
<list[12]>	
<list[13]>	
<list[12]>	
...	...

This is similar to the previous case; we have exploded the first level and obtained again a list column, but this time there will be common names among the elements, so we can unnest wider.

```
pol %>%
  unnest_longer(pol) %>%
  unnest_wider(pol)

Error in 'unnest_wider()':
In column: 'pol'.
In row: 1749.
Caused by error:
! Can't unnest elements with missing names.
Supply 'names_sep' to generate automatic names.
```

There is an error. It is worth reading the message carefully. It says that row 1749 has been found to have a value but not a name, and this confuses the function when creating the new columns, because by default it uses element names as column names. It suggests the solution: use attribute **names_sep** and specify a custom separator for column names. Just pick one, for example, the colon symbol.

```
pol %>%
  unnest_longer(pol) %>%
  unnest_wider(pol, names_sep= ":") -> pol1
```

pol:birth_date	pol:death_date	pol:family_name	pol:gender	pol:given_name	...
1944-10-15	2018-11-20	Collins	male	Michael	...
1969-01-31	NA	Huizenga	male	Bill	...
1959-09-28	NA	Clawson	male	Curtis	...
1930-08-14	2001-10-26	Solomon	male	Gerald	...
1960-05-28	NA	Rigell	male	Edward	...
1951-05-20	NA	Crapo	male	Michael	...
1926-05-12	NA	Hutto	male	Earl	...
1937-11-07	2015-11-19	Ertel	male	Allen	...
1916-09-01	2007-11-24	Minish	male	Joseph	...
1957-08-04	NA	Andrews	male	Robert	...
...	...	...	...	...	...

Good, it looks like we are headed in the correct direction. Several columns have already been transformed into ordinary columns; others are still listed columns to be unnested. But first, let us look at the column names to better understand the previous error.

```
names(pol1)
 [1] "pol:birth_date"        "pol:death_date"
 [3] "pol:family_name"       "pol:gender"
 [5] "pol:given_name"        "pol:id"
 [7] "pol:identifiers"       "pol:image"
 [9] "pol:images"            "pol:links"
[11] "pol:name"              "pol:other_names"
[13] "pol:sort_name"         "pol:contact_details"
[15] "pol:honorific_prefix"  "pol:classification"
[17] "pol:srgb"              "pol:seats"
[19] "pol:type"              "pol:1"
[21] "pol:2"                 "pol:3"
[23] "pol:area_id"           "pol:legislative_period_id"
[25] "pol:on_behalf_of_id"   "pol:organization_id"
[27] "pol:person_id"         "pol:role"
[29] "pol:start_date"        "pol:end_date"
[31] "pol_id"
```

Column names have been created by the union of the name and the value of the list element, separated by the colon, as we specified. One, *pol_id*, does not have both parts; that was the culprit for the error.

Since we are now interested in remaining list columns, there is a convenient solution that helps us find them all at once. It starts with function **is.list()**, returning TRUE if its argument is a list. Combined with selection helper **where()** that returns only variables/columns for which its argument returns TRUE, and the select(), we have a compact and very efficient solution for retrieving columns based on their type.

```
poll %>% select(where(is.list))
```

pol:identifiers	pol:images	pol:links	pol:other_names	pol:contact_details
<list[16]>	<list[2]>	<list[6]>	<list[2]>	<NULL>
<list[21]>	<list[2]>	<list[15]>	<list[4]>	<list[3]>
<list[15]>	<list[2]>	<list[9]>	<list[2]>	<list[1]>
<list[17]>	<list[2]>	<list[4]>	<list[2]>	<NULL>
<list[20]>	<list[2]>	<list[13]>	<list[4]>	<list[1]>
...	...	...	...	...

Of 31 columns, just five are still list columns. In order to fully transform the data frame, we should transform each one of these columns. For example, we consider ***pol:links***, with links to web sites each politician has stated. List elements have different sizes because politicians may declare a different number of web sites.

From the data frame *poll* we select some of the ordinary columns and the *pol:links*, then we proceed to unnesting this last one. The elements of each list of the *pol:links* should be exploded in more rows corresponding to each politician.

```
poll %>% select(1:5, 'pol:links') %>%
  unnest_longer('pol:links')
```

pol:birth_date	pol:death_date	pol:family_name	pol:gender	pol:given_name	pol:links
1944-10-15	2018-11-20	Collins	male	Michael	<list[2]>
1944-10-15	2018-11-20	Collins	male	Michael	<list[2]>
1944-10-15	2018-11-20	Collins	male	Michael	<list[2]>
1944-10-15	2018-11-20	Collins	male	Michael	<list[2]>
1944-10-15	2018-11-20	Collins	male	Michael	<list[2]>
1944-10-15	2018-11-20	Collins	male	Michael	<list[2]>
1969-01-31	NA	Huizenga	male	Bill	<list[2]>
1969-01-31	NA	Huizenga	male	Bill	<list[2]>
1969-01-31	NA	Huizenga	male	Bill	<list[2]>
1969-01-31	NA	Huizenga	male	Bill	<list[2]>
...	...	...	...	...	...

We have made another step forward. Now each politician has a number of rows associated equal to the number of its links; for example, the first one, (the late) Michael Collins, has six rows, the second, Bill Huizenga, has 15, and so on.

At this point, there is just one step left; the column *pol:links* is still a list column, but now all elements have the same size, and evidently, the links are represented with two information. We can unnest wider this time, expecting just two new columns in place of the current one.

```
pol1 %>% select(1:5, 'pol:links')   %>%
   unnest_longer('pol:links') %>%
   unnest_wider('pol:links')
```

pol: birth_date	pol: death_date	pol: family_name	pol: gender	pol: given_name	note	url
1944-10-15	2018-11-20	Collins	male	Michael	Wikimedia Commons	https://commons.wikimedia.org/ wiki/Category:Mac_Collins
1944-10-15	2018-11-20	Collins	male	Michael	Wikipedia (de)	https://de.wikipedia.org/wiki/Mac_ Collins
1944-10-15	2018-11-20	Collins	male	Michael	Wikipedia (en)	https://en.wikipedia.org/wiki/Mac_ Collins
1944-10-15	2018-11-20	Collins	male	Michael	Wikipedia (simple)	https://simple.wikipedia.org/wiki/ Mac_Collins
1944-10-15	2018-11-20	Collins	male	Michael	Wikipedia (sv)	https://sv.wikipedia.org/wiki/Mac_ Collins
1944-10-15	2018-11-20	Collins	male	Michael	website	http://www.house.gov/maccollin s
1969-01-31	NA	Huizenga	male	Bill	Wikimedia Commons	https://commons.wikimedia.org/ wiki/Category:Bill_Huizenga
1969-01-31	NA	Huizenga	male	Bill	Wikipedia (de)	https://de.wikipedia.org/wiki/Bill_ Huizenga
1969-01-31	NA	Huizenga	male	Bill	Wikipedia (en)	https://en.wikipedia.org/wiki/Bill_ Huizenga
1969-01-31	NA	Huizenga	male	Bill	Wikipedia (fa)	https://fa.wikipedia.org/wiki/%D8 %A8%DB%8C%D9%84_%D9%87%D9 %88%DB%8C%D8%B2%D9%86%DA %AF%D8%A7
...	...	...	...	...	...	...

The result is exactly as expected. Instead of the *pol:links* list column, we now have ordinary columns *note* and *url* for each politician link. Similarly to what we have done with this list column, we should proceed with the other list columns that remain if we want to completely transform the data frame.

11.2.1 Memory Problem when Reading Very Large Datasets

JSON datasets could be very large, as could the CSV ones. But working with a very large dataset might be challenging because of the limited computational power and RAM memory of an ordinary personal computer or laptop. A problem arises because R, by default, tries to load the whole dataset into RAM memory, which might be bad for the functioning of the computer if the dataset is huge.

It is a popular rule of thumb to consider that the memory space required by a dataset to be read, without incurring in malfunctioning, should not exceed half the available RAM size. The problem is that the memory space required for reading is larger than the simple data size, possibly considerably larger. For example, a normal laptop with 16GB of RAM could run into problems by reading a dataset of just few GB, a size easily exceeded by many datasets available as Open Data.

As a real case, *Yelp*, the renowned web site for reviews of restaurants and many others, releases an open dataset of reviews for several cities (*Yelp Open Dataset*, https://www.yelp.com/dataset). The Yelp dataset is only licensed for personal, didactic, or academic usage, so it cannot be used in a handbook like this one but being an excellent resource for experimenting with a very large JSON dataset, we suggest how to do for avoiding memory problem and leave it as an exercise to be done autonomously.

Among the available datasets Yelp provides, the larger one, containing the actual customers' reviews, is larger than 5GB. Reading it with the normal `read_json()` function could easily turn into problems like excessively slowing the computer and ultimately getting it stuck. It is not guaranteed, but it is likely.

In any case, with very large dataset there exist a different way of reading them that bypass the standard way employed by R of storing the whole dataset in RAM. The solution is reading the dataset by smaller chunks of data. For this reason, library *jsonlite* provides function **stream_in()** that reads line by line from the input. Combining it with functions **textConnection()** and **readLines()**, the problem of reading a very large dataset could be managed. The key attribute is **n**, the number of lines to read from source in a single connection, 100 000 typically is a good trade-off to avoid memory problems without excessively increase the reading time. For example, a script could be the following:

```
file_name<- "datasets/YELP_reviews/
            yelp_dataset_full/yelp_academic_dataset_review.json"

reviews<- jsonlite::stream_in(textConnection(
                    readLines(file_name, n=100000)), verbose=F)
```

It will not be fast, anyway; to read a very large dataset is a huge effort for a normal laptop, doing it by chunks of 100 000 rows may easily take several minutes or more. Anyway, better than getting stuck with a saturated RAM.

11.3 Python: Dictionary Data Format

As previously said, the Python **dict** format, abbreviation for *dictionary*, corresponds to the *list* format of R, with just little differences. The logic, organization, general methods, and difficulties are the same as discussed in the chapter introduction. The syntax and libraries are different, with some details to consider. Let us start with the first basic example of a dict.

We've already encountered before how to define a dict in its basic form, because included in the syntax of several functions we used. It makes use of **curly brackets** to define the pairs *key:value*.

```
# Define an empty dict
a1= {}

# Define keys with corresponding values
a1['a']='A'
a1['b']='B'
a1['c']='C'
a1['d']='D'
a1

{'a': 'A', 'b': 'B', 'c': 'C', 'd': 'D'}
```

Here we have four elements with keys a, b, c, d, and values A, B, C, D. Very easy, in this form it is basically just an array with elements associated to names, instead of being indexed only by position. Values can be retrieved by name, too.

```
a1['c']
a1['b']

'C'
'B'
```

As we know, the dict format is particularly useful in the definition of nested or hierarchical structures, meaning that element values could be dict, producing several levels in the data organizations. The following dict is the complete example we used in the introduction of the chapter to show the particular organization of the list/dict data format. We have three levels of nesting.

```
a2 = {
  1: { 'name': 'Polycarp',
       'surname': 'Arthmail',
       'city': 'Des Moines',
       'state': 'IA',
       'department': 'Divinity School',
       'address': { 'street': '45 Francis Avenue',
                    'zipcode': '02138',
                    'city': 'Cambridge',
                    'state': 'MA'}
                },
  2: { 'name': 'Lada',
       'surname': 'Damon',
       'city': 'Hanover',
       'state': 'NH',
       'department': 'Chemistry',
       'address': { 'street': '12 OXFORD STREET',
                    'zipcode': '02138',
                    'city': 'Cambridge',
                    'state': 'MA'}},
  3: { 'name': 'Stribog',
       'surname': 'Castor',
       'city': 'Madison',
```

```
         'state': 'WI',
         'department': 'East Asian Studies',
         'address': { 'street': '9 Kirkland Place',
                      'zipcode': '02138',
                      'city': 'Cambridge',
                      'state': 'MA'}
                },
   4: { 'name': 'Cassandra',
        'surname': 'Shpynx',
        'city': 'Sausalito',
        'state': 'CA',
        'department': 'Organismic & Evolutionary Biology',
        'address': { 'street': '26 Oxford Street ',
                     'zipcode': '02138',
                     'city': 'Cambridge',
                     'state': 'MA'}}
                  }
```

In this case, to select elements, we have various combinations.

```
# 1st level
a2[4]

{'name': 'Cassandra',
 'surname': 'Shpynx',
 'city': 'Sausalito',
 'state': 'CA',
 'department': 'Organismic & Evolutionary Biology',
 'address': {'street': '26 Oxford Street ',
             'zipcode': '02138',
             'city': 'Cambridge',
             'state': 'MA'}}

# 2nd level
a2[3]['department']

'East Asian Studies'

# 3rd level
a2[2]['address']['street']

'12 OXFORD STREET'
```

11.3.1 Methods

Several useful methods are available for working with dicts. The following Table 11.1 shows them. Let us see some examples with these methods.

```
a2.keys()
dict_keys([1, 2, 3, 4])
```

Table 11.1 Methods for Python dict data format.

Method	Description
`clear()`	Delete all elements
`copy()`	Make a copy of the dict
`get()`	Returns the value corresponding to a key
`items()`	Returns a list of pairs *key:values*
`keys()`	Returns the keys associated to a certain level
`values()`	Returns a list of values corresponding to a certain level
`pop()`	Remove the element associated to a certain key
`popitem()`	Remove the last inserted pair *key:value*
`update()`	Update the dict with new pairs *key:value*

The result shows all keys of the top-level. To list inner levels, we should specify which one. For example, all keys of element *address* included into element *3*.

```
a2[3]['address'].keys()

dict_keys(['street', 'zipcode', 'city', 'state'])

print(a2[1]['name'], a2[1]['surname'])
print(a2[2]['name'], a2[2]['surname'])
print(a2[3]['name'], a2[3]['surname'])
print(a2[4]['name'], a2[4]['surname'])

Polycarp Arthmail
Lada Damon
Stribog Castor
Cassandra Shpynx
```

Method `get()` has the same effect of square brackets.

```
# Same as a2[2]
a2.get(2)

# Same as a2[2]['name']
a2.get(2).get('name')

'Lada'
```

With `values()` we can do the same but obtaining values instead of keys.

```
a2[2].values()
```

```
dict_values(['Lada', 'Damon', 'Hanover', 'NH', 'Chemistry',
          {'street': '12 OXFORD STREET', 'zipcode': '02138',
           'city': 'Cambridge', 'state': 'MA'}])
```

With **items()** we obtain the pairs *key:values*.

```
a2[2].items()

dict_items([('name', 'Lada'), ('surname', 'Damon'), ('city', 'Hanover'),
          ('state', 'NH'), ('department', 'Chemistry'),
          ('address', {'street': '12 OXFORD STREET', 'zipcode': '02138',
                       'city': 'Cambridge', 'state': 'MA'})])
```

A *for cycle* could be useful to show part of the dict structure.

```
for key in a2:
  print(a2[key]['name'], a2[key]['surname'])

Polycarp Arthmail
Lada Damon
Stribog Castor
Cassandra Shpynx
```

It could also handle the two components of the pair *key:value*, providing a nice visualization.

```
for k, v in a2.items(): print(k, '->', v)

1 -> {'name': 'Polycarp', 'surname': 'Arthmail', 'city': 'Des Moines', 'state':
'IA', 'department': 'Divinity School', 'address': {'street': '45 Francis
Avenue', 'zipcode': '02138', 'city': 'Cambridge', 'state': 'MA'}}


2 -> {'name': 'Lada', 'surname': 'Damon', 'city': 'Hanover', 'state': 'NH',
'department': 'Chemistry', 'address': {'street': '12 OXFORD STREET',
'zipcode': '02138', 'city': 'Cambridge', 'state': 'MA'}}


3 -> {'name': 'Stribog', 'surname': 'Castor', 'city': 'Madison', 'state': 'WI',
'department': 'East Asian Studies', 'address': {'street': '9 Kirkland Place',
'zipcode': '02138', 'city': 'Cambridge', 'state': 'MA'}}


4 -> {'name': 'Cassandra', 'surname': 'Shpynx', 'city': 'Sausalito', 'state':
'CA', 'department': 'Organismic & Evolutionary Biology', 'address': {'street':
'26 Oxford Street ', 'zipcode': '02138', 'city': 'Cambridge', 'state': 'MA'}}
```

Again, to explore the inner organization, the particular list element should be specified.

```
for k, v in a2[2]['address'].items(): print(k, '->', v)

street -> 12 OXFORD STREET
zipcode -> 02138
city -> Cambridge
state -> MA
```

These are basic operations on a Python dict, with the useful addiction of the *for cycle* to explore parts of the hierarchy. Now we move on to the issue that interests us most: the transformations from a *dictionary* to a pandas data frame.

11.3.2 From Dictionary to Data Frame With a Single Level of Nesting

Similar to what discussed for R, the transformation of a dict into data frame ranges from very easy to somewhat complicated, depending on the complexity of the hierarchical structure of data. We start from the easiest case by simplifying the organization of the previous dict in order to have just one level of nesting.

```
a3 = { 1: { 'name': 'Polycarp',
        'surname': 'Arthmail',
        'city': 'Des Moines',
        'state': 'IA',
        'department': 'Divinity School'
        },
    2: { 'name': 'Lada',
        'surname': 'Damon',
        'city': 'Hanover',
        'state': 'NH',
        'department': 'Chemistry'
        },
    3: { 'name': 'Stribog',
        'surname': 'Castor',
        'city': 'Madison',
        'state': 'WI',
        'department': 'East Asian Studies'
        },
    4: { 'name': 'Cassandra',
        'surname': 'Shpynx',
        'city': 'Sausalito',
        'state': 'CA',
        'department': 'Organismic & Evolutionary Biology'
        }
    }
```

11.3.2.1 Functions `pd.Dataframe()` and `pd.Dataframe.from_dict()`

Pandas function `pd.Dataframe()` is the most straightforward. It transforms lists of homogeneous values and same size into data frame columns. If the original dict has this simple organization, then the transformation into data frame is effortless. This is the case of the data frame *a3*.

```
pd.DataFrame(a3)
```

	1	2	3	4
name	Polycarp	Lada	Stribog	Cassandra
surname	Arthmail	Damon	Castor	Shpynx
city	Des Moines	Hanover	Madison	Sausalito
state	IA	NH	WI	CA
department	Divinity School	Chemistry	East Asian Studies	Organismic & Evolutionary Biology

The data frame is completely transformed, just organized in an ill-suited way, with the row index values that should serve better as column names (column index). Generating the *transpose*, fixes the little problem and we obtain a perfectly usable data frame.

```
pd.DataFrame(a3).T
```

	name	surname	city	state	department
1	Polycarp	Arthmail	Des Moines	IA	Divinity School
2	Lada	Damon	Hanover	NH	Chemistry
3	Stribog	Castor	Madison	WI	East Asian Studies
4	Cassandra	Shpynx	Sausalito	CA	Organismic & Evolutionary Biology

A variant of `pd.Dataframe()` that includes the transposition of rows and columns, plus some additional options, is **`pd.Dataframe.from_dict()`**. Its main attributes are:

- `orient`: values could be *columns, index* or *tight*, where **columns** means that we want the result as data frame *columns*, **index** if we want the result to be *rows*, **tight** for particular dicts with keys having the form *['index', 'columns', 'data', 'index_names', 'column_names']*.
- `dtype`: a specific data type we want columns to be converted into.
- `columns`: the columns names that should be used if the option `orient='index'` has been chosen.

We can try again with data frame *a3*, first with *columns* then with *index*.

```
pd.DataFrame.from_dict(a3, orient='columns')
```

and

```
pd.DataFrame.from_dict(a3, orient='index')
```

Outcomes are the same of the previous case.

11.3.3 From Dictionary to Data Frame with Several Levels of Nesting

This is the general case and the most common. Things gets more complicated, but the logic resembles the one we have learnt with unnesting wider and longer for R, the syntax changes, some aspects are different, but ultimately, we should retrieve a familiar approach,

11.3.3.1 Function `pd.json_normalize()` and Join Operation

We consider data frame *a2*, the one with an additional level of hierarchy, for which the simple operation previously seen is not sufficient. However, let us start as we did before, either using function `pd.Dataframe()` and creating the transpose, or using `pd.Dataframe.from_dict()` with attribute *orient='index'*. They are equivalent.

```
# Equivalent to pd.DataFrame.from_dict(a2, orient='index')
pd.DataFrame(a2).T
```

	name	surname	city	state	department	address
1	Polycarp	Arthmail	Des Moines	IA	Divinity School	{'street': '45 Francis Avenue', 'zipcode': '02…
2	Lada	Damon	Hanover	NH	Chemistry	{'street': '12 OXFORD STREET', 'zipcode': '021…
3	Stribog	Castor	Madison	WI	East Asian Studies	{'street': '9 Kirkland Place', 'zipcode': '021…
4	Cassandra	Shpynx	Sausalito	CA	Organismic & Evolutionary Biology	{'street': '26 Oxford Street ', 'zipcode': '02…

The result is not that bad, some columns are already transformed into ordinary pandas columns, but one, *address*, has dicts as elements. It is a *dict column* and we need to work on it to obtain a data frame with all ordinary columns. Here the two environments, R and Python, differ in the technical steps, but the logic is the same. Elements of column *address* are clearly well-suited to be transformed in columns, they have *equal names* (e.g. *street*, *zipcode*, etc.) that could easily become columns *street*, *zipcode* and so on. In R, we would have unnested wider, here in Python we have to **normalize** the dict column. *Dict elements are **normalized** when names are transformed into data frame columns, and the operation is well-suited when they have names in common.* The little complication is that the result cannot be obtained directly inside the original data frame, but it is obtained separately, the specific column is transformed into columns in a separate data frame. Therefore, the original data frame and the newly created columns should be joined together.

The procedure in logical steps:

1. Transform the dict into data frame with `pd.Dataframe()` or `pd.DataFrame.from_dict()`, some columns will be ordinary columns, others will be dict columns.
2. Each dict column should be normalized, in order for its pairs *key:value* to be transformed into ordinary columns, with pandas function **pd.json_normalize()**.
3. The result is a distinct data frame composed of columns that should be reunited to the original data frame with a *join operation*, for example by means of the common **pd.merge()** or the less common **pd.join()**.

Now the steps as instructions.
STEP 1. Convert the dict into a pandas data frame.

```
# Equivalent to pd.DataFrame(a2).T
df= pd.DataFrame.from_dict(a2, orient='index')
```

The result is the data frame we have just obtained at the beginning of this subsection.

```
df.columns
Index(['name', 'surname', 'city', 'state', 'department', 'address'],
      dtype='object')
```

STEP 2. Column *address* should be normalized.

```
norm= pd.json_normalize(df.address)
```

	street	zipcode	city	state
0	45 Francis Avenue	02138	Cambridge	MA
1	12 OXFORD STREET	02138	Cambridge	MA
2	9 Kirkland Place	02138	Cambridge	MA
3	26 Oxford Street	02138	Cambridge	MA

Data frame *norm* has the ordinary columns corresponding to the elements of the dict column *address*.

STEP 3. Join between data frame *df* and data frame *norm*. They do not have keys in common so attributes `left_on` and `right_on` cannot be used, but the index could be used. However, the index does not correspond in the two data frames, with *norm* having the implicit row index starting from 0, while *df* has the names of the top-level as row index (i.e. 1,2,3,4). We can solve it easily by resetting the *df*'s index. For convenience, we also drop the original *address* column.

```
df_norm= df.reset_index().\
        merge(norm, left_index=True, right_index=True).\
        drop(columns='address')
```

index	name	surname	city_x	state_x	department	street	zipcode	city_y	state_y
0 1	Polycarp	Arthmail	Des Moines	IA	Divinity School	45 Francis Avenue	02138	Cambridge	MA
1 2	Lada	Damon	Hanover	NH	Chemistry	12 OXFORD STREET	02138	Cambridge	MA
2 3	Stribog	Castor	Madison	WI	East Asian Studies	9 Kirkland Place	02138	Cambridge	MA
3 4	Cassandra	Shpynx	Sausalito	CA	Organismic and Evolutionary Biology	26 Oxford Street	02138	Cambridge	MA

An alternative version makes use of pandas function **join()** in place of merge(), which is a more specialized join function that *directly uses indexes of the two data frames for joining.* A second variation is using function **pop()** in Step 2 to remove the *dict* column *address*, instead of using drop(). The two solutions are equivalent.

However, a complication arises, function join() does not handle the case of columns with same name by adding default suffixes. In this case, columns *city* and *state* have same names but refer to different information in the two data frames. The result is an error. The suffixes must be explicitly specified with attributes **lsuffix** and **rsuffix**.

```
# STEP 2
norm2= pd.json_normalize(df.pop('address'))

# STEP 3
df_norm2 = df.reset_index().join(norm2, lsuffix='_x', rsuffix='_y')
```

index	name	surname	city_x	state_x	department	street	zipcode	city_y	state_y
0 1	Polycarp	Arthmail	Des Moines	IA	Divinity School	45 Francis Avenue	02138	Cambridge	MA
1 2	Lada	Damon	Hanover	NH	Chemistry	12 OXFORD STREET	02138	Cambridge	MA
2 3	Stribog	Castor	Madison	WI	East Asian Studies	9 Kirkland Place	02138	Cambridge	MA
3 4	Cassandra	Shpynx	Sausalito	CA	Organismic and Evolutionary Biology	26 Oxford Street	02138	Cambridge	MA

Function pd.explode() With the previous example, we have seen the case of a data frame with a dict column whose elements have names in common. In that case the transformation by *normalization (creating new columns)* is the most appropriate.

Now we consider the alternative case of *dict columns whose elements do not have names in common* or *have names associated to multiple values (vectors).* In this case, normalizing the dict column would produce many new ordinary columns with sparse values, not the result we may want. We need a different operation.

To discuss this case, we need to complicate a little the previous dict *a2* by adding a new element *language* whose *values are vectors, not single values.* To obtain ordinary data frame columns with elements having vectors as values, we should not normalize, we do not need more columns, those are vectors containing values, not names. *We need more rows, one separate row for each single value,* it is a different operation. In R, it was *unnest longer*; in Python it takes the name of **exploding** *the compact form into multiple rows*, and the function to use is `pd.explode()`.

```
a4 = {
  1: { 'name': 'Polycarp',
       'surname': 'Arthmail',
       'city': 'Des Moines',
       'state': 'IA',
       'language': ['Aramaic','Hebrew','Greek'],
       'department': 'Divinity School',
       'address': { 'street': '45 Francis Avenue',
                   'zipcode': '02138',
                   'city': 'Cambridge',
                   'state': 'MA'}
                 },
  2: { 'name': 'Lada',
       'surname': 'Damon',
       'city': 'Hanover',
       'state': 'NH',
       'language': ['German','Hungarian','Italian'],
       'department': 'Chemistry',
       'address': { 'street': '12 OXFORD STREET',
                   'zipcode': '02138',
                   'city': 'Cambridge',
                   'state': 'MA'}},
  3: { 'name': 'Stribog',
       'surname': 'Castor',
       'city': 'Madison',
       'state': 'WI',
       'language': ['Mandarin','Tagalog', 'Japanese'],
       'department': 'East Asian Studies',
       'address': { 'street': '9 Kirkland Place',
                   'zipcode': '02138',
                   'city': 'Cambridge',
                   'state': 'MA'}
                 },
  4: { 'name': 'Cassandra',
       'surname': 'Shpynx',
       'city': 'Sausalito',
       'state': 'CA',
       'language': ['French','Persian'],
       'department': 'Organismic & Evolutionary Biology',
       'address': { 'street': '26 Oxford Street ',
                   'zipcode': '02138',
```

```
                    'city': 'Cambridge',
                    'state': 'MA'}}
                    }
```

We have data frame *a4* and at the second level, there is element *language* with a vector of values. First, let us see what happens when we transform the *dict a4* into a data frame.

```
df1= pd.DataFrame.from_dict(a4, orient='index')
df1.columns

Index(['name', 'surname', 'city', 'state', 'language', 'department',
       'address'],
      dtype='object')
```

Differently from the previous case, element *language* has been transformed into a column. Let us see how it looks like.

```
df1[['name', 'language']]
```

	name	language
1	Polycarp	[Aramaic, Hebrew, Greek]
2	Lada	[German, Hungarian, Italian]
3	Stribog	[Mandarin, Tagalog, Japanese]
4	Cassandra	[French, Persian]

It is a data frame column, but values are Python lists, which complicate things when we execute normal data wrangling operations like sorting, selection, grouping, and so forth. So, we need to work on column *language* too, in addition to column *address,* as we have seen before. This is why, in the procedure, there is an additional step for *exploding* those vectors of values into separate rows. Here are the steps.

STEP 1. Convert the *dict* into a pandas data frame.

```
df1= pd.DataFrame.from_dict(a4, orient='index')
```

	name	surname	city	state	language	department	address
1	Polycarp	Arthmail	Des Moines	IA	[Aramaic, Hebrew, Greek]	Divinity School	{'street': '45 Francis Avenue', 'zipcode': '02...
2	Lada	Damon	Hanover	NH	[German, Hungarian, Italian]	Chemistry	{'street': '12 OXFORD STREET', 'zipcode': '021...

(Continued)

	name	surname	city	state	language	department	address
3	Stribog	Castor	Madison	WI	[Mandarin, Tagalog, Japanese]	East Asian Studies	{'street': '9 Kirkland Place', 'zipcode': '021...
4	Cassandra	Shpynx	Sausalito	CA	[French, Persian]	Organismic & Evolutionary Biology	{'street': '26 Oxford Street ', 'zipcode': '02...

STEP 2 (NEW). Explode vector values of column *language* into distinct rows.

```
df1= df1.explode('language', ignore_index=True)
```

Now the data frame has size 11×7, from the original 4×7. Let us look at column *language*.

```
df1[['name', 'language']]
```

	name	language
0	Polycarp	Aramaic
1	Polycarp	Hebrew
2	Polycarp	Greek
3	Lada	German
4	Lada	Hungarian
5	Lada	Italian
6	Stribog	Mandarin
7	Stribog	Tagalog
8	Stribog	Japanese
9	Cassandra	French
10	Cassandra	Persian

The list values have been exploded into separate rows.

STEP 3 and STEP 4. At this point, we are in a situation similar to Step 2 of the previous example; we have to normalize column *address* and join the result with *df1*.

```
norm= pd.json_normalize(df1['address'])
```

	street	zipcode	city	state
0	45 Francis Avenue	02138	Cambridge	MA
1	45 Francis Avenue	02138	Cambridge	MA
2	45 Francis Avenue	02138	Cambridge	MA

	street	zipcode	city	state
3	12 OXFORD STREET	02138	Cambridge	MA
4	12 OXFORD STREET	02138	Cambridge	MA
5	12 OXFORD STREET	02138	Cambridge	MA
6	9 Kirkland Place	02138	Cambridge	MA
7	9 Kirkland Place	02138	Cambridge	MA
8	9 Kirkland Place	02138	Cambridge	MA
9	26 Oxford Street	02138	Cambridge	MA
10	26 Oxford Street	02138	Cambridge	MA

In this specific case, the row index of *df1* is equivalent to *norm*'s index, so there is no need to reset; we can just join them.

```
df_norm1= df1.merge(norm, left_index=True, right_index=True).\
        drop(columns='address')
```

	name	surname	city_x	state_x	language	department	street	zipcode	city_y	state_y
0	Polycarp	Arthmail	Des Moines	IA	Aramaic	Divinity School	45 Francis Avenue	02138	Cambridge	MA
1	Polycarp	Arthmail	Des Moines	IA	Hebrew	Divinity School	45 Francis Avenue	02138	Cambridge	MA
2	Polycarp	Arthmail	Des Moines	IA	Greek	Divinity School	45 Francis Avenue	02138	Cambridge	MA
3	Lada	Damon	Hanover	NH	German	Chemistry	12 OXFORD STREET	02138	Cambridge	MA
4	Lada	Damon	Hanover	NH	Hungarian	Chemistry	12 OXFORD STREET	02138	Cambridge	MA
5	Lada	Damon	Hanover	NH	Italian	Chemistry	12 OXFORD STREET	02138	Cambridge	MA
6	Stribog	Castor	Madison	WI	Mandarin	East Asian Studies	9 Kirkland Place	02138	Cambridge	MA
7	Stribog	Castor	Madison	WI	Tagalog	East Asian Studies	9 Kirkland Place	02138	Cambridge	MA

(Continued)

	name	surname	city_x	state _x	language	department	street	zipcode	city_y	state _y
8	Stribog	Castor	Madison	WI	Japanese	East Asian Studies	9 Kirkland Place	02138	Cambridge	MA
9	Cassandra	Shpynx	Sausalito	CA	French	Organismic & Evolutionary Biology	26 Oxford Street	02138	Cambridge	MA
10	Cassandra	Shpynx	Sausalito	CA	Persian	Organismic & Evolutionary Biology	26 Oxford Street	02138	Cambridge	MA

11.3.4 Python: Use Cases with JSON Datasets

The Python package **json** is the most common to handle JSON datasets. The installation is standard, with packet managers like *pip*, *conda*, or *mamba*.

```
import json
```

The standard function for reading JSON files is **pd.read_json()**. Alternatively, a JSON file could be read with the general method for reading files in Python, using function **open()** to access the content of the file, and the specific **json.load()** to load the content. We will see examples with both methods. As case studies, we use again some of the JSON datasets of the R section, to highlight similarities and differences.

The Nobel Prize For this case study, the JSON dataset is the collection of Nobel laureates from the *Nobel Prize Foundation*. Let us read it with the standard pd.read_json().

```
nobel= pd.read_json("datasets/Nobel/prize.json")
```

	prizes
0	{'year': '2022', 'category': 'chemistry', 'lau...
1	{'year': '2022', 'category': 'economics', 'lau...
2	{'year': '2022', 'category': 'literature', 'la...
3	{'year': '2022', 'category': 'peace', 'laureat...
4	{'year': '2022', 'category': 'physics', 'laure...
...	...
659	{'year': '1901', 'category': 'chemistry', 'lau...

	prizes
660	{'year': '1901', 'category': 'literature', 'la…
661	{'year': '1901', 'category': 'peace', 'laureat…
662	{'year': '1901', 'category': 'physics', 'laure…
663	{'year': '1901', 'category': 'medicine', 'laur…

We have read it correctly, and the resulting data frame has a single column *prizes*, whose elements are dicts, one for each Nobel prize, for year and category. Those dicts have most/all names in common among rows, so this is the perfect situation for normalizing the column.

```
nobel= pd.json_normalize(nobel.prizes)
```

	year	category	laureates	overallMotivation
0	2022	chemistry	[{'id': '1015', 'firstname': 'Carolyn', 'surna…	NaN
1	2022	economics	[{'id': '1021', 'firstname': 'Ben', 'surname':…	NaN
2	2022	literature	[{'id': '1017', 'firstname': 'Annie', 'surname…	NaN
3	2022	peace	[{'id': '1018', 'firstname': 'Ales', 'surname'…	NaN
4	2022	physics	[{'id': '1012', 'firstname': 'Alain', 'surname…	NaN
…	…	…	…	…
659	1901	chemistry	[{'id': '160', 'firstname': 'Jacobus H.', 'sur'…	NaN
660	1901	literature	[{'id': '569', 'firstname': 'Sully', 'surname'…	NaN
661	1901	peace	[{'id': '462', 'firstname': 'Henry', 'surname'…	NaN
662	1901	physics	[{'id': '1', 'firstname': 'Wilhelm Conrad', 's'…	NaN
663	1901	medicine	[{'id': '293', 'firstname': 'Emil', 'surname':…	NaN

This is a particular case, because being the original data frame composed of a single column (i.e. *prizes*), we do not need the step with the join operation; there are no separate data frames to join, it is just a single one. We can proceed. Let us consider column *laureates*.

Its elements have dicts, with information referred to all Nobel laureates for that particular year and category. They have common names, but they are also Python vectors of dicts (pay attention to the square brackets enclosing the dicts), so do we need to normalize or explode these values? Let us try with normalize.

```
pd.json_normalize(nobel.laureates)
```

	0	1	2
0	{'id': '1015', 'firstname': 'Carolyn', 'surnam…	{'id': '1016', 'firstname': 'Morten', 'surname…	{'id': '743', 'firstname': 'Barry', 'surname':…

(Continued)

	0	1	2
1	{'id': '1021', 'firstname': 'Ben', 'surname': …	{'id': '1022', 'firstname': 'Douglas', 'surnam…	{'id': '1023', 'firstname': 'Philip', 'surname…
2	{'id': '1017', 'firstname': 'Annie', 'surname'…	None	None
…	…	…	…

The outcome is not what we want; this way, we have put Nobel laureates in distinct columns, which is useless for us. What we want instead is that each Nobel laureate should go in a new row, similar to a long-form transformation. We need to *explode* the column.

```
nobel_expl= nobel.explode('laureates', ignore_index=True)
nobel_expl[['year','category','laureates']]
```

	year	category	laureates
0	2022	chemistry	{'id': '1015', 'firstname': 'Carolyn', 'surnam…
1	2022	chemistry	{'id': '1016', 'firstname': 'Morten', 'surname…
2	2022	chemistry	{'id': '743', 'firstname': 'Barry', 'surname':…
3	2022	economics	{'id': '1021', 'firstname': 'Ben', 'surname': …
4	2022	economics	{'id': '1022', 'firstname': 'Douglas', 'surnam…
…	…	…	…
1033	1901	literature	{'id': '569', 'firstname': 'Sully', 'surname':…
1034	1901	peace	{'id': '462', 'firstname': 'Henry', 'surname':…
1035	1901	peace	{'id': '463', 'firstname': 'Frédéric', 'surnam…
1036	1901	physics	{'id': '1', 'firstname': 'Wilhelm Conrad', 'su…
1037	1901	medicine	{'id': '293', 'firstname': 'Emil', 'surname': …

Rows increased to 1038, and now for each year and category, we have one row for each Nobel laureate. We are moving in the right direction, and now it is clear what we should do next: *normalize* column *laureates* of data frame *nobel_expl*.

```
norm= pd.json_normalize(nobel_expl.laureates)
norm[['firstname','surname']]
```

	firstname	surname
0	Carolyn	Bertozzi
1	Morten	Meldal
2	Barry	Sharpless

	firstname	surname
3	Ben	Bernanke
4	Douglas	Diamond
...	...	...
1033	Sully	Prudhomme
1034	Henry	Dunant
1035	Frédéric	Passy
1036	Wilhelm Conrad	Röntgen
1037	Emil	von Behring

Finally, this time we have to *join* the two data frames *nobel_expl* and *norm*.

```
nobel_laureates= nobel_expl.join(norm).drop(columns='laureates')
```

	year	category	id	firstname	surname	motivation	share
0	2022	chemistry	1015	Carolyn	Bertozzi	"for the development of click chemistry and bi…	3
1	2022	chemistry	1016	Morten	Meldal	"for the development of click chemistry and bi…	3
2	2022	chemistry	743	Barry	Sharpless	"for the development of click chemistry and bi…	3
3	2022	economics	1021	Ben	Bernanke	"for research on banks and financial crises"	3
4	2022	economics	1022	Douglas	Diamond	"for research on banks and financial crises"	3
...	...	...	...	...	...	...	...
1033	1901	literature	569	Sully	Prudhomme	"in special recognition of his poetic composit…	1
1034	1901	peace	462	Henry	Dunant	"for his humanitarian efforts to help wounded…	2
1035	1901	peace	463	Frédéric	Passy	"for his lifelong work for international peace…	2
1036	1901	physics	1	Wilhelm Conrad	Röntgen	"in recognition of the extraordinary services …	1
1037	1901	medicine	293	Emil	von Behring	"for his work on serum therapy, especially its…	1

US Politicians This is the JSON dataset from *Everypolitician* containing public information regarding MEPs of the 116th Congress of the United States of America.

If we try reading the dataset with the common `pd.read_json()`, an error is raised.

```
df=pd.read_json("datasets/Everypoliticians/ep-popolo-v1.0.json")

ValueError: All arrays must be of the same length
```

This is an example where for reading the JSON file, the generic method should be employed.

```
with open('datasets/Everypoliticians/ep-popolo-v1.0.json') as json_data:
    pol = json.load(json_data)
```

This way, we have read it correctly. We can explore the structure with command line methods, as seen before. The top-level keys are seven; element *persons* is the nested dict with information on MEPs.

```
pol.keys()

dict_keys(['posts', 'persons', 'organizations', 'meta',
           'memberships', 'events', 'areas'])
```

Exploring further, we can extract information on single elements of *organizations*, for example, an excerpt of the information about the party at index 2.

```
pol.get('organizations')[2]
{'classification': 'party', 'id': 'democrat-liberal',
 'identifiers': [{'identifier': 'Q6540770', 'scheme': 'wikidata'}],
 'links': [{'note': 'website', 'url': 'http://www.liberalparty.org/'}],
 'name': 'Democrat-Liberal',
 'other_names': [{'lang': 'en', 'name': 'Liberal Party of New York',
 'note': 'multilingual', 'source': 'wikidata-label'},
...
```

The output is extremely verbose; this dataset has a rich structure that is not easily inspected visually.

We proceed as seen in previous examples, but this time we have to work on each top-level element separately. Trying to convert the whole *dict* into data frame raises an error. We work on *persons*.

```
df= pd.DataFrame(pol['persons'])
df
```

	birth_date	...	family _name	gender	given _name	links	contact_details
0	1944-10-15	...	Collins	male	Michael	[{'note': 'Wikimedia Commons', 'url': 'https:/...	NaN
1	1969-01-31	...	Huizenga	male	Bill	[{'note': 'Wikimedia Commons', 'url': 'https:/...	[{'type': 'fax', 'value': '202-226-0...
2	1959-09-28	...	Clawson	male	Curtis	[{'note': 'Wikimedia Commons', 'url': 'https:/...	[{'type': 'twitter','value': 'RepCurtClawson'}]
...	...	...	...	...	...	...	...
1737	1954-07-12	...	McCollum	female	Betty	[{'note': 'Wikimedia Commons', 'url': 'https:/...	[{'type': 'fax', 'value': '202-225-19...
1738	1954-06-19	...	Cooper	male	Jim	[{'note': 'Wikimedia Commons', 'url': 'https:/...	[{'type': 'fax', 'value': '202-226-10...

The result has 15 columns. Some columns have elements with single values, like, for example, column *family_name*. Column *links*, instead, have dict elements, with lists of links and related information, for each politician. Do we need to normalize or explode it?

Let us first see what the outcome is if we normalize, meaning that we create new columns from the dict elements.

```
pd.json_normalize(df['links'])
```

	0	1	2	...	127	128
0	{'note': 'Wikimedia Commons', 'url': 'https://...	{'note': 'Wikipedia (de)', 'url': 'https://de...	{'note': 'Wikipedia (en)', 'url': 'https://en...	...	None	None
1	{'note': 'Wikimedia Commons', 'url': 'https://...	{'note': 'Wikipedia (de)', 'url': 'https://de...	{'note': 'Wikipedia (en)', 'url': 'https://en...	...	None	None
...	...		...	...	...	...	...

The result is not what we want; the normalize operation has separated into distinct columns the elements of the dict, which were dict in their turn. We did not obtain columns related to names. The correct operation is to *first explode the elements into distinct lines*, meaning each politician's link goes in a new row, *then normalize*.

```
df_expl= df.explode('links', ignore_index=True)
df_expl[['family_name', 'links']]
```

	family_name	links
0	Collins	{'note': 'Wikimedia Commons', 'url': 'https://...
1	Collins	{'note': 'Wikipedia (de)', 'url': 'https://de...
2	Collins	{'note': 'Wikipedia (en)', 'url': 'https://en...
3	Collins	{'note': 'Wikipedia (simple)', 'url': 'https:/...
4	Collins	{'note': 'Wikipedia (sv)', 'url': 'https://sv...
...	...	...
16787	Cooper	{'note': 'facebook', 'url': 'https://facebook...
16788	Cooper	{'note': 'instagram', 'url': 'repjimcooper'}
16789	Cooper	{'note': 'twitter', 'url': 'https://twitter.co...
16790	Cooper	{'note': 'website', 'url': 'http://cooper.hous...
16791	Cooper	{'note': 'youtube', 'url': 'RepJimCooper'}

We have obtained 16792 rows, with multiple rows for each politician, corresponding to the different links referred to by each one of them. Now we can *normalize* column *links* of data frame *df_expl*.

```
norm= pd.json_normalize(df_expl['links'])
norm
```

	note	url
0	Wikimedia Commons	https://commons.wikimedia.org/wiki/Category:Ma...
1	Wikipedia (de)	https://de.wikipedia.org/wiki/Mac_Collins
2	Wikipedia (en)	https://en.wikipedia.org/wiki/Mac_Collins
3	Wikipedia (simple)	https://simple.wikipedia.org/wiki/Mac_Collins
4	Wikipedia (sv)	https://sv.wikipedia.org/wiki/Mac_Collins
...	...	...
16787	facebook	https://facebook.com/JimCooper
16788	instagram	repjimcooper
16789	twitter	https://twitter.com/RepJimCooper
16790	website	http://cooper.house.gov
16791	youtube	RepJimCooper

We have separated the former *links* column into new columns corresponding to names, and finally we can join the two data frames, *df_expl* and *norm*.

```
politicians= df_expl.join(norm).drop(columns='links')
```

	birth _date	death _date	family _name	gender	given _name	...	note	url
0	1944-10-15	2018-11-20	Collins	male	Michael	...	Wikimedia Commons	https://commons .wikimedia.org/wiki/ Category:Ma...
1	1944-10-15	2018-11-20	Collins	male	Michael	...	Wikipedia (de)	https://de.wikipedia.org/ wiki/Mac_Collins
2	1944-10-15	2018-11-20	Collins	male	Michael	...	Wikipedia (en)	https://en.wikipedia .org/wiki/Mac_Collins
...	...	...	...	...	...	...	...	...
16789	1954-06-19	NaN	Cooper	male	Jim	...	twitter	https://twitter.com/ RepJimCooper
16790	1954-06-19	NaN	Cooper	male	Jim	...	website	http://cooper.house.gov
16791	1954-06-19	NaN	Cooper	male	Jim	...	youtube	RepJimCooper

We could proceed in the same way with other dict columns of the original data frame.

Questions

11.1 (R/Python)

A list/dictionary data organization is...
  A Readable and represents hierarchies of information
  B Not readable; only processable with computational tools
  C Similar to a tabular data structure
  D Similar to a matrix
  (R: A)

11.2 (R/Python)

The JSON format is...
  A Similar to data frames
  B Similar to a pdf
  C Similar to a matrix
  D None of the above
  (R: D)

11.3 (R)

If *list1* is a list object, what do we obtain with `list1["ADDRESS"]`?
  A The values of column ADDRESS
  B The value of element ADDRESS
  C The values of the list with key/name ADDRESS
  D It is a syntax error
  (R: C)

11.4 (R)

If *list1* is a list object, what is the difference between `list1["ADDRESS"]` and `list1$ADDRESS`?
  A They are the same

B The first shows the values of list ADDRESS, and the second shows the values of the column ADDRESS

C They both refer to the column ADDRESS

D One of the two returns an error

(R: A)

11.5 (R)

As a rule of thumb, function `unnest_wider()` is appropriate when…

A Different lists have no keys in common

B Different lists have several keys in common and same number of values

C When we want to perform a wide-form transformation of a list

D When lists are named lists

(R: B)

11.6 (R)

Function `unnest_wider()` transforms a list column into…

A Distinct rows for each unique key/name

B A combined single list

C As many columns as the number of keys/names

D Distinct columns for each unique key/name

(R: D)

11.7 (R)

As a rule of thumb, function `unnest_longer()` is appropriate when…

A Different lists have no keys in common

B Different lists have several keys in common and same number of values

C When we want to perform a long-form transformation of a list

D When lists are named lists

(R: A)

11.8 (R)

Function **unnest_longer()** transforms a list column into…

A Distinct rows for all keys/names

B A combined single list

C As many rows as the number of unique keys/names

D Distinct columns for each unique key/name

(R: A)

11.9 (R)

Considering the following sequence of instruction, which is the reason for repeating `unnest_longer()` and `unnest_wider()` operations?

```
df %>%
  unnest_longer(name1) %>% unnest_wider(name1) %>%
  unnest_longer(name2) %>% unnest_wider(name2)
```

A We try different approaches until we produce a meaningful result

B *name1* and *name2* are two different list columns to unnest

C First, we unnest list column *name1*, then *name2*, which was nested in *name1*

D First, we unnest list column *name1*, which was nested in *name2,* then *name2*

(R: C)

11.10 (Python)

If *list1* is a dict object, what do we obtain with `list1['name']['name1']['name2']`?

A The value of the element *name* at 3rd level, included in list *name1*, included in list *name2*

B The value of the element *name2* at 3rd level, included in list *name1*, included in list *name*

C The values of the elements *name*, *name1*, and *name2*

D It is a syntax error

(R: B)

11.11 (Python)

As a rule of thumb, function `pd.json.normalize()` is appropriate when...

A A dict column has lists with no keys in common

B A dict column has lists with several keys in common and same number of values

C When we want to perform a wide-form transformation of a dict

D With different dict columns

(R: B)

11.12 (Python)

Function `pd.json.normalize()` transforms a dict column into...

A In the same data frame, there are distinct rows for each unique key

B A combined single dict

C In a new data frame, there are distinct rows for each unique key

D Distinct columns for each unique key

(R: C)

11.13 (Python)

As a rule of thumb, function `pd.explode()` is appropriate when...

A A dict column has lists with no keys in common

B A dict column has lists with several keys in common and the same number of values

C When we want to perform a wide-form transformation of a dict

D With different dict columns

(R: A)

11.14 (Python)

Function `pd.explode()` transforms a dict column into...

A In the same data frame, there are distinct rows for each unique key

B A combined single dict

C In a new data frame, there are distinct rows for each unique key

D Distinct columns for each unique key

(R: A)

Index

:= 313
.after 37, 38
.before 37, 38
.by_group 51, 233
.iloc 73–77
.keep 45
.loc 73–77
[:alpha:] 151
[:digit:] 151
[:punct:] 151
[:symbol:] 151
%$% 57
%do% 280
%in% 104–105
%within% 136
|> 57

a

across() 324–325, 327
addition 6, 30, 51, 79, 101, 119, 131, 153, 159,
    182, 201, 231, 244, 321, 361, 363, 381, 394,
    410, 433
advanced plain text editor 8
agg() 244
aggfunc 214, 251
aggregate() 244, 247, 248
aggregate data 242, 298
aggregated data frame 236, 242, 263
aggregation operation 222, 227–232, 247–251,
    256
all() 146–147, 232
alpha-2 350
alpha-3 350, 353
Anaconda 6

anonymous function 307, 315, 317, 319, 321,
    322, 327, 333
anti join 365–369, 386–389
any() 146–147, 176
anyNA() 146
append() 299
apply() 261, 264, 316–319, 334, 337–341
arrange() 50, 51, 222, 233, 237, 312
array slicing 69–70
arsenal 8, 165
as_date() 132
as_mapper() 321
as_tibble 320
as.character() 404
as.data.frame() 320
as.double() 150
as.factor() 150
as.integer() 150
as.list() 150
as.logical() 150
as.numeric() 129, 150, 151
as.POSIXct() 129, 130
assign() 80–81, 340, 341
astype() 182, 341
astype("boolean") 183
astype("category") 183
attribute 26, 27, 33, 37, 38, 41, 45, 46, 51, 60,
    62–67, 70, 76, 79, 86, 120, 167, 169, 172,
    181, 197–199, 202–204, 206, 208, 209,
    212–214, 228, 229, 233, 237, 251, 252, 254,
    261, 263, 272, 275, 276, 288, 294, 302, 308,
    315, 317, 319, 320, 322–324, 341, 354, 372,
    373, 377, 378, 404, 408, 419, 422, 428–431
axis 68, 79, 85, 173, 177, 212

Data Science Fundamentals with R, Python, and Open Data, First Edition. Marco Cremonini.
© 2024 John Wiley & Sons, Inc. Published 2024 by John Wiley & Sons, Inc.
Companion website: www.wiley.com/go/DSFRPythonOpenData

b

backticks   27, 29, 119, 172
base method   115, 116, 147, 159–161, 164, 165, 188, 242, 316–321
Berlin Open Data   129, 166, 186
bind_cols()   328
bind_rows()   161
Boolean mask   102, 104–106, 115–119, 138, 144, 145, 147, 177, 238, 239, 324, 385–387, 408
Boolean operator   100
Bureau of Transportation Statistics   222, 271, 272, 286, 297
by copy   175, 180–182, 335
by view   175, 180–182
ByteIO   245

c

calculated column   44, 45, 80, 234, 242–244, 259–261, 271, 340
case_when()   272, 276–277, 282
cat()   278
categorical elements   54
Categorical()   90
caveat   84, 160, 315
character classes   151
cheatsheet   129, 136, 151
class()   15, 39
clear()   425
col_level   89, 203
Colab   7
colMeans()   146
cols   199, 324
colSums()   146–147, 177
column creation   42–43, 69–81, 234, 307
column deletion   43, 45
column selection   24–36, 59–66, 128, 324, 325
command line   2, 3, 6, 398, 413, 440
commercial   1, 165
community   1
compare()   189, 190
comparedf()   165
competing standards   27, 350
Comprehensive R Archive Network (CRAN)   2–4
concat()   83, 189
conda   6, 436
conditional mapping   321–323

conditional operations   236, 271, 272, 284, 286, 289
conditions and iterations   271–302
contains()   35
copy()   170, 425
copy(deep=True)   170, 175, 180, 184, 286–289, 296, 297, 299, 301, 302, 335, 336, 338–341, 377
Copyright   24, 101, 128, 129, 197, 271, 307, 347, 348, 394, 395
count()   248, 312
counting rows   228, 231, 232, 247–251
country code   52, 349–353, 355, 356, 367, 368, 374–377, 387
Creative Commons   128, 307, 347
creativity   347
CSV format   8–10
curly brackets   68, 249, 312, 393, 422
custom data frame   108, 137, 366
custom function   307, 311, 314, 328, 329, 332

d

data frame   15, 23–91, 207–213, 234–236, 347–389, 427–436
data masking   44–45, 312–315
data science   1–10, 18, 42, 59, 99, 154, 159, 307, 316, 347, 394
data type transformations   141–154, 156, 173–182, 316, 327
data()   15
Dataframe.from_dict()   427–430
DataFrame()   73
DataFrameGroupBy   247, 262–264
dataset   8–10, 13, 15, 18, 19, 24–36, 61–62, 101, 128–129, 143–144, 175–176, 197, 222, 271–272, 307, 347–348, 394–395, 421–422, 436
datetime type   52, 90, 115, 155, 160, 166, 167
datetime.datetime.strftime()   169
datetime.datetime.strptime()   167–169
day()   134, 169
dayfirst   166, 167, 187
days()   133, 134
def   330
dependencies   4, 6
deprecated   19, 200, 320, 324

desc() 50
describe() 18, 61
descriptive statistics 13, 15–19, 24, 26, 44, 59, 61, 394
dict 67, 68, 182, 249, 393–395, 422, 423, 425–427, 429–433, 440, 441, 443
dictionary 67–68, 183, 249, 393
dictionary data format 393–443
didactic dataset 15, 316
difference() 65
discover knowledge 347
disjoint condition 107–114
distinct() 360, 362
distribution 1, 5, 6, 26, 128, 307, 347, 410
dmy() 131, 132, 157–160
dmy_h() 131
dmy_hm() 131
dmy_hms() 131
dollar symbol 39, 42
dot notations 321
double brackets 399
dplyr 29
drop() 79, 173
drop_duplicates() 382
droplevel() 212, 298
dt.datetime.strptime() 167
dt.month 117
dt.month_name() 90
dt.strftime() 169
dtypes 18
duplicated() 360, 362
duplicated keys 358–363, 378–384
duplicated rows 358, 360, 362, 363, 365, 382–384

e
ends_with() 35, 201
English charity 395
error 4, 9, 14, 26–30, 36, 37, 57, 63, 77, 79, 84, 117, 120, 128, 129, 131–133, 136, 138, 139, 142, 143, 156, 158, 160, 161, 164, 167, 173, 175, 176, 179, 183, 184, 187, 222, 284, 285, 293–295, 312, 313, 317, 321, 325, 326, 333, 340, 348–350, 354, 356, 404, 408, 414, 418, 419, 431, 440
error message 142, 184, 414
escape 10
EU members 348

European Union 348
Eurostat 128, 150, 182–186, 195, 307, 327
Everypolitician 395, 417, 440
everything() 35, 324
execution time 296–297, 326–330, 334, 336–337
explode() 431–436

f
factor 54, 150
fillna() 179
filter() 101, 102, 104, 105, 114, 116, 119, 238–242, 312, 321, 323–324, 408
first() 232
for() 278–280, 291–294
for cycle 278, 280, 283, 291, 292, 295, 316, 329, 339, 426, 427
foreach() 280
format() 53, 225
forward looking 152
forward pipe 55–57
fromJSON() 410
full join 351, 357, 374–375
full_join() 356–357
function 309–312
fundamentals 1, 3, 6, 38, 44, 49, 100, 127, 228, 232, 271, 347, 354

g
gather() 200
get() 425
ggplot 16
glimpse() 15, 17, 25
Google Colaboratory 7
Google Translate 129, 155, 159, 164, 186, 187
GOV.UK 200–202
Gregorian calendar 54, 127
group_by() 222, 224–225, 227
groupby() 247
group_indices() 226, 227
group_keys() 226
group_rows() 226, 227
group_vars() 226, 227

h
handling missing values 141–154, 173–182
head() 15, 18, 256, 257
hierarchical structures 394, 423, 427

i

IBM   24, 28, 38, 49, 59, 85
id_cols   197, 199
id_vars   203
if_all()   323, 324
if_any()   323–324
if_else()   272, 275
If-elif-else   285–286, 296
If-else   272, 277–278, 285–286
if()   277–278, 285
ifelse()   272–275
import   59
indentation   284
index level   86–88, 206, 254
indexed data frame   207–208, 375–378
indexer   79, 181
indicator   139, 140, 173, 347
indirection   312
info()   18, 60
Inner join   351, 356, 357, 359, 363–366, 372–376
inner_join()   354–356
inplace   79, 80, 85
insert()   80–81
installation   2, 4–7
installer   5, 6
integrated development environment (IDE)   1, 2
International Standard Organization (ISO)   350
interval()   136
IQR()   232
is_bool()   183
is_categorical()   183
is_datetime64_dtype()   183
is_dict_like()   183
is_list_like()   183
is_numeric_dtype()   183
is_string_dtype()   183
is.character()   150, 408
is.double()   150
is.factor()   150
is.integer()   150
is.list()   150, 420
is.logical()   150, 408
is.na()   144–147, 276
is.numeric()   150, 408
isin()   384–386
isna()   176–178
items()   301–302, 425, 426

iterations   271–302
iterator   278

j

JavaScript Object Notation (JSON)   394
join data frames   347–389
join operation   347, 349–353, 369–389, 429–436
join_by   354
join()   300–301, 332, 336, 431
json_normalize()   429–436
json.load()   436
jsonlite   410
JupyterLab   5–7

k

Kaggle   24
key:value   68, 196, 197, 393
keys of a join operation   347, 349–350
keys()   425
keyword arguments   341
keyword NA (Not Available)   16, 17, 44, 142, 326
keyword NaN (Not a Number)   19
keyword NaT (Not a Time)   19
keywords for missing values   142–143
kwargs   341

l

label:value   393
lambda function   261, 264, 307, 321, 333–334
lapply()   316–319
last()   232
last_col()   35
layout   2, 3
left data frame   357, 359, 365, 366, 372, 375, 380
left join   351, 357, 359, 375
left_index   377
left_join()   354, 357
left_on   372, 377
length()   15, 278
levels of indexing   399
library()   3, 15
list data format   395–410
list_cbind()   320
list_rbind()   320
list()   395
lists as element values   399
locale configuration   167–168

logical associations 347, 348, 356
logical condition 99–121, 133–136, 171–172, 323–324
logical conjunction 100
logical correspondence 148, 149
logical disjunction 100
logical equivalence 104
logical group 222, 227
logical operator 99–101
logical steps 106, 109, 111, 181, 430
long form 139, 195
lsuffix 431
lubridate 129–132, 134, 156, 159, 162, 165, 169, 170

m
mad() 232
magrittr 55, 57–59
mamba 436
map_at() 323
map_chr() 320
map_dbl() 320
map_dfc() 320
map_dfr() 320
map_if() 321–323
map_int() 320
map_lgl() 320, 408
map() 319–321, 406
Markdown 5
mask() 290
matched keys 350, 374
max() 230
mdy_h() 131
mdy_hm() 131
mdy_hms() 131, 132
mdy() 131
mean() 44, 228–230
median() 232, 244
melt() 203
memory problem 421–422
memory space 4–6, 312, 422
merge() 357–358, 371–374, 430
min() 230–231
missing values as replacement 142, 173–174
mixing data frames and lists 399
module 19, 24, 167, 244, 245, 296
month() 134, 169

months() 133, 134
multi-index 85, 206, 297–300
multicolumn operation 307–341
multicolumn transformation 324–325
mutate() 42, 44, 222, 324–325

n
n() 228
n_distinct() 232
NA_character_ 142, 326
NA_complex_ 142, 326
NA_integer_ 142, 326
na_matches 354
NA_real_ 142, 326
na_values 176
na.omit() 149
na.rm 44, 48, 146, 229
na.strings 143
name:value 393, 396
NamedAgg() 251
names_from 197
names_to 199
names() 15, 30, 398
NAs introduced by coercion 151
National Centers for Environmental Information (NOAA) 410
ncol() 15, 278
negation 100
nested data structure 397
nested iterations 280–281, 294–296
nested levels 393
nested lists as data frame column values 400
nesting 427, 429
New York City
New York City Open Data 37, 56, 197
nlargest() 259
The Nobel Prize Foundation 395, 415, 436
normalize 429
notebook format 5
Notepad++ 8
np.array 69, 70, 96, 289, 292–294, 334
np.max 214
np.mean 214
np.min 214
np.nan 173, 175
np.nanmax() 334
np.nanmin() 334

`np.select()` 287–289
`np.where()` 286–287
`nrow()` 15
`nsmallest()` 259
`nth()` 232
NULL 43
NumPy 5, 7–8, 59, 69–70

o

`object.size()` 225
official codes 350
omit rows 149–150
open-source 1–10
`openpyxl` 173
operations on groups 221–264
order of precedence 101
Organization for Economic Co-operation and
      Development (OECD) 139, 140, 173, 176,
      195
orient 428
`origin` 130
Our World in Data 195, 348
outer join 374, 386

p

package 4, 15, 29
package manager 2–6
pandas 5–8, 59, 70–73, 169–171
parameter placeholder 57–59
parameters passing by reference 312
parameters passing by value 312
`parse_date_time()` 162–165
parsing dates 130–132
pattern 46, 81
pattern matching 8, 137, 172, 324, 327
`pd.read_csv()` 27, 28, 61, 176, 244, 245
`pd.read_excel()` 173
`pd.replace()` 175
`pip` 6, 436
pipe 55–59, 110
`pivot_longer()` 197, 199, 200, 203
`pivot_table()` 213
`pivot_wider()` 197, 200, 202, 204
`pivot()` 204–206, 213
pivoting 195–216
`popitem()` 425
Posit 1

positional index 63
`print()` 278
proprietary 1, 8
public domain 395
`pull()` 400
purrr 315, 319
purrr-style 321
Python language 5–8

q

`quantile()` 232
`query()` 119–121, 202

r

R language 1, 2
RAM 3, 4, 422
randint 285, 286
`rank()` 238–242
`rbind()` 55
`read_csv()` 26, 222, 244
`read_csv2()` 28
`read_delim()` 27
`read_excel()` 139, 143, 154, 173
`read_json()` 410
`read_tsv()` 150
`read.csv()` 27, 143
`read.csv2()` 27
`read()` 244
readability 23, 195, 242, 352, 371, 412
`readLines()` 422
readr 5, 26, 27, 143
readxl 139
`reduce()` 321
regex 46, 184
regular expression 46, 81
`reindex()` 67–68
relocate columns 36–38, 67–68
`relocate()` 37
rename columns 53
`rename()` 37, 67–68
`replace_na()` 148
`replace()` 148, 179, 335
replacing missing values 147–149, 179–180
repurrrsive 401
`reset_index()` 88
right data frame 351, 357
right join 351, 357, 375

`right_index` 377
`right_join()` 357
`right_on` 372
row selection 101–121
`rowMeans()` 146
`rowSums()` 146
RStudio 1–5, 15, 16, 37, 129, 136, 151
RStudio Cloud 1
RStudio Desktop 1–3
RStudio viewer 15, 398, 402, 403
`rsuffix` 431

S
`sample_n()` 52
`sapply()` 316–319
scalable 221, 297
scale 99, 127, 316, 410
`sd()` 232, 244
`select()` 29, 30, 40
selection by exclusion 32–35, 64–66
selection by range 31–32
selection helper 35–36, 63, 77–78
semi join 363–365, 384–386
separate columns 24, 46, 83
`separate()` 46, 48
separator 9
`set_index()` 75, 86
shape 18, 60
simple exploratory data analysis 13–19
`slice_head()` 236
`slice_max()` 236
`slice_min()` 236
`slice_tail()` 236
slicing 38–45 69–81, 236–238
`sort_index()` 85, 254
`sort_values()` 85, 252, 264
sorting by an external list 51–55, 89–91
sorting by multiple columns 50–51
sorting data frame 49–55, 85–91
sorting within groups 232–234, 261–264
`spread()` 200
`stack()` 206, 211–213
`starts_with()` 35, 201
stats 44, 149
Stockholm International Peace Research Institute (SIPRI) 348
`str_c()` 137

`str_count()` 137
`str_detect()` 137, 138, 152, 156, 282, 324
`str_ends()` 137
`str_replace()` 137, 282
`str_replace_all()` 137, 140, 153, 156, 321
`str_starts()` 137
`str_sub()` 137
`str_to_lower()` 137
`str_to_title()` 137
`str_to_upper()` 137
`str_trim()` 137, 153
`str_view()` 137
`str.cat()` 84, 172
`str.contains()` 78, 172
`str.endswith()` 78, 172
`str.join()` 172
`str.len()` 172
`str.length()` 137
`str.lower()` 172
`str.match()` 172
`str.removeprefix()` 172
`str.removesuffix()` 172
`str.replace()` 172
`str.slice()` 81, 82, 84
`str.split()` 81–83
`str.startswith()` 77, 120, 202
`str.strip()` 172
`str.upper()` 172, 181
`str()` 15, 17, 150, 395, 400, 411, 413
`stream_in()` 422
string manipulation 58, 84, 120, 136, 148, 172, 182, 282, 319
`stringr` 136
`sub()` 59
Sublime Text 8
subsetting 39–42, 99–121, 323–324
suffix 354
`sum()` 177, 231–232, 250
`summarize()` 222, 227
`summary()` 15, 17, 25
superseded 116, 320
symbols for date formats 163
syntax error 28, 139
`Sys.setlocale` 132
`Sys.time()` 279, 280, 283, 284, 310, 329, 330

t

tabular   8, 16, 26, 28, 29, 195, 394
tabular data   9, 23
tail()   15, 18, 257
tally()   226, 228
territorial entities   103, 349, 350
textConnection()   422
tibble   15, 27
tidy   23, 24
tidy evaluation   312
tidyr   46, 148, 197, 401
tidyverse   4, 5, 15, 16, 24, 26, 29, 37, 46, 50, 55,
        57, 101, 129, 136, 148, 154, 197
tilde symbol   321
time()   168
timestamp   169–171, 187
to_datetime()   165–167
to_dict()   183
to_frame()   259
to_list()   183
to_numeric()   183
to_string()   183
toJSON()   410
transform()   259
transformation function   150, 182
transpose   428
trick   143, 158, 323
trimws()   153
truth table   100, 104
type list   400, 401, 408
typed missing value   142

u

UK Government   348
UNdata   197
unique code   362
unique()   15, 18, 19, 102, 110
unite()   48
unite columns   45–49, 81–85
United Kingdom Open Data   197
United Nations   195, 197, 198, 271, 280, 296, 328,
        336
United States Environmental Protection Agency
        (EPA)   24, 52, 89, 101, 102, 114, 128, 133,
        169
United States of America   395, 417, 440
Unix Epoch Time   129, 130

unmatched keys   356, 357, 366–368, 374, 384,
        386, 388
unnest_auto()   405
unnest_longer()   401, 403, 405–408
unnest_wider()   401, 402
unnesting   402, 407, 408, 410, 411, 413, 418, 420,
        429
unstack()   206, 208–210
untidy   24, 195
update()   425
US Census Bureau   103–105
usecols   61
user-defined function   308–315, 330–333
utility functions   13, 15–19
utils   225

v

value_name   203
value_vars   203
values_from   197
values_to   200
values()   425
var_name   203
variable embracing   312
variant   57–58, 319–320, 386–389
verification function   150, 182
very large dataset   421–422
View()   15
view()   15
Vizgr.org   394
Vroom   29

w

warning   35, 79, 108, 151
weekday()   169
where()   286–287, 289–291, 420
which()   148
while cycle   292–294
while()   291–295
wide form   195
Wide-long Transformation   206–207
Wikipedia Open Data Policy   394, 395
World Bank   347, 348
wrong indentation   295

X

x.max()   334
x.min()   334
xlrd   173

y

year()   134, 169
yearfirst   166, 167

years()   133, 134
Yelp   422
Yelp Open Dataset   422

Z

zipfile   244

Printed and bound by CPI Group (UK) Ltd, Croydon, CR0 4YY

23/04/2025

14660911-0003